# Bology

## Interactive Reader

# HOLT McDOUGAL

**HOUGHTON MIFFLIN HARCOURT**

# Table of Contents

## Unit 1 Introducing Biology

## Unit 2 Cells

# Unit 3  Genetics

# Unit 4 Evolution

# Unit 5 Ecology

# Unit 6  Classification and Diversity

# Unit 9 Human Biology

## To the Student

The *Interactive Reader* is a shorter version of your biology textbook. It contains only the most essential biology knowledge but includes all of the same biology vocabulary as the full-length textbook. You can interact with this book—by writing answers right after the questions, by underlining or highlighting important sentences, or by writing your own thoughts about biology directly next to the text.

Each chapter begins with a list of Key Concepts and gives you a chance to both review the words that you learned earlier and to preview new words that you will learn.

Throughout each chapter, you'll find the following features:

- **Instant Replay** questions quickly check your understanding of what you read. You can write your answers on the page.
- **Mark It Up** boxes remind you to highlight sentences with vocabulary words.
- **Academic Vocabulary** words are defined at the bottom of some pages. These words are useful to know for all subject areas, not just for biology.
- **Vocabulary Check** at the end of each section tests your knowledge of the most important vocabulary terms.
- **The Big Picture** tests how well you have mastered the most important biology concepts.
- **The Chapter Review** tests your understanding of the key material in the chapter.

# 1 Biology in the 21st Century

## GETTING READY TO LEARN

### Preview Key Concepts

**1.1 The Study of Life**
Biologists study life in all its forms.

**1.2 Unifying Themes of Biology**
Unifying themes connect concepts from many fields of biology.

**1.3 Scientific Thinking and Processes**
Science is a way of thinking, questioning, and gathering evidence.

**1.4 Biologists' Tools and Technology**
Technology continually changes the way biologists work.

**1.5 Biology and Your Future**
Understanding biology can help you make informed decisions.

### Review Academic Vocabulary

Write the correct word for each definition.

diversity     function     inquiry     structure     issue

**1.** _____ : an activity or job

**2.** _____ : a topic of discussion or debate

**3.** _____ : variety

**4.** _____ : the way parts are put together

**5.** _____ : asking questions or investigating

### Preview Biology Vocabulary

Four key terms from this chapter share the same word part. Read the definitions and guess what the word part means.

| TERM | DEFINITION |
|------|------------|
| biology | the scientific study of life |
| biosphere | all life on Earth and where it lives |
| biodiversity | the different types of life on Earth |
| biotechnology | the use of living things |

What I think *bio*– means: _____

# The Study of Life

**KEY CONCEPT** Biologists study life in all its forms.

## Earth is home to an incredible diversity of life.

Living things are found almost everywhere on Earth. There is life in the deepest parts of the ocean, in hot springs, and even in Antarctic ice. Living things can be all shapes and sizes. The blue whale is the largest animal living on Earth. Other living things are so small they can only be seen through a microscope.

This organism is made of a single cell and is too small to be seen with just the human eye.

### The Biosphere

Everything that lives on Earth, and every place where those things live, is part of the **biosphere.** Prairies, forests, deserts and other land environments are all part of the biosphere. Oceans, lakes, and other water environments are also part of the biosphere. Even the inside of your nose, where bacteria and fungi live, is a part of the biosphere.

### Biodiversity

The word *diversity* means "variety." If you have lots of different kinds of t-shirts, you have a variety of t-shirts, or a diversity of t-shirts. The word part *bio-* means "related to life." **Biodiversity** is the variety, or all the different types, of life on Earth. There is more biodiversity in warm areas of Earth. More living things can survive in consistently warm areas. These areas have a larger food supply for more forms of life. The region around the equator* has the most consistently warm temperatures on Earth, so there is the greatest biodiversity near the equator.

**VISUAL VOCAB**

Across the **biosphere,** the variety of life is called **biodiversity.**

Biodiversity is **greater** closer to the equator.

biosphere = everywhere life exists

**\* ACADEMIC VOCABULARY**

**equator** the imaginary circle around the middle of the Earth

These are all different species of North American birds.

Cardinal  Screech owl  Brown pelican  Peregrine falcon  Snowy egret

A **species** is a particular type of living things that can breed and reproduce. Humans are one species, and monarch butterflies are another species. About 2 million different living species have been identified. Biologists think that there could be millions more species that have not yet been discovered. Over half of all known species are insects.

**INSTANT REPLAY** Where on Earth would you find the greatest variety of species?

_____

_____

# All organisms share certain characteristics.

**Biology** is the scientific study of all forms of life, or all types of organisms. An **organism** is any individual living thing. All organisms have some things in common.

1. **Cells**  All organisms are made up of one or more cells. The **cell** is the basic unit of life. Many living things are made of just one cell. Other living things, such as humans, are made up of many cells.

2. **Need for energy**  All organisms need a source of energy. Some organisms, such as plants, use energy from sunlight to make their own food. Animals get their energy by eating other organisms. Energy is used in metabolism. **Metabolism** is all of the chemical processes that happen in an organism. These chemical processes break down molecules and build up other molecules that an organism needs.

3. **Response to environment**  Organisms react to light, temperature, touch, sound, and other parts of their environment. For example, plants grow toward light. The pupils of your eyes get smaller when you are in bright light.

This example of an animal cell is similar to many cells in your body.

**4. Reproduction and development** Members of a species must be able to reproduce, or make new organisms. The new organisms, or offspring, must be able to grow and develop into mature* organisms that can have more offspring. When organisms reproduce, they pass on their genetic information to the offspring. The genetic information is in a molecule called **DNA,** or deoxyribonucleic acid. DNA contains molecular instructions for growth and development.

This drawing shows the structure of DNA. This shape is called a double helix.

 Highlight four characteristics that all organisms share.

---

## 1.1 Vocabulary Check

| | |
|---|---|
| biosphere | organism |
| biodiversity | cell |
| species | metabolism |
| biology | DNA |

**Mark It Up**

Go back and highlight each sentence that has a vocabulary word in **bold.**

**Fill in the blanks with the correct term from the list above.**

1. _____ is the scientific study of all living things.

2. Genetic material that is passed on to offspring is called _____.

3. A _____ is a particular type of living things that can breed and reproduce.

4. The smallest unit of life is the _____.

5. All organisms use energy for _____, which is the breakdown and buildup of molecules necessary for life.

## 1.1 The Big Picture

6. Put the following three terms in order from smallest to largest: species, biosphere, cell. _____

7. List at least three characteristics that all living things share.

_____

_____

_____

# 1.2 Unifying Themes of Biology

**KEY CONCEPT** Unifying themes connect concepts from many fields of biology.

When you hear the word theme, you might think of the music that starts your favorite TV show every week. Or you might think of something that happens over and over again. In biology, themes are ideas that come up time after time. They connect, or unify, different areas of biology.

## All levels of life have systems of related parts.

Think about the different parts of a car—doors, tires, engine, seats, and so on. Even if you have all the different pieces of a car, it will not work unless all the pieces are put together in the right way. A car is a system. A **system** is a group of related parts that work together to make a whole.

There are many systems in biology. Some systems are tiny. A single heart cell, for example, is a system. Different cell parts and different chemicals all work together to make the heart cell function. Your heart, blood, arteries, and veins all work together in another system, your circulatory system.

An **ecosystem** is a biological system that includes living things, such as plants and animals, and nonliving things, such as water and rocks. A forest and a desert are both ecosystems. An ecosystem can also be a small area. A single tree or a pond is also an ecosystem.

The circulatory system and respiratory system work together to absorb oxygen from the air.

 **INSTANT REPLAY** Circle three examples of ecosystems.

## Structure and function are related in biology.

Think about a car again. The structure, or shape, of each car part is related to its function, or how it works. For example, the round shape of a tire allows it to roll. The treads help it not to slip.

Structure and function are connected in living things, too. The structure of your ear allows you to hear—something that you cannot do with your knees or hands. The structure of your hands allows you to hold a pencil or a baseball bat—something you cannot do with your ears.

Nerve cell

Your sharp front teeth help you bite into food, and your flat back teeth help you grind up the food.

Structure and function are connected on all levels. The structure of your nerve cells, for example, is different from the structure of your red blood cells and white blood cells. The differences in structure allow each type of cell to do its job.

Blood cells

The structure of nerve cells allows them to send and receive electrical signals. The structure of blood cells is very different. Each cell's structure affects its function.

What is another example—not given above—of a relationship between structure and function in the human body?

_____

_____

## Organisms must maintain homeostasis to survive in diverse environments.

How can people be outside when the temperature is below freezing, but still have a body temperature that stays around 37°C (98.6°F)? Although temperature and other conditions in the environment are always changing, the conditions inside of an organism usually stay the same. The ability of an organism to keep its internal conditions about the same is called **homeostasis.**

It is very important that the conditions inside organisms stay the same, because cells can survive only in certain ranges of conditions. Changes in temperature, blood sugar, or other conditions in an organism's body can be life threatening.

Systems in your body help to keep you in homeostasis. If your body temperature gets higher than normal, for example, your body will start sweating to help you cool down. This is an example of negative feedback. Your body sends information that it is too hot; sweating helps return your temperature to its normal state. In negative feedback, a change in a system causes a response to return the system to normal. Behavior also helps to maintain homeostasis. If you feel too cold, for example, you may put on warmer clothes.

Why is homeostasis important for survival?

_____

_____

# Evolution explains the unity and diversity of life.

**Evolution** is the change in living things over time. Evolution is not a change in an individual. Instead, evolution is the change in the genetic makeup of a population—a group of individuals—of a species over time.

## Adaptation

There is a lot of variation among the individuals in a species. Some variation can be inherited, or passed on to offspring through DNA. Some characteristics help an organism to survive and reproduce in a particular environment. An inherited characteristic that gives an advantage is called an **adaptation.** Organisms with an adaptation for a particular environment are more likely to survive and have offspring. Their offspring will also have the adaptation, and so they will be more likely to survive and reproduce. Over time, more individuals in the population will have the adaptation. This process is called natural selection.

The meaning of the word *adaptation* in evolution is different from the common meaning of the word. For example, if you say that you are adapting to a new classroom or to a new town, you are not talking about evolution. Instead, you are talking about becoming familiar with something new. Evolutionary adaptations are changes that occur over many generations* in response to changes in the environment.

## Unity and Diversity

Fish, birds, mushrooms, bacteria, and humans share many similarities. For example, they are all made of cells, and they all pass on genetic information through DNA. Their cells contain many similar structures with similar functions. These are examples of the similarities, or the unity, of life.

Although living things share many similarities, they also have many differences. Fish, birds, mushrooms, bacteria, and humans live in different environments, get energy from different sources, and reproduce in very different ways. The diversity of life means the differences among living things.

There is both diversity, or differences, and unity, or similarities, in living things.

---

**\* ACADEMIC VOCABULARY**

**generation** a single stage of offspring in the history of a family: You and your brothers and sisters are one generation; your parents are another generation.

Evolution explains both the unity and the diversity of life. Over billions of years, living things have changed, resulting in a huge variety of species. Still, all species have things in common, because they all share common ancestors.

 What is the difference between the biological meaning of *adaptation* and the common meaning of *adaptation*?

_____

_____

| 1.2 | Vocabulary Check |
|---|---|

| | **Mark It Up** |
|---|---|

| system | evolution |
|---|---|
| ecosystem | adaptation |
| homeostasis | |

Go back and highlight each sentence that has a vocabulary word in **bold**.

**Choose the correct term from the list for each description.**

1. conditions inside an organism do not change _____

2. an inherited characteristic that gives an organism an advantage _____

3. change over time of the genetic makeup of a population _____

4. all the living and nonliving things in an area and their interactions _____

5. a group of parts that function as a whole _____

| 1.2 | The Big Picture |
|---|---|

6. How are the words *system* and *ecosystem* related? _____

_____

7. How are structure and function related in living things? _____

_____

8. What could happen if an organism could not maintain homeostasis?

_____

_____

9. What does it mean that there is both unity and diversity of life?

_____

_____

_____

# Scientific Thinking and Processes

**KEY CONCEPT** Science is a way of thinking, questioning, and gathering evidence.

## Like all science, biology is a process of inquiry.

Science is a process of inquiry, or investigation. Science is one way we try to understand the world around us. All sciences have certain things in common, but there is no one way of doing science.

**Observations** Science begins with **observation,** or collecting information about a topic. Some observations are made directly with our senses. Other observations might involve using tools and technology.

**Data** When observations are recorded, saved, or written down, they are called **data.** Sights, sounds, and smells are examples of qualitative data. They describe a "quality" of an observation. Mass, volume, and temperature are examples of quantitative data. They can be measured.

**Hypotheses** Scientists use observations and data to form a hypothesis. A **hypothesis** (plural, *hypotheses*) is a possible answer to a scientific question. A hypothesis must be able to be tested.

 What part of science do you think the young woman in the picture is involved in? Why?

_____

Making observations involves gathering information about a topic.

**Observing** Scientists make observations and study earlier research.

**Forming hypotheses** Scientists ask questions and try to explain observations.

**Testing hypotheses** Scientists collect data that they use to support or reject a hypothesis.

**Analyzing data** Scientists analyze their data to draw conclusions about their research.

**Evaluating results** Scientists evaluate the data and conclusions presented by other scientists.

## Biologists use experiments to test hypotheses.

Scientific experiments allow scientists to test hypotheses and find out how something happens. In an **experiment,** scientists change one factor, or variable, to see how it affects the outcome of a situation. The factor that is changed in an experiment is called the **independent variable.** For example, suppose a scientist is testing how much of a medicine is necessary to treat high blood pressure. The independent variable is the dose of medicine, or how much medicine a patient gets. Then, the scientist sees how changes in the independent variable affect the dependent variable. The **dependent variable** is what the scientist measures as the outcome or result of the experiment. In this example, the dependent variable is blood pressure. The change in blood pressure *depends* on the amount of medicine given.

The independent variable should be the only part of a controlled experiment that changes. All other conditions should not change. The factors that do not change are called **constants.** For example, the form of medicine would be a constant—it would always be a pill.

**What is the difference between the dependent variable and the independent variable in an experiment?**

_____

_____

**VOCABULARY**

In common usage, the term *constant* means "unchanging." In experimental research, a constant is a condition or factor that is controlled so that it does not change.

## A theory explains a wide range of observations.

Many words have several different meanings. Depending on how a word is used, its meaning can change completely. For example, the word *right* could mean *correct,* or it could refer to a direction. Similarly, the word *theory* has different meanings. In everyday conversation, the word *theory* can mean a wild idea, or something that is imagined to be true. In science, the meaning of *theory* is very different.

Recall that a hypothesis is a proposed answer to a scientific question. A **theory** is a proposed explanation for a wide range of observations and experimental results that is supported by a wide range of evidence. Both gravity and natural selection are scientific theories.

Science is an ongoing process. Theories can change based on new evidence. New theories that better explain observations and experimental results can replace older theories. Our understanding of the world around us has changed very much over the past few decades*, and the study of biology has changed and expanded as well.

**What is the difference between a scientific theory and a hypothesis?**

_____

_____

**\* ACADEMIC VOCABULARY**

**decades** periods of ten years

### 1.3    Vocabulary Check

| | |
|---|---|
| observation | independent variable |
| data | dependent variable |
| hypothesis | constant |
| experiment | theory |

**Mark It Up**

Go back and highlight each sentence that has a vocabulary word in **bold.**

1. In the list above, circle the word that means what a scientist changes in an experiment.

2. Put a box around the word that means a factor that does not change.

3. Underline the word that means a written record of observations.

### 1.3    The Big Picture

4. Why are most factors held constant in a scientific experiment?

_____

5. How are hypotheses and theories related?

_____

_____

6. What is science? Write a definition for the word.

_____

_____

# 1.4 Biologists' Tools and Technology

**KEY CONCEPT** Technology continually changes the way biologists work.

Cars, computers, and cell phones are examples of technology. Technology has helped biologists learn a lot about life. Today, technology even allows scientists to observe activity inside the human brain.

## Imaging technologies provide new views of life.

Cells are too small to see with just your eyes. Before the microscope was invented, no one knew about cells. Many different technologies have extended humans' abilities to view life.

### Microscopes

A **microscope** provides an enlarged image of an object. Light microscopes, like the one in the drawing to the right, can be used to see cells as small as bacteria. Light microscopes can be used to view living things. Other types of microscopes are used to see even smaller things. Electron microscopes can be used to see things as small as protein molecules. However, electron microscopes cannot be used to view living things.

### Medical Imaging

Different types of technology are used to see inside organisms—without cutting the organism open. X-rays pass through soft skin and can show images of bones and teeth. A tool called magnetic resonance imaging (MRI) can be used to see things that are softer than bone. A functional MRI can even show images of brain activity.

This light microscope can be used to see cells.

**INSTANT REPLAY** What did scientists discover with the help of microscopes?

## Complex systems are modeled on computers.

Computers can be used to study living systems that cannot be studied directly. Computer models are also used when actual experiments are not safe, ethical, or practical. For example, computer models can be used to study heart attacks. Computer models can also help to study large systems. For example, they can help predict how fast a disease might spread, and how many people will get sick.

## The tools of molecular genetics give rise to new biological studies.

When your parents were in high school, no one would have imagined the DNA technologies in use today. In just the last 40 years, we have learned how the genetic code works, studied the functions of genes, and have even changed genes. A **gene** is a segment of DNA that stores genetic information. The study of genes has led to new fields of biology.

- **Molecular genetics** is the study and manipulation of DNA on a molecular level. Manipulation of DNA means the ability to change the DNA of organisms.
- **Genomics** is the study of the entire DNA sequences of humans and other organisms. The entire DNA sequence of an organism is called its genome.

  Where do you think biology will be in another 40 years?

 What two new fields of biology use DNA technologies?

_____

---

| 1.4 | Vocabulary Check |
|---|---|

**Mark It Up**

Go back and highlight each sentence that has a vocabulary word in **bold**.

microscope     molecular genetics
gene             genomics

1. What is the study of the entire DNA sequence of an organism?

   _____

2. A _____ is a segment of DNA.

---

| 1.4 | The Big Picture |
|---|---|

3. Give an example of how technology has changed human understanding of life. _____

4. A person who is working to insert a new gene into an organism might be in the field of _____

**KEY CONCEPT** Understanding biology can help you make informed decisions.

## Your health and the health of the environment depend on your knowledge of biology.

Do energy drinks really give you energy? Is bottled water healthier than tap water? Are you at risk for any genetic diseases or health problems? What are the benefits of exercise? How does sleep affect your brain? What are the effects of alcohol, illegal drugs, and tobacco? What are the health risks of pollution in your area? An understanding of biology can help you make choices and decisions that affect your health.

Biologists and other scientists research environmental issues such as pollution, biodiversity, land conservation, and natural resource use. But decisions about the future are made by everyone, not just by scientists. An understanding of many areas of biology—from genetics to ecosystem studies—can help you make informed* decisions.

 What is one health issue that biology can help you to better understand?

## Biotechnology offers great promise but also raises many issues.

**Biotechnology** is the use of living things and biological processes. Some forms of biotechnology have been around for centuries*, such as the use of microorganisms to make bread and cheese. Today, other uses of biotechnology include DNA testing and DNA fingerprinting. DNA fingerprinting has helped to free people who were accused of a crime that they did not commit. Two other examples of biotechnology are described on the next page.

* ACADEMIC VOCABULARY

**informed** based on facts
**centuries** periods of one hundred years

1. **Genetically modified organisms** Through centuries of breeding, humans have slowly modified, or changed, many different plant and animal species. For example, carrots and poodles are genetically modified organisms because they have been selectively bred over many years. Today's technologies allow for genetic changes in short periods of time. Now we can move, or transfer, genes from one species into another species. Organisms that have genes from a different species are called **transgenic** organisms.

   Transgenic bacteria can make human insulin to treat people with diabetes. Transgenic, or genetically modified, food is a topic of debate all around the world. Genetic changes could make foods more nutritious. Genetic changes could also make plants grow well without the use of pesticides. However, there are many questions about genetically modified foods that no one knows the answers to yet. Are they safe to eat? Could they spread genes to wild plants? An understanding of the possible benefits and risks of transgenic organisms requires knowledge of biology.

2. **Genetic screening** Another form of biotechnology is human genetic screening. Genetic screening could help to see if a person is at risk for a genetic disorder. Genetic screening also raises questions about ethics*. Who should be allowed to see a person's genetic information? Should parents be allowed to use genetic screening to choose the characteristics of their children?

| THE GENE WORD FAMILY | |
|---|---|
| Gene | segment of DNA that stores genetic information |
| Genome | entire DNA sequence of an organism |
| Genomics | study of genomes |
| Molecular genetics | study and manipulation of DNA molecule |
| Genetic screening | testing DNA to see if a person is at risk for a genetic disorder |
| Transgenic | an organism that has a gene from a different species |

What is one benefit and one risk of biotechnology?

_____

_____

## Biology presents many unanswered questions.

About 50 years ago, the structure of DNA was discovered. By 2003 the entire human DNA sequence was known. Today, however, there are still more questions than answers. Can cancer be cured? Does life exist on other planets? How are memories kept in the brain?

A huge number of questions in biology are not just unanswered—they have not been asked. Before the microscope was invented, no one studied anything microscopic. Before biologists knew what the genetic material was, no one used genetic screening or DNA testing. As technology and biology advance, what do you think will be discovered in the next 20 years?

**INSTANT REPLAY** Will all biology questions be answered some day? Explain your answer.

_____

_____

## 1.5 Vocabulary Check

**Mark It Up**

Go back and highlight each sentence that has a vocabulary word in **bold**.

biotechnology

transgenic

1. If *bio-* means "life," then *biotechnology* means _____ is applied to technology.

2. If *trans-* means "over or across," then *transgenic* organisms have genes that have been brought _____ from other organisms.

## 1.5 The Big Picture

3. How could your understanding of biology help you to make decisions about your health and the environment? _____

_____

_____

4. An issue is a topic of discussion, or something that can raise concerns. Why is biotechnology sometimes called an issue? _____

_____

5. Why are some biology questions still unanswered? _____

_____

_____

# Chapter 1 Review

1. What are four characteristics that living things share? _____
_____

2. Write the terms *organism*, *biosphere*, and *cell* onto the diagram in order of biggest system to smallest system. The biggest circle should be labeled with the biggest system and the smallest circle with the smallest system.

   a. _____

   b. _____

   c. _____

   a.

   b.

   c.

3. Draw an example of a relationship between structure and function in a living thing.

4. Which of the following is an example of homeostasis?
   a. genetically modified organisms that produce insulin
   b. unchanging body temperature even in hot and cold environments
   c. the inheritance of an evolutionary adaptation
   d. front teeth that bite into food and back teeth that grind up food

5. What is the difference between a scientific hypothesis and a scientific theory? _____
_____

6. Choose the word that completes the following sentence:
   Biological evolution is the result of _____ changes in a population of a species.
   a. ecosystem          c. genetic
   b. metabolism         d. molecular

7. How has technology changed the way biologists study living things? Give an example. _____
_____

8. What is one reason a computer model might be used in biological research? _____

9. Write a definition of the word *biology* that a younger student would understand. _____

10. Describe one benefit and one risk involved in the use of transgenic organisms. _____
_____

# 2 Chemistry of Life

## GETTING READY TO LEARN

### Preview Key Concepts

**2.1 Atoms, Ions, and Molecules**
All living things are based on atoms and their interactions.

**2.2 Properties of Water**
Water's unique properties allow life to exist on Earth.

**2.3 Carbon-Based Molecules**
Carbon-based molecules are the foundation of life.

**2.4 Chemical Reactions**
Life depends on chemical reactions.

**2.5 Enzymes**
Enzymes are catalysts for chemical reactions in living things.

### Review Academic Vocabulary

Write the correct word for each definition.

cell     organism     DNA     atom     molecule

1. _____ : any individual living thing

2. _____ : genetic material

3. _____ : smallest unit of life

4. _____ : smallest unit of matter

5. _____ : combination of atoms held together by bonds

### Preview Biology Vocabulary

Six key terms from this chapter share the same word parts. Read the definitions and guess what the word part means.

| TERM | DEFINITION | WHAT I THINK THE WORD PART MEANS |
|------|------------|----------------------------------|
| endothermic | Describes a chemical reaction that absorbs more energy than it releases | |
| exothermic | Describes a chemical reaction that releases more energy than it absorbs | |
| cohesion | attraction among molecules of the same substance | |
| adhesion | attraction among molecules of different substances | |
| Solution | Mixture of substances that is the same throughout | |
| solute | A dissolved substance | |

# Atoms, Ions, and Molecules

**KEY CONCEPT** All living things are based on atoms and their interactions.

## Living things consist of atoms of different elements.

Every physical* thing that you can think of, living or not living, is made of very small particles called atoms. An **atom** is the smallest basic unit of matter, or of any physical substance*. A frog, a car, and your body are all made of atoms.

### Atoms

An atom is made up of three types of smaller particles: protons, neutrons, and electrons. Protons and neutrons form the center of an atom, called the nucleus. Electrons are much smaller and form the outer part of the atom. Protons have a positive electrical charge, and electrons have a negative electrical charge. Neutrons have no charge; they are neutral. Atoms have an equal number of protons and electrons, so they are electrically neutral.

Protons and electrons form the nucleus of an atom.

The electrons move around the nucleus in a three-dimensional space.

### Elements

An **element** is one particular type of atom. An element cannot usually be broken down into a simpler substance. Hydrogen, oxygen, aluminum, and gold are all familiar elements. But what makes one element different from other elements? The atoms of each element have a unique number of protons. There are 91 elements that occur naturally on Earth. Only about 25 of those elements are found in living things.

Imagining something as tiny as an atom can be hard. Scientists have come up with different models to try to show what an atom looks like or to show how atoms interact. In the figure on the next page, Bohr's atomic model shows that electrons surround the nucleus in regions called energy levels. Each energy level can hold a different number of electrons. The simplified model shows atoms as balls that differ in size and color.

---

**\* ACADEMIC VOCABULARY**

**physical** related to something real, that can be touched or seen, not an idea
**substance** something physical, or a kind of matter

**BOHR'S ATOMIC MODEL**

Hydrogen atom (H)

nucleus:
1 proton (+)
0 neutrons

outermost energy
level: 1 electron (–)

Oxygen atom (O)

nucleus:
8 protons (+)
8 neutrons

outermost energy
level: 6 electrons (–)

inner energy level:
2 electrons (–)

**SIMPLIFIED MODEL**

Hydrogen atom (H)

Oxygen atom (O)

Just 4 elements make up 96 percent of the human body's mass*. These elements are carbon (C), oxygen (O), nitrogen (N), and hydrogen (H). The other 4 percent of your body consists of mostly calcium (Ca), phosphorous (P), potassium (K), sulfur (S), sodium (Na), and iron (Fe).

## Compounds

The atoms of elements found in organisms are often linked, or bonded, to other atoms. A **compound** is a substance made of atoms of different elements bonded together in a certain ratio. Water ($H_2O$) is a compound of two hydrogen atoms and an oxygen atom. The properties of a compound can be different from the properties of the elements that make up the compound. For example, hydrogen and oxygen are both gases on Earth, but together they can form water. Similarly, a diamond is made of the element carbon, but carbon can also be part of sugars, proteins, and millions of other compounds.

How are atoms, elements, and compounds related?

_____

_____

The positive sodium ion ($Na^+$) and negative chloride ion ($Cl^-$) attract each other and form an ionic bond.

# Ions form when atoms gain or lose electrons.

An **ion** is an atom that has gained or lost one or more electrons. Some ions have a positive charge ($^+$) and some ions have a negative charge ($^-$). The charge gives the ion special properties.

ionic bond

Na⁺          Cl⁻

Sodium ion          Chloride ion

Ions are important in living things. For example, calcium ions ($Ca^{2+}$) are needed for every muscle movement in your body. Chloride ions ($Cl^-$) are important for a type of chemical signal in your brain.

Positive ions, such as sodium ($Na^+$), are attracted to negative ions, such as chloride ($Cl^-$). An **ionic bond** forms between a positively charged ion and a negatively charged ion. Salt, or sodium chloride (NaCl) is held together by an ionic bond.

 How does an atom become an ion?

_____

## Atoms share pairs of electrons in covalent bonds.

Some atoms do not easily gain or lose electrons. Instead, the atoms of many elements will share pairs of electrons. A **covalent bond** forms when atoms share a pair of electrons. A **molecule** is two or more atoms held together by covalent bonds. For example, oxygen ($O_2$) and water ($H_2O$) are molecules.

 What kind of bond unites the atoms in a water molecule?

_____

| 2.1 | Vocabulary Check |
|---|---|

**Mark It Up**

Go back and highlight each sentence that has a vocabulary word in **bold**.

atom                ionic bond
element            covalent bond
compound       molecule
ion

1. Name two types of bonds. _____

2. The smallest basic unit of matter is called a(n) _____.

3. One type of atom, such as hydrogen, is called a(n) _____.

4. A(n) _____ is an atom that has gained or lost an electron.

5. _____ and _____ are two words that mean a substance made of atoms that are bonded together.

| 2.1 | The Big Picture |
|---|---|

6. What is the difference between an ion and an atom?

_____

_____

7. Name five elements that make up the molecules in living organisms.

_____

_____

# Properties of Water

**KEY CONCEPT** Water's unique properties allow life to exist on Earth.

## Life depends on hydrogen bonds in water.

Unlike most things, water expands, or gets bigger, when it freezes. Because of this, ice is less dense than water. Therefore, ice floats in water. When a lake freezes, fish can still survive because the ice floats. The ice layer on the surface of the lake insulates* it and allows the water underneath to stay liquid.

### Water and Hydrogen Bonds

Water molecules have special properties. The oxygen has a slightly negative charge, and the hydrogens have slightly positive charges. This makes the molecule polar—like a magnet, a water molecule has positive and negative ends. The positive charge from the hydrogen atom of one water molecule can attract a negative charge from another molecule. This attraction is called a **hydrogen bond.** Hydrogen bonds occur among water molecules and also in proteins, in DNA, and in other molecules.

### Properties Related to Hydrogen Bonds

Each individual hydrogen bond is not very strong, but all together, hydrogen bonds give water properties that are important to life.

Hydrogen bonds form between neighboring water molecules. They cause water molecules to stick together.

- **High specific heat** Hydrogen bonds give water a high specific heat. This means that water resists changes in temperature, which is important in helping cells to maintain homeostasis.
- **Cohesion** The attraction among molecules of the same substance is **cohesion.** Cohesion from hydrogen bonds makes water molecules stick to each other. Cohesion is why water forms beads, or droplets, like those you see on a car that has just been washed.
- **Adhesion** The attraction among molecules of different substances is called **adhesion.** In other words, water molecules stick to other things. Adhesion helps plants move water from their roots to their leaves because the water molecules stick to the sides of the tubes that carry water through the plant.

 How does a hydrogen bond form?

_____

# Many compounds dissolve in water.

To take part in life processes, many molecules and ions must be dissolved in water-based fluids, such as blood or plant sap. When one substance dissolves in another, a solution forms. A **solution** is a mixture of substances that is equally mixed throughout. A solution has two parts:

- The **solvent** is the substance that there is more of, and that dissolves the other substance.
- The **solute** is the substance that dissolves in the solvent.

The amount of solute dissolved in a certain amount of solvent is the solution's concentration. A tiny bit of drink mix in one cup of water has very little flavor. Four spoonfuls of drink mix in one cup of water tastes stronger because it has a higher concentration.

Polar molecules—molecules with positive and negative ends—dissolve in water. But some compounds are nonpolar, like fats and oils. Nonpolar molecules do not have charged parts—no positive or negative ends—so they are not attracted to polar molecules like water. Nonpolar molecules will dissolve in nonpolar solvents. For example, vitamin E is nonpolar and dissolves in fats in human bodies.

**VISUAL VOCAB**

The **solvent** is the substance that is present in the greatest amount, and is the substance that dissolves solutes.

solvent

solution

solute

A **solute** is the substance that dissolves.

**VOCABULARY**

In everyday use, the word *solution* means "an answer." This meaning of solution is different, and means "a mixture."

 What are the two parts of a solution?

_____

# Some compounds form acids or bases.

Some compounds break up into ions when they dissolve in water.

- An **acid** is a compound that releases a proton when it dissolves in water. A proton is a hydrogen ion ($H^+$). An acid increases the concentration of $H^+$ ions in a solution.
- A **base** removes $H^+$ ions from a solution. After a base dissolves in water, the solution has a low $H^+$ concentration.

The acidity of a solution is the concentration of $H^+$ ions. Acidity is measured on the **pH** scale. In the figure of the pH scale, you can see that pH is usually between 0 and 14. A solution with a pH of 0 is very acidic, with a high $H^+$ concentration. A solution with a pH of 14 is very basic, with a low $H^+$ concentration. Solutions with a pH of 7 are neutral—neither acidic nor basic. Most organisms, including humans, need to keep their pH close to 7. However, some organisms need very different pH ranges to live.

**THE pH SCALE**

stomach acid pH between 1 and 3

blood pH 7.4

pure water pH 7

bile (digestive juice) pH between 8 and 9

| pH 0 | 1 | 2 | 3 | 4 | 5 | 6 | 7 | 8 | 9 | 10 | 11 | 12 | 13 | pH 14 |

← more acidic          neutral          more basic →

The concentration of $H^+$ ions varies depending on how acidic or basic a solution is.

high $H^+$ concentration

low $H^+$ concentration

---

**INSTANT REPLAY**

What is the difference between an acid and a base?

_____

## 2.2 Vocabulary Check

| Mark It Up |
| --- |
| Go back and highlight each sentence that has a vocabulary word in **bold**. |

hydrogen bond   solution   acid

cohesion   solvent   base

adhesion   solute   pH

1. A _____ is a mixture made of two parts, the _____, which is the bigger part, and the _____, which dissolves.

2. Attraction among molecules of the same type is called _____.

3. Attraction among molecules of different types is called _____.

4. The _____ scale measures the concentration of $H^+$ ions.

5. A high concentration of $H^+$ ions makes something a(n) _____ and a low concentration of $H^+$ ions makes something a(n) _____.

6. _____ give water special properties such as cohesion.

## 2.2 The Big Picture

7. Why are hydrogen bonds important for life? _____
   _____

8. What is the pH level for most human cells?
   _____

# 2.3 Carbon-Based Molecules

**KEY CONCEPT** Carbon-based molecules are the foundation of life.

## Carbon atoms have unique bonding properties.

Most molecules that make up living things are based on carbon atoms. The structure of a carbon atom allows it to form up to four covalent bonds. It can bond to other carbons or to different atoms. As shown in the figure below, carbon-based molecules have three basic structures: straight chains, branched chains, and rings.

---

### CARBON CHAINS AND RINGS

**Straight chain**

$$H-\underset{\underset{H}{|}}{\overset{\overset{H}{|}}{C}}-\underset{\underset{H}{|}}{\overset{\overset{H}{|}}{C}}-\underset{\underset{H}{|}}{\overset{\overset{H}{|}}{C}}-\overset{\overset{H}{|}}{C}=\overset{\overset{H}{}}{\underset{\underset{H}{}}{C}}$$

A simplified structure can also be shown as:

$$CH_3-CH_2-CH_2-CH=CH_2$$

**Branched chain**

$$CH_3-CH-CH_2-CH_3$$
$$\underset{\underset{CH_3}{|}}{\overset{\overset{CH_3}{|}}{\phantom{CH_3}}}$$
$$CH_2$$

**Ring**

(ring structure with O, CH, C, CH, CH, C, O—CH₃, OH)

Each line represents a covalent bond. Each letter represents an atom. Notice that there are four bonds for every carbon atom (C). When a carbon (C) is attached to a hydrogen (H) sometimes there is no line drawn to represent the bond, but the bond is still there.

---

Think of a chain made up of connected loops, or links. Each link is a subunit that makes up the bigger chain. Many carbon-based molecules have subunits that make up a bigger molecule.

Each subunit is called a **monomer**. When monomers are linked together, they form molecules called polymers. A **polymer** is a large molecule made of many monomers bonded together. A polymer can also be called a macro-molecule. *Macro-* means "large," so a macromolecule is a large molecule. The monomers that make up a polymer can all be the same, or they can be different, depending on the type of macromolecule.

### VISUAL VOCAB

Each smaller molecule is a subunit called a **monomer.**

*mono-* = one
*poly-* = many

monomer

polymer

A **polymer** is a molecule that contains many monomers bonded together.

How are polymers and monomers related?

_____

# Four main types of carbon-based molecules are found in living things.

All organisms are made of four types of carbon-based molecules: carbohydrates, lipids, proteins, and nucleic acids.

## Carbohydrates

Fruits and grains both contain large amounts of carbohydrates. **Carbohydrates** are molecules made of carbon, hydrogen, and oxygen. Sugars and starches are both types of carbohydrates. These carbohydrates can be broken down to produce energy in cells. Some carbohydrates are part of cell structure in plants.

The most basic carbohydrates are simple sugars. Many simple sugars have five or six carbon atoms. Fructose and glucose are both sugars that have six carbon atoms. The sugar that you might use in the kitchen is made of two sugar molecules bonded together.

Many glucose molecules bonded together form polymers such as starch and cellulose. These polymers are called polysaccharides. Starches are carbohydrates made by plants. Starch can be broken down as a source of energy by plant and animal cells. Cellulose is also made by plants. Cellulose makes up cell walls, the tough outer covering of plant cells. The stringy fibers of vegetables like celery are made of cellulose. The structure of starch molecules is different from the structure of cellulose molecules. The different structures give them their different properties.

Glucose is a six-carbon sugar. Glucose is often represented by a hexagon, a six-sided figure. Each point on the hexagon represents a carbon, except the point that has an O, for oxygen.

### CARBOHYDRATE STRUCTURE

**Polymer (starch)**

monomer

Starch is a polymer of glucose monomers that often has a branched structure.

**Polymer (cellulose)**

monomer

Cellulose is a polymer of glucose monomers that has a straight, rigid structure.

## Lipids

**Lipids** are molecules that include fats, oils, and cholesterol. Lipids are nonpolar, so they do not dissolve in water. Like carbohydrates, most lipids are made of carbon, oxygen, and hydrogen atoms. Some lipids are broken down and used as energy in cells. Other lipids form part of the cell's structure.

Fats and lipids store large amounts of energy in organisms. Animal fats are found in foods such as meat and butter. Plant fats are found in nuts and oils, like olive oil or peanut oil. Fats and lipids are made of molecules called fatty acids. **Fatty acids** are chains of carbon atoms bonded to hydrogen atoms. In many lipids, the fatty acid chains are attached on one end to another molecule called glycerol. Because of the shape of the fatty acid chains, some fats are liquid at room temperature, like olive oil, and other fats are solid, like butter.

All cell membranes are made mostly of another type of lipid, called a phospholipid (FAHS-foh-LIHP-ihd). A phospholipid has glycerol, two fatty acid "tails," and a phosphate group that forms the "head" of the molecule. The phosphate group includes phosphorous and oxygen atoms. This part of the molecule is polar, so it is attracted to water. The fatty acid end of the molecule is nonpolar, and is not attracted to water.

Cholesterol (kuh-LEHS-tuh-RAWL) is a lipid with a ring structure. Although high cholesterol is a health risk, your body needs a certain amount of cholesterol to function. Cholesterol is part of cell membranes. Cholesterol is also an important part of steroid hormones. Cholesterol-based steroids help your body respond to stress and also control sexual development and the reproductive system.

### FATTY ACIDS

Fatty acid

Fatty acids are long chains of carbon atoms attached to hydrogen atoms.

Butter is made up of fatty acids.

### PHOSPHOLIPID STRUCTURE

Phospholipid

$PO_4^-$

head                tails

A phospholipid has nonpolar fatty acid "tails" and a polar "head" that contains a phosphate group.

## Proteins

Proteins are the most varied of the carbon-based molecules in organisms. There are many different types of proteins. They are involved in many different body functions including movement, eyesight, and digestion.

A **protein** is a polymer made of monomers called amino acids. **Amino acids** are molecules that contain carbon, hydrogen, oxygen, nitrogen, and sometimes sulfur. Organisms use 20 different amino acids to build different types of proteins. Your body can make 12 of the amino acids it needs. The other 8 amino acids come from the foods you eat, such as meat, beans, and nuts.

This part is different for each amino acid monomer.

This part is the same for each amino acid monomer.

Look at the figure at right to see the amino acid called serine. All amino acids have part of their structure that is the same. Another part of their structure is different for each amino acid. The part that is different is called the side group, or R-group. Amino acids are bonded together to form proteins.

---

**AMINO ACID AND PROTEIN STRUCTURE**

All amino acids have a carbon atom bonded to a hydrogen atom, an amino group (NH₂), and a carboxyl group (COOH). Different amino acids have different side groups (**R**).

**Monomer (amino acid)**

peptide bonds

Peptide bonds form between the amino group of one amino acid and the carboxyl group of another amino acid.

**Polymer (protein)**

peptide bonds

A polypeptide is a chain of precisely ordered amino acids linked by peptide bonds. A protein is made of one or more polypeptides.

---

Proteins are different based on the number and order of amino acids. A protein's function depends on the specific order of the amino acids, which affects the shape of the protein. The side groups of each amino acid can interact with each other and affect the protein's shape. For example, hydrogen bonds can form between different side groups.

Hemoglobin is the protein in your red blood cells that transports oxygen. Hemoglobin is made of 574 amino acids. Hydrogen bonds help make the structure of this protein. If just one of the amino acids in hemoglobin changes, the structure of the protein can change in a way that prevents the protein from working properly. A change in one amino acid in hemoglobin causes the disorder called sickle cell anemia.

Typically, red blood cells are shaped like a saucer (left). A change in just one amino acid in hemoglobin can cause cells to have the curved shape characteristic of sickle cell anemia.

## Nucleic Acids

There are two general types of nucleic acids: DNA and RNA. **Nucleic acids** are polymers that are made up of monomers called nucleotides. A nucleotide is made up of a sugar, a phosphate group, and a nitrogen-containing molecule called a base. Nucleic acids contain the instructions to build proteins.

Nucleic acids are different from the other three macromolecules you read about. Carbohydrates, lipids, and proteins have many different structures and functions. Nucleic acids have just one function. They code for proteins. You will learn more about nucleic acids in Unit 3.

 **What are four main types of macromolecules found in living things?**

_____

_____

## 2.3 Vocabulary Check

| | |
|---|---|
| monomer | protein |
| polymer | amino acid |
| carbohydrate | lipid |
| fatty acid | nucleic acid |

**Mark It Up**

Go back and highlight each sentence that has a vocabulary word in **bold**.

1. Name four types of macromolecules. _____

_____

2. A protein is made up of monomers called _____.

3. The carbon chain that makes up part of a lipid is called a _____.

4. A six-carbon sugar is an example of a _____ that can join with other molecules to form a _____ such as starch or cellulose.

## 2.3 The Big Picture

1. What are three different shapes, or structures, of carbon-based molecules?_____

2. Complete the following chart.

| MONOMER | POLYMER | EXAMPLE | FUNCTION |
|---------|---------|---------|----------|
| Glucose | | | |
| | Protein | | |
| | | DNA | |

3. What is a phospholipid?

_____

4. Living things are sometimes called "carbon-based life forms." Do you think this is a good way to describe life? Explain your answer.

_____

# 2.4 Chemical Reactions

**KEY CONCEPT** Life depends on chemical reactions.

## Bonds break and form during chemical reactions.

Plant and animal cells break down sugars to make energy. All cells build protein molecules by bonding amino acids together. These processes are examples of chemical reactions. **Chemical reactions** change substances into different substances by breaking and forming chemical bonds.

### Reactants and Products

The oxygen molecules ($O_2$) that you breathe in are part of a series of chemical reactions. These chemical reactions use oxygen and glucose ($C_6H_{12}O_6$), and produce carbon dioxide ($CO_2$), water ($H_2O$), and energy that your body can use. This process is called cellular respiration.

$$6O_2 + C_6H_{12}O_6 \longrightarrow 6CO_2 + 6H_2O$$

Reactants   Direction   Products

- **Reactants** are the substances that are changed during a chemical reaction. Oxygen and glucose are the reactants in the reaction shown above.
- **Products** are the substances made by a chemical reaction. Carbon dioxide and water are the products of the above reaction.

### Bond Energy

In order for reactants to change into products, the bonds of the reactants must break, and new bonds must form in the products. Breaking a bond requires energy. **Bond energy** is the amount of energy that it takes to break a bond between two atoms. Bonds between different types of atoms have different bond energies. A certain amount of energy is needed to break the bond between two oxygen atoms. A different amount of energy is needed to break the bond between carbon and hydrogen. Energy is released when bonds form.

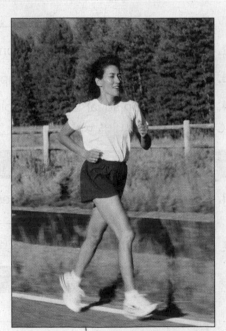

The breakdown of glucose provides chemical energy for all activities, including running.

### Chemical Equilibrium

Some chemical reactions only go one way, from reactants to products, until all the reactants are used up. However, many reactions in living things are reversible. These reactions can move in both directions at the same time. One reaction that goes both directions allows your blood to carry carbon dioxide. Carbon dioxide reacts with water in your blood to form a compound called carbonic acid ($H_2CO_3$).

$$CO_2 + H_2O \rightleftharpoons H_2CO_3$$

The arrows in this equation show that the reaction goes in both directions. Usually, the direction depends on the amounts of each compound. If there is a high concentration of carbon dioxide—like around your cells—the reaction moves toward the right and carbonic acid forms. If there is a low concentration of carbon dioxide—like in your lungs—the reaction goes toward the left and carbonic acid breaks down.

When a reaction takes place at an equal rate in both directions, the concentration, or amounts, of the reactants and products stays the same. **Equilibrium** (EE-kwuh-LIHB-ree-uhm) is when both the reactants and products are made at the same rate.

 In which part of a chemical reaction do bonds break? In which part do they form?

---

# Chemical reactions release or absorb energy.

Energy is both absorbed* and released during a chemical reaction. Some chemical reactions give off more energy than they take in. Other chemical reactions take in more energy than they give off. **Activation energy** is the amount of energy that needs to be absorbed for a chemical reaction to start.

**ACTIVATION ENERGY**

**Activation energy** is the amount of energy that needs to be absorbed for a chemical reaction to start. When enough activation energy is added to the reactants, bonds in the reactants break and the reaction begins.

**ENDOTHERMIC REACTION** Energy Absorbed

An **endothermic** chemical reaction absorbs more energy than it releases. The products have a higher bond energy than the reactants, and the difference in bond energy is absorbed from the surroundings. Photosynthesis is an endothermic reaction.

**EXOTHERMIC REACTION** Energy Released

An **exothermic** chemical reaction releases more energy than it absorbs. The products have a lower bond energy than the reactants, and the difference in bond energy is released to the surroundings. Cellular respiration is an exothermic reaction.

* ACADEMIC VOCABULARY

**absorb** to take in or use

Both **exothermic** and **endothermic** reactions take place in organisms. For example, cellular respiration—the process that uses glucose and oxygen to provide usable energy—is exothermic. It also provides heat that keeps your body warm. Photosynthesis, on the other hand, is endothermic. It absorbs more energy from sunlight than it releases.

 **What is the difference between an exothermic reaction and an endothermic reaction?** _____

_____

## 2.4 Vocabulary Check

**Mark It Up**

Go back and highlight each sentence that has a vocabulary word in **bold**.

| | |
|---|---|
| chemical reaction | equilibrium |
| reactant | activation energy |
| product | exothermic |
| bond energy | endothermic |

**Use the words above to fill in the blanks in the section summary below.**

Making and breaking chemical bonds are examples of **1.** _____. Bonds are broken in the **2.** _____, the chemicals that are changed during the process. Bonds are made in the **3.** _____, the chemicals that result from the process. If a reaction takes place at an equal rate in both directions, it is in **4.** _____. The amount of energy needed to break a bond is called the **5.** _____.

The **6.** _____ is the amount of energy needed to start a reaction. If a reaction absorbs more energy than it releases it is called an **7.** _____ reaction. If a reaction releases more energy than it absorbs it is called an **8.** _____ reaction.

## 2.4 The Big Picture

9. Look at the chemical reaction below. Draw a circle around the reactant(s). Underline the product(s).

   hydrogen peroxide      water       oxygen

   $H_2O_2$ ⟶      $H_2O$   +   $O_2$

10. Imagine a seesaw, like on a children's playground. Which of the following drawings of a seesaw best represents equilibrium? Explain.

# 2.5 Enzymes

**KEY CONCEPT** Enzymes are catalysts for chemical reactions in living things.

## A catalyst lowers activation energy.

Activation energy for a chemical reaction is like the energy that is needed to push a rock up a hill. Once enough energy is added to get the rock to the top of the hill, the rock can roll down the other side by itself.

Under normal conditions, a reaction requires a certain amount of activation energy, and it occurs at a certain rate. Even after a chemical reaction starts, it may happen very slowly. A **catalyst** (KAT-l-ihst) is a substance that decreases the activation energy needed to start a chemical reaction. As a result, a catalyst also increases the rate of the chemical reaction, or makes the products form faster. A catalyst takes part in a chemical reaction, but it does not get changed or used up. Therefore, a catalyst is not considered a reactant or a product.

Activation energy is like the energy you would need to push a rock up a hill.

### CATALYSTS AND ACTIVATION ENERGY

Under normal conditions, a certain amount of activation energy is needed to start a chemical reaction. A catalyst decreases the activation energy needed.

 How does a catalyst affect activation energy?

_____

_____

## Enzymes allow chemical reactions to occur under tightly controlled conditions.

substrates (reactants)

enzyme

Chemical reactions that happen inside organisms must take place under very specific conditions. They have to occur at the temperature of the organism's body. Often, they have to occur with low concentrations of reactants. Reactions must take place very quickly, so they usually need a catalyst. **Enzymes** are catalysts for chemical reactions in living things.

Like other catalysts, enzymes lower the activation energy of chemical reactions and make the reactions happen more quickly. Enzymes are involved in almost every process in organisms. They are needed to break down food, to build proteins, and for your immune system to work.

product

Almost all enzymes are proteins. Like other proteins, enzymes are made of long chains of amino acids. Each enzyme binds a particular reactant, or **substrate.** The substrate fits into a part of the enzyme, like a key fits into a lock. Just like a specific key opens a specific lock, each enzyme acts on a specific substrate. The place on the enzyme where the substrate fits—the lock that the key fits into—is called the active site. Like other proteins, enzymes also depend on structure to function properly. Enzyme structure is important because the shape of an enzyme allows only certain molecules to bind to an enzyme's active site.

An enzyme binds to substrates at the active site. It catalyzes a reaction and then releases the new product that has been formed.

 INSTANT REPLAY    How does the structure of an enzyme affect its function?

_____

| 2.5 | Vocabulary Check |
|---|---|

**Mark It Up**

Go back and highlight each sentence that has a vocabulary word in **bold.**

catalyst          substrate
enzyme

1. A catalyst for reactions in living things is a(n) _____.

2. A(n) _____ is a reactant that binds to a catalyst.

3. An enzyme is a kind of _____.

| 2.5 | The Big Picture |
|---|---|

4. What are two ways a catalyst affects a chemical reaction?

_____

_____

5. A catalyst is not a product or a reactant of a chemical reaction. Why not?

_____

# Chapter 2 Review

1. The pH of four different solutions (a, b, c, and d) are recorded below. Which solution is most acidic?
   a. pH = 3
   b. pH = 7
   c. pH = 10
   d. pH = 14

2. The drawing below represents an atom. Use arrows to show where each of these three parts of an atom are located in the atom's structure.

   **electron**
   **proton**
   **neutron**

3. Why does the order of amino acids affect the structure of a protein?

   _____

4. How does a catalyst affect the activation energy of a chemical reaction?

   _____

5. How are the words *catalyst* and *enzyme* related?

   _____

   _____

6. What kind of bond gives water its important properties of adhesion, cohesion, and high specific heat?

   _____

7. What is the difference between an amino acid and a nucleic acid?

   _____

   _____

8. Photosynthesis is a chemical reaction that uses more energy than it releases. This type of reaction is
   a. endothermic
   b. exothermic
   c. at equilibrium
   d. ionic

9. Complete the chart below about bonds.

| TYPE OF BOND | EXAMPLE OF A MOLECULE WITH THIS TYPE OF BOND | DRAWING OF THIS TYPE OF BOND |
|---|---|---|
| Ionic bond | | |
| Covalent bond | | |
| Hydrogen bond | | |

# CHAPTER

# 3 Cell Structure and Function

## GETTING READY TO LEARN

### Preview Key Concepts

**3.1 Cell Theory**
Cells are the basic unit of life.

**3.2 Cell Organelles**
Eukaryotic cells share many similarities.

**3.3 Cell Membrane**
The cell membrane is a barrier that separates a cell from the external environment.

**3.4 Diffusion and Osmosis**
Materials move across membranes because of concentration differences.

**3.5 Active Transport, Endocytosis, and Exocytosis**
Cells use energy to transport materials that cannot diffuse across a membrane.

### Review Academic Vocabulary

lipid          protein          enzyme          substrate

1. _____ : polymer of amino acids

2. _____ : biological catalysts

3. _____ : examples include fats and cholesterol

4. _____ : what an enzyme works on

### Preview Biology Vocabulary

Try to guess the meaning of each boldfaced word from its context.

| PHRASE | MY GUESS |
|---|---|
| 1. The cell membrane, like a tea bag, is characterized by **selective permeability**. | |
| 2. The smell of baking bread spreads throughout your home by **diffusion**. | |
| 3. Cells in your immune system gobble up invading bacteria and recycle old cell parts through **phagocytosis**. | |

# 3.1 Cell Theory

**KEY CONCEPT** Cells are the basic unit of life.

## Early studies led to the development of the cell theory.

Cells are the very smallest parts of life. All living things are made of cells. However, most cells cannot be seen without a microscope. How did scientists find out about cells when they couldn't see them?

### Discovery of Cells

Over many years, many scientists observed and studied cells under the microscope. As early scientists improved both microscopes and lenses, they could learn more and more about cells. Some of these findings are listed in the table below.

| SCIENTIST (YEAR) | FINDING |
|---|---|
| Hooke (1665) | identified and named cells |
| Leeuwenhoek (1674) | observed living cells; could see greater detail due to better lenses |
| Schleiden (1838) | noted that plants are made of cells |
| Schwann (1839) | concluded that all living things are made of cells |
| Virchow (1855) | proposed that all cells come from other cells |

### Cell Theory

The discoveries of these early scientists came together into the **cell theory.** Today's scientists agree with this cell theory. It says three things:

- All living things are made of cells.
- All cells come from other living cells.
- The cell is the most basic unit of life. There is nothing living that is smaller than a cell.

Underline the part of the cell theory that says where cells come from.

## Prokaryotic cells lack a nucleus and most internal structures of eukaryotic cells.

Cells come in different shapes and carry out different jobs. However, they all share some features. Cells are very small. They are surrounded by a membrane that controls what enters and leaves the cell. They have **cytoplasm,** a jellylike material that contains the building blocks needed for life. And they are made of similar molecules. One of these molecules is DNA, the genetic information.

There are two main types of cells, prokaryotic cells and eukaryotic cells. **Prokaryotic cells** are extremely small. Their DNA floats in the cytoplasm, and they have no distinct* internal parts. Prokaryotes, such as bacteria, are made of only one cell. **Eukaryotic cells** have a nucleus, which is a membrane that separates DNA from the cytoplasm. The nucleus is a type of **organelle,** a small part that carries out a specific job in a cell. Eukaryotic cells have many types of organelles. Like the nucleus, most organelles are covered by a membrane. Eukaryotes, such as plants and animals, are made of one cell or many cells.

 In the text above, circle two things that eukaryotic cells have inside them that prokaryotic cells do not have.

> **VISUAL VOCAB**
>
> **Prokaryotic cells** do not have a nucleus or other membrane-bound organelles.
>
> cytoplasm    DNA    cell membrane
>
> nucleus    organelle
>
> **Eukaryotic cells** have a nucleus and other membrane-bound organelles.

**\* ACADEMIC VOCABULARY**

**distinct**  distinguishable as a separate entity

### 3.1    Vocabulary Check

cell theory          eukaryotic cells
cytoplasm            organelle
prokaryotic cells

> **Mark It Up**
>
> Go back and highlight each sentence that has a vocabulary word in **bold.**

1. Name two types of cells. _____, _____

2. In both types of cells, the jellylike substance is _____.

3. Parts that carry out specific jobs within a cell are _____.

### 3.1    The Big Picture

4. List the three parts of the cell theory. _____
_____
_____

# 3.2 Eukaryotic Cells and Cell Organelles

**KEY CONCEPT** Eukaryotic cells share many similarities.

## Cells have an internal structure.

Your skeleton is made of bones that help keep all your body parts in place. Eukaryotic cells have a skeleton, too. It is called the cytoskeleton. The cytoskeleton is a network of protein fibers. They look like a lot of tiny strings that crisscross a cell. The **cytoskeleton** is the framework of a cell. It gives a cell shape, support, and strength. The cytoskeleton can change as a cell needs to change.

cytoskeleton

The cytoskeleton supports and shapes the cell.

**INSTANT REPLAY** What might a cell look like if it had no cytoskeleton?

_____

_____

## Several organelles are involved in making and processing proteins.

Proteins are a very important type of molecule that are used in all life functions. Basic life functions include reproduction, repair, and growth of injured cells or body parts. Life functions also include the regulation of circulation and digestion systems. You need proteins to digest the foods you eat or to move your muscles when you ride a bike. Proteins are at work when your heart beats or your eye blinks. Some hormones such as insulin, which controls your blood sugar levels, are also proteins.

Proteins are very important, and many organelles work together to make them. These organelles include the nucleus, endoplasmic reticulum, ribosomes, the Golgi apparatus, and vesicles. Ribosomes are found in both eukaryotic and prokaryotic cells. However, the other organelles—those surrounded by a membrane—are found only in eukaryotic cells.

**Nucleus** The **nucleus** stores and protects the DNA of the cell. DNA contains the genes that are the instructions for making proteins.

The nucleus stores and protects DNA.

**Endoplasmic Reticulum (ER)** The **endoplasmic reticulum (ER)** is a network of thin, folded membranes that helps in the production of proteins and other molecules. The membranes are like a maze; they fold back on themselves and have little spaces inside the folds. There are two types of ER, smooth and rough. The rough ER looks bumpy because it has ribosomes attached to it.

**Ribosomes** Ribosomes are tiny organelles that link amino acids together to form proteins. They are found on the surface of the ER and floating freely in the cytoplasm.

**Golgi apparatus** Each **Golgi apparatus** is a stack of layers of membranes. In the Golgi apparatus, proteins are changed, put into packages, and carried to other places in the cell.

**Vesicles** Vesicles are small sacs. They carry different molecules to where they are needed. Vesicles are generally short-lived and are formed and recycled as needed.

The Golgi apparatus modifies, packages, and transports proteins.

 What is the job of the nucleus?

_____

_____

## Other organelles have various functions.

Some organelles do jobs other than making proteins.

**Mitochondria** Mitochondria are bean-shaped organelles that produce chemical energy that is usable by a cell. They have two membranes. The inner membrane has lots of folds that form compartments. Mitochondria also have their own ribosomes and DNA. At one time, mitochondria may have been independent prokaryotes that were taken in by larger cells.

Mitochondria generate usable energy for the cell.

**Vacuoles** Vacuoles are sacs of fluids that store materials in a cell. These materials include water, food molecules, ions, and enzymes. Many plant cells have a large central vacuole. When filled with fluid, the central vacuole exerts pressure that can help support the plant.

**Lysosomes** Lysosomes are organelles that contain enzymes. They protect a cell by attacking incoming bacteria or viruses. They also break down old cell parts.

**Centrioles** Centrioles are shaped like cylinders. They are made of tiny tubes in a circle. They move when animal cells divide in two. Centrioles help form cilia and flagella, structures that help cells to move or to move liquids past a cell. Centrioles are surrounded by the centrosome. The centrosome is a small region of cytoplasm that organizes proteins into fibers that help cells divide.

Centrioles are separated during cell division. They help form cilia and flagella.

 Highlight the organelle that produces usable energy for a cell.

# SUMMARY OF CELL STRUCTURE

Eukaryotic cells have highly organized structures, including membrane-bound organelles. Plant and animal cells share many of the same types of organelles, but both also have organelles that are unique to their needs.

## PLANT CELL

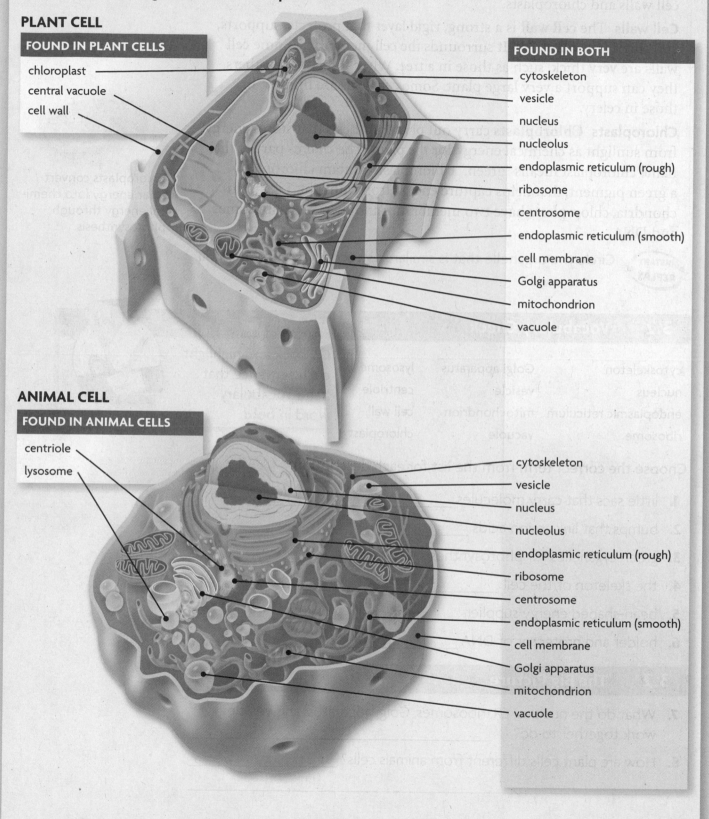

**FOUND IN PLANT CELLS**

- chloroplast
- central vacuole
- cell wall

**FOUND IN BOTH**

- cytoskeleton
- vesicle
- nucleus
- nucleolus
- endoplasmic reticulum (rough)
- ribosome
- centrosome
- endoplasmic reticulum (smooth)
- cell membrane
- Golgi apparatus
- mitochondrion
- vacuole

## ANIMAL CELL

**FOUND IN ANIMAL CELLS**

- centriole
- lysosome

- cytoskeleton
- vesicle
- nucleus
- nucleolus
- endoplasmic reticulum (rough)
- ribosome
- centrosome
- endoplasmic reticulum (smooth)
- cell membrane
- Golgi apparatus
- mitochondrion
- vacuole

# Plant cells have cell walls and chloroplasts.

Plant cells have two parts that animal cells do not have. Plant cells have cell walls and chloroplasts.

**Cell walls**  The **cell wall** is a strong, rigid layer that protects, supports, and shapes the plant cell. It surrounds the cell membrane. Some cell walls are very thick, such as those in a tree. When joined with others, they can support a very large plant. Some cell walls are thinner, like those in celery.

**Chloroplasts**  **Chloroplasts** carry out photosynthesis that stores energy from sunlight as chemical energy for the plant. The *chloro-* part of the name chloroplast means "green." Chloroplasts contain chlorophyll, a green pigment, that helps capture energy from sunlight. Like mitochondria, chloroplasts have two membranes and their own ribosomes and DNA.

Chloroplasts convert solar energy into chemical energy through photosynthesis.

  Circle the organelle that is similar in structure to mitochondria.

## 3.2  Vocabulary Check

**Mark It Up**

Go back and highlight each sentence that has a vocabulary word in **bold**.

| cytoskeleton | Golgi apparatus | lysosome |
| nucleus | vesicle | centriole |
| endoplasmic reticulum | mitochondrion | cell wall |
| ribosome | vacuole | chloroplast |

Choose the correct term from the list for each description.

1. little sacs that carry molecules _____
2. bumps that link amino acids _____
3. green organelles for photosynthesis _____
4. the skeleton of the cell _____
5. bean-shaped energy supplier _____
6. holder and protector of DNA _____

## 3.2  The Big Picture

7. What do the nucleus, ER, ribosomes, Golgi apparatus, and vesicles work together to do? _____
8. How are plant cells different from animals cells? _____
_____

# 3.3 Cell Membrane

**KEY CONCEPT** The cell membrane is a barrier that separates a cell from the external environment.

## Cell membranes are composed of two phospholipid layers.

The **cell membrane** is the package that a cell comes in. It is a thin layer that separates the inside of the cell from the outside of the cell. It controls what comes into and goes out of the cell. The cell membrane is made up of a double layer of phospholipids. A **phospholipid** is made of three parts: a phosphate group, a glycerol, and two fatty acid chains.

The phosphate group and glycerol make up the "head." The fatty acids make up the "tail." In the cell membrane, phospholipids are arranged tail-to-tail so that the heads face outward. The phosphate group has an electrical charge, so the heads on the outside are polar. They interact with water. All through the two layers of phospholipids are other molecules. Some are proteins; some are cholesterol; some are carbohydrates.

**VISUAL VOCAB**

A **phospholipid** is composed of three basic parts:

— charged phosphate group

— glycerol

— two fatty acid chains

**CELL MEMBRANE**

The cell membrane is made of two phospholipid layers embedded with other molecules, such as proteins, carbohydrates, and cholesterol.

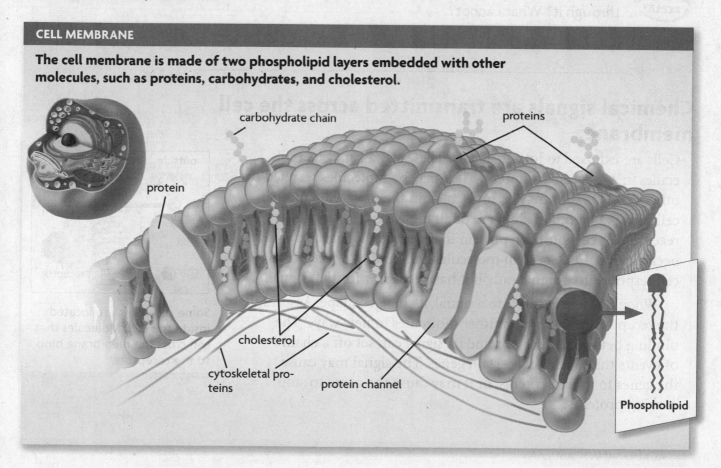

carbohydrate chain

proteins

protein

cholesterol

cytoskeletal proteins

protein channel

Phospholipid

### Fluid Mosaic Model

Scientists have developed the **fluid mosaic model** to describe the cell membrane. The membrane is fluid because the phospholipids in each layer can move and slide. It acts like a film of oil on the surface of water. The membrane is like a mosaic because of all the different molecules embedded* among the phospholipids. Together, they look like a mosaic.

### Selective Permeability

The cell membrane has **selective permeability**. This means that it allows some materials, but not all, to cross it, or permeate it. In other words, the cell membrane is semipermeable. You might own a semipermeable jacket. The jacket is waterproof; it does not allow water in from the outside. But water vapor from your sweat can exit through the fabric. Just like the jacket, a semipermeable cell membrane lets only some materials through.

In a cell, small nonpolar molecules can usually cross the membrane by themselves. Small polar molecules can be carried by proteins. Large molecules can be moved in vesicles.

 Name another semipermeable object. What can pass through it? What cannot?

_____

_____

A selectively permeable membrane allows some, but not all, molecules to cross.

## Chemical signals are transmitted across the cell membrane.

Cells are exposed to lots of signals. These signals may be molecules in a cell's environment. They may be molecules secreted by other cells. Or they may be molecules on the surface of another cell. How can a cell make sense of all these signals? Cells have receptors. A **receptor** is a protein that detects a signal and acts because of it. Only certain molecules will bind to a receptor. A cell responds to a signal only if it has a receptor for that signal.

When a receptor binds to a signal, it changes shape. As a result, the receptor interacts with other molecules in new ways. The binding between a receptor and its signal can set off a chain of events that will affect certain genes. The signal may cause the genes to make proteins, or it may cause the genes to stop making proteins.

Some receptors are located inside the cell. Molecules that can cross the membrane bind to the receptors.

* ACADEMIC VOCABULARY

**embedded** to be completely enclosed in; to make an integral part of something

Cells have receptors both inside the cell and in the cell membrane. Recall that some molecules can easily cross the cell membrane, but others cannot. Molecules that can cross the membrane bind to receptors inside the cell. Molecules that cannot cross the membrane bind to receptors in the membrane. When the signal binds to a receptor, the receptor changes its shape. Other molecules inside the cell respond to the changing shape of the receptor. The signal molecule itself never enters the cell.

Molecules that cannot enter the cell bind to receptors in the membrane. When bound, the receptor transmits the signal inside the cell by changing shape.

 How does a receptor in the membrane transmit a message to the cell? _____

_____

_____

## 3.3    Vocabulary Check

cell membrane          selective permeability
phospholipid           receptor
fluid mosaic model

**Mark It Up**

Go back and highlight each sentence that has a vocabulary word in **bold**.

Circle the correct word from the choices below.

1. Which material has selective permeability, a sponge or a shovel?

2. Which contains the other, cell membrane or phospholipid?

3. Which receives signals, a fluid mosaic model or a receptor?

## 3.3    The Big Picture

4. What does the cell membrane do for the cell? _____

_____

5. Describe how the phospholipids are arranged in the cell membrane.

_____

_____

6. Do cells respond to every signal? Explain. _____

_____

7. Explain how a tea bag is an example of selective permeability. _____

_____

# Diffusion and Osmosis

**KEY CONCEPT** Materials move across membranes because of concentration differences.

## Diffusion and osmosis are types of passive transport.

Cells are constantly taking in and sending out substances. But cells do not have to use energy to move all those molecules. **Passive transport** is the movement (transport) of molecules without a cell using energy (passive).

Passive transport is the movement of molecules across the membrane from areas of higher concentration to areas of lower concentration. It does not require energy input from the cell.

### Concentration

Concentration is the amount of molecules of one type in an area. If there are few molecules, the area has a low concentration. If there are many molecules, the area has a high concentration. Concentration can vary from one region to another. A **concentration gradient** is the difference in the concentration of a substance from one location to another. Molecules move from one place to another because of this difference in concentration.

**Diffusion** is the movement of molecules from a place of higher concentration to a place of lower concentration. When molecules diffuse, they are described as moving down their concentration gradient*. The diffusion of molecules across the cell membrane is a type of passive transport. It happens because of the natural motion of particles. Diffusion does not need energy from a cell.

The diffusion of water molecules is called **osmosis.** The process of osmosis is exactly the same as diffusion but refers only to water molecules. Water molecules diffuse across a membrane from a place of higher water concentration to a place of lower water concentration.

### Solutions

If you dissolve salt in water, you have made a solution. The more salt you put in the water, the higher the concentration of salt becomes, and the lower the concentration of water becomes. The salt is the solute, and the water is the solvent.

Cells are usually surrounded by fluid. The type of solution that a cell is in can have a big effect on the cell. There are three types of solutions: isotonic, hypotonic, and hypertonic. These terms are comparisons. They compare the concentration of one solution to the concentration of another solution.

* ACADEMIC VOCABULARY

**gradient** a slope or incline; the change in a quantity per unit distance

- A solution is **isotonic** to a cell if it has the same concentration of solutes that the cell has. *Iso-* means "equal." In an isotonic solution, water moves into and out of a cell at equal rates. As a result, cell size remains constant.
- A solution is **hypertonic** if it has a higher concentration of solutes than a cell. *Hyper-* means "more." This means the cell has a higher concentration of water than the surrounding fluid. As a result, water diffuses out of the cell, and the cell shrivels.
- A solution is **hypotonic** if it has a lower concentration of solutes than a cell. *Hypo-* means "less." This means the cell has a lower concentration of water than the surrounding fluid. As a result, water diffuses into the cell, and the cell grows larger.

Notice how water moves from the area of higher water concentration to the area of lower water concentration in two of the pictures below.

## EFFECTS OF OSMOSIS

**Osmosis is the diffusion of water across a semipermeable membrane from an area of higher water concentration to an area of lower water concentration.**

### 1 ISOTONIC SOLUTION

isotonic

isotonic

A solution is isotonic to a cell if it has the same concentration of solutes as the cell. Equal amounts of water enter and exit the cell, so its size stays constant.

### 2 HYPERTONIC SOLUTION

hypertonic

hypotonic

A hypertonic solution has more solute than a cell. Overall, more water exits a cell that is in a hypertonic solution, causing the cell to shrivel or even die.

### 3 HYPOTONIC SOLUTION

hypotonic

hypertonic

A hypotonic solution has less solute than a cell. Overall, more water enters a cell that is in a hypotonic solution, causing the cell to expand or even burst.

INSTANT REPLAY

In each picture above, mark a plus (+) where the water concentration is higher, and a minus (−) where it is lower.

## Some molecules diffuse through selective transport proteins.

If some molecules can't diffuse through the cell membrane by themselves, they can get help. Transport proteins give them a ride through the membrane. This process is called **facilitated diffusion.** The word *facilitate* means "to make easier." Different transport proteins make it easier for certain molecules to get through the cell membrane without a cell using energy. Facilitated diffusion is another type of passive transport.

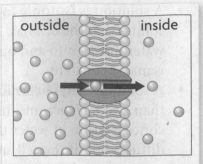

Facilitated diffusion enables molecules that cannot directly cross the phospholipid bilayer to diffuse through transport proteins in the membrane.

 In facilitated diffusion, do molecules move down their concentration gradient? Explain. _____

_____

_____

| 3.4 | **Vocabulary Check** | **Mark It Up** |
| --- | --- | --- |

passive transport      isotonic

concentration gradient    hypertonic

diffusion             hypotonic

osmosis           facilitated diffusion

**Mark It Up**

Go back and highlight each sentence that has a vocabulary word in **bold.**

**1.** Which two words mean nearly the same thing? _____

_____

**2.** Which word includes a "helper?" _____

**3.** Which word describes a slope? _____

## 3.4  The Big Picture

**4.** How does passive transport benefit a cell? _____

_____

**5.** Why do cells need facilitated diffusion? _____

_____

**6.** Why does a cell swell in a hypotonic solution? _____

_____

_____

# 3.5 Active Transport, Endocytosis, Exocytosis

**KEY CONCEPT** Cells use energy to transport materials that cannot diffuse across a membrane.

## Proteins can transport materials against a concentration gradient.

You have seen that the cell membrane controls the passive transport of materials into and out of a cell. However, cells often need large amounts of materials that cannot diffuse across the membrane. Cells can use energy to move molecules from an area of lower concentration to an area of higher concentration. This process is called **active transport.** As the figure shows, active transport uses energy to drive molecules through transport proteins. This process plays an important role in helping cells to maintain homeostasis.

What is the difference between active transport and passive transport? _____

_____

During active transport, a cell uses energy to move substances against a concentration gradient—that is, from a lower to a higher concentration.

## Endocytosis and exocytosis transport materials across the membrane in vesicles.

Sometimes a material is too large to cross the membrane. Cells can use energy to transport these materials in vesicles. A cell uses **endocytosis** to take in large materials or liquids. The prefix *endo-* means "in." In endocytosis, the cell membrane starts to fold in, forming a pocket around a substance. The pocket breaks off inside the cell, making a vesicle. The contents of the vesicle are then broken down or released into the cell.

**Phagocytosis** (FAG-uh-sy-TOH-sihs) is a type of endocytosis in which the cell membrane grows out to surround large particles. The word literally means "cell eating." Phagocytosis plays an important role in the immune system when white blood cells "eat" bacteria and other invaders.

1  The cell membrane folds inward, enclosing the substance in a pocket.

2  The pocket pinches off inside the cell, forming a vesicle.

3  The vesicle fuses with a lysosome, where enzymes break it down.

**Exocytosis** is the opposite of endocytosis. The prefix *exo-* means "out." It is the process that moves substances out of the cell. In exocytosis, a vesicle surrounds materials that need to be removed. The vesicle then goes to the cell membrane, fuses with it, and lets go of the contents. Exocytosis is the cell's way of getting rid of wastes or secreting molecules.

**1** The cell forms a vesicle around material that needs to be removed or secreted.

**2** The vesicle is transported to the cell membrane.

**3** The vesicle membrane fuses with the cell membrane and releases the contents.

 What functions do endocytosis and exocytosis carry out for the cell?

_____

_____

## 3.5 Vocabulary Check

**Mark It Up**

Go back and highlight each sentence that has a vocabulary word in **bold**.

active transport     phagocytosis
endocytosis     exocytosis

1. Draw the last step of exocytosis at right.

> **1.**
>
> **2.**

2. Draw the first step of endocytosis at right.

## 3.5 The Big Picture

3. The biggest difference between active transport and passive transport is the need for the cell to use _____.

4. Draw a Venn diagram in the space to the right to compare and contrast exocytosis and endocytosis.

# Chapter 3 Review

1. What are the three major parts of the cell theory? _____

   _____

   _____

2. Label the organelles shown below, and write a brief description of their functions.

   _____ _____ _____ _____

   _____ _____ _____ _____

   _____ _____ _____ _____

3. Which of the following is an example of selective permeability?

   **a.** a magnet          **c.** a milk jug

   **b.** a window screen    **d.** a bottle rocket

4. The head of a phospholipid interacts with water because it is _____.

5. Diffusion is an example of

   **a.** passive transport    **c.** active transport

   **b.** membrane receptors   **d.** transport proteins

6. A _____ solution has a higher concentration of solutes than a cell.

7. A _____ is a protein that recognizes and responds to a signal.

8. Label each of the figures below with one of the following terms: exocytosis, active transport, endocytosis, or facilitated diffusion. Draw a star beside the processes that require a cell to use energy.

   _____ _____ _____ _____

# 4 Cells and Energy

## GETTING READY TO LEARN

### Preview Key Concepts

**4.1 Chemical Energy and ATP**
All cells need chemical energy.

**4.2 Overview of Photosynthesis**
The overall process of photosynthesis produces sugars that store chemical energy.

**4.3 Photosynthesis in Detail**
Photosynthesis requires a series of chemical reactions.

**4.4 Overview of Cellular Respiration**
The overall process of cellular respiration converts sugar into ATP using oxygen.

**4.5 Cellular Respiration in Detail**
Cellular respiration is an aerobic process with two main stages.

**4.6 Fermentation**
Fermentation allows the production of a small amount of ATP without oxygen.

### Review Academic Vocabulary

Write the correct word for each definition.

carbohydrate      mitochondria      enzyme

1. _____ : convert food into usable energy

2. _____ : molecule broken down as a source of energy

3. _____ : decreases activation energy for reactions

### Preview Biology Vocabulary

Two key terms from this chapter share the same word part. Read the definitions and guess what the word part means.

| TERM | DEFINITION | WHAT I THINK THE WORD PART MEANS |
|------|------------|----------------------------------|
| **aerobic** | describes reactions that require oxygen | |
| **anaerobic** | describes reactions that do not require oxygen | |

# 4.1 Chemical Energy and ATP

**KEY CONCEPT** All cells need chemical energy.

## The chemical energy used by most cell processes is carried by ATP.

Chemical energy is used by all organisms and is needed for all life processes. The chemical energy that all cells use is in the form of ATP, which stands for **a**denosine **tri**phosphate. **ATP** is a molecule that carries energy that cells can use. This energy comes from the breakdown of food molecules. The energy from the food is transferred by ATP. When ATP gets broken down, the energy is released.

ATP has three phosphate groups. The bond that holds the third phosphate molecule is easily broken. When the third phosphate is removed, energy is released. Then, the molecule becomes ADP, which stands for **a**denosine **di**phosphate. ADP does not carry energy that cells can use. The difference between ATP and ADP is

- ATP has three phosphate groups and is high energy
- ADP has two phosphate groups and is lower energy

**ADP** is a lower-energy molecule. If another phosphate is added to ADP, it becomes ATP again, and is high energy. The energy that comes from breaking down food is used to convert ADP into ATP.

**VISUAL VOCAB**

**ATP** transfers energy to cell processes.

adenosine    **tri**phosphate

tri = 3

**ADP** is a lower-energy molecule that can be converted into ATP.

adenosine    **di**phosphate

di = 2

phosphate added

adenosine triphosphate

phosphate removed

energy

energy from breakdown of molecules

energy

energy released for cell functions

adenosine diphosphate

What is the role of ATP in living things?

_____

## Organisms break down carbon-based molecules to produce ATP.

Foods that you eat do not contain ATP that your cells can use. First, the food must be digested. Digestion breaks down the food into smaller molecules—such as carbohydrates, lipids, and proteins—that your cells can use to make ATP.

The amount of ATP produced depends on the type of molecule that is broken down. A molecule of the simple sugar glucose produces about 36 molecules of ATP. A typical fat molecule produces about 146 molecules of ATP. A protein molecule produces about 36 molecules of ATP, similar to a sugar. However, protein is usually not used for energy. Instead, proteins are broken down into amino acids that are used to build more proteins.

The foods you eat are digested into carbon-based molecules such as carbohydrates, lipids, and proteins.

Plant cells also need ATP. But plants do not eat food the way animals must. Instead, plants make their own food. Through the process of photosynthesis, plants use energy from sunlight to make sugars. Plant cells then break down these sugars to produce ATP, just like animal cells do. The process of photosynthesis is described in Sections 4.2 and 4.3.

In the section above, circle the names of three carbon-based molecules that your cells can use to make ATP.

## A few types of organisms do not need sunlight and photosynthesis as a source of energy.

Some organisms, such as plants, use sunlight and photosynthesis to make their own source of energy. Other organisms, like us, need sunlight and photosynthesis for our source of energy, too, because we eat plants. We also eat other animals—but those animals ate plants that got their energy from sunlight and photosynthesis. Most organisms need sunlight and photosynthesis either directly or indirectly for energy.

But some organisms do not need sunlight. In the deep ocean, for example, there are areas too deep for sunlight to reach, but some organisms are able to live there. These organisms live near cracks in the ocean floor that release chemical compounds, such as sulfides. The organisms that live there use these chemicals as their energy source.

**Chemosynthesis** (KEE-mo-SIHN-thih-sihs) is a process by which some organisms use chemical energy—instead of light energy—as an energy source to make their own food. These organisms still need ATP for energy. The way they make their ATP is very similar to how other organisms make ATP.

 **INSTANT REPLAY** What is the source of energy for organisms that use chemosynthesis?

_____

| 4.1 | **Vocabulary Check** |
|---|---|

**Mark It Up**

Go back and highlight each sentence that has a vocabulary word in **bold.**

ATP                    chemosynthesis

ADP

**Choose the correct term from the list for each description.**

1. high-energy molecule with 3 phosphates _____

2. lower-energy molecule with 2 phosphates _____

3. use of chemicals as an energy source _____

| 4.1 | **The Big Picture** |
|---|---|

4. Label the ATP and ADP molecules in the diagram below.

5. The word beginning *chemo-* means "chemical." *Synthesis* means "making something through chemical reactions." How does the meaning of the word parts relate to the meaning of the term *chemosynthesis*?

_____

# Overview of Photosynthesis

**KEY CONCEPT** The overall process of photosynthesis produces sugars that store chemical energy.

## Photosynthetic organisms are producers.

Some organisms are called producers because they produce their own sources of chemical energy. Other organisms also use the chemical energy that producers make. Plants are producers. Plants capture energy from sunlight, and store it as chemical energy in the form of sugars. These sugars are made through **photosynthesis.** Remember from Section 3.2 that chloroplasts are organelles in plant cells where photosynthesis takes place.

**Chlorophyll** (KLAWR-uh-fihl) is a molecule in chloroplasts that absorbs some of the energy in visible* light. Plants use energy in visible light for photosynthesis. Visible light looks white, but it is made up of different wavelengths, or colors, of light.

Plants have two kinds of chlorophyll, called chlorophyll *a* and chlorophyll *b*. These two types of chlorophyll absorb red and blue wavelengths of light. Neither type of chlorophyll absorbs much green light. Plants are green because green wavelengths of light are reflected by chlorophyll.

 What is the role of chlorophyll in photosynthesis?

## Photosynthesis in plants occurs in chloroplasts.

Chloroplasts are plant cell organelles. Two main parts of chloroplasts are needed for photosynthesis:

- The grana (singular, *granum*) are stacks of compartments called **thylakoids** (THY-luh-KOYDZ). Thylakoids are shaped like coins, flat and circular. The thylakoid compartments are enclosed by membranes. These membranes contain chlorophyll.
- The stroma is fluid that is all around the grana inside the chloroplast.

There are two stages of photosynthesis, which are called the light-dependent reactions and the light-independent reactions.

The **light-dependent* reactions** capture energy from sunlight. These reactions happen in the thylakoids and their membranes. Chlorophyll

chloroplast

Chloroplasts in plant cells contain a light-absorbing molecule called chlorophyll, not shown here.

* ACADEMIC VOCABULARY

**dependent** needs something to function

**visible** able to be seen

absorbs energy from sunlight. The energy moves along the thylakoid membrane and is transferred to molecules that carry energy, such as ATP. During this process, water ($H_2O$) molecules are broken down, and oxygen ($O_2$) molecules are released.

The **light-independent\* reactions** use the energy from the light-dependent reactions to make sugars. These reactions happen in the stroma. During this process, carbon dioxide ($CO_2$) and energy from the light-dependent reactions are used to build sugars, usually glucose ($C_6H_{12}O_6$).

The equation for the whole process of photosynthesis is shown below. You can see that there are many arrows between the reactants—$6CO_2$ and $6H_2O$—and the products—$C_6H_{12}O_6$ and $6O_2$. Although there is only one arrow, there are many steps in the process.

$$6CO_2 \quad + \quad 6H_2O \quad \xrightarrow{\text{light, enzymes}} \quad C_6H_{12}O_6 \quad + \quad 6O_2$$

Carbon Dioxide    Water    light, enzymes    a sugar    oxygen

## OVERVIEW OF PHOTOSYNTHESIS

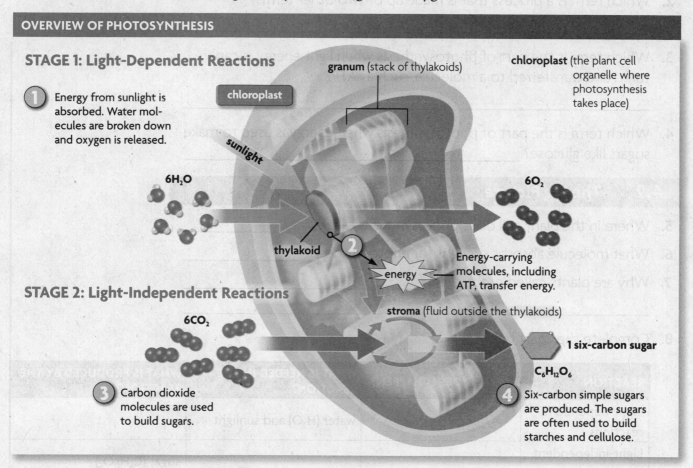

**STAGE 1: Light-Dependent Reactions**

**granum** (stack of thylakoids)

**chloroplast** (the plant cell organelle where photosynthesis takes place)

chloroplast

1 Energy from sunlight is absorbed. Water molecules are broken down and oxygen is released.

sunlight

$6H_2O$

$6O_2$

thylakoid

2 energy

Energy-carrying molecules, including ATP, transfer energy.

**STAGE 2: Light-Independent Reactions**

**stroma** (fluid outside the thylakoids)

$6CO_2$

1 six-carbon sugar

$C_6H_{12}O_6$

3 Carbon dioxide molecules are used to build sugars.

4 Six-carbon simple sugars are produced. The sugars are often used to build starches and cellulose.

INSTANT REPLAY    Circle the four main steps of photosynthesis shown on the diagram.

\* ACADEMIC VOCABULARY

**independent** can function without something

Simple sugars, such as glucose, are not the only carbohydrates that come from photosynthesis. Plants use simple sugars to build starch and cellulose molecules. Another important product of photosynthesis is oxygen. You will read more about that in Sections 4.4 and 4.5.

## 4.2 Vocabulary Check

photosynthesis          light-dependent reactions
chlorophyll             light-independent reactions
thylakoid

**Mark It Up**

Go back and highlight each sentence that has a vocabulary word in **bold**.

1. Which two terms are things that are found in the chloroplast?

   _____

2. Which term is a process that is made up of two other terms?

   _____

3. Which term is the part of photosynthesis when light energy is captured and transferred to a molecule, such as ATP?

   _____

4. Which term is the part of photosynthesis when energy is used to make sugars like glucose? _____

## 4.2 The Big Picture

5. Where in the plant cell does photosynthesis take place? _____

6. What molecule absorbs sunlight for photosynthesis? _____

7. Why are plants called *producers*? _____

   _____

8. Complete the chart below.

| REACTION | WHERE DOES IT HAPPEN? | WHAT IS NEEDED IN THE REACTION? | WHAT IS PRODUCED BY THE REACTION? |
|---|---|---|---|
| Light-dependent reactions | | water ($H_2O$) and sunlight | |
| Light-independent reactions | | | sugar ($C_6H_{12}O_6$) |

# 4.3 Photosynthesis in Detail

**KEY CONCEPT** Photosynthesis requires a series of chemical reactions.

## The first stage of photosynthesis captures and transfers energy.

In Section 4.2 you read a summary of photosynthesis. Now, we will look at the process more closely. During the light-dependent reactions, energy is captured from sunlight and moved along the thylakoid membrane. This process involves two groups of molecules called **photosystems.** The two photosystems are called photosystem I* and photosystem II*. Both photosystems absorb energy from sunlight.

### Photosystem II and Electron Transport

In photosystem II, several things happen.

- Chlorophyll and other light-absorbing molecules absorb energy from sunlight. The energy is transferred to electrons (e⁻) that leave the chlorophyll. These high-energy electrons enter the **electron transport chain,** which is made of proteins in the thylakoid membrane.
- Water molecules are split apart into oxygen, hydrogen ions, and electrons. The oxygen is released—the same oxygen you breathe. The electrons from water take the place of the electrons that left the chlorophyll.
- Electrons in the electron transport chain move from protein to protein. Their energy pumps hydrogen ions (H⁺) across the thylakoid membrane, from outside the thylakoid to inside. The transport of H⁺ ions across the membrane makes the inside of the thylakoid have a higher concentration of H⁺ ions than on the outside of the thylakoid membrane. When there is a difference in the concentration of a substance—like there is here with H⁺ ions—it is called a concentration gradient.

### Photosystem I and Energy-Carrying Molecules

In photosystem I, several things happen.

- The electrons from photosystem II move on to photosystem I. In addition, chlorophyll absorbs energy from sunlight, which results in even more high-energy electrons.
- The electrons are added to NADP⁺, a molecule that is similar to ADP. This makes NADPH, a molecule that acts a lot like ATP.

> **NOTE:**
> The photosystems are named I and II because they were discovered in that order. The numbers do not refer to the order of the process. In other words, photosystem I does not happen first.

thylakoid

**Light-dependent reactions take place in and across the thylakoid membrane.**

* ACADEMIC VOCABULARY

**I and II** part of a number system called Roman numerals, I = 1 and II = 2

- The concentration gradient in the thylokoid, described previously, provides the energy to make ATP. The $H^+$ ions will diffuse, or flow, back out of the thylakoid through a channel* in the membrane. This channel is part of an enzyme called **ATP synthase.** As the $H^+$ ions flow through ATP synthase, phosphate groups are added to ADP to make ATP. The energy from both ATP and NADPH is used later to make sugars.

**LIGHT-DEPENDENT REACTIONS**

**Photosystem II and electron transport**

**1** Energy is absorbed from sunlight.

**3** Hydrogen ions are transported across the thylakoid membrane.

inside the thylakoid

thylakoid membrane

stroma

chlorophyll

**2** Water molecules are broken down.

$2e^-$ $2H^+$

$H_2O$ $\frac{1}{2}O_2$

electron transport chain in the thylakoid membrane

**Photosystem I and energy-carrying molecules**

**4** Energy is absorbed from sunlight.

**6** Hydrogen ions diffuse through a protein channel.

ATP synthase

$2e^-$

NADP$^+$

NADPH

ADP

+P

$H^+$

ATP

**5** NADPH is produced when electrons are added to NADP$^+$.

**7** ADP is changed into ATP when hydrogen ions flow through ATP synthase.

Circle the part of the figure above that shows ADP turning into ATP when $H^+$ ions flow through ATP synthase.

# The second stage of photosynthesis uses energy from the first stage to make sugars.

The second stage of photosynthesis is the light-independent reactions. This stage also happens in the chloroplast—but in the stroma, not in the thylakoids. This stage is light-independent because it does not need light. These reactions use energy from ATP and NADPH to run the chemical reactions that make up the Calvin cycle. The chemical reactions of the **Calvin cycle** use carbon dioxide ($CO_2$) and energy from ATP and NADPH to make sugars.

stroma (fluid)

**Light-independent reactions take place in the stroma.**

* ACADEMIC VOCABULARY

**channel** a passage, or a space that can be moved through

**THE CALVIN CYCLE**

1. Carbon dioxide ($CO_2$) molecules enter the cycle and are added to five-carbon molecules. Six-carbon molecules are formed.

2. Energy is added. The six-carbon molecules split to form three-carbon molecules. More energy is added and the molecules are rearranged into higher-energy molecules.

3. A high-energy three-carbon molecule exits for every 3 $CO_2$ molecules that enter. After 2 three-carbon molecules have exited, they bond to form 1 six-carbon sugar.

4. Three-carbon molecules are changed back to five-carbon molecules by energy from ATP.

Photosynthesis is important for many reasons. Plants produce food for themselves and for other organisms. They use the sugars from photosynthesis to build carbohydrates necessary for plant growth and development. Photosynthesis also removes carbon dioxide from Earth's atmosphere and produces the oxygen that you breathe.

 **INSTANT REPLAY** Circle the product of the Calvin cycle in the diagram above.

## 4.3    Vocabulary Check

photosystem                    ATP synthase
electron transport chain       Calvin cycle

**Mark It Up**
Go back and highlight each sentence that has a vocabulary word in **bold**.

1. Which part of photosynthesis produces sugars? _____

2. What molecule adds a phosphate group to ADP to make ATP? _____

3. What groups of molecules are involved in photosynthesis? _____

4. What is the name for the set of proteins in the thylakoid membrane that electrons move through? _____

## 4.3    The Big Picture

5. In which stage of photosynthesis does electron transport begin? In which stage is sunlight needed? _____

6. What is the main product of the Calvin cycle? _____

7. What are the reactants of photosynthesis? What are the products?

_____

# 4.4 Overview of Cellular Respiration

**KEY CONCEPT** The overall process of cellular respiration converts sugar into ATP using oxygen.

## Cellular respiration makes ATP by breaking down sugars.

You probably know that you need to breathe oxygen to survive. But how does your body use that oxygen? That oxygen helps your body to release chemical energy that is stored in sugars and other carbon-based molecules. The energy is released to produce ATP. This process of using oxygen to produce ATP by breaking down carbon-based molecules is called **cellular respiration.** Cellular respiration makes most of the ATP that a cell needs. Cellular respiration is an aerobic process. **Aerobic** (air-OH-bihk) means that it needs oxygen to happen.

Cellular respiration takes place in mitochondria. These organelles are sometimes called the cell's "powerhouses" because this is where most of the cell's ATP is made. Mitochondria do not make ATP directly from food. ATP is made through many chemical reactions.

Before cellular respiration can happen, food has to be broken down into smaller molecules. Food gets broken down into smaller molecules like glucose. Then, glucose gets broken down. Remember that glucose is a six-carbon sugar. **Glycolysis** (gly-KAHL-uh-sihs) breaks glucose into two molecules that each have three carbons.

Mitochondria (middle) are found in both animal (top) and plant (bottom) cells. They make ATP through cellular respiration.

glucose            2 three-carbon molecules

Glycolysis breaks glucose into 2 three-carbon molecules.

Glycolysis is an anaerobic process. **Anaerobic** means that it does not need oxygen to happen. Glycolysis happens in the cell's cytoplasm. The three-carbon molecules from glycolysis then enter the mitochondria. The products of glycolysis—the three-carbon molecules—enter the mitochondria and are used in cellular respiration.

 **INSTANT REPLAY** Why is cellular respiration called an aerobic process?

_____

# Cellular respiration is like a mirror image of photosynthesis.

A mirror image is like an opposite—the same thing, but in reverse. Cellular respiration and photosynthesis are not really opposites, but it can be helpful to think about them in that way. Photosynthesis makes sugars and cellular respiration breaks down sugars. The chemical equations of the two processes are basically opposites.

The structures of mitochondria and chloroplasts are very similar. Remember that part of photosynthesis happens inside the stroma—the fluid in the chloroplast—and part of photosynthesis happens inside the membrane of the thylakoid. Similarly, part of cellular respiration happens in the fluid inside the mitochondria, called the matrix. The other part of cellular respiration happens in the inner membrane of the mitochondria.

After glycolysis, the three-carbon molecules enter the mitochondria and begin the process of cellular respiration. There are two main parts of cellular respiration:

**COMPARING PROCESSES**

Photosynthesis

REACTANTS — PRODUCTS

light energy

$CO_2$ → Sugars ($C_6H_{12}O_6$)

$H_2O$ → $O_2$

Cellular Respiration

PRODUCTS — REACTANTS

$CO_2$ ← Sugars ($C_6H_{12}O_6$)

$H_2O$ ← $O_2$

ATP, heat energy

The products of photosynthesis—sugars and $O_2$—are the reactants in cellular respiration.

**Stage 1: Krebs cycle**  The molecules from glycolysis enter a series of reactions called the Krebs cycle. The **Krebs cycle** produces a small amount of ATP and other molecules that carry energy to the next part of cellular respiration. It also makes carbon dioxide as a waste product.

**Stage 2: Electron Transport**  Energy is moved through a chain of proteins and a large number of ATP molecules are made. Oxygen enters the process here. The oxygen is used to make water molecules, which are waste products.

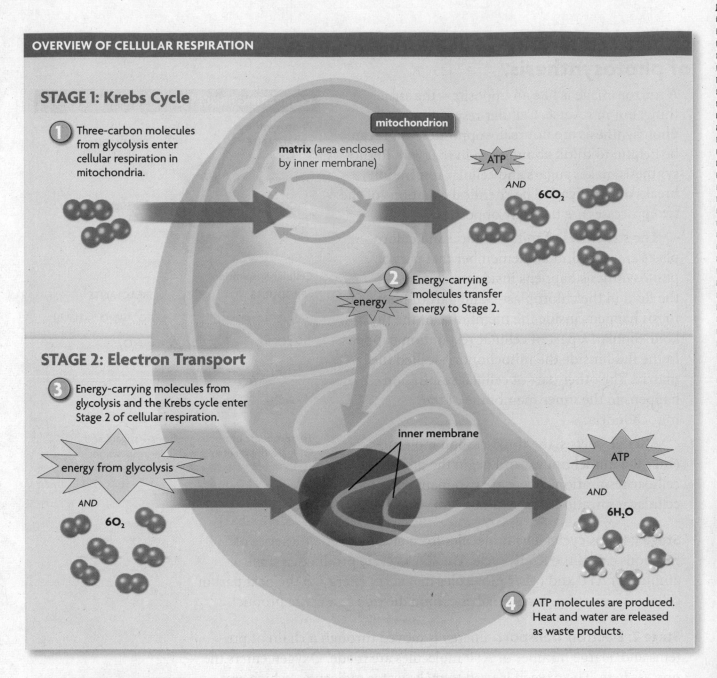

## STAGE 1: Krebs Cycle

**1** Three-carbon molecules from glycolysis enter cellular respiration in mitochondria.

**mitochondrion**

**matrix** (area enclosed by inner membrane)

ATP

AND

$6CO_2$

**2** Energy-carrying molecules transfer energy to Stage 2.

energy

## STAGE 2: Electron Transport

**3** Energy-carrying molecules from glycolysis and the Krebs cycle enter Stage 2 of cellular respiration.

energy from glycolysis

AND

$6O_2$

**inner membrane**

ATP

AND

$6H_2O$

**4** ATP molecules are produced. Heat and water are released as waste products.

Up to 38 ATP molecules are made from the breakdown of one glucose molecule. The equation for cellular respiration is shown below. You can see that there are many arrows between the reactants—$C_6H_{12}O_6$ and $6O_2$—and the products—$6CO_2$ and $6H_2O$. These arrows are there to tell you that there are many steps in the process. For example, the equation for cellular respiration includes glycolysis. Many enzymes also play important roles in the production of ATP.

$$C_6H_{12}O_6 \ + \ 6O_2 \longrightarrow \longrightarrow \longrightarrow \longrightarrow \quad 6CO_2 \ + \ 6H_2O$$

a sugar     oxygen                     carbon dioxide    water

Follow the steps of cellular respiration shown on in the figure on the previous page.

 Circle the products of cellular respiration in the figure on the previous page.

## 4.4 Vocabulary Check

**Mark It Up**

Go back and highlight each sentence that has a vocabulary word in **bold.**

cellular respiration anaerobic

aerobic Krebs cycle

glycolysis

1. Which two terms are opposites? _____

2. Which term is a process that must happen in the cell's cytoplasm before cellular respiration? _____

3. Which term is a process that happens within the mitochondria as part of cellular respiration? _____

4. Which term is the name for this chemical equation:

$$C_6H_{12}O_6 \; + \; 6O_2 \rightarrow \rightarrow \rightarrow \rightarrow 6CO_2 \; + \; 6H_2O$$

a sugar      oxygen              carbon dioxide    water

_____

## 4.4 The Big Picture

5. In which organelle does cellular respiration take place?

_____

6. What are the products and the reactants for cellular respiration?

_____

7. Where is most of the ATP made during cellular respiration?

_____

# 4.5 Cellular Respiration in Detail

**KEY CONCEPT** Cellular respiration is an aerobic process with two main stages.

## Glycolysis is needed for cellular respiration.

In Section 4.4 you read a summary of cellular respiration. Now, we will look at the process more closely, starting with glycolysis. The process of glycolysis happens in all cells, including yours. It does not require oxygen. If oxygen is available, the products of glycolysis are used in cellular respiration.

Glycolysis alone produces a small amount of ATP. But other products of glycolysis are used later in cellular respiration to make lots of ATP. These other products are NADH, which carries energy, and pyruvate. NADH is an energy-carrying molecule similar to NADPH in photosynthesis. In cellular respiration, NADH carries energy to an electron transport chain. Pyruvate (py-ROO-vayt) is the three-carbon molecule that is broken down in the mitochondria during cellular respiration.

Glycolysis breaks glucose into 2 three-carbon molecules called pyruvate. NADH and ATP are also produced.

Notice that two ATP are used in the process of glycolysis. Four ATP are made. The net gain is 4 ATP made − 2 ATP used = 2 ATP molecules. In summary, for each molecule of glucose that is broken down, the products of glycolysis are:

- 2 ATP
- 2 NADH
- 2 pyruvate

The ATP is energy for the cell. The NADH and pyruvate are needed for cellular respiration.

 On the chemical formula above, circle the three products of glycolysis: ATP, NADH, and pyruvate.

# The Krebs cycle is the first main part of cellular respiration.

Cellular respiration makes many more ATP molecules than does glycolysis. The process begins with pyruvate entering the mitochondria. Pyruvate then gets broken down. Next, the process continues with the Krebs cycle. There are many steps in the Krebs cycle, highlighted below.

The Krebs cycle takes place in the mitochondrion matrix.

## THE KREBS CYCLE

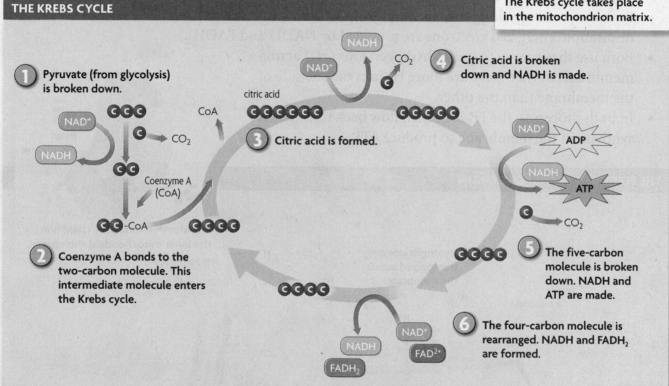

**1** Pyruvate (from glycolysis) is broken down.

**2** Coenzyme A bonds to the two-carbon molecule. This intermediate molecule enters the Krebs cycle.

**3** Citric acid is formed.

**4** Citric acid is broken down and NADH is made.

**5** The five-carbon molecule is broken down. NADH and ATP are made.

**6** The four-carbon molecule is rearranged. NADH and FADH$_2$ are formed.

The main function of the Krebs cycle is to produce energy-carrying molecules, such as NADH. Another energy-carrying molecule that the Krebs cycle produces is called FADH$_2$. These molecules transfer energy to the electron transport chain, the next main part of cellular respiration.

For each pyruvate, the products of the Krebs cycle are:

- 3 CO$_2$
- 1 ATP
- 4 NADH
- 1 FADH$_2$

Carbon dioxide (CO$_2$) is given off as a waste product. The ATP is energy for the cell. NADH and FADH$_2$ are energy-carrying molecules that are used in the next part of cellular respiration.

 What are NADH and FADH$_2$ used for in the cell?

# The electron transport chain is the second main part of cellular respiration.

The electron transport chain in cellular respiration is similar to the electron transport chain in photosynthesis. Some of the similarities include:

- Both are made of proteins that are in a membrane. In cellular respiration, the electron transport chain takes place in and across the inner membrane of a mitochondrion.
- Both move energy along the electron transport chain. In cellular respiration, energized electrons are provided by NADH and $FADH_2$.
- Both use that energy to pump hydrogen ions ($H^+$) across a membrane, so that there are more $H^+$ ions on one side of the membrane than the other.
- In both processes, the $H^+$ ions then flow back through ATP synthase in the membrane to produce ATP.

inner membrane

The electron transport chain is in the inner mitochondrial membrane.

## THE ELECTRON TRANSPORT CHAIN

**2** Hydrogen ions are transported across the membrane.

proteins in the inner membrane

inner membrane of mitochodrion

matrix

**1** Electrons are removed from NADH and $FADH_2$.

NADH

FADH₂

NAD⁺

FAD²⁺

$H^+$

$\frac{1}{2} O_2$

2e⁻

2H⁺

$H_2O$

ATP synthase

+P

ADP

ATP

**3** ADP is changed into ATP when hydrogen ions flow through ATP synthase.

**4** Water is formed when oxygen picks up electronss and hydrogen ions.

rons that have
e products of the
ysis—are:

## ...hesis

piration are
nergy from sun-
hemical energy to
at the table below,
een the processes.

| ...ULAR RESPIRATION |
| --- |
| ...hondrion |
| ...s ($C_6H_{12}O_6$) and $O_2$ |
| ...ins within inner ...chondrial membrane |
| ...s cycle in matrix of ...chondria breaks down ...on-based molecules |
| ...and $H_2O$ |

...hich each process

...mentation removes
...ctrons from NADH and
...ycles $NAD^+$ for glycolysis.

...spiration?

...electron transport

...ellular respiration,

...p to make ATP?

# 4.6 Fermentation

**KEY CONCEPT** Fermentation allows the production of a small amount of ATP without oxygen.

## Fermentation allows glycolysis to continue.

The amount of oxygen that you breathe in is enough for your cells during most activities. But if you are doing high levels of activity, your body cannot bring in enough oxygen for your cells. Even though you breathe faster, there is still not enough oxygen for cellular respiration.

Glycolysis happens all the time, even when there is no oxygen. If there is oxygen, the products of glycolysis are used in cellular respiration. If there is no oxygen, your cells can keep producing small amounts of ATP through the anaerobic processes of glycolysis and fermentation.

**Fermentation** does not make ATP, but it allows glycolysis to continue. Remember that the products of glycolysis are pyruvate, ATP, and NADH. In the process of glycolysis, NAD⁺ is turned into NADH. In order for glycoysis to keep going, there need to be molecules of NAD⁺ that can be turned into NADH. This is what fermentation does. It provides a supply of NAD⁺ that allows glycolysis to continue.

Suppose that a molecule of glucose was just split by glycolysis in one of your muscle cells. If there is no oxygen available, lactic acid fermentation will happen. **Lactic acid** fermentation happens in your muscle cells, in the cells of other vertebrates*, and in some microorganisms. Lactic acid is what makes your muscles burn during hard exercise. Here is what happens in your muscle cells without oxygen:

1. Pyruvate and NADH from glycolysis enter fermentation. Pyruvate is turned into lactic acid. NADH is turned into NAD⁺ .
2. The NAD⁺ molecules are recycled back to glycolysis. This allows glycolysis to continue.

---

* ACADEMIC VOCABULARY

**vertebrate** an animal with a backbone, such as a human, a bird, or a fish

When your muscles are burning during excercise, it is because your cells are using fermentation. By itself, fermentation does not make ATP. But it allows glycolysis to keep going, and glycolysis does make some ATP. After the hard exercise is over, and oxygen is available, cellular respiration will start again.

 **What molecule does fermentation provide to glycolysis?**

_____

## Fermentation and its products are important in several ways.

Fermentation also helps produce food. Cheese, bread, and yogurt are just a few of the foods that are made by fermentation. There are other types of fermentation, too, in addition to lactic acid fermentation. Alcoholic fermentation is used by many yeasts* and some plants. Yeast makes bread rise by breaking down sugar through glycolysis and alcoholic fermentation. The carbon dioxide gas released causes the dough to rise.

Bacteria that use fermentation are important in the digestive systems* of animals. These microorganisms make their ATP without oxygen—because they are in an animal's digestive system.  Without these organisms, neither you nor other animals would be able to fully digest foods.

 **List three foods made through fermentation processes.**

_____

* ACADEMIC VOCABULARY

**yeast**  a single-celled organism

**digestive system**  the parts of an animal where food gets broken down, including the intestines and the stomach

### 4.6    The Big Picture

1.  Fermentation alone does not make ATP. How does fermentation help a cell make ATP? _____

_____

2.  What is lactic acid? _____

_____

# Chapter 4 Review

1. What cellular process makes most of a cell's ATP? _____
   _____

2. Do humans need photosynthesis to survive? Explain your answer.
   _____

3. Put the words *Krebs cycle, glycolysis,* and *electron transport chain* in
   the flow chart below to show the order of the main steps of cellular
   respiration.

   | | | |
   |---|---|---|
   | | → | → |

4. Which of the descriptions below best describes cellular respiration?
   a. chemical energy is released when glucose is broken down into
      carbon dioxide
   b. sunlight energy is stored in carbon-based molecules like glucose
   c. $6CO_2 + 6H_2O \longrightarrow \longrightarrow \longrightarrow \longrightarrow C_6H_{12}O_6 + 6O_2$
   d. when oxygen is available, fermentation occurs

5. Which of the descriptions below best describes photosynthesis?
   a. $C_6H_{12}O_6 + 6O_2 \longrightarrow \longrightarrow \longrightarrow \longrightarrow 6CO_2 + 6H_2O$
   b. sunlight energy is stored in carbon-based molecules like glucose
   c. an ATP-making process that occurs in mitochondria
   d. chemical energy is released when glucose is broken down into
      carbon dioxide

**For questions 6 and 7, refer to the diagram to the right.**

Animal cell     Plant cell

6. Where in the cell does cellular respiration occur?
   Circle the organelle in both cells and write the
   name of the organelle next to your circles.

7. Where in the cell does photosynthesis occur?
   Draw a box around the organelle and write the
   name of the organelle next to your box.

# 5 Cell Growth and Division

## GETTING READY TO LEARN

### Preview Key Concepts

**5.1 The Cell Cycle**
Cells have distinct phases of growth, reproduction, and normal functions.

**5.2 Mitosis and Cytokinesis**
Cells divide during mitosis and cytokinesis.

**5.3 Regulation of the Cell Cycle**
Cell cycle regulation is necessary for healthy growth.

**5.4 Asexual Reproduction**
Many organisms reproduce by cell division.

**5.5 Multicellular Life**
Cells work together to carry out complex functions.

### Review Academic Vocabulary

Write the correct word for each definition.

homeostasis        nucleus        centrosome        cell membrane

1. _____ : forms spindle fibers

2. _____ : described by the fluid mosaic model

3. _____ : maintaining constant internal conditions

4. _____ : largest organelle in a cell

### Preview Biology Vocabulary

See how many key terms from this chapter you already know. Rewrite each phrase, using a different word or words for the **words in bold.**

| PHRASE | REWRITTEN WITH DIFFERENT WORDS |
|---|---|
| 1. The formation of skin and nerves and muscles in a developing embryo is an example of **cell differentiation.** | The formation of skin and nerves and muscles in a developing embryo is an example of _____. |
| 2. Bacteria reproduce asexually through **binary fission.** | Bacteria reproduce asexually through _____ _____ |
| 3. Organisms that reproduce sexually use **mitosis** for growth, development, and repair. | Organisms that reproduce sexually use _____ _____ for growth, development, and repair. |

# 5.1 The Cell Cycle

**KEY CONCEPT** Cells have distinct phases of growth, reproduction, and normal functions.

## The cell cycle has four main stages.

Cells grow and divide in a regular pattern, or cycle*. If you cut your finger, your cells grow and divide to make more cells. This is how your finger heals.

The **cell cycle** is a regular pattern of growth, DNA duplication*, and cell division* that occurs in eukaryotic cells. Recall that your cells are eukaryotic cells, and they have a nucleus. There are four main stages of the cell cycle:

- gap 1—normal growth
- synthesis—DNA is copied
- gap 2—more growth
- mitosis—nuclear division

> Together, these three stages make up a part of the cell cycle called interphase.

Each stage is described below.

**Gap 1 (G₁)** In G₁ cells do their normal functions. For example, your muscle cells contract, and intestinal cells absorb nutrients.

**Synthesis (S)** *Synthesis* means "the combining of parts to make a whole." During the S stage, a cell puts together, or synthesizes, a whole copy of its nuclear DNA. In eukaryotes, DNA is in the nucleus. At the end of this stage, there are two complete sets of DNA in a cell's nucleus.

**Gap 2 (G₂)** In G₂ cells grow and continue their normal functions. If the cell is healthy, it will continue to the next stage.

**Mitosis (M)** There are two parts of this stage: mitosis and cytokinesis. **Mitosis** (my-TOH-sihs) is the division of the cell nucleus and the DNA inside it. **Cytokinesis** (sy-toh-kuh-NEE-sihs) is the division of the contents of the rest of the cell—the cytoplasm.

These four main stages are shown in the graph at the top of page 75.

**VISUAL VOCAB**

**Mitosis** is the division of the cell nucleus and its contents.

parent cell

mitosis

cytokinesis

daughter cells

**Cytokinesis** divides the cell cytoplasm.

*Daughter cells* is a term to describe these resulting cells, but it does not mean that they are female.

**\* ACADEMIC VOCABULARY**

**cycle** a pattern of events that is repeated

**duplication** the process of doubling, or copying

**division** separating

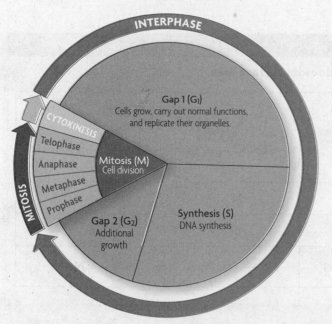

Cells grow and copy their DNA during interphase. During M stage, both the nucleus (in mitosis) and cytoplasm (in cytokinesis) are divided.

 On the figure above, circle the terms for the four stages of the cell cycle.

## Cells divide at different rates.

Different types of eukaryotic cells take different amounts of time to go through the cell cycle. The table at right lists the life span—or how long until a cell dies—for different types of human cells. Also, cells divide at different rates depending on a person's age. Children's cells divide faster than do cells in adults. In adults, many cells divide only if there is an injury or cell death.

 How long does it take for a cell to go through the cell cycle?

_____

| CELL LIFE SPAN | |
|---|---|
| **CELL TYPE** | **APPROXIMATE LIFE SPAN** |
| Skin cell | 2 weeks |
| Red blood cell | 4 months |
| Liver cell | 300–500 days |
| Intestine—internal lining | 4–5 days |
| Intestine—muscle and other tissues | 16 years |

This chart shows the life span of five different types of human cells. Each type of cell divides at a different rate.

## Cell size is limited.

A cell must be big enough to fit all of the molecules and organelles it needs to live. A cell also must be small enough to quickly transport nutrients and wastes into and out of the cell across the cell membrane. As a cell gets bigger, its volume* increases faster than its surface area*. If a cell gets too big, there is not enough surface area of the cell membrane to transport nutrients and wastes for such a big volume. The upper limit on cell size depends on its surface area-to-volume ratio. The surface area-to-volume ratio is the size of the surface area compared to the size of the volume.

**\* ACADEMIC VOCABULARY**

**volume**  the amount of space in a three-dimensional object
**surface area**  the total amount of area on the surfaces of an object

## RATIO OF SURFACE AREA TO VOLUME IN CELLS

**As a cell grows, its volume increases more rapidly than does its surface area.**

| Relative size | | | |
|---|---|---|---|
| | 1  | 2 | 3  |
| **Surface area** (length × width × number of sides) | 6 | 24 | 54 |
| **Volume** (length × width × height) | 1 | 8 | 27 |
| **Ratio of surface area to volume** | $\frac{6}{1}$ = 6:1 | $\frac{24}{8}$ = 3:1 | $\frac{54}{27}$ = 2:1 |

**INSTANT REPLAY** Can a cell get too big? Explain.

_____

## 5.1    Vocabulary Check

**Mark It Up**

Go back and highlight each sentence that has a vocabulary word in **bold**.

cell cycle                    cytokinesis

mitosis

**Fill in the blanks with the correct term from the list above.**

1. _____ is the division of the nucleus and its contents.

2. The _____ is a pattern of growth, DNA duplication, and division.

3. The division of the cell cytoplasm is called _____.

## 5.1    The Big Picture

4. During which stage of the cell cycle is DNA copied? _____

5. Do all cells take the same amount of time to divide? Explain. _____

_____

6. How does the surface area-to-volume ratio limit cell size? _____

_____

## Chromosomes condense* at the start of mitosis.

DNA is a double-stranded molecule, like a twisted ladder. A **chromosome** is one long piece of DNA. Every one of your body cells has 46 chromosomes. The DNA in each chromosome has many genes.

During interphase, when the cell is not dividing, the chromosomes are loose—kind of like 46 pieces of spaghetti. During mitosis, the DNA is condensed* and organized. This helps the chromosomes to stay untangled while the cell divides.

The figure below shows how the DNA strand turns into the very condensed form of a chromosome during mitosis.

---

**CHROMOSOME STRUCTURE**

**DNA condenses tightly during the early stages of mitosis.**

histone

chromatid

**telomere**

centromere

**telomere**

**DNA double helix**
Each continuous, double-stranded DNA molecule makes one chromosome.

**DNA and histones**
DNA wraps around proteins called **histones,** forming **chromatin.**

**Chromatin**
Interactions between parts of the histones further compact the DNA.

**Supercoiled DNA**
The chromatin coils more and more tightly around organizing proteins.

**Condensed, duplicated chromosome**
The condensed, duplicated chromosomes can be lined up and separated during mitosis.

---

Look at the picture of the condensed, duplicated chromosome. Recall that the chromosomes are copied during the S stage that happens before mitosis. This condensed, duplicated chromosome looks like an "X." The right half of the X and the left half are copies of each other.

**\* ACADEMIC VOCABULARY**

**condense** to make something smaller or more compact

They are identical. Each half of a duplicated chromosome is called a **chromatid** (KROH-muh-tihd). Together, the two identical chromatids are called sister chromatids. The sister chromatids are held together at a place called the **centromere** (SEHN-truh-MEER).

 Explain how a chromatid and a duplicated chromosome are related.

## Mitosis and cytokinesis produce two genetically identical daughter cells.

By the end of interphase, a cell is ready to divide. Mitosis divides the DNA, and cytokinesis divides the rest of the cell. The result is two identical cells. Mitosis happens in all of your body cells—except cells that form eggs or sperm. Your cells divide for growth, development, and repair. Single-celled organisms use cell division to reproduce.

Mitosis and cytokinesis are continuous processes. They do not happen in steps. However, scientists have divided the processes into steps to make them easier to understand and discuss. The four main phases of mitosis are prophase, metaphase, anaphase and telophase. Cytokinesis begins at the end of anaphase or in telophase. These steps are shown in the figure to the right.

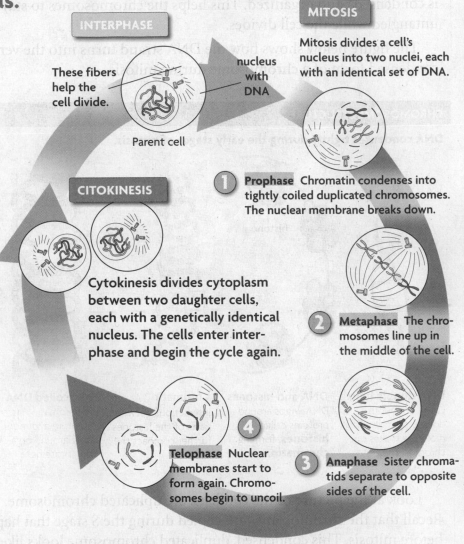

**INTERPHASE**

These fibers help the cell divide.

nucleus with DNA

Parent cell

**MITOSIS**

Mitosis divides a cell's nucleus into two nuclei, each with an identical set of DNA.

**1 Prophase** Chromatin condenses into tightly coiled duplicated chromosomes. The nuclear membrane breaks down.

**2 Metaphase** The chromosomes line up in the middle of the cell.

**3 Anaphase** Sister chromatids separate to opposite sides of the cell.

**4 Telophase** Nuclear membranes start to form again. Chromosomes begin to uncoil.

**CITOKINESIS**

Cytokinesis divides cytoplasm between two daughter cells, each with a genetically identical nucleus. The cells enter interphase and begin the cycle again.

 What is one reason your body cells need to divide?

## 5.2    Vocabulary Check

chromosome      centromere

histone      prophase

chromatin      metaphase

telomere      anaphase

chromatid      telophase

**Mark It Up**

Go back and highlight each sentence that has a vocabulary word in **bold**.

1. Label the diagram below with the terms *chromosome*, *chromatid*, *centromere*, and *telomere*.

2. Draw and label each phase of mitosis—*prophase, metaphase, ana-phase,* and *telophase*—in the circles below:

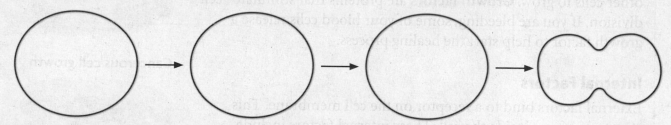

3. On the diagram above, in question 2, circle the part of the process in which cytokinesis occurs.

4. The word part *telo-* means "end." How does this word part relate to the meaning of the terms *telomere* and *telophase*? _____

_____

## 5.2    The Big Picture

1. During which stage of the cell cycle is DNA copied? _____

2. How many chromatids are there in one duplicated chromosome? _____

3. Two identical daughter cells result from mitosis and cytokinesis. In what ways are they "identical"? _____

# 5.3 Regulation of the Cell Cycle

**KEY CONCEPT** Cell cycle regulation is necessary for healthy growth.

## Internal and external factors regulate cell division.

If the cell cycle goes out of control, cancer can result. Cancer is uncontrolled cell division. To regulate means "to control." Regulation of the cell cycle is important for healthy cell growth. Internal means "inside" and external means "outside." Information from both inside and outside the cell—internal and external factors—help regulate the cell cycle.

### External Factors

There are external physical and chemical signals that help regulate the cell cycle. For example, a cell that is surrounded by other cells stops dividing. Many cells also release chemical signals that tell other cells to grow. **Growth factors** are proteins that stimulate* cell division. If you are bleeding, some of your blood cells release a growth factor to help start the healing process.

**Normal cell growth**

**Cancerous cell growth**

### Internal Factors

External factors bind to a receptor on the cell membrane. This starts a response inside the cell. These internal factors include enzymes and proteins that help a cell move through the cell cycle.

### Apoptosis

Just as cells need to grow and divide, other cells need to die. Internal or external signals can start an orderly process of cell death. The cell is broken down and its parts are reused in building other molecules. This process of programmed cell death is called **apoptosis** (AP-uhp-TOH-sihs).

Normal animal cells (top) stop dividing when they touch each other. Cancer cells (bottom) do not respond to normal signals and, as a result, form clumps of cells.

**INSTANT REPLAY** Why is regulation of the cell cycle important?

_____

* ACADEMIC VOCABULARY

**stimulate** to cause something to happen

# Cell division is uncontrolled in cancer.

**Cancer** is the common name for a group of diseases that involve uncontrolled cell division. Cancer cells keep dividing and form clumps called tumors. A **benign** tumor is relatively harmless because the cells stay clumped together and it can be removed. A **malignant** tumor has cancer cells that break away from the tumor. These cells **metastasize** (mih-TAS-tuh-syz), which means they travel to other parts of the body and can form more tumors. When a cancer metastasizes, it is much harder to get rid of.

Cancer cells come from normal cells that have damaged genes. Substances that are known to cause or lead to cancer are called **carcinogens** (kahr-SIHN-uh-juhnz). Tobacco smoke and certain air pollutants are carcinogens.

Cancer cells break away from malignant tumors. They can then be carried in the blood-stream to other parts of the body where they form new tumors.

 **INSTANT REPLAY** What is the difference between a benign tumor and a malignant tumor?

_____

_____

## 5.3 Vocabulary Check

growth factor     malignant

apoptosis     metastasize

cancer     carcinogen

benign

**Mark It Up**

Go back and highlight each sentence that has a vocabulary word in **bold**.

**Choose the correct term from the list for each description.**

1. substance that causes cancer _____

2. programmed cell death _____

3. a tumor that does not metastasize _____

## 5.3 The Big Picture

1. What are two ways that cell division is regulated in healthy cells?

_____

_____

2. What is one main difference between a normal cell and a cancer cell?

_____

_____

# 5.4 Asexual Reproduction

**KEY CONCEPT**  Many organisms reproduce by cell division.

## Binary fission is similar in function to mitosis.

Reproduction is a process of making new organisms from one or more parent organisms. It happens in two ways, sexually and asexually. Sexual reproduction involves the joining of egg and sperm, and results in unique* offspring. **Asexual reproduction** is the production of offspring from a single parent. The offspring are, for the most part, genetically identical to each other and to the parent.

### Binary Fission and Mitosis

Recall that prokaryotes include organisms such as bacteria. Most prokaryotes reproduce through binary fission. **Binary fission** (BY-nuh-ree FIHSH-uhn) is asexual reproduction of a single-celled organism by division into two parts. Binary fission does not follow the same steps as mitosis; the processes are different. But binary fission and mitosis have similar results—two daughter cells that are genetically identical to the parent cell.

### Advantages of Asexual Reproduction

Asexual reproduction can quickly result in large numbers of offspring. All cells can have offspring. In contrast, sexual reproduction is slower. Only females can have offspring, and many sexually reproducing organisms must find a mate.

### Disadvantages of Asexual Reproduction

Asexually reproduced offspring are genetically identical—so they will respond to their environment in the same way. If conditions stay the same, this is not a problem. If the environment changes, and the organisms cannot live with the changes, the entire population could die off. In contrast, offspring from sexual reproduction are genetically different from the parents. Genetic diversity increases the chance that some individuals will survive even in changing conditions.

**VISUAL VOCAB**

Binary fission is the asexual reproduction of a single-celled organism by division into two roughly equal parts. *Binary* means "in parts of two." *Fission* means "dividing" or "separating."

parent cell

DNA duplicates

cell begins to divide

daughter cells

**BACTERIA GROWTH**

One bacterium can result in a total of 1024 cells after only 10 rounds of cell division.

 **INSTANT REPLAY**   What types of organisms reproduce by binary fission?

_____

* ACADEMIC VOCABULARY

**unique**  unlike any other

# Some eukaryotes reproduce through mitosis.

Growing a new plant from a cutting is an example of asexual reproduction through mitosis. Sea stars, flatworms, strawberries, potatoes, sea anemones, yeast, and many other eukaryotic organisms can also reproduce asexually, through mitosis. Many organisms can reproduce both sexually and asexually. The form of reproduction may depend on the conditions around the organism.

 How do eukaryotes reproduce asexually?

_____

## 5.4 Vocabulary Check

**Mark It Up**

Go back and highlight each sentence that has a vocabulary word in **bold**.

asexual reproduction

binary fission

**Circle the correct word to complete each sentence.**

1. Asexual reproduction results in genetically *different / identical* daughter cells.

2. Binary fission is when a single-celled organism divides into *two / four* daughter cells.

## 5.4 The Big Picture

1. Through what process do most prokaryotes reproduce asexually?

_____

2. Through what process do eukaryotes reproduce asexually? _____

3. List one advantage and one disadvantage of asexual reproduction.

_____

_____

# 5.5 Multicellular Life

**KEY CONCEPT** Cells work together to carry out complex functions.

## Multicellular organisms depend on interactions among different cell types.

In multicellular organisms like you, different types of cells communicate and work together. There are different levels of organization.

- **Tissues** are groups of cells that work together to perform a similar function. For example, plants have photosynthetic tissue made of cells that contain chlorophyll.
- **Organs** are groups of tissues that work together to perform specific functions. For example, different tissues work together to form a plant leaf, the plant's food-producing organ.
- **Organ systems** are groups of organs that work together. For example, the shoot system of a plant is the part of the plant that is above ground. The stems supports the plant, the leaves capture sunlight, and flowers help in reproduction.

---

### LEVELS OF ORGANIZATION

**Cells work together in groups that form larger, specialized structures.**

| CELL | TISSUE | ORGAN | SYSTEMS |
|------|--------|-------|---------|
| A multicellular organism has different types of cells. | Similar types of cells that work together form different types of tissues. | Different types of tissues work together in an organ. | Organs work together in organ systems. Here, you can see the plant's root system and shoot system, each made of different organs, which are made of different tissues. |

Parenchyma

Collenchyma

---

INSTANT REPLAY

What is an example of an organ and an organ system from the human body?

_____

## Specialized cells perform specific functions.

Your body began as a single fertilized egg. If that egg cell simply divided to make lots of identical cells, it would not form a baby. To form all of the different tissues that make up your body, cells need to specialize, or develop specific functions. For example, some cells become skin cells and others become stomach cells. **Cell differentiation**\* is the process by which cells that are not specialized develop into their specialized forms.

So why do stomach cells function differently than skin cells? They do not have different DNA. Almost all cells in your body have the same full set of DNA. Different types of cells simply use different genes contained in the DNA. Skin cells use one part of the DNA information—for skin cells—and stomach cells use a different part of the DNA information—for stomach cells.

 If all cells in your body have the same DNA, how can you have different types of cells?

## Stem cells can develop into different cell types.

Once a cell differentiates, it stays in its specialized form. For example, once a cell becomes a stomach cell, it cannot turn into another type of cell. **Stem cells** are a special type of body cell that can develop into different types of cells. Stem cells can:

- divide and renew themselves for a long period of time,
- remain undifferentiated, and
- develop into many different types of specialized cells.

When a stem cell divides, it forms either two stem cells or one stem cell and one specialized cell.

stem cell

2 new stem cells

1 new stem cell  +  1 specialized cell

## Stem Cell Classification

Stem cells can be classified, or grouped, by their ability to differentiate into cell types of different tissues. Some kinds of stem cells can differentiate into any cell, and others can only differentiate into a few different kinds of cells. In general, the more differentiated a stem cell already is, the fewer types of cells it can form. Stem cells can also be classified by where they come from—either adult cells or embryonic* cells.

| STEM CELL CLASSIFICATION | | | |
|---|---|---|---|
| Type of cell | fertilized egg | embryonic stem cell | adult stem cell (example from blood) |
| Can give rise to | all cells | almost any cell | closely related cells |
| Example | new organism | neurons, skin, muscle, kidney, cartilage, bone, liver, pancreas | red blood cells, platelets, white blood cells |

## Adult Stem Cells

Adult stem cells are found all over the body—in the brain, liver, bone marrow, skeletal muscle, dental pulp, and even fat. These cells are partly undifferentiated. For years, much evidence suggested that adult stem cells could only make closely related cells. Newer research suggests that adult stem cells may be able to make many different types of cells.

## Embryonic Stem Cells

Most embryonic stem cells come from donated stem cells grown in a lab. These embryos are grown from eggs that are fertilized outside a woman's body. The stem cells come from a three-to-five-day-old cluster of cells. These cells are entirely undifferentiated and can form any type of cell in the human body.

In the figure, circle the embryonic stem cells.

**HARVESTING EMBRYONIC STEM CELLS**

inner cell mass

fertilized egg

muscle cells

neurons

red blood cells

First, an egg is fertilized by a sperm cell in a petri dish. The egg divides, forming an inner cell mass. These cells are then removed and grown with nutrients. Scientists try to control how the cells specialize by adding or removing certain molecules.

* ACADEMIC VOCABULARY

**embryonic** related to an embryo

## Research and Treatment Hope

Stem cells have been used to treat patients with various types of cancer for many years. They offer hope for treating many more diseases. For example, stem cells could potentially be used to replace nonworking cells in organs. This could help cure diabetes or repair heart damage. In addition, stem cells offer a new way to develop drugs. The current process for drug development is very expensive and takes a long time. Testing new products on specific cell types grown from stem cells could make the process faster and cheaper.

## 5.5 Vocabulary Check

**Mark It Up**

Go back and highlight each sentence that has a vocabulary word in **bold**.

tissue          cell differentiation

organ           stem cell

organ system

1. Underline the word in the list above that means "a group of similar cells that work together to perform a similar function."

2. Circle the word in the list above that means "a cell that is undifferentiated, and can turn into different types of cells."

3. Make a box around the word that means "the process by which cells that are unspecialized turn into their specialized forms."

## 5.5 The Big Picture

1. Fill in the boxes below to show the different levels of organization in multicellular organisms.

work together in groups to form

which work together to form

which work together to form

cells

2. Are there differences in the DNA in different types of human body cells? Explain. _____

_____

_____

# Chapter 5 Review

1. In a multicellular organism, what makes cells different—for example, what makes a muscle cell different from a brain cell? _____

   _____

2. What process is shown in the diagram below?

   a. cell differentiation
   b. mitosis
   c. apoptosis
   d. sexual reproduction

3. Write the terms *tissue*, *organ*, and *organ system* onto the diagram in order of largest level of organization to smallest level of organization. The biggest circle should be labeled with the biggest level of organization and the smallest circle with the smallest level.

   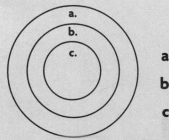

   a. _____

   b. _____

   c. _____

4. Circle the correct words to complete the sentence below.

   Asexual reproduction results in offspring that are genetically **different / identical** and sexual reproduction results in offspring that are genetically **different / identical.**

5. A stem cell is a cell that is
   a. undifferentiated
   b. differentiated
   c. only found in embryos
   d. only found in the brain stem

6. A breakdown in the cell cycle can lead to uncontrolled cell division. What is a disease that can result from this breakdown?

   _____

7. Draw a duplicated chromosome, and label the drawing with the following terms: *centromere*, *telomere*, and *chromatid*.

8. What are the four stages of the cell cycle? _____

# 6 Meiosis and Mendel

## GETTING READY TO LEARN

### Preview Key Concepts

**6.1 Chromosomes and Meiosis**
Gametes have half the number of chromosomes that body cells have.

**6.2 Process of Meiosis**
During meiosis, diploid cells undergo two cell divisions that result in haploid cells.

**6.3 Mendel and Heredity**
Mendel's research showed that traits are inherited as discrete units.

**6.4 Traits, Genes, and Alleles**
Genes encode proteins that produce a diverse range of traits.

**6.5 Traits and Probability**
The inheritance of traits follows the rules of probability.

**6.6 Meiosis and Genetic Variation**
Independent assortment and crossing over during meiosis result in genetic diversity.

## Review Academic Vocabulary

Write the correct word for each definition.

mitosis     data     chromosome     experiment

1. _____ : recorded observations

2. _____ : results in identical daughter cells

3. _____ : long, continuous piece of DNA

4. _____ : allows scientists to test hypothesis

## Preview Biology Vocabulary

To see how many key terms you already know from this chapter, choose the word that makes sense in each sentence.

trait     gene     egg     Punnett square

1. The shape of your ears is a(n) _____.

2. A(n) _____ is a grid system that helps predict information about the offspring of two parent organisms.

3. A(n) _____ is a sex cell in a female organism.

4. A segment of DNA that codes for a protein is a(n) _____.

# 6.1 Chromosomes and Meiosis

**KEY CONCEPT**  Gametes have half the number of chromosomes that body cells have.

## You have body cells and gametes.

All of the different cells in your body can be divided into two groups: somatic cells and germ cells.

- **Germ cells** are the cells in your reproductive organs—the ovaries or testes—that develop into eggs or sperm.
- **Somatic cells** (soh-MAT-ihk), or body cells, are all the other cells in your body.

Somatic cells make up most of your tissues and organs. The DNA in your somatic cells will not be passed on to your children. Only the DNA in the egg or sperm cells gets passed on to offspring. Egg cells and sperm cells are called **gametes.**

Egg cells and sperm cells are called gametes.

Each species has a characteristic number of chromosomes per cell. For example:

- **Humans** have 23 pairs of chromosomes. In other words, there are 23 × 2 = 46 chromosomes in all body cells.
- **Fruit flies** have 4 pairs of chromosomes, or 8 chromosomes per cell.
- **Yeast** have 16 pairs of chromosomes, or 32 chromosomes per cell.

The organism currently known to have the most chromosomes is a fern. It has more than 1200 chromosomes. Chromosome number is not related to the size or complexity of an organism.

Do gametes come from germ cells or somatic cells?

_____

## Your cells have autosomes and sex chromosomes.

Suppose you had 23 pairs of gloves. You would have a total of 23 × 2 = 46 gloves. You could divide them into two sets: 23 right-hand and 23 left-hand gloves. Similarly, your body cells have 23 pairs of chromosomes, for a total of 46. These can be divided into two sets: 23 from your mother and 23 from your father. Just as you use both gloves if it is cold outside, your cells use both sets of chromosomes to function properly.

Each pair of chromosomes is called a homologous pair. Here, *homologous* means "having the same structure." **Homologous chromosomes** are two chromosomes—one from the mother and one from the father—that are the same size and have copies of the same genes.

Although each chromosome in a homologous pair has copies of the same genes, the two copies may differ. For example, each chromosome in a pair might have a gene that influences eye color. But the gene on one chromosome of the pair may lead to brown eyes and the gene on the other chromosome may lead to green eyes.

One of your 23 pairs of chromosomes is your pair of **sex chromosomes.** These chromosomes control the sex of an organism. Humans, and all mammals, have two different sex chromosomes called X and Y.

- Females have two X chromosomes.
- Males have one X chromosome and one Y chromosome.

The rest of your chromosomes—the other 22 pairs—are called **autosomes.** These chromosomes contain genes for all of the rest of an organism's life functions.

 If a person's pair of sex chromosomes is XY, is the person male or female? _____

# Body cells are diploid; gametes are haploid.

**Sexual reproduction** involves two gametes—an egg and a sperm—joining together. **Fertilization** happens when the egg and sperm actually combine. The nucleus of the egg combines with the nucleus of the sperm to form one nucleus. This new nucleus must have the correct number of chromosomes—46 for humans. Therefore, the egg and sperm each must each have half that number of chromosomes—23 for humans.

### Diploid and Haploid Cells

Gametes—eggs and sperm—are **haploid** (HAP-loyd) cells. Haploid cells have one copy of each chromosome—again, 23 for humans. A sperm and egg join together to form a **diploid** (DIHP-loyd) cell—for a total of 46 chromosomes for humans. Body cells are all diploid. Only gametes are haploid.

### Meiosis

The germ cells in your reproductive organs form gametes through a process called meiosis. **Meiosis** (my-OH-sihs) is a process that divides a diploid cell into a haploid cell. In Chapter 5 you learned about mitosis, another process that divides a cell. The figure on the next page shows some of the differences between mitosis and meiosis.

**VISUAL VOCAB**

**Diploid** cells have two copies of each chromosome: one copy from the mother and one from the father.

Body cells are diploid (2n).

Gametes (sex cells) are haploid (n).

**Haploid** cells have only one copy of each chromosome.

## COMPARING MITOSIS AND MEIOSIS

| MITOSIS | | MEIOSIS | |
|---|---|---|---|
| | Produces genetically identical cells | Produces genetically unique cells | |
| | Results in diploid cells | Results in haploid cells | |
| | Takes place throughout an organism's lifetime | Takes place only at certain times in an organism's life cycle | |
| | Involved in asexual reproduction | Involved in sexual reproduction | |

Remember that mitosis results in two identical diploid cells. Mitosis is used for development, growth, and repair. In contrast, meiosis results in four haploid cells that are unique. Meiosis happens only in germ cells to make gametes. Meiosis will be presented in detail in the next section.

 **INSTANT REPLAY** What is the difference between the cells that result from mitosis and the cells that result from meiosis?

_____

| 6.1 | Vocabulary Check |
|---|---|

**Mark It Up**

Go back and highlight each sentence that has a vocabulary word in **bold**.

| | |
|---|---|
| somatic cell | sexual reproduction |
| gamete | fertilization |
| homologous chromosome | haploid |
| sex chromosome | diploid |
| autosome | meiosis |

1. when the nucleus of an egg joins the nucleus of a sperm _____

2. a body cell _____

3. an egg or sperm cell _____

4. any chromosome except a sex chromosome _____

| 6.1 | The Big Picture |
|---|---|

5. If a diploid cell with 8 chromosomes goes through meiosis, how many chromosomes will the resulting haploid cells have? _____

6. Circle the sex of a person with the sex chromosomes XX: male / female

SECTION

# 6.2 Process of Meiosis

**KEY CONCEPT** During meiosis, diploid cells undergo two cell divisions that result in haploid cells.

## Cells go through two rounds of division in meiosis.

Meiosis begins with a diploid cell that already has duplicated chromosomes. There are two rounds of cell division—meiosis I and meiosis II. The phases of meiosis are similar to the phases of mitosis. To keep the two processes separate in your mind, focus on the big picture. Mitosis results in identical diploid cells, and meiosis results in unique haploid cells.

### Homologous Chromosomes and Sister Chromatids

Recall that homologous chromosomes are two separate chromosomes: one from your mother and one from your father. Homologous chromosomes carry the same genes in the same order. However, the copies of the genes may differ. Homologous chromosomes are not copies of each other. In contrast, recall that a duplicated chromosome is made of two sister chromatids, attached at the centromere. Sister chromatids are identical copies of each other.

Homologous chromosomes (shown duplicated) are two separate chromosomes—one inherited from the mother, and one from the father.

### The Process of Meiosis

Before meiosis begins, DNA has already been copied. Homologous chromosomes are separated in the first half of meiosis—meiosis I. This results in two haploid cells with duplicated chromosomes. These cells are haploid because they each have only one of every pair of homologous chromosomes. Sister chromatids are separated in the second half of meiosis—meiosis II. This results in four haploid cells with undoubled chromosomes. Like mitosis, scientists describe this process in phases. Follow the process of meiosis illustrated on the next page. The figure is simplified, showing only four chromosomes.

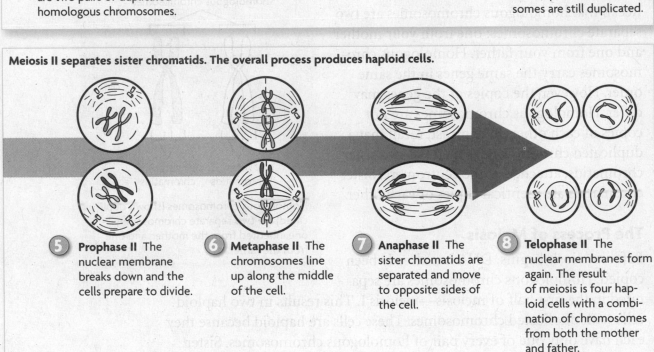

**MEIOSIS**

**Meiosis I separates homologous chromosomes.**

from mother

from father

**1 Prophase I** The nuclear membrane breaks down. The duplicated chromosomes condense and homologous chromosomes begin to pair up. Notice that there are two pairs of duplicated homologous chromosomes.

**2 Metaphase I** The chromosomes line up along the middle of the cell.

**3 Anaphase I** The paired homologous chromosomes separate. Sister chromatids remain attached.

**4 Telophase I** Cytokinesis separates the cells. Each cell contains only one of each pair of chromosomes—not both. In other words, the cells are now haploid. The chromosomes are still duplicated.

**Meiosis II separates sister chromatids. The overall process produces haploid cells.**

**5 Prophase II** The nuclear membrane breaks down and the cells prepare to divide.

**6 Metaphase II** The chromosomes line up along the middle of the cell.

**7 Anaphase II** The sister chromatids are separated and move to opposite sides of the cell.

**8 Telophase II** The nuclear membranes form again. The result of meiosis is four haploid cells with a combination of chromosomes from both the mother and father.

Now that you've seen how meiosis works, let's review two key differences between the processes of meiosis and mitosis.

- Meiosis has two cell divisions. Mitosis has only one cell division.
- Meiosis results in haploid cells. Mitosis results in diploid cells.

On the diagram above, circle the part in the process of meiosis when the cells first become haploid.

# Haploid cells develop into mature gametes.

**Gametogenesis** (guh-MEE-tuh-JEHN-ih-sihs) is the production of gametes—eggs or sperm. Gametogenesis includes both meiosis and other changes that the haploid cells must go through. The **sperm** cell, the male gamete, is much smaller than the **egg,** the female gamete. After meiosis, a cell that develops into a sperm will form a compact shape with a long tail, or flagellum, that the cell uses to move. For egg production, only one of the cells from meiosis becomes an egg. It receives most of the cytoplasm and organelles. The other cells produced by meiosis become **polar bodies,** smaller cells that contain little more than DNA, and are eventually broken down.

GAMETOGENESIS

Sperm Production — germ cell (diploid)

meiosis

mature gametes (haploid)

4 sperm cells

Egg Production — germ cell (diploid)

meiosis

mature gamete (haploid)

1 egg    polar bodies

 INSTANT REPLAY

How do mature gametes differ from the immature haploid cells?

_____

_____

## 6.2    Vocabulary Check

**Mark It Up**

Go back and highlight each sentence that has a vocabulary word in **bold.**

gametogenesis        egg
sperm                polar body

**Choose the correct term from the list above to complete the sentences below.**

1. Sperm and eggs are formed through the process of _____.

2. For egg formation, one of the cells resulting from meiosis becomes an egg and the others become _____.

## 6.2    The Big Picture

3. What is the end result of meiosis? _____
_____

4. What are two differences between meiosis and mitosis? _____
_____
_____

# SECTION 6.3 Mendel and Heredity

**KEY CONCEPT** Mendel's research showed that traits are inherited as discrete units.

## Mendel laid the groundwork for genetics.

**Traits** are characteristics* that are inherited, such as eye color, leaf shape, or tail length. Scientists recognized that traits are hereditary, or passed from one generation to the next, long before they understood how traits are passed on. **Genetics** is the study of biological inheritance patterns and variation in organisms.

The study of genetics started in the 1800s with an Austrian monk named Gregor Mendel. He recognized that there are separate units of inheritance—what we now call genes—that come from each parent. Mendel studied inheritance in pea plants.

 Highlight the sentence above that tells who Gregor Mendel was.

## Mendel's data revealed patterns of inheritance.

Three things about Mendel's experiments helped him develop his laws of inheritance.

 **He controlled the breeding of the pea plants he studied.** Pea flowers have both male and female parts. They usually self-pollinate. In other words, a plant mates with itself. As shown in the figure to the right, Mendel controlled the matings of his pea plants. He chose which plants to cross. In genetics, the mating of two organisms is called a **cross.**

**He used "either-or" characteristics.** Mendel studied seven different pea traits, including flower color and pea shape. All of the characteristics he studied had only two forms, so all plants either had one form or the other. For example, all of the flowers were purple or white. All of the peas were wrinkled or round.

Mendel controlled the fertilization of his pea plants by removing the male parts, or stamens.

He then fertilized the female part, or pistil, with pollen from a different pea plant.

**MENDEL'S PROCESS**

---

\* ACADEMIC VOCABULARY

**characteristic** something that is recognizable, or that distinguishes someone or something

**3** **He used purebred plants.** If a line of plants self-pollinates for long enough, the plants become genetically uniform, or **purebred.** The offspring of a purebred parent inherits all of the parent organism's characteristics—they are all the same as the parent. Because Mendel started with purebred plants, he knew that any variation in the offspring was a result of his crosses.

## Results

Mendel found that when he crossed purebred plants, one of the forms of a trait was hidden in the offspring. But the form would reappear in the next generation.

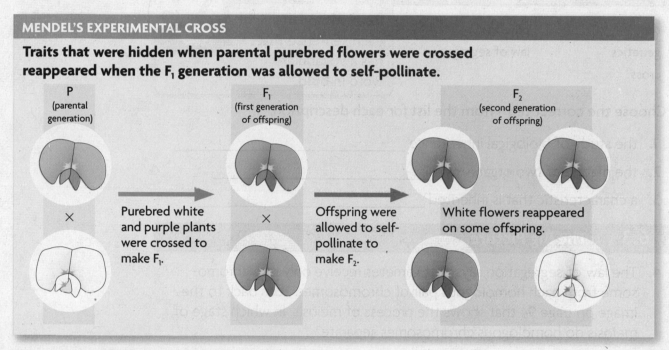

**MENDEL'S EXPERIMENTAL CROSS**

**Traits that were hidden when parental purebred flowers were crossed reappeared when the $F_1$ generation was allowed to self-pollinate.**

**P**
(parental generation)

×

Purebred white and purple plants were crossed to make $F_1$.

**$F_1$**
(first generation of offspring)

×

Offspring were allowed to self-pollinate to make $F_2$.

**$F_2$**
(second generation of offspring)

White flowers reappeared on some offspring.

Mendel studied many plants and made many crosses. He found similar patterns in all of his results. In the figure above, you can see that the white flowers disappeared in the first generation of offspring. In the second generation, however, he found that about one-fourth of the plants had the form of the trait that had disappeared in the first generation. The other three-fourths of the plants had purple flowers. In other words there was a 3:1 ratio of purple-flowered:white flowered plants in the second generation.

## Conclusions

These observations helped Mendel form his first law, called the **law of segregation.** There are two main parts of this law.

- Organisms inherit two copies of each gene, one from each parent.
- Only one copy of a gene goes into an organism's gametes. The two copies of a gene separate—or segregate—during gamete formation.

 Highlight the two parts of Mendel's law of segregation listed above.

### 6.3    Vocabulary Check

**Mark It Up**

Go back and highlight each sentence that has a vocabulary word in **bold.**

trait            purebred
genetics         law of segregation
cross

Choose the correct term from the list for each description.

1.  the study of biological inheritance _____

2.  the mating of two organisms _____

3.  a characteristic that is inherited _____

### 6.3    The Big Picture

4.  The law of segregation says that gametes receive only one chromosome from each homologous pair of chromosomes. Turn back to the image on page 94 that shows the process of meiosis. In which stage of meiosis do homologous chromosomes separate?

    _____

    _____

5.  Give two examples of human traits that are not mentioned in the section above. _____

    _____

    _____

# Traits, Genes, and Alleles

**KEY CONCEPT**  Genes encode proteins that produce a diverse range of traits.

## The same gene can have many versions.

As you learned, the units of inheritance that Mendel studied are now called genes. You can think of a **gene** as a piece of DNA that stores instructions to make a certain protein. Each gene is located at a particular place on a chromosome called a locus. Just like a house has an address on a street, a gene has a locus on a chromosome.

Many things come in different forms. For example, bread can be wheat, white, or rye. Most genes have many forms, too. An **allele** (uh-LEEL) is any of the different forms of a gene. The gene for pea shape, for example, has two alleles—one for round peas and another for wrinkled peas.

Your cells, like the pea plant's cells, have two alleles for each gene—one on each chromosome of a homologous pair. The term **homozygous** (HOH-moh-ZY-guhs) means the two alleles of a gene are the same—for example, both alleles are for round peas. The term **heterozygous** (HEHT-uhr-uh-ZY-guhs) means the two alleles are different—for example, one allele is for wrinkled peas and one is for round peas.

 Draw a circle around each of the alleles shown in the Visual Vocab to the right.

## Genes influence the development of traits.

For Mendel's peas, if a plant was heterozygous for pea shape, the pea shape would be round. This is because the allele for round peas is **dominant,** or expressed when two different alleles are present. A **recessive** allele is expressed only when there are two copies of the recessive allele. A dominant allele is not better or stronger or more common; it is simply the allele that is expressed when there are two different alleles. Mendel studied traits that had just two alleles, one that was dominant and one that was recessive. Most traits involve much more complicated patterns of inheritance.

Alleles are represented with letters—capital letters for dominant alleles and lowercase letters for recessive alleles. For example, the dominant allele for round pea shape can be

**VISUAL VOCAB**

**Homozygous** alleles are identical to each other.

homozygous alleles

wrinkled   wrinkled

heterozygous alleles

wrinkled   round

**Heterozygous** alleles are different from each other.

The drawing on p. 93 shows a homologous pair of duplicated chromosomes. Notice that here the chromosomes are drawn unduplicated. These are two homologous pairs of unduplicated chromosomes.

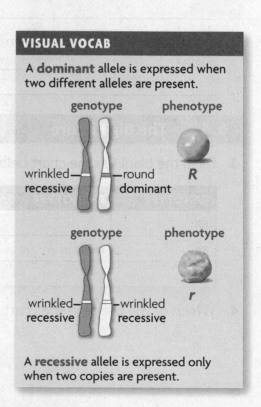

**VISUAL VOCAB**

A **dominant** allele is expressed when two different alleles are present.

genotype           phenotype

wrinkled—   —round
recessive        dominant          *R*

genotype           phenotype

wrinkled—   —wrinkled
recessive        recessive          *r*

A **recessive** allele is expressed only when two copies are present.

written as *R*, for round. The recessive allele, for wrinkled pea shape, can be represented with the same letter, but lowercase—*r*.

A **genotype** is the set of alleles an organism has for a trait. For example, a genotype could be homozygous dominant (*RR*), heterozygous (*Rr*), or homozygous recessive (*rr*). A **phenotype** is what the resulting trait looks like—for example, round or wrinkled. A **genome** is all of an organism's genetic material—all of the genes on all of the chromosomes.

 What is the difference between a genotype and a phenotype?

_____

_____

| 6.4 | Vocabulary Check |
|---|---|

**Mark It Up**

Go back and highlight each sentence that has a vocabulary word in **bold**.

gene    recessive

allele    genotype

homozygous  phenotype

heterozygous  genome

dominant

1. What is the difference between a gene and an allele? _____

_____

_____

2. What is the difference between a dominant allele and a recessive allele? _____

_____

| 6.4 | The Big Picture |
|---|---|

3. Fill in the blanks in the chart below regarding pea shape.

| GENOTYPE | PHENOTYPE | HOMOZYGOUS OR HETEROZYGOUS |
|---|---|---|
| *RR* | | homozygous dominant |
| *Rr* | round peas | |
| *rr* | | homozygous recessive |

4. Which of the alleles in the chart above is dominant? _____

# 6.5 Traits and Probability

**KEY CONCEPT** The inheritance of traits follows the rules of probability.

## Punnett squares illustrate genetic crosses.

A **Punnett square** is a grid* system for predicting all possible genotypes resulting from a cross. The outside edges, or axes*, of the grid represent the possible genotypes of gametes from each parent. The grid boxes show the possible genotypes of offspring from those two parents.

Let's briefly review what you've learned about meiosis and segregation to examine how the Punnett square works. Both parents have two alleles for each gene. These alleles are represented on the axes of the Punnett square. During meiosis, the chromosomes—and therefore the alleles—are separated. Each gamete can receive only one of the alleles, but not both. When fertilization happens, gametes from each parent join together and form a diploid cell with two copies of each chromosome. The new cell has two alleles for each gene. This is why each box shows two alleles. One is from each parent.

**VISUAL VOCAB**

The **Punnett square** is a grid system for predicting possible genotypes of offspring.

Parent 1 alleles

Parent 2 alleles

possible genotypes of offspring

 **What do the letters on the axes of the Punnett square represent?** _____

## A monohybrid cross involves one trait.

Thus far, we have studied crosses of one trait. **Monohybrid crosses** are crosses that examine the inheritance of only one specific trait—for example, flower color. If we know the genotypes of the parents, we can use a Punnett square to predict the genotypes of the offspring.

The Punnett squares on the next page show the results of three different crosses:

- Homozygous dominant crossed with homozygous recessive (*FF* × *ff*)
- Heterozygous crossed with heterozygous (*Ff* × *Ff*)
- Heterozygous crossed with homozygous recessive (*Ff* × *ff*)

**grid** a layout of squares, like on graph paper

**axes** lines that act as points of reference

All offspring receive a dominant allele, *F*, from one parent and a recessive allele, *f*, from the other parent. So all offspring—100 percent—have the heterozygous genotype *Ff*. And 100 percent of offspring have purple flowers.

From each parent, half of the offspring receive a dominant allele, *F*, and half receive a recessive allele, *f*. Therefore, one-fourth of the offspring have an *FF* genotype, one-half are *Ff*, and one-fourth are *ff*. In other words, the genotypic ratio is 1:2:1 of *FF* : *Ff* : *ff*. Remember that both *FF* and *Ff* genotypes have a purple phenotype. The phenotypic ratio is 3:1 of purple:white flowers.

All of the offspring receive a recessive allele, *f*, from the homozygous recessive parent. Half receive a dominant allele, *F*, from the heterozygous parent, and half receive the recessive allele, *f*. The resulting genotypic ratio is 1:1 of *Ff:ff*. The phenotypic ratio is 1:1 of purple:white.

Suppose that we had a purple-flowered pea plant but did not know its genotype. It could be *FF* or *Ff*. We could figure out its genotype by crossing the purple-flowered plant with a white-flowered plant. We know that the white-flowered plant is *ff*, because it has the recessive phenotype. If the purple-flowered plant is *FF*, the offspring will all be purple. If the purple-flowered plant is *Ff*, half of the offspring will have purple flowers, and half will have white flowers. Crossing a homozygous recessive organism with an organism of unknown genotype is called a **testcross.**

What are the genotypes of offspring from an *FF* × *ff* cross?

## A dihybrid cross involves two traits.

So far, we have examined monohybrid crosses, or crosses that examine only one trait. Mendel also performed **dihybrid crosses,** or crosses that examine the inheritance of two different traits.

For example, Mendel crossed a purebred plant that had yellow round peas with a purebred plant that had green wrinkled peas. He wanted to see if the two traits—pea shape and color— were inherited together. The first generation of offspring all looked the same, and they were all heterozygous for both traits. The second generation of offspring is shown in the figure to the right. In addition to green wrinkled and yellow round peas, there were also green round and yellow wrinkled peas. In other words, Mendel found that pea shape and color were independent of each other—they were not inherited together. Mendel's second law of genetics is the **law of independent assortment,** which states that alleles of different genes separate independently of one another during gamete formation, or meiosis. Different traits are inherited separately.

VOCABULARY

*Mono-* means "one," and *di-* means "two." A *monohybrid cross* looks at one trait and a *dihybrid cross* looks at two traits.

**DIHYBRID CROSS**

This dihybrid cross is heterozygous-heterozygous.

F₁ generation

| | YR | Yr | yR | yr |
|---|---|---|---|---|
| YR | YYRR | YYRr | YyRR | YyRr |
| Yr | YYRr | YYrr | YyRr | Yyrr |
| yR | YyRR | YyRr | yyRR | yyRr |
| yr | YyRr | Yyrr | yyRr | yyrr |

F₂ generation

 **What is the difference between a monohybrid cross and a dihybrid cross?** _____

_____

## Heredity patterns can be calculated with probability.

**Probability** is the likelihood, or chance, that a particular event will happen. It predicts the average number of times something happens, not the exact number of times.

$$\text{Probability} = \frac{\text{number of ways a specific event can occur}}{\text{number of total possible outcomes}}$$

Suppose you flip a coin. There is a $\frac{1}{2}$ chance it will land on heads, and a $\frac{1}{2}$ chance that it will land on tails. Suppose you flip two coins. For each one, the chance it will land on heads is $\frac{1}{2}$. But for both to land on heads, the chance is $\frac{1}{2} \times \frac{1}{2} = \frac{1}{4}$.

These probabilities can be applied to meiosis, too. Suppose a germ cell has heterozygous alleles for a trait, for example, *Ff*. A gamete has a $\frac{1}{2}$ chance of getting an *F* and a $\frac{1}{2}$ chance of getting an *f*. If two heterozygous plants are crossed, what is the chance that the offspring will be *FF*? There is a $\frac{1}{2}$ chance that the sperm will carry an *F* and a $\frac{1}{2}$ chance that the egg will carry an *F*. Therefore, there is a $\frac{1}{2} \times \frac{1}{2} = \frac{1}{4}$ chance that the offspring will be *FF*. Probability can be used to determine all of the possible genotypic outcomes of a cross.

**PROBABILITY AND HEREDITY**

The coins are equally likely to land heads up or tails up.

Two sides of coin 2

$\frac{1}{2}$ H    $\frac{1}{2}$ T

$\frac{1}{2}$ H

Two sides of coin 1

$\frac{1}{2}$ T

$\frac{1}{4}$ HH    $\frac{1}{4}$ HT

$\frac{1}{4}$ HT    $\frac{1}{4}$ TT

If you flip two coins, what is the probability that they will both land on tails?

_____

---

## 6.5    Vocabulary Check

**Mark It Up**

Go back and highlight each sentence that has a vocabulary word in **bold**.

Punnett square          dihybrid cross
monohybrid cross        law of independent assortment
testcross               probability

**Choose the correct term from the list for each description.**

1. crossing an organism of unknown genotype with a homozygous recessive organism _____

2. a cross to examine one trait only _____

3. a cross to examine two different traits _____

## 6.5    The Big Picture

4. Fill in the Punnett square and list the genotype and phenotype ratios.

Genotype ratio: _____

Phenotype ratio: _____

|     | F   | f   |
| --- | --- | --- |
| f   |     | Ff  |
| f   |     |     |

# SECTION 6.6 Meiosis and Genetic Variation

**KEY CONCEPT** Independent assortment and crossing over during meiosis result in genetic diversity.

## Sexual reproduction creates unique gene combinations.

Sexual reproduction produces a lot of variety within a species. This genetic variety comes from the events of meiosis and from the fertilization of gametes, which is a random process. Recall that humans have 23 pairs of chromosomes, and that each pair assorts independently from the others. As a result, there are about 8 million different combinations of chromosomes that can be produced during meiosis of one human cell.

Suppose a human sperm cell that has one of 8 million different possible combinations fertilizes a human egg cell that has one of 8 million different possible combinations. Since any sperm cell can fertilize any egg, more than 64 trillion possible combinations can result.

For all sexually reproducing organisms, sexual reproduction results in unique combinations of the two parents' genes. Therefore, their offspring have unique phenotypes. This variety helps some organisms of a species survive and reproduce in conditions where other organisms of the species cannot.

 **INSTANT REPLAY** What are two parts of sexual reproduction that produce genetic variation?

_____

_____

## Crossing over during meiosis increases genetic diversity.

Crossing over is a process that occurs during meiosis and also contributes to genetic variation. **Crossing over** is the exchange* of chromosome pieces between homologous chromosomes. This happens during prophase I of meiosis I. The process is shown in the figure to the right. Crossing over can happen many times—even within the same pair of homologous chromosomes.

\* ACADEMIC VOCABULARY

**exchange** to give and receive, or to trade something

> **VOCABULARY**
>
> Recall Mendel's law of independent assortment described on p. 103.

### CROSSING OVER

**Crossing over exchanges pieces of DNA between homologous chromosomes.**

1. Two homologous chromosomes pair up with each other during prophase I in meiosis.

2. In this position, some chromatids are very close to each other and pieces cross.

3. Some of these pieces break off and reattach to the other homologous chromosome.

Recall that a single chromosome has many genes, each with its own locus, or place, on the chromosome. Two genes on the same chromosome may be close together or far apart. For example, in the figure to the right, genes A and B are close together, but they are both far apart from genes C and D. When crossing over occurs, it is likely that genes A and B will be separated from genes C and D. But it is unlikely that genes A and B will be separated from each other—or that C and D will be separated—because they are so close together. Genes located close together tend to be inherited together, which is called **genetic linkage.**

**INSTANT REPLAY** In the figure above, which genes are likely to be separated by crossing over? _____

## 6.6 Vocabulary Check

**Mark It Up**

Go back and highlight each sentence that has a vocabulary word in **bold.**

crossing over            genetic linkage

1. Draw a picture that shows two chromosomes crossing over.

2. Draw a picture that shows genetic linkage of two genes on a chromosome.

## 6.6 The Big Picture

3. How is genetic diversity beneficial to a species? _____

_____

4. How does crossing over contribute to genetic diversity? _____

_____

_____

# Chapter 6 Review

1. Which pair of sex chromosomes makes a person male: XX or XY ?

2. Which cells in a multicellular organism undergo meiosis? _____
   _____

3. What is the final product of meiosis?

   **a.** identical diploid cells

   **b.** unique diploid cells

   **c.** identical haploid cells

   **d.** unique haploid cells

4. In pea plants, the allele for tall stems, *T*, is dominant to the allele for short stems, *t*. Draw and fill in a Punnett square that shows the cross of a heterozygous plant, *Tt*, with a homozygous dominant plant, *TT*.

5. List all the possible genotypes of the offspring from your Punnett square in question 4. Next to each genotype write the corresponding phenotype—short stems or tall stems.

6. What part of meiosis is responsible for Mendel's law of segregation?

   **a.** DNA condensing into tightly packaged chromosomes

   **b.** homologous chromosomes crossing over

   **c.** alleles assorting independently into gametes

   **d.** homologous pairs of chromosomes separating into different gametes

7. Which human cells are haploid? _____

8. Explain in words or with drawings how the processes of *fertilization* and *crossing over* contribute to genetic diversity.

CHAPTER

# 7 Extending Mendelian Genetics

## GETTING READY TO LEARN

### Preview Key Concepts

**7.1 Chromosomes and Phenotype**
The chromosomes on which genes are located can affect the expression of traits.

**7.2 Complex Patterns of Inheritance**
Phenotype is affected by many different factors.

**7.3 Gene Linkage and Mapping**
Genes can be mapped to specific locations on chromosomes.

**7.4 Human Genetics and Pedigrees**
A combination of methods is used to study human genetics.

### Review Academic Vocabulary

dominant          recessive          phenotype          autosome

1. _____ : physical expression of genes

2. _____ : may be masked by another gene

3. _____ : chromosomes other than X and Y

4. _____ : expressed even if only one copy is present

### Preview Biology Vocabulary

Try to guess the meaning of each boldfaced word from its context.

| PHRASE | MY GUESS |
|---|---|
| 1. If a woman is a **carrier** of red-green colorblindness, she is able to see red and green but her son may not. | |
| 2. Human skin color is a **polygenic trait** that results from the expression of four different genes. | |
| 3. Doctors can use a **karyotype** to see where a patient's chromosome has broken off. | |

108

# 7.1 Chromosomes and Phenotype

**KEY CONCEPT** The chromosomes on which genes are located can affect the expression of traits.

About 99.9 percent of everyone's DNA is identical. But look around you and you'll see a huge variety of traits, such as hair color and texture, eye color and shape, height and weight. Mendel's peas are a good place to start learning about genetics. But the great variety in living things is not just a result of dominant and recessive alleles. There are many complexities of genetic inheritance.

## Two copies of each autosomal gene affect phenotype.

Recall that autosomes are all of an organism's chromosomes except the sex chromosomes. Sexually reproducing organisms have two of each chromosome, one from the mother and one from the father. The two chromosomes have the same genes, but may have different alleles. Different alleles can produce different phenotypes.

Most traits are the result of genes on autosomes. Many human genetic disorders* are also caused by autosomal genes. The chance that a person will have one of these disorders can be predicted, just as we predicted the phenotypes of Mendel's peas.

### Disorders Caused by Recessive Alleles

Two copies of the allele must be present for a person to have a disorder caused by recessive alleles. Someone who is homozygous for the recessive allele will have the disorder. Someone who is heterozygous does not have the disorder but is a carrier. A **carrier** is someone who does not have a disorder but carries the recessive allele, and therefore can pass the allele on to offspring. If both parents are heterozygotes, neither will have the disorder, but they can still have children with the disorder.

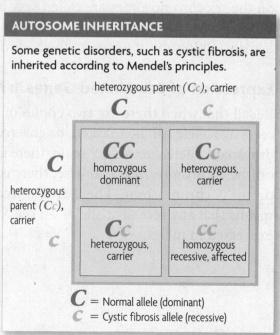

**AUTOSOME INHERITANCE**

Some genetic disorders, such as cystic fibrosis, are inherited according to Mendel's principles.

heterozygous parent (*Cc*), carrier

|  | *C* | *c* |
|---|---|---|
| *C* | *CC* homozygous dominant | *Cc* heterozygous, carrier |
| *c* | *Cc* heterozygous, carrier | *cc* homozygous recessive, affected |

heterozygous parent (*Cc*), carrier

*C* = Normal allele (dominant)
*c* = Cystic fibrosis allele (recessive)

* ACADEMIC VOCABULARY

**disorder** disease

### Disorders Caused by Dominant Alleles

Dominant genetic disorders are less common than recessive disorders. Because the disorder is caused by a dominant allele, there is a 50 percent chance that a child will have it even if only one parent has one of the alleles. If both parents are heterozygous for a dominant disorder, they both have symptoms of the disorder, and there is a 75 percent chance that a child will inherit the disorder.

 What is the genotype of a carrier of a recessive disorder?

_____

## Males and females can differ in sex-linked traits.

So far, we have examined the expression of autosomal genes. The expression of genes on sex chromosomes—the X and Y chromosomes—is different. Recall that for humans and other mammals, females have an XX genotype and males have an XY genotype. A female can pass on only an X chromosome to offspring. A male can pass on either an X or a Y chromosome to offspring.

In humans and many other organisms, the Y chromosome is smaller and has many fewer genes than the X chromosome. In addition to sex determination, genes on the X chromosome affect many traits. Genes on the sex chromosomes are called **sex-linked genes**. When people talk about sex-linked genes, they are usually talking about genes on the X chromosome.

**SEX CHROMOSOME INHERITANCE**

The gametes from an XY male determine the sex of the offspring.

### Expression of Sex-Linked Genes in Males

Recall that when there are two copies of an allele, the expression of a recessive allele can be masked, or covered up, by the expression of a dominant allele. For an XY male, there is only one copy of each gene on the Y chromosome. Likewise, there is only one copy of each gene on the X chromosome. There are no second copies of the alleles. This means that any recessive alleles on the X or Y chromosomes will be expressed in males.

## Expression of Sex-Linked Genes in Females

All of the body cells in a female have two X chromosomes. But each cell uses only one of the two X chromosomes. The other X chromosome gets "turned off." Which of the two X chromosomes remains active and which gets turned off is random. In other words, some cells use one X chromosome, and other cells use the other X chromosome.

**X chromosome inactivation** is the process by which one of the two X chromosomes in every cell in female mammals gets turned off. Even though only one of the two alleles is expressed in each cell, overall, both alleles for each gene on the X chromosomes affect a female's phenotype.

 Why do males have only one allele for all genes on the X chromosome? _____

_____

---

### 7.1    Vocabulary Check

**Mark It Up**

Go back and highlight each sentence that has a vocabulary word in **bold**.

carrier                    X chromosome inactivation

sex-linked gene

1. Which term describes something that happens in female mammals?
   _____

2. Which term describes an organism that is a heterozygote for a recessive autosomal disorder?
   _____

3. Which term describes a gene that will always be expressed in male mammals?
   _____

---

### 7.1    The Big Picture

4. Look back at the figure of autosome inheritance. The two parents are carriers of a recessive disorder called cystic fibrosis. What is the probability that any of the offspring of these two parents will have the disorder? _____

5. Look back at the figure of sex chromosome inheritance. Explain why a female can pass on only an X chromosome to offspring? _____

_____

_____

**KEY CONCEPT** Phenotype is affected by many different factors.

## Phenotype can depend on interactions* of alleles.

In many cases, alleles are not simply dominant or recessive. Alleles may interact in many different ways. For example, alleles might have a range of dominance. There might be more than just two alleles for a gene. Or there might be many different genes that all affect one trait.

### Incomplete Dominance

Sometimes, neither allele is completely dominant or completely recessive. In this case, the heterozygous phenotype is somewhere between the two homozygous phenotypes. In other words, the alleles show **incomplete dominance.** One example of incomplete dominance is the flowers of the four o'clock plant. When plants that are homozygous for red flowers are crossed with plants that are homozygous for white flowers, the offspring have pink flowers. Neither of the phenotypes of the parents can be seen separately in the offspring.

**VISUAL VOCAB**

When alleles are neither dominant nor recessive, such as with incomplete dominance, uppercase letters with either subscripts— $F_2$—or superscripts—$F^2$—are used to represent the different alleles.

| GENOTYPE | $F_1F_1$ | $F_1F_2$ | $F_2F_2$ |
|---|---|---|---|
| PHENOTYPE | red flowers | pink flowers | white flowers |

The flower colors of the four o'clock plant show incomplete dominance. Heterozygous plants have a phenotype in between the two homozygous plants.

### Codominance

Sometimes, both alleles of a gene are expressed completely, and neither is dominant or recessive. In this case, alleles show **codominance.** With incomplete dominance, recall that the heterozygous flowers were pink—a blend of the two homozygous phenotypes. Codominance is different because both traits are expressed separately. The heterozygous phenotype would have some red areas and some white areas.

---

**\* ACADEMIC VOCABULARY**

**interaction** two or more things working together

Human blood types are an example of codominance. Blood type is also a multiple-allele trait, because there are three different alleles. The three alleles are called $I^A$, $I^B$, and $i$. Both $I^A$ and $I^B$ produce a protein called an antigen on the surface of red blood cells. $I^A$ and $I^B$ are codominant. Allele $i$ is recessive and does not produce an antigen. Four different phenotypes are possible, shown in the figure to the right.

**INSTANT REPLAY** What is the difference between incomplete dominance and codominance? _____

_____

_____

| CODOMINANCE | | |
|---|---|---|
| PHENOTYPE (BLOOD TYPE) | | GENOTYPES |
| A | antigen A | $I^AI^A$ or $I^Ai$ |
| B | antigen B | $I^BI^B$ or $I^Bi$ |
| AB | both antigens | $I^AI^B$ |
| O | no antigens | $ii$ |

# Many genes may interact to produce one trait.

As you have seen, some phenotypes are a result of incomplete dominance, codominance, and multiple alleles. But most traits in plants and animals, including humans, are the result of several genes that interact.

## Polygenic Traits

Traits produced by two or more genes are called **polygenic traits.** For example, eye color and skin color are both determined by the interaction of multiple genes. At least three genes affect eye color. Each gene has two alleles. Scientists think that there may be even more genes that affect eye color.

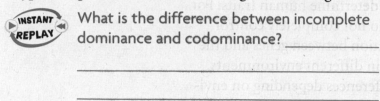

**VISUAL VOCAB**

Traits that are produced by two or more genes are called **polygenic traits.**

| many | genes |
| poly | genic |

## Epistasis

Fur color in mice and other mammals is also a polygenic trait. In mice, at least five different genes interact to produce the fur color phenotype. One of the genes is called an epistatic gene. This gene can prevent the expression of all of the other genes. Albinism—the lack of pigment* in skin, hair, and eyes—is the result of epistasis. If a mouse is homozygous for the alleles that prevent pigmentation, the fur will be white no matter what alleles the mouse has for the other four genes. Albinism occurs in humans, too.

| GENE NAME | DOMINANT ALLELE | RECESSIVE ALLELE |
|---|---|---|
| BEY1 | brown | blue |
| BEY2 | brown | blue |
| GEY | green | blue |

At least three different genes interact to produce the range of human eye colors.

**INSTANT REPLAY** What is the difference between a multiple-allele trait and a polygenic trait? _____

_____

# The environment interacts with genotype.

Phenotype is not determined only by genes. The environment—the conditions surrounding an organism—also affect phenotype. For example, the sex of sea turtles depends on the temperature of the environment in which the egg develops. Female turtles make nests on beaches and bury their eggs in the sand. Eggs that are in warmer parts of the nest become female. Eggs in cooler parts become male.

Genes and environment also interact to determine human traits. For example, genes influence height, but they do not completely control height. One way scientists study the interaction between genes and the environment is by comparing twins raised in different environments. Identical twins can have height and size differences depending on environmental conditions such as nutrition and health care.

 Why might genetically identical twins have different phenotypes?

_____

_____

## 7.2    Vocabulary Check

**Mark It Up**

Go back and highlight each sentence that has a vocabulary word in **bold**.

incomplete dominance          polygenic trait
codominance

**Match the correct term from the list to each example below.**

1. Eye color, which is determined by at least three genes, is an example of

   _____

2. The flowers of a heterozygous four o'clock plant are pink, which is between the flower color of each homozygous plant. This is an example of _____

3. Human blood type is determined by a protein, called an antigen, on the surface of red blood cells. Someone with both the $I^A$ and $I^B$ alleles will have both the A and B antigens on their red blood cells. This is an example of _____

## 7.2    The Big Picture

4. List at least three patterns of inheritance that are different than the dominant-recessive pattern of Mendel's peas. _____

   _____

# 7.3 Gene Linkage and Mapping

**KEY CONCEPT** Genes can be mapped to specific locations on chromosomes.

## Gene linkage was explained through fruit flies.

You may have seen fruit flies in the kitchen, buzzing around ripe fruit. Fruit flies are also used in genetic research because they have variations that are easy to observe, for example, in eye color, body color, and wing shape.

A scientist named Thomas Hunt Morgan and his students did experiments similar to Mendel's experiments, but with fruit flies. They found that some traits were inherited together. They called these traits linked traits. They concluded that linked traits are caused by linked genes—genes that are on the same chromosome. Chromosomes, not genes, assort independently during meiosis. So genes on the same chromosome move together. But they also found that linked genes were not always inherited together. They concluded that this is because of crossing over between homologous chromosomes.

**Connecting CONCEPTS**

**Crossing Over** Recall from **Chapter 6** that segments of non-sister chromatids can be exchanged during meiosis.

**INSTANT REPLAY** What are linked genes? _____

_____

## Linkage maps estimate distances between genes.

Recall from Chapter 6 that homologous chromosomes cross over, or exchange pieces, during meiosis. The closer together two genes are, the less likely it is that they will be separated by crossing over. The farther apart two genes are, the more likely it is that they will be separated during meiosis.

One of Morgan's students kept track of the number of times that linked genes were inherited separately. In other words, he kept track of the frequency of cross-overs. He converted the percentage of cross-overs into a measurement called map units. Using this information, he made **linkage maps** that showed the relative locations of genes on a chromosome. You can see an example of a linkage map in the figure to the right.

**A LINKAGE MAP FOR GENES A, B, AND C**

- Gene A and gene B get separated, or cross over, 6.0 percent of the time.

- Gene B and gene C get separated 12.5 percent of the time.

- Gene A and gene C get separated 18.5 percent of the time.

The chromosome is drawn as a line. The locations of the genes are shown as points on the line. The cross-over frequencies can be used to figure out the order, or relative locations, of genes on the same chromosome.

Linkage maps show the relative locations of genes, but not the actual physical distances between the genes.

 Why does the frequency of cross-overs give information about the relative locations of genes? _____

_____

_____

| 7.3 | Vocabulary Check |
| --- | --- |

**Mark It Up**

Go back and highlight each sentence that has a vocabulary word in **bold**.

linkage map

1. Use the following data to label the linkage map below for genes R, S, and T.

   • Gene R and gene S cross over 5.0 percent of the time.

   • Gene S and gene T cross over 10.0 percent of the time.

   • Gene R and gene T cross over 15.0 percent of the time.

| 7.3 | The Big Picture |
| --- | --- |

2. How were fruit flies used in genetic research? _____

_____

_____

3. How are linked genes different from sex-linked genes? _____

_____

_____

# 7.4 Human Genetics and Pedigrees

**KEY CONCEPT** A combination of methods is used to study human genetics.

## Human genetics follows the patterns seen in other organisms.

Fruit flies and pea plants may seem simple. And they are certainly different than humans. But human genetics follows the same patterns of heredity. The process of meiosis happens the same way in humans as in fruit flies. Humans, like other organisms that reproduce sexually, have the same relationships between alleles: dominant-recessive interactions, polygenic traits, and sex-linked genes, among others.

Although many traits are complex, single-gene traits are helpful in understanding human genetics. A downward-pointed hairline—called a widow's peak—is a single-gene trait with a dominant-recessive inheritance pattern. Many human genetic disorders are, too. Much of what is known about human genetics comes from studying genetic disorders.

 In what ways are human genetics similar to fruit fly or pea plant genetics? _____

_____

_____

## Females can carry sex-linked disorders.

Recall from Section 7.1 that some genetic disorders are caused by genes on autosomes. Both males and females can be carriers of a recessive autosomal disorder. That is, they can have one recessive allele but have no symptoms of the disorder.

In contrast, only females can be carriers of a sex-linked disorder. Recall that the X chromosome has far more genes than the Y chromosome, including some that cause genetic disorders. A sex-linked disorder usually refers to a gene on the X chromosome.

Females have an XX genotype. Because they have two X chromosomes, they can be heterozygous and have one recessive allele, but not have symptoms of the disorder. A male has an XY genotype. A male who has an allele for a disorder located on the X chromosome will not have a second, normal allele to mask it.

> **VOCABULARY**
>
> The term *carrier* means "a person who transports something." In genetics, a carrier is a person who "transports" a recessive allele but does not express the recessive phenotype.

 Why can't males be carriers of sex-linked disorders? _____

_____

# A pedigree is a chart for tracing genes in a family.

A **pedigree** chart can help trace the phenotypes and genotypes in a family to determine the chance that a child might have a certain genetic disorder. The genotypes can often be figured out using enough family phenotypes. Using phenotypes to figure out the possible genotypes in a family is like solving a puzzle. You have to use logic* and clues to narrow the possibilities for each person's genotype.

## Tracing Autosomal Genes

Consider the widow's peak, the pointed shape of a person's hairline, mentioned earlier in this section. The widow's peak is an autosomal trait. A pointed hairline is dominant to a straight hairline.

- People with a widow's peak have either homozygous dominant (*WW*) or heterozygous (*Ww*) genotypes.
- Two parents without a widow's peak are both homozygous recessive (*ww*), and cannot have children who have a widow's peak.
- Two parents who both have a widow's peak can have a child who does not (*ww*) if both parents are heterozygous (*Ww*).

The inheritance of this trait is shown in the figure below.

| | |
|---|---|
| ☐ | Male without phenotype |
| ◼ | Male with phenotype |
| ◪ | Male carrier |

| | |
|---|---|
| ○ | Female without phenotype |
| ● | Female with phenotype |
| ◓ | Female carrier |

**TRACING AUTOSOMAL GENES: WIDOW'S PEAK**

**Parental generation**

1 ☐ — 2 ○
*ww*    *Ww*

*W* = Dominant
*w* = Recessive

- Male 1 must be *ww* and female 2 must be heterozygous (*Ww*), because they have a daughter (5) with the recessive trait.

**F₁ generation**

3 ☐ — 4 ◓   5 ○   6 ◼ — 7 ●
*ww*   *Ww*   *ww*   *Ww*   *WW* or *Ww*

- Children 4 and 6 have the widow's peak trait. They must be heterozygous, because they can inherit only one dominant allele.

**F₂ generation**

8 ● 9 ○ 10 ◼   11 ◼ 12 ● 13 ◼
*Ww* *ww* *Ww*   *WW* or *Ww*   *WW* or *Ww*   *WW* or *Ww*

- Children 8 and 10 have the widow's peak trait. They must be heterozygous, because they can inherit only one dominant allele.

* ACADEMIC VOCABULARY

**logic** reason, critical thinking

## Tracing Sex-Linked Genes

For sex-linked genes, you have to think about dominant and recessive alleles, but you also have to think about inheritance of the sex chromosomes. One example of a sex-linked trait is red-green colorblindness, a condition that causes a person to not be able to see the difference between some colors.

| PHENOTYPE | GENOTYPES | |
|---|---|---|
| | **MALE** | **FEMALE** |
| Red-green colorblind | $X^m Y$ | $X^m X^m$ |
| Normal vision | $X^M Y$ | $X^M X^m$ or $X^M X^M$ |

By using a process of elimination*, you can often figure out the possible genotypes for a given phenotype.

- Colorblind females must be homozygous recessive ($X^m X^m$).
- Males who are colorblind must have the recessive allele ($X^m Y$).
- Females who are heterozygous for the alleles ($X^M X^m$) are not colorblind, but are carriers of the trait.

The inheritance of colorblindness is shown in the figure below.

☐ Male without phenotype  ◯ Female without phenotype

■ Male with phenotype  ● Female with phenotype

◩ Male carrier  ◖ Female carrier

TRACING SEX-LINKED GENES: COLORBLINDNESS

**Parental generation**

1 $X^M Y$ — 2 $X^M X^m$

$X^M$ = Dominant
$X^m$ = Recessive

- Male 1 must be $X^M Y$ and female 2 must be a carrier ($X^M X^m$) because they have two colorblind sons.

**F₁ generation**

3 $X^M Y$  4 $X^M X^m$  5? $X^M X^M$ or $X^M X^m$  6 $X^m Y$  7 $X^m Y$  8? $X^M X^M$ or $X^M X^m$

- Female 4 must be a carrier ($X^M X^m$) because she has a colorblind son. Males 6 and 7 must be $X^m Y$. Females 5 and 8 are not colorblind, but it is not possible to determine whether they are carriers.

**F₂ generation**

9? $X^M X^M$ or $X^M X^m$  10 $X^M Y$  11? $X^M X^M$ or $X^M X^m$  12 $X^m Y$  13 $X^M X^m$  14 $X^M X^m$  15 $X^M Y$

- Children 13 and 14 must be carriers because their father is colorblind. Females 9 and 11 are not colorblind, but it is not possible to determine whether they are carriers.

**What is one difference between tracing the inheritance of autosomal traits and tracing the inheritance of sex-linked traits?**

_____

_____

***ACADEMIC VOCABULARY**

**process of elimination** getting to the best answer by ruling out possible answers that are not correct

# Several methods help map human chromosomes.

The human genome, or all of the DNA in a human cell, is so large that it is difficult to map human genes. In addition to pedigrees, other methods more directly study human chromosomes. A **karyotype** (KAR-ee-uh-TYP), for example, is a picture of all of the chromosomes in a cell. Chemicals are used to stain the chromosomes. The stains produce a pattern of bands on the chromosomes. These patterns can be used to tell different chromosomes apart. Karyotypes can also show if there are extra chromosomes or missing parts of chromosomes. Down syndrome, for example, results from an extra copy of at least part of chromosome 21, and can be identified on a karyotype. The large-scale mapping of all human genes truly began with the Human Genome Project, which you will read more about in Chapter 9.

 What is one example of a genetic disorder that can be seen on a karyotype? _____

## 7.4  Vocabulary Check

**Mark It Up**

Go back and highlight each sentence that has a vocabulary word in **bold**.

pedigree                    karyotype

Label the drawings below with the proper term.

1.

2.

_____        _____

## 7.4  The Big Picture

3. Why can the genetics of fruit flies be applied to humans?

_____

4. What is the genotype of a female carrier of a sex-linked genetic disorder? _____

5. What are pedigree charts used for? _____

_____

6. What types of information can a karyotype provide?

_____

# Chapter 7 Review

1. A certain disorder is recessive and sex-linked. Circle all of the genotypes of people who have the disorder.

   $X^R X^r$      $X^r X^r$      $X^R Y$      $X^r Y$

2. A certain disorder is recessive and autosomal. Circle all of the genotypes of people who have the disorder.

   *RR*      *Rr*      *rr*

3. Explain how the expression of genes on sex chromosomes differs from the expression of genes on autosomal chromosomes. _____

   _____

   _____

4. If two genes are linked, what does that mean about their physical location on chromosomes? _____

5. Which of the following shows the genotype for a normal human male?

   a. X

   b. YY

   c. XX

   d. XY

6. The frequency of a certain biological process—in which pieces of homologous chromosomes are exchanged—is used to figure out gene linkage maps. What is the name of this process? _____

7. It is known that two fruit fly traits are linked. One trait is determined by gene A and the other by gene B. The two traits are usually, but not always, inherited together. What is the best explanation for this observation?

   a. the genes are not linked

   b. the genes are on different chromosomes

   c. the genes are far enough apart for crossing over to occur

   d. the genes are too close for crossing over to occur

8. Some traits follow two-allele dominant-recessive inheritance patterns. Name at least two other genetic inheritance patterns. _____

   _____

   _____

# 8 From DNA to Proteins

## GETTING READY TO LEARN

### Preview Key Concepts

**8.1 Identifying DNA as the Genetic Material**
DNA was identified as the genetic material through a series of experiments.

**8.2 Structure of DNA**
DNA structure is the same in all organisms.

**8.3 DNA Replication**
DNA replication copies the genetic information of a cell.

**8.4 Transcription**
Transcription converts a gene into a single-stranded RNA molecule.

**8.5 Translation**
Translation converts an mRNA message into a polypeptide, or protein.

**8.6 Gene Expression and Regulation**
Gene expression is carefully regulated in both prokaryotic and eukaryotic cells.

**8.7 Mutations**
Mutations are changes in DNA that may or may not affect phenotype.

### Review Academic Vocabulary

Write the correct word for each definition.

enzyme    ribosome    protein

1. _____ : biological catalyst

2. _____ : site of protein synthesis

3. _____ : shape determines its function

### Preview Biology Vocabulary

See how many key terms from this chapter you already know. Rewrite each phrase, using a different word or words for the **words in bold**.

| PHRASE | REWRITTEN WITH DIFFERENT WORDS |
|---|---|
| 1. DNA **replication** allows every new cell to have a complete set of DNA. | DNA _____ allows every new cell to have a complete set of DNA. |
| 2. **Mutagens** such as UV light can result in skin cancer. | _____ such as UV light can result in skin cancer. |
| 3. **RNA** is found in both the nucleus and the cytoplasm. | _____ is found in both the nucleus and the cytoplasm. |

# 8.1 Identifying DNA as the Genetic Material

**KEY CONCEPT** DNA was identified as the genetic material through a series of experiments.

DNA was identified as the genetic material relatively recently—in the 1950s. This section reviews three research projects that all added up to this discovery: 1) Griffith's research, 2) Avery's research, and 3) Hershey and Chase's research. Together, these scientists' findings led to the conclusion that DNA is the genetic material.

## Griffith finds a "transforming principle."

In 1928 a British microbiologist named Frederick Griffith investigated two forms of the bacterium that causes pneumonia*. He injected the two different forms into mice. One form of the bacterium killed the mice, but the other form did not.

Griffith used heat to kill a sample of the deadly disease-causing bacteria and then mixed the dead bacteria with a sample of live, harmless bacteria. He injected this mixture into mice. Even though the disease-causing bacteria that he injected were heat-killed, the mice still died.

Griffith concluded that some material must have been transferred from the heat-killed bacteria to the harmless bacteria. Whatever that material was, it contained information that changed the harmless bacteria into disease-causing bacteria. Griffith called this mystery material the "transforming principle."

*Transform* means "to change." Why do you think Griffith called the mystery material the "transforming principle"? _____

_____

_____

_____

### GRIFFITH'S EXPERIMENTS

**The S form of the bacterium is deadly; the R form is not.**

live
S bacteria

live
R bacteria

dead mouse

live mouse

heat-killed
S bacteria

heat-killed S bacteria
+ live R bacteria

live mouse

dead mouse

---

* ACADEMIC VOCABULARY

**pneumonia** a disease that affects the lungs

## Avery identifies DNA as the transforming principle.

Oswald Avery worked with other biologists for over ten years trying to figure out what Griffith's transforming principle was. They thought the transforming principle could be protein or it could be DNA. Avery's group found a way to separate this mystery material from samples of bacteria. They ran several tests on the material. Their tests and findings are shown in the chart below.

| AVERY'S RESEARCH | |
| --- | --- |
| **TEST** | **RESULT** |
| 1. Standard chemical test for protein and DNA | found presence of DNA, but no protein |
| 2. Tests to determine the amounts of nitrogen (N) and phosphorous (P) | the proportions of N and P matched the makeup of DNA, but not protein |
| 3. Tests to see which enzymes could break down the substance | enzymes that break down DNA broke down this substance, but enzymes that break down protein did not break down the substance |

Avery and his group concluded that DNA must be the transforming principle, or genetic material. Some scientists questioned this conclusion. Scientists also wondered whether DNA was the genetic material for all organisms or just for bacteria.

 On the chart above, highlight three reasons Avery concluded that the mystery material was DNA, not protein.

## Hershey and Chase confirm that DNA is the genetic material.

In 1952 the work of Alfred Hershey and Martha Chase provided evidence that DNA is indeed the genetic material. Hershey and Chase studied a type of virus that infects bacteria, called a **bacteriophage** (bak-TEER-ee-uh-FAYJ), or "phage" for short.

A phage infects a bacterium by inserting its genetic material into the bacterium. Hershey and Chase wanted to find out what material the phage inserted into a bacterium—was it protein or was it DNA? They conducted two experiments. In the first experiment, Hershey and Chase marked the phages' proteins with radioactive labels. When the phages infected the bacteria, no significant radioactivity was found inside the bacteria. In the second experiment, Hershey and Chase marked the phages' DNA with radioactive labels. When the phages infected the

DNA

protein coat

Bacteriophages are viruses that infect bacteria.

bacteria, high levels of radioactivity were found inside the bacteria. These results finally convinced scientists that the genetic material is DNA and not protein.

 What is the material that phages insert into bacteria?

_____

<table>
<tr><td>**8.1**</td><td>**Vocabulary Check**</td></tr>
</table>

**Mark It Up**

Go back and highlight each sentence that has a vocabulary word in **bold.**

bacteriophage

1. How did Hershey and Chase's research with bacteriophages help confirm that DNA is the genetic material? _____

_____

<table>
<tr><td>**8.1**</td><td>**The Big Picture**</td></tr>
</table>

2. Complete the following chart about the three main research projects that led to the identification of DNA as the genetic material.

| RESEARCHERS' NAMES | SUMMARY OF RESEARCH | SUMMARY OF CONCLUSIONS |
|---|---|---|
| Griffith | | found a "transforming principle" |
| Avery | | |
| Hershey and Chase | identified the substance that phages inject into bacteria | |

3. Which of the three experiments gave evidence that protein was not the genetic material? _____

_____

_____

# 8.2 Structure of DNA

**KEY CONCEPT** DNA structure is the same in all organisms.

## DNA is composed of four types of nucleotides.

Since the 1920s scientists have known the chemical parts of the DNA molecule. DNA is a very long polymer, or chain of repeating units. The units, or monomers, that make up DNA are called **nucleotides** (NOO-klee-oh-TYDZ). Each nucleotide has three parts: a phosphate group, a base, and a sugar.

There are four different types of DNA nucleotides: cytosine (C), thymine (T), adenine (A), and guanine (G). All of the nucleotides contain a phosphate group and a deoxyribose sugar. They differ in their nitrogen-containing bases, as shown in the table below.

Notice that thymine (T) and cytosine (C) have nitrogen-containing bases with a single-ring structure. Adenine (A) and guanine (G) are bases with a double-ring structure. A single molecule of human DNA is made of billions of nucleotides.

**VISUAL VOCAB**

The small units, or monomers, that make up a strand of DNA are called **nucleotides.** Nucleotides have three parts.

phosphate group    nitrogen-containing base

deoxyribose (sugar)

- phosphate group: one phosphorus with four oxygens
- deoxyribose: ring-shaped sugar
- nitrogen-containing base: a single or double ring built around nitrogen atoms and carbon atoms

**THE FOUR NITROGEN-CONTAINING BASES OF DNA**

| PYRIMIDINES = SINGLE RING | | | PURINES = DOUBLE RING | | |
|---|---|---|---|---|---|
| Name of Base | Structural Formula | Model | Name of Base | Structural Formula | Model |
| thymine | (structure) | T | adenine | (structure) | A |
| cytosine | (structure) | C | guanine | (structure) | G |

 Circle the names of the four nucleotides shown in the table above.

## Watson and Crick developed an accurate* model of DNA's three-dimensional structure.

For a long time, scientists hypothesized that DNA in all organisms was made up of equal amounts of the four nucleotides. Then Erwin Chargaff found that the proportion of the bases differs from organism to organism. In the DNA of each organism, the amount of A equals the amount of T, and the amount of C equals the amount of G.

Then in the early 1950s, the scientists Rosalind Franklin and Maurice Wilkins used x-rays to make a kind of photograph of DNA molecules. These photographs did not show what DNA looks like, but they showed patterns that gave clues about DNA's structure.

Around the same time, the scientists James Watson and Francis Crick were working together to figure out DNA structure, too. Based on the work of other scientists, they hypothesized that DNA might have a spiral, or helix (HEE-lihks), shape. Watson and Crick saw Franklin's photos and used the information to complete their model of DNA structure.

In April 1953 Watson and Crick published their DNA model in a paper in the journal *Nature*. They found that nucleotides fit together in a **double helix.** Two strands of DNA wrap around each other like a twisted ladder.

 **What new information did Watson and Crick contribute to science?** _____

_____

Watson and Crick's model showed DNA in the shape of a double helix.

## Nucleotides always pair in the same way.

Each side of the DNA double helix is a long strand of phosphates and sugars, connected by covalent bonds. The two sides of the double helix are held to each other by hydrogen bonds that form between the bases in the middle. Each individual hydrogen bond is weak, but together they are strong enough to hold the shape of DNA. The bases of the two DNA strands always bond according to the **base pairing rules:** T pairs with A, and C pairs with G.

The bases pair in this way because of hydrogen bonds. Notice that A and T form two hydrogen bonds, whereas C and G form three.

To help remember the rules of base pairing, notice that the letters G and C have a similar shape. Once you know that G and C pair together, you know that A and T also pair together. If the sequence of bases on one DNA strand is CTGA, the other DNA strand will be GACT.

* ACADEMIC VOCABULARY

**accurate**  correct

## BASE PAIRING RULES

**The base pairing rules describe how nucleotides form pairs in DNA. T always pairs with A, and G always pairs with C.**

hydrogen bond          covalent bond

This ribbonlike part represents the phosphate groups and deoxyribose sugar molecules that make up DNA's "backbone."

The nitrogen-containing bases bond in the middle to form the rungs of the DNA ladder.

 **INSTANT REPLAY** What sequence of bases would pair with GTACG?

_____

## 8.2    Vocabulary Check

**Mark It Up**

Go back and highlight each sentence that has a vocabulary word in **bold.**

nucleotide          base pairing rules

double helix

1. Label the drawing at the right with the terms *nucleotide, base pairing rules,* and *double helix*. Write each term and draw a line that connects the term to the appropriate part of the drawing.

## 8.2    The Big Picture

2. What are the three different parts of a nucleotide? _____

_____

3. What are the names of the four nucleotides? _____

_____

4. Use the base pairing rules to write the sequence that would pair with the following sequence: TCACGTA _____

# 8.3 DNA Replication

**KEY CONCEPT** DNA replication copies the genetic information of a cell.

## Replication copies the genetic information.

According to the rules of base pairing, A pairs with T and C pairs with G. If the base sequence of one strand of DNA is known, the sequence of the other strand is also known. One strand can act as a template*, or pattern, for another strand. During the process of DNA **replication,** a cell uses both strands of DNA as templates to make a copy of the DNA.

Recall that your body cells each contain 46 chromosomes made up of DNA. The DNA is copied once during the cell cycle, in the S phase. After a cell divides, the resulting cells each have a complete set of DNA.

What do the base pairing rules have to do with replication?

_____

_____

## Proteins carry out the process of replication.

DNA does not copy itself. Enzymes and other proteins do the actual work of replication. Here we will look at the process of replication in eukaryotes. The process is similar in prokaryotes.

First, some enzymes pull apart, or unzip, the double helix to separate the two strands of DNA. Other proteins keep the strands apart while the strands serve as templates. There are nucleotides floating around in the nucleus. These nucleotides can pair up, according to the base pairing rules, with the nucleotides on the open strands. A group of enzymes called **DNA polymerases** (PAHL-uh-muh-rays) bond the new nucleotides together. When the process is finished, there are two complete molecules of DNA, each exactly like the original double strand as shown in the figure on the next page.

**VISUAL VOCAB**

**DNA polymerases** are enzymes that form bonds between nucleotides during replication.

The ending *-ase* signals that this is an enzyme.

DNA polymer **ase**

This part of the name tells what the enzyme does—makes DNA polymers.

What is the job of the DNA polymerases? _____

_____

* ACADEMIC VOCABULARY

**template** a pattern that can be used to make a copy of something

**When a cell's DNA is copied, or replicated, two complete and identical sets of genetic information are produced. Then cell division can occur.**

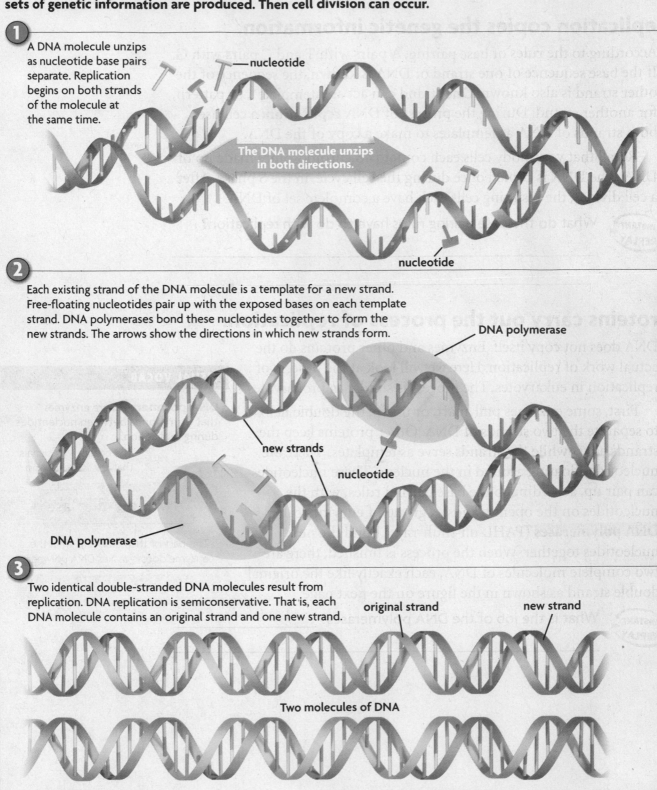

**1** A DNA molecule unzips as nucleotide base pairs separate. Replication begins on both strands of the molecule at the same time.

nucleotide

The DNA molecule unzips in both directions.

nucleotide

**2** Each existing strand of the DNA molecule is a template for a new strand. Free-floating nucleotides pair up with the exposed bases on each template strand. DNA polymerases bond these nucleotides together to form the new strands. The arrows show the directions in which new strands form.

DNA polymerase

new strands

nucleotide

DNA polymerase

**3** Two identical double-stranded DNA molecules result from replication. DNA replication is semiconservative. That is, each DNA molecule contains an original strand and one new strand.

original strand

new strand

Two molecules of DNA

## Replication is fast and accurate.

Your DNA has replicated trillions of times since you grew from a single cell. And DNA replication is happening in your cells right now. Replication happens very fast. As you can see in the figure, the process starts at many different places along a eukaryotic chromosome.

DNA replication is also very accurate. There are very few errors—only about one error per 1 billion nucleotides. Replication has a built-in "proofreading" process. If the wrong nucleotide gets added, DNA polymerase can find the error, remove the incorrect nucleotide, and replace it with the correct one.

A

B

C

D

Replication starts at many different places along a eukaryotic chromosome. The DNA helix is unzipped at many points. The replication "bubbles" grow larger as replication progresses in both directions, resulting in two complete copies.

 **INSTANT REPLAY** What does it mean that replication has a "proofreading" function? _____

_____

---

### 8.3 Vocabulary Check

**Mark It Up**

Go back and highlight each sentence that has a vocabulary word in **bold.**

replication          DNA polymerase

1. What is the end product of replication? _____

_____

2. What is the role of DNA polymerase in replication? _____

_____

---

### 8.3 The Big Picture

3. What does it mean that a DNA strand is *used as a template* in replication? _____

_____

4. Give at least two examples of how enzymes and other proteins help in the process of replication. _____

_____

5. What is one reason that there are very few errors in DNA replication?

_____

_____

# 8.4 Transcription

**KEY CONCEPT** Transcription converts a gene into a single-stranded RNA molecule.

## RNA carries DNA's instructions.

The **central dogma** describes how information from DNA gets used to make proteins. The central dogma involves three processes.

Replication copies DNA.

Transcription converts a DNA message into an intermediate molecule, called RNA.

Translation interprets an RNA message into a string of amino acids, called a polypeptide. Either a single polypeptide or many polypeptides working together make up a protein.

These processes are similar in prokaryotes and eukaryotes, but there are important differences. Here, we will look at these processes in eukaryotic cells.

**RNA** stands for ribonucleic acid. RNA, like DNA, is made of nucleotides with three parts: a sugar, a phosphate group, and a nitrogen-containing base. RNA is different from DNA in three important ways.

1.  The sugar in RNA is ribose, not deoxyribose as in DNA. Ribose has one more oxygen atom than deoxyribose.

2.  RNA has four bases: A, C, G, and U. RNA has the base uracil (U) instead of thymine (T). Uracil (U) pairs with adenine (A).

3.  RNA is a single strand of nucleotides, not a double strand like DNA. The single-stranded structure of RNA allows an RNA molecule to fold up into complex three-dimensional shapes.

**Connecting CONCEPTS**

**DNA Structure** As you learned in **Section 8.2**, nucleotides are made of a phosphate group, a sugar, and a nitrogen-containing base. In DNA, the four bases are adenine, cytosine, guanine, and thymine. In RNA, uracil (below) replaces thymine and pairs with adenine.

What are three ways RNA differs from DNA? _____

_____

## Transcription makes three types of RNA.

**Transcription** is the process of copying a sequence of DNA to produce a complementary* strand of RNA. Only a piece of DNA, or a gene, gets transcribed into RNA, not the whole strand of DNA. Just as DNA polymerases help with replication, an enzyme called **RNA polymerase** helps with transcription.

* ACADEMIC VOCABULARY

**complementary** matching

## TRANSCRIPTION

**Transcription produces an RNA molecule from a DNA template. Like DNA replication, this process takes place in the nucleus in eukaryotic cells and involves both DNA unwinding and nucleotide base pairing.**

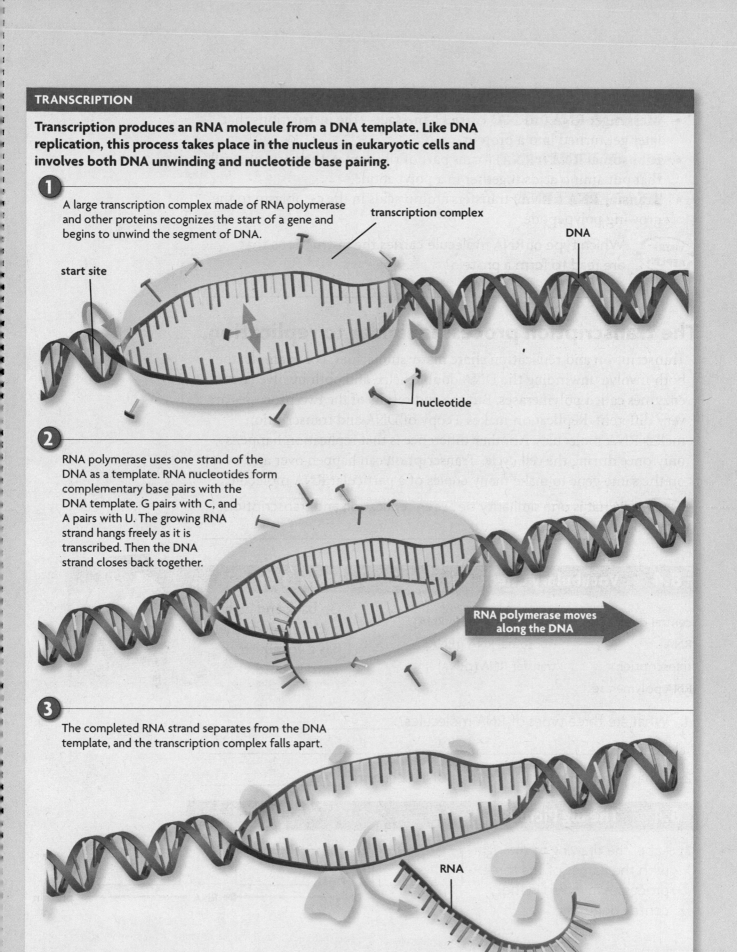

**1** A large transcription complex made of RNA polymerase and other proteins recognizes the start of a gene and begins to unwind the segment of DNA.

start site

transcription complex

DNA

nucleotide

**2** RNA polymerase uses one strand of the DNA as a template. RNA nucleotides form complementary base pairs with the DNA template. G pairs with C, and A pairs with U. The growing RNA strand hangs freely as it is transcribed. Then the DNA strand closes back together.

RNA polymerase moves along the DNA

**3** The completed RNA strand separates from the DNA template, and the transcription complex falls apart.

RNA

Transcription makes three different types of RNA molecules.

- **Messenger RNA (mRNA)** carries a message—the instructions that later get turned into a protein.
- **Ribosomal RNA (rRNA)** forms part of ribosomes, the parts of a cell that put amino acids together in a polypeptide.
- **Transfer RNA (tRNA)** transfers amino acids in the cytoplasm to the growing polypeptide.

 Which type of RNA molecule carries the instructions that are read to form a protein?

_____

## The transcription process is similar to replication.

Transcription and replication share many similarities. For example, they both involve unwinding the DNA double helix, and both involve large enzymes called polymerases. But the end results of the two processes are very different. Replication makes a copy of DNA and transcription makes RNA molecules. Another difference is that replication happens only once during the cell cycle. Transcription can happen over and over on the same gene to make many copies of a particular RNA molecule.

 What is one similarity between replication and transcription?

_____

| 8.4 | Vocabulary Check |
|---|---|

| | |
|---|---|
| central dogma | messenger RNA (mRNA) |
| RNA | ribosomal RNA (rRNA) |
| transcription | transfer RNA (tRNA) |
| RNA polymerase | |

**Mark It Up**

Go back and highlight each sentence that has a vocabulary word in **bold.**

1. What are three types of RNA molecules? _____

_____

2. What process makes RNA from a DNA sequence? _____

| 8.4 | The Big Picture |
|---|---|

3. Label the drawing to the right with the names of the three processes involved in the central dogma.

DNA ⟶ RNA ⟶ protein

# 8.5 Translation

**KEY CONCEPT** Translation converts an mRNA message into a polypeptide, or protein.

Translation is a process that converts a message from one language into another. For example, a book may be translated from Spanish into English. Translation happens in cells, too. Cells translate an mRNA message into amino acids, the building blocks of proteins.

## Amino acids are coded by mRNA base sequences.

**Translation** is the process that reads an mRNA message and turns it into a polypeptide. One or more polypeptides make a protein. An mRNA message can be translated into 20 different amino acids. How can just four nucleotides—A, U, C, and G—be translated into so many different amino acids? Just as the 26 letters of the alphabet can be used to form many more than 26 words, the four letters of RNA are put together in different combinations to form many different "words."

### GENETIC CODE: mRNA CODONS

**The genetic code matches each mRNA codon with its amino acid or function.**

Suppose you want to determine which amino acid is encoded by the CAU codon.

1. Find the first base, C, in the left column.

2. Find the second base, A, in the top row. Find the box where these two intersect.

3. Find the third base, U, in the right column. CAU codes for histidine, abbreviated as His.

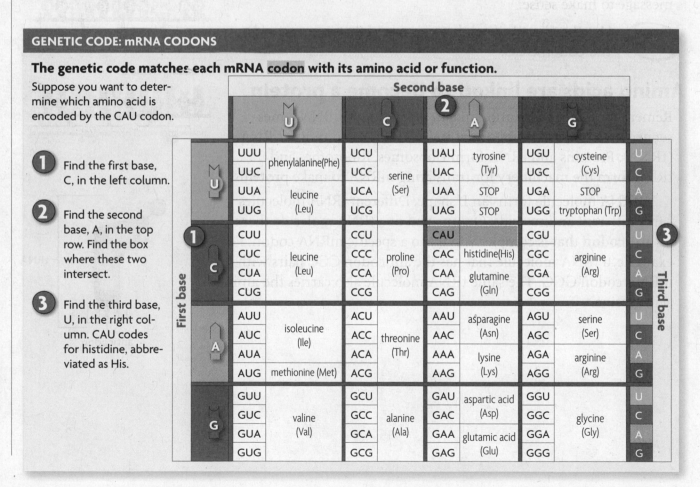

In the language of the genetic code, a "word" is made of three nucleotides and is called a **codon.** A codon codes for an amino acid. Multiple codons can code for the same amino acid. For example, the codons UCU, UCC, UCA, and UCG all code for serine.

In addition to codons that code for amino acids, there is a **start codon** that signals the start of translation. The start codon is AUG, and codes for the amino acid methionine. There are also three **stop codons** that signal the end of an amino acid chain.

For words to make sense, they must be read starting at the correct place, or with the correct reading frame. For example, the sentence "THE CAT ATE THE RAT" makes sense. "T HEC ATA TET HER AT," which is made of the same letters, has a different reading frame and does not make sense. The same is true for codons. There are no spaces between codons, but the correct start site and the correct reading frame must be used for the message to make sense.

 Use the chart to find the amino acid that is encoded by the codon GGG.

## Amino acids are linked to become a protein.

Remember that transcription makes three kinds of RNA—messenger RNA (mRNA), ribosomal RNA (rRNA), and transfer RNA (tRNA). Proteins and rRNA form ribosomes. Ribosomes and tRNA form the machinery for translating mRNA to make proteins.

A tRNA molecule forms an L shape. Different tRNA molecules carry different amino acids. On one end of a tRNA molecule there is an **anticodon** that is complementary to a specific mRNA codon. For example, a tRNA molecule that has the anticodon CCC pairs with the mRNA codon GGG. The same tRNA molecule also carries the amino acid glycine.

Codons are read as a series of three nonoverlapping nucleotides. A change in the reading frame changes the resulting protein.

**Reading frame 1**

C G A U A C A G U A G C

Arg   Tyr   Ser   Ser

**Reading frame 2**

C G A U A C A G U A G C

Asp   Thr   Val

amino acid

tRNA

anticodon

## TRANSLATION

**Translation converts an mRNA transcript into a polypeptide. The process consists of three repeating steps.**

cytoplasm

amino acid

nucleus

ribosome

tRNA

mRNA

Translation occurs in the cytoplasm of both eukaryotic (illustrated) and prokaryotic cells. It starts when a tRNA carrying a methionine attaches to a start codon.

**1** The exposed codon in the first site attracts a complementary tRNA bearing an amino acid. The tRNA anticodon pairs with the mRNA codon, bringing it very close to the other tRNA molecule.

methionine

leucine

Met

Leu

incoming tRNA

anticodon

U A C

A U G

mRNA

start codon

The anticodon on the tRNA is complementary to the mRNA codon.

**2** The ribosome forms a peptide bond between the two amino acids and breaks the bond between the first tRNA and its amino acid.

peptide bond

Met

Leu

**3** The ribosome pulls the mRNA strand the length of one codon. The first tRNA is shifted into the exit site, where it leaves the ribosome and returns to the cytoplasm to recharge. The first site is again empty, exposing the next mRNA codon.

Met

Leu

Cys

The ribosome continues to translate the mRNA strand until it reaches a stop codon. Then it releases the new protein and disassembles.

Leu

Cys

Cys

Arg

Met

stop codon

The process of translation happens in the cytoplasm of both prokaryotic and eukaryotic cells. The illustration on the previous page shows the process of translation in just one ribosome. In a cell, many ribosomes may translate the same gene at the same time to make many copies of the same protein.

What is the final product of the process of translation?

_____

| 8.5 | Vocabulary Check | Mark It Up |
|---|---|---|

translation        stop codon
codon              anticodon
start codon

**Mark It Up**

Go back and highlight each sentence that has a vocabulary word in **bold**.

**1.** What does a start codon do? a stop codon?

_____

_____

**2.** What is the relationship between a codon and an anticodon?

_____

_____

### 8.5    The Big Picture

**3.** Fill in the blanks to complete the concept map for the process of translation.

**4.** Refer to the genetic code table to find the amino acid that is encoded by the mRNA codon CCA. What bases would be found in the complementary tRNA anticodon?

_____

# 8.6 Gene Expression and Regulation

**KEY CONCEPT** Gene expression is carefully regulated in both prokaryotic and eukaryotic cells.

## Prokaryotic cells turn genes on and off by controlling transcription.

A cell does not need to produce all of its proteins all the time. Instead, gene expression, or how much a gene is used to make a protein, is regulated*. This regulation allows an organism to make the right amounts of the proteins it needs, when it needs them.

Let's examine the *lac* operon shown below. All of the genes of the *lac* operon are transcribed together, not separately. They are all under the control of one promoter. A **promoter** is a DNA segment that allows a region of DNA to be transcribed. It helps RNA polymerase to find the place where a gene starts.

An **operon** is a region of DNA that contains a promoter, an operator, and one or more genes that code for all the proteins necessary for a particular task. Bacterial genes tend to be organized into operons. The *lac* operon includes all the genes that code for the enzymes that bacteria need to digest the sugar lactose.

**VOCABULARY**

The word *promote* comes from the Latin prefix *pro-*, meaning "forward," and the Latin word *movere*, meaning "to move."

**The *lac* operon**

The promoter helps RNA polymerase to start transcription.

When lactose is present, bacteria need the enzymes to break it down. But if no lactose is present, bacteria do not need to waste resources making enzymes to break down a sugar that isn't there. Like a switch, the operon is turned on when the enzymes are needed. Then the genes are transcribed. When the enzymes are not needed, the operon is turned off and transcription is blocked.

**INSTANT REPLAY** If lactose is present, would the *lac* operon in a bacterial cell be on or off? Explain. _____

_____

* ACADEMIC VOCABULARY

**regulated** controlled

# Eukaryotic cells regulate gene expression at many points.

Every cell in your body has the same set of DNA, but your cells are not all the same. Your cells are different because different genes are expressed in different types of cells. Eukaryotic cells regulate gene expression by controlling transcription and by mRNA processing.

- **Controlling transcription** Like prokaryotes, eukaryotes have promoter sequences that help start transcription. Other DNA sequences can speed up or slow down the rate of transcription of a gene.

- **mRNA processing** In eukaryotes, the mRNA produced by transcription needs to go through some changes, or processing, before translation. Some segments of the mRNA, called **exons,** code for protein. Other segments of the mRNA, called **introns,** do not code for proteins. They are in between the exons. Part of mRNA processing is the removal of introns.

**mRNA PROCESSING**

**An mRNA molecule is usually processed during or immediately after DNA transcription.**

In eukaryotic cells, DNA contains noncoding stretches called introns and coding stretches called exons.

DNA

intron | exon | intron | exon | intron | exon

gene

Protein-coding DNA is transcribed into mRNA.

mRNA

exon | intron | exon | intron | exon

The mRNA goes through three major processing steps: the removal of introns and the addition of a cap and tail.

mRNA

cap

tail

The exons are joined together, and the mRNA molecule enters the cytoplasm, where it can be translated.

processed mRNA

The mRNA is processed in the nucleus of a eukaryotic cell. Introns are removed and exons are joined together before the mRNA leaves the nucleus. Almost no prokaryotic cells have introns in their DNA.

 What is the difference between an intron and an exon?

_____

_____

**Vocabulary Check**

promoter       exon

operon       intron

**Mark It Up**

Go back and highlight each sentence that has a vocabulary word in **bold**.

**Circle the correct words to complete the sentences below.**

1. One part of a(n) *promoter / operon* is a(n) *promoter / operon*.

2. The *introns / exons* are removed in mRNA processing, and the *introns / exons* are joined together and later translated.

**8.6    The Big Picture**

3. What is the importance of regulating gene expression? _____ _____ _____

4. What are two ways in which eukaryotic cells regulate gene expression? _____

5. If all cells in a multicellular organism have the same set of DNA, what accounts for the differences among different types of cells in a multicellular organism? _____ _____ _____

# 8.7 Mutations

**KEY CONCEPT** Mutations are changes in DNA that may or may not affect phenotype.

## Some mutations affect a single gene, while others affect an entire chromosome.

In biology a **mutation** means a change in an organism's DNA. A mutation can happen during replication and affect a single gene. A mutation can also happen during meiosis and affect a whole chromosome.

### Gene Mutations

There are different types of gene mutations.

- A **point mutation** is when an incorrect nucleotide is put into a DNA molecule during replication. If the error is not fixed by DNA polymerase, the DNA is permanently changed. For example, the figure to the right shows a CTC codon that is changed to a CTA codon. As a result, the wrong amino acid is added—aspartic acid instead of glutamic acid.

- A **frameshift mutation** is the addition or removal of a nucleotide in the DNA sequence. This results in a change in the reading frame. Recall the importance of the reading frame from Section 8.5. Think back to the sentence "THE CAT ATE THE RAT." If the letter *E* is removed, or deleted, from the first "THE," the reading frame is shifted. The result is "THC ATA TET HER AT…" The reading frame is also shifted if a nucleotide is added, or inserted.

**TYPES OF MUTATIONS**

**A mutation is a change in an organism's DNA.**

Normal

DNA    G A T C T C A G G C T A

mRNA   C U A G A G U C C G A U

protein    Leu    Glu    Ser    Asp

Point mutation

DNA    G A T C T A A G G C T A

mRNA   C U A G A U U C C G A U

protein    Leu    Asp    Ser    Asp

mutated base

A

### Chromosomal Mutations

Errors in meiosis can result in changes in large parts of a chromosome. Recall that crossing over is a normal process in which chromosomes exchange pieces. Errors in crossing over or in other parts of meiosis can result in chromosomes with two copies of the same gene. Pieces of non-homologous chromosomes might even be exchanged.

 What is the difference between a gene mutation and a chromosomal mutation? _____

_____

## Mutations may or may not affect phenotype.

Whether a mutation affects an organism depends on many different things.

- **Type of mutation** A point mutation only affects one codon. A frameshift mutation usually has a bigger effect because it changes the whole reading frame and can affect many codons.

- **Impact on the amino acid sequence** A change in one codon can still have a big effect. For example, if a codon for an amino acid is changed into a stop codon, transcription would end at the wrong place. A point mutation may also have no effect. Recall that more than one codon can code for the same amino acid. For example, CGU, CGC, CGA, and CGG all code for arginine. A point mutation that changes the last nucleotide of this codon would have no effect on the resulting amino acid.

- **Impact on the resulting protein** Some changes might not affect the resulting protein's shape or function. Other changes might prevent the protein from functioning. For example, a mutation could change the active site of an enzyme and prevent the enzyme from binding to its substrate.

- **Type of cell** Recall that mutations that occur in germ cells can be passed on to offspring. Mutations in body cells cannot be passed on to offspring.

cysteine

stop

This point mutation changed a codon for cysteine into a stop codon.

 Give one example of a mutation that would not affect an organism's phenotype. _____

_____

_____

## Mutations can be caused by several factors.

Mutations happen. But cells have tools to repair them. For example, DNA polymerase has a "proofreading" function to fix errors. However, mutations can happen faster than the body's repair system can work. Some mutations are the result of errors that happen normally in the cell. Other mutations are caused by things in the environment.

- **Replication errors** DNA polymerase proofreads replication, but a small number of errors are not fixed. Over time, there are more and more errors. Eventually these mutations affect how the cell works. There is evidence that a build-up of mutations is a major cause of aging.

- **Mutagens** Some conditions and substances in the environment can cause DNA mutations—such as UV light and some chemicals. Things in the environment that can change DNA are called **mutagens.**

  If mutations cause changes that affect the control over cell division, cancer may result.

 What are two examples of mutagens? _____

_____

_____

---

| 8.7 | **Vocabulary Check** |
|---|---|

**Mark It Up**

Go back and highlight each sentence that has a vocabulary word in **bold.**

| | |
|---|---|
| mutation | frameshift mutation |
| point mutation | mutagen |

**1.** What is the difference between a *mutation* and a *mutagen*?

_____

_____

**2.** What is the difference between a *point mutation* and a *frameshift mutation?* _____

_____

---

| 8.7 | **The Big Picture** |
|---|---|

**3.** Is a mutation that happens during meiosis likely to affect a single gene or an entire chromosome? Explain. _____

_____

_____

**4.** Give an example of one mutation that will affect an organism's phenotype and one mutation that will not affect phenotype. _____

_____

_____

# Chapter 8 Review

1. According to the base-pairing rules for DNA, which base pairs with each base listed below?

   A pairs with _____, C pairs with _____, G pairs with _____,

   and T pairs with _____

2. What is the name of the process by which information from DNA is copied into RNA?

   a. replication

   b. transcription

   c. translation

   d. mutation

3. What is the central dogma? _____

   _____

   _____

4. What are two differences between DNA and RNA? _____

   _____

5. List three types of RNA molecules. _____

   _____

6. Which of the following is an example of a codon?

   a. AUG

   b. ACTG

   c. RNA

   d. DNA

7. In a multicellular organism, what accounts for the differences between different types of cells? _____

   _____

8. Which type of mutation will probably have a larger effect: a point mutation or a frameshift mutation? Explain your answer.

   _____

   _____

9. What is the shape of a DNA molecule? _____

   _____

# CHAPTER

# 9 Frontiers of Biotechnology

## GETTING READY TO LEARN

### Preview Key Concepts

**9.1 Manipulating DNA**
Biotechnology relies on cutting DNA at specific places.

**9.2 Copying DNA**
The polymerase chain reaction rapidly copies segments of DNA.

**9.3 DNA Fingerprinting**
DNA fingerprints identify people at the molecular level.

**9.4 Genetic Engineering**
DNA sequences of organisms can be changed.

**9.5 Genomics and Bioinformatics**
Entire genomes are sequenced, studied, and compared.

**9.6 Genetic Screening and Gene Therapy**
Genetics provides a basis for new medical treatments.

## Review Academic Vocabulary

Write the correct word for each definition.

allele     nucleotide     DNA polymerase     genome

1. _____ : all of the genes making up an organism

2. _____ : enzyme that forms bonds between neighboring nucleotides

3. _____ : monomer that makes up DNA and RNA

4. _____ : alternate form of a gene

## Preview Biology Vocabulary

To see how many key terms you already know from this chapter, choose the word that makes sense in each sentence.

gene therapy     clone     bioinformatics

1. A genetically identical copy of a gene or organism is a _____.

2. _____ is the use of computer databases to organize and analyze biological data.

3. The replacement of a defective or missing gene is called _____.

**146** Interactive Reader

# SECTION 9.1 Manipulating DNA

**KEY CONCEPT** Biotechnology relies on cutting DNA at specific places.

## Scientists use several techniques to manipulate* DNA.

DNA is a large molecule, but it is still too small to see or to pick up with your hands. How can scientists work with DNA without being able to handle it directly? Chemicals, computers, and enzymes are just a few of the tools that are used in genetics research. For example, chemicals can be used to change, or mutate, a DNA sequence. Computers are used to organize large amounts of data from genetics research. Enzymes that come from bacteria are used to cut and copy pieces of DNA.

What are three tools used in genetics research?

_____

_____

## Restriction enzymes cut DNA.

Recall that a chromosome is a long string of DNA that contains many different genes. To study just one gene, scientists cut apart DNA and separate out the different pieces. Some enzymes, called **restriction enzymes,** are like molecular "scissors" that cut apart DNA. A restriction enzyme cuts DNA at a specific nucleotide sequence. The place where a restriction enzyme cuts the DNA is called a restriction site. There are many different restriction enzymes. Each one cuts at a different restriction site. Two different restriction enzymes will cut the same strand of DNA in different ways.

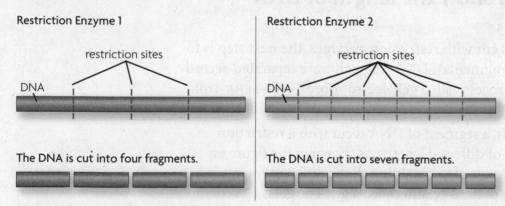

**Restriction Enzyme 1**

restriction sites

DNA

The DNA is cut into four fragments.

**Restriction Enzyme 2**

restriction sites

DNA

The DNA is cut into seven fragments.

Restriction enzyme 1 cuts the DNA strand in three places. Restriction enzyme 2 cuts the same strand of DNA in six places.

---

* ACADEMIC VOCABULARY

**manipulate** to work with and change, or alter, something

Some restriction enzymes cut straight across the DNA molecule, leaving "blunt ends." Other restriction enzymes leave "sticky ends," as shown in the figure below. A piece of DNA with sticky ends can join with another piece of DNA that has matching sticky ends because the base pairs are complementary. This feature makes sticky ends very helpful in genetics research.

**RESTRICTION ENZYMES CUT DNA**

**Some restriction enzymes leave behind nucleotide tails, or "sticky ends," when they cut DNA.**

A restriction enzyme called *Taq*I cuts DNA when it finds its restriction site. *Taq*I's restriction site is
TCGA
AGCT

What are "sticky ends"?

_____

_____

# Restriction maps show the length of DNA fragments*.

After a piece of DNA is cut with restriction enzymes, the next step is to separate the different fragments*. DNA fragments are separated according to their sizes by a process called **gel electrophoresis** (ih-LEHK-troh-fuh-REE-sihs).

In gel electrophoresis, a segment of DNA is cut with a restriction enzyme into fragments of different lengths, as shown in the figure on the next page. The DNA sample, containing all the different fragments, is loaded into a thin piece of hard gelatin called a gel. The gel is placed into a machine that has a positive electrode* at one end and a negative electrode at the other end. DNA molecules have a negative charge, so they are

**\* ACADEMIC VOCABULARY**

**fragment** a smaller piece of a whole

attracted to the positive end. The fragments move through the gel in that direction after the electrical current is turned on. Then the different fragments from the sample are separated by size. Smaller pieces of DNA move through the gel faster than do the larger pieces. The distances the pieces of DNA travel can be used to estimate their sizes. The bands that show up on the gel do not give any information about the DNA sequence. They indicate only the length of the DNA.

Gel electrophoresis is used in many different parts of genetics research. For example, it can be used to diagnose genetic diseases by comparing the patterns of bands on a gel from an unknown sample of DNA with a known sample. The pattern of bands on a gel can be thought of as a map. This type of map is called a **restriction map,** and shows the lengths between each restriction site in a piece of DNA.

 Which DNA fragment travels farther in a gel: large or small?

**GEL ELECTROPHORESIS**

A segment of DNA is cut with a restriction enzyme into fragments of different lengths.

DNA sample

Different sizes of DNA fragments show up as bands on a gel. Smaller fragments move farther down the gel.

DNA fragments          Restriction map on gel

direction of travel

---

\* ACADEMIC VOCABULARY

**electrode** the positive or negative end of electrical equipment

---

**9.1    Vocabulary Check**

restriction enzyme     restriction map
gel electrophoresis

**Mark It Up**

Go back and highlight each sentence that has a vocabulary word in **bold.**

**Choose the correct term from the list for each description**

1. cuts DNA at specific sequences _____

2. tool that separates DNA fragments _____

3. shows the sizes of DNA fragments between restriction sites

_____

---

**9.1    The Big Picture**

4. Circle the piece that would travel the farthest in gel electrophoresis.

_____    _____    _____

# 9.2 Copying DNA

**KEY CONCEPT** The polymerase chain reaction rapidly copies segments of DNA.

## PCR uses polymerase to copy DNA segments*.

A scientist needs more than just a single piece of DNA or a single copy of a gene to study the DNA. To get a larger amount of DNA, the DNA is copied. **Polymerase chain reaction (PCR)** is a technique that produces millions, or even billions, of copies of a specific DNA sequence in just a few hours. Recall that DNA polymerase is a key enzyme in DNA replication. PCR also uses DNA polymerase to make copies of DNA—but in a test tube, not in a cell.

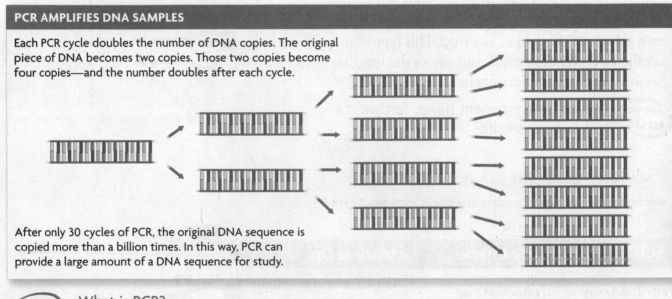

**PCR AMPLIFIES DNA SAMPLES**

Each PCR cycle doubles the number of DNA copies. The original piece of DNA becomes two copies. Those two copies become four copies—and the number doubles after each cycle.

After only 30 cycles of PCR, the original DNA sequence is copied more than a billion times. In this way, PCR can provide a large amount of a DNA sequence for study.

 What is PCR?

_____

_____

## PCR is a three-step process.

PCR uses four materials: the DNA to be copied, DNA polymerases, lots of each of the four DNA nucleotides—A, C, G, and T—and two primers. A **primer** is a short piece of DNA that acts as the starting place for a new strand. A primer is needed because DNA polymerase cannot start a new strand; it can only add to a strand that has already been started. There are three main steps in PCR. These steps happen over and over in a cycle, as shown in the figure on the following page.

---

**\* ACADEMIC VOCABULARY**

**segment** a portion, or a part

**THE PROCESS OF PCR**

1. **Separating** The container with all of the reactants is heated for a few seconds to separate the strands of DNA.

DNA strands

2. **Binding** The container is cooled and the primers bind to the DNA strands.

primer 1
primer 2

polymerase

nucleotides

3. **Copying** The container is heated to the temperature at which the polymerases work best. The polymerases add nucleotides until the DNA segment has been copied.

**What is the purpose of PCR?**

_____

_____

---

## 9.2 Vocabulary Check

**Mark It Up**

Go back and highlight each sentence that has a vocabulary word in **bold.**

polymerase chain reaction (PCR)

primer

1. What does a primer do? _____

_____

2. What is the end result of PCR? _____

_____

---

## 9.2 The Big Picture

3. The development of PCR was considered a major advance for genetics research. What can PCR do that is so important for genetics research?

_____

_____

4. What is the role of polymerase in PCR?

_____

# 9.3 DNA Fingerprinting

**KEY CONCEPT** DNA fingerprints identify people at the molecular level.

## A DNA fingerprint is a type of restriction map.

Except for identical twins, each person's set of DNA, or genome, is unique. A **DNA fingerprint** shows parts of an individual's DNA that can be used to identify a person. A DNA fingerprint is a type of restriction map, like the ones you read about in Section 9.1. A DNA sample is cut with a restriction enzyme, and the fragments are separated with gel electrophoresis. The pattern of bands that results is the DNA fingerprint.

The greatest differences in DNA are in certain areas of the genome called noncoding regions. These are parts of DNA that do not code for proteins and are not parts of genes. Noncoding regions often have areas in which a particular DNA sequence is repeated a number of times. One person might have seven repeats of the sequence and another person might have three repeats of the sequence. These differences can be seen when the two samples are cut with restriction enzymes and separated by gel electrophoresis.

---

**DNA FINGERPRINTING**

**A DNA fingerprint shows differences in the number of repeats of certain DNA sequences.**

This DNA sequence of 33 base pairs can be repeated many times in a sample of a person's DNA.

C T A A A G C T G G A G G T G G G C A G G A A G G A C C G A G G T

Person A and person B have different numbers of repeated DNA sequences in their DNA.

A DNA fingerprint finds differences in DNA by separating the fragments on a gel.

Person A    4 repeats        3 repeats

6 repeats        7 repeats

Person B    2 repeats        5 repeats

3 repeats        4 repeats

Person A    Person B

number of repeating DNA sequences

7 6 5 4 3 2 1

direction of travel

DNA fragments with different numbers of repeated DNA sequences show up as different bands on a gel.

---

**What is identified in DNA fingerprinting?**

_____

# DNA fingerprinting is used for identification.

DNA fingerprinting has been widely used to identify people since the 1990s. All people have the same repeated DNA sequences. But the number of repeats differs greatly among people.

DNA fingerprinting uses more than one section of noncoding DNA. For example, five different regions of DNA might be used to make a DNA fingerprint. The more regions that are used, the less likely it is that two people will have the same DNA fingerprint. There is a very small chance—one in many millions—that two people have the same DNA fingerprint.

DNA fingerprinting is used for many different purposes.

- In legal cases, as evidence against a suspect or as evidence of a suspect's innocence. DNA fingerprinting has helped free many people who were convicted of crimes they did not commit.
- To prove family relationships, such as paternity*, or to provide information necessary for immigration requests.
- To study biodiversity and to identify genetically engineered crops.

 **INSTANT REPLAY** Why is more than one section of noncoding DNA used in DNA fingerprinting?

_____

_____

## 9.3 | Vocabulary Check

**Mark It Up**

Go back and highlight each sentence that has a vocabulary word in **bold**.

DNA fingerprint

1. What is DNA fingerprinting?

_____

_____

2. What are two different uses of DNA fingerprinting? _____

_____

3. What part of the human genome is used for DNA fingerprinting? _____

_____

# 9.4 Genetic Engineering

**KEY CONCEPT**  DNA sequences of organisms can be changed.

## Entire organisms can be cloned.

A **clone** is a genetically identical copy of a gene or organism. Cloning is quite common in some organisms. For example, many plants can clone themselves from their roots. Bacteria make clones of themselves when they reproduce by dividing in two.

Mammals cannot clone themselves. But scientists have developed a technique to clone mammals in the laboratory. The nucleus of a cell from the animal to be cloned is put into an egg cell that has had its nucleus removed. If the procedure is successful, the egg will develop into a living copy of the original animal.

Although a clone is genetically identical to the original animal, it will likely look different and act different from the original. As you have learned, many factors, including environment, affect the expression of genes. A clone may also not be as healthy as the original animal, possibly because it has "old" DNA.

Cloning may be used for different purposes. For example, scientists are studying how to use organs from cloned mammals for transplant into humans.

 What is one organism in which cloning is common?

_____

## New genes can be added to an organism's DNA.

A copied gene is also called a clone. Scientists can insert a cloned gene from one organism into another organism. This process of changing an organism's DNA to give the organism new traits is called **genetic engineering.** Genetic engineering uses **recombinant DNA** (ree-KAHM-buh-nuhnt), or DNA that contains genes from more than one organism. In many cases, foreign DNA is inserted into a plasmid to make recombinant DNA. **Plasmids** are closed loops of DNA in a bacterial cell.

**VISUAL VOCAB**

foreign DNA

plasmid (bacterium DNA)

plasmid

bacterial chromosome

Bacterium

**Recombinant DNA** is DNA that combines genes from more than one organism.

Foreign DNA is inserted into plasmids to make recombinant DNA.

**Foreign DNA can be inserted into a plasmid to make recombinant DNA.**

A plasmid and the foreign DNA with the gene are cut with the same restriction enzyme.

The sticky ends of the plasmid and the foreign gene match.

The plasmid and the foreign gene are bonded together to form recombinant DNA.

Because the genetic code is shared by all organisms, a gene from one organism can be transcribed and translated in another organism.

What is the term for a plasmid that contains a foreign gene?

# Genetic engineering produces organisms with new traits.

After a gene is added to a plasmid, the recombinant plasmid can be put into bacteria. The bacteria will express the new gene and make that gene's product. The bacteria with the recombinant plasmid are called transgenic. A **transgenic** organism has one or more genes from another organism inserted into its genome. Transgenic bacteria with the gene for human insulin make human insulin that is used to treat people with diabetes.

## Genetic Engineering in Plants and Animals

Scientists have made transgenic plants that have new traits, such as resistance to frost or disease. Some genetically engineered crops, also called genetically modified (GM) crops, are now common in the United States.

Scientists have made some transgenic animals, too. Transgenic mice are often used as models of human development and disease. One type of transgenic mouse is used to study cancer.

Another type of genetic manipulation involves "turning off" a particular gene in an organism. These organisms are called knockouts. For example, **gene knockout** mice have a gene that does not function because the gene has been deactivated. Knockouts help researchers to see what happens when a particular gene does not work. Knockout mice are used to study many different things, including genetic disorders and gene function.

## Concerns About Genetic Engineering

There are some concerns about possible negative effects of genetically engineered organisms on human health and the environment. Some scientists think that too little research has been done on the possible side effects of eating GM foods over a long period of time. Scientists also have concerns about the effects of GM plants on the environment and on biodiversity.

 What is one example of a transgenic organism?

_____

---

### 9.4    Vocabulary Check

**Mark It Up**

Go back and highlight each sentence that has a vocabulary word in **bold**.

clone            plasmid

genetic engineering     transgenic

recombinant DNA      gene knockout

Choose the correct term from the list to complete each sentence.

1. An organism with recombinant DNA is called _____.

2. The purposeful disruption of the function of a particular gene in an organism is called a _____.

3. Genetic engineering makes use of a circular piece of bacterial DNA called a _____.

---

### 9.4    The Big Picture

4. Bacteria and humans are very different. But recombinant bacteria that have a human gene for insulin can produce human insulin. What characteristic of the genetic code makes it possible for bacteria to make a human protein? _____

5. Imagine that your friend's cat was cloned. Would the clone be exactly like the original cat? Explain your answer. _____

_____

**KEY CONCEPT**  Entire genomes are sequenced, studied, and repaired.

## Genomics involves the study of genes, gene functions, and entire genomes.

A gene is a segment of DNA. A genome is all of an organism's DNA. And **genomics** is the study of genomes. Scientists compare genomes both within and across species. Comparing DNA from many organisms at one time can help scientists identify disease-causing genes, learn about evolutionary relationships, and discover how genes interact.

### DNA Sequencing

Studies of genomics begin with gene sequencing. **Gene sequencing** means finding the order, or sequence, of nucleotides in genes or genomes. Gene sequences give scientists important clues about how genes function. Some organisms, such as fruit flies, yeast, and mice, are used as models for human gene functions and genetic disorders.

| COMPARING GENOME SIZES | |
| --- | --- |
| Organism | Approximate Total DNA (millions of bases) |
| *E. coli* | 4.6 |
| Yeast | 12.1 |
| Fruit fly | 165 |
| Banana | 873 |
| Chicken | 1200 |
| Humans | 3000 |
| Vanilla | 7672 |
| Crested newt | 18,600 |
| Lungfish | 139,000 |

Source: University of Nebraska

Different organisms have different sized genomes.

### The Human Genome Project

In 1990 an international project to study the human genome began. The two main goals of the **Human Genome Project** are:

1. to map and sequence all of the DNA base pairs in the human chromosomes, and

2. to identify all of the genes within the sequence.

In 2003, scientists completed the first goal. They finished sequencing the human genome. But knowing the sequence of the billions of base pairs is just a beginning. Today, scientists continue to work to identify genes and figure out the functions of genes.

Underline the two main goals of the Human Genome Project.

# Technology allows the study and comparison of both genes and proteins.

Some traits—like the ones Mendel studied with his pea plants—are controlled by a single gene. But most genes are not single units that work alone. Instead, most biological processes and physical traits are the result of the interactions among many genes. Technology is very important for organizing and analyzing large amounts of data about genes, genomes, and proteins.

## Bioinformatics

Gene sequencing and other parts of genomic research produce huge amounts of data. These data are useful only if they are organized so that they can be analyzed. **Bioinformatics** is the use of computer databases to organize and analyze biological data. This has become a very important part of the study of genes and proteins. For example, a scientist can now search databases to find a gene that codes for a known protein.

## DNA Microarrays

**DNA microarrays** are tools that allow scientists to study many genes, and their expression, at once. A microarray is a very small chip with thousands of genes laid out in a grid.

This chip can be used to scan tissue samples to identify which genes are expressed. The mRNA present in the tissue sample is converted into a complementary, single strand of DNA that is labeled with a fluorescent dye. This labeled DNA is added to the microarray and binds to its complementary DNA in the microarray. Wherever the labeled DNA binds to the DNA on the microarray, a glowing dot appears. The pattern of glowing dots on a microarray—those that are fluorescent—shows which genes are being expressed. This tool can be used in many ways. For example, the pattern of gene expression in healthy cells can be compared with the pattern of gene expression in cancer cells.

> **VOCABULARY**
>
> The word part *micro-* means "small," and an *array* is an organized arrangement. A *DNA microarray* is a tiny organized arrangement of many genes.

## Proteomics

Genomics is the study of genomes. **Proteomics** (PROH-tee-AH-mihks) is the study of the proteins that result from an organism's genome. Proteomics also includes the study of how proteins work and how they interact. The study of proteins can be very complicated. For example, a single gene can code for more than one protein, depending on how the mRNA is processed.

The study of proteins is very important for many areas of biology. For example, proteomics is important to the study of evolutionary histories and in the study of human disease. By better understanding the proteins that are involved in different diseases, such as cancer or heart disease, scientists might be able to develop new treatments that target the specific proteins.

 **INSTANT REPLAY** What is the difference between proteomics and genomics?

_____

_____

## 9.5 Vocabulary Check

**Mark It Up**

Go back and highlight each sentence that has a vocabulary word in **bold**.

genomics

gene sequencing

Human Genome Project

bioinformatics

DNA microarray

proteomics

**Choose the correct term from the list for each description.**

1. the use of computers to organize data _____

2. determining the order of nucleotides in DNA _____

3. the study of genomes _____

4. the study of proteins resulting from a genome _____

5. a tool used to study the expression of many genes at once

_____

## 9.5 The Big Picture

6. What are the two goals of the Human Genome Project? _____

_____

_____

7. Give one example of a technology that is used to study genes and genomes. _____

_____

# 9.6 Genetic Screening and Gene Therapy

**KEY CONCEPT** Genetics provides a basis for new medical treatments.

## Genetic screening can detect genetic disorders.

**Genetic screening** is the process of testing a sample of a person's DNA to determine that person's risk of having a genetic disorder or passing on a genetic disorder. Genetic screening is not used to check for every possible genetic problem. But there are tests for many specific genetic disorders.

Identifying a genetic disease can help save lives by preparing a person with preventative treatment. It can also lead to some difficult choices. Suppose a person is at risk for passing on a genetic disease to his or her children. How should the person use that information? Should it influence the decision to have or not to have children? What would you do?

 What is the purpose of genetic screening?

_____

_____

## Gene therapy is the replacement of faulty* genes.

The goal of **gene therapy** is to treat a genetic disease by replacing a gene or adding a new gene into a person's genome. But how can a gene be inserted into a person's genome? One method that scientists have tried is to get the gene into stem cells in the patient's bone marrow. Because stem cells continue to divide, they will continue to express the inserted gene.

Gene therapy has had some successes, but much of gene therapy is still experimental. For example, scientists are working to insert a gene into a person's genome that will make the person's immune system attack cancer cells. Although gene therapy is still experimental, research in this field continues because it has great potential for treating disease.

 What is the purpose of gene therapy?

_____

_____

**\* ACADEMIC VOCABULARY**

**faulty** having error

## 9.6 Vocabulary Check

genetic screening
gene therapy

**Mark It Up**

Go back and highlight each sentence that has a vocabulary word in **bold**.

**Choose the correct term from the list for each description.**

1. the replacement of a defective or missing gene, or the addition of a new gene into a person's genome _____

2. the process of testing DNA to determine a person's risk of having or passing on a genetic disorder _____

## 9.6 The Big Picture

3. Which would come first, genetic screening or gene therapy? Explain.

_____

_____

# Chapter 9 Review

1. What is the name of the substance that is used to cut DNA at particular sequences?

   _____

2. The drawing below shows the result of gel electrophoresis. Circle the band that represents the largest fragment of DNA.

3. How do the DNA base pairing rules apply to PCR?

   _____

4. Which of the following can be used to identify a person?
   a. a gene
   b. proteomics
   c. a DNA fingerprint
   d. a restriction enzyme

5. What is the name of the item shown in the drawing below?

   _____

6. Which of the following is a true statement about clones?
   a. they look identical
   b. they have identical DNA
   c. there are no differences between clones
   d. no clones exist in nature

7. How are restriction enzymes used to make recombinant DNA?

   _____

8. What is the Human Genome Project?

   _____

# 10 Principles of Evolution

## GETTING READY TO LEARN

### Preview Key Concepts

**10.1 Early Ideas About Evolution**
There were theories of biological and geologic change before Darwin.

**10.2 Darwin's Observations**
Darwin's voyage provided insights into evolution.

**10.3 Theory of Natural Selection**
Darwin proposed natural selection as a mechanism for evolution.

**10.4 Evidence of Evolution**
Evidence of common ancestry among species comes from many sources.

**10.5 Evolutionary Biology Today**
New technology is furthering our understanding of evolution.

### Review Academic Vocabulary

Write the correct word for each definition.

competition        hybridization        phenotype

1. _____ : two or more organisms try to get the same resource

2. _____ : physical characteristics of an organism

3. _____ : the crossing of two different species

### Preview Biology Vocabulary

See how many key terms from this chapter you already know. Rewrite each phrase, using a different word or words for the **words in bold.**

| PHRASE | REWRITTEN WITH DIFFERENT WORDS |
|---|---|
| 1. In birds, wings and hollow bones are each an **adaptation**. | In birds, wings and hollow bones are each an _____ _____. |
| 2. You may have traits from each of your parents due to **heritability**. | You may have traits from each of your parents _____. |
| 3. The hand bones in humans and the flipper bones in seals are examples of **homologous structures**. | The hand bones in humans and the flipper bones in seals are examples of _____ _____ |

# 10.1 Early Ideas About Evolution

**KEY CONCEPT** There were theories of biological and geologic change before Darwin.

## Early scientists proposed ideas about evolution.

**Evolution** is the process of biological change by which descendants* come to differ from their ancestors. Much of today's understanding of evolution is based on Charles Darwin's work in the 1800s. But Darwin did not come up with the idea of evolution himself. Many other scientists contributed important ideas to the study of evolution. Several historical ideas—about species, geology, and the mechanisms of evolution—are described below. Like all science, the modern understanding of biological evolution builds on hundreds of years of study and research.

### Species

In the 1700s, a botanist named Carolus Linnaeus came up with a system to organize and name all of the different known types of organisms, or species. A **species** is a group of organisms that can reproduce and have fertile* offspring. Linneaus' classification system grouped organisms according to physical similarities. His system also shows evolutionary relationships, and is still in use today.

In Linnaeus' time, there was a common belief that the organisms that lived on earth were fixed, or that species did not change. Linneaus proposed that species could change. For example, he observed in experiments that two different plant species could cross, and make a new type of plant.

There is great diversity in different species of birds.

---

* ACADEMIC VOCABULARY

**descendant** offspring, or an organism that is related to another organism from the past
**fertile** able to breed and have offspring

In the 1700s, it was also a common belief that Earth was only 6000 years old. But several geologists began to challenge this idea. The geologists believed they had evidence that Earth was much older. The evidence of the old age of Earth was important to Darwin's development of his ideas.

### Mechanisms of Evolution

Many scientists in the 1700s did not believe that species could go extinct*. But many scientists thought species could change, or evolve. There were many different ideas, however, about the mechanism of evolution, or how evolution happens. For example, different scientists had different ideas about how environmental changes affect evolution, how changes get passed on to offspring, and what causes biological variation.

 How does history affect the development of scientific ideas?

_____

_____

_____

## Theories of geologic change set the stage for Darwin's theory.

The study of fossils led some scientists to conclude that species do go extinct. **Fossils** are traces of organisms that existed in the past. The locations of fossils in different rock layers provide clues about Earth's past. But how did those rock layers form? Geologists held different ideas about geologic change.

- **Catastrophism** (kuh-TAS-truh-FIHZ-uhm) is the idea that past natural disasters—like floods and volcanic eruptions—shaped landforms, and caused species to become extinct in the process.
- **Gradualism** (GRAJ-oo-uh-LIHZ-uhm) is the idea that landforms were shaped by very slow changes over a long period of time, and not by natural disasters.

The formation of mountains, shown here, results from slow changes over long periods of time.

* ACADEMIC VOCABULARY

**geology**  the study of rocks, minerals, and landforms

**extinct**  no longer existing

- **Uniformitarianism** (YOO-nuh-FAWR-mih-TAIR-ee-uh-NIHZ-uhm) is the idea that the same processes that shaped landforms in the past also shape landforms today. In other words, the geologic processes that shape Earth are uniform, or the same, through time. Uniformitarianism became the favored theory of geologic change and played an important role in the development of Darwin's theory.

 Which idea about geologic change became the accepted theory? _____

_____

**VISUAL VOCAB**

**Uniformitarianism** proposes that present geologic processes are the key to the past.

Every layer of rock was formed by the uniform laying down of sediment that still occurs today.

## 10.1  Vocabulary Check

**Mark It Up**

Go back and highlight each sentence that has a vocabulary word in **bold**.

evolution          catastrophism
species            gradualism
fossil             uniformitarianism

1. Name three ideas about geologic change. _____

_____

2. What is the term for a group of organisms that can reproduce and have fertile offspring? _____

3. What is the term for the process of biological change by which organisms come to differ from their ancestors? _____

## 10.1  The Big Picture

4. How are catastrophism and gradualism different? _____

_____

5. How did the ideas of scientists before Darwin influence Darwin's ideas? _____

_____

_____

# 10.2 Darwin's Observations

**KEY CONCEPT** Darwin's voyage provided insights into evolution.

## Darwin observed differences among island species.

Darwin spent over 20 years researching biological evolution. He made important observations during his travels on a ship that sailed the coast of South America and the Pacific islands. Darwin was amazed by the variation of traits among similar species that he saw in his travels. The word *variation* has many common uses, but in biology, **variation** means the differences in the physical traits among individuals in a group of organisms.

Darwin noticed that there was variation between species on different islands. This was especially noticeable in the Galápagos Islands, a chain of islands off of the coast of Ecuador in South America. For example, he noticed that birds called finches had different kinds of beaks in areas with different food sources. He found finches with thick beaks in areas with large hard-shelled nuts, and finches with smaller beaks in areas where fruits were available.

These differences seemed to match the environment and the diet of the finches. Darwin realized that species may somehow be able to adapt to their surroundings. An **adaptation** is a feature that allows an organism to better survive in its environment.

Albemarle Island

Abingdon Island

Darwin also studied different species of Galapagos tortoises that are adapted to different environments.

 What adaptations did Darwin notice in finches? _____

_____

## Darwin observed fossil and geologic evidence supporting an ancient Earth.

During his travels, Darwin found that some fossils looked similar to living species. This suggested that the living species might have some relationship to the fossil forms. In order for such changes to occur, Darwin figured that Earth must be much older that 6000 years.

Darwin found much evidence supporting the ideas of uniformitarianism. For example, he found fossil shells of marine* organisms high up in the Andes mountains. Later he experienced an earthquake and saw land that had been underwater get shifted up above the sea level. He put together observations like these, and concluded that daily geologic processes can add up to much bigger changes over a long period of time.

 **What is one example of evidence from Darwin's travels that supports an ancient Earth?** _____

_____

**\* ACADEMIC VOCABULARY**

**marine** related to the ocean

## 10.2 Vocabulary Check

**Mark It Up**

Go back and highlight each sentence that has a vocabulary word in **bold**.

variation          adaptation

**For each term, write brief definitions of its common and biological meanings.**

1. variation
   common meaning: _____
   biological meaning: _____

2. adaptation
   common meaning: _____
   biological meaning: _____

## 10.2 The Big Picture

3. What is one example of biological variation that Darwin observed in his travels? _____

4. What is one example of geologic evidence supporting uniformitarianism that Darwin observed in his travels? _____

_____

# 10.3 Theory of Natural Selection

**KEY CONCEPT**   Darwin proposed natural selection as a mechanism for evolution.

## Several key insights* led to Darwin's idea for natural selection.

The variation of similar species among islands, fossil evidence, and geologic events convinced Darwin that evolution occurs. But he still wondered *how* evolution occurs. Here, you will read about some of Darwin's reasoning that led him to his idea for natural selection.

**Artificial Selection**   Darwin noticed that plants and animals that are raised by humans had variations in traits that were not seen in their wild relatives. Think of all the different breeds of dogs that you have seen. In a process called **artificial selection,** humans select individuals with the traits they desire, and then breed them to produce more individuals with those traits.

**Heritability**   In order for artificial selection to occur, traits must be heritable.  **Heritability** (HER-ih-tuh-BIHL-uh-tee) is the ability of a trait to be passed down from one generation to the next. Things that are acquired in an organism's life, like a broken bone, are not heritable.

**Natural Section**   Darwin reasoned that a process similar to artificial selection could happen in nature. In artificial selection, humans are the source of selection. In natural selection, the environment is the source of selection. **Natural selection** is a process in which individuals that have inherited beneficial* adaptations produce more offspring than do other individuals.

Humans have changed animal species, such as these different dog breeds, through artificial selection.

**Struggle for Survival** Darwin was influenced by the work of an economist named Thomas Malthus. Malthus proposed that resources like food, water, and shelter were limits to human population growth. Darwin reasoned that a similar struggle happened in nature.

Darwin saw great variation within populations of organisms. A **population** is all the individuals of a species that live in an area. He saw individuals with adaptations that matched their environment. Darwin proposed that these adaptations arose over many generations in a process he called "descent with modification."

 What is the difference between artificial and natural selection? _____

_____

The white fur of this rabbit allows it to blend in with its environment.

## Natural selection explains how evolution can occur.

Darwin was not the only scientist studying evolution during this time. Another scientist named Alfred Wallace independently developed an explanation of how evolution occurs. Wallace's explanation was very similar to Darwin's. In the late 1850s, the ideas of Darwin and Wallace were presented to the scientific community.

There are four main principles to the theory of natural selection: variation, overproduction, adaptation, and descent with modification.

- **Variation** Individuals of a species differ due to genetic variation. Heritable differences are the basis for natural selection.
- **Overproduction** Organisms have more offspring than can survive. This results in competition among offspring for resources.
- **Adaptation** Some individuals have certain variations that allow them to survive better than other individuals in their environment. These individuals are "naturally selected" to live longer and produce more offspring that also have those adaptations.
- **Descent with modification** Over time, natural selection will result in species with adaptations that are beneficial for survival and reproduction in a particular environment. More individuals will have the trait in every following generation, as long as the environmental conditions stay the same.

> **VOCABULARY**
> The term *descent* is used in evolution to mean the passing of genetic information from generation to generation.

Let's apply these four principles to an example of natural selection. About 11,000 years ago, jaguars faced a shortage of food due to a changing climate. There were fewer mammals to eat, and jaguars had to eat reptiles to survive. Variations in jaw and tooth size allowed some individuals to more easily eat shelled reptiles.

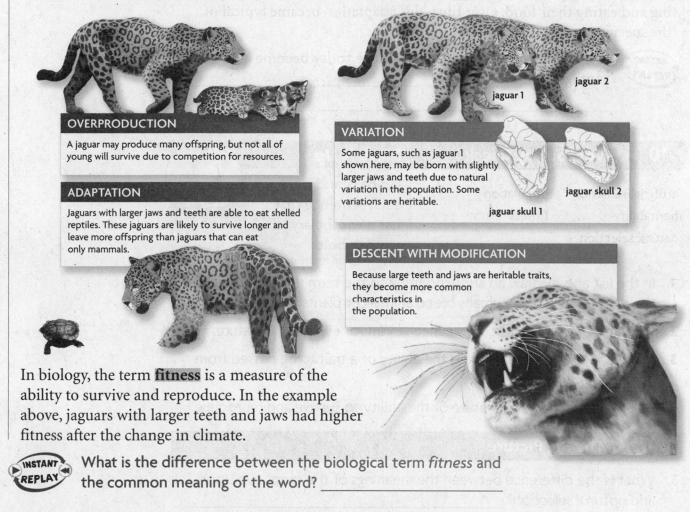

**OVERPRODUCTION**

A jaguar may produce many offspring, but not all of young will survive due to competition for resources.

**ADAPTATION**

Jaguars with larger jaws and teeth are able to eat shelled reptiles. These jaguars are likely to survive longer and leave more offspring than jaguars that can eat only mammals.

**VARIATION**

Some jaguars, such as jaguar 1 shown here, may be born with slightly larger jaws and teeth due to natural variation in the population. Some variations are heritable.

jaguar skull 1

jaguar skull 2

jaguar 1

jaguar 2

**DESCENT WITH MODIFICATION**

Because large teeth and jaws are heritable traits, they become more common characteristics in the population.

In biology, the term **fitness** is a measure of the ability to survive and reproduce. In the example above, jaguars with larger teeth and jaws had higher fitness after the change in climate.

**INSTANT REPLAY** What is the difference between the biological term *fitness* and the common meaning of the word? _____

_____

# Natural selection acts on existing variation.

Natural selection cannot make new alleles. It can only work with variation that already exists. In other words, natural selection acts on phenotypes, or physical traits, and not on genetic material itself.

**Changing environments** As an environment changes, different traits become beneficial. Think about the jaguars. When mammals were their main food source, small teeth and jaws were beneficial. But when the environment changed, larger teeth and jaws became beneficial to better eat reptiles. Because the environment constantly changes, a trait that is an advantage today may be a disadvantage in the future.

**Adaptations as compromises** Adaptations can sometimes be thought of as compromises. One example of an adaptive compromise is the panda bear's "thumb." Modern pandas have five digits that are like your fingers and a sixth digit that functions like a thumb. This digit is actually a wrist bone. Ancestral pandas with bigger wrist bones had an advantage in holding and eating their food. Over time, this adaptation became typical of the species.

 Why might a trait that is an advantage today become a disadvantage in the future? _____

_____

---

### 10.3 Vocabulary Check

| | |
|---|---|
| artificial selection | population |
| heritability | fitness |
| natural selection | |

**Mark It Up**

Go back and highlight each sentence that has a vocabulary word in **bold**.

1. In the list above, draw an arrow pointing to the term that describes the process by which humans breed animals or plants for certain traits.

2. Circle the term that describes a mechanism for evolution in nature.

3. Underline the term that means the ability of a trait to be passed from one generation to the next.

4. Box the term that is a measure of the ability to survive and reproduce.

---

### 10.3 The Big Picture

5. What is the difference between the meanings of the terms *evolution* and *natural selection*? _____

_____

_____

6. What are four main principles to the theory of natural selection?

_____

_____

_____

# 10.4 Evidence of Evolution

**KEY CONCEPT** Evidence of common ancestry among species comes from many sources.

## Evidence for evolution in Darwin's time came from several sources.

Genetic inheritance was not known in Darwin's time. But Darwin supported his ideas with evidence from many other sources—fossils, geography, embryology, and anatomy. His evidence was very strong, and left no doubt in the minds of scientists that all organisms share a common ancestor. Today, the concept of evolution ties together all fields of biology.

### Fossils

Before Darwin, scientists studying fossils knew that organisms changed over time. Fossilized organisms were different in different layers of rocks. The bottom layers of rock are the oldest, and contain fossils of more ancient organisms. The upper layers of rock are the youngest, and contain fossils of more recent organisms. Findings in the fossil record support Darwin's idea of descent with modification.

Trilobites are extinct organisms that lived in ancient oceans.

### Geography

During Darwin's travels, he noticed that plants and animals on islands looked similar to species on the mainland, but not exactly the same. He hypothesized that organisms from the mainland had migrated to the islands. Different islands had different food sources, climates, and predators. The different environmental conditions favored different traits in these migrant organisms. For example, the finches on the different Galápagos islands have different shapes of beaks that evolved in response to the different island habitats. This is an important part of **biogeography,** the study of the distribution of organisms around the world.

### Embryology

Embryology is the study of embryos and their development. Darwin noticed that the embryos of different species may look very similar, although the adult species look very different. For example, fish, birds, reptiles, and mammals all have gill slits as embryos. These slits develop into gills in fish, but develop into ears and throats in mammals. The similar features of embryos in very different organisms suggest evolution from a distant common ancestor.

### Anatomy

Some of Darwin's best evidence came from comparing the body parts of different species. He found that some organisms have body parts that are similar in structure, but might be used differently.

- **Homologous structures** (huh-MAHL-uh-guhs) are features that are similar in structure, but appear in different organisms and may have different functions. For example, think of the front limbs of humans, bats, and moles. The front limbs of these organisms share similar bone structure, but each organism uses these limbs differently. Homologous structures appear across many different species, and offer strong evidence for common descent.

- **Analogous structures** (uh-NAL-uh-guhs) are structures that perform a similar function, but are not similar in origin. For example, both birds and butterflies have wings. They both use their wings to fly, but their wings do not share a common origin. Bird wings have bones, and butterfly wings do not.

The wings of birds and butterflies are analogous structures.

Just because two organisms share similar structures does not mean they are closely related. Homologous structures show common ancestry, while analogous structures do not.

 **What is the difference between a homologous structure and an analogous structure?** _____

_____

## Structural patterns are clues to the history of a species.

**Vestigial structures** (veh-STIHJ-ee-uhl) are small leftover organs or structures that had a function in an early ancestor. For example, snakes and whales have tiny pelvic bones. Even though neither organism walks, their ancestors were four-legged animals. These pelvic bones are vestigial structures.

The appendix is an example of a vestigial structure in humans. The appendix is a remnant of an organ that helped to digest certain plant material eaten by human ancestors. The human appendix has lost the ability to digest this material, and actually has no known function.

A whale's pelvic bone is a vestigial structure—a leftover from an early ancestor.

Vestigial structures do not become smaller in one individual organism. These structures became smaller over many generations. Today, biologists consider vestigial structures among the most important examples demonstrating how evolution works.

 **What are vestigial structures?** _____

_____

_____

## 10.4 Vocabulary Check

biogeography                analogous structure

homologous structure        vestigial structure

**Complete each sentence with the correct term from the list above.**

1. The forelimbs of humans, bats, and moles are examples of

   _____

2. Bird wings and butterfly wings are examples of

   _____

3. Pelvic bones in whales are an example of

   _____

## 10.4 The Big Picture

4. What were four lines of evidence Darwin used to support his argument for evolution? _____

   _____

5. How do vestigial structures demonstrate common ancestry? _____

   _____

   _____

# 10.5 Evolutionary Biology Today

**KEY CONCEPT** New technology is furthering our understanding of evolution.

## Fossils provide a record of evolution.

**Paleontology** (PAY-lee-ahn-TAHL-uh-jee) is the study of fossils or extinct organisms. The fossil record is not complete. One reason for this is because most organisms do not form fossils after they die. Fossils form only in particular environmental conditions. However, fossil evidence that does not support evolution has never been found.

Darwin wondered why he did not find fossils that showed transitions between different groups of organisms. Since Darwin's time, many of these transitional fossils have been found. For example, fossils have been found of a transitional species in the evolution of whales. This organism had a whalelike body, but still had the limbs of land animals. Fossils continue to provide new information and evidence for current ideas about evolution.

**VOCABULARY**

Paleontology is the study of prehistoric life forms. *Paleo-* means "ancient," and *-ology* means "the study of."

### WHALE EVOLUTION

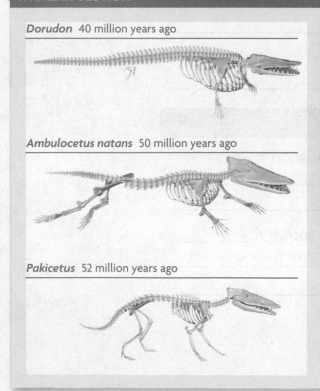

*Dorudon* 40 million years ago

*Ambulocetus natans* 50 million years ago

*Pakicetus* 52 million years ago

Modern-day whale

Fossil evidence supports the idea that whales descended from hoofed mammals. *Pakicetus* had a whale-shaped skull and teeth adapted for hunting fish. *Ambulocetus natans* lived on both land and water. *Dorudon* had tiny hind legs that were useless on land, similar to modern-day whales.

INSTANT REPLAY

What is a transitional fossil? _____

_____

## Molecular and genetic evidence support fossil and anatomical evidence.

The fields of genetics and molecular biology have added strong support to Darwin's theory of natural selection. All living things have DNA, share the same genetic code, and make most of the same proteins from the same 20 amino acids. Comparisons of DNA and protein sequences can be used to show evolutionary relationships between different organisms. The more related two organisms are, the more similar the sequences will be. Because there are thousands of genes in even simple organisms, DNA contains a huge amount of information on evolutionary history.

Some particular genes are found in many organisms—from fruit flies to humans—and therefore give evidence of a very distant common ancestor. For example, homeobox genes, which control development, are found in a wide range of organisms. These genes are even found in organisms that lived 600 million years ago. You will read more about homeobox genes in Chapter 23.

| MOLECULAR EVIDENCE | |
| --- | --- |
| **Hippopotamus** | TCC TGGCA GTCCA GTGGT |
| **Humpback whale** | CCC TGGCA GTGCA GTGCT |

Molecular evidence also supports the idea that whales descended from hoofed mammals. As shown above, the DNA sequences of a whale and a hippopotamus are very similar.

 How does genetic evidence give information about evolutionary relationships? _____

_____

_____

## Evolution unites all fields of biology.

Scientists continue to actively study evolution through natural selection. The theory of natural selection combined with genetics is sometimes called the modern synthesis of evolutionary theory.

New tools are providing more data than ever before. Modern tools from different fields of study add to what has been discovered through fossil evidence. For example, as shown in the figure above, the comparisons of milk protein genes support the fossil evidence for the relationship between whales and hippopotamuses. New discoveries are limited only by the time and resources of scientists.

The basic principles of evolution are used in all fields of science, including medicine, geology, geography, chemistry, and ecology. For example, the idea of common descent helps biologists understand where new diseases come from and how they might be best treated.

**VOCABULARY**

*Synthesis* means the combination of different ideas to form a new thing.

As much as we know about life on Earth, there is so much more waiting to be discovered. As the great geneticist Theodosius Dobzhansky (1900–1975) once noted, "Nothing in biology makes sense except in the light of evolution."

**INSTANT REPLAY** What is the modern synthesis of evolutionary biology?

_____

_____

_____

## 10.5 Vocabulary Check

**Mark It Up**

Go back and highlight each sentence that has a vocabulary word in **bold**.

Paleontology

**1.** Write a definition for the term *paleontology*. _____

_____

_____

## 10.5 The Big Picture

**2.** Why are transitional fossils important information for tracing the course of evolution? _____

_____

_____

**3.** This chart shows the sequence of a particular gene in three different organisms. Which two organisms do you think are most closely related? Explain your answer.

| ORGANISM | GENE SEQUENCE |
| --- | --- |
| Organism A | TCAGGAACTA |
| Organism B | ACAGGAAGTA |
| Organism C | TGTAAGTATA |

_____

_____

**4.** Name three fields of science in which the principles of evolution are used. _____

_____

# Chapter 10 Review

1. Fill in the chart below with examples of different lines of evidence for evolution.

| Field of Study | Fossils | Geography | Embryology | Anatomy |
|---|---|---|---|---|
| Evidence | | | | |

2. The panda's "thumb" is actually a sixth "finger" made from a wrist bone, not from the same bone parts as the human thumb. These bones are an example of which type of structures?
   a. analogous structures
   b. homologous structures
   c. vestigial structures
   d. evolutionary structures

3. Which idea best describes our modern understanding of geologic change?
   a. gradualism
   b. catastrophism
   c. uniformitarianism
   d. biogeography

4. Explain why the following sentence is true: "An evolutionary advantage today may be an evolutionary disadvantage in the future." _____

   _____

   _____

5. Write a brief definition of the term *natural selection*. _____

   _____

6. What is a heritable trait? _____

   _____

7. Based on what we know today about genetics, what accounts for variation in a population? _____

   _____

# 11 The Evolution of Populations

## GETTING READY TO LEARN

### Preview Key Concepts

**11.1 Genetic Variation Within Populations**
A population shares a common gene pool.

**11.2 Natural Selection in Populations**
Populations, not individuals, evolve.

**11.3 Other Mechanisms of Evolution**
Natural selection is not the only mechanism through which populations evolve.

**11.4 Hardy-Weinberg Equilibrium**
Hardy-Weinberg equilibrium provides a framework for understanding how populations evolve.

**11.5 Speciation Through Isolation**
New species can arise when populations become isolated.

**11.6 Patterns in Evolution**
Evolution occurs in patterns.

### Review Academic Vocabulary

Write the correct word for each definition.

allele    equilibrium    gene    natural selection    phenotype

**1.** _____ : region of DNA that codes for a protein

**2.** _____ : trait produced by one or more genes

**3.** _____ : one of the mechanisms of evolution

**4.** _____ : alternative form of a gene

**5** _____ : a state of balance; an unchanging system

### Preview Biology Vocabulary

To see how many key terms you already know from this chapter, choose the word that makes sense in each sentence.

coevolution    extinction    speciation

**1.** Two or more species arise from a common ancestor through _____.

**2.** During _____, two or more species evolve in response to each other.

**3.** _____ is the elimination of a species from the Earth.

# 11.1 Genetic Variation Within Populations

**KEY CONCEPT** A population shares a common gene pool.

## Genetic variation in a population increases the chance that some individuals will survive.

A population of organisms may have a wide range of phenotypes. Imagine a large population of frogs. They might all look the same at first, but look closer and you will see that they differ in leg length, tongue shape, skin color, body size, and many other traits.

> Recall from section 6.4 that all of the physical characteristics, or traits, of an individual organism make up its phenotype.

The more variation in phenotypes, the more likely that some individuals can survive in a changing environment. For example, imagine that during most summers, green-skinned frogs are easily hidden in the green plants around a pond. But if there is a very dry summer, brown-skinned frogs might have an advantage and be better hidden in the dry grasses.

A population with a lot of genetic variation likely has a wide range of phenotypes. Genetic variation is stored in a population's gene pool. A **gene pool** is made up of all of the alleles of all of the individuals in a population. Each allele in a gene pool exists at a certain rate, or frequency. An **allele frequency** is a measure of how common an allele is in a population.

---

**ALLELE FREQUENCY**

An allele frequency is the ratio of one allele to the total number of the alleles for that gene in the gene pool.

**CALCULATING ALLELE FREQUENCIES**

G codes for green      g codes for brown
Gs in gene pool        5 gs in gene pool

**12** total alleles for skin color trait in gene pool

Frequency of allele $G = \frac{7}{12} = 0.583 \approx 58.3\%$

Frequency of allele $g = \frac{5}{12} = 0.417 \approx 41.7\%$

---

Why does genetic variation increase the chance that some organisms in a population will survive? _____

_____

# Genetic variation comes from several sources.

Genetic variation comes from two main sources: mutation and recombination.

- **Mutation**  A mutation is a random change in DNA. This change can result in a new allele. If the mutation happens in a cell that makes gametes—sperm or eggs—then the mutation can be passed on to offspring. Mutations increase the genetic variation in a gene pool.
- **Recombination**  New combinations of alleles form during meiosis—the type of cell division that forms gametes. When gametes are made, each parent's alleles are arranged in new ways. This can result in many different genetic combinations.

Some scientists are also researching other possible sources of genetic variation. One of these other possible sources is called hybridization. This occurs when organisms breed with organisms of another closely-related species, resulting in new combinations of alleles.

 **INSTANT REPLAY**  Circle the two main sources of genetic variation.

| 11.1 | Vocabulary Check |
|---|---|

gene pool          allele frequency

**Mark It Up**

Go back and highlight each sentence that has a vocabulary word in **bold**.

**1.** What is a gene pool? _____

_____

**2.** What is an allele frequency? _____

_____

| 11.1 | The Big Picture |
|---|---|

**3.** A certain population of lizards has a very small gene pool, with little variation. How does this affect the chance that individuals of the population will survive changes in the environment? _____

_____

_____

**4.** Describe two main source of genetic variation. _____

_____

_____

# 11.2 Natural Selection in Populations

**KEY CONCEPT** Populations, not individuals, evolve.

## Natural selection acts on distributions of traits.

Some people are very short, and some are very tall, but most are somewhere in the middle. Traits such as height show a **normal distribution**—the frequency is highest for the middle, or mean phenotype, and lowest at the two ends, or extreme phenotypes.

Environmental conditions can change, and a certain phenotype can become an advantage. Individuals with this phenotype are then better able to survive and reproduce. Therefore, the alleles related to the favorable phenotypes increase in frequency.

What phenotype has the greatest frequency in a trait that follows a normal distribution?

**NORMAL DISTRIBUTION**

mean

Frequency

Range of variable

## Natural selection can change the distribution of a trait in one of three ways.

**Microevolution** is the observable change in the allele frequencies of a population over time. Natural selection is one process that can lead to microevolution. Three ways that natural selection can change the distribution of a trait are through directional, stabilizing, and disruptive selection.

### Directional Selection

Selection that favors a phenotype at one end, or extreme, of a range is called **directional selection.** One example of directional selection is the evolution of antibiotic-resistant bacteria. When medical antibiotics were first developed, bacteria had varying levels of drug resistance. After medical antibiotics came into use, bacteria that were resistant had a great advantage, and could survive and reproduce.

**DIRECTIONAL SELECTION**

Antibiotic drugs put pressure on bacteria populations.

mean          mean

Frequency

Low drug resistance          High drug resistance

Key: ----- Normal distribution    ——— Distribution after selection

## Stabilizing Selection

Selection that favors the middle, or intermediate, phenotype is called **stabilizing selection.** During stabilizing selection, both extreme phenotypes are selected against. For example, the gall fly is a fly that lays its eggs inside the stem of a plant. Its larvae produce a chemical that makes the plant stem form a bump, called a gall. Large galls—and the larvae inside—get eaten by woodpeckers, and small galls get attacked by wasps. But middle-sized galls are not bothered. As a result, there is a higher frequency of flies that form middle-sized galls.

**STABILIZING SELECTION**

→ Woodpeckers and wasps put pressure on gall-fly populations.

mean

wasp → ← woodpecker

Frequency

Small gall size — Large gall size

## Disruptive Selection

Selection that favors both extreme phenotypes is called **disruptive selection.** One example of disruptive selection occurs in a bird species called the lazuli bunting. This bird has feathers that range from dull brown to bright blue. For one year-old males, dull brown birds and bright blue birds are most successful at attracting mates. Dominant adult males are aggressive toward bright blue and bluish-brown males. However, bright blue birds attract mates anyway due to their color. Year-old males with bluish-brown "middle" phenotypes are less successful.

**DISRUPTIVE SELECTION**

→ Dominant adult males put pressure on young bluish-brown males in the bunting population.

mean

Frequency

Brown — Blue

Key: ----- Normal distribution ——— Distribution after selection

Each of these three types of selection—directional, stabilizing, and disruptive—changes the distribution of a trait. Directional selection moves the distribution towards one extreme or the other. Stabilizing selection moves the distribution more towards the middle. And disruptive selection pushes the distribution toward both extremes.

Name three ways natural selection can change the distribution of a trait. _____

_____

_____

**Mark It Up**

Go back and highlight each sentence that has a vocabulary word in **bold**.

| | |
|---|---|
| normal distribution | stabilizing selection |
| microevolution | disruptive selection |
| directional selection | |

**Choose the correct term for each graph below.**

1.

_____

2.

_____

3. Question #2 above is an example of _____

## 11.2   The Big Picture

4. Which unit of organisms evolves—an individual, a population, or a species? Explain. _____

_____

5. Give one example of how natural selection can change the distribution of a trait. _____

_____

# 11.3 Other Mechanisms of Evolution

**KEY CONCEPT** Natural selection is not the only mechanism through which populations evolve.

## Gene flow is the movement of alleles between populations.

In addition to natural selection, other factors can lead to the evolution of populations. For example, when an organism joins a new population and reproduces, its alleles become part of that population's gene pool. The movement of alleles from one population to another is called **gene flow.**

For many animals, gene flow occurs when individuals move between populations. As shown in the map, a young bald eagle might mate and reproduce 2500 kilometers from where it hatched. Gene flow also occurs in plant and fungi populations when seeds or spores are spread to new areas.

 Water in a stream "flows." What "flows" during gene flow? _____

_____

## Genetic drift is a change in allele frequencies due to chance.

Imagine you have a huge bag full of hundreds of candies—exactly half are mints and half are lemon drops. If you randomly grab 50 candies, it is likely that they will be about half mints and half lemon drops. If you reach into the bag and just pick out a few candies, you might get exactly half mints and half lemon drops. But, just by chance, you might also get all lemon drops, or all mints, or another combination—different from half and half.

This map shows the locations where young banded eagles were found during the first summer after hatching.

With the larger "population" of 50 candies, it is likely that both types of candy are equally represented. But with the small sample size of just a few candies, it is more likely that the few candies will not represent the proportions of the whole bag.

Allele frequencies in small populations can also be affected by chance. Changes in allele frequencies that are due to chance are called **genetic drift.** Two processes commonly cause populations to become small enough for genetic drift to occur: the bottleneck effect and the founder effect.

- The **bottleneck effect** is genetic drift that occurs after a population has been greatly reduced in size. A natural disaster, for example, can leave only a few survivors of a population. The few survivors do not represent the genetic diversity of the original population.
- The **founder effect** is genetic drift that occurs after a small number of individuals begin to live in a new area.

### VISUAL VOCAB

The **bottleneck effect** describes the effect of a destructive event that leaves only a few survivors in a population.

| Initial population | Bottleneck effect | Surviving population |

### THE FOUNDER EFFECT

**The founder effect** can occur if a small number of individuals colonize a new area.

The gene pool for a population of flowers has genetic diversity that results in three different color phenotypes.

A bird carries a few seeds to a new location. These seeds "found" a new population.

Alleles for the lightest flower color increase in the new small population through genetic drift.

Genetic drift can cause problems for populations because it results in a loss of genetic variation. Small populations have only a small amount of the genetic variation from the original larger population. With little genetic variation, a population is less likely to have some individuals that are able to survive a changing environment.

What are two ways that genetic drift can occur? _____

_____

_____

## Sexual selection occurs when certain traits increase mating success.

Some traits help an organism find a mate. **Sexual selection** occurs when a trait increases mating success, and gets passed on to the next generation. These traits can be very showy—like bright coloring or large antlers. Research suggests that some showy traits may be linked with genes for good health and fertility.

What traits are involved in sexual selection? _____

_____

| 11.3 | Vocabulary Check |
|------|------------------|

**Mark It Up**

Go back and highlight each sentence that has a vocabulary word in **bold**.

gene flow      founder effect

genetic drift      sexual selection

bottleneck effect

**Match the correct term from the list above with each description below.**

1. two processes of genetic drift _____ _____

2. the movement of alleles between populations _____

3. selection for traits that increase mating success _____

| 11.3 | The Big Picture |
|------|-----------------|

4. Look back at the figures on p. 187. How does genetic drift affect the genetic diversity of a population?

_____

_____

5. A plant seed may get carried very far on a windy day, and sprout in another field full of the same type of plant. What mechanism of evolution is this an example of? Explain. _____

_____

_____

# 11.4 Hardy-Weinberg Equilibrium

**KEY CONCEPT** Hardy-Weinberg equilibrium provides a framework for understanding how populations evolve.

## Hardy-Weinberg equilibrium describes populations that are not evolving.

Biologists often use models to learn more about complex situations. Hardy-Weinberg equilibrium is a model that can be used to study how a population is changing. It was developed in 1908 and is named after the two people who developed it. Here, *equilibrium* refers to genotype frequencies that stay the same from generation to generation. If genotype frequencies of a population stay in equilibrium then the population is not evolving. Populations that meet five conditions listed below are said to be in **Hardy-Weinberg equilibrium.**

- **Very large population**  No genetic drift can occur.
- **No emigration\* or immigration\***  No gene flow can occur.
- **No mutations**  No new alleles can be added to the gene pool.
- **Random mating**  No sexual selection can occur.
- **No natural selection**  All traits must equally help in survival.

Real populations rarely meet all five conditions. But the model is a useful tool for understanding changes in populations. Real data can be compared with data predicted by the model.

 What does is mean if a population meets all five conditions listed above? _____

_____

_____

**\* ACADEMIC VOCABULARY**

**emigration**  moving out of a population
**immigration**  moving into a population

# The Hardy-Weinberg equation is used to predict genotype frequencies in a population.

The Hardy-Weinberg equation can be used to predict genotype frequencies for simple dominant-recessive traits in a population. The equation predicts the values that would be present if the population is in equilibrium.

Let's use the Hardy-Weinberg equation to calculate predicted genotype frequencies for a tail shape trait in a population of 1000 fish.

- 640 fish have forked tail fins, which is the dominant trait. Forked-fin fish have $TT$ or $Tt$ genotypes.
- 360 fish have smooth tail fins, and the homozygous recessive $tt$ genotype.

The letter $p$ stands for the frequency of the dominant allele and $q$ stands for the frequency of the recessive allele. The Hardy-Weinberg equation is:

$$p^2 + 2pq + q^2 = 1$$

## USING THE HARDY-WEINBERG EQUATION

**Use the Hardy-Weinberg equation to calculate predicted genotype frequencies for this population.**

In a population of 1000 fish, 640 have forked tail fins and 360 have smooth tail fins. Tail fin shape is determined by two alleles: $T$ is dominant for forked and $t$ is recessive for smooth.

**1** Find $q^2$, the frequency of smooth-finned fish (recessive homozygotes).

$$q^2 = \frac{360 \text{ smooth-finned fish}}{1000 \text{ fish in population}} = 0.36$$

**2** To find the predicted value of $q$, take the square root of $q^2$.

$$q = \sqrt{0.36} = 0.6$$

**3** Use the equation $p + q = 1$ to find the predicted value of $p$. Rearrange the equation to solve for $p$.

$$p = 1 - q$$
$$p = 1 - 0.6 = 0.4$$

These are the predicted allele frequencies: $p = 0.4$ and $q = 0.6$.

**4** Calculate the predicted genotype frequencies from the predicted allele frequencies.

$$p^2 = 0.4^2 = 0.16$$ → 16% of fish have forked fins ($TT$)
$$2pq = 2 \times (0.4) \times (0.6) = 0.48$$ → 48% of fish have forked fins ($Tt$)
$$q^2 = 0.6^2 = 0.36$$ → 36% of fish have smooth fins ($tt$)

### VARIABLES

$p$ = frequency of allele $T$ (dominant allele)

$q$ = frequency of allele $t$ (recessive allele)

$p^2$ = frequency of fish with $TT$ (dominant homozygous genotype)

$2pq$ = frequency of fish with $Tt$ (heterozygous genotype)

$q^2$ = frequency of fish with $tt$ (recessive homozygous genotype)

 **INSTANT REPLAY** What do $p$ and $q$ stand for in the Hardy-Weinberg equation?

_____

_____

# There are five factors that can lead to evolution.

In nature, evolution should be expected in all populations most of the time. The Hardy-Weinberg model shows there are five factors that can lead to evolution.

## INITIAL POPULATION

Here are the alleles associated with body color in a hypothetical population.

## GENETIC DRIFT

After a bottleneck event, only gray and blue alleles remained in the small population. Through genetic drift, gray alleles increase in frequency. Allele frequencies can change due to chance alone.

## GENE FLOW

Black alleles increase in frequency because of immigration; gray alleles decrease in frequency because of emigration. The movement of alleles from one population to another changes allele frequencies.

arriving

leaving

## MUTATION

A new allele, associated with light blue body color, is formed through mutation. This could affect sexual selection if this body color improves mating success. It could affect natural selection if this body color increases the chance for survival. New alleles can form through mutation, creating genetic variation needed for evolution.

new allele

## SEXUAL SELECTION

Blue alleles are associated with blue body color, which improves mating success. Blue alleles therefore increase in frequency. Alleles associated with improved mating success increase in frequency.

## NATURAL SELECTION

White alleles are associated with white body color, which allows individuals to blend in with their environment and avoid predation. White alleles therefore increase in frequency. Alleles associated with increased survival increase in frequency.

Evolution is continuous. Environments are always changing, although often very slowly relative to a human's lifetime. Evolution is a response to these changes. As environments change, populations either adapt or go extinct. When a population becomes extinct, a different species can take its place, and the cycle continues.

**INSTANT REPLAY** What are five factors that can lead to evolution? _____

_____

_____

_____

## 11.4 Vocabulary Check

**Mark It Up**

Go back and highlight each sentence that has a vocabulary word in **bold**.

Hardy-Weinberg equilibrium

1. What does it mean for a population to be in Hardy-Weinberg equilibrium? _____

_____

## 11.4 The Big Picture

2. Is it common for natural populations to be in Hardy-Weinberg equilibrium? Explain. _____

_____

_____

3. In a population of organisms, the frequency of the homozygous recessive genotype is 0.3, the frequency of the heterozygous genotype is 0.6, and the frequency of the homozygous dominant genotype is 0.1. Fill in the correct numbers for each variable below:

$p^2 =$ _____

$2pq =$ _____

$q^2 =$ _____

4. Describe one of the five factors that can lead to evolution. _____

_____

_____

**SECTION**

# 11.5 Speciation Through Isolation

**KEY CONCEPT** New species can arise when populations are isolated.

## The isolation* of populations can lead to speciation.

The more gene flow there is between two populations, the more similar the populations will be because they will have similar alleles in their gene pools. But if there is very little gene flow between two populations, these populations are likely to become genetically different as changes in the gene pools add up over time.

If gene flow between two populations stops, the populations are said to be isolated. Over time, isolated populations become more and more genetically different. Members of the two populations may begin to look and behave differently from one another.

These changes can result in **reproductive isolation,** which is when members of different populations can no longer mate successfully. Members of the two populations might not be physically able to mate with each other, or they might not produce offspring that can survive and reproduce. Reproductive isolation is the last step in **speciation,** the process of one species becoming two or more separate species.

 How does reproductive isolation result in speciation? _____

_____

## Populations can become isolated in several ways.

Several things can prevent mating between populations, leading to reproductive isolation. Things that prevent mating are called barriers, because they block mating. Three types of barriers to mating are behavioral, geographic, and temporal.

- Behavioral barriers result in **behavioral isolation,** isolation caused by differences in courtship and mating behaviors. Over 2000 species of fireflies are isolated in this way. Each species produces a different pattern of flashes that attracts mates of their own species.

- Geographic, or physical, barriers result in **geographic isolation,** such as when a river or mountain divides a population into two or more groups. For example, populations of snapping shrimp have become isolated by a strip of land, called the Isthmus of Panama, that formed between the Atlantic and Pacific Oceans. If shrimp from different sides are placed together, they will not mate.

- Temporal barriers result in **temporal isolation,** when timing prevents reproduction between populations. Reproduction periods may change to a different time of year or day. For example, two pine tree species in California are separated in this way. One species sheds its pollen in February, while the other sheds its pollen in April.

**GEOGRAPHIC BARRIER**

NORTH AMERICA

*Isthmus of Panama*

SOUTH AMERICA

ATLANTIC OCEAN

PACIFIC OCEAN

Equator

0    500    1,000 miles
0    500    1,000 kilometers

N W E S

Although snapping shrimp in the Atlantic and Pacific oceans look similar, they are distinct species that have evolved through geographic isolation, separated by the Isthmus of Panama.

Circle three types of reproductive barriers.

---

## 11.5 Vocabulary Check

reproductive isolation
speciation
behavioral isolation
geographic isolation
temporal isolation

**Mark It Up**

Go back and highlight each sentence that has a vocabulary word in **bold.**

**Fill in the blanks with the correct term from the list above.**

1. Reproductive isolation caused by a river is an example of _____.

2. Reproductive isolation caused by differences in the time of day that mating happens is one type of _____.

## 11.5 The Big Picture

3. How does reproductive isolation affect the gene pools of two or more populations? _____

_____

4. How do these effects on the gene pools lead to speciation? _____

_____

# 11.6 Patterns in Evolution

**KEY CONCEPT** Evolution occurs in patterns.

## Evolution through natural selection is not random.

In everyday conversation, the word random can have different meanings. In science, if something is *random* or happens by *chance*, it means that it cannot be predicted. Mutation and genetic drift are random events, because they cannot be predicted. These random events are sources of genetic diversity.

Natural selection, which acts on genetic diversity, is not random. Individuals with traits that are better adapted for their environment are more likely to survive and reproduce than individuals without those traits. Two ways that natural selection can direct a population's traits are through convergent evolution and divergent evolution.

**PATTERNS IN NATURAL SELECTION**

Generation 1     Generation 2     Generation 3

In this hypothetical population, a certain body color is favored by natural selection. Over time, more and more individuals in the population will have this advantageous phenotype.

- **Convergent evolution** is when unrelated species evolve similar characteristics. The wings on birds and insects are examples of convergent evolution.

- **Divergent evolution** is when closely related species evolve in different directions, and become increasingly different. The kit fox and the red fox, for example, are closely related species but look very different. The red fox has dark reddish fur and the kit fox has light sandy colored fur. These differences are the result of adaptations to two different environments.

Natural selection pushes a population's traits in a particular direction. But when the environment changes, different traits may become advantageous, and natural selection may take a different direction.

**VISUAL VOCAB**

To **converge** means to come together.

To **diverge** means to move apart.

**INSTANT REPLAY**    Why are mutation and genetic drift random events? _____

_____

# Species can shape each other over time.

Specialized relationships can form between different species through coevolution. **Coevolution** is the process in which two or more species evolve in response to changes in each other. In some cases, coevolution is beneficial to all species involved. In other cases, coevolution is the result of competition between species.

## Beneficial Relationships

One example of a beneficial relationship is the coevolution of a plant species called the bull-thorn acacia and a species of stinging ant. The acacia plant has large hollow thorns in which the ants live. The ants also feed on the plant's nectar*. The ants protect the plant by stinging small animals that try to eat the plant's leaves. The hollow thorns and nectar production of the acacia and the stinging of the ants evolved due to the relationship between the species.

## Competitive Relationships

Coevolution can also occur in competitive relationships. For example, over many generations, the shells of certain snails called murex snails have evolved to become thicker and spinier. In response, the crabs that eat these snails have evolved more and more powerful claws strong enough to crack the snails' shells. This coevolutionary competition can go on and on, generation after generation.

The crab is the natural predator of the snail.

Natural selection favors snails with thicker shells and spines.

Through natural selection, crabs evolve more powerful claws that can pierce the snails' thick, spiny shells.

In response, natural selection favors snails with even thicker shells and spines.

**INSTANT REPLAY** What are two types of relationships that can result from coevolution? _____

_____

* ACADEMIC VOCABULARY

**nectar** a sweet sap produced by plants

## Species can become extinct.

**Extinction** is the permanent loss of species from Earth. Like speciation, extinction is a natural process. Biologists divide extinction events into two categories—background extinctions and mass extinctions.

- **Background extinctions** Extinctions that occur continuously, but at a low rate are called background extinctions. Usually only one or a few species are affected in a particular area.
- **Mass extinctions** Extinctions that destroy many species, often all across Earth, are called mass extinctions. Mass extinctions are thought to occur suddenly in geologic time, because of a dramatic event like an ice age or an asteroid impact. The fossil record shows that there have been at least five mass extinctions in the last 600 million years.

 What is the difference between background extinctions and mass extinctions? _____

_____

## Speciation often occurs in patterns.

The fossil record shows a repeating pattern in the history of life. There have been short periods with lots of evolutionary activity, followed by long periods of stability. The theory of **punctuated equilibrium** describes this pattern: long periods of little change (*equilibrium*) are interrupted (*punctuated*) by shorter periods of intense evolutionary events, such as speciation. The idea of punctuated equilibrium was presented in 1972, and is a revision of Darwin's idea that new species arise through ongoing, slow changes.

Sometimes, evolution can split one species into a number of different species, each adapted to a different environment, in a process called **adaptive radiation.** To radiate means to spread out. Adaptive radiation results in many different species spread out in different environments.

One example of adaptive radiation is the spread of mammals that happened after a mass extinction 65 million years ago at the end of the Cretaceous period. At the time, mammals had already existed for over 100 million years, living among the dinosaurs. These mammals were tiny and usually ate insects.

**VISUAL VOCAB**

**Adaptive radiation** is the rapid evolution of many diverse species from ancestral species.

descendent species

time

ancestral species

The extinction of the dinosaurs left a lot of environments open for other types of animals. In the first 10 million years after the dinosaurs' extinction, more than 4000 mammal species evolved, including whales, bats, rodents*, and primates*.

**INSTANT REPLAY** How is the spread of mammals an example of adaptive radiation? _____

_____

**\* ACADEMIC VOCABULARY**

**primates** the group of animals that includes monkeys, apes, and humans

**rodents** the group of animals that includes mice, rats, and squirrels

## 11.6 Vocabulary Check

convergent evolution     extinction

divergent evolution     punctuated equilibrium

coevolution     adaptive radiation

**Mark It Up**

Go back and highlight each sentence that has a vocabulary word in **bold.**

**Match the correct term from the list above to each example below.**

1. the evolutionary relationship between the bull-thorn acacia and a species of stinging ant _____

2. the evolution of wings in birds and insects _____

3. the permanent loss of dinosaurs from Earth _____

## 11.6 The Big Picture

4. Explain why evolution through natural selection is not random. _____

_____

_____

5. Describe the theory of punctuated equilibrium. _____

_____

_____

_____

# Chapter 11 Review

1. What are two main sources of genetic variation? _____
   _____

2. How does genetic variation affect the chance that a population will survive changing environmental conditions? _____
   _____
   _____

3. Which of the following is an example of genetic drift? _____
   a. founder effect
   b. punctuated equilibrium
   c. microevolution
   d. speciation

4. What pattern of selection is shown in the graph below?
   a. directional
   b. stabilizing
   c. disruptive
   d. punctuated

5. In a rainstorm, a few individuals of a population were carried to a new area. The new population has some, but not all, of the variation in the original population. How will having less genetic variation affect the new population? _____
   _____

6. How can the isolation of populations lead to speciation? _____
   _____
   _____

7. Is it likely for a natural population to be in Hardy-Weinberg equilibrium? Explain your answer. _____
   _____

8. According to the fossil record, speciation can occur in patterns. Name and describe one of these patterns. _____
   _____
   _____

# 12 The History of Life

## GETTING READY TO LEARN

### Preview Key Concepts

**12.1 The Fossil Record**
Fossils are a record of life that existed in the past.

**12.2 The Geologic Time Scale**
The geologic time scale divides Earth's history based on major past events.

**12.3 Origin of Life**
The origin of life on Earth remains a puzzle.

**12.4 Early Single-Celled Organisms**
Single-celled organisms existed 3.8 billion years ago.

**12.5 Radiation of Multicellular Life**
Multicellular life evolved in distinct phases.

**12.6 Primate Evolution**
Humans appeared late in Earth's history.

## Review Academic Vocabulary

Write the correct word for each definition.

adaptive radiation      aerobic      anaerobic      extinction

**1** _____ : requiring oxygen

**2.** _____ : one species evolving into many descendant species

**3.** _____ : elimination of species from Earth

**4.** _____ : not requiring oxygen

## Preview Biology Vocabulary

Three key terms from this chapter share the same word part. Read the definitions and guess what the word part means.

| TERM | DEFINITION | WHAT I THINK -*zoic* MEANS |
|------|-----------|----------------------------|
| Cenozoic | geologic era that began 65 million years ago and continues today | |
| Mesozoic | geologic era during which time dinosaurs roamed Earth | |
| Paleozoic | geologic era during which time every major animal group alive today evolved | |

# 12.1 The Fossil Record

**KEY CONCEPT** Fossils are a record of life that existed in the past.

## Fossils can form in several ways.

There are many different kinds of fossils besides the giant dinosaur skeletons we see in museums. Different kinds of fossils form in different ways. For example:

- Fossils can form when minerals carried in water are deposited around or replace a hard structure, like a bone or shell.
- Flowing water can remove all of the original bone or tissue and leave an imprint. Minerals can then fill in the space, remaking the original shape of the organism.
- Traces of an organism's activity—such as nests or footprints—can be preserved.
- Organisms can be preserved in tree resin* that hardens into amber if the tree gets buried underground.
- An entire organism can become encased in material such as ice or volcanic ash or immersed in bogs.

### FOSSILIZATION BY MINERALS IN SEDIMENT

**The most common process of fossilization happens in areas where sediment\* constantly settles, such as in a river or lakebed.**

An organism dies in a location, such as a riverbed, where sediments can rapidly cover its body.

Over time, pressure from additional sediment compresses the body, and minerals slowly replace all hard structures, such as bone.

Earthquakes or erosion may expose the fossil millions of years after formation, or it may be uncovered by paleontologists, hikers, or road-building crews.

---

**\* ACADEMIC VOCABULARY**

**resin** sticky substance secreted by plants after a wound
**sediment** small rock particles

There are many different kinds of fossils, and each kind requires specific conditions for a fossil to actually form. As a result, only a tiny percentage of living things that ever existed became fossils. Most remains decompose or are destroyed before they can form fossils. Even if a fossil forms, a natural event like an earthquake can later destroy the fossil.

 Describe the most common process of fossilization. _____

_____

## Radiometric dating provides an accurate estimate of a fossil's age.

In the 1700s, geologists realized that lower layers of rocks were older than the layers above. In the same way, the fossils within the lower layers are older than the fossils within the layers above. **Relative dating** is used to estimate the time when an organism lived by comparing the placement of its fossils to the placement of other fossils. Relative dating can be used to learn which organisms are older or younger, but it does not give actual ages.

**Radiometric dating** is used to determine a fossil's actual age. This process makes use of isotopes that are found in materials. **Isotopes** are atoms of an element that have the same number of protons but a different number of neutrons. Some isotopes are unstable and decay, or break down, over time into a different form or element.

The rate at which an isotope decays can be measured in terms of half-lives. A **half-life** is the amount of time it takes for half of the isotope in a sample to break down into its different form. The actual age of a sample can be determined by how much the isotope within the sample has broken down.

Different elements have different half-lives. Elements with shorter half-lives can be used to date more recent objects. Elements with longer half-lives can be used to date more ancient objects.

**Connecting** CONCEPTS

**Chemistry of Life** Recall from Chapter 2 that all atoms of a given element have the same number of protons. Isotopes have the same number of protons, but different numbers of neutrons. Two different isotopes of carbon are shown below.

● neutrons ● protons

| CARBON-12 NUCLEUS | CARBON-14 NUCLEUS |
|---|---|
| 6 protons | 6 protons |
| 6 neutrons | 8 neutrons |

| DECAY OF ISOTOPES | | |
|---|---|---|
| Isotope (parent) | Product (daughter) | Half-life (years) |
| rubidium-87 | strontium-87 | 48.8 billion |
| uranium-238 | lead-206 | 4.5 billion |
| chlorine-36 | argon-36 | 300,000 |
| carbon-14 | nitrogen-14 | 5730 |

Radiometric dating has been used to determine the age of Earth. The results of many different samples consistently estimates Earth's age at about 4.5 billion years.

 How is radiometric dating measured? _____

_____

relative dating       isotope

radiometric dating    half-life

**Fill in the blanks with the correct term from the list above.**

1. A(n) _____ is a measurement of the time it takes for half of an unstable isotope to decay.

2. An atom of an element with the same number of protons but different numbers of neutrons is called a(n) _____.

3. _____ involves comparing the ages of different fossils according to their order in rock layers.

4. _____ uses measurements of half-lives to determine the actual age of a material.

| 12.1 | The Big Picture |
| --- | --- |

5. Why do only a tiny percentage of living things ever become fossils?

_____

_____

6. How does the information given by relative dating differ from the information given by radiometric dating? _____

_____

_____

# 12.2 The Geologic Time Scale

**KEY CONCEPT** The geologic time scale divides Earth's history based on major past events.

## Index fossils are another tool to determine the age of rock layers.

You have read that both relative dating and radiometric dating can help scientists determine the ages of rock layers. **Index fossils** are another tool for determining the ages of fossils and rock layers. Index fossils are fossils of organisms that existed only during specific spans of time and lived in large geographic areas. If an index fossil is found in a layer of rock, it means that the rock layer and other fossils found in that layer are the same age as the index fossil.

An extinct marine organism called a fusulinid (FYOO-zuh-LY-nihd) is one example of an index fossil. These organisms were very common beginning about 360 million years ago, but disappeared after a mass extinction 248 million years ago. The presence of fusulinids means that a rock layer is between 248 and 360 million years old. If other organisms are in the same rock layer as the fusulinids, it means that they lived during the same time period.

Fusulinids are an index fossil. They lived between 248 and 360 million years ago.

What does it mean if fusulinids are in a rock layer? _____

_____

## The geologic time scale organizes Earth's history.

As you just read, Earth is about 4.5 billion years old. Scientists used fossil and geologic records to organize this huge amount of time into smaller sections based on major geologic changes. The entire history of Earth is represented by the **geologic time scale.**

The geologic time scale is made of three basic units of time:

- **Eras** last tens to hundreds of millions of years and have two or more periods.
- **Periods** are the most commonly used units of time on the geologic time scale, and they last tens of millions of years.
- **Epochs** (EHP-uhks) are the smallest unit of geologic time, and they last several million years.

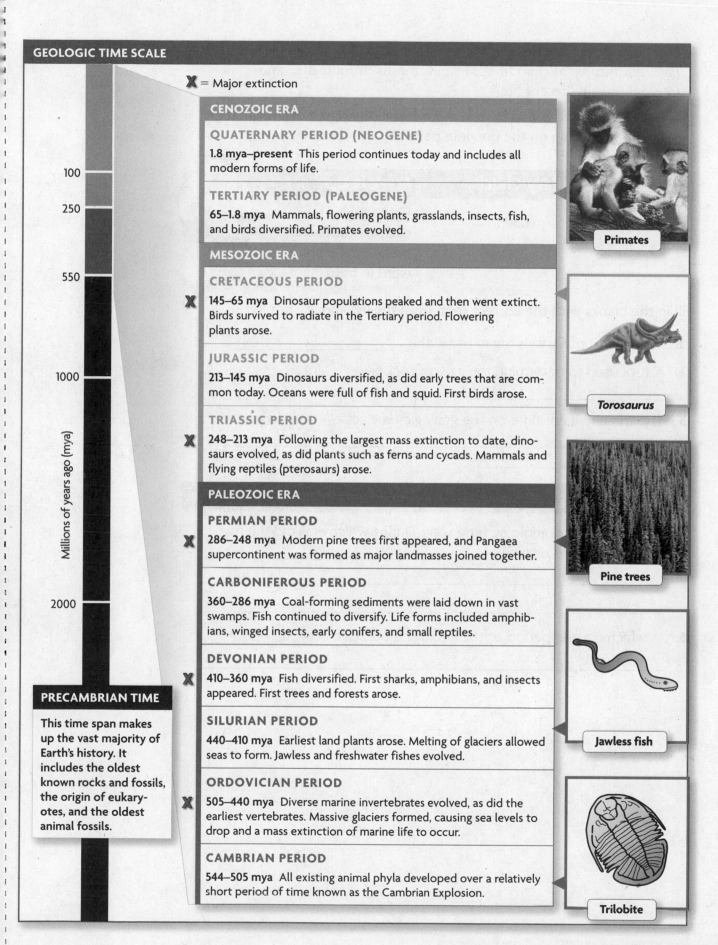

## GEOLOGIC TIME SCALE

**X** = Major extinction

### CENOZOIC ERA

#### QUATERNARY PERIOD (NEOGENE)

**1.8 mya–present** This period continues today and includes all modern forms of life.

#### TERTIARY PERIOD (PALEOGENE)

**65–1.8 mya** Mammals, flowering plants, grasslands, insects, fish, and birds diversified. Primates evolved.

**Primates**

### MESOZOIC ERA

#### CRETACEOUS PERIOD

**X 145–65 mya** Dinosaur populations peaked and then went extinct. Birds survived to radiate in the Tertiary period. Flowering plants arose.

#### JURASSIC PERIOD

**213–145 mya** Dinosaurs diversified, as did early trees that are common today. Oceans were full of fish and squid. First birds arose.

**Torosaurus**

#### TRIASSIC PERIOD

**X 248–213 mya** Following the largest mass extinction to date, dinosaurs evolved, as did plants such as ferns and cycads. Mammals and flying reptiles (pterosaurs) arose.

### PALEOZOIC ERA

#### PERMIAN PERIOD

**X 286–248 mya** Modern pine trees first appeared, and Pangaea supercontinent was formed as major landmasses joined together.

**Pine trees**

#### CARBONIFEROUS PERIOD

**360–286 mya** Coal-forming sediments were laid down in vast swamps. Fish continued to diversify. Life forms included amphibians, winged insects, early conifers, and small reptiles.

#### DEVONIAN PERIOD

**X 410–360 mya** Fish diversified. First sharks, amphibians, and insects appeared. First trees and forests arose.

#### SILURIAN PERIOD

**440–410 mya** Earliest land plants arose. Melting of glaciers allowed seas to form. Jawless and freshwater fishes evolved.

**Jawless fish**

#### ORDOVICIAN PERIOD

**X 505–440 mya** Diverse marine invertebrates evolved, as did the earliest vertebrates. Massive glaciers formed, causing sea levels to drop and a mass extinction of marine life to occur.

#### CAMBRIAN PERIOD

**544–505 mya** All existing animal phyla developed over a relatively short period of time known as the Cambrian Explosion.

**Trilobite**

### PRECAMBRIAN TIME

This time span makes up the vast majority of Earth's history. It includes the oldest known rocks and fossils, the origin of eukaryotes, and the oldest animal fossils.

Millions of years ago (mya)

100
250
550
1000
2000

The names of the three eras came from early ideas about fossils. *Paleozoic* means "ancient life," *Mesozoic* means "middle life," and *Cenozoic* means "recent life."

 Circle the names of the three eras in the figure of the geologic time scale on the previous page.

## 12.2    Vocabulary Check

index fossil                    period
geologic time scale      epoch
era

> **Mark It Up**
>
> Go back and highlight each sentence that has a vocabulary word in **bold**.

**Fill in the blanks with the correct term from the list above.**

1. The history of Earth is organized in the _____.

2. A tool used to determine the ages of rock layers is a(n) _____.

3. The three units of time on the geologic time scale—from largest to smallest—are _____, _____, and _____.

## 12.2    The Big Picture

4. Look back at the geologic time scale. During which eras did the five mass extinctions occur? _____

   _____

   _____

5. In which era and period of the geologic time scale do you live? _____

   _____

# 12.3 Origin of Life

**KEY CONCEPT** The origin of life on Earth remains a puzzle.

## Earth was very different billions of years ago.

Hypotheses exist about the origin of Earth and its living things—but many questions remain. Most scientists agree on two main points:

- Earth is billions of years old.
- The conditions of the early planet and its atmosphere were very different from conditions today.

Today, the most widely accepted hypothesis of Earth's origins is that the solar system formed from a cloud of dust and gas called a **nebula.** Gravity pulled the material in the nebula together into a large disk that circled the sun. Over millions of years, this material became the planets.

For the first 700 million years, Earth was most likely molten*. Over time, the molten materials separated into Earth's layers. Gases were released and formed an atmosphere of ammonia, water vapor, methane, and carbon dioxide. Most scientists agree that free oxygen was not a big part of the atmosphere until after the first forms of life evolved.

Between 4 and 3.8 million years ago, Earth began to cool. Water vapor from the atmosphere condensed and fell as rain. Earth then had liquid water and energy from lightning and the sun, which may have played a role in the origin of life on Earth.

 **INSTANT REPLAY** Underline the two main points that scientists agree on about Earth's origins.

## Several sets of hypotheses propose how life began on Earth.

Hypotheses about how life began focus on three things: the formation of early organic molecules, the formation of early cells, and the structure of early genetic material.

* ACADEMIC VOCABULARY

**molten** in liquid form

## Early Organic Molecules

Organic molecules, like sugars and amino acids, are the building blocks of life. There are two main hypotheses about how organic compounds could have appeared on Earth.

- **Miller-Urey experiment** In the 1950s, two scientists designed an experiment that simulated, or reproduced, early Earth conditions in their laboratory. Their experiment showed that organic molecules could have formed on the early Earth from inorganic molecules.

- **Meteorite hypothesis** A meteorite that fell in Australia in 1969 was found to contain organic molecules. More than 90 amino acids were identified, including 19 that are found on Earth. This finding suggests that organic molecules might have arrived on Earth through meteorites or may have been present when Earth formed.

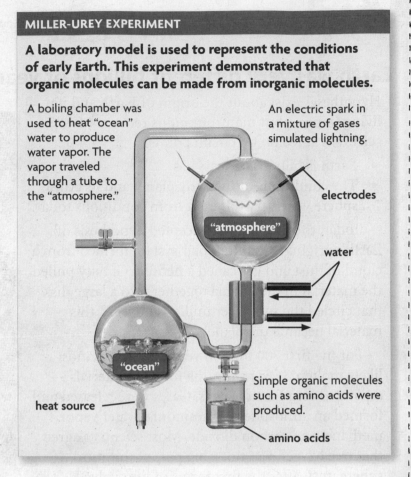

**MILLER-UREY EXPERIMENT**

**A laboratory model is used to represent the conditions of early Earth. This experiment demonstrated that organic molecules can be made from inorganic molecules.**

A boiling chamber was used to heat "ocean" water to produce water vapor. The vapor traveled through a tube to the "atmosphere."

An electric spark in a mixture of gases simulated lightning.

electrodes

water

"atmosphere"

"ocean"

heat source

Simple organic molecules such as amino acids were produced.

amino acids

## Early Cell Structure

One hypothesis about early cell structure focuses on how organic molecules could have been brought together. Another hypothesis focuses on how cell membranes could have formed.

- **Bringing together organic molecules** Hot gases rise from cracks deep on the ocean floor. The gases form rocky structures after mixing with the cool ocean water. One hypothesis is that these rocky structures had small compartments where basic organic molecules could have been held together in a small space. Once together, these molecules could have formed into the first cells.

- **Forming a lipid membrane** Lipid molecules will form into membrane-enclosed spheres just because of the properties of the molecules. One hypothesis is that at some point lipids formed a double membrane. These membranes could then form around a variety of organic molecules. These cell-like structures could have later given rise to the first true cells.

Today's cells have a lipid bilayer.

## Early Genetic Material

RNA, rather than DNA, may have been the genetic material in early living things. Short chains of RNA can form from inorganic molecules. RNA molecules called **ribozymes** can catalyze chemical reactions. Unlike DNA, RNA in the form of a ribozyme can make copies of itself.

RNA does not catalyze chemical reactions as well as proteins do, and RNA does not store genetic information as well as DNA does. Over time, proteins and DNA may have replaced some of the functions of RNA, eventually leading to today's system of genetic material.

 **What was produced in the Miller-Urey experiment?**

_____

**Connecting** CONCEPTS

**Enzymes** Recall from **Chapter 2** that a catalyst helps start and speeds up a chemical reaction.

---

### 12.3 Vocabulary Check

nebula

ribozyme

**Mark It Up**

Go back and highlight each sentence that has a vocabulary word in **bold**.

**1.** Write a definition for the term *nebula*. _____

_____

_____

**2.** Write a definition for the term *ribozyme*. _____

_____

_____

---

### 12.3 The Big Picture

**3.** List two ways in which the conditions on an early Earth differed from conditions today. _____

_____

_____

**4.** What are two hypotheses about the formation of organic molecules on Earth? _____

_____

_____

# 12.4 Early Single-Celled Organisms

**KEY CONCEPT** Single-celled organisms existed 3.8 billion years ago.

## Microbes have changed the physical and chemical composition of Earth.

The earliest microbes, or single-celled organisms, were prokaryotes that did not need oxygen to survive. After some microbe populations evolved the ability to photosynthesize, these microbes changed the atmosphere by giving off oxygen. Microbes also changed Earth's surface by depositing minerals.

The earliest fossils of photosynthetic life are 3.5 billion years old. These are fossils of **cyanobacteria** (sy-uh-noh-bak-TEER-ee-uh), which are bacteria that conduct photosynthesis. The oxygen released by photosynthesis entered the ocean and the atmosphere, which allowed for the evolution of organisms that use oxygen.

What were the first single-celled organisms like? _____

_____

**Connecting CONCEPTS**

**Cells** Recall from **Chapter 3** that prokaryotes do not have a membrane-bound nucleus or organelles.

## Eukaryotic cells may have evolved through endosymbiosis.

The fossil record shows that eukaryotic cells had evolved by 1.5 billion years ago. Unlike a prokaryote, a eukaryote has a nucleus and other membrane-bound organelles. Eukaryotic cells all used oxygen to survive. The first eukaryotes were made of only one cell. Multicellular, or many-celled, eukaryotic organisms eventually evolved.

Most scientists agree that the evolution of eukaryotes involved endosymbiosis. **Endosymbiosis** (EHN-doh-SIHM-bee-OH-sihs) is a relationship in which one organism lives within the body of another, and both benefit. Early mitochondria and chloroplasts may have been small prokaryotic cells that were taken up by larger prokaryotes. The large cell benefits from the products of the small cell—such as energy or sugars—and the smaller cell benefits from the stable environment.

A eukaryote has a nucleus and other membrane-bound organelles.

**VOCABULARY**

*Endosymbiosis* can be broken down into *endo-*, meaning "within," *sym-*, meaning "together," and *biosis*, meaning "way of life."

bacterium

early nuclear envelope

cell

Bacterium enters cell.

Over generations, bacteria evolve as mitochondria.

The theory of endosymbiosis is based on several characteristics of both mitochondria and chloroplasts:

- Unlike other organelles, mitochondria and chloroplasts have their own DNA.
- They can copy themselves within the cell in which they are found.
- They are about the same size as prokaryotes.
- Their DNA forms a circle, like prokaryotes.
- Their gene structures are similar to those of prokaryotes.

**INSTANT REPLAY** Describe one piece of evidence that supports the theory of endosymbiosis. _____

_____

# The evolution of sexual reproduction led to increased diversity.

Recall from Chapter 5 that during asexual reproduction, a single parent organism produces offspring that are genetically identical to itself. The first prokaryotes and the first eukaryotes reproduced asexually. Asexual reproduction allows organisms to have many offspring quickly.

Sexual reproduction requires more time and energy—because an organism needs to find a mate. Also, only half of an organism's genes get passed on. One advantage of sexual reproduction, however, is that it increases genetic variation within the population. Sexual reproduction allows new combinations of genes to come together.

Sexual reproduction may also have resulted in an increase in the rate of natural selection. Sexual reproduction produces more genetic variation. More variation allows a population to adapt more quickly to new conditions.

Early eukaryotes may have had some variations that made living near other eukaryotic cells beneficial. Over time, populations may have evolved from cells living close to each other and cooperating. This cooperation may have been the first step in the evolution of multicellular life.

 What is one main advantage of sexual reproduction? _____

_____

## 12.4 Vocabulary Check

### Mark It Up

Go back and highlight each sentence that has a vocabulary word in **bold**.

cyanobacteria
endosymbiosis

**1.** What are cyanobacteria?

_____

**2.** What type of cell evolved through endosymbiosis?

_____

## 12.4 The Big Picture

**3.** How did oxygen begin to build up in the atmosphere and the ocean?

_____

_____

**4.** What are two structures in eukaryotes that likely evolved through endosymbiosis? _____

_____

**5.** Why might sexual reproduction have resulted in an increase in the rate of evolution by natural selection? _____

_____

_____

**KEY CONCEPT** Multicellular life evolved in distinct phases.

## Life moved onto land during the Paleozoic era.

Multicellular organisms first appeared during the **Paleozoic** (PAY-lee-uh-ZOH-ihk) era, which began 544 million years ago. The earliest part of the Paleozoic era is the Cambrian period. This part of Earth's history is often called the **Cambrian explosion.** During this time, there was an "explosion" of animal species. In other words, a huge diversity of animals evolved.

At the start of the Paleozoic, all life was in the ocean. By the middle of the era, life moved onto land. Near the end of the era, in the Carboniferous period, the remains of millions of organisms were buried in sediment. Over time, these remains became the coal and petroleum that we use today.

Underline one key event of the Paleozoic era. _____

_____

## Reptiles radiated during the Mesozoic era.

The **Mesozoic** (MEHZ-uh-ZOH-ihk) era began 248 million years ago and ended 65 million years ago. This era is often called the Age of Reptiles, because dinosaurs lived during this time.

The Mesozoic is divided into three periods: the Triassic, Jurassic, and Cretaceous. The first mammals evolved during the Triassic. A mass extinction ended the Triassic, and was followed by the radiation of the dinosaurs in the Jurassic. In the Cretaceous, dinosaur diversity was at its greatest. A meteorite struck Earth at the end of the Cretaceous, leading to a mass extinction and the end of the dinosaurs.

Why is the Mesozoic era often called the Age of Reptiles? _____

_____

_____

## Mammals radiated during the Cenozoic era.

The **Cenozoic** (SEE-nuh-ZOH-ihk) era began 65 million years ago and continues today. This era is sometimes called the Age of Mammals, because many kinds of mammals evolved during this time.

The Cenozoic is divided into two periods: the Tertiary (65–1.8 million years ago) and the Quaternary (1.8 million years ago until today). The earliest ancestors of humans evolved near the end of the Tertiary. But *Homo sapiens,* modern humans, did not evolve until about 100,000 years ago in the Quaternary.

 What are the two periods of the Cenozoic era?

_____

| 12.5 | Vocabulary Check |
|---|---|

**Mark It Up**

Go back and highlight each sentence that has a vocabulary word in **bold.**

Paleozoic          Mesozoic

Cambrian explosion     Cenozoic

Fill in the blanks with the correct term from the list above.

1. List the three eras, from most ancient to most recent. _____
_____

2. What happened during the Cambrian explosion? _____
_____

| 12.5 | The Big Picture |
|---|---|

3. In which era did life move onto land? _____

4. In which era did dinosaurs live? _____

5. In which era did the earliest human ancestors evolve? _____

# 12.6 Primate Evolution

**KEY CONCEPT** Humans appeared late in Earth's history.

## Humans share a common ancestor other with primates.

Compared to all of geologic time—4.5 billion years—the evolution of humans has occurred only very recently. Humans are one of the **primates,** a category of mammals that includes lemurs, monkeys, apes, and humans. These mammals share particular traits, including:

- flexible hands and feet
- forward-looking eyes, which allow for excellent three-dimensional vision
- large brains relative to body size
- arms that can rotate in a circle

Many primates also have thumbs that can move against their fingers. In addition to sharing these physical traits, primates are also similar to each other at the molecular level.

Lemurs are one type of primate, a category of mammals that share particular traits.

### Primate Evolution

There are two main groups of primates that share a common ancestor:

- **prosimians** (proh-SIHM-ee-uhnz), which are the oldest living primate group
- **anthropoids** (AN-thruh-POYDZ), which are the humanlike primates

The anthropoids are divided into two groups of monkeys and the hominoids. The hominoids are further divided into the gibbons, orang-utans, gorillas, chimpanzees, and humans. Humans are **hominids,** a group that includes modern humans and extinct species in the human line of ancestry. Hominids walk upright, have long lower limbs, thumbs that work against the other four fingers, and relatively large brains.

The evolutionary histories of organisms can be represented by a branching tree. Each place a branch splits represents a speciation event.

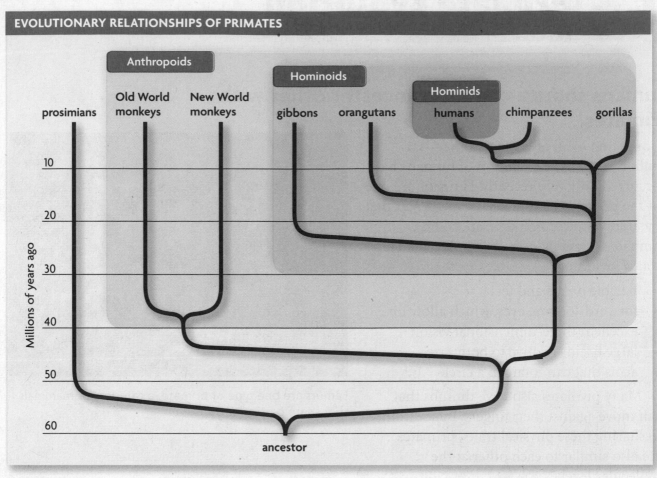

## EVOLUTIONARY RELATIONSHIPS OF PRIMATES

Anthropoids

Hominoids

Hominids

prosimians | Old World monkeys | New World monkeys | gibbons | orangutans | humans | chimpanzees | gorillas

Millions of years ago

10
20
30
40
50
60

ancestor

The gorilla lineage split with the human/chimpanzee lineage about 10 million years ago.

## Walking Upright

Animals that can walk on two legs are called **bipedal** (BY-PEHD-l). This trait has important adaptive advantages. It leaves hands free for other activities—like gathering food, carrying infants, and using tools. The evolution of upright walking required changes in the skeletal structure of human ancestors. These changes can be seen in intermediate fossils between hominoids that walked on all fours and early hominids that walked on two legs.

 List two traits that all primates share.

_____

_____

**VISUAL VOCAB**

**Bipedal** is an adjective that describes two-legged or upright walking. *Bi-* means "two," and *ped* means "foot."

# There are many fossils of extinct hominids.

You have read that hominids include all the species in the human lineage. Fossil evidence has provided much information about extinct hominids. Most hominid species are classified into two groups: the genus *Australopithecus* and the genus *Homo*.

## The Genus *Australopithecus*

*Australopithecus afarensis* (AF-uh-REHN-sihs) lived to 4 to 3 million years ago. Its brain was smaller than modern humans, but it had humanlike limbs.

## The Genus *Homo*

*Homo habilis* is the earliest known member of the genus *Homo*, and lived 2.4 to 1.5 million years ago. This was the earliest known hominid to make stone tools. *Homo habilis* had a larger brain than *Australopithecus afarensis*. This species may have lived alongside *Australopithecus afarensis* for about 1 million years.

*Homo neanderthalensis*, commonly called Neanderthals, lived from 200,000 to 30,000 years ago, possibly alongside *Homo sapiens*.

---

**EXAMPLES OF HOMINID SKULLS**

**Hominid evolution shows a progression in brain size.**

| 4–3 MILLION YEARS AGO | 2.4–1.5 MILLION YEARS AGO | 200,000–30,000 YEARS AGO | 200,000 YEARS AGO–PRESENT |
|---|---|---|---|
| *Australopithecus afarensis* | *Homo habilis* | *Homo neanderthalensis* | *Homo sapiens* |

| | | | |
|---|---|---|---|
| *Australopithecus afarensis* had a brain volume of 430 cm³. | *Homo habilis* had a brain volume of about 700 cm³. | *Homo neanderthalensis'* brain volume may have reached 1500 cm³. | Modern *Homo sapiens* have a brain volume average of about 1300 cm³. |

INSTANT REPLAY

Name two extinct *Homo* species. _____

_____

## Modern humans arose about 200,000 years ago.

The first *Homo sapiens,* the species that includes modern humans, lived around 200,000 years ago. Many of the features of the earliest *Homo sapiens* were different from humans today. After becoming a separate species, *Homo sapiens* continued to evolve. Fossil sites give evidence for trends in human evolution. Two key trends can be seen in the role of culture and the size of the human brain:

- **The role of culture** Although tools are used by some other animals, they are key signs of culture in human evolution. A comparison of tools from fossil sites shows a steady trend: over time, the tools human ancestors used became more complex and more useful.

- **The evolution of the human brain** There is genetic evidence that the genes controlling the size and complexity of the human brain evolved very rapidly. The rapid evolution of the large brain size provided a strong selective advantage for the hominids.

 What are two trends in human evolution? _____

_____

| 12.6 | **Vocabulary Check** |
|---|---|

**Mark It Up**

Go back and highlight each sentence that has a vocabulary word in **bold**.

primate        hominid

prosimian      bipedal

anthropoid

1. Write the terms *hominid, primate,* and *anthropoid* onto the diagram in order of biggest category to smallest category. The biggest circle should be labeled with the biggest category and the smallest circle with the smallest category.

2. Draw an arrow pointing to the circle with the group of organisms that is bipedal.

3. Which term is a category of organisms that includes prosimians?

_____

| 12.6 | **The Big Picture** |
|---|---|

4. What is the adaptive advantage of walking upright? _____

_____

5. What is one kind of evidence that provides information about human ancestors? _____

6. When did the first *Homo sapiens* evolve? _____

# Chapter 12 Review

1. What characteristics of humans and other primates suggest they share a common ancestor? _____
_____
_____

2. Write the terms *epoch, era,* and *period* onto the diagram in order of biggest unit of time to smallest unit of time. The biggest circle should be labeled with the biggest unit and the smallest circle with the smallest unit.

3. What is radiometric dating used for? _____
_____

4. The early Earth atmosphere had little free oxygen. But about 2 billion years ago, oxygen began to accumulate in the air and ocean. What was the source of that oxygen?

   **a.** meteorites

   **b.** photosynthetic organisms

   **c.** multicellular organisms

   **d.** ribozymes

5. Briefly describe the theory of endosymbiosis. _____
_____
_____
_____

6. The radiation of mammals followed what major events on Earth?

   **a.** the Cambrian explosion, and the movement of life onto land

   **b.** the evolution of multicellular life, and the increase in free oxygen

   **c.** the Carboniferous period, and events that produced coal

   **d.** a mass extinction, and the end of dinosaurs

7. Sexual reproduction increases genetic variation. Why is genetic variation advantageous? _____
_____
_____

# CHAPTER 13 Principles of Ecology

## GETTING READY TO LEARN

### Preview Key Concepts

**13.1 Ecologists Study Relationships**
Ecology is the study of the relationships among organisms and their environments.

**13.2 Biotic and Abiotic Factors**
Every ecosystem includes both living and nonliving factors.

**13.3 Energy in Ecosystems**
Life in an ecosystem requires a source of energy.

**13.4 Food Chains and Food Webs**
Food chains and food webs model the flow of energy in an ecosystem.

**13.5 Cycling of Matter**
Matter cycles in and out of an ecosystem.

**13.6 Pyramid Models**
Pyramids model the distribution of energy and matter in an ecosystem.

### Review Academic Vocabulary

Write the correct word for each definition.

experiment    organism    observation    population

1. _____ : hypothesis is tested under controlled conditions

2. _____ : using the senses to study the world

3. _____ : all individuals of one species living in a certain area

4. _____ : any individual living thing

### Preview Biology Vocabulary

See how many key terms from this chapter you already know. Rewrite each phrase, using a different word or words for the **words in bold**.

| PHRASE | REWRITTEN WITH DIFFERENT WORDS |
|---|---|
| 1. Rocks and air are examples of **abiotic factors**. | Rocks and air are examples of _____. |
| 2. A plant **is a producer**. | A plant _____ |
| 3. A rabbit is **an herbivore**. | A rabbit is _____ |

220

# 13.1 Ecologists Study Relationships

**KEY CONCEPT** Ecology is the study of the relationships among organisms and their environment.

## Ecologists study relationships at different levels of organization.

**Ecology** is the study of the interactions among living things, and between living things and their surroundings. Ecologists study nature on different levels, from a local to a global scale.

- **Organism** An organism is one individual living thing.
- **Population** A population is a group of the same species that lives in one area.
- **Community** A **community** is a group of different species that live together in one area.
- **Ecosystem** An **ecosystem** includes all of the organisms as well as the climate, soil, water, rocks, and other nonliving things in an area. An entire ecosystem may live within a single decaying log. But the log may be part of a larger ecosystem, such as a forest.
- **Biome** A **biome** (BY-ohm) is a major regional or global community of organisms. A biome is usually defined by the climate and by the plant communities that live in an area.

Organism

Population

Community

Ecosystem

### LEVELS OF ORGANIZATION

**The Florida Everglades is an example of the subtropical savanna biome. Many organisms live in this aquatic ecosystem.**

Biome

Ecologists study relationships within and between each level of organization. For example, one ecologist might study a single population of Pacific salmon. Another ecologist might study how the current loss of Pacific salmon affects other species. Yet another ecologist might study the effects of this loss on a global scale.

 What are five different levels of organization at which an ecologist might study biological relationships?

_____

_____

## Ecological research methods include observation, experimentation, and modeling.

Ecological research involves many different methods and tools. Three main components of ecological research are observation, experimentation, and modeling.

### Observation

Observation is the act of carefully watching something over time. Observation may be part of short-term or long-term studies. Long-term studies are important because many environmental changes happen slowly over time.

Observation can involve directly watching populations of organisms. It can also involve indirectly observing populations by tracing signs of the organism's presence, such as tracks. Scientists also use radio collars to follow the movements of some animals. These collars allow scientists to track organisms that move long distances, such as coyotes.

Observation involves carefully watching something over a certain period of time.

### Experimentation

Scientists may perform experiments in a lab or in the natural area where the organisms live. There are benefits and drawbacks to each type of experiment. A lab experiment allows for more control of variables. But at the same time, it does not include the complex interactions that happen in nature. An experiment in a natural setting gives a better picture of how organisms really interact. However, a natural setting also makes it difficult to identify the effects of individual variables.

## Modeling

Some questions cannot be easily investigated through observations or experiments. Models can be used to explore organisms and whole ecosystems in ways that would not be possible in a natural setting. One way of thinking about modeling is that it can be used to answer questions that start with "What would happen if…?"

Models use real data to predict outcomes for different situations. For example, a wide variety of data was combined into a model of Yellowstone National Park. This model was then used to decide how best to reintroduce grey wolves into the park.

What are three components of ecological research?

_____

---

| 13.1 | Vocabulary Check |
|---|---|

**Mark It Up**

Go back and highlight each sentence that has a vocabulary word in **bold**.

ecology            ecosystem
community          biome

**Fill in the blanks with the correct term from the list above.**

1. _____ is the study of interactions among living things, and between living things and their surroundings.

2. A major regional or global community of organisms is a(n) _____.

3. A(n) _____ is all of the living things as well as the nonliving things in an area.

4. A group of different species that all live together in one area is a(n) _____.

---

| 13.1 | The Big Picture |
|---|---|

5. Put the following in order from largest to smallest level of organization: *community, biome, population, individual, ecosystem.*

_____

_____

6. Describe the benefits and drawbacks of experiments in a laboratory compared with experiments in a natural setting.

_____

_____

_____

# 13.2 Biotic and Abiotic Factors

**KEY CONCEPT** Every ecosystem includes both living and nonliving factors.

## An ecosystem includes both biotic and abiotic factors.

All ecosystems are made up of living and nonliving components.* These parts are called biotic and abiotic factors.

- **Biotic** (by-AHT-ihk) factors are living things, such as plants, animals, fungi, and bacteria.
- **Abiotic** (AY-by-AHT-ihk) factors are nonliving things, such as temperature, moisture, wind, rocks, and sunlight.

In an ecosystem, biotic and abiotic factors work together in a complex web.

 Give one example of a biotic factor and one example of an abiotic factor.

_____

_____

## Changing one factor in an ecosystem can affect many other factors.

Every organism depends on a combination of biotic and abiotic resources to live. All species—including humans—are affected by changes to the biotic and abiotic factors in an ecosystem.

**Biodiversity** (BY-oh-dih-VUR-sih-tee) is the variety of living things in an ecosystem. Some areas of Earth, including tropical rain forests, have very high biodiversity. Tropical rain forests cover less than 7 percent of Earth's ground surface, but contain over 50 percent of Earth's plant and animal species.

A single change in an ecosystem can have a variety of effects. Some changes may have very little effect. But in some cases, the loss of one species can have a very large effect on an entire ecosystem. A **keystone species** is a species that has an unusually large effect on its ecosystem.

**VISUAL VOCAB**

Like a keystone that holds up an arch, a **keystone species** holds together a dynamic ecosystem.

keystone

\* ACADEMIC VOCABULARY

**component** part

**KEYSTONE SPECIES**

creation of wetland ecosystem

increased waterfowl population

increased fish population

keystone species

nesting sites for birds

One example of a keystone species is the beaver. Beavers cut down trees and build dams on rivers. This changes the ecosystem by turning a river into areas of ponds and marshes. Many different species can live in the pond and marsh environments that are made by beavers.

 What do beavers make that results in a wetland ecosystem?

_____

| 13.2 | **Vocabulary Check** | **Mark It Up** |

biotic        biodiversity
abiotic       keystone species

Go back and highlight each sentence that has a vocabulary word in **bold.**

**Circle the correct term from each pair to complete the sentences below.**

1. Wind and rocks are two examples of *biotic / abiotic* factors.

2. Fungi and plants are two examples of *biotic / abiotic* factors.

3. A keystone species has a *large / small* effect on an ecosystem.

4. Biodiversity is the *quantity / variety* of organisms in an area.

| 13.2 | **The Big Picture** |

5. What are two categories of factors that make up an ecosystem?

_____

# 13.3 Energy in Ecosystems

**KEY CONCEPT** Life in an ecosystem requires a source of energy.

## Producers provide energy for other organisms in an ecosystem.

In Section 13.2 you read that ecosystems are made up of both biotic and abiotic factors. Another important part of an ecosystem is the flow of energy. All organisms need a source of energy in order to survive.

- **Producers** are organisms that make their own food. Plants and other photosynthesizing organisms are producers. Producers are also called **autotrophs.**

- **Consumers** are organisms that get their energy by eating other organisms, including plants and animals. Consumers are also called **heterotrophs.**

Producers provide the basis for an ecosystem's energy. Some consumers eat producers. For example, moose and elk eat plants. Some consumers eat other consumers. For example, the grey wolf eats moose and elk. But all consumers depend on producers. Without producers, moose and elk could not survive and without moose and elk, the wolf could not survive.

> **VOCABULARY**
>
> The suffix –*troph* comes from a Greek word meaning "nourishment," or food.
> - The prefix *auto*– means "self."
> - The prefix *hetero*– means "different."

Plants are producers, or autotrophs.

Animals are consumers, or heterotrophs.

Circle the names of three consumers in the **paragraph above.**

## Almost all producers obtain energy from sunlight.

Most producers on Earth use sunlight as their energy source. Photosynthesis is the process by which plants and some protists, such as green algae, use energy from the Sun to make sugars. Plants use these sugars as energy for cellular respiration.

Not all producers rely on the Sun for energy. In 1977 scientists first visited deep-sea vents on the floor of the ocean. They were very surprised to find many different organisms living in an ocean floor ecosystem, far from the reach of sunlight.

The producers in this ocean floor ecosystem are prokaryotes that make their own food, using chemicals as an energy source, not the Sun. This process is called **chemosynthesis** (KEE-moh-SIHN-thih-sihs). Chemosynthetic organisms also live in hot springs.

 Underline two places that chemosynthetic organisms live.

| 13.3 | Vocabulary Check |
|------|------------------|

producer          heterotroph
autotroph         chemosynthesis
consumer

**Mark It Up**

Go back and highlight each sentence that has a vocabulary word in **bold**.

Fill in the blanks with the correct term from the list above.

1. Which two words describe an organism that eats other organisms as food? _____

2. Which two words describe an organism that makes its own food?

_____

| 13.3 | The Big Picture |
|------|-----------------|

3. List two different energy sources for producers. Circle the one that is the source for most producers.

_____

# 13.4 Food Chains and Food Webs

**KEY CONCEPT** Food chains and food webs model the flow of energy in an ecosystem.

## A food chain is a model that shows a sequence of feeding relationships.

As you have read, energy flows through an ecosystem from producers to consumers. A simple way to represent this flow of energy is with a food chain. A **food chain** shows the feeding relationships for a single chain of producers and consumers.

Grasses are producers. They get energy through photosynthesis.

Rabbits are consumers. They eat producers, such as grasses.

Hawks are also consumers. They eat other consumers, such as rabbits.

### Types of Consumers

As you can see in the food chain above, not all consumers are alike. Different types of consumers have different food sources.

- **Herbivores,** such as the rabbit above, are organisms that eat only plants.
- **Carnivores,** such as the hawk above, are organisms that eat only animals.
- **Omnivores** are organisms that eat both plants and animals. Most humans are omnivores.
- **Detritivores** (dih-TRY-tuh-vohrz) are organisms that eat dead plant and animal matter. Earthworms, for example, are detritivores.
- **Decomposers** are detritivores that break down plant and animal matter into simpler compounds. Fungi, for example, are decomposers. Decomposers return nutrients to the ecosystem.

Some organisms eat only one or a few specific types of organisms. For example, a bird called the Florida snail kite eats mostly one particular type of snail. Organisms that have a very selective diet are called **specialists.** Because specialists eat only one or a few particular organisms, they are very sensitive to changes in the populations of organisms they eat. For example, if the snail population drops, the Florida snail kite does not have another main food source.

Other organisms, called **generalists,** eat a variety of different organisms. For example, the grey wolf eats many different animals, including elk, moose, deer, beavers, and mice.

A bird called the Florida snail kite is a specialist. It eats mostly one type of snail, like the organism shown above.

### Trophic Levels

The figure on page 228 shows a food chain of grasses (producers)—rabbit (herbivore)—hawk (carnivore). You can think of each link in a food chain as a level of feeding, or a **trophic level.** Energy flows up the food chain from the lowest trophic level to the highest.

- Producers are the first, or bottom, trophic level.
- The next trophic level is made of primary consumers—herbivores that eat producers.
- The next trophic level is made of secondary consumers—carnivores that eat herbivores.
- Continuing up the food chain, tertiary consumers are carnivores that eat secondary consumers.

Omnivores, such as most humans, can be listed at different trophic levels in different food chains. A person is at the level of primary consumer when eating vegetables. A person is at the level of secondary consumer when eating beef or chicken.

> VOCABULARY
>
> *Primary* means first in order.
> *Secondary* means second in order.
> *Tertiary* means third in order.

**INSTANT REPLAY** At what trophic level are herbivores found?

_____

# A food web shows a complex network of feeding relationships.

A food chain shows a simple sequence of feeding relationships. But most feeding relationships are not very simple. For example, a generalist such as the grey wolf may be a part of several food chains that involve elk, deer, mice, and other organisms. This complex network of feeding relationships and the related flow of energy can be represented by a **food web.**

**A food web shows the network of feeding relationships between trophic levels in an ecosystem. Food webs can be quite complex, because many organisms feed on a variety of other species.**

This rabbit is a primary consumer and gets its energy by eating plants.

This fox is a secondary consumer and gets its energy by eating rabbits, squirrels, mice, or sparrows.

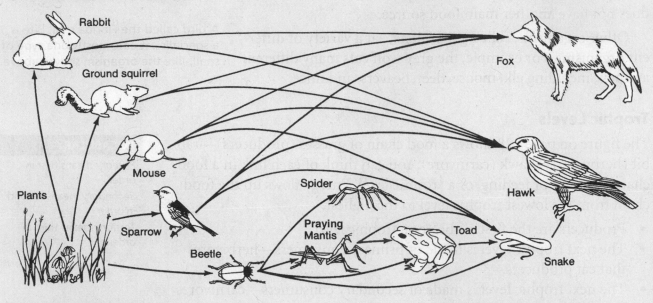

Rabbit

Ground squirrel

Fox

Mouse

Spider

Hawk

Plants

Sparrow

Praying Mantis

Toad

Beetle

Snake

Plants are producers and get their energy from the Sun.

This hawk may be a secondary consumer, a tertiary consumer, or even at a higher trophic level, depending on what it eats.

The stability of a food web depends on producers. Notice that the feeding chains of all organisms can be traced back to producers. In the food web above, a variety of prairie plants are the base of the food web.

Also notice that some organisms can be involved with the food web at different trophic levels, depending on what they eat. When the hawk eats a mouse, it is a secondary consumer. But when it eats a snake—that ate a beetle that ate plants—it is a tertiary consumer. At each link in a food web, some energy is stored within an organism but most energy is lost to the environment as heat.

In the food web shown above, at what trophic level does the spider feed?

_____

## 13.4 Vocabulary Check

food chain     decomposer

herbivore     specialist

carnivore     generalist

omnivore     trophic level

detritivore     food web

**Mark It Up**

Go back and highlight each sentence that has a vocabulary word in **bold**.

1. What is the difference between a food chain and a food web?

_____

_____

2. What is the difference between a specialist and a generalist?

_____

_____

3. What is the difference between a detritivore and a decomposer?

_____

_____

## 13.4 The Big Picture

4. Fill in the chart below to describe your place in the food web.

| LIST THE LAST THREE TYPES OF FOOD THAT YOU ATE. | WHAT TYPE OF CONSUMER WERE YOU? | AT WHAT TROPHIC LEVEL DID YOU EAT? |
|---|---|---|
|  |  |  |

# 13.5 Cycling of Matter

**KEY CONCEPT** Matter cycles in and out of an ecosystem.

## Water cycles through the environment.

Water moves continuously through the water cycle. The water cycle, or the **hydrologic cycle** (HY-druh-LAHJ-ihk), is the circular pathway of water on Earth—from the atmosphere, to the surface, below ground, and back into the atmosphere again. On Earth's surface, living things—including you—are part of the water cycle.

---

**HYDROLOGIC CYCLE**

**The hydrologic cycle is the circular pathway of water on Earth.**

precipitation condensation

transpiration

surface runoff

evaporation

lake

groundwater

seepage

water storage in ocean

---

During precipitation, water falls to the ground as rain or snow. Water may trickle through the ground in the process of seepage. Liquid water becomes vapor in the process of evaporation. When water evaporates from plants, it's called transpiration. Water vapor becomes liquid water again during condensation.

---

**INSTANT REPLAY** Name two ways that water can enter the atmosphere.

_____

---

**\* ACADEMIC VOCABULARY**

**vapor** the gaseous state of a substance

# Elements essential* for life also cycle through ecosystems.

Oxygen, carbon, nitrogen, hydrogen, phosphorus, and sulfur are some of the elements necessary for life. Like water, these elements also cycle through ecosystems. The movement of a particular chemical through the living and nonliving parts of an ecosystem is called a **biogeochemical cycle** (BY-oh-JEE-oh-KHEM-ih-kuhl). Here you will read about four biogeochemical cycles: the oxygen cycle, the carbon cycle, the nitrogen cycle, and the phosphorus cycle.

## The Oxygen Cycle

Most organisms use oxygen for cellular respiration. Recall from Chapter 4 that plants and other photosynthesizing organisms release oxygen as a waste product.

## The Carbon Cycle

Carbon is a main component of carbohydrates, proteins, fats, and all of the other molecules that make up living things. Carbon can be found in many different forms—as gas in the atmosphere, dissolved in water, in fossil fuels such as oil and coal, in rocks such as limestone, and in the soil.

Plants convert carbon dioxide from the air into carbohydrates. Carbohydrates get passed through the living world as one organism eats another. Processes such as respiration and the burning of fossil fuels return carbon to the atmosphere.

### OXYGEN CYCLE

In the oxygen cycle, oxygen is produced through photosynthesis. Living organisms take in this oxygen and release it as carbon dioxide through respiration.

### CARBON CYCLE

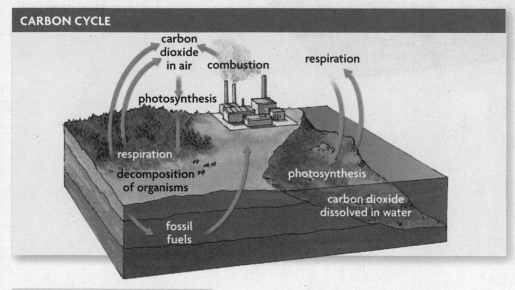

Carbon dioxide from the atmosphere is used by plants during photosynthesis. Respiration releases carbon dioxide back into the atmosphere. The burning of fossil fuels, such as oil and gas, releases carbon dioxide into the atmosphere as well. Carbon dioxide also returns to the atmosphere as dead organisms decompose.

* ACADEMIC VOCABULARY

**essential** necessary, required for

## The Nitrogen Cycle

About 78 percent of the atmosphere is made of nitrogen gas. Organisms need nitrogen to live, but most organisms cannot use nitrogen in a gas form. Instead, most organisms can only use nitrogen when it is in the form of ions such as ammonium ($NH_4^+$) or nitrate ($NO_3^-$). Certain types of bacteria can turn nitrogen gas into ammonia through a process called **nitrogen fixation.**

Much of the nitrogen cycle happens underground. After nitrogen fixation, other bacteria turn the product, ammonia, into nitrates. Nitrates are used by plants to make amino acids and proteins. Nitrogen moves through the living world as one organism eats another. Some types of bacteria also use nitrates, and release nitrogen gas back into the atmosphere.

**NITROGEN CYCLE**

nitrogen in atmosphere

animals

plants

denitrifying bacteria

nitrogen-fixing bacteria in roots

decomposers

nitrates

nitrifying bacteria

ammonification

nitrogen-fixing bacteria in soil

ammonium

nitrites

nitrifying bacteria

Nitrogen gas in the atmosphere is changed into ammonia by nitrogen-fixing bacteria. Ammonia becomes ammonium, which nitrifying bacteria change into nitrates. Plants use nitrates to make amino acids and proteins. This nitrogen is passed through the food web. Denitrifying bacteria change nitrates back into nitrogen gas, which is released into the atmosphere.

## The Phosphorus Cycle

The oxygen, carbon, and nitrogen cycles all have some part that involves atmospheric gases. The phosphorus cycle is different. Most of the phosphorus cycle takes place at ground level.

Phosphate is released by the slow breakdown of rocks. Plants take up phosphate through their roots. Phosphorus then moves through the food web. When dead organisms are broken down by decomposers, phosphorus is released back into the environment.

 Underline the main difference between the phosphorus cycle and the other cycles in this section.

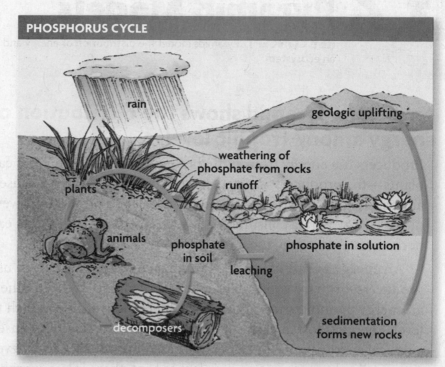

**PHOSPHORUS CYCLE**

rain

geologic uplifting

weathering of phosphate from rocks

runoff

plants

animals

phosphate in soil

phosphate in solution

leaching

decomposers

sedimentation forms new rocks

The weathering of rocks releases phosphates into soil and water. Plants take up phosphates, which are then passed through the food web. Phosphates are released back into the soil when these organisms die. Some phosphates sink to the bottom of water bodies, where they may become rock over thousands of years.

## 13.5    Vocabulary Check

**Mark It Up**

Go back and highlight each sentence that has a vocabulary word in **bold.**

hydrologic cycle
biogeochemical cycle
nitrogen fixation

1. List four biogeochemical cycles:

   _____ _____ _____ _____

2. Nitrogen fixation changes _____ into _____.

3. The hydrologic cycle is the path of what substance? _____

## 13.5    The Big Picture

4. What two main biological processes are responsible for the cycling of oxygen? _____

# 13.6 Pyramid Models

**KEY CONCEPT** Pyramids model the distribution of energy and matter in an ecosystem.

## An energy pyramid shows the distribution of energy among trophic levels.

Producers use energy from sunlight to make food. Herbivores eat plants—the producers—to get energy. Some of the energy is used by the animals to grow and some is used for cellular respiration. However, most of the energy that is consumed is lost as heat. Carnivores then eat the herbivores. And again, most of the energy is lost as heat.

An **energy pyramid** is a diagram that compares the energy used by producers, primary consumers, and other trophic levels. In other words, an energy pyramid shows how much energy is available at each trophic level. Energy is lost at each trophic level of a food chain. Because of this, a typical energy pyramid has a large base of producers. Each level above gets smaller, because as energy is lost as heat, there is less energy available as food for organisms. The longer the food chain, the more energy is lost between the bottom and top links.

An energy pyramid shows the energy flow between trophic levels in an ecosystem. Between each level, up to 90 percent of the energy is lost as heat into the environment.

energy lost as heat

energy transferred

Where are producers located on the energy pyramid?

_____

# Other pyramid models illustrate an ecosystem's biomass and distribution of organisms.

An energy pyramid shows energy loss at each trophic level. Pyramid diagrams can also be used to represent other components of an ecosystem. Two other types of pyramid models are a biomass pyramid and a pyramid of numbers.

## Biomass Pyramids

**Biomass** is a measure of the total amount, or dry mass, of organisms in a given area. A biomass pyramid is a diagram that compares the biomass of different trophic levels within an ecosystem. It shows the mass of producers that are needed to support primary consumers, the mass of primary consumers required to support secondary consumers, and so on. Notice that each trophic level has a smaller biomass than the one below it.

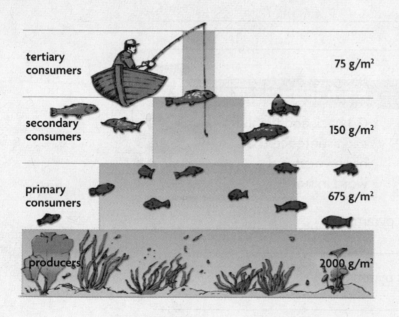

tertiary consumers — 75 g/m²

secondary consumers — 150 g/m²

primary consumers — 675 g/m²

producers — 2000 g/m²

The biomass pyramid shows the total dry mass of organisms found at each trophic level.

## Pyramids of Numbers

A pyramid of numbers gives a count of the numbers of individual organisms at each trophic level in an ecosystem. This type of pyramid gives a good picture of the large numbers of producers that are required to support just a few top-level consumers. Notice that it takes a huge number of producers to support just a few mountain lions.

| | |
|---|---|
| tertiary consumers | 5 |
| secondary consumers | 5000 |
| primary consumers | 500,000 |
| producers | 5,000,000 |

In a pyramid of numbers, each level represents the actual number of organisms at each trophic level.

**What is represented by a pyramid of numbers?**

_____

_____

_____

---

### 13.6 Vocabulary Check

biomass
energy pyramid

**Mark It Up**

Go back and highlight each sentence that has a vocabulary word in **bold**.

1. What is represented by an energy pyramid? _____

_____

2. What is represented by a biomass pyramid? _____

_____

---

### 13.6 The Big Picture

3. Which trophic level contains the most energy? _____

4. What happens to most energy at each trophic level? _____

_____

_____

# Chapter 13 Review

1. What do ecologists study? _____
   _____

2. Label the energy pyramid with the following terms: *tertiary consumers, producers,
   secondary consumers, primary consumers.*

   _____

3. On the energy pyramid, draw an arrow
   pointing to the trophic level that has the
   most available energy.

   _____

4. The source of energy for most autotrophs is
   a. chemicals.
   b. oxygen.
   c. carbon dioxide.
   d. sunlight.

5. Explain why the following statement is true: *The stability of an ecosystem depends on producers.* _____
   _____
   _____

6. What is biodiversity?
   a. total number of organisms in an area
   b. total variety of organisms in an area
   c. abiotic factors in an ecosystem
   d. one species whose presence affects many other species

7. Use the following terms to label the drawings below: *herbivore,
   producer, carnivore.*

8. How do elements such as carbon and nitrogen get moved through the
   living world? _____
   _____
   _____

# 14 Interactions in Ecosystems

## GETTING READY TO LEARN

### Preview Key Concepts

**14.1 Habitat and Niche**
Every organism has a habitat and a niche.

**14.2 Community Interactions**
Organism interact as individuals and as populations.

**14.3 Population Density and Distribution**
Each population has a density, a dispersion, and a reproductive strategy.

**14.4 Population Growth Patterns**
Populations grow in predictable patterns.

**14.5 Ecological Succession**
Ecological succession is a process of change in the species that make up a community.

### Review Academic Vocabulary

Write the correct word for each definition.

abiotic      ecosystem      population      species

1. _____ : collection of living and nonliving things in an area

2. _____ : all the individuals of one species living in an area

3. _____ : nonliving

4. _____ : group of organisms that can breed and produce fertile offspring

### Preview Biology Vocabulary

Try to guess the meaning of each boldfaced word from its context.

| PHRASE | MY GUESS |
|---|---|
| 1. A **mutualism** exists between bees and the flowering plants that they pollinate. | |
| 2. The **population density** of deer in a certain area is 20 deer per square kilometer. | |
| 3. After the **population crash** in 1964, hardly any reindeer remained on St. Matthew Island. | |

# 14.1 Habitat and Niche

**KEY CONCEPT**  Every organism has a habitat and a niche.

## A habitat differs from a niche.

A **habitat** includes all of the living and nonliving components of the environment in which an organism lives. For example, the plants, the fish, the birds, the shade, and the water are all parts of the habitat shown at the right.

Each organism interacts with its environment in a different way. The fish, for example, use a different part of the habitat's resources than the ducks. The part of an environment that a species uses to survive and reproduce is called an **ecological niche** (nihch). A niche includes all of the physical, chemical, and biological factors that a species uses.

You can think of a habitat as *where* a species lives and a niche as *how* a species lives within its habitat. A niche includes

A habitat includes all of the living and nonliving parts of the environment in which an organism lives.

- **Food**  The type of food a species eats and where it fits in the food web are parts of the species' niche.
- **Nonliving conditions**  A niche includes nonliving, or abiotic, conditions such as the range of temperature a species needs to live.
- **Behavior**  The time of day a species is active and when it reproduces are also part of the species' niche.

The different species shown above all share the same habitat. But each species occupies a different niche.

**List at least one living and nonliving component of the habitat shown above.** _____

_____

## Resource availability gives structure to a community.

Many different species may share the same habitat. But if two species use the same resources within a habitat, there will be competition between the two species.

## Competition for the Same Niche

In the late 1800s, the North American grey squirrel was introduced to Great Britain. The grey squirrel used the same food resources, habitat, and space as the native European red squirrel. In other words, the two species competed for the same resources. Currently, the red squirrel population is declining. The grey squirrel population is pushing the red squirrel population out of its niche.

The principle of **competitive exclusion** states that when two species are competing for the same resources, one species will be better suited to the niche, and the other species will either be pushed into another niche or will become extinct. Competitive exclusion can also result in two species sharing different parts of a niche. Or, natural selection can lead to an evolutionary response in one of the species.

## Similar Adaptations to Similar Niches

**Ecological equivalents** are species that occupy similar niches but live in different geographical regions. Ecological equivalents live in niches with similar resources, and have similar adaptations. But because ecological equivalents live in different regions, they do not compete for resources.

 **Why don't ecological equivalents compete for resources?**

_____

> **VOCABULARY**
>
> _Equivalent_ means "equal." Ecological equivalents are species that occupy very similar, or equal, niches.

---

## 14.1 Vocabulary Check

**Mark It Up**

Go back and highlight each sentence that has a vocabulary word in **bold.**

habitat                     competitive exclusion
ecological niche      ecological equivalent

**Fill in the blanks with the correct term from the list above.**

1. _____ results when two species are competing for the same resources.

2. Species that live in similar niches in different regions are _____.

3. Two species may live in a similar _____ but occupy different _____.

## 14.1  The Big Picture

4. Look back at the illustration on page 241. Is it likely that there will be competitive exclusion between the fish and the ducks? Explain.

_____

# 14.2 Community Interactions

**KEY CONCEPT** Organisms interact as individuals and as populations.

## Competition and predation are two important ways in which organisms interact.

There are many different types of interactions between species in an ecosystem. Two important interactions are competition and predation.

- **Competition** occurs when two organisms fight for the same limited resources. Members of different species may compete for the same resources. Members of the same species may also compete with each other for the same resources.
- **Predation** occurs when one organism captures and feeds upon another organism. Lions and hawks are well known as predators. But herbivores are predators, too. A deer, for example, preys on grass.

Lions are predators, animals that hunt and feed on other organisms.

 Why can a deer be considered a predator?

_____

_____

## Symbiosis is a close relationship between species.

**Symbiosis** is a close ecological relationship between two or more organisms of different species. One example of symbiosis is the relationship between certain bees and flowering plants. Bees collect pollen or nectar from flowers, and in the process they pollinate the flower. In this case, both species benefit. There are three major types of symbiosis: mutualism, commensalism, and parasitism.

- **Mutualism** is an interaction in which both organisms benefit.
- **Commensalism** is a relationship in which one organism benefits and the other organism neither benefits nor is harmed.
- **Parasitism** is a relationship in which one species benefits and the other is harmed. The species that gets harmed is called the host and the species that benefits is called the parasite.

Predation is also a relationship in which one species benefits and the other is harmed. Parasitism is different from predation because a parasite does not immediately kill its host. Some parasites may lead to the death of the host after days or even years. Other parasites, like fleas or lice, harm the host but do not necessarily kill it.

 **INSTANT REPLAY** Which type of symbiosis benefits one organism and harms the other? _____

| 14.2 Vocabulary Check | Mark It Up |
|---|---|

competition      mutualism

predation        commensalism

symbiosis        parasitism

**Mark It Up**

Go back and highlight each sentence that has a vocabulary word in **bold.**

**Fill in the blanks with the correct term from the list above.**

1. What are three types of symbiosis? _____

_____

2. What type of interaction occurs between organisms fighting for the same resources? _____

3. What type of interaction occurs when one organism captures and feeds on another organism? _____

## 14.2 The Big Picture

4. Your body is currently involved in many different symbiotic relationships. For example, microscopic organisms called mites live at the base of each of your eyelashes. The mites benefit from the relationship by eating dead skin cells and oils released by your skin. You are not harmed, nor does this benefit you. What type of symbiosis is this?

_____

5. With both predation and parasitism, one organism benefits and the other is harmed. What is the main difference between parasitism and predation? _____

_____

_____

# 14.3 Population Density and Distribution

**KEY CONCEPT** Each population has a density, a dispersion, and a reproductive strategy.

## Population density is the number of individuals that live in a defined area.

You may have noticed that cities have more dense populations of people and rural areas have more widely spread out, or dispersed, populations. Different populations of other organisms also have different population densities. **Population density** is a measurement of the number of individuals living in a defined space.

$$\frac{\text{\# of individuals}}{\text{area (units}^2)} = \text{population density}$$

For example, if scientists counted 200 deer in an area of 10 square kilometers, the density of the deer population would be 20 deer per square kilometer. Wildlife biologists study population densities to learn about the lifestyles of different species and about environmental changes that are affecting the health of different populations.

**What two measurements are needed to calculate population density?** _____

_____

## Geographic dispersion of a population shows how individuals in a population are spaced.

**Population dispersion** is the way in which individuals of a population are distributed, or spread out, in an area. Three types of population dispersion are

- **Clumped dispersion** Individuals live close together in groups. This might help for mating, for protection, or to use food resources.
- **Uniform dispersion** Individuals live at specific distances from one another. This may be because of competition for limited resources.
- **Random dispersion** Individuals are spread randomly in an area.

> **VOCABULARY**
>
> *Uniform* can mean a particular set of clothes. Here, *uniform* is used as an adjective and means "the same."

**Population dispersion** is the way in which individuals of a population are spread out in an area. Dispersion patterns help us understand species interactions.

Uniform dispersion

Clumped dispersion

Many fish species swim together in large groups to avoid predators, showing clumped dispersion.

Uniform dispersion

Many bird species are territorial, each protecting its own space, showing uniform dispersion.

Random dispersion

Three-toed sloths have almost no competitors and few predators. They show a random dispersion.

 **INSTANT REPLAY** What are three types of population dispersion? _____

_____

## Survivorship curves help to describe the reproductive strategy of a species.

A survivorship curve is a diagram that shows the number of organisms that survive over time, starting from birth. There are three basic patterns of survivorship curves.

- **Type I** This curve is typical of humans and other large mammals. There are few deaths of infant organisms and most will survive to old age. These organisms tend to have parents that care for their young.

- **Type II** This curve is typical of birds, small mammals, and some reptiles. At all points of life, these organisms have equal chances of living or dying, either from disease or predation.

- **Type III** This curve is typical of invertebrates*, fish, amphibians*, and plants. These organisms have large numbers of offspring, or produce many eggs or seeds. Many of the offspring will die from predation, but a few will survive to adulthood.

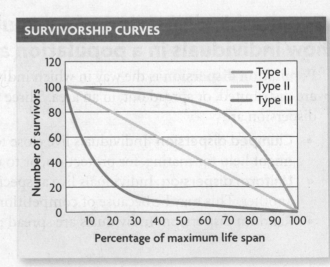

SURVIVORSHIP CURVES

Each type of curve represents a different reproductive strategy. Some organisms have few offspring and most will survive. Other organisms may lay thousands of eggs, only a few of which will survive to maturity.

 **INSTANT REPLAY** Why is Type I survivorship typical of humans and other large mammals? _____

_____

\* **ACADEMIC VOCABULARY**

**invertebrates** animals, such as insects, without a backbone

**amphibians** animals, such as frogs, that need water to reproduce

## 14.3 Vocabulary Check

population density                survivorship curve
population dispersion

**Mark It Up**

Go back and highlight each sentence that has a vocabulary word in **bold**.

Fill in the blanks with the correct term from the list above.

1. _____ is the number of individuals per unit of area.

2. A _____ shows the number of organisms that survive over time.

## 14.3 The Big Picture

3. Which type of population dispersion—clumped, uniform, or random—would be beneficial for a species in which competition for resources is high? Explain. _____

_____

_____

4. What is one example of an organism with clumped dispersion?

_____

_____

5. What do the three types of survivorship curves represent? _____

_____

_____

# 14.4 Population and Growth Patterns

**KEY CONCEPT** Populations grow in predictable patterns.

## Changes in a population's size are determined by immigration, births, emigration, and deaths.

The size of a population is usually changing. If there are plenty of resources such as food and water, a population may grow. If there are few resources, the population may decrease in size. Four factors affect the size of a population: immigration, births, emigration, and deaths.

- **Immigration** is the movement of individuals into a population from another population.
- **Births** increase the number of individuals in a population.
- **Emigration** is the movement of individuals out of a population and into another population.
- **Deaths** decrease the size of a population.

  Circle two factors that increase a population's size.

## Population growth is based on available resources.

The rate of growth for a population depends on the resources available. Two different types of population growth are exponential growth and logistic growth.

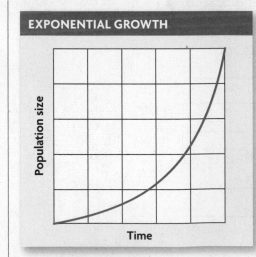

**Exponential growth** occurs when a population size increases greatly over a period of time. This type of population growth occurs when there are plenty of resources available.

**Logistic growth** begins with a period of slow growth, followed by exponential growth. As the population grows, resources become more and more limited. The population eventually levels off at a size the environment can support.

The **carrying capacity** of an environment is the maximum number of individuals of a particular species that the environment can support. If the environment changes, the carrying capacity can change, too. For example, a disease might destroy a population's main food source. This situation may cause the population to crash. A **population crash** is a large decrease in the size of a population over a short time period.

If there are unlimited resources, what type of population growth is likely to occur? _____

## Ecological factors limit population growth.

Many factors affect the carrying capacity of an environment for a population. The factor that has the greatest effect on limiting population growth is called the **limiting factor.** For example, if a lack of space is the biggest factor limiting population growth, then space would be the limiting factor. Two main categories of limiting factors are density-dependent factors and density-independent factors.

### Density-Dependent Limiting Factors

**Density-dependent limiting factors** are limiting factors that are affected by the population density, or the number of individuals living in a given area.

- **Competition**  The more dense the population is, the greater the competition among individuals is for resources such as food.
- **Predation**  The density of the prey population affects the number of predators that can survive. If there is an increase in the number of prey, then the area can support more predators. If there is a decrease in the number of prey, then the number of predators will drop, too.
- **Parasitism and disease**  Parasites and disease spread more quickly through dense, or crowded, populations. This can result in a decrease in the population size.

### Density-Independent Limiting Factors

**Density-independent limiting factors** are limiting factors that affect the size of any population, no matter what density of individuals live in an area.

- **Unusual weather**  Weather can affect the size of a population regardless of its density.
- **Natural disasters**  Volcanoes, hurricanes, and other natural disasters can wipe out populations regardless of density.

- **Human activities** Destruction of habitat, pollution, and the introduction of nonnative species are all human activities that affect population size regardless of density.

 What is the difference between a density-dependent and a density-independent limiting factor? _____

_____

## 14.4 Vocabulary Check

**Mark It Up**

Go back and highlight each sentence that has a vocabulary word in **bold**.

immigration          population crash
emigration           limiting factor
exponential growth   density-dependent limiting factor
logistic growth      density-independent limiting factor
carrying capacity

**Circle the correct term from each pair to complete the sentences below.**

1. *Immigration / emigration* is the movement of organisms out of one population into another population.

2. A limiting factor that does not depend on the number of individuals in an area is a *density-dependent / density-independent* limiting factor.

3. A type of population growth that begins slowly, then grows quickly, and finally levels off is *exponential growth / logistic growth*.

4. If the carrying capacity of an environment drops suddenly, it can result in a *population crash / limiting factor*.

## 14.4 The Big Picture

5. List two factors that increase a population's size and two factors that decrease a population's size. _____

_____

6. How does the availability of resources affect whether a population's growth is exponential or logistic? _____

_____

7. Give one example of a density-dependent limiting factor and one example of a density-independent limiting factor. _____

_____

_____

# 14.5 Ecological Succession

**KEY CONCEPT** Ecological succession is a process of change in the species that make up a community.

## Succession occurs following a disturbance in an ecosystem.

**Succession** is a sequence of changes that recreates a damaged community or creates a new community in an area that was not inhabited before.

### Primary Succession

**Primary succession** is the development of an ecosystem in an area that was not inhabited before. This type of succession might begin on cooled lava, after a volcano erupts. Or it might begin on bare rock that is exposed when a glacier melts. The first organisms that move into an area like this are called **pioneer\* species.**

Lichens and some mosses are pioneer species. They live on rock, and can break rock down into smaller pieces. Dead lichens and mosses mix with rock pieces to form a thin soil. Over time, seeds get blown in and grow in the soil. The soil continues to thicken, and eventually can support trees.

*Connecting* **CONCEPTS**

**Symbiosis** A lichen is a symbiotic relationship between fungi and algae. The fungi collect water and the algae make food through photosynthesis.

**PRIMARY SUCCESSION**

Melting glaciers, volcanic eruptions, landslides, and strip mines can all begin the process of primary succession.

| 0–15 years Moss, lichens, grasses | 15–80 years Shrubs, cottonwoods, alder thicket | 80–115 years Transition to forest, alder, spruce | 115–200 years Hemlock-spruce forest |
|---|---|---|---|

**\* ACADEMIC VOCABULARY**

**pioneer** the first to do a certain thing

## Secondary Succession

**Secondary succession** is the regrowth of a damaged ecosystem in an area that still has healthy soil. This may occur after a small event, such as a tree falling, or after a larger event, such as a hurricane.

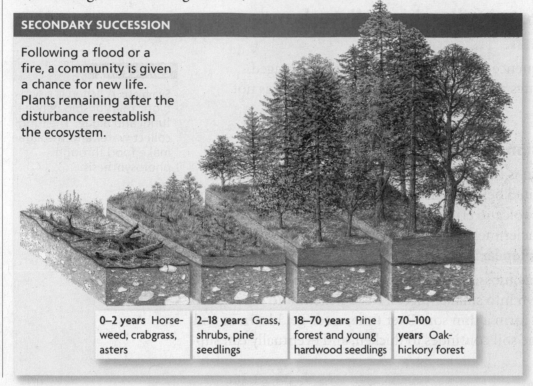

**SECONDARY SUCCESSION**

Following a flood or a fire, a community is given a chance for new life. Plants remaining after the disturbance reestablish the ecosystem.

| 0–2 years Horse-weed, crabgrass, asters | 2–18 years Grass, shrubs, pine seedlings | 18–70 years Pine forest and young hardwood seedlings | 70–100 years Oak-hickory forest |

INSTANT REPLAY

Circle two examples of pioneer species.

---

## 14.5   Vocabulary Check

**Mark It Up**

Go back and highlight each sentence that has a vocabulary word in **bold**.

succession              pioneer species
primary succession      secondary succession

**Fill in the blanks with the correct term from the list above.**

1. The first species to inhabit an area is a _____.

2. Succession in an area that was not previously inhabited is called

   _____.

---

## 14.5   The Big Picture

3. What trend do you see in the changes in plant communities over the course of ecological succession? _____

   _____

# Chapter 14 Review

1. One way organisms interact is through competition. What do organisms compete for? _____

2. Limiting factors limit the growth of a population. A natural disaster, such as a hurricane, is a density-independent limiting factor. What makes this limiting factor density-independent?

   _____

   _____

   _____

3. A lesser long-nosed bat has a symbiotic relationship with the saguaro cactus. Bats help to pollinate the cacti through the indirect transfer of pollen as the bats fly from one cactus to another to feed on cactus flower nectar. What type of symbiosis is this?

   **a.** mutualism

   **b.** commensalism

   **c.** parasitism

   **d.** predation

4. What conditions allow for exponential growth of a population? _____

   _____

5. Two species of birds make their nests and eat the fruits of the same kind of tree. One of the bird species is active in the late evening, and makes nests and eats fruits near the top of the tree. The other bird species is active in the dawn and early morning. It makes nests and eats fruits in the bottom tree branches. These two species inhabit

   **a.** the same habitat and the same niche

   **b.** the same habitat but different niches

   **c.** different habitats but the same niche

   **d.** different habitats and different niches

6. If no other changes occurred, how would emigration affect the population density of a group of organisms? _____

   _____

7. What biological process occurs after there has been a disturbance—such as a flood, or a tornado—in an established ecosystem?

   _____

   _____

# 15 The Biosphere

## GETTING READY TO LEARN

### Preview Key Concepts

**15.1 Life in the Earth System**
The biosphere is one of Earth's four interconnected systems.

**15.2 Climate**
Climate is a key abiotic factor that affects the biosphere.

**15.3 Biomes**
Biomes are land-based, global communities of organisms.

**15.4 Marine Ecosystems**
Marine ecosystems are global.

**15.5 Estuaries and Freshwater Ecosystems**
Freshwater ecosystems include estuaries as well as flowing and standing water.

### Review Academic Vocabulary

Write the correct word for each definition.

adaptation     biome     biomass     ecosystem

1. _____ : total amount, or dry mass, of organisms in an area

2. _____ : global community of organisms characterized by plant communities and climate

3. _____ : collection of living and nonliving things in an area

4. _____ : trait that allows organisms to better survive in their environments

### Preview Biology Vocabulary

Two key terms from this chapter share the same word part. Read the definitions and guess what the word part means.

| TERM | DEFINITION | WHAT I THINK *PLANKTON* MEANS |
|------|-----------|-------------------------------|
| zoo**plankton** | tiny, free-floating animals that live in the water | |
| phyto**plankton** | tiny, free-floating, photosynthetic organisms | |

# 15.1 Life in the Earth System

**KEY CONCEPT** The biosphere is one of Earth's four interconnected systems.

## The biosphere is the portion of Earth that is inhabited by life.

Everything that lives on Earth, and every place where those things live, is part of the **biosphere.** The biosphere includes all of the living and nonliving parts of all of Earth's ecosystems. The living parts of the biosphere make up the **biota.**

The biosphere is one of four major systems on Earth. The other three Earth systems are

- the **hydrosphere,** all of Earth's water, ice, and water vapor;
- the **atmosphere,** the air that surrounds the entire planet;
- and the **geosphere,** the physical features of Earth's surface—including the continents, rocks, the sea floor, and everything below Earth's surface.

These four Earth systems are interconnected. A plant growing in the biosphere uses water from the hydrosphere, carbon dioxide from the atmosphere, and minerals in the soil that came from the geosphere. The four Earth systems all interact in Earth's ecosystems.

> **VISUAL VOCAB**
>
> The **biosphere** includes living organisms and the land, air, and water on Earth where living things reside.
>
> biosphere
>
> biota
>
> The collection of living things in the biosphere may also be called the **biota.**

 **INSTANT REPLAY** Which Earth system includes all of the water on Earth?

_____

## Biotic and abiotic factors interact in the biosphere.

The four Earth systems include both living and nonliving—or biotic and abiotic—factors. Because they are all connected, a change in one sphere can affect the others. For example, when carbon dioxide levels increase in the atmosphere, plants can grow more quickly. As plants use more carbon dioxide, the levels of carbon dioxide in the atmosphere will drop. When the carbon dioxide levels drop, plant growth will slow. This is an example of a give-and-take, or a feedback loop, between the living and nonliving parts of Earth. New fields of science are investigating the relationships between the four Earth systems.

 **INSTANT REPLAY** What do the words _biotic_ and _abiotic_ mean? _____

_____

**Mark It Up**

Go back and highlight each sentence that has a vocabulary word in **bold**.

biosphere          atmosphere

biota              geosphere

hydrosphere

**Fill in the blanks with the correct term from the list above.**

1. the living part of the biosphere _____

2. the air that surrounds Earth _____

3. the water system on Earth _____

4. the features of Earth's surface and below _____

5. the part of Earth where life exists _____

| 15.1 | The Big Picture |

6. This drawing illustrates the interaction between the four main Earth systems. Label the part of the drawing that represents each system: *biosphere, hydrosphere, atmosphere,* and *geosphere.*

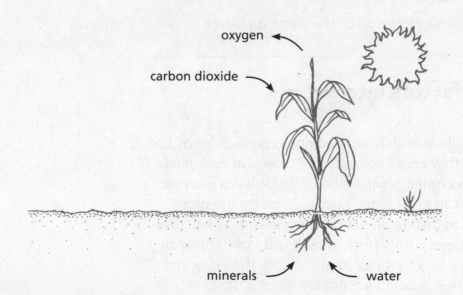

oxygen

carbon dioxide

minerals          water

# 15.2 Climate

**KEY CONCEPT** Climate is a key abiotic factor that affects the biosphere.

## Climate is the prevailing* weather of a region.

The weather may change from day to day. One day it might rain, and another day it might be sunny. In contrast, climate does not change from day to day. The **climate** is the long-term pattern of weather conditions in a region. Climate includes average temperature and precipitation, such as rain or snowfall. Climate also includes the changes that happen at different times of the year, like rainy seasons, dry seasons, winter, or summer.

A **microclimate** is the climate in a small, specific place within a larger area. For example, there may be many microclimates within a grassy meadow. The tops of the grasses might be dry and warm because they are exposed to sunlight. At the base of the grasses, near the ground, it may be shaded, damp, and cool. Different types of organisms may live in different microclimates within the same area. For example, frogs may live in the cool damp areas of the meadow and grasshoppers may live in the sunny dry tops of the grasses.

 What is a microclimate? _____

_____

## Earth has three main climate zones.

Earth can be divided into three main climate zones: polar, tropical, and temperate.

- The polar climate zone is found at the far northern and southern regions of Earth. Because Earth's surface is curved, this area receives the least direct sunlight.
- The tropical climate zone is near the equator. This area receives the most direct sunlight.
- The temperate climate zone includes the area in between the tropical and polar zones.

The amount of direct sunlight that hits different parts of Earth is a main factor in the type of climate in that region. Other factors also influence climate. For example, the movement of air and water affects temperature and rainfall. Features such as mountains and oceans also affect climate.

* ACADEMIC VOCABULARY

**prevailing** frequent, common

## CLIMATE ZONES

**The uneven heating of Earth by the Sun results in three different climate zones.**

sunlight

polar

temperate

tropical

temperate

polar

### POLAR CLIMATE

The polar climate zone is located in far northern and far southern parts of the planet, where the temperature is typically cold and often below freezing.

### TROPICAL CLIMATE

The tropical climate zone, which surrounds the equator, is characterized by warm, moist conditions.

### TEMPERATE CLIMATE

The temperate climate zone is located in the broad area lying between the polar and tropical climate zones. This zone has summer and winter seasons of about equal length.

**INSTANT REPLAY** In which climate zone do you live? _____

---

## 15.2    Vocabulary Check

**Mark It Up**

Go back and highlight each sentence that has a vocabulary word in **bold**.

climate       microclimate

**1.** How is a microclimate different from a climate? _____

_____

_____

## 15.2    The Big Picture

**2.** What are the three main climate zones? _____

_____

**3.** What are two main factors that determine the type of climate in a region? _____

_____

# 15.3 Biomes

**KEY CONCEPT** Biomes are land-based, global communities of organisms.

## Earth has six major biomes.

A biome is a region that is defined by the climate and the plant communities that live in the area. There are six major biomes:

- Tropical rain forest
- Grassland
- Desert
- Temperate forest
- Taiga
- Tundra

These broad biomes can be divided into more specific zones. For example, there are different kinds of grasslands and different kinds of temperate forests.

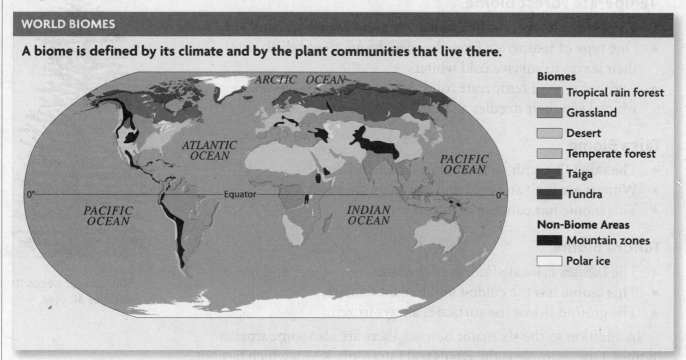

**WORLD BIOMES**

**A biome is defined by its climate and by the plant communities that live there.**

ARCTIC OCEAN

ATLANTIC OCEAN

PACIFIC OCEAN

Equator

PACIFIC OCEAN

INDIAN OCEAN

**Biomes**
- Tropical rain forest
- Grassland
- Desert
- Temperate forest
- Taiga
- Tundra

**Non-Biome Areas**
- Mountain zones
- Polar ice

## Tropical Rain Forest Biome

- This biome has warm temperatures and lots of rain.
- Most organisms live in the uppermost branches of the forest, which is called the **canopy.**
- Very little sunlight makes it through the canopy.
- Animals that live in the canopy use loud vocalizations to communicate.

## Grassland Biome

- A **grassland** is an area in which the main plant life is grass.
- There are both tropical and temperate grasslands.
- In tropical grasslands, hoofed animals such as gazelles and zebras are most common.
- In temperate grasslands, many animals, such as prairie dogs, live underground.

## Desert Biome

- A **desert** is very dry and gets little rain.
- Plants and animals have adaptations to survive the dry climate.
- There are four types of deserts: hot, semi arid, coastal, and cold.

These are leaves of deciduous trees.

## Temperate Forest Biome

- This biome has very different summer and winter seasons.
- One type of temperate forest has **deciduous** trees, which drop their leaves to survive cold winters.
- Another type of temperate forest has many **coniferous** trees, which keep their needles all year.

## Taiga Biome

- The **taiga** (TY-guh) is located in cooler climates.
- Winters are long and cold and summers are short.
- This biome has coniferous forests.

## Tundra Biome

- The **tundra** is located north of the taiga.
- This biome has the coldest and longest winters.
- The ground below the surface is always frozen.

This conifer keeps its needles all year.

In addition to the six major biomes, there are also some smaller biomes. One example is the **chaparral** (SHAP-uh-RAL), which has hot, dry summers and cool, moist winters. This biome is found along the southern coast of California and several other parts of the world. The main chaparral plants are small evergreen shrubs.

 In the map of world biomes on page 259, circle the biome in which you live.

# Polar ice caps and mountains are not considered biomes.

Polar ice caps are ice-covered areas that have no soil and no specific plant community. In mountains, the climate and the plant and animal communities change at different altitudes.* Recall that biomes are defined partly by the plant community that lives in the region. Because polar ice caps do not have specific plant communities and mountains have different plant communities at different altitudes, these two regions are not considered biomes.

 **Why aren't polar ice caps and mountains considered biomes?**

_____

* ACADEMIC VOCABULARY

**altitude**  height above sea level

## 15.3    Vocabulary Check

| | |
|---|---|
| canopy | coniferous |
| grassland | taiga |
| desert | tundra |
| deciduous | chaparral |

> **Mark It Up**
>
> Go back and highlight each sentence that has a vocabulary word in **bold**.

**Fill in the blanks with the correct term from the list above.**

1. The two coldest biomes are _____.

2. Two types of trees are _____.

3. The top layer of rain forest trees is called the _____.

4. The driest biome is the _____.

## 15.3    The Big Picture

5. Pick one of the six main biomes and describe it in the chart below.

| | |
|---|---|
| **Name of the biome** | |
| **Location** | |
| **Description** | |

# 15.4 Marine Ecosystems

**KEY CONCEPT** Marine ecosystems are global.

## The ocean can be divided into zones.

The ocean can be divided into zones according to distance from shore and water depth. The four major ocean zones are the intertidal zone, neritic zone, bathyal zone, and abyssal zone.

- The **intertidal zone** is the shoreline area between high and low tide lines. This zone contains tidal pools.

- The **neritic zone** (nuh-RIHT-ihk) is the next closest area to shore. This zone may be very shallow in some places and up to 200 meters deep in other places.

- The **bathyal zone** (BATH-ee-uhl) extends from the edge of the neritic zone to the ocean bottom. This zone ranges from about 200 to 2000 meters deep.

- The **abyssal zone** (uh-BIHS-uhl) is the deepest zone. No sunlight reaches this zone, so photosynthetic organisms do not live here. Instead, chemosynthetic organisms form the base of the food web.

**OCEAN ZONES**

**The ocean is divided into four major zones.**

intertidal zone

neritic zone

bathyal zone

abyssal zone

### Life in the Neritic Zone

The neritic zone makes up only a small percentage of the total ocean area, but it contains a large percentage of ocean life. Huge quantities of tiny free-floating organisms called **plankton** live in the neritic zone. There are both animal plankton and photosynthesizing plankton. Animal plankton are called **zooplankton** and photosynthesizing plankton are called **phytoplankton.**

Most of the photosynthesis that occurs on Earth is done by blue-green algae and other phytoplankton. Around 70 percent of the oxygen in each breath you take was produced by phytoplankton in the ocean. These organisms form the base of the food web in this zone.

 **INSTANT REPLAY** What is the difference between zooplankton and phytoplankton? _____

_____

# Coastal waters are unique habitats.

The neritic zone is nutrient-rich, and sunlight reaches through the water. This zone supports two main ocean habitats: coral reefs and kelp forests.

- **Coral reefs** are found mainly within the tropical climate zone. Water temperatures are warm all year. There may be hundreds of species of corals, fishes, sponges, and sea urchins in a single coral reef.
- **Kelp forests** are found in cold waters, such as California's Monterey Bay. Thick communities of kelp, a type of seaweed, make up this habitat. A wide range of species lives here, from tiny invertebrates to large sea lions.

Sponges and fish live in coral reefs.

**INSTANT REPLAY**  In which ocean zone are coral reefs and kelp forests found?

_____

_____

## 15.4    Vocabulary Check

**Mark It Up**

Go back and highlight each sentence that has a vocabulary word in **bold**.

intertidal zone        zooplankton

neritic zone           phytoplankton

bathyal zone           coral reef

abyssal zone           kelp forest

plankton

**Fill in the blanks with the correct term from the list above.**

1. List the four ocean zones, from closest to shore to farthest from shore. _____

   _____

   _____

2. Which term is a tiny, free-floating organism? _____

## 15.4    The Big Picture

3. What organisms form the base of the food web in the neritic zone?

   _____

4. What organisms form the base of the food web in the abyssal zone?

   _____

5. What is one main difference between the coral reef and kelp forest habitats? _____

   _____

# 15.5 Estuaries and Freshwater Ecosystems

**KEY CONCEPT** Freshwater ecosystems include estuaries as well as flowing and standing water.

## Estuaries are dynamic* environments where rivers flow into the ocean.

The area where a river flows into an ocean is called an **estuary.** Estuaries include many different ecosystems, such as salt marshes, mud flats, open water, mangrove forests, and tidal pools. Estuaries are sometimes called nurseries of the sea. Just like a nursery center takes care of babies, estuaries are very important areas where many different species of ocean organisms raise their young.

### Estuary Characteristics

- Fresh water from the river mixes with the salt water from the ocean in estuary environments.
- Estuaries are rich in nutrients that wash in from land.
- Estuaries have great biodiversity.
- Migrating birds use estuaries as stops along their migration paths.
- Estuaries provide a protected area where many different species lay eggs and raise young.

**VOCABULARY**

Recall from Chapter 13 that *biodiversity* is the variety of species in an area. Estuaries have a high biodiversity.

### Estuaries Protect Coastlines

Estuaries are located between the ocean and the coast. They help to protect shorelines from storms, winds, and flooding. In some coastal areas of the United States, over 80 percent of the estuaries have been destroyed by land development and human activities. The destruction of estuaries harms ocean life. Their destruction also leaves the coastline unprotected, and more likely to be damaged by storms.

Why are estuaries sometimes called "nurseries of the sea?"

_____

_____

**\* ACADEMIC VOCABULARY**

**dynamic** active, constantly changing

## Freshwater ecosystems include moving and standing water.

Rivers and streams are ecosystems with moving water. Lakes and ponds are ecosystems with standing water, or water that stays in the same place. The water that fills these freshwater ecosystems comes from rain, snow, and springs that drain into the rivers and lakes from the surrounding land. The region of land that drains into a freshwater ecosystem is called a **watershed.**

### Wetlands

In addition to rivers, streams, lakes, and ponds, wetlands are also important freshwater ecosystems. A wetland is an area of land that stays soaked in water for at least part of the year. Wetlands include bogs, marshes, and swamps. These are important habitats for many different species. Wetlands also help to filter water and maintain a clean water supply.

### Adaptations of Freshwater Organisms

Different freshwater ecosystems can differ in water temperature, oxygen levels, pH, the speed of water flow, and many other conditions. Each type of freshwater ecosystem is home to species with adaptations for the particular conditions in that ecosystem.

What is a wetland? _____

_____

## Ponds and lakes share common features.

Just like the ocean can be divided into zones, so can lakes and ponds. Lakes and ponds can be divided into three zones: *littoral, limnetic,* and *benthic.*

- The **littoral zone** is along the shoreline, between the high and low water marks where rooted plants can grow. Snails, water lilies, and other organisms live here.
- The **limnetic zone** is the open water further out from shore. Large amounts of plankton live here, and are food for populations of fish.

- The **benthic zone** is the lake or pond bottom, where less sunlight reaches. Bacteria and other decomposers live in the mud and sand in the benthic zone.

INSTANT REPLAY  In which zone do many plankton live? _____

| 15.5 | Vocabulary Check | Mark It Up |

estuary          limnetic zone

watershed        benthic zone

littoral zone

**Mark It Up**

Go back and highlight each sentence that has a vocabulary word in **bold.**

**Match the correct term from the list above to each description below.**

1. bottom zone of a lake that receives little sunlight _____

2. region of land that drains into a river or lake _____

3. area where a river meets the ocean _____

4. open water zone of a lake _____

5. edge of a lake where rooted plants can grow _____

## 15.5    The Big Picture

6. Describe the estuary environment in a way that a younger student could understand. _____

_____

7. List at least one freshwater ecosystem with moving water and one with standing water. _____

_____

_____

8. Decomposers live in the mud and sand on the bottom of lakes and ponds. In which zone do they live—*littoral, limnetic,* or *benthic*?

_____

# Chapter 15 Review

1. Label Earth's three main climate zones at the right.

2. How do the three climate zones differ?

   _____

   _____

   _____

3. In which climate zone is the tundra biome located? _____

   _____

4. What is one way in which deciduous and coniferous trees differ?

   _____

5. Which ocean zone contains the greatest biodiversity and the most ocean life?

   a. the intertidal zone

   b. the neritic zone

   c. the bathyal zone

   d. the abyssal zone

6. What is one way in which oxygen moves between the biosphere and the atmosphere in an ecosystem?

   a. through decomposition and nitrogen fixation

   b. through biotic adaptations

   c. through photosynthesis and respiration

   d. oxygen is abiotic, and does not cycle through the biosphere

7. How has human activity affected estuary ecosystems? _____

   _____

   _____

8. Give an example of how the biosphere, atmosphere, hydrosphere, and geosphere interact in Earth's ecosystems. _____

   _____

   _____

# 16 Human Impact on Ecosystems

## GETTING READY TO LEARN

### Preview Key Concepts

**16.1 Human Population Growth and Natural Resources**
As the human population grows, the demand for Earth's resources increases.

**16.2 Air Quality**
Fossil fuel emissions affect the biosphere.

**16.3 Water Quality**
Pollution of Earth's freshwater supply threatens habitat and health.

**16.4 Threats to Biodiversity**
The impact of a growing human population threatens biodiversity.

**16.5 Conservation**
Conservation methods can help protect and restore ecosystems.

### Review Academic Vocabulary

Write the correct word for each definition.

biodiversity    carrying capacity    keystone species    limiting factor

1. _____ : number of individuals an environment can support

2. _____ : variety of life in an area

3. _____ : something that limits the size of a population

4. _____ : organism with an unusually large effect on its ecosystem

### Preview Biology Vocabulary

See how many key terms from this chapter you already know. Rewrite each phrase, using a different word or words for the **words in bold.**

| PHRASE | REWRITTEN WITH DIFFERENT WORDS |
|--------|-------------------------------|
| 1. Some sources of energy, such as coal and oil, **are nonrenewable resources.** | Some sources of energy, such as coal and oil, _____ _____. |
| 2. Other sources of energy, such as wind and solar energy, **are renewable resources.** | Other sources of energy, such as wind and solar energy, _____ _____. |
| 3. Certain chemicals and waste products found in a lake are examples of **pollution.** | Certain chemicals and waste products found in a lake are examples of _____ _____ |

# 16.1 Human Population Growth and Natural Resources

**KEY CONCEPT** As the human population grows, the demand for Earth's resources increases.

## Earth's human population continues to grow.

Humans depend on Earth's nutrient and energy cycles. We use Earth's energy to power our televisions, lights, cars, airplanes, and everything else in our homes and cities. Your cotton T-shirt and this paper page come from plants that need Earth's nutrient cycles to grow. Humans, too, are part of Earth's cycles. The way that we use resources and produce waste affects Earth's energy and nutrient cycles.

Today there are more than 6 billion people on Earth, and the human population continues to grow. How many people can Earth support? Is there enough space to feed and shelter 10 billion people? 20 billion? We do not know of a limit to the amount of people Earth can hold. But some limit must exist. Earth cannot support an unlimited number of people.

**WORLD POPULATION**

Technologies developed by humans have allowed for continued human population growth. For example, developments in agriculture, medicine, and transportation have increased the number of people Earth can support.

- **Agriculture** The development of gas powered equipment and other technologies made it possible to produce great amounts of food.
- **Medicine** Advancements in medicine have lowered infant deaths and limited the spread of disease.
- **Transportation** Trains, trucks, boats, and airplanes help move food and materials around the world.

Give one example of how technology has helped to support a growing population. _____

_____

## The growing human population exerts pressure on Earth's natural resources.

Over millions of years, natural processes change dead organisms into the substances that we use today as oil and coal. Oil and coal are the two main resources that we use for energy. These are **nonrenewable resources** because we use them much faster than they form.

Not all resources are nonrenewable. **Renewable resources** are ones that cannot be used up, or can be replaced as fast as they are used. Some resources, like wind and solar energy, cannot be used up. Other resources, such as wood, can be renewable if they are regrown as quickly as they are used.

Wood and other resources can become nonrenewable if they are not used carefully. Drinking water, for example, is threatened by pollution and overuse.

The number of people that Earth can support depends on the use of Earth's resources. The United States uses more resources and produces more waste than any other country on Earth. This country's population throws away around 1 ton of waste per person each year. What would happen if all of Earth's 6 billion people made so much waste?

What's for lunch? Oil and gas were used to transport your food. The wood used to make paper bags may or may not be renewable. Pesticides sprayed on fruits and vegetables may end up in your water supply.

Name one example of a nonrenewable resource and one example of a renewable resource. _____

_____

## Effective management of Earth's resources will help meet the needs of the future.

Humans need natural resources to survive, but the way these resources are used threatens the well-being of the human population. The responsible use of resources can help to keep these resources for future generations.

The amount of land necessary to produce enough food, water, shelter, and energy, and to hold the waste of an individual or a population is called an **ecological footprint.** Individuals and populations vary in their use of resources and production of waste. Therefore, the size of ecological footprints also varies.

The average U.S. citizen's ecological footprint is larger than 24 football fields and is one of the largest in the world. Nations such as China and India have smaller ecological footprints, but many more "feet." These countries' populations are more than three times the size of the U.S. population.

 Which region has the second largest ecological footprint?

_____

_____

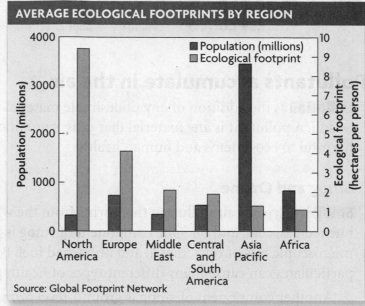

**AVERAGE ECOLOGICAL FOOTPRINTS BY REGION**

Legend: ■ Population (millions)  ■ Ecological footprint

Source: Global Footprint Network

Different regions of the world have varying levels of impact on their environment. This graph shows the average ecological footprint of populations around the world.

## 16.1   Vocabulary Check

**Mark It Up**

Go back and highlight each sentence that has a vocabulary word in **bold**.

nonrenewable resource          ecological footprint
renewable resource

Fill in the blanks with the correct term from the list above.

1. A(n) _____ cannot be used up, or is remade as fast as it is used.

2. The size of a(n) _____ depends on the amount of resources used and waste produced.

## 16.1   The Big Picture

3. Can the supply of oil and gas ever run out? Explain your response.

_____

_____

4. What is one way individuals can decrease the size of their ecological footprints? _____

_____

# 16.2 Air Quality

**KEY CONCEPT** Fossil fuel emissions affect the biosphere.

## Pollutants accumulate in the air.

**Pollution** is the addition of any undesirable material to the air, water, or soil. A pollutant is any material that causes pollution. Pollutants are harmful to ecosystems and human health.

### Smog and Ozone

**Smog** is a type of air pollution that forms from the waste products of burned gas, coal, and oil. One component of smog is **particulates,** microscopic bits of dust, metal, and unburned fuel. Breathing air with particulates can cause many different types of health problems.

Another component of smog is ground-level ozone. The ozone that is formed from pollution stays near the ground and is harmful to human health and to ecosystems. Ozone is also found in the upper atmosphere. There, ozone plays an important role in protecting Earth from ultraviolet rays found in sunlight.

### Acid Rain

Chemicals produced from the burning of coal and oil can become part of Earth's cycles, including the water cycle. **Acid rain** is produced when pollutants in the water cycle cause the pH of rain to drop below normal.

Recall that pH 7 is neutral. All rain is slightly acidic and has a pH of around 5.6. When pollutants become part of the water cycle, they can react with water and oxygen and cause acid rain, which has a pH lower than 5.6. Acid rain falls in many areas of the United States. It threatens water supplies and harms ecosystems.

> **VISUAL VOCAB**
>
> **Acid rain** is a type of rain produced when pollutants in the water cycle cause rain pH to drop below normal levels.
>
> Acid rain          Normal rain
> pH 4.6              pH 5.6
>
> — H+ ions —

 How are the effects of ground level ozone different from the effects of ozone in the upper atmosphere?

## Air pollution is changing Earth's biosphere.

Carbon dioxide is a natural part of Earth's atmosphere. The levels of carbon dioxide rise and fall over time as a natural part of Earth's climate cycles. Times of high carbon dioxide levels are also times of warmer global climates. Lower carbon dioxide levels are times of cooler global climates.

## The Greenhouse Effect

It can be cold outside but warm inside a car that is parked in a sunny place. It can also be warm inside a greenhouse on a cold day. Like the greenhouse glass that helps to trap heat, Earth's atmosphere contains gases that help to slow the loss of heat. These gases are called greenhouse gases, and the process by which they slow the loss of heat is called the **greenhouse effect.**

Carbon dioxide, water vapor, and methane are three of the most common greenhouse gases. You can think of these gases as forming a blanket that helps to keep Earth warm. The greenhouse effect keeps Earth warm enough to support life.

carbon dioxide ($CO_2$)

methane ($CH_4$)    water ($H_2O$)

Carbon dioxide, water vapor, and methane are three of the most common greenhouse gases.

## Global Warming

Over the last 100 years, the average global temperature has risen. Global temperature changes are a normal part of Earth's climate cycle. But changes in temperature usually happen over tens of thousands of years—not over 100 years.

The trend of increasing global temperatures is called **global warming.** The warming is a result of increases in greenhouse gases. The increases in greenhouse gases come from automobiles, industry, and other human activities.

Global warming already threatens ecosystems around the world. Increased flooding, stronger tropical storms, and a loss of biodiversity are a few of the threats that may be caused by global warming. The polar ice cap is melting, and may affect global weather patterns. The future of global warming is uncertain, but continued global warming could greatly change our planet.

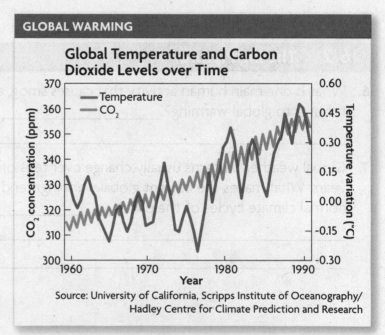

**GLOBAL WARMING**

**Global Temperature and Carbon Dioxide Levels over Time**

Source: University of California, Scripps Institute of Oceanography/ Hadley Centre for Climate Prediction and Research

As automobile use and industry have grown, so have the levels of carbon dioxide and other greenhouse gases in the atmosphere. This graph shows average global temperature changes (blue) against atmospheric carbon dioxide levels (gray) measured at Mauna Loa Observatory in Hawaii.

 How has air pollution contributed to global warming?

_____

_____

**Mark It Up**

Go back and highlight each sentence that has a vocabulary word in **bold**.

| | |
|---|---|
| pollution | acid rain |
| smog | greenhouse effect |
| particulates | global warming |

**Match each clue below with the correct term from the list above.**

1. one component of smog _____

2. a trend of increasing global temperatures _____

3. keeps heat from escaping Earth _____

4. rain with reduced pH due to pollution _____

5. a kind of air pollution _____

## 16.2 The Big Picture

6. What is one main human activity that causes smog, acid rain, and contributes to global warming? _____

_____

7. Global weather patterns usually change over tens of thousands of years. What makes the current global warming trend different from normal climate cycles of the past? _____

_____

_____

# 16.3 Water Quality

**KEY CONCEPT** Pollution of Earth's freshwater supply threatens habitat and health.

## Water pollution affects ecosystems.

Pollution can have major effects on water ecosystems. Chemical contaminants, sewage, trash, and other wastes can end up in rivers, lakes, and other waters all over the world.

One way scientists determine the health of an ecosystem is by studying particular organisms, called **indicator species.** These species give a sign, or indication, of the health of an ecosystem. Frogs, for example, are sometimes used as indicator species for water quality. In polluted waters, frogs may have tumors or grow extra arms or legs.

 What is an indicator species? _____

_____

## Biomagnification causes accumulation of toxins in the food chain.

Pollutants that dissolve in water will exit an organism through its wastes. Other types of pollutants do not dissolve in water, and will stay in the body fat of an organism. These pollutants will move from organism to organism up the food chain. **Biomagnification** is the process by which pollutants move up the food chain. The pollutants will accumulate, or collect, in organisms highest up the food chain.

For example, pollutants wash into a lake. Phytoplankton take in small amounts of these pollutants. Zooplankton feed on phytoplankton, and take in the pollutants from all of the phytoplankton they eat. Small fish eat many zooplankton, and therefore take in even larger amounts these pollutants. Larger fish eat the smaller fish, and the pollutants build up even more.

**BIOMAGNIFICATION**

**The movement of fat-soluble pollutants through a food chain results in higher concentrations in the top consumer.**

herring gull eggs
124 ppm

lake trout
4.83 ppm

smelt
1.04 ppm

zooplankton
0.123 ppm

phytoplankton
0.025 ppm

ppm = parts per million

The top predator receives the largest dose of the pollutant. For example, the beluga whale is a top predator in certain ocean environments. A beluga whale population in eastern Canada has such extreme levels of toxic chemicals that dead whales are sometimes treated as hazardous waste. Humans are also top-level consumers and can be affected by biomagnification.

 **INSTANT REPLAY** Look back at the biomagnification figure on page 275. Which of the organisms shown has the highest concentration of pollutants? _____

_____

## 16.3    Vocabulary Check

**Mark It Up**

Go back and highlight each sentence that has a vocabulary word in **bold**.

indicator species

biomagnification

1. *To indicate* means "to give a sign." What does an indicator species indicate? _____

_____

2. *To magnify* means "to increase, or make larger." What gets magnified in biomagnification? _____

_____

## 16.3    The Big Picture

3. Why are the top level consumers in a food chain most affected by biomagnification? _____

_____

_____

4. Does biomagnification affect humans? Explain your response. _____

_____

_____

_____

# 16.4 Threats to Biodiversity

**KEY CONCEPT** The impact of a growing human population threatens biodiversity.

## Preserving biodiversity is important to the future of the biosphere.

Recall that biodiversity is the variety of organisms in an ecosystem. Biodiversity gives stability to an ecosystem. In other words, it helps an ecosystem adjust to changes. Biodiversity is also important for medicine and technology. Nearly half of all prescribed medicines are based on plant substances. Natural substances are also important models for many technologies. But biodiversity is not just measured in dollars. Biodiversity ensures the future health of Earth.

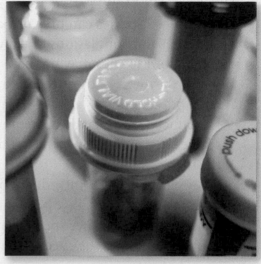

Nearly half of all prescribed medicines are based on plant substances.

Many human actions threaten biodiversity. Loss of habitat and pollution are harming animal and plant populations around the world. Rain forests have the most biodiversity and are the most threatened ecosystems in the world. Preserving rain forests is an important part of preserving the biodiversity of our planet.

 How does biodiversity affect the stability of ecosystems?

_____

_____

## Loss of habitat eliminates species.

As the human population grows, humans are destroying more and more natural areas. Human activities also form barriers, such as roads and highways, which prevent organisms from moving between different parts of their habitats.

Barriers break a habitat into pieces, causing **habitat fragmentation.** As a result, organisms cannot move freely through their habitat. Some areas have built bridges and tunnels to connect habitats that are separated by roads.

 How does habitat fragmentation affect organisms?

_____

_____

## Introduced species can disrupt stable relationships in an ecosystem.

Native species are organisms with evolutionary histories in a particular habitat. In contrast, an **introduced species** is any organism that was brought to an ecosystem as the result of human actions. Introduced species can disrupt an ecosystem in many ways. For example,

The release of pets, such as snakes, into the wild is one way that non-native species get introduced into ecosystems.

- Introduced species can prey on native species. This predation decreases the populations of native species.

- Introduced species may not have predators in the habitat where they were introduced. As a result, they may have very large populations.

- Introduced species may be better competitors than native species in a particular niche, pushing the native species out of the niche.

Some species have been introduced because of irresponsible human activities. Other species have been introduced by accident, as humans travel the globe. Still other species have been introduced on purpose, but without any idea that the species could cause harm.

### Effect on Native Species

The Florida Everglades is an ecosystem with plants and animals that have evolved together for tens of thousands of years. A snake called a Burmese python is an introduced species in this ecosystem. The python eats small animals, and may threaten endangered species in the Everglades. The snakes are native to Southeastern Asia, and are sold in the United States as pets. Irresponsible owners have released some of these snakes into the Everglades.

Introduced species of plants also disrupt ecosystems. A plant called kudzu was introduced to the U.S. in the late 1800s as a houseplant. It was also planted outdoors. This plant was meant to be helpful in controlling erosion. However, it is now a problem in many of the eastern states. It grows very fast and covers native plants, blocking them from sunlight.

## Economic Damage

Introduced species also cause economic damage. The common house mouse, for example, was introduced to Australia in the late 1700s. These mice can cause big problems for farmers by eating through their crops. During 1993–1994, it was estimated that mice cost Australian farmers $65 million in lost crops.

Mice are an introduced species in Australia that have caused economic damage.

 **INSTANT REPLAY** What is one example of an introduced species? _____

_____

---

### 16.4 Vocabulary Check

habitat fragmentation
introduced species

**Mark It Up**

Go back and highlight each sentence that has a vocabulary word in **bold**.

1. How does habitat fragmentation affect an ecosystem? _____

_____

_____

2. How is an introduced species different from a native species? _____

_____

_____

---

### 16.4 The Big Picture

3. What is the importance of biodiversity to humans and to ecosystems?

_____

_____

4. How does the loss of habitat affect biodiversity? _____

_____

_____

5. How can an introduced species affect an ecosystem? _____

_____

_____

# 16.5 Conservation

**KEY CONCEPT** Conservation methods can help protect and restore ecosystems.

## Sustainable development manages resources for present and future generations.

Currently, most use of natural resources is unsustainable. This unsustainable use of resources meets current needs, but is harmful to future generations. **Sustainable development** is a practice in which natural resources are used and managed in a way that meets current needs and does not harm future generations. Changes to current practices can lead to a more sustainable use of resources.

 What are two components of sustainable development?

_____

## Conservation practices focus on a few species but benefit entire ecosystems.

Some laws, such as the Endangered Species Act, protect individual species. For the protected species to survive, its habitat must be protected. Because the habitat is protected, other species that live in the same habitat also benefit. The species that is legally protected is called an **umbrella species,** because its protection allows many other species to be protected.

The manatee, for example, is a protected mammal that lives in the Gulf of Mexico and the Atlantic Ocean along the southeastern coast of the United States. Efforts to protect the manatee involve protecting the waters in which they live and the seagrass that is their main food source. As a result, the entire ecosystem benefits from efforts to save a single species.

 How does the protection of the manatee benefit coastal ecosystems? _____

_____

**VISUAL VOCAB**

When an **umbrella species** is protected, the other species in the same habitat, or under the same "umbrella," also benefit.

**HABITAT**

## Protecting Earth's resources helps protect our future.

All living things, including humans, share Earth and its resources. Humans can have a very negative impact on our environment by polluting, destroying habitats, and introducing species.

But humans also have the ability and the technology to change the extent of the damage to our planet. Our economies and our lives depend on a healthy, sustainable Earth. We can

- control population growth by controlling birth rates
- develop technology to produce more food and less waste
- change our practices to limit the damage to ecosystems
- take action to protect ecosystems

Public actions also help to preserve and protect the future of our planet. Currently, for example, there are laws that protect air, water, and particular species. There are also national parks that protect natural areas from development.

Bald eagle populations recovered after laws helped to protect this species.

 **What type of public action helped protect the bald eagle?**

_____

_____

## 16.5  Vocabulary Check

sustainable development
umbrella species

**Mark It Up**

Go back and highlight each sentence that has a vocabulary word in **bold**.

1. Write a brief definition of *sustainable development*. _____

_____

2. Write a brief definition of *umbrella species*. _____

_____

## 16.5  The Big Picture

3. How is it possible that the protection of one species can benefit an entire ecosystem? _____

_____

4. What is one way public action is helping to protect Earth's resources?

_____

_____

# Chapter 16 Review

1. Which energy source is more sustainable—renewable resources or nonrenewable resources? Explain your response. _____
   _____
   _____

2. Wood can be a renewable resource. Under what conditions might wood become a *nonrenewable* resource? _____
   _____

3. How does a growing human population threaten Earth's resources?
   _____
   _____

4. Toxins accumulate in high-level consumers through _____.

   a. smog

   b. particulates

   c. indicator species

   d. biomagnification

5. How can the protection of just one species, such as the manatee, benefit other species in the same habitat? _____
   _____
   _____

6. The opposite of a native species is

   a. an introduced species

   b. an indicator species

   c. a predator

   d. an umbrella species

7. What is the main goal of sustainable development? _____
   _____
   _____

# 17 The Tree of Life

## GETTING READY TO LEARN

### Preview Key Concepts

**17.1 The Linnaean System of Classification**
Organisms can be classified based on physical similarities.

**17.2 Classification Based on Evolutionary Relationships**
Modern classification is based on evolutionary relationships.

**17.3 Molecular Clocks**
Molecular clocks provide clues to evolutionary history.

**17.4 Domains and Kingdoms**
The current tree of life has three domains.

## Review Academic Vocabulary

Write the correct word for each definition.

convergent evolution      eukaryotic      prokaryotic      species

1. _____ : cell containing a nucleus and membrane-bound organelles

2. _____ : cell not containing a nucleus or membrane-bound organelles

3. _____ : process in which two unrelated species evolve similar traits while adapting to similar environments

4. _____ : group of organisms that can breed and produce fertile offspring

## Preview Biology Vocabulary

Try to guess the meaning of each boldfaced word from its context.

| PHRASE | MY GUESS |
|---|---|
| 1. The scientific name for humans, written in **binomial nomenclature**, is *Homo sapiens*. | |
| 2. Scientists can use genetic and fossil evidence to study the **phylogeny** for a group of species. | |
| 3. Each **taxon** in the Linnaean classification system gets more and more specific, from kingdom to species. | |
| 4. The evolutionary relationships among certain species can be shown visually in a **cladogram**. | |

# 17.1 The Linnaean System of Classification

**KEY CONCEPT** Organisms can be classified based on physical similarities.

## Linnaeus developed the scientific naming system still used today.

Do you know what an Irish daisy is? What about a lion's tooth flower? A dandelion? Irish daisy, lion's tooth, and dandelion are all common names for the same flower. You can imagine how confusing it could be for scientists to try to talk about a particular organism if everyone has a different name for it.

In the 1750s, the Swedish botanist Carolus Linnaeus developed a system for classifying* and naming living things. Linnaeus' system gave naturalists a common language, which made it easier for them to talk about their findings with one another.

### Taxonomy

**Taxonomy** is the science of naming and classifying organisms. Linnaean taxonomy classifies organisms based on their physical similarities. A group of organisms in a classification system is called a **taxon** (plural, *taxa*). The species is the basic taxon of the Linnaean system. A species is a group of organisms that can breed and produce offspring that can reproduce. With a few changes, the Linnaean system of naming is still used today.

### Scientific Names

**Binomial nomenclature** (by-NOH-mee-uhl NOH-muhn-KLAY-chuhr) is a system that gives each species a two-part scientific name using Latin words. The first part of the name is the genus. The second part describes the species.

- **Genus** A **genus** (plural, genera) includes one or more species that are thought to be closely related. For example, the genus *Quercus* includes more than 500 species of oak trees. Genus names always begin with a capital letter. They are written in italics or underlined.

**Cardinal**

The cardinal is a species of bird. A species is the basic taxon of the Linnean system.

### VISUAL VOCAB

**Binomial nomenclature** is a standard naming system that gives each species a two-part name using Latin words.

| two | name | naming | system |
| --- | --- | --- | --- |

**bi** nomial **nomen** clature

(1) *Genus* (2) *species*

---

\* ACADEMIC VOCABULARY

**classifying** organizing into groups

- **Species descriptor**  The second part of the name describes the species. The species descriptor is also written in italics or underlined. It is written in lowercase letters. *Quercus alba* is the scientific name for white oak trees.

The species descriptor is never written alone because the same descriptor may be used for many different genera. For example, *Quercus alba* is the scientific name for white oak trees and *Tyto alba* is the scientific name for barn owls. The descriptor *alba* means "white." Alone, *alba* does not refer to any particular species.

There can be many different common names for one particular species. Irish daisy, lion's tooth, and dandelion are all common names. But there is only one scientific name for this plant: *Taraxacum officinale*. Not only can there be many names for an organism in one language, but there are many more names for an organism in different languages. Scientific names help scientists around the world talk about particular organisms without confusion.

 Find the scientific name for dandelion in the paragraph above. Circle the genus. Draw a box around the species descriptor.

## Linnaeus' classification system has seven levels.

The Linnaean system of classification has seven levels: kingdom, phylum (plural, *phyla*), class, order, family, genus, and species. The most general level is kingdom. A kingdom contains one or more phyla. A phylum contains one or more classes, and so on.

 Underline the seven levels of Linnaeus' classification system.

## The Linnaean classification system has limitations.

Linnaeus' system is based on physical similarities between organisms. However, organisms that are physically similar are not always closely related. Recall that unrelated species can evolve similar traits through convergent evolution, as they adapt to similar environments.

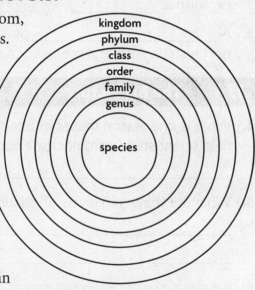

Each level in the Linnaean system of classification is nested, or included, in the level above it.

Today, scientists use molecular and genetic research to help classify living things. Genetic similarities give strong evidence that organisms are related. Genetic information has resulted in some organisms getting reclassified into different groups.

What is one limitation of Linnaeus' classification system?

_____

_____

## 17.1 Vocabulary Check

taxonomy                    binomial nomenclature

taxon                        genus

**Mark It Up**

Go back and highlight each sentence that has a vocabulary word in **bold**.

Fill in the blanks with the correct term from the list above.

1. Binomial nomenclature has two parts: the _____ and the species descriptor.

2. _____ is the science of naming and classifying organisms.

3. A _____ is a group of organisms in a classification system, such as a species or a genus.

## 17.1 The Big Picture

4. What is one reason that scientific names, instead of common names, help scientists to communicate about organisms? _____

_____

5. What are the seven levels of classification, from biggest to smallest?

_____

_____

6. Linnaeus' classification system is based on physical similarities. What type of information has been used more recently to determine relationships between organisms? _____

_____

_____

# 17.2 Classification Based on Evolutionary Relationships

**KEY CONCEPT** Modern classification is based on evolutionary relationships.

## Cladistics is classification based on common ancestry.

Today, scientists agree that organisms should be classified based on evolutionary relationships and not just physical similarities. Sometimes, physical similarities can give evidence for evolutionary relationships. Other times, physical similarities do not mean that organisms are related. For example, both birds and bats have wings, but they are not closely related.

### Phylogeny

The evolutionary history for a group of species is called a **phylogeny** (fy-LAHJ-uh-nee). A phylogeny is made using more than just physical similarities. It is made using evidence from living species, the fossil record, and molecular data, such as DNA and protein sequences. Phylogenies can be shown as branching tree diagrams. Each branch represents a species or another taxon. An evolutionary tree shows how different groups of species are related to each other.

### Cladistics

The most common method used to make evolutionary trees is called cladistics. **Cladistics** (kluh-DIHS-tihks) is classification based on evolutionary relationships, or common ancestry. A **cladogram** is an evolutionary tree that suggests how species may be related.

Over evolutionary time, certain traits in a group of species, or a clade, stay the same. Each species also has traits that have changed over time. **Derived characters** are traits that are shared by some species but not by others. These traits can be used to figure out evolutionary relationships. The more closely related species are, the more derived characters they will share.

What does a cladogram show? _____

_____

> **VOCABULARY**
>
> At the root of the words *cladistics* and *cladogram* is the word *clade*. A clade is a group of species that shares a common ancestor.

## Interpreting a Cladogram

The main features of a cladogram are shown in the cladogram for tetrapods below. Tetrapods are vertebrates that share a common ancestor with four limbs. Some tetrapods, such as snakes, no longer have the four limbs that their known ancestors have.

**Derived characters** Derived characters are shown as hash marks. All species above a hash mark share the derived character it represents. There are six derived characters labeled on the tetrapod cladogram.

**Nodes** Each place where a branch splits is called a node. Nodes represent the most recent common ancestor shared by a clade. There are five nodes on the tetrapod cladogram.

**Identifying clades** You can identify a clade by using the "snip rule." Whenever you "snip" a branch under a node, a clade falls off. There are five clades in the tetrapod cladogram.

---

**CLADOGRAM FOR TETRAPODS**

A **cladogram** shows the likely evolutionary relationships among a group of species based on common ancestry and derived characters.

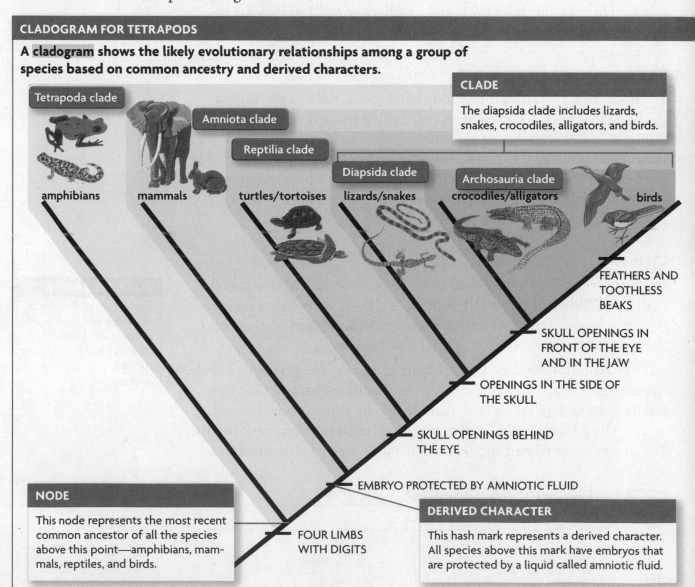

**CLADE**

The diapsida clade includes lizards, snakes, crocodiles, alligators, and birds.

Tetrapoda clade

Amniota clade

Reptilia clade

Diapsida clade

Archosauria clade

amphibians    mammals    turtles/tortoises    lizards/snakes    crocodiles/alligators    birds

FEATHERS AND TOOTHLESS BEAKS

SKULL OPENINGS IN FRONT OF THE EYE AND IN THE JAW

OPENINGS IN THE SIDE OF THE SKULL

SKULL OPENINGS BEHIND THE EYE

EMBRYO PROTECTED BY AMNIOTIC FLUID

**NODE**

This node represents the most recent common ancestor of all the species above this point—amphibians, mammals, reptiles, and birds.

FOUR LIMBS WITH DIGITS

**DERIVED CHARACTER**

This hash mark represents a derived character. All species above this mark have embryos that are protected by a liquid called amniotic fluid.

# Molecular evidence reveals species' relatedness.

An evolutionary tree is always a work in progress. With new evidence, trees can be changed to show how species are likely related.

Today, molecular evidence, such as DNA sequences, is used to help learn about species relatedness. In some cases, molecular data agree with classification based on physical similarities. In other cases, molecular data lead scientists to classify species in a different way.

**What can lead scientists to change an evolutionary tree?**

_____

_____

| 17.2 | Vocabulary Check |
| --- | --- |

**Mark It Up**

Go back and highlight each sentence that has a vocabulary word in **bold**.

phylogeny        cladogram

cladistics        derived character

Use the correct term from the list above to answer questions about the diagram below.

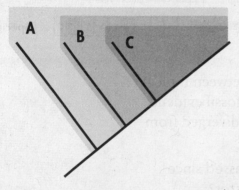

1. What type of diagram is shown above? _____

2. The _____ for a group of species is represented by this type of diagram.

3. Make a mark on the diagram above to represent a derived character shared by species A, B, and C.

4. What method is used to make this type of branching tree shown above? _____

| 17.2 | The Big Picture |
| --- | --- |

5. What types of information are used to make a cladogram? _____

_____

_____

# 17.3 Molecular Clocks

**KEY CONCEPT** Molecular clocks provide clues to evolutionary history.

## Molecular clocks use mutations to estimate evolutionary time.

Recall from Chapter 8 that a mutation is a change in an organism's DNA. Mutations happen regularly over evolutionary time. With more time, more mutations build up. Therefore, the more time that has passed since two species branched from a common ancestor, the more molecular differences they will have. Species that are closely related will have fewer differences. A **molecular clock** is a model that uses mutation rates to measure evolutionary time.

**MOLECULAR EVOLUTION**

Mutations add up at a fairly constant rate in the DNA of species that evolved from a common ancestor.

DNA sequence from a common ancestor

Ten million years later— one mutation in each lineage

The DNA sequences from two descendant species show mutations that have accumulated (black).

Another ten million years later— one more mutation in each lineage

The mutation rate of this sequence equals one mutation per ten million years.

Species A

Species B

To estimate mutation rates, scientists must find links between molecular data and real time. For example, geologic events and fossil evidence can help scientists to figure out how long ago two species diverged from a common ancestor.

 Look at the figure above. How much time has passed since species A and B branched from a common ancestor?

_____

## Mitochondrial DNA and ribosomal RNA provide two types of molecular clocks.

DNA and RNA are found in several parts of cells. The DNA in the nucleus of cells is called nuclear DNA. Mitochondria, the energy factories of cells, contain mitochondrial DNA. Ribosomes, the organelles that make proteins, contain ribosomal RNA.

Different molecules have different mutation rates. Scientists can choose which molecule to use as a molecular clock depending on what they are measuring. Molecules with faster mutation rates can be used as molecular clocks for recent evolutionary time. Molecules with slower mutation rates can be used as molecular clocks when studying longer periods of evolutionary time.

**Animal Cell**

nucleus

ribosome

mitochondrion

Mitochondrial DNA and ribosomal RNA are both used as molecular clocks.

- **Mitochondrial DNA** (mtDNA) has a mutation rate that is faster than nuclear DNA. It is therefore useful for studying closely-related species that have diverged from a common ancestor recently in evolutionary time.

- **Ribosomal RNA** (rRNA) has regions that have a very slow mutation rate. This makes it useful for studying distantly-related species, such as those in different kingdoms, which have diverged from a common ancestor much longer ago.

Similarly, you use different "clocks" depending on how much time you are measuring. You probably use hours to measure your day, but you wouldn't use hours to measure your age—you would use years.

INSTANT REPLAY

Which molecule is more useful for studying distant evolutionary time—mitochondrial DNA or ribosomal RNA?

_____

_____

## 17.3 Vocabulary Check

**Mark It Up**

Go back and highlight each sentence that has a vocabulary word in **bold**.

molecular clock        ribosomal RNA
mitochondrial DNA

Match the description below with the correct term from the list above.

**1.** slow mutation rate _____

**2.** fast mutation rate _____

## 17.3 The Big Picture

**3.** What does a molecular clock measure? _____

_____

**4.** Why might a scientist choose mitochondrial DNA instead of ribosomal RNA as a molecular clock? _____

_____

# 17.4 Domains and Kingdoms

**KEY CONCEPT** The current tree of life has three domains.

## Classification is always a work in progress.

The tree of life is a model that shows the most current understanding of how all living things are related. Over time, the organization of the tree of life has changed. With new findings and new discoveries, scientists changed how organisms are classified.

Until the mid-1800s, all living things were divided into two kingdoms: Plantae (plants) and Animalia (animals). Then, a third kingdom, called Protista, was added for single-celled organisms. A fourth kingdom, called Monera, was added in the early 1900s to give prokaryotes a kingdom of their own. In the mid-1900s, kingdom Fungi was added for organisms such as mushrooms and molds. In 1977, kingdom Monera was divided into two groups of prokaryotes—Bacteria and Archaea. Each of these changes was based on new scientific findings.

> **Connecting CONCEPTS**
>
> **Classification** Recall from Section 17.1 that the kingdom is the largest category in the Linnaean classification system.

| HISTORY OF THE KINGDOM SYSTEM | | | | |
|---|---|---|---|---|
| **1753 Two kingdoms** | **1866 Three kingdoms** | **1938 Four kingdoms** | **1959 Five kingdoms** | **1977 Six kingdoms** |

Genetic studies show that the two groups of prokaryotes, bacteria and archaea, are very different from each other. In terms of genes, they are more different from each other than animals are from plants.

 In which of the six kingdoms are humans categorized? _____

## The three domains in the tree of life are Bacteria, Archaea, and Eukarya.

The six kingdoms can be divided into three domains. A domain is a grouping larger than a kingdom. Prokaryotes are divided into two domains: Bacteria and Archaea. All eukaryotes are placed into a third domain, called Eukarya.

| Prokaryote | Eukaryote |
|---|---|

A prokaryotic cell does not have a membrane-bound nucleus or organelles. A eukaryotic cell has a membrane-bound nucleus and organelles.

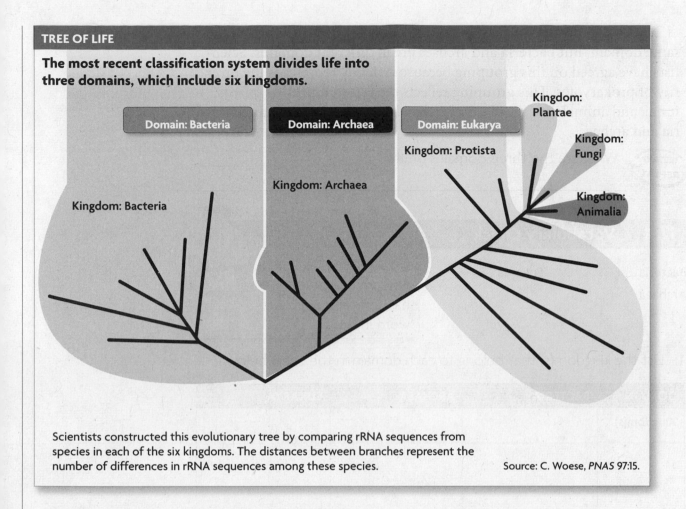

## TREE OF LIFE

**The most recent classification system divides life into three domains, which include six kingdoms.**

Domain: Bacteria

Domain: Archaea

Domain: Eukarya

Kingdom: Plantae

Kingdom: Fungi

Kingdom: Animalia

Kingdom: Protista

Kingdom: Archaea

Kingdom: Bacteria

Scientists constructed this evolutionary tree by comparing rRNA sequences from species in each of the six kingdoms. The distances between branches represent the number of differences in rRNA sequences among these species.

Source: C. Woese, *PNAS* 97:15.

- **Bacteria** The domain **Bacteria** includes the single-celled prokaryotes in the kingdom Bacteria. This domain is one of the largest groups of organisms on Earth. In fact, there are more bacteria in your mouth than there are people that have ever lived! Bacteria are often classified by their shape or whether they cause disease.
- **Archaea** The domain **Archaea** (ahr-KEE-uh) contains single-celled prokaryotes in the kingdom Archaea. Archaea and bacteria are both single-celled prokaryotes, but the two groups of organisms have many differences. For example, they have very different cell wall chemistry. Archaea are often classified for the extreme environments they can live in, such as deep sea vents and hot geysers.
- **Eukarya** The domain **Eukarya** (yoo-KAR-ee-uh) is made up of all organisms with eukaryotic cells. Some eukaryotes are single-celled, like most protists. Other eukaryotes are multicellular, like you. The domain Eukarya includes the kingdoms Protista, Plantae, Fungi, and Animalia.

Notice that protists, plants, fungi, and animals are all grouped in the same domain. But bacteria and archaea are in different domains. Scientists have agreed on this grouping because it clearly represents the diversity of prokaryotes. This grouping reflects the fact that protists, plants, fungi, and animals are more closely related to each other than are bacteria and archaea.

**INSTANT REPLAY** What are the three domains of life? _____

_____

## 17.4 Vocabulary Check

**Mark It Up**

Go back and highlight each sentence that has a vocabulary word in **bold.**

Bacteria      Eukarya

Archaea

**1.** List the kingdom(s) that belong to each domain in the chart below.

| DOMAIN | BACTERIA | ARCHAEA | EUKARYA |
|--------|----------|---------|---------|
| Kingdom(s) | | | |

## 17.4 The Big Picture

**2.** Why has the classification of different groups of living things changed over the years? _____

_____

**3.** How is a kingdom different from a domain? _____

_____

# Chapter 17 Review

1. The scientific name for the grey wolf is *Canis lupis.* Draw a circle around the genus. Draw a square around the species descriptor.

2. Based on the information in the cladogram, which of the following pairs of organisms is most closely related?
   a. 1 & 4
   b. 1 & 5
   c. 2 & 5
   d. 4 & 5

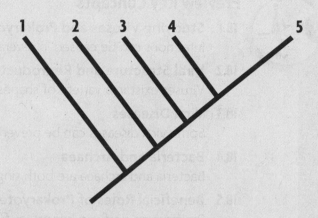

3. What information does a cladogram give?
   a. the physical similarities among species
   b the evolutionary relationships among species
   c. the number of years ago that species evolved
   d. the taxonomy of species

4. What key information does modern classification rely upon that was not available in Linnaeus' time? _____

_____

5. Arrange the following terms in order from largest grouping of organisms to smallest grouping of organisms: *family, class, domain, phylum, species, kingdom, genus, order* _____

_____

6. Name two types of molecules that are commonly used as molecular clocks. _____

7. Which kingdoms are included in each of the three domains? _____

_____

_____

8. Do you think that the current organization in the tree of life will ever change? Defend your answer. _____

_____

_____

# 18 Viruses and Prokaryotes

## GETTING READY TO LEARN

### Preview Key Concepts

**18.1 Studying Viruses and Prokaryotes**
Infections can be caused in several ways.

**18.2 Viral Structure and Reproduction**
Viruses exist in a variety of shapes and sizes.

**18.3 Viral Diseases**
Some viral diseases can be prevented with vaccines.

**18.4 Bacteria and Archaea**
Bacteria and archaea are both single-celled prokaryotes.

**18.5 Beneficial Roles of Prokaryotes**
Prokaryotes perform important functions for organisms and ecosystems.

**18.6 Bacterial Diseases and Antibiotics**
Understanding bacteria is necessary to prevent and treat disease.

### Review Academic Vocabulary

Write the correct word for each definition.

archaea        homeostasis        lipid

1. _____ : prokaryotes belonging to one of the three domains of life

2. _____ : nonnpolar molecule made of carbon, hydrogen, and oxygen

3. _____ : condition of constant internal conditions

### Preview Biology Vocabulary

To see how many key terms you already know from this chapter, choose the word that makes sense in each sentence.

antibiotic        toxin        vaccine

1. A doctor may prescribe a(n) _____ if you have a bacterial infection.

2. You may have received a(n) _____ in the form of a shot to prevent getting the flu.

3. Any poison produced by an organism, including the oil produced by poison ivy, is a(n) _____ .

# 18.1 Studying Viruses and Prokaryotes

**KEY CONCEPT** Infections can be caused in several ways.

## Viruses, bacteria, viroids, and prions can all cause infection.

Any living organism or particle* that can cause an infectious disease is called a **pathogen.** An infectious disease is an illness that can be passed from one organism to another. Bacteria, viruses, viroids, and prions can all be pathogens. Although many types of bacteria are helpful—and even necessary—for your health, some types of bacteria can make you sick.

**RELATIVE SIZES OF CELLS AND INFECTIOUS PARTICLES**

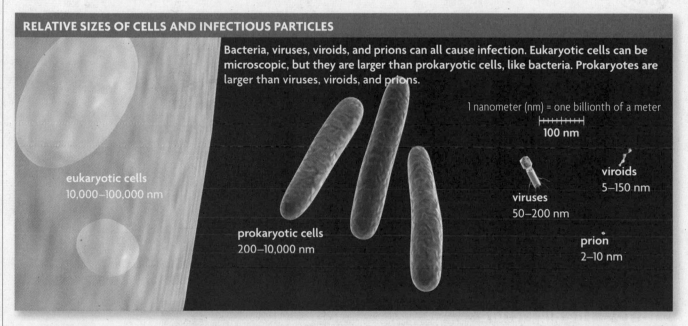

Bacteria, viruses, viroids, and prions can all cause infection. Eukaryotic cells can be microscopic, but they are larger than prokaryotic cells, like bacteria. Prokaryotes are larger than viruses, viroids, and prions.

1 nanometer (nm) = one billionth of a meter

100 nm

eukaryotic cells
10,000–100,000 nm

prokaryotic cells
200–10,000 nm

viruses
50–200 nm

viroids
5–150 nm

prion
2–10 nm

**Bacteria** These single-celled organisms are prokaryotes. Bacteria are living things—they contain DNA, use nutrients and energy, grow and reproduce, and respond to their environment.

**Viruses** A **virus** is an infectious particle made only of a piece of DNA or RNA surrounded by a protein coat. Viruses have some characteristics of living things, but not all. For example, they cannot reproduce on their own. They need living cells to help them reproduce and to make proteins.

**Viroids** A **viroid** is a piece of single-stranded RNA without a protein coat. Viroids cause diseases in plants, and are passed through seeds or pollen. Like a virus, a viroid cannot reproduce without the help of living cells.

**\* ACADEMIC VOCABULARY**

**particle** a little piece of something

**Prions** A **prion** (PREE-ahn) is an infectious particle made only of proteins. Recall from Chapter 2 that proteins have a three-dimensional shape. Prions cause proteins to fold incorrectly, so they end up with the wrong shape and do not work properly. Prions are different from other pathogens because they have no genetic material, but can still cause disease. Prion diseases are always deadly, because the body has no immune response against a protein. The illness commonly called mad cow disease is caused by prions.

This drawing shows the three-dimensional structure of the blood protein hemoglobin. The proper function of a protein is based on its shape. Prions affect the shape of proteins. As a result, the proteins will not work properly.

Circle the names of four pathogens presented above.

---

## 18.1 Vocabulary Check

virus           viroid

pathogen       prion

**Mark It Up**

Go back and highlight each sentence that has a vocabulary word in **bold**.

Match each clue below to the correct term from the list above.

1. made of protein only _____

2. made of DNA or RNA and a protein coat _____

3. causes infectious disease _____

4. made of RNA only _____

---

## 18.1 The Big Picture

5. Fill in the table below with the following terms: *bacteria, viruses, viroids,* and *prions.*

| PATHOGENS | |
|---|---|
| **LIVING CELLS** | **NOT LIVING CELLS** |
| | |

# 18.2 Viral Structure and Reproduction

**KEY CONCEPT**  Viruses exist in a variety of shapes and sizes.

## Viruses differ in shape and in ways of entering host cells.

Not all viruses are the same. They can be simple or complex in structure, and they have different ways of getting into host cells. Host cells are cells that are infected by a virus. Viruses can only reproduce after they have infected host cells.

### The Structure of Viruses

Viruses are made up of two main parts: a piece of genetic material, and a protein covering, or coat, called a **capsid.** Unlike eukaryotes and prokaryotes, the genetic material of viruses may be either DNA or RNA.

The shape of a virus plays an important role in how it works. The proteins on the surface of a viral capsid match a particular host—like a key fits a lock. Each type of virus can infect only certain hosts. Some viruses can infect several species. Others can infect only a single species.

### VIRAL SHAPES

**The different proteins that make up a viral capsid give viruses a variety of shapes.**

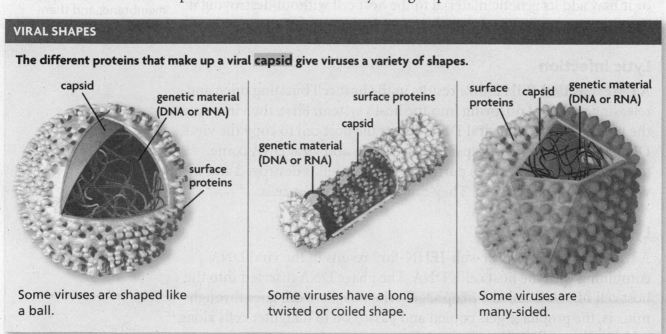

capsid

genetic material (DNA or RNA)

surface proteins

Some viruses are shaped like a ball.

surface proteins

capsid

genetic material (DNA or RNA)

Some viruses have a long twisted or coiled shape.

surface proteins

capsid

genetic material (DNA or RNA)

Some viruses are many-sided.

### Viruses that Infect Bacteria

**Bacteriophages** (bak-TEER-ee-uh-FAYJ-ihz) are a group of viruses that infect bacteria. Bacteriophages are often called "phages" for short. Phages attach to the outside of a bacterium, and inject their DNA into the cell.

### Viruses that Infect Eukaryotes

Viruses that infect eukaryotes enter a host cell differently than phages enter host bacterial cells. For example, viruses that infect eukaryotes may get taken into a cell through endocytosis. Once inside the eukaryotic cell, the virus finds the nucleus, where the host cell's DNA is located.

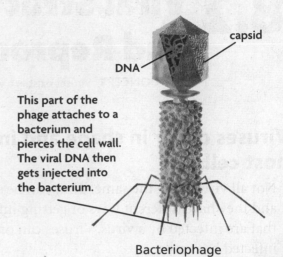

capsid

DNA

This part of the phage attaches to a bacterium and pierces the cell wall. The viral DNA then gets injected into the bacterium.

Bacteriophage

 **INSTANT REPLAY** What are the two main structural parts of a virus?

_____

## Viruses cause two types of infections.

Once inside a host cell, there are two basic pathways of infection that are similar for all viruses. A virus may end up destroying the host cell, or it may add its genetic material to the host cell without destroying it. These two pathways are shown for bacteriophages on the next page.

Endocytosis is a process in which a substance is surrounded by the cell membrane, and then released into the cell.

### Lytic Infection

A **lytic infection** (LIHT-ihk) results in the host cell bursting open and releasing new viral offspring into the host's system. First, the virus enters the host cell. Then, the viral DNA directs the host cell to copy the viral DNA and produce more capsids. The capsids and viral DNA come together to make new virus particles. The host cell is destroyed and the viral offspring are released. They can then infect other cells.

### Lysogenic Infection

A **lysogenic infection** (LY-suh-JEHN-ihk) results in the viral DNA combining with the host cell's DNA. The phage DNA inserted into the host cell's DNA is called a **prophage.** When the host cell goes through mitosis, the prophage gets copied and passed on to daughter cells along with the host cell's DNA. The prophage can remain a permanent part of the host cell's DNA. Or, it can enter the lytic cycle and produce new viruses.

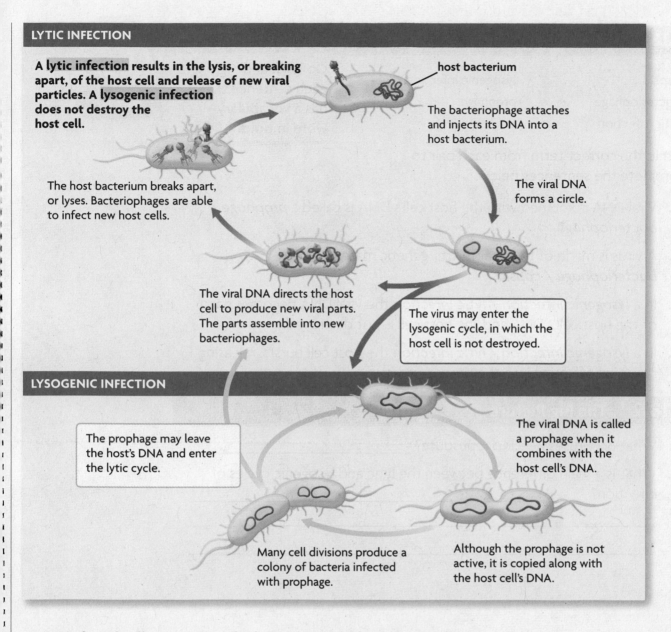

## LYTIC INFECTION

A **lytic infection** results in the lysis, or breaking apart, of the host cell and release of new viral particles. A **lysogenic infection** does not destroy the host cell.

host bacterium

The bacteriophage attaches and injects its DNA into a host bacterium.

The viral DNA forms a circle.

The host bacterium breaks apart, or lyses. Bacteriophages are able to infect new host cells.

The viral DNA directs the host cell to produce new viral parts. The parts assemble into new bacteriophages.

The virus may enter the lysogenic cycle, in which the host cell is not destroyed.

## LYSOGENIC INFECTION

The prophage may leave the host's DNA and enter the lytic cycle.

The viral DNA is called a prophage when it combines with the host cell's DNA.

Many cell divisions produce a colony of bacteria infected with prophage.

Although the prophage is not active, it is copied along with the host cell's DNA.

An infected cell may stay in the lysogenic cycle for a long time. A trigger, such as stress, can push the virus into the lytic cycle. The virus will then use the cell to produce new viruses.

In which cycle of infection are new viral particles released—lytic or lysogenic? _____

capsid

bacteriophage

lytic infection

lysogenic infection

prophage

### Mark It Up

Go back and highlight each sentence that has a vocabulary word in **bold**.

Circle the correct term from each pair to complete the sentences below.

1. Viral DNA combined with the host cell's DNA is called a *prophage / bacteriophage.*

2. A virus is made of two main parts, genetic material and a *bacteriophage / capsid.*

3. In a *lysogenic infection / lytic infection* the viral DNA becomes part of the host cell's DNA and the host cell is not destroyed.

4. In a *lysogenic infection / lytic infection* the host cell bursts, releasing new viral offspring into the host's system.

## 18.2 The Big Picture

5. What do viruses need to reproduce? _____

6. What is a main difference between the lytic and lysogenic cycles of infection? _____

_____

_____

# 18.3 Viral Diseases

**KEY CONCEPT** Some viral diseases can be prevented with vaccines.

## Viruses cause many infectious diseases.

Your body has defenses against viruses. Skin is your body's first defense. A virus cannot get through your skin unless there is an opening such as a cut or a scrape. A virus can also enter your body through other openings, such as the mouth, nose, genital areas, eyes, and ears. Some viral infections are deadly and others are barely noticeable. Several human illnesses caused by viruses are listed below.

### The Common Cold

More than 200 viruses cause the illness that we call the *common cold*. It is hard to find a cure for the common cold because it is caused by so many different viruses that mutate rapidly.

### Influenza

The influenza virus is often called the *flu* for short. The flu spreads quickly. There are often flu **epidemics,** or rapid outbreaks that affect many people. Subtypes of the flu can infect birds, horses, pigs, whales, and seals. Currently, only three subtypes infect humans. The flu can be controlled with a **vaccine** (vak-SEEN), a substance that gets the body's immune system to prepare a response against a virus. Flu viruses mutate rapidly, so a new vaccine must be made every year.

### SARS

SARS (severe acute respiratory disease) has symptoms similar to the flu, including fever and coughing. SARS first appeared in Asia in 2002. By the following summer it had spread to other countries.

### HIV

HIV (human immunodeficiency virus) is a type of virus called a **retrovirus.** *Retro-* means "backward." A retrovirus copies its genetic material "backwards." Usually, DNA is used to make a copy of RNA, but a retrovirus contains RNA that gets used to make DNA. The DNA then becomes part of the host cell's DNA.

Usually, DNA is used to make RNA. But retroviruses can use RNA to make DNA.

HIV can remain part of the host cell's DNA for many years with no symptoms. When the virus becomes active, it makes more viral particles. The host cells burst, and the new viruses can infect other cells. This stage of the disease destroys the host's white blood cells.

White blood cells are a very important part of the human immune response. The loss of white blood cells leads to AIDS, or acquired immune deficiency syndrome. Once a person's white blood cells are destroyed, she or he may be unable to fight off the common microorganisms that humans come into contact with every day.

HIV mutates very quickly, which makes it a challenge to treat. However, there are medicines that can help to slow the spread of the virus once a person is infected.

 Name three infectious diseases that are caused by viruses.

_____

| VIRAL DISEASE | | | |
|---|---|---|---|
| VIRAL INFECTION | SYMPTOMS OF DISEASE | TRANSMISSION OF DISEASE | U.S. VACCINE RECOMMENDATION |
| Chickenpox | *rash, itchy skin, fever, fatigue** | contact with rash, droplet inhalation | for children between 12 and 18 months |
| Hepatitis A | *yellow skin, fatigue, abdominal pain* | contact with contaminated feces | for people traveling to infected locations and protection during outbreaks |
| Mumps | *painful swelling in salivary glands, fever* | droplet inhalation | for children between 12 and 15 months and again at 4 to 6 years |
| Rabies | *anxiety, paralysis, fear of water* | bite from infected animal | for veterinarians and biologists in contact with wildlife |
| West Nile | *fever, headache, body ache* | bite from infected mosquito | no available vaccine |

## Vaccines are made from weakened pathogens.

In the United States, most children are vaccinated against diseases such as measles, mumps, and chicken pox. Every year, millions of people are vaccinated against influenza.

* ACADEMIC VOCABULARY

**fatigue** a feeling of tiredness

A vaccine contains the weakened virus or parts of the virus that it is supposed to protect against. A vaccine triggers the body's immune system response. Because the vaccine contains a weakened virus, it does not cause illness. But if the virus enters the body again, the body will be prepared to start an immune response before the virus can cause damage.

**INSTANT REPLAY** What main substance would an influenza vaccine contain?

_____

| 18.3 | Vocabulary Check | **Mark It Up** |

**Mark It Up**

Go back and highlight each sentence that has a vocabulary word in **bold**.

epidemic          retrovirus

vaccine

**Write a short definition for each vocabulary term.**

1. epidemic: _____

_____

2. vaccine: _____

_____

3. retrovirus _____

_____

## 18.3 The Big Picture

4. What is the body's first defense against infection? _____

5. How does a vaccine protect a person against infection? _____

_____

_____

6. Why is a person with AIDS more easily infected by pathogens than a person without AIDS? _____

_____

_____

# 18.4 Bacteria and Archaea

**KEY CONCEPT** Bacteria and archaea are both single-celled prokaryotes.

## Prokaryotes are widespread on Earth.

Bacteria and archaea live just about everywhere on Earth—even inside rocks and in polar ice caps. A drop of your saliva may contain 40 million bacterial cells. A gram of soil may contain 5 billion bacterial cells from over 10,000 types of bacteria. Prokaryotes are an important part of the communities in which they live.

Prokaryotes can be divided into groups based on their need for oxygen.

- An **obligate anaerobe** (AHB-lih-giht AN-uh-ROHB) cannot survive in the presence of oxygen.
- An **obligate aerobe** (AHB-lih-giht AIR-ohb) needs oxygen to survive.
- A **facultative aerobe** (FAK-uhl-tay-tihv AIR-ohb) can survive whether or not oxygen is present.

What is the difference between an obligate anaerobe and an obligate aerobe? _____

_____

> **VOCABULARY**
>
> Something that is *obligatory* is something that *must* happen. Something that is *facultative* is something that *may* happen but does not have to happen.

## Bacteria and archaea are structurally similar but have different molecular characteristics.

All prokaryotes either belong to the domain Archaea or the domain Bacteria. The two groups of organisms have similar appearances but have many differences in their genetics and biochemistry.

### Structural Comparison

- **Cell shape** Archaea come in many shapes. Bacteria have three common forms: rod-shaped, spiral-shaped, and spherical-shaped.
- **No organelles** Prokaryotes have no nucleus or other membrane-bound organelles.
- **DNA** Prokaryotic DNA is in the shape of a loop, or a circle, and is located in the cytoplasm.
- **Plasmids** Prokaryotes can also have plasmids. A **plasmid** is a small piece of DNA that replicates separately from the main chromosome.
- **Movement** Many bacteria and archaea use flagella to move. A **flagellum** (fluh-JEHL-uhm) is a long structure outside of the cell that is used to move. The flagella of bacteria and archaea look similar but they are structurally different.
- **Pili** Many prokaryotes have structures called pili, which are shorter and thinner than flagella. Pili help prokaryotes to stick to surfaces.

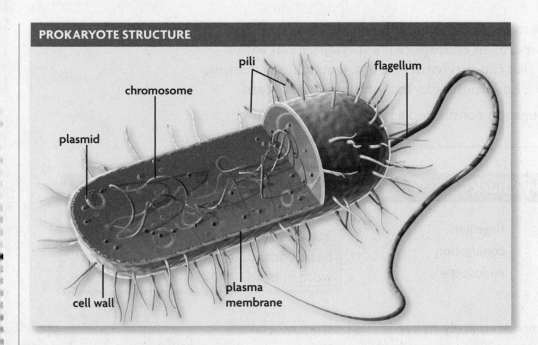

Molecular Comparison

Archaea and bacteria are very different on a molecular level. Molecular evidence suggests that archaea have at least as much in common with eukaryotes as they do with bacteria. The cell walls and cell membranes of archaea and bacteria have very different chemical components. For example, archaea have a type of lipid in their membranes that is not found in any other living organism.

 What is one way in which archaea and bacteria differ?

_____

# Bacteria have various strategies for survival.

You might use a thoughtful plan, or a strategy, for playing a game. In science, a *strategy* also means an adaptation that improves a species' chance for survival. The exchange of genetic material through conjugation and the formation of endospores are two bacterial strategies for survival.

Bacteria reproduce asexually. However, through a process called **conjugation** (KAHN-juh-GAY-shuhn), two or more bacterial cells can exchange DNA. This process allows bacteria to adapt quickly to different environmental conditions.

**VISUAL VOCAB**

In **conjugation,** genetic material transfers between prokaryotes, producing genetic variation. DNA passes through a structure called a conjugation bridge which connects the cells.

conjugation bridge

When conditions are very bad for growth and survival, some bacteria can produce an endospore. An **endospore** is a specialized cell with a thick, protective wall that can survive drying out, temperature changes, and even disinfectants. Endospores can last for hundreds of years.

Why is conjugation considered a survival strategy?

_____

## 18.4 Vocabulary Check

**Mark It Up**

Go back and highlight each sentence that has a vocabulary word in **bold**.

obligate anaerobe      flagellum

obligate aerobe      conjugation

facultative aerobe      endospore

plasmid

1. Which type of bacterium is likely to live at the bottom of a lake, where there is no oxygen? _____

2. Look back at the figure of prokaryote structure on page 307.
   - Draw an arrow that points to the flagellum.
   - Circle a plasmid.

3. Name one process and one structure that are bacterial strategies for survival. _____

## 18.4 The Big Picture

4. Where can bacteria and archaea live? _____

_____

5. Bacteria and archaea look very similar. In what main way do they differ?

_____

_____

_____

# 18.5 Beneficial Roles of Prokaryotes

**KEY CONCEPT** Prokaryotes perform important functions for organisms and ecosystems.

## Prokaryotes provide nutrients to humans and other animals.

Bacteria are important parts of animal digestive systems. Both the bacteria and the host animal benefit from this relationship. The bacteria benefit from a stable home and source of food. The host animal benefits because the bacteria help break down foods and produce vitamins and other nutrients.

Prokaryotes are also important to human nutrition because they are used to make many common foods. Cheese, sour cream, yogurt, butter, pickles, soy sauce, sauerkraut, vinegar, and many other foods all depend on fermentation by prokaryotes to produce their flavors.

You may have heard about food poisoning caused by bacteria. Although some types of bacteria in food can be harmful, eating food produced by bacteria is not dangerous—as long as it's the right kind of bacteria!

**INSTANT REPLAY** Many types of foods are made using bacteria. Which of the foods listed above have you tried? _____

_____

## Prokaryotes play important roles in ecosystems.

You cannot see prokaryotes with your bare eyes, so it may be easy to forget about them. But they play very important roles in every ecosystem. For example, some prokaryotes produce oxygen through photosynthesis. Others help cycle carbon, nitrogen, hydrogen, and phosphorous through the environment.

One example of prokaryotes' roles in nutrient cycles is shown in this drawing. Bacteria in the soil help to cycle nitrogen through the environment.

**NITROGEN CYCLE**

**Much of the nitrogen cycle occurs underground, where bacteria transform nitrogen into a form that can be used by plants.**

nitrogen in atmosphere

animals

plants

denitrifying bacteria

decomposers

nitrogen-fixing bacteria

nitrifying bacteria

Prokaryotes can break down many natural substances. They can also break down many substances made by humans. Because of this ability, scientists use prokaryotes in a process called bioremediation. **Bioremediation** (BY-oh-rih-MEE-dee-AY-shuhn) is a process that uses living things to break down pollutants. For example, some types of bacteria can digest oil. These bacteria are used to help clean up oil spills and other industrial accidents.

 **What is one example of a pollutant that bacteria can help to break down?**

_____

_____

| 18.5 | **Vocabulary Check** | **Mark It Up** |

**Mark It Up**

Go back and highlight each sentence that has a vocabulary word in **bold.**

bioremediation

1. *Remediation* means "fixing a problem." The prefix *bio-* means "life." Explain how these word parts contribute to the meaning of *bioremediation.* _____

_____

| 18.5 | **The Big Picture** |

2. What are two ways that prokaryotes provide nutrients to humans?

_____

_____

3. What is one important role that prokaryotes play in ecosystems?

_____

_____

# 18.6 Bacterial Diseases and Antibiotics

**KEY CONCEPT** Understanding bacteria is necessary to prevent and treat disease.

## Some bacteria cause disease.

Some bacteria can cause disease in plants and animals. Bacteria can cause illness in two basic ways:

1. Bacteria can attack the cells in one of the body's tissues. For example, the disease tuberculosis, sometimes called TB, is caused by bacteria that invade the lungs and use the tissue for nutrients.

2. Bacteria can make poisons, called toxins, that can be carried in the blood to other parts of the body. A **toxin** is a poison released by an organism. For example, the most common source of food poisoning is from toxins released by a type of bacteria.

| COMMON BACTERIAL INFECTIONS | | | |
|---|---|---|---|
| **INFECTION** | **BACTERIUM** | **SYMPTOMS** | **CAUSES** |
| **Acne** | *Propionibacterium* | chronic cysts, blackheads | increased oil production in skin |
| **Anthrax** | *Bacillus anthracis* | fever, trouble breathing | inhaling endospores |
| **Lyme disease** | *Borrelia burgdorferi* | rash, aching, fever, swelling of joints | bite from infected tick |
| **Tetanus** | *Clostridium tetani* | severe muscle spasms, fever, lockjaw | wound contaminated with soil |
| **Tooth decay** | *Streptococcus mutans* | tooth cavities | large populations of bacteria in mouth |

 Look at the table above. Which of these common bacterial infections have you heard of? _____

_____

## Antibiotics are used to fight bacterial disease.

**Antibiotics** are chemicals that kill or slow the growth of bacteria. Many antibiotics work by stopping bacteria from making cell walls. Antibiotics do not affect animal cells because animal cells do not have cell walls. Similarly, antibiotics do not affect viruses, because viruses do not have cell walls.

Antibiotics are very important medical treatments. However, they should only be used when necessary. Recall that bacteria are a very important part of your digestive system. These "good" bacteria are also affected by antibiotics. The overuse of antibiotics can kill the bacteria in your digestive system, resulting in illness.

How do many antibiotics prevent the growth of bacteria?

_____

_____

## Bacteria can evolve resistance to antibiotics.

Antibiotics can be life-saving medicines. However, the inappropriate and incomplete use of antibiotics has resulted in strains of bacteria that are not affected by antibiotics. In other words, these strains of bacteria are resistant to antibiotics. Antibiotic-resistant bacteria are a major public health issue.

Resistance occurs as a result of natural selection. Any bacteria that are resistant will survive and reproduce. Resistance can then be passed on to offspring and spread to other bacteria. Three factors that have contributed to resistance are described below.

**ANTIBIOTIC RESISTANCE**

A bacterium carries genes for antibiotic resistance on a plasmid.

A copy of the plasmid is transferred through conjugation.

Resistance is quickly spread through many bacteria and their offspring.

- **Overuse** Anytime antibiotics are used, there is a chance to select for resistant bacteria. The unnecessary use of antibiotics—such as when bacteria are not the cause of an illness—increases the possibility that resistant bacteria will become more common.

- **Underuse** Antibiotics may make a person feel better after just one or two days. But the whole prescription of antibiotics must be taken. Otherwise, it is possible that only the weakest bacteria will be killed, and the ones with some resistance may survive.

- **Misuse** A large portion of the antibiotics used in the United States are fed to livestock, such as cows, to increase their growth. Antibiotics may therefore be added to the food of healthy animals. The misuse of antibiotics in agriculture can lead to antibiotic resistance of bacteria in the animals' food.

In summary, anytime antibiotics are used when they are not necessary, or when they are used improperly, it increases the chances for antibiotic-resistant bacteria to become more common. An illness caused by antibiotic-resistant bacteria is difficult or impossible to treat because the bacteria do not respond to antibiotics.

 Explain the role of natural selection in the production of antibiotic-resistant bacteria. _____

_____

_____

## 18.6 Vocabulary Check

**Mark It Up**

Go back and highlight each sentence that has a vocabulary word in **bold.**

toxins          antibiotics

Fill in the blanks with the correct term from the list above.

1. Some bacterial infections can be treated with _____.

2. The _____ produced by some bacteria cause diseases in plants and animals.

## 18.6 The Big Picture

3. Give one example of a disease, illness, or infection caused by bacteria and describe its symptoms. _____

_____

4. Can colds be treated with an antibiotic? Explain your response. _____

_____

_____

5. Imagine that your friend has a ten-day prescription of antibiotics for an illness. Your friend feels better after only two days and wants to stop taking the medicine. Explain why your friend should complete the full prescription of antibiotics. _____

_____

_____

# Chapter 18 Review

1. What are four types of pathogens? _____
   _____

2. Is a virus a living organism? Explain your response. _____
   _____
   _____

3. List one way that bacteria are "helpful" to humans and one important
   role they play in ecosystems. _____
   _____
   _____

4. What do retroviruses do that is different from other viruses?
   **a.** use DNA to make RNA
   **b.** use RNA to make DNA
   **c.** use DNA to make DNA
   **d.** use RNA to make RNA

5. What biological process is involved in the formation of strains of bacteria that are resistant to antibiotics? _____

6. All prokaryotes belong to one of two domains: _____
   or _____.

7. How does a vaccine protect against illness? _____
   _____
   _____

8. Label the cell wall, a chromosome, a plasmid, and the flagellum on this
   diagram of a typical prokaryote.

# 19 Protists and Fungi

## GETTING READY TO LEARN

### Preview Key Concepts

**19.1 Diversity of Protists**
Kingdom Protista is the most diverse of all the kingdoms.

**19.2 Animal-like Protists**
Animal-like protists are single-celled heterotrophs that can move.

**19.3 Plantlike Protists**
Algae are plantlike protists.

**19.4 Funguslike Protists**
Funguslike protists decompose organic matter.

**19.5 Diversity of Fungi**
Fungi are heterotrophs that absorb their food.

**19.6 Ecology of Fungi**
Fungi recycle nutrients in the environment.

### Review Academic Vocabulary

Write the correct word for each definition.

decomposer     heterotroph     plankton

1. _____ : microscopic free-floating organisms

2. _____ : organism that obtains energy by consuming
other organisms

3. _____ : organism that eats and breaks down dead
organic matter

### Preview Biology Vocabulary

Try to guess the meaning of each boldfaced word from its context.

| PHRASE | MY GUESS |
|---|---|
| **1.** A mushroom is the **fruiting body** of many types of fungi. | |
| **2.** Some types of **algae** are microscopic, forming the base of aquatic food webs. | |
| **3.** The algal part of **lichen** produces sugars which the fungi eat, and the fungus part provides a habitat for the algae. | |

# 19.1 Diversity of Protists

**KEY CONCEPT** Kingdom Protista is the most diverse of all the kingdoms.

## Protists can be animal-like, plantlike, or funguslike.

The kingdom Protista includes a huge diversity of organisms in hundreds of phyla. Members of this kingdom are often simply called protists. A **protist** is a eukaryote that is not an animal, a plant, or a fungus. Although protists share some similarities with animals, plants, and fungi, they are different enough from each group that they do not fit in any of them.

Protists can be classified into three categories based on how they get their food. These categories do not show evolutionary relationships among protists. However, they are a helpful way to organize this very diverse group of organisms.

A paramecium is an animal-like protist.

- **Animal-like protists** Some protists get their food like animals do—by eating other organisms. However, animal-like protists differ from animals. All animal-like protists are single-celled and all animals are multicellular.
- **Plantlike protists** Some protists get their food like plants do— through photosynthesis. However, plantlike protists differ from plants. Plantlike protists do not have roots, stems, or leaves. Plantlike protists may be single-celled or multicellular, or live in colonies of cells. True plants are all multicellular.
- **Funguslike protists** Some protists get their food in the same way that fungi do—by decomposing dead organisms. However, funguslike protists differ from fungi because they can move for part of their lifecycle, and fungi cannot.

> **VOCABULARY**
> A *colony of cells* means "a group of cooperating cells."

What are three categories of protists? _____

_____

_____

# Protists are difficult to classify.

Recall from Chapter 17 that prokaryotes are divided into two domains: Archaea and Bacteria, and all eukaryotes belong to the domain Eukarya. The domain Eukarya contains four kingdoms: one for animals, one for plants, one for fungi, and one for protists.

The kingdom Protista contains any organism that does not fit well into the kingdoms for animals, plants, or fungi. However, the organisms classified as protists are not all closely related. Information about the molecular biology of protists may lead to changes in the organization of the kingdom.

**Six kingdoms**

Animalia  Plantae
Protista
Archaea
Fungi  Bacteria

## RELATIONSHIPS OF PROTISTS TO OTHER EUKARYOTES

**All protists currently belong to kingdom Protista, but some protists are more closely related to other kingdoms than to members of their own kingdom.**

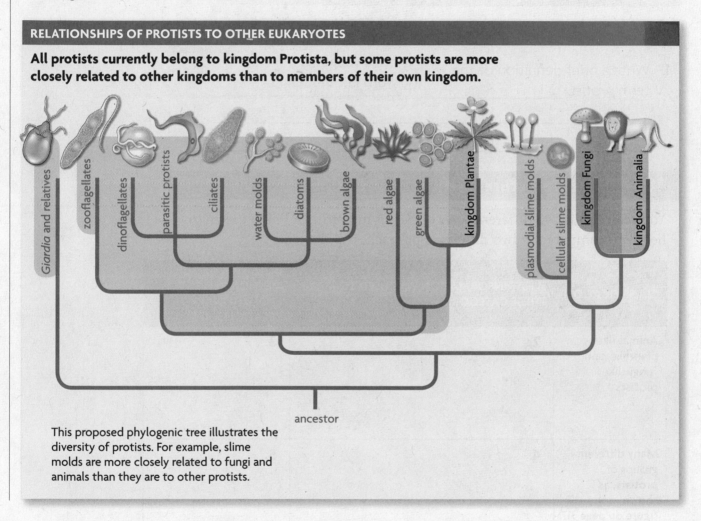

*Giardia* and relatives · zooflagellates · dinoflagellates · parasitic protists · ciliates · water molds · diatoms · brown algae · red algae · green algae · kingdom Plantae · plasmodial slime molds · cellular slime molds · kingdom Fungi · kingdom Animalia

ancestor

This proposed phylogenic tree illustrates the diversity of protists. For example, slime molds are more closely related to fungi and animals than they are to other protists.

The figure on the previous page shows evolutionary relationships among protists and other eukaryotes based on molecular evidence. Notice that some protists are more closely related to plants, animals, or fungi than they are to other protists. For example, a group of protists called slime molds are more closely related to animals and to fungi than to other protists and to plants.

 Look at the phylogenetic tree on page 317. Circle all of the groups of organisms that are protists.

## 19.1 Vocabulary Check

**Mark It Up**

Go back and highlight each sentence that has a vocabulary word in **bold**.

protist

1. Write a brief definition of the term *protist.* _____

_____

_____

## 19.1 The Big Picture

You read about two different ways of classifying protists. Fill in the chart below to compare the two different approaches.

| CLASSIFICATION | WHAT INFORMATION WAS USED TO MAKE THESE CATEGORIES? | DOES THIS GROUPING METHOD REFLECT EVOLUTIONARY RELATIONSHIPS? |
|---|---|---|
| Animal-like, plantlike, and funguslike protists | 2. | 3. |
| Many different groups of protists, as shown in the figure on page 317. | 4. | 5. |

# 19.2 Animal-like Protists

**KEY CONCEPT** Animal-like protists are single-celled heterotrophs that can move.

## Animal-like protists move in various ways.

The many groups of animal-like protists are often called **protozoa.** Like animals, protozoa move around and eat other organisms. The main difference between animals and protozoa is that all animals are multicellular while all protozoa are single-celled.

Snakes slither, fish swim, insects fly, and rabbits hop on four legs. Animal-like protists also move in many different ways. Three common ways that protozoa move are described below.

### Protozoa with Flagella

Many protozoa use flagella to move. Recall from Chapter 18 that flagella are tail-like structures that help single-celled organisms move. The flagella of protists—which are eukaryotes—look similar to the flagella of prokaryotes, but they are structurally very different.

### Protozoa with Pseudopods

Some protozoa move by changing shape, and forming pseudopods. A **pseudopod** (SOO-duh-PAHD) is a temporary* extension of the cell that helps protozoa move. To form a pseudopod, the cell flows outward, and forms an extension of the cell. The extension attaches to the surface that the cell is on, and the rest of the cell is pulled towards the pseudopod.

Some protozoa, like the amoeba (uh-MEE-buh) at the right, also use pseudopods to feed. The extension of the cell surrounds food particles, which get taken into the cell for digestion.

Amoeba

pseudopod

Amoebas make up one group of protozoa that moves by using pseudopods.

### Protozoa with Cilia

Some protozoa, like the paramecium at the right, move by using cilia. **Cilia** are short, hairlike structures on the cell surface. Cilia help an organism to move and capture food.

 **INSTANT REPLAY** What are three structures that protozoa use to move?

_____

_____

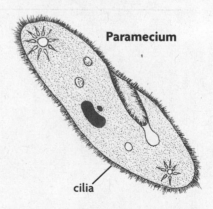

Paramecium

cilia

A paramecium is a single-celled protist covered with thousands of cilia that are used for movement.

**\* ACADEMIC VOCABULARY**

**temporary** for a short amount of time; not permanent

# Some animal-like protists cause disease.

Some protozoa cause infectious diseases. Malaria, for example, is a disease that is caused by an animal-like protist. Malaria can cause fever and vomiting, and in some cases it can even lead to death. It is passed to humans and other animals through the bite of a certain kind of mosquito. Other types of protists are responsible for causing the disease known as sleeping sickness, as well as intestinal diseases.

 What is one disease that is caused by a type of protozoa?

_____

## 19.2 Vocabulary Check

**Mark It Up**

Go back and highlight each sentence that has a vocabulary word in **bold**.

protozoa            cilia

pseudopod

1.  Which group of protists is called protozoa? _____

2.  *Pseudo-* means "fake" and *-pod* means "foot." How do these word parts relate to the meaning of *pseudopod*? _____

    _____

    _____

3.  Name two functions of cilia. _____

## 19.2 The Big Picture

4.  Describe the difference between flagella and cilia. _____

    _____

    _____

KEY CONCEPT   Algae are plantlike protists.

## Plantlike protists can be single-celled or multicellular.

Photosynthetic plantlike protists are called **algae.** Unlike plants, plantlike protists do not have roots, stems, leaves, or other plant tissues.

All plants are multicellular. Plantlike protists may be single-celled or multicellular. Multicellular algae likely arose from organisms such as the *Volvox* at the right.

Plantlike protists are found in many habitats—from the desert to tundra. Most are organisms that live in water. Through photosynthesis, plantlike protists that live in the ocean produce about half of the oxygen that we breathe.

Some plantlike protists also have characteristics that are animal-like. Euglena, for example, have chloroplasts and conduct photosynthesis. They also can move around easily and can sense light with an eye spot.

**INSTANT REPLAY**   What biological process accounts for the oxygen that algae produce?

**Volvox**

*Volvox* are actually hundreds of individual algae cells that join together to form a colony in the shape of a hollow ball. Offspring form smaller daughter colonies inside the parent colony.

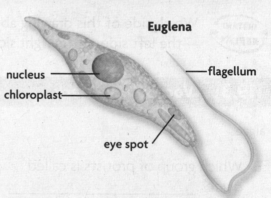

**Euglena**

nucleus
chloroplast
flagellum
eye spot

A euglena has both animal-like structures—such as an eyespot and flagella—and plantlike structures, such as chloroplasts.

## Many plantlike protists can reproduce both sexually and asexually.

Most protists can undergo both asexual and sexual reproduction. All algae can reproduce asexually. For example, multicellular algae can break apart, and each piece can form a new organism. For single-celled algae, asexual reproduction is more complex and involves a parent cell dividing by mitosis.

Sexual reproduction occurs in algae as well. Some species go back and forth from generation to generation, reproducing sexually and then asexually. Other species reproduce asexually for a few generations until conditions change, and then they reproduce sexually.

**VOCABULARY**

Recall from Chapter 6 that *haploid* cells have one copy of each chromosome and *diploid* cells have two copies of each chromosome.

**LIFE CYCLE OF SINGLE-CELLED GREEN ALGAE**

**Some single-celled green algae, such as *Chlamydomonas*, undergo sexual as well as asexual reproduction.**

Meiosis occurs within the zygote, producing four haploid cells that will grow and mature.

haploid cells (1*n*)

**meiosis**

**mitosis**

During asexual reproduction, the cell divides by mitosis.

zygote (2*n*)

**Sexual reproduction**

**Asexual reproduction**

Gametes fuse, forming a diploid zygote.

mature cell (1*n*)

The daughter cells develop flagella and become zoospores, which become mature haploid cells.

gametes (1*n*)

**mitosis**

During sexual reproduction mitosis produces many haploid gametes.

 **INSTANT REPLAY**  Which side of this drawing above shows asexual reproduction —the left side or the right side? _____

---

**19.3    Vocabulary Check**

**Mark It Up**

Go back and highlight each sentence that has a vocabulary word in **bold**.

algae

**1.** Which group of protists is called *algae*? _____

---

**19.3    The Big Picture**

**2.** Where do most plantlike protists live? _____

**3.** Name two ways that algae can reproduce. _____

_____

**4.** How is a euglena both plantlike and animal-like? _____

_____

_____

_____

# 19.4 Funguslike Protists

**KEY CONCEPT** Funguslike protists decompose organic matter.

## Slime molds and water molds are funguslike protists.

Like fungi, funguslike protists are decomposers. Fungi and funguslike protists also have similar life cycles. However, funguslike protists can move during part of their life cycle and fungi cannot. Funguslike protists play an important role in ecosystems by recycling nutrients such as carbon and nitrogen back into the soil. Two kinds of funguslike protists are slime molds and water molds.

- **Slime molds** are protists that have both funguslike and animal-like traits. They are common on dead leaves and under logs. Two main types of slime molds are plasmodial slime molds and cellular slime molds. Plasmodial slime molds live as a mass of cytoplasm that is actually one large cell with many nuclei. Cellular slime molds are made up of many cells that form a sluglike body.

- **Water molds** are protists that are made of branching strands of cells. They are common in freshwater habitats. Many water molds are decomposers, but some are parasites of plants or fish.

How are funguslike protists similar to fungi? _____

_____

_____

| 19.4 | Vocabulary Check |
|---|---|

**Mark It Up**

Go back and highlight each sentence that has a vocabulary word in **bold**.

slime mold

water mold

1. Where do slime molds commonly live? _____

2. Where do water molds commonly live? _____

| 19.4 | The Big Picture |
|---|---|

3. What important role do funguslike protists play in ecosystems? _____

_____

_____

# 19.5 Diversity of Fungi

**KEY CONCEPT** Fungi are heterotrophs that absorb their food.

## Fungi are adapted to absorb their food from the environment.

Fungi are everywhere. They are in the soil, the water, and the air. They also live in and on plants and animals. Fungi can be divided into three groups: single-celled yeasts, molds, and true fungi. Molds and true fungi are multicellular. The basic structure of a true fungus is shown below.

A **fruiting body** is a reproductive structure of a fungus that grows above ground. Mushrooms are one type of fruiting body.

spore-producing structures

The bodies of multicellular fungi are made of long strands called **hyphae** (HY-fee).

A **mycelium** (my-SEE-lee-uhm) is an underground network of hyphae.

For many years, biologists classified fungi as plants. However, there are a few main differences between these two groups. One difference is that plants make their own food through photosynthesis, and fungi get their food by absorbing it from their environment. This food can come from many different sources—including tree bark, bread, and even flesh. As fungi grow, hyphae extend into their food source. The hyphae release substances that break down the food so it can be absorbed across their cell walls.

Another main difference is that fungal cell walls are made of a substance called **chitin** (KYT-uhn). This substance is also found in the shells of insects, but is not found in plants.

What is one main difference between fungi and plants? _____

_____

_____

_____

# Fungi come in many shapes and sizes.

The kingdom Fungi is very diverse. For example, some fungi live in water and have spores with flagella to move around. Others grow out from tree trunks and form "shelves." Some are parasites of other organisms. Others cause disease in plants. Fungi are commonly divided into four main groups—primitive fungi, sac fungi, bread molds, and club fungi.

- **Primitive fungi** The simplest type of fungi are called the primitive fungi. Most live in the water and have spores with flagella that help them to move.
- **Sac fungi** These fungi all form a sac that contains spores for reproduction. The yeasts that are used to make bread rise and as the source of the antibiotic penicillin are both sac fungi.
- **Bread molds** Most bread molds get their food by decomposing dead or decaying organic matter. However, at least one group of bread molds gets food through a symbiotic relationship. **Mycorrhizae** (my-kuh-RY-zuh) are fungi that live in a mutualistic relationship with the roots of certain plants. These fungi change nitrogen into a form that plants can use. The plant gets usable nitrogen. The fungus gets food and a place to live.
- **Club fungi** These fungi have fruiting bodies shaped like clubs. This group includes mushrooms, rusts and smuts, which are two types of fungi that cause diseases in plants.

 Circle the name of the plant part where mycorrhizae live.

# Fungi reproduce sexually and asexually.

Recall that yeasts are single-celled fungi. Some yeasts can reproduce sexually in a process that involves meiosis. However, most yeasts reproduce asexually. One type of asexual reproduction is called fission, which produces two identical daughter cells. In another type of asexual reproduction, called budding, a small bud of cytoplasm that contains a copy of the nucleus pinches off of the parent cell.

Multicellular fungi have more complicated reproductive cycles. Each major group of fungi has unique reproductive structures.

- Bread molds reproduce sexually when the food supply is low and asexually when there is plenty of food. They reproduce asexually by producing spores in **sporangia,** which are spore-forming structures at the tips of their hyphae.

**VISUAL VOCAB**

**Sporangia** are structures that produce spores.

spores — sporangia

- Club fungi are named for their club-shaped structures called basidia, where spores are produced during sexual reproduction. Basidia are found on the underside of mushrooms, inside the leaflike gills that you can easily see.
- Sac fungi also produce sexually when the food supply is low and asexually when there is plenty of food. They have a saclike case, called an ascus, which forms during sexual reproduction. An ascus forms at the tip of each hypha within the fruiting body. Spores form inside the ascus.

When the spores are ready, fungi release them and they are carried in the air to a new location. Fungal spores have even been found more than 150 kilometers (93 miles) above the surface of Earth. If spores land in a favorable environment, they can grow into new hyphae.

**Name two processes by which yeasts can reproduce asexually.**

_____

---

## 19.5 Vocabulary Check

chitin        fruiting body

hyphae      mycorrhizae

mycelium    sporangia

### Mark It Up

Go back and highlight each sentence that has a vocabulary word in **bold**.

1. Label the diagram at the right with the correct vocabulary terms.

_____

_____

---

## 19.5 The Big Picture

2. How do all fungi take in food? _____

_____

3. Name the four main categories of fungi. _____

_____

_____

# 19.6 Ecology of Fungi

**KEY CONCEPT** Fungi recycle nutrients in the environment.

## Fungi may be decomposers, pathogens, or mutualists.

Fungi play a major role in every ecosystem on Earth.

### Fungi as Decomposers

Fungi and bacteria are the main decomposers in all ecosystems. Fungi can break down dead material, such as leaves, wood, and animals. Through decomposition, fungi return nutrients such as carbon, nitrogen, and minerals back into the soil. Plants and animals could not survive without the activity of decomposers. However, the decomposing activity of certain fungi can also cause damage to trees as well as the insides of wooden structures such as houses and boats.

### Fungi as Pathogens

Some fungi can be pathogens, or organisms that cause disease. Fungi can cause disease in animals, including humans. For example, fungi cause athlete's foot and ringworm. Fungi can also cause more serious diseases such as lung illnesses. Fungal infections are hard to treat because fungi are eukaryotes, so their cellular structure is similar to ours. It is difficult to make medicine that will harm fungal cells but not damage human cells.

Fungi can also cause disease in plants. For example, a fungal disease called Dutch elm disease began in the United States in the 1930s. Today, the disease has destroyed more than half of the elm trees in the northern United States. Fungal diseases also affect food crops. Many crops are treated with chemical sprays called fungicides. Today, crops that are genetically engineered to be resistant to fungal diseases are becoming more and more common in agriculture.

### Fungi as Mutualists

Recall that mutualism is a symbiotic relationship in which both organisms benefit. Fungi form mutualistic relationships with several types of organisms including algae and plants.

- **Lichens** A **lichen** (LY-kuhn) is a mutualistic relationship between a fungus and algae or photosynthetic bacteria. The algae or bacteria carry out photosynthesis, making sugars that feed both organisms. The fungal hyphae provide habitat for the algae or bacteria. Lichens can grow on rocks, trees, soil, and other surfaces.

- **Mycorrhizae** You read in section 19.5 that mycorrhizae are mutualistic associations between plant roots and soil fungi. The fungus benefits because it uses sugars produced by the plant. The plant benefits because it gets nutrients from the soil that it could not get without the fungus.

- **Fungal gardens and insects** Some insects also have mutualisms with fungi. A certain type of ant that lives in Central and South America, called the leafcutter ant, actually grows fungi in a type of garden. The ants cut tiny pieces of leaves with their jaws and carry the pieces to an underground nest. In the nests, they mix the leaf pieces with pieces of a certain type of fungus. The fungus absorbs nutrients from the leaf pieces and the ants eat parts of the fungus.

Densely packed fungal hyphae

Layer of algae

Loosely packed fungal hyphae

Densely packed fungal hyphae

A **lichen** is a symbiotic relationship between an alga and a fungus.

**INSTANT REPLAY** Complete the following equations:

fungus + _____ = lichen

fungus + _____ = mycorrhizae

## Fungi are studied for many purposes.

**Food** Many species of fungi are edible, such as the mushrooms we eat on pizza and the yeast we use to bake bread. Substances produced by fungi are also used in soft drinks and some candy.

**Medicine** Fungi are also studied for use in medicines. In their natural habitats, fungi compete with bacteria. Substances naturally produced by fungi may be useful for treating bacterial infections.

This morel is an edible mushroom.

**Model system**  Yeasts are used as a model system for the study of molecular biology. Recall that yeasts are eukaryotes, like plants and animals. Because of this, yeasts have many of the same genes and proteins found in plants and animals. They are also small, grow quickly, and are easy to grow in the laboratory. The molecular biology learned through the study of yeasts can be applied to multicellular organisms.

**INSTANT REPLAY**  What is one reason that yeast is used as a model system for research in molecular biology? _____

_____

_____

## 19.6  Vocabulary Check

**Mark It Up**

Go back and highlight each sentence that has a vocabulary word in **bold**.

lichen

**Fill in the blanks to complete the sentence below.**

1.  A lichen is a _____ relationship between fungi and _____.

## 19.6  The Big Picture

2.  What are three roles that fungi may have in an ecosystem? _____

_____

_____

3.  What are three ways fungi are used by humans? _____

_____

_____

# Chapter 19 Review

1. What is a protist? _____
   _____

2. Protists move in several ways. Name the structure each organism
   below uses to move.

   _____  _____  _____

3. Slime molds and water molds obtain their food in a way similar to
   which group of organisms—plants, animals, or fungi? _____

4. Algae obtain their food in a way similar to which group of organisms—
   plants, animals, or fungi? _____

5. What is one important role fungi play in ecosystems?
   a. they are decomposers
   b. they are autotrophs
   c. they are photosynthetic
   d. they are prokaryotes

6. What is one similarity among animals, plants, protists, and fungi?
   a. they are all prokaryotes
   b. they are all heterotrophs
   c. they all include single-celled organisms
   d. they are all eukaryotes

7. Describe one example of a mutualistic relationship between a fungus
   and another organism. _____
   _____
   _____

8. What type of fungus is used to make bread? _____

# 20 Plant Diversity

## GETTING READY TO LEARN

### Preview Key Concepts

**20.1 Origins of Plant Life**
Plant life began in the water and became adapted to land.

**20.2 Classification of Plants**
Plants can be classified into nine phyla.

**20.3 Diversity of Flowering Plants**
The largest phylum in the plant kingdom is the flowering plants.

**20.4 Plant in Human Culture**
Humans rely on plants in many ways.

### Review Academic Vocabulary

Write the correct word for each definition.

algae        chlorophyll        herbivore        photosynthesis

1. _____ : process in which plants and some algae produce sugar

2. _____ : photosynthetic plantlike protists

3. _____ : light-absorbing pigment molecule

4. _____ : organism that eats only plants

### Preview Biology Vocabulary

To see how many key terms you already know from this chapter, choose the word that makes sense in each sentence.

cone        fruit        pollen grain        seed

1. A _____ contains a cell that will divide to form sperm, and may also contribute to seasonal allergies.

2. A tall tree can grow from a tiny _____

3. A _____ is the reproductive structure of most gymnosperms, such as pine trees.

4. The mature ovary of a flower, called a _____, can take many forms, such as a juicy peach.

# 20.1 Origins of Plant Life

**KEY CONCEPT** Plant life began in the water and became adapted to land.

## Land plants evolved from green algae.

**Plants** are multicellular eukaryotes. Most plants live on land and use photosynthesis to make their own food. All green algae share certain characteristics with plants.

- Both green algae and plants are photosynthetic. They have chlorophyll that absorbs energy from the sun to use during photosynthesis.
- Both green algae and plants have the same type of chlorophyll. Chlorophyll is what makes these algae and most plants green.
- Both green algae and plants use starch to store food for later use.
- Like plants, most green algae have cell walls with cellulose.

**Plant Ancestor** One species of green algae is the ancestor of all plants. It was most likely a member of the class Charophyceae. Three important plant characteristics that probably developed first in this algae are a multicellular body, a method of cell division in which cells communicate using chemicals, and reproduction by sperm that travels to an egg to fertilize it.

**The Evolution of Plants** Scientists think that the early charophyceans lived in shallow water that sometimes dried out. Natural selection favored individuals that survived being dry. These individuals lived long enough to reproduce. Their offspring also survived dry conditions. The first true plants probably grew along lakes and streams. Over time, the descendants, or offspring, lived in places that were always dry.

 What are three characteristics that green algae share with plants? _____

_____

## Plants have adaptations for life on land.

Living on land is not the same as living in water. Algae are surrounded by water, which supports their weight. Sperm and spores can travel through water to reach an egg. Water also prevents sperm, eggs, and young offspring from drying out. Plants have evolved adaptations to retain moisture, transport water, grow upright, and reproduce without free-standing water.

**Retaining Moisture** Plants will die if they dry out completely. The surfaces of plants are covered with a cuticle. The **cuticle** is a waxlike, waterproof layer that holds in moisture. It can also keep out air. Tiny holes in the cuticle, called **stomata** (singular stoma), open to allow air in and close to keep in moisture.

stoma

**Transporting Resources** A plant must move water and nutrients from the soil through the plant body. Sugars must move out of the leaves. A **vascular system** is a collection of special tissues that move substances through the plant.

**Growing Upright** Plant height is limited by a plant's ability to support its own weight. A material called **lignin** (LIGH-nihn) supports a tall plant. It causes cell walls of some vascular tissues to become hard. Lignin makes plant stems stiff and makes wood hard.

**Reproducing on Land** Plants living on land need a way to reproduce without water. Pollen and seeds are adaptations that allow seed plants to reproduce without any free-standing water. A **pollen grain** contains a cell that will divide to form sperm. It is carried by wind or animals to the female part of a plant. A **seed** is a storage container for the plant embryo. It has a hard coat and protects the embryo from drying out. The embryo can develop when conditions are right.

 **INSTANT REPLAY** Describe one adaptation plants use to survive on dry land.

_____

_____

_____

# Plants evolve with other organisms in their environment.

Plants have evolved alongside other organisms for millions of years. During this time, they have developed close relationships with these other living things.

**Mutualisms** A mutualism is an interaction between two species that is good for both species. For example, plant roots provide a habitat for certain fungi and bacteria. In return, the fungi and bacteria help the plant get nutrients from the soil. Also, many flowering plants have nectar and fruit that attract animal species. These animals spread the plant's pollen or seeds and get a meal in return.

Vascular tissues form "pipelines" that carry materials to different parts of the plant.

**Plant-Herbivore Interactions** Plants have a variety of adaptations that discourage animals from eating them. The spines on a cactus and the thorns on a rose stem are examples. Another type of adaptation is producing chemicals that taste bad or are toxic to keep animals away.

 Underline an example of a mutualism.

| 20.1 | **Vocabulary Check** | **Mark It Up** |

Go back and highlight each sentence that has a vocabulary word in **bold**.

plant          stomata
lignin         seed
cuticle        vascular system
pollen grain

**Choose the correct term from the list for each description.**

1. waterproof layer _____

2. contains a cell that becomes a sperm _____

3. moves water, nutrients, and sugar through a plant _____

4. helps a plant stem stand up _____

## 20.1   The Big Picture

5. What evidence makes scientists think that land plants evolved from green algae? _____
_____
_____
_____

6. What challenges did early plants face living on dry land? _____
_____
_____

7. Why is it important for some plants to attract animals? _____
_____
_____

# 20.2 Classification of Plants

**KEY CONCEPT** Plants can be classified into nine phyla.

## Mosses and their relatives are seedless nonvascular plants.

Mosses and their relatives grow close to the ground because they do not have vascular systems. They also need water so sperm can swim to the eggs. Three phyla belong to this category: Hepatophyta (the liverworts), Anthocerophyta (the hornworts), and Bryophyta (the mosses).

**Liverworts** Most liverworts live in damp environments. They get moisture from the soil. There are two basic forms: thallose and leafy. The thallose liverworts look like the lobes of a liver and give the group its name. Leafy liverworts have stemlike and leaflike structures.

**Hornworts** Hornworts are found in tropical forests and along streams all over the world. The main plant body of a hornwort is flat and lobelike. The name hornwort refers to the long spore-producing structures that look like horns.

The main body of a thallose liverwort is the lobe-like structure that grows flat on the ground. Eggs are produced in the umbrella-like structures.

**Mosses** Mosses do not have true leaves. Instead, they have a leaflike structure only one cell thick. Some species have cuticles, and most have stomata. Mosses use structures called rhizoids (RY-zoydz) to anchor themselves to soil, rocks, or tree trunks. Mosses are often the first plants to grow on bare land. They can survive in deserts and tundras by remaining dormant* until water is available

**INSTANT REPLAY** What are two characteristics shared by liverworts, hornworts, and mosses? _____

_____

_____

## Club mosses and ferns are seedless vascular plants.

The two phyla of seedless vascular plants are Lycophyta, the club mosses, and Pterophyta, the ferns. These plants need water to reproduce. But their vascular system allows them to grow higher above the ground and get materials from the soil.

---

**\* ACADEMIC VOCABULARY**

**dormant** a state in which no growth occurs

**Club Mosses** Club mosses are the oldest living group of vascular plants. But they are not true mosses. Ancient species looked like trees and were even bigger. Only the smaller species survived when the climate cooled.

**Whisk Ferns, Horsetails, and Ferns** Whisk ferns grow mostly in the tropics and subtropics. They do not have true roots and leaves.

Horsetails grow in wetland areas and along rivers and streams. Their leaves grow in a circle around the stem. Horsetails' cell walls contain a rough compound called silica, the main ingredient in glass, and colonial settlers used the plant to scrub pots.

Ferns are the most successful members of this phylum. Their large leaves are called fronds. Some small ferns can be houseplants. The larger tree ferns live in the tropics and can grow over three stories tall.

Fern leaves are called fronds.

 Describe one way that a mature seedless vascular plant would look different from a seedless nonvascular plant. _____

## Seed plants include cone-bearing plants and flowering plants.

Seed plants have three special advantages over their seedless ancestors.

1. **Seed plants can reproduce without free-standing water.** Seed plants produce pollen grains. Each pollen grain contains a cell that can become a sperm. Pollen can be carried by the wind or on the body of an animal, such as a bee. **Pollination** occurs when pollen comes in contact with the female reproductive parts of the same plant species. Therefore, seed plants can live in drier places.

2. **Seeds nourish\* and protect plant embryos.** Inside a seed is a food supply for the developing plant embryo. The outside of a seed is a protective coat. This allows a seed to survive cold weather or a lack of water. A seed can remain dormant for months, or even years, while waiting for the right growing conditions.

3. **Seeds allow plants to disperse to new places.** Wind, water, or animals can carry seeds far from the plant that produced them. Many plants have adaptations to help their seeds disperse. Maple tree seeds have "wings" that help the wind carry them.

**\* ACADEMIC VOCABULARY**

**nourish** provide nutrients for

There are two main types of seed plants.

- A **gymnosperm** (JIHM-nuh-spurm) is a seed plant whose seeds are not inside a fruit.
- An **angiosperm** (AN-jee-uh-spurm) is a seed plant that has seeds enclosed in some type of fruit.

Most gymnosperms have cones and are evergreen, such as pine trees. A woody **cone** is the reproductive structure of most gymnosperms. Male cones produce pollen and female cones produce eggs. The three living phyla of gymnosperms are Cycadophyta, the cycads; Ginkgophyta, *Ginkgo biloba;* and Coniferophyta, the conifers.

**Cycads** Cycads provided food for the dinosaurs. They look like palm trees with large cones. Today they grow in tropical areas in the Americas, Asia, Africa, and Australia. Many species are endangered because of their slow growth and habitat loss.

**Ginkgo** When dinosaurs lived, ginkgoes were an abundant plant. Today, only one species survives, *Ginkgo biloba*. It is native to China. One reason it has survived there is that Buddhist monks have grown and tended it since 1100. The ginkgo may be the oldest living species of seed plant.

**Conifers** The most diverse and common gymnosperms alive today are the conifers. These include pines, redwood, spruce, cedar, fir, and juniper. All conifers have needlelike leaves and most are green all year-round. Conifers grow quickly and supply most of the timber used for paper, cardboard, housing lumber, and plywood. They also live a long time and can grow very tall and massive. A bristlecone pine in California is 4700 years old. And a giant sequoia tree is 1.2 million kilograms.

Most conifers, such as these, are green all year round.

**Flowering Plants** Angiosperms belong to a phylum of their own, called Anthophyta. A **flower** is the reproductive structure of these plants. It protects the plants gametes and fertilized eggs. A **fruit** is the mature ovary of a flower. It can be juicy and good to eat, like a peach, or it can be the fluff around a dandelion seed.

**INSTANT REPLAY** List three advantages that seed plants have over nonseed plants. _____

_____

_____

_____

## 20.2    Vocabulary Check

pollination      cone
gymnosperm       flower
angiosperm       fruit

**Choose the correct term from the list for each description.**

1. reproductive structure of most gymnosperms _____

2. mature ovary of a flower _____

3. seed plant with seeds enclosed in some type of fruit _____

4. pollen meets female reproductive parts of the same plant species

   _____

## 20.2    The Big Picture

5. Explain why nonvascular plants must grow close to the ground. _____
   _____
   _____
   _____
   _____

6. How does pollen help a seed plant reproduce without water? _____
   _____
   _____

7. What two characteristics of a seed help an embryo survive harsh
   conditions? _____
   _____
   _____

# 20.3 Diversity of Flowering Plants

**KEY CONCEPT** The largest phylum in the plant kingdom is the flowering plants.

## Flowering plants have adaptations that allow them to dominate in today's world.

When the dinosaurs went extinct 65 million years ago, so did many seedless plants. This left space for flowering plants to spread out and multiply. New types of seed plants developed. This new diversity was tied to the diversification of land animals, such as insects and birds. Today there are at least 250,000 identified flowering plant species.

**Flowers and Pollination** You have probably seen a bee or butterfly near the center of a flower. These insects and other animals eat pollen or nectar, which is a sugary solution produced by some flowers. As the animal eats, it gets pollen on itself. When it moves to another flower, some of the pollen brushes off onto the new flower. Thus, animal pollinators directly transfer pollen from one flower to another. This is a more efficient method of pollination than having to rely on the wind.

Butterflies and bats are animal pollinators.

**Fruits and Seed Dispersal** A fruit surrounds and protects the seed or seeds. Some fruits are food for animals. Animals digest the fruit but not the seeds inside. The seeds pass through the animal and are deposited away from the parent plant. Other fruits are burrs that stick to an animal when it passes by and drop off later in a new location.

How can animals be involved in flowering plant reproduction?

_____

_____

## Botanists classify flowering plants into two groups based on seed type.

**VOCABULARY**
*Mono-* and *di-* are prefixes meaning "one" and "two." *Cot* is a shortened form of the word *cotyledon.* Therefore, monocots have one cotyledon and dicots have two.

The seeds of flowering plants have either one cotyledon or two. A **cotyledon** (KAHT-uhl-EED-uhn) is an embryonic leaf inside a seed.

**Monocots**   A flowering plant whose embryo has one seed leaf is called a monocotyledon, or **monocot** (MAHN-uh-KAHT). Monocots have long, narrow leaves with parallel veins, flower parts that are usually in multiples of three, and scattered bundles of vascular tissue in the stem. Corn, wheat, rice, and lilies are monocots.

**Dicots**   A flowering plant whose embryo has two cotyledons is called a dicotyledon, or **dicot** (DY-Kaht). Dicots have leaves with netlike veins, flower parts that are usually in multiples of four or five, and rings of vascular tissue in the stem. Peanuts and most deciduous trees, which lose their leaves in the fall, are dicots.

 To compare monocots and dicots, circle the words that describe each type of flowering plant.

## Flowering plants are also categorized by stem type and lifespan.

**Herbaceous or Woody Stems**   Wood is a fibrous, or stringy, material made of dead cells that are part of the vascular system of some plants. Stems of woody plants are therefore stiff. Trees and shrubs have woody stems. Plants that do not produce wood, such as cacti and marigolds, are called herbaceous plants.

Monocots, such as lilies, have flower parts in multiples of three.

**Lifespans**   Three basic types of lifespans occur in flowering plants.

- Annuals grow from a seed, produce flowers, and die in one year. Corn, lettuce, and some garden flowers are annuals.
- Biennials take two years to complete a life cycle. During the first year, the plant produces a short stem, leaves that grow close to the ground, and an underground food reserve. In the second year, the food reserves are used to produce a taller stem, leaves, flowers, and seeds. Carrots are biennials.

- Perennials live for more than two years. Most woody plants, such as trees, are perennials. The stems and leaves of herbaceous perennials, such as some grasses, die at the end of the fall and grow back in the spring.

What is the difference among annuals, biennials, and perennials?

_____

_____

## 20.3 Vocabulary Check

| cotyledon | dicot |
| monocot | wood |

1. In the list above, circle the two words that best describe an oak tree.

2. Put a box around the word that describes a flowering plant that has flower parts in threes.

3. Underline the word that names part of a seed.

## 20.3 The Big Picture

4. How have the pollination methods of flowering plants made them so successful? _____

_____

_____

5. Name three ways in which flowering plants can be categorized. _____

_____

_____

6. What are the four main differences between monocots and dicots?

_____

_____

_____

_____

# 20.4 Plants in Human Culture

**KEY CONCEPT**  Humans rely on plants in many ways.

## Agriculture provides stable food supplies for people in permanent settlements.

Humans use plants for nearly everything in daily life. The paper for a book's pages comes from wood, ink contains plant oil, clothes come from cotton plants, and much of our food comes from plants. Today, crop plants are an important part of our economy.

**Hunting and Gathering**  Plants have always been used for food, shelter, clothing, and medicine. While **botany** is the study of plants, **ethnobotany** is the study of how people of different cultures use plants. For most of human history, people have hunted animals and gathered plants to survive. This required people to change locations if weather, disease, or overuse affected the food supply.

**Farming**  About 10,000 years ago people started planting seeds for harvest. They chose plants with the best traits, saved their seeds, and planted them the next year. Corn, rice, and wheat were developed from wild grasses in this way. Farming provided a reliable source of food. Extra food was sold to earn money. In this way, farming became part of a culture's economy.

**VOCABULARY**

*Ethnobotany* comes from the Greek words *ethnos,* which means "people," and *botané,* which means "plants."

  Why is farming a more reliable way to provide food than gathering plants? _____

_____

## Plant products are important economic resources.

During the early Middle Ages, spices such as pepper, cinnamon, and cloves were so valuable that they were used as money. Plants are still important economic resources all over the world. The values of rice, corn, wheat, soybeans, coffee, sugar, cotton, and forest products are traded in world markets. They are worth billions of dollars.

  Underline the plants that are important economic resources in today's global market.

# Plant compounds are essential to modern medicine.

**Pharmacology** is the study of drugs and their effects on the body. Many drugs used today are developed from plants. Salicin, which comes from willow trees, is the active ingredient in aspirin. Taxol is used as a cancer treatment. It comes from the Pacific yew tree and had long been used by Native Americans for many other conditions.

**Alkaloids** are strong plant chemicals that contain nitrogen. Some alkaloids interfere with cell division and help fight cancer. Taxol is an alkaloid. Childhood leukemia is treated with alkaloids from the Madagascar periwinkle flower. Scientists also work to develop synthetic* drugs based on natural compounds.

 Underline two drugs used today that come from plants.

* ACADEMIC VOCABULARY

**synthetic** human-made

## 20.4 Vocabulary Check

| | |
|---|---|
| botany | pharmacology |
| ethnobotany | alkaloid |

Choose the correct term from the list above for each description.

**Mark It Up**

Go back and highlight each sentence that has a vocabulary word in **bold**.

1. compound that can interfere with cell division _____

2. study of plants _____

3. study of drugs and their effect on the body _____

4. how people in different cultures use plants _____

## 20.4 The Big Picture

5. How did changing from hunting and gathering to farming affect local populations? _____

_____

6. Why is it important to study how other cultures use plants for medicines? _____

_____

# Chapter 20 Review

1. What two adaptations help plants retain moisture while still allowing air to move in and out? _____

2. Which of the following is evidence that land plants evolved from green algae?
   a. Green algae can survive being dry.
   b. Green algae are photosynthetic.
   c. Green algae use pollen grains to produce sperm.
   d. Green algae use stomata to keep water out.

3. Describe one major difference between mosses and ferns. _____

   _____

4. Which of the following is found ONLY in a seed plant?
   a. cuticle
   b. cotyledon
   c. vascular system
   d. sperm

5. How do flowers contribute to the reproductive success of angiosperms? _____

   _____

6. Does the illustration below show a monocot or a dicot? _____

7. Why is the underground food reserve important to a biennial plant?

   _____

8. How might ethnobotany play a role in pharmacology? _____

   _____

9. Explain why some alkaloids can help fight cancer. _____

   _____

# 21 Plant Structure and Function

## GETTING READY TO LEARN

### Preview Key Concepts

**21.1 Plant Cells and Tissues**
Plants have specialized cells and tissue systems.

**21.2 The Vascular System**
The vascular system allows for the transport of water, minerals, and sugars.

**21.3 Roots and Stems**
Roots and stems form the support system of vascular plants.

**21.4 Leaves**
Leaves absorb light and carry out photosynthesis.

### Review Academic Vocabulary

Write the correct word for each definition.

cuticle　　lignin　　osmosis　　tissue　　vascular system

1. _____ : waxy layer that holds in moisture

2. _____ : a way that water can diffuse across a membrane

3. _____ : tissues that transport resources throughout a plant

4. _____ : cells that work together to perform a similar function

5. _____ : strengthens the cell walls of some plants

### Preview Biology Vocabulary

Try to guess the meaning of each boldfaced word from its context.

| PHRASE | MY GUESS |
|---|---|
| 1. During **transpiration,** the outward flow of water creates a vacuum that pulls water upward through a plant. | |
| 2. **Fibrous roots** spread like a mat beneath the soil surface, anchoring the plant into the ground. | |
| 3. **Taproots** are able to get water from deep in the ground and can sometimes store food. | |
| 4. A leaf **blade** can come in many shapes and sizes. | |

# 21.1 Plant Cells and Tissues

**KEY CONCEPT** Plants have specialized cells and tissue systems.

## Plant tissues are made of three basic cell types.

Did you know that a plant's roots, stems or trunks, and leaves are considered the organs of the plant? As in other organisms, a plant's organs are made of tissues, and tissues are made of cells. Plants have three main organs, made of three tissue systems, mostly made up of three basic cell types.

**Parenchyma cells** A **parenchyma cell** (puh-REHNG-kuh-muh) stores starch, oil, and water. It is the most common type of cell and is found throughout the plant. These cells have thin walls and large water-filled vacuoles in the middle. Photosynthesis occurs in green chloroplasts within parenchyma cells in leaves. Inside roots and stems, a parenchyma cell's chloroplasts and colorless plastids store starch. Parenchyma cells can divide throughout their entire lives, and they help heal wounds to the plant and grow new parts.

Parenchyma cells have thin cell walls that can change shape.

**Collenchyma cells** A **collenchyma cell** (kuh-LEHNG-kuh-muh) provides support as the plant grows. These cells have either thin or thick walls. Most collenchyma cells are found in young tissues or leaves and shoots. Often they form stringlike strands, as in celery. The special feature of collenchyma cells is that they are flexible because they do not contain lignin. They change size as a leaf grows.

Collenchyma cells have walls that range from thin to thick.

**Sclerenchyma cells** A **sclerenchyma cell** (skluh-REHNG-kuh-muh) is the strongest of the basic cell types. They are very stiff and tough because of a second cell wall that contains lignin. But this means they cannot change size. Therefore, they are found in plant parts that are no longer growing. Many sclerenchyma cells die and fall apart when they mature, but they leave their rigid cell walls behind for support.

Sclerenchyma cells have very thick and rigid walls that support the plant, even when the cells die.

Underline a special trait of the cell walls of parenchyma, collenchyma, and sclerenchyma cells.

# Plant organs are made of three tissue systems.

A tissue is a group of cells working together to perform a certain task. Plants have three tissue systems: dermal, ground, and vascular tissue systems. The cells are often connected by plasmodesmata (PLAZ-muh-DEHZ-muh-tuh). These are strands of cytoplasm that pass through openings in cell walls. The cells of a plant tissue can share water, nutrients, and chemical signals through the plasmodesmata.

**Dermal tissue system**  Dermal tissue covers the outside of a plant and protects it. Epidermis is dermal tissue made of live parenchyma cells. Epidermal cells may secrete* a waxy material that becomes the cuticle on leaves and some stems. Dermal tissue made of dead parenchyma makes up the outer bark of woody plants.

Epidermis is dermal tissue made of live parenchyma cells.

**Ground tissue system**  Under the dermal tissue is the system of ground tissue, which makes up much of the inside of a plant. Ground tissue provides support and stores materials in roots and stems. In leaves, ground tissue contains chloroplasts for photosynthesis.

**Vascular Tissue System**  The ground tissue surrounds the system of vascular tissue, which transports water, mineral nutrients, and organic compounds to all parts of the plant. The vascular system is made of hollow tubes. **Xylem** (ZY-luhm) is vascular tissue that carries water and nutrients up from the roots to the rest of the plant. **Phloem** (FLOH-EHM) is vascular tissue that carries sugars produced by photosynthesis from the leaves to the rest of the plant.

 Underline three functions of ground tissue in plants.

Xylem     Phloem

* ACADEMIC VOCABULARY

**secrete** to form and give off a substance

parenchyma cell          ground tissue
collenchyma cell         vascular tissue
sclerenchyma cell        xylem
dermal tissue            phloem

**Mark It Up**

Go back and highlight each sentence that has a vocabulary word in **bold**.

**Choose the correct term from the list for each description.**

1. lignin makes it the strongest cell type _____

2. transports water, nutrients, and organic compounds throughout the plant _____

3. cell type that can divide throughout its life _____

4. transports products of photosynthesis _____

## 21.1   The Big Picture

5. Put the following three terms in order of their location in a plant, from inside to outside: ground tissue, dermal tissue, vascular tissue.

   _____

6. Name and describe the function of dermal tissue made of live parenchyma cells and dermal tissue made of dead parenchyma cells.

   _____

   _____

   _____

# 21.2 The Vascular System

**KEY CONCEPT** The vascular system allows for the transport of water, minerals, and sugars.

## Water and dissolved minerals move through xylem.

Your heart pumps blood through your body. But a tree has no heart to act as a pump. Water and dissolved minerals move up from the roots to the rest of the plant through xylem, a type of vascular tissue. Xylem is called a complex tissue because it contains other cells in addition to parenchyma, collenchyma, and sclerenchyma cells.

### Tracheids and Vessel Elements

A tracheid (TRAY-kee-ihd) is one type of specialized cell in xylem. These cells are long and narrow. Water flows from one cell to another through openings in the cell walls. Some vascular plants have another type of cell called a vessel element. These are shorter and wider than tracheids. Both cell types must mature and die before water can move through them. When a vessel element dies, the cell wall at either end breaks apart. The cells then connect end to end and form long tubes.

### How Water Moves In a Plant

**Cohesion-tension theory** The cohesion-tension theory states that the physical properties of water allow water to rise through a plant. Water molecules have a strong attraction for one another and for other surfaces. Water molecules that are next to each other form hydrogen bonds, and this creates a force called cohesion. Hydrogen bonds between a water molecule and another substance, such as the wall of xylem tissue, create a force called adhesion. Cohesion and adhesion create tension that moves water up through xylem.

**Capillary action** The tendency of water to move upward in a hollow tube is called capillary action. Capillary action is possible because of the tension created by cohesion and adhesion. But capillary action cannot lift water to the top branches by itself. Transpiration is the loss of water vapor, or evaporation, from leaves. The outward flow of water creates a vacuum* in the leaf xylem that pulls water upward.

Name the two forces that create the tension that moves water up through xylem.

_____

\* **ACADEMIC VOCABULARY**

**vacuum** an empty space

# Phloem carries sugar from photosynthesis throughout the plant.

Phloem tissue is a living, complex tissue made of cells called sieve elements. Phloem fluids, called sap, flow through holes at the ends of the cells. The products of photosynthesis move from the leaves to the stems and roots. Minerals traveling up through the xylem can also move into the phloem.

**Sources and sinks** Phloem sap can move in any direction. The **pressure-flow model** explains how sap moves through a plant from a sugar source to a sugar sink. A source is any part of a plant that has a high concentration of sugars. This is usually the leaves, but can also be the roots. A sink is the plant part that uses or stores the sugar, such as growing shoots and stems, fruit, or storage roots.

phloem

xylem

sugars

**1** Sugars move from their source, such as photosynthesizing leaves, into the phloem.

**2** Water moves from the xylem into the phloem by osmosis, due to the higher concentration of sugars in the phloem. The water flow helps move sugars through the phloem.

water

**3** The sugars move into the sink, such as a root or fruit, where they are stored.

**Loading the source** At a source, sugar moves into the phloem until the sugar reaches a high concentration. That means that at a source, there is a low concentration of water relative to sugars. To understand this, imagine that you have put a half cup of sugar into one cup of iced tea instead of just a spoonful. In the plant, water will then flow into the phloem by osmosis to reduce the high concentration of sugars.

**Unloading into the sink** The loading of sugars and the flow of water into the source creates high pressure. As sugar is unloaded into the sink, the concentration of sugar in the sink is lessened and the pressure decreases. This difference in pressure keeps the sugary sap flowing in the direction of the sink.

Explain the difference between a sugar source and a sugar sink in a plant and give one example of each.

_____

_____

_____

## 21.2 Vocabulary Check

**Mark It Up**

Go back and highlight each sentence that has a vocabulary word in **bold**.

cohesion-tension theory

transpiration

pressure-flow model

Choose the correct term from the list for each description.

**1.** explains how sap moves through a plant _____

**2.** creates upward force in a plant through evaporation _____

**3.** helps explain how water moves through xylem _____

## 21.2 The Big Picture

**4.** Describe the physical properties of water that support the cohesion-tension theory. _____

_____

_____

**5.** Why is it important that phloem sap be able to move in any direction through a plant? _____

_____

_____

# 21.3 Roots and Stems

**KEY CONCEPT** Roots and stems form the support system of vascular plants.

## Roots anchor plants and absorb mineral nutrients from soil.

Roots can make up over half of the body of plant. They anchor the plant to the soil and absorb, transport, and store water and minerals the plant needs.

**Parts of a root** Roots contain vascular, ground, and dermal tissue systems. There are four main parts of a root.

1. The **vascular cylinder\*** is in the center of the root and is made of xylem and phloem tissue. It is surrounded by ground tissue and covered with dermal tissue.

2. **Root hairs** are tiny projections on dermal tissue cells above the root tips. This is where most of the water is absorbed.

3. The **root cap** protects the growing part of the root as it pushes through the soil.

4. The **meristem** is made of cells that are the source of new cells for root growth. Apical (AY-pik-kul) meristems make the tips of roots and stems grow longer. Woody roots and stems also have lateral meristems, which make these plant parts thicker.

vascular cylinder

apical meristem

root cap

**Types of roots** A **fibrous root** system has thin strands, most of which are the same size. These strands spread out beneath the soil surface. A **taproot** system has a long, thick root with smaller branches that reach deep into the ground to get water. Some taproots, such as radishes and carrots, store food.

**Water and mineral uptake** When roots take up nutrients, they also absorb water. This is because mineral nutrients are usually dissolved in water. Plants use energy to move nutrients into the roots through active transport. The increased concentration of nutrients in the roots causes water to move into the root tip by osmosis.

 Circle the names of the four main parts of a root.

---

\* ACADEMIC VOCABULARY

**cylinder** a three-dimensional rounded shape that is longer than it is wide

## Stems support plants, transport materials, and provide storage.

Stems support flowers and leaves, but they do other things, too. Most of a plant's vascular system is in a stem, and stems can also store food and water. For example, a cactus stem can photosynthesize and store water. And while most stems grow above ground, potatoes and ginger are examples of underground stems.

Stems can be herbaceous or woody. Herbaceous stems are usually soft because they do not have many rigid xylem cells. Most herbaceous stems do not grow taller than two meters and they are often green and conduct photosynthesis. Herbaceous plants can be monocots or dicots.

Most plants with woody stems are dicots, such as oak trees or pine trees. Tree trunks are woody stems. The center of a woody stem, called heartwood, is the oldest part of the xylem. It provides support but no longer transports water. The sapwood around the heartwood does transport water.

**Stem growth** The meristem cells, which divide to create more cells, are active throughout the life of a plant. Growth that makes stems grow taller or roots grow longer is called **primary growth.** This type of growth occurs in apical meristems at the ends of stems and roots. Growth that makes the stems and roots of woody plants wider is called **secondary growth.** This type of growth takes place in lateral meristems in the outer layers of a tree trunk.

**VISUAL VOCAB**

**Primary growth** lengthens roots and stems.

**Secondary growth** widens roots and stems.

**Tree rings** The story of a tree's life can be read from its tree rings, which are formed through secondary growth. Each annual ring, which includes both a light and dark band, represents one year of growth. The age of a tree can be determined by counting the rings.

Tree rings also tell how much a tree grew each season. If there is a good supply of water during the spring, new xylem cells are wide and have thin walls. These cells will be light in color. A thick light-colored band means there was a lot or rain during that part of the year. When water is limited later in the year, the xylem cells are smaller and have thicker walls, so they appear darker in color.

bands

bark

heartwood

sapwood

one year
of growth
(dark band
plus light band)

Explain the difference between primary and secondary growth.

_____

_____

## 21.3    Vocabulary Check

vascular cylinder    fibrous root

root hair    taproot

root cap    primary growth

meristem    secondary growth

### Mark It Up

Go back and highlight each sentence that has a vocabulary word in **bold**.

**Fill in the blanks with the correct term from the list above.**

1. New cells form in the _____ as a plant grows.

2. A _____ can help a plant get water from deep underground.

3. The _____ protects the growing part of a root.

4. _____ growth takes place in the lateral meristems.

5. A _____ is a tiny projection that helps absorb water.

## 21.3    The Big Picture

6. What stimulates the absorption of water in a plant's roots? _____
   _____
   _____

7. What information might a tree's growth rings provide about the
   weather conditions during the tree's life? _____
   _____

# 21.4 Leaves

**KEY CONCEPT**  Leaves absorb light and carry out photosynthesis.

## Most leaves share some similar structures.

"Leaves of three, let it be." This is a saying of experienced hikers who know how to avoid poison ivy. Plant species have their own unique leaf shapes, specially adapted for light gathering and retaining water in their particular environment.

Leaves grow out from a plant's stem. Their basic parts are the blade and the petiole. The **blade** is usually wide and flat and it collects sunlight. The **petiole** is a thin stalk that connects the blade to the stem.

**Leaf tissues**  Like roots and stems, leaves have an outer covering of dermal tissue, which is covered by a waxy cuticle. Deep inside the leaf, the vascular tissue is surrounded by ground tissue. Between the top and bottom layers of a leaf is a type of parenchyma tissue called **mesophyll** (MEHZ-uh-FIHL).

**Stomata and guard cells**  The underside of a leaf has stomata for transpiration and gas exchange. During the day, a pair of **guard cells** around each stoma absorbs water and swells up into a semicircle shape, opening the stoma. Water evaporates and carbon dioxide can enter. When more water is lost than is taken up, the guard cells deflate, and the stomata close.

**Leaf characteristics**  Leaves come in many shapes and sizes. A simple leaf has just one blade connected to the petiole. A compound leaf has many blades on one petiole. These groups of blades are called leaflets.

**VISUAL VOCAB**

The **blade** of a leaf collects sunlight for photosynthesis. It connects to the plant's stem by a **petiole**.

- blade
- petiole

---

**LEAF CHARACTERISTICS USED TO IDENTIFY PLANTS**

Certain leaf characteristics—such as the leaf type, the vein pattern, and the shape of the leaf margin—can be used to identify plants.

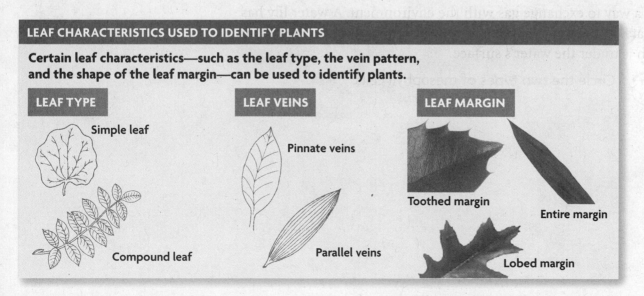

**LEAF TYPE**
- Simple leaf
- Compound leaf

**LEAF VEINS**
- Pinnate veins
- Parallel veins

**LEAF MARGIN**
- Toothed margin
- Entire margin
- Lobed margin

Other traits of leaves used to identify plants include the pattern of veins and the leaf edge, or margin.

 Name three leaf characteristics used to identify a plant.

_____

_____

## Most leaves are specialized systems for photosynthesis.

Photosynthesis occurs mainly in the leaves of a plant. You will recall that the process requires carbon dioxide, water, and light. Leaves have structures and adaptations that allow photosynthesis to occur, even in very different environments.

**Photosynthetic structures** Photosynthesis occurs in the mesophyll tissue of a leaf. There are two kinds of mesophyll. Palisade mesophyll is a layer of tall, rectangular cells that absorb light that enters the leaf. Beneath this layer is the spongy mesophyll, which is a layer of loosely packed cells with many air spaces between them. The air spaces connect to the outside of the plant through the stomata, allowing for gas exchange.

This cross section of a leaf shows structures for photosynthesis.

**Leaf adaptations** Leaves are adapted for photosynthesis in the plant's particular environment. For example, in the desert, it is important to prevent water loss. Cacti leaves are the sharp spines that protect them and reduce water loss. Plants that live in water have plenty of water but need a way to exchange gas with the environment. A water lily has stomata on the upper surface of its leaves, instead of on the bottom, which is under the water's surface.

 Circle the two types of mesophyll cells.

## 21.4 Vocabulary Check

blade            mesophyll
petiole          guard cell

**Choose the correct term from the list for each description.**

1. a thin stalk of a leaf _____

2. tissue in which photosynthesis occurs _____

3. main body of a leaf _____

4. helps to open and close stoma _____

## 21.4 The Big Picture

5. Explain how palisade and spongy mesophylls function for photosynthesis. _____
_____
_____

6. Why are guard cells important? _____
_____

7. In what kind of environment might you find a leaf with a very thick cuticle? Explain. _____
_____
_____

# Chapter 21 Review

1. Which basic cell type provides support as a plant grows?
   _____

2. Which basic plant cell type is the strongest? _____

3. Which of the following is a function of the dermal tissue system?
   a. stores starch and water for the plant
   b. protects the plant
   c. supports roots and stems
   d. produces lignin for support

4. Describe the functions of xylem and phloem.
   _____
   _____

5. Explain how transpiration helps move water up through a plant.
   _____
   _____

6. How are forces of cohesion and adhesion created in a plant?
   _____
   _____
   _____

7. Secondary growth takes place in the
   a. root cap mersistems.
   b. apical meristems.
   c. lateral meristems.
   d. leaf meristems.

8. What characteristics of mesophyll make it possible for most of a plant's photosynthesis to occur here? _____
   _____

9. What would happen if the guard cells never closed the stomata?
   _____

10. What environmental conditions affect a leaf's adaptations?
    _____

CHAPTER

# 22 Plant Growth, Reproduction, and Response

## GETTING READY TO LEARN

### Preview Key Concepts

**22.1 Plant Life Cycles**
All plants alternate between two phases in their life cycles.

**22.2 Reproduction in Flowering Plants**
Reproduction of flowering plants takes place within flowers.

**22.3 Seed Dispersal and Germination**
Seeds disperse and begin to grow when conditions are favorable.

**22.4 Asexual Reproduction**
Plants can produce genetic clones of themselves through asexual reproduction.

**22.5 Plant Hormones and Responses**
Plant hormones guide plant growth and development.

### Review Academic Vocabulary

Write the correct word for each definition.

diploid     haploid     meiosis     mitosis     zygote

1. _____ : fertilized female gamete

2. _____ : diploid cell divides into four haploid cells

3. _____ : cell divides its nucleus and contents

4. _____ : containing only one copy of each chromosome

5. _____ : containing two copies of each chromosome

### Preview Biology Vocabulary

Two key terms from this chapter share the same word part. Read the definitions and guess what the word part means.

| TERM | DEFINITION | WHAT I THINK -*phyte* MEANS |
|------|------------|------------------------------|
| sporo**phyte** | spore-producing plant | |
| gameto**phyte** | gamete-producing plant | |

McDougal Littell Biology

**359**

# 22.1 Plant Life Cycles

**KEY CONCEPT** All plants alternate between two phases in their life cycles.

## Plant life cycles alternate* between producing spores and gametes.

Recall that animals produce gametes—sperm and eggs—through meiosis. After fertilization, a new diploid organism is produced. Diploid cells have two copies of each chromosome ($2n$).

Plants also produce gametes, But a plant reproductive cycle has a few more steps. A plant's diploid plant body produces spores through meiosis. A spore develops into a haploid plant body. Haploid cells have one copy of each chromosome ($1n$). A life cycle that alternates between diploid and haploid phases is called **alternation of generations.**

**The Diploid Phase** A fertilized egg, called a zygote, begins the diploid phase of the plant life cycle. A zygote divides by mitosis and grows into a mature* **sporophyte** (SPAWR-uh-FYT), or spore-producing plant. Spores are produced by specialized cells that divide by meiosis, which reduces the number of chromosomes to half.

**The Haploid Phase** A spore is the beginning of the haploid phase. It divides by mitosis and grows into a mature **gametophyte** (guh-MEE-tuh-FYT), or gamete-producing plant. Sperm and eggs are produced here through mitosis. Once fertilization takes place, the cycle continues with a new sporophyte.

> **VOCABULARY**
> The suffix *–phyte* comes from the Greek word *phuton*, meaning "plant."

**ALTERNATION OF GENERATIONS**

Plant life cycles alternate between a sporophyte phase, which produces spores, and a gametophyte stage, which produces gametes.

sporophyte ($2n$)

zygote ($2n$)

fertilization

SPOROPHYTE PHASE

meiosis

GAMETOPHYTE PHASE

gametes ($1n$)

spores ($1n$)

gametophyte ($1n$)

 **INSTANT REPLAY** Circle the starts of the diploid and haploid phases of a life cycle.

## Life cycle phases look different among various plant groups.

The sporophyte and gametophyte generations look different for nonvascular plants, seedless vascular plants, and seed plants.

***

* ACADEMIC VOCABULARY

**alternate** to do one thing and then another, back and forth

**mature** fully grown

## Life Cycle of Nonvascular Plants: Moss

The gametophyte phase is dominant in nonvascular plants. When you look at a green, carpetlike patch of moss, you are looking at gametophytes.

**Sporophyte** Moss sporophytes are stalklike structures that grow up from the gametophyte. At the tip of a moss sporophyte is a capsule. It contains sacs called sporangia that produce spores. When the spores are mature, the capsule opens and releases them. If a spore lands in a suitable spot, it can grow into a gametophyte.

**Gametophyte** Each male structure in the gametophyte produces hundreds of sperm and each female structure produces one egg. In the presence of water, sperm swim to and fertilize an egg, and the sporophyte phase begins again.

capsule

sporophyte (2*n*)

gametophyte (1*n*)

## Life Cycle of Seedless Vascular Plants: Ferns

The sporophyte is the dominant phase for all vascular plants. When you look at a fern with it's big green leaves, you are looking at a sporophyte.

**Sporophyte** On the underside of a fern leaf, called a frond, you might see brown dots. These are sori, which are groups of sporangia. Recall that the sporangia are sacs that produce spores. The spores are released and, if they land in a suitable spot, develop into a gametophyte.

**Gametophyte** A fern gametophyte, called a prothallus, is about the size of your little fingernail. It anchors itself to the soil. Special structures produce sperm and eggs. In the presence of water, sperm are released and swim toward an egg. After fertilization, a zygote forms on the prothallus. This is the beginning of the new sporophyte generation. As the zygote grows, the prothallus rots away. The mature sporophyte is the familiar fern plant, which will produce spores, and the cycle will begin again.

sori

sporophyte (2*n*)

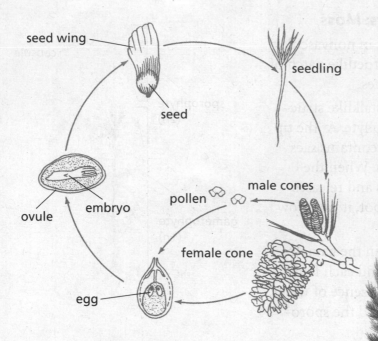

## Life Cycle of Seed Plants: Conifers

Remember that the sporophyte is the familiar form for all vascular plants, including seed plants. One difference between seedless plants and seed plants is that seed plants produce two types of spores that develop into male and female gametophytes. Another difference is that the gametophytes of seed plants are microscopic.

**Sporophyte** Pine trees are typical conifer sporophytes. A pine tree has male and female cones. The female cones are often bigger and more scaly than male cones. Each scale of a female cone has two ovules that produce spores. Male spores are produced in male cones.

**Gametophyte** Only one spore in each ovule will develop into a microscopic female gametophyte, which will produce an egg. Male spores develop into pollen grains, the male gametophytes of seed plants.

- **Pollination** Male cones release clouds of pollen in the spring. When a pollen grain lands on a female cone, it sticks. Pollination occurs when the pollen grain reaches the small opening of an ovule. Eggs have been produced in the ovule, and sperm develop from one cell of the pollen grain. A pollen tube grows from the pollen grain toward an egg. In pine trees, this can take a year even though the distance is only several millimeters.

- **Fertilization** The sperm travel down the pollen tube toward the egg. One sperm will fertilize an egg, forming a zygote. The zygote will develop into an embryo. Meanwhile, the ovule develops into a protective seed.

- **A New Cycle** When the seeds are mature, the scales of the cone open up and release them. The pine tree seedling that grows from the seed is the sporophyte of a new generation.

 What is a major difference between the gametophytes of a seedless plant and a seed plant?

_____

_____

| 22.1 | Vocabulary Check |
|---|---|

**Mark It Up**

Go back and highlight each sentence that has a vocabulary word in **bold**.

alternation of generations
sporophyte
gametophyte

**Choose the correct term from the list for each description.**

1. includes a 2*n* phase and 1*n* phase _____

2. it has one copy of each chromosome _____

3. the most visible part of a vascular plant _____

| 22.1 | The Big Picture |
|---|---|

4. In plants, why is mitosis the process that produces gametes, instead of meiosis?_____

_____

_____

5. How are seedless plants spread to new areas?

_____

_____

6. To which generation of a conifer's life cycle do the pine cones belong?

_____

# 22.2 Reproduction in Flowering Plants

**KEY CONCEPT** Reproduction of flowering plants takes place within the flowers.

## Flowers contain reproductive organs protected by specialized leaves.

Most people prefer sweet-smelling, colorful flowers for their gardens. These same characteristics attract animal pollinators.

**The Outside of a Flower** You may have noticed that different flower parts are arranged in layers. The outermost layer of a flower is made of sepals. **Sepals** are modified leaves that protect the flower. They are often green but can be brightly colored. Just inside the sepals is a layer of **petals,** which are also modified leaves. Brightly colored petals can attract animal pollinators. When sepals and petals are the same color, they are called tepals. This occurs in monocot flowers, such as lilies. Flowering plants that use wind pollination usually have small sepals and petals, or even none at all.

**The Inside of a Flower** In some species, flowers have either male or female structures. But most flowers have both. A **stamen** is the male structure of a flower. It has a stalk, called a filament, that supports an anther. Anthers produce pollen grains. The innermost part of the flower is the female structure, called a **carpel.** There are often several carpels that join together, forming a pistil. Each carpel has three parts. The stigma is the top part. It's sticky and holds pollen grains when they land there. The style is a tube that leads from the stigma to the ovary. At the base of the flower is the **ovary,** where female gametophytes are produced.

**INSTANT REPLAY** How can colorful sepals and petals help a flower reproduce?

_____

_____

## Flowering plants can be pollinated by wind or animals.

When a pollen grain reaches the stigma of the same plant species, that flower has been pollinated. The way a flower looks gives clues about how it is pollinated. Wind-pollinated flowers are usually small and produce large amounts of pollen. This requires a lot of energy.

Insects, birds, and other animals often pollinate flowers that have bright colors or sweet smells. When an animal visits a flower to collect pollen or nectar for food, it is dusted with pollen grains. As the animal looks for food in another flower, pollen from the first flower may brush onto the stigma of the other flower. This method of pollination is more direct and more efficient than wind pollination.

 What is the advantage of animal pollination for a flowering plant?

_____

_____

## Fertilization takes place within the flower.

The flower parts you have just learned about are part of the sporophyte. The gametophytes are tiny and enclosed in the flower.

**Male Gametophytes** Anthers produce pollen grains, the male gametophytes of seed plants. Cells within the anthers divide by meiosis to produce four male haploid spores. Each spore divides again, by mitosis, to produce two haploid cells. These two cells form a single pollen grain.

**Female Gametophytes** One female gametophyte forms in each ovule of an ovary. First, one cell in the ovule divides by meiosis to produce four female spores. The nucleus of one of these spores divides by mitosis three times. This spore now has eight haploid nuclei ($1n$). Membranes grow between the nuclei to form seven cells. A large cell in the middle has two nuclei, called polar nuclei. One of the other cells develops into an egg. These seven cells form the female gametophyte, also called an embryo sac.

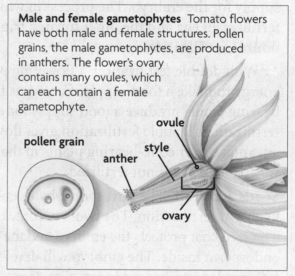

**Male and female gametophytes** Tomato flowers have both male and female structures. Pollen grains, the male gametophytes, are produced in anthers. The flower's ovary contains many ovules, which can each contain a female gametophyte.

pollen grain

anther

style

ovule

ovary

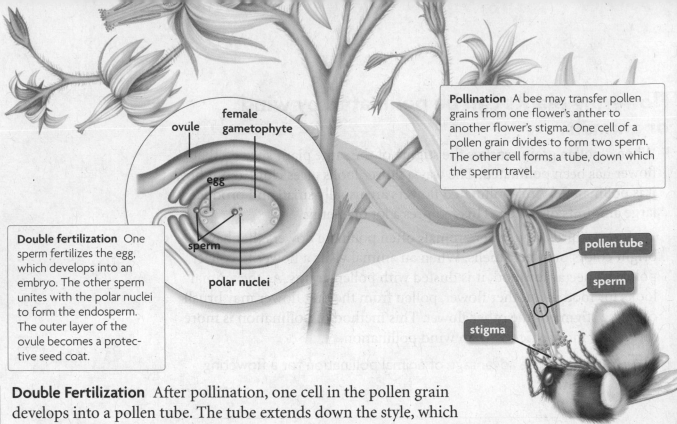

**Pollination** A bee may transfer pollen grains from one flower's anther to another flower's stigma. One cell of a pollen grain divides to form two sperm. The other cell forms a tube, down which the sperm travel.

ovule

female gametophyte

egg

sperm

polar nuclei

pollen tube

sperm

stigma

**Double fertilization** One sperm fertilizes the egg, which develops into an embryo. The other sperm unites with the polar nuclei to form the endosperm. The outer layer of the ovule becomes a protective seed coat.

**Double Fertilization** After pollination, one cell in the pollen grain develops into a pollen tube. The tube extends down the style, which leads to the ovule. The other cell in the pollen grain divides by mitosis to produce two sperm ($1n$). Both sperm travel down the pollen tube. One sperm fertilizes the egg. The other sperm joins with the two polar nuclei. This cell now has a triploid ($3n$) nucleus, and will become the **endosperm,** a food supply for the embryo. The process in which one sperm fertilizes an egg and the other forms a triploid cell is called **double fertilization.**

With double fertilization, a flowering plant only uses energy to make a food supply if an egg is fertilized. Cone-bearing plants produce a food supply for every egg before fertilization. Double fertilization gives flowering plants an advantage over cone-bearing plants in that energy is not wasted if an egg is not fertilized.

**Seeds and Fruit** The next sporophyte generation begins at fertilization. The ovule becomes a seed. The seed coat protects the embryo and the endosperm inside. The embryo will develop one or two cotyledons, or seed leaves. Cotyledons can also provide food for the new plant until photosynthesis begins.

The **endosperm** nourishes the developing plant embryo inside of the seed coat. The prefix *endo-* means "inside," and *sperm* comes from the Greek word *sperma*, which means "seed."

endosperm

seed coat

embryo

**Seeds and fruit** Many seeds develop inside the ovary of each tomato flower. While the seeds develop, the ovary tissue develops into the juicy flesh of a tomato. A few seeds will find their way into the soil to grow into new tomato plants.

The ovary around the seed develops into a fruit. Apples, watermelons, and cherries are fruits. But so are many vegetables, grains, and nuts. Tomatoes and cucumbers are fruits that contain many seeds. A peanut shell is also a fruit. The next section explains how a fruit helps a seed disperse, or move, to a new area.

What happens to the polar nuclei in an embryo sac?

_____

_____

## 22.2 Vocabulary Check

**Mark It Up**

Go back and highlight each sentence that has a vocabulary word in **bold**.

| | |
|---|---|
| sepal | ovary |
| petal | endosperm |
| stamen | double fertilization |
| carpel | |

**Fill in the blanks with the correct term from the list above.**

1. A _____ is the male structure of a flower.

2. The _____ is the food supply for the developing embryo.

3. The female structure of a flower is called a _____.

4. A _____ is a modified leaf that protects a developing flower.

## 22.2 The Big Picture

5. Put the following terms in the correct order to show the journey of a sperm to an egg: pollen tube, egg, anther, stigma

_____

6. What advantage does double fertilization provide to flowering plants?

_____

_____

_____

# 22.3 Seed Dispersal and Germination

**KEY CONCEPT** Seeds disperse and begin to grow when conditions are favorable.

## Animals, wind, and water can spread seeds.

Fruits help disperse seeds. Seed dispersal is important because a plant that grows right next to its parent may compete for the same space, sunlight, water, and nutrients. Fruits come in different shapes and sizes with different adaptations for spreading seeds.

**Tasty Fruits** Animals are attracted to fleshy fruits that taste good, such as apples and berries. An animal eats the fruit and digests the flesh. But the protective seed coat allows the seeds to pass through the animal's digestive tract. The animal deposits the seeds, along with fecal* fertilizer. The seed may sprout on this little mound of fertilizer.

**Sticky Fruits** Some fruits can ride away from the parent plant on the body of an animal. Burrs can stick to an animal that passes by. The burr will fall off later, after getting a free ride from the animal.

**Traveling Fruits** Seeds dispersed by the wind often have fruits that act like parachutes* or wings. Clumps of cotton from cottonwood trees are fruits with a seed attached. Some plants that grow near water produce fruits that float. Coconuts can float for thousands of miles across an ocean.

 What is the function of fruit?

_____

_____

## Seeds begin to grow when environmental conditions are favorable.

**Dormancy** It may be days or years until seeds begin to grow into new plants. An embryo that is not growing is in a state of **dormancy.** Dormancy can end with the right temperature, moisture, oxygen, and light levels. But some seeds must pass through an animal's digestive tract to make the seed coat soft. Seed dormancy allows the next generation of plants to grow when conditions are favorable.

---

**\* ACADEMIC VOCABULARY**

**fecal** waste material produced by a living organism

**parachute** an object that helps something float through the air

**368** McDougal Littell Biology

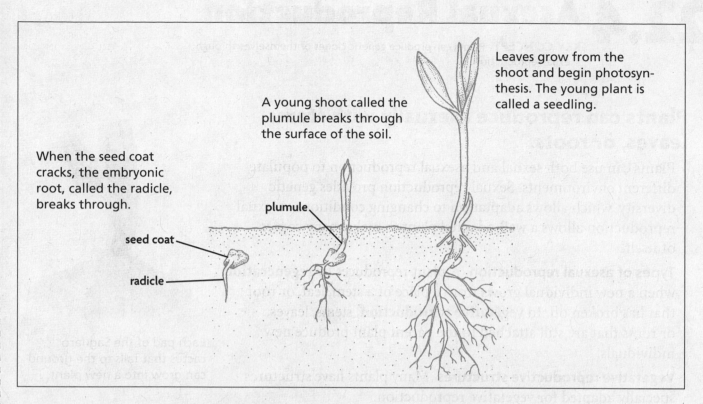

Leaves grow from the shoot and begin photosynthesis. The young plant is called a seedling.

A young shoot called the plumule breaks through the surface of the soil.

When the seed coat cracks, the embryonic root, called the radicle, breaks through.

plumule

seed coat

radicle

**Germination** During **germination,** the embryo breaks out of the seed and begins to grow. It starts when the embryo takes up water, the seed swells, and the seed coat cracks. The endosperm provides sugars for the growing embryo.

Underline the benefit that dormancy provides to a plant.

## 22.3  Vocabulary Check

dormancy
germination

1. Circle the word that means "stopped growing."

2. Underline the word that means "begin to grow."

## 22.3  The Big Picture

3. What are three ways that flowering plants disperse their seeds?

_____

4. Why must you water a garden that has newly planted seeds?

_____

# 22.4 Asexual Reproduction

**KEY CONCEPT** Plants can produce genetic clones of themselves through asexual reproduction.

## Plants can reproduce asexually with stems, leaves, or roots.

Plants can use both sexual and asexual reproduction to populate different environments. Sexual reproduction provides genetic diversity, which allows adaptation to changing conditions. Asexual reproduction allows a well-adapted plant to make many copies of itself.

**Types of asexual reproduction** A plant reproduces by **regeneration** when a new individual grows from a piece of a stem, leaf, or root that has broken off. In **vegetative reproduction,** stems, leaves, or roots that are still attached to the parent plant produce new individuals.

Each pad of the Saguaro cactus that falls to the ground can grow into a new plant.

**Vegetative reproductive structures** Many plants have structures specially adapted for vegetative reproduction.

- Stems that grow horizontally along the ground are called runners, or stolons. At certain points on a stolon, a new plant grows.
- Horizontal* underground stems are called rhizomes. New plants grow from buds in the rhizome's joints.
- A tuber is an underground stem modified for storage. Potatoes are tubers. The "eyes" of a potato are buds that can sprout new plants.
- Bulbs are underground storage stems surrounded by modified leaves and covered with a papery skin. Tulips and onions are bulbs. When conditions are right, bulbs divide to produce new plants.

 Underline four structures used for vegetative reproduction.

## People can produce plants with special traits using vegetative structures.

People use a process called vegetative propagation to grow plants with special traits, such as seedless fruits. This process uses a plant's ability to reproduce from pieces of parent plant. There are few ways to do this.

**\* ACADEMIC VOCABULARY**

**horizontal** across or side to side, as opposed to up and down

If a cutting from a stem or leaf is buried in soil or placed in water, it will produce new roots. Cuttings are often made from houseplants. Making cuttings is quick and doesn't cost much. In grafting, the vegetative structures of two or more plants are joined together. For example, an incision is made in one tree, then a branch or bud from another tree is attached. Grafting allows a plant grower to reproduce two or more special traits in a new plant.

**What are the two main types of asexual reproduction?**

_____

_____

## 22.4 Vocabulary Check

**Mark It Up**

Go back and highlight each sentence that has a vocabulary word in **bold**.

regeneration

vegetative reproduction

**Choose the correct term from the list for each description.**

1. a new plant grows from a rhizome _____

2. a piece of a leaf can produce a new plant _____

## 22.4 The Big Picture

3. Provide two reasons why a plant grower would use vegetative reproduction. _____

_____

_____

4. If genetic diversity is so important, why do plants have the ability to use asexual reproduction? _____

_____

5. How are rhizomes and tubers alike and how are they different? _____

_____

_____

# 22.5 Plant Hormones and Responses

**KEY CONCEPT** Plant hormones guide plant growth and development.

## Plant hormones regulate* plant functions.

A **hormone** is a chemical messenger produced in one part of an organism that affects the activity of cells in another part. Hormones direct and regulate many activities that are important to survival and reproduction.

Hormones begin their work when they move from the cells that make them to their target cells. Target cells have receptors that recognize the hormone. When a hormone meets the right receptor, it causes a response. There are several groups of plant hormones based on what they do and their chemical properties.

- **Gibberellins** (jihb-uh-REHL-ihnz) produce big changes in size. They end seed dormancy, start germination, and help a young seedling grow quickly. Gibberellins are also responsible for the large size of many fruits and the fast upward growth of some flower stalks.

- **Ethylene** (EHTH-uh-LEEN) is produced by fruits and causes them to ripen. Commercial* growers use ethylene. Tomatoes can be picked before they are ripe. After they are shipped to the markets, the tomatoes are exposed to ethylene gas, which turns them a ripe red outside. However, it does not produce the same sugars that are made when a tomato ripens on the vine.

- **Cytokinins** (sy-tuh-KY-nihnz) stimulate cytokinesis, which is the final stage of cell division. They are produced in growing roots and developing seeds and fruits. They are also involved in lateral, or sideways, growth of branches.

Gibberellins are involved in the rapid growth of sunflowers.

* ACADEMIC VOCABULARY

**regulate** to control something

**commercial** business involved in buying and selling goods

- **Auxins** (AWK-sihnz) make plant cells in the apical meristem, or growing tip, become longer. This causes the main stem to grow upward. However, a high amount of auxins in the roots can prevent plant growth. This is why auxins are often found in herbicides, chemicals used to kill unwanted plants. As you will learn in the next section, auxins also control some forms of **tropism,** which is the movement of a plant in response to an environmental stimulus.

**Name four plant hormones and describe what they do.**

_____

_____

_____

# Plants can respond to light, touch, gravity, and seasonal changes.

If you've ever been outside on a very hot summer day, you may have responded by moving to a shady place. Plants cannot change locations, but they do have ways of responding to their environment.

**Phototropism**   When light hits a plant stem, auxins build up on the shaded side. Auxins cause cells to grow longer. The longer cells on the shaded side cause the stem to bend toward the light. The response of a plant to grow toward light is called **phototropism.**

**Thigmotropism**   A plant's growth response to touch is called **thigmotropism.** This can be seen in climbing plants and vines. The plants grow in coils around anything they touch. Contact with the object causes the same type of cell growth found in other tropisms. Wind is a type of touch, too. Plants on a windy hillside will grow as if pushed in the direction of the wind.

**Gravitropism**   When a seed germinates underground, roots grow down into the soil, and the shoot grows upward toward the surface. This up-and-down growth is called **gravitropism,** because the plant is responding to Earth's gravity. Positive gravitropism is growth in the direction that gravity pulls, downward. Upward growth is negative gravitropism because it is against the force of gravity.

**Rapid Responses**   Some plants have very rapid, or fast, responses that are often adaptations to help protect plants from predators. For example, the mimosa, or sensitive plant, quickly folds it leaves together a few seconds after it is touched. The Venus flytrap flower, which catches and "digests" insects, can close it leaves on an insect in less than a second.

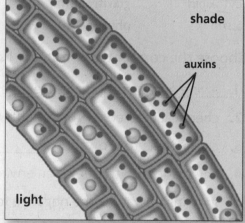
Auxins build upon the shaded side, causing cells to lengthen and the stem to bend toward light.

**Photoperiodism** What stimulates a shrub to flower or a tree to drop its leaves? The response in which plants can take signals from the changing lengths of day and night throughout the year is called **photoperiodism.** Shorter days and longer nights during the fall help trigger the leaves of many deciduous trees to change color.

Name two functions of rapid response in plants.

_____

_____

## 22.5 Vocabulary Check

**Mark It Up**

Go back and highlight each sentence that has a vocabulary word in **bold.**

| | |
|---|---|
| hormone | tropism |
| gibberellin | phototropism |
| ethylene | thigmotropism |
| cytokinin | gravitropism |
| auxin | photoperiodism |

**Choose the correct term from the list for each description.**

1. a vine grows around a fence pole _____

2. chemical messenger that affects cellular activity _____

3. causes cells to grow longer _____

4. any plant growth due to an environmental stimulus _____

5. growing upward is the negative form of this _____

## 22.5 The Big Picture

7. Why are receptors important to plant hormones? _____
_____

8. What is the function of cytokinins found in developing seeds and fruits?_____
_____

9. What is the relationship between auxins and phototropism? _____
_____

# Chapter 22 Review

1. What roles do the sporophyte and gametophyte play in a plant's life cycle? _____

   _____

2. List the basic steps of the alternation of generations in plants and label the plant parts at each step as either 1*n* or 2*n*.

   _____

   _____

   _____

   _____

3. Which of the following is associated ONLY with double fertilization?
   a. pollen tube
   b. haploid spore
   c. endosperm
   d. ovule

4. Name two male parts of a flower and describe the function of each.

   _____

   _____

5. Why is it important that seeds disperse away from the parent plant?

   _____

   _____

6. Seed _____ allow(s) a plant to germinate under favorable environmental conditions.
   a. coats
   b. burrs
   c. dispersal
   d. dormancy

7. Name four types of vegetative structures. _____

   _____

8. What is the difference between phototropism and photoperiodism?

   _____

   _____

   _____

# 23 Invertebrate Diversity

## GETTING READY TO LEARN

### Preview Key Concepts

**23.1 Animal Characteristics**
Animals are diverse but share common characteristics.

**23.2 Animal Diversity**
More than 95 percent of all animal species are invertebrates.

**23.3 Sponges and Cnidarians**
Sponges and cnidarians are the simplest animals.

**23.4 Flatworms, Mollusks, and Annelids**
Flatworms, mollusks, and annelids belong to closely related phyla.

**23.5 Roundworms**
Roundworms have bilateral symmetry and shed their outer skeleton to grow.

**23.6 Echinoderms**
Echinoderms are on the same evolutionary branch as vertebrates.

### Review Academic Vocabulary

Write the correct word for each definition.

sporophyte    gametophyte    germination    phototropism    auxin

1. _____ : beginning of the haploid phase of a plant

2. _____ : embryo breaking out of a seed coat

3. _____ : plant hormone

4. _____ : bending toward the light

5. _____ : spore divides and matures into this

### Preview Biology Vocabulary

Try to guess the meaning of each boldfaced word from its context.

| PHRASE | MY GUESS |
|---|---|
| 1. Unlike insects, spiders, or snails, all birds, fish, and mammals are **vertebrates**. | |
| 2. Sponges have no muscles or nerve cells to move, so they are **sessile**. | |

# 23.1 Animal Characteristics

**KEY CONCEPT** Animals are diverse but share common characteristics.

Humans are animals. So are jellyfish, cockroaches, tapeworms, sea stars, and dogs. Animals come in many different shapes and sizes. They also share a common ancestry and physical and genetic characteristics.

## Animals are the most physically diverse kingdom of organisms.

Animals are an amazingly diverse group of organisms. For example, the huge blue whale is two times longer than a school bus. Rotifers, tiny organisms that live in water, are smaller than the period at the end of this sentence.

Some animals look like soft tubes. Others have muscular bodies inside hard shells. Some have many specialized tissues and organs, and others have no distinct tissues at all. Some animals walk, burrow, swim, or fly. Others spend their adult lives stuck in a single spot.

Animal body plans have many shapes and sizes.

 Underline some of the diversity found in the animal kingdom.

## All animals share a set of characteristics.

Animals share certain characters, which are features that can be inherited. These characters set animals apart from other multicellular organisms. The characters also suggest that all animals have a common ancestor that lived millions of years ago.

**All animals are multicellular heterotrophs.** Unlike plant cells, animal cells cannot make their own food. They do not have chloroplasts for photosynthesis. Therefore, all animals are heterotrophs, meaning they must eat other organisms to get the nutrients they need. All animals are also eukaryotes, or multicellular organisms.

**Animal cells are supported by collagen.** Animal cells do not have rigid cell walls. Instead, collagen gives these cells their shape. **Collagen** is a protein found only in animals. Skin, bone, ligaments, fingernails, and hair contain collagen. Individual collagen proteins combine, like a rope, to form fibers that are strong and flexible.* These fibers form a network that cells use for support. Collagen is also an important part of the jointed skeleton that many animals have.

* ACADEMIC VOCABULARY

**flexible** able to bend

**Animals are diploid and usually reproduce sexually.** All animals can produce diploid offspring. This means that the offspring have one set of chromosomes from each parent. But some animals do not always use sexual reproduction. For example, a *Hydra* can also make a copy of itself by developing a bud that grows into a new *Hydra*. The two *Hydras* then split apart. This type of asexual reproduction is known as budding.

**Most animals have *Hox* genes.** In animals, **homeotic** genes control the early development of cells into specific types of organs and tissues. Within each homeotic gene is a sequence* of nucleotides called **homeobox,** or *Hox* genes. The *Hox* genes control where organs and tissues develop from the animal's head to its tail.

 Highlight the characteristics that all animals share.

* ACADEMIC VOCABULARY

**sequence** arranged in a certain order

## 23.1 Vocabulary Check

| Mark It Up |
|---|
| Go back and highlight each sentence that has a vocabulary word in **bold**. |

collagen homeobox

homeotic

**Choose the correct term from the list above for each description.**

1. determine the position of organs and tissues in an organism
   _____ genes

2. protein that forms support network for cells _____

3. affect early development in animals _____ genes

## 23.1 The Big Picture

4. All animals are heterotrophs. Explain why this is the case. _____

_____

5. What do all animal body parts that contain collagen have in common?

_____

6. What is the difference between homeotic genes and *Hox* genes? _____

_____

# 23.2 Animal Diversity

**KEY CONCEPT**  More than 95 percent of all animal species are invertebrates.

When you think of an animal, a vertebrate such as dog or bird may come to mind. However, most animals are invertebrates and look nothing like a dog or a bird. Biologists look for certain characteristics that help them sort animals into separate groups. Then they can arrange those groups into a family tree.

## Each animal phylum has a unique body plan.

A **vertebrate** is an animal with an internal segmented backbone. Humans are vertebrates, and they tend to pay more attention to other vertebrates, such as cats and dogs. But vertebrates make up less than five percent of all known animal species. Most animals are **invertebrates,** which means they have no backbones.

**Animal phyla**  Scientists use shared characters to separate animals into more than 30 major groups. Each group, or **phylum** (plural, *phyla*), has a specific set of physical characteristics. This is true both in phyla where species look very much alike and in phyla where they look very different from one another.

**INVERTEBRATE SPECIES BY GROUP**

**Arthropods, which include insects, make up the largest group of invertebrates.**

3%  5%

6%

86%

- Arthropods
- Mollusks
- Worms
- Sponges, cnidarians, echinoderms, and others

**Homeobox genes and body plans**  If you look at pictures of fish, birds, and land animals, you will see how different their body plans are. Some have fins, others have wings, and still others have four legs. Differences in body plans come from different directions given by the homeobox, or *Hox*, genes.

The *Hox* genes tell embryonic cells what part of the body they are going to become, such as the head, middle, or tail. The first *Hox* genes appeared millions of years ago and were copied over and over. Along the way, some genes mutated and produced new and different forms.

A mutation in a *Hox* gene can change an animal's entire body plan. As a result, animal bodies would become more diverse over time. Scientists think that mutations in *Hox* genes may be one reason why there are so many different animal species.

**INSTANT REPLAY**  What influences the different body plans seen in various animal groups? _____

_____

_____

# Animals are grouped using a variety of criteria.*

Animals are placed in separate groups based on certain characteristics. Three criteria used to group animals are body plan symmetry, number of tissue layers, and developmental patterns.

**Body plan symmetry** If you draw a line down the middle of a square, both sides are equal in shape and size. The dividing line is called the central axis. Symmetry refers to how alike an object is on each side of its central axis. Most animal body plans fall into one of two types of symmetry.

- **Bilateral symmetry** The animal can be divided equally along one line only. This line splits an animal into two sides that are mirror images of each other.
- **Radial symmetry** The body parts are arranged in a circle around a central axis.

Bilateral animals have distinct heads and tails, called the anterior (head) and posterior (tail) ends. They also have distinct backs and bellies, called the dorsal (back) and ventral (belly) surfaces.

**Tissue layers** Bilateral animals have three distinct layers of tissue. The layers are the ectoderm, endoderm, and mesoderm. The ectoderm is the outer layer that develops into the skin, brain, and nervous system. The endoderm is an inner layer that lines the animal's gut. The mesoderm is a middle layer that develops into internal tissues and organs.

Most radial animals have only the endoderm and the ectoderm. Without the mesoderm layer, they do not have complex internal tissues and organs.

**Developmental patterns** Animals are separated into two major groups: the protostomes and the deuterostomes. These groups have several differences.

- **Cleavage* pattern** In most **protostomes,** early cell divisions lead to an eight-celled embryo in a twisted arrangement. In **deuterostomes,** the eight-celled embryos have cells that are lined up on top of each other.
- **Gut cavity formation** In protostomes, the gut cavity is formed from separations in the mesoderm. In deuterostomes, it forms from pouches, or bags, created by folds in the gut tube.

## VISUAL VOCAB

Humans have bilateral symmetry, while sand dollars have radial symmetry.

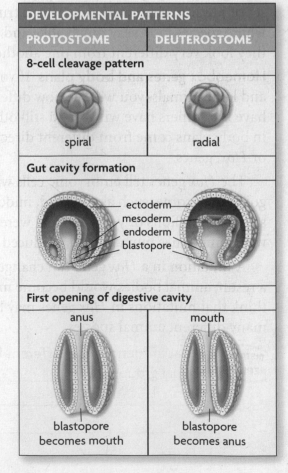

| DEVELOPMENTAL PATTERNS | |
|---|---|
| **PROTOSTOME** | **DEUTEROSTOME** |
| **8-cell cleavage pattern** | |
| spiral | radial |
| **Gut cavity formation** | |
| ectoderm — mesoderm — endoderm — blastopore | |
| **First opening of digestive cavity** | |
| anus — blastopore becomes mouth | mouth — blastopore becomes anus |

- **First opening of the digestive cavity** In deuterostomes, the anus is formed first, and the mouth is formed second. In protostomes, the mouth is formed first, and the anus is formed second.

What are the differences in tissue layers of bilateral and radial animals? _____

## A comparison of structure and genetics reveals the evolutionary history of animals.

Scientists have compared ribosomal DNA and *Hox* genes to help them understand how invertebrate groups are related. They have also used genetics to reorganize some of these groups and to compare their physical characteristics.

The presence of tissues can also be used to separate one group from another. Sponges, which do not have tissues, are the simplest members of the animal kingdom. They are followed by animals with two tissue layers, such as jellyfish and corals.

Finally, radial and bilateral symmetry is another characteristic that separates groups. The two major groups with these characteristics are the protostomes and the deuterostomes.

Scientists compare genetic sequences to help them make the tree of animal groups more accurate.

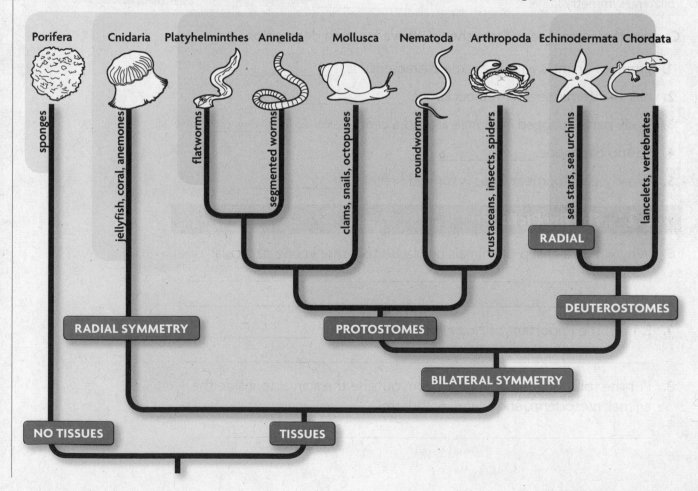

- Protostomes have two subgroups. One includes flatworms, annelids, and mollusks. The other subgroup includes roundworms and arthropods.
- Deuterostomes include animals such as sea stars and sand dollars in one group and vertebrates such as birds and mammals in the other.

**New evolutionary relationships** A new organization of the animal kingdom shows relationships between animals that scientists did not know about before. Groups with similar characteristics may have evolved these traits at different times after the groups branched out from a common ancestor. As more species are studied, scientists will be able to put together a clearer picture of the invertebrate tree.

 Highlight the structural and genetic evidence that scientists use to understand the evolutionary history of animals.

## 23.2 Vocabulary Check

### Mark It Up

Go back and highlight each sentence that has a vocabulary word in **bold**.

vertebrate      radial symmetry

invertebrate      protostome

phylum      deuterostome

bilateral symmetry

**Choose the correct term from the list above for each description.**

1. group of animals with the same characteristics _____

2. has an internal segmented backbone _____

3. body parts arranged in a circle around a central axis _____

4. has no backbone _____

5. in early development, anus is formed first _____

## 23.2 The Big Picture

6. Why would a group of animals be placed together in one particular phylum? _____

_____

7. Explain the important of *Hox* genes to an organism. _____

_____

8. Put the following terms in order from outside the animal to inside the animal: mesoderm, endoderm, ectoderm. _____

_____

# 23.3 Sponges and Cnidarians

**KEY CONCEPT** Sponges and cnidarians are the simplest animals.

## Sponges have specialized cells but no tissues.

Because of their body plan, sponges may be the most primitive animals on Earth. Sponge fossils more than 570 million years old have been found in Australia. This makes them one of the oldest groups of animals that scientists have found so far.

**Sponge characteristics** Sponges have no muscle or nerve cells. They are **sessile,** meaning they cannot move. Sponges attach to hard surfaces. They give off toxic substances to keep other sponges from growing near them and to protect them from predators.

**Sponge reproduction** Sponges can reproduce both sexually and asexually. Some species release eggs and sperm into the water, where fertilization occurs. Other species release only sperm, and the egg is fertilized inside the female sponge. Like *Hydras,* sponges can also make copies of themselves by budding.

**Sponge anatomy** Sponges do not have mouths. They are **filter feeders,** which means they eat by straining food particles from the water. Water is pulled in through tiny pores in their body wall. Used water is pushed out through a larger hole, called the osculum. The water flows through the sponge's body in a network of tubelike channels.

Sponges come in many colors and shapes. They may look like tubes or lie flat on the ocean floor. All sponges are made of two layers of cells over a frame of hard fibers, called spongin. Sponges do not have tissues, but do have a few kinds of specialized cells.

- **Pinacocytes** are thin and like leather. They form the outer layer.
- **Choanocytes,** or "collar cells," form the inner layer. Each cell has a flagellum, which it moves to pull in water that contains food particles.
- **Amoebocytes** are mobile cells between the cell layers. They absorb and digest food and circulate nutrients, oxygen, and waste materials.

> **VOCABULARY**
>
> *Sessile* comes from a Latin word meaning "to sit." The opposite of sessile is mobile. *Mobile* comes from a Latin word meaning "to move."

Sponges are among the simplest animals alive.

**INSTANT REPLAY** How does a sponge's body plan show that it is a very primitive animal? _____

_____

_____

# Cnidarians are the oldest living animals that have specialized tissues.

Unlike sponges, cnidarians can move using simple nerves and muscles.

**Cnidarian characteristics** Cnidarians have two body forms. The **polyp** is a tube with the mouth and tentacles facing upward. The other form is the umbrella-shaped **medusa** with the mouth and tentacles facing downward. Both forms have radial symmetry.

**Cnidarian reproduction** Polyps reproduce asexually by budding. Medusas release sperm and eggs into the water for sexual reproduction.

**Cnidarian anatomy** Cnidarians have two tissue layers with a jellylike material called **mesoglea** between them. The outer layer has three kinds of cells.

- **Contracting cells** cover the cnidarian and contain muscle fibers.
- **Nerve cells** form a network over the entire animal. They send sensory information and help muscles work together.
- **Cnidocytes** contain stinging structures for defense and to capture prey. Most of these cells are on the tentacles.

A **nematocyst** is a stinging structure found in sea anemones and jellyfish. It is a capsule containing a thin, coiled tube with a poisonous point at one end. Prey captured by a nematocyst is pushed through the animal's mouth and into a saclike digestive space called the **gastrovascular cavity.**

Cnidarians, like this medusa jellyfish, are able to move and capture prey.

**Cnidarian classes** There are four major groups of cnidarians.

- **Anthozoa** include sea anemones and corals. Most of these animals have a polyp form, and there is no medusa stage.
- **Hydrozoa** include fire corals. They alternate between polyp and medusa forms.
- **Scyphozoa** are jellyfish. Most of these animals have a medusa form, with a short polyp stage or none at all.
- **Cubozoa** include tropical box jellyfish. Most have a medusa form. They have a boxlike body and well-developed eyes.

**INSTANT REPLAY** Name three types of cells in a cnidarian's outer tissue layer and describe what they do. _____

_____

_____

_____

## 23.3 Vocabulary Check

**Mark It Up**

Go back and highlight each sentence that has a vocabulary word in **bold**.

sessile       mesoglea

filter feeder      nematocyst

polyp       gastrovascular cavity

medusa

1. Underline the word that means "straining food particles from water."

2. Circle the words that describe cnidarian body forms.

3. Draw a box around the word that means attached to one place.

4. Draw a wavy line under the word that describes a place for digestion in some cnidarians.

5. Highlight a word that means a stinging structure.

## 23.3 The Big Picture

6. What sponge characteristics help explain why they are sessile? _____

_____

7. Explain how sponges accomplish filter feeding. _____

_____

_____

_____

_____

8. What characteristics of cnidarians allow them to catch their own food? _____

_____

9. How do the polyp and medusa forms reproduce? _____

_____

_____

# 23.4 Flatworms, Mollusks, and Annelids

**KEY CONCEPT** Flatworms, mollusks, and annelids belong to closely related phyla.

Most flatworms, mollusks, and annelids are classified in the same group. These animals have either a feeding structure made of hollow tentacles or a larva that swims using cilia.

## Flatworms are simple bilateral animals.

Flatworms do not have stomachs or lungs. The gut is incomplete or missing. They are flat and thin because they have no circulatory system. Oxygen moves into their cells by diffusion, so all the cells must be close to the outside environment. The three classes of flatworms include the planarians, flukes, and tapeworms.

**Planarians** Planarians live independently. They have a head, eyespots, and a simple brain made of nerve tissue. The mouth is on the belly surface and leads to a gut cavity. A muscular tube called the pharynx extends from the mouth to collect food. Planarians can move using cilia or bands of muscle that twist their bodies.

Planarians have a solid body that lacks a complete gut.

**Flukes** Flukes are parasites. They feed on the body fluids of other animals, called hosts. Both invertebrates and vertebrates can be hosts. The pharynx extends from the mouth to a gut cavity. Many species need more than one host to complete their life cycles.

**Tapeworms** Tapeworms are parasites that live in vertebrate guts. The small head has suckers or hooks used to attach to the host. They have no gut cavity. Tapeworms absorb nutrients from the host's digested food. Many tapeworms have life cycles that involve many hosts.

How does each type of flatworm obtain food? _____

_____

# Mollusks are diverse animals.

Mollusks have a complete digestive tract. A **complete digestive tract** has a mouth and an anus at opposite ends of a tube. This allows for frequent digestion, which means the animals can be more active.

**Mollusk anatomy** Mollusks can be as different as oysters and squids. They can be sessile filter feeders, herbivores, or predators. All mollusks share at least one of three characteristics: a radula, mantle, or ctenidia.

- **Radula** The **radula** is a feeding organ that mollusks scrape over their food. Hard teeth on the radula pick up food particles.
- **Mantle** The mantle is an area of tissue that covers internal organs. In most mollusks, it secretes a hard shell to protect the animal.
- **Ctenidia** The ctenidia are flat gills found in mollusks that live in the water. They absorb oxygen from the water.

  Blood is pumped through the gills and the **hemocoel.** The hemocoel consists of spaces between cells in the animal's tissues. This circulatory system extends into a large muscular foot. Snails use the foot to crawl, and clams use it to dig.

The anatomy of a garden snail includes a radula and a mantle, both of which are features shared by most mollusks.

**Classes of mollusks** There are seven classes of mollusks, but most of the species are found in only three of the classes.

- **Gastropoda** includes snails, nudibranches, abalones, and limpets. More than half of the mollusk species are in this class.
- **Pelecypoda** are bivalves, and include clams, oysters, mussels, and scallops. Their soft body is covered by two shells connected by a hinge.
- **Cephalopoda** includes squids, octopuses, nautiluses, and cuttlefish. They have the most well-developed nervous system and eyes of all the mollusks.

**Mollusk reproduction** Mollusks reproduce in several ways. Garden snails, for example, are hermaphrodites, or animals that have both male and female reproductive organs in one body. However, reproduction still requires two snails. A packet of sperm is transferred from one snail to another and is used to fertilized eggs.

What three characteristics do many mollusks share? _____

_____

# Annelids have segmented bodies.

Segmentation is a feature of the three annelid groups: earthworms, marine worms, and leeches. **Segmentation** refers to the repeated sections of an annelid's long body. Each section contains a set of body structures.

**Annelid anatomy** A segment usually contains part of the digestive tract, nerve cord, blood vessels, organs to collect and excrete waste, muscle, and a coelom. The **coelom** is a fluid-filled space surrounded by muscle and divided by structures called septa (singular *septum*). The coelom works as a type of skeleton to help annelids move.

Annelids have body plans characterized by segmentation.

**Annelid diet** Earthworms and marine worms eat organic waste material. Some leeches are predators; other leeches feed on animal blood.

**Annelid reproduction** Annelids reproduce sexually or asexually. Asexual reproduction occurs when a piece of an annelid's back end breaks off to form a new individual. Others, such as earthworms, are hermaphrodites.

 Highlight the details of annelid anatomy.

---

## 23.4 Vocabulary Check

complete digestive tract      segmentation

radula      coelom

hemocoel

1. Circle the feeding organ that has hard teeth.

2. Underline the fluid-filled space divided by septa.

3. Put a box around a tube that has a mouth and an anus.

## 23.4 The Big Picture

4. What is the benefit of a complete digestive tract? _____

_____

5, Why wouldn't snails that live on land have ctenidia? _____

_____

6. Explain the importance of the hemocoel. _____

_____

# 23.5 Roundworms

**KEY CONCEPT**  Roundworms have bilateral symmetry and shed their outer skeleton to grow.

Roundworms are found in almost every ecosystem on Earth. These include mountaintops, deep ocean trenches, hot springs, and Arctic ice.

## Roundworms shed their stiff outer skeleton as they grow.

Roundworms are also called nematodes. They are not only one of the most numerous species on Earth, they also have the most diversity among species. Some roundworms are less than a millimeter long while others grow to over 10 meters in length.

Roundworms are in the same group as Arthropods, which include crustaceans, spiders, and insects. Like mollusks and annelids, these animals are protostomes and have bilateral symmetry. They also have a tough exoskeleton called a cuticle. The **cuticle** is made of chitin. It must be shed, or fall off, whenever the animal grows larger.

**Roundworm anatomy**  A roundworm is shaped like a tube. It has a flat-fronted head and a pointed tail. Muscle is laid out from one end of the animal to the other.

A fluid-filled space called a **pseudocoelom** separates the muscles from the central gut tube. The prefix *pseudo-* means "false." This term means that the structure is not really a coelom, because it is not completely surrounded by muscle. Roundworms do not have a circulatory or respiratory system. They do have a digestive system, which includes a mouth, pharynx, intestine, and anus.

**Roundworm reproduction**  Most roundworms reproduce sexually and lay eggs. Some roundworms even give birth to live young.

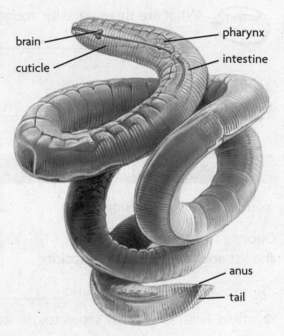

Roundworms are shaped like a tube and must shed their stiff cuticles as they grow.

  List some of the characteristics of a roundworm's internal anatomy. _____

_____

_____

## Many roundworms are parasites.

Roundworms are parasites of almost every plant and animal species. They can cause a lot of damage to crops. Roundworms that infect humans include hookworms, pinworms, and Guinea worms.

- A hookworm lives in the digestive tract of its host, where it feeds on the host's blood. It infects a human when a person walks barefoot on contaminated* soil. Recall that roundworms can be less than a millimeter in length.

- A pinworm lives in the gut of its host. Infections usually occur when a person eats or drinks something that contains pinworm eggs.

- Guinea worms live in the gut and connective tissues of its host. People can become infected when they drink dirty water containing the worms. World health organizations have helped to get rid of this parasite in most areas of the world.

 What are three parasitic roundworms that infect human hosts?

_____

| **23.5** | **Vocabulary Check** |
| --- | --- |

cuticle                    pseudocoelom

**Choose the correct term from the list above for each description.**

**Mark It Up**

Go back and highlight each sentence that has a vocabulary word in **bold.**

1. exoskeleton made of chitin _____

2. fluid-filled space that separates muscle from the gut tube

   _____

| **23.5** | **The Big Picture** |
| --- | --- |

3. Why do roundworms shed their cuticles? _____

_____

_____

4. How can hookworm infections be prevented? _____

_____

# 23.6 Echinoderms

**KEY CONCEPT** Echinoderms are on the same evolutionary branch as vertebrates.

Have you ever visited a tidal pool? You might have seen brightly colored sea stars and spiky sea urchins, which are two kinds of echinoderms.

## Echinoderms have radial symmetry.

Adult echinoderms have radial symmetry. However, echinoderm larvae have bilateral symmetry. Scientists think that echinoderms had bilateral ancestors and that radial symmetry is a derived character.

**Echinoderm anatomy** All echinoderms have an internal skeleton made of tiny plates called **ossicles.** The ossicles contain calcium and are in the surface of the skin. Catch connective tissue holds the plates together. This tissue allows an echinoderm to change from being very flexible to being very stiff in a few seconds.

Echinoderms have a **water vascular system.** This is a series of water-filled canals, or tubes, that run through each arm from the ring canal that surrounds the central disk. They store water for circulation and fill tiny suckers along the arms called tube feet. The feet can reach out or pull back, depending on changes in water pressure. Tube feet are used to grab objects and to move around.

Each arm of a sea star contains digestive and reproductive glands.

A sea star has a complete digestive system with a mouth, stomach, small length of intestine, and an anus. Sea stars can also regenerate, or regrow, their arms if part of the central disk is still there.

**Echinoderm reproduction** Most echinoderms reproduce sexually. Sea stars release eggs and sperm into the water. The fertilized egg develops into a free-floating larva. As it matures, the larva goes through a series of changes until it reaches its adult form.

 Explain how ossicles form an internal skeleton. _____

_____

# There are five classes of Echinoderms.

Echinoderms have many types of body plans. They range from the spiny round sea urchin to the oblong sea cucumber.

**Feather stars and sea lilies**  A feather star can move with its arms, but is usually attached to a surface. Sea lilies are sessile. Both animals are filter feeders.

**Sea stars**  Some sea stars are filter feeders. Others eat whatever food they find, while still others are predators.

**Brittle stars and basket stars**  Brittle stars have long skinny arms without tube feet. They are scavengers or predators. Basket stars are filter feeders.

**Sea urchins, sea biscuits, and sand dollars**  Sea biscuits and sand dollars eat waste matter. They are covered with tiny projections that help the animals move around and dig into the ocean floor. Sea urchins are covered with long, sharp spines. Most sea urchins graze on algae.

**Sea cucumbers**  Sea cucumbers are long fleshy bilateral animals. Instead of arms, they have thick, fleshy tentacles that catch food.

 Highlight the different feeding methods of sea stars.

## 23.6  Vocabulary Check

ossicle                    water vascular system

Choose the correct term from the list for each description.

1. canals that run through each arm of an echinoderm _____

2. tiny plate that makes up an echinoderm's skeleton _____

## 23.6  The Big Picture

3. How does the water vascular system help an echinoderm move?

_____

_____

4. Describe two main differences in the body plans of sea stars and sea cucumbers. _____

_____

# Chapter 23 Review

**1.** What are four characteristics that all animals share? _____

_____

**2.** What can happen to a species' body plan if there is a mutation in a
*Hox* gene? _____

_____

**3.** Label the animals shown below as either radial or bilateral.

**a.**

**b.**

_____                    _____

**4.** The ectoderm develops into the _____
  **a.** skin, internal tissues, and layer that lines an animal's gut.
  **b.** skin, brain, and nervous system.
  **c.** skin, internal tissues, and nervous system.
  **d.** skin, internal organs, and brain.

**5.** What are three developmental characteristics that can tell you whether an animal is a protostome or a deuterostome? _____

_____

**6.** How can the presence of tissues be used to group animals? _____

_____

_____

_____

**7.** What can genetics tell us about the evolutionary relationships among
animals? _____

_____

**8.** Describe two differences between polyps and medusas. _____

_____

**9.** Name three characteristics that identify mollusks. _____

_____

**10.** How can roundworms affect people? _____

_____

# 24 A Closer Look at Arthropods

## GETTING READY TO LEARN

### Preview Key Concepts

**24.1 Arthropod Diversity**
Arthropods are the most diverse of all animals.

**24.2 Crustaceans**
Crustaceans are a diverse group of ancient arthropods.

**24.3 Arachnids**
Arachnids include spiders and their relatives.

**24.4 Insect Adaptations**
Insects show an amazing range of adaptations.

**24.5 Arthropods and Humans**
Arthropods and humans interact in many ways.

### Review Academic Vocabulary

Write the correct word for each definition.

invertebrate    phylum    coelom    filter feeder    segmentation

1. _____ : repeated sections of an animal's body

2. _____ : animals that strain food particles from water

3. _____ : group of animals that share similar characteristics

4. _____ : fluid-filled space surrounded by muscle

5. _____ : animals without backbones

### Preview Biology Vocabulary

To see how many key terms you already know from this chapter, choose the word that makes sense in each sentence.

pupa    abdomen    insecticide    arachnid

1. In an insect, the rear portion of its body is called the _____.

2. A(an) _____ has eight legs, the ability to produce silk, and fanglike pincers.

3. Inside a cocoon, the _____ begins to change into its adult form.

4. Farmers use a type of poison, or _____, to control insects that damage crops.

# 24.1 Arthropod Diversity

**KEY CONCEPT** Arthropods are the most diverse of all animals.

Arthropods are the most successful animal phylum on Earth. More than three-fourths of all known animals—more than 1 million species—are arthropods. Their diversity is the result of millions of years of adaptations.

## Arthropod features are highly adapted.

**Arthropods** are invertebrates with an exoskeleton made of chitin. They have a series of paired, jointed appendages and segmented body parts.

### Arthropod Characteristics

An arthropod's body is completely covered by a protective exoskeleton. An **exoskeleton** is an external skeleton that supports the animal's tissues against gravity. It is made of proteins and chitin. **Chitin** is a long organic molecule made of sugars. It is arranged in layers that point in different directions. These layers make chitin very tough and strong.

Arthropods also have jointed appendages, which is an important adaptation that helps them live in different environments. An **appendage** is an extension of an organism's body, such as a wing or leg. It can be used for walking, flying, sensing, holding food, or chewing. Appendages can be shaped like rakes, tweezers, nutcrackers, hammers, or paddles.

Arthropods come in many sizes and body shapes. Some can be seen only with a microscope, while others are very large. For example, tropical stick insects may be 30 centimeters (1 ft) in length. No matter what the size, all arthropod bodies are segmented. In arthropods, **segmentation** refers to a body that is divided into sections. Each section has a different function.

Trilobite fossils show the exoskeleton, segmentation, and jointed appendages.

### Arthropod Groups

There are five main arthropod groups.

- **Trilobites** are extinct but were an important part of Paleozoic marine ecosystems for nearly 300 million years. Their bodies were divided into three long vertical sections.
- **Crustaceans** are found in the oceans, freshwater streams, and on land. King crabs, lobsters, microscopic copepods, and armored pill bugs are in this group.
- **Chelicerates** include horseshoe crabs, scorpions, spiders, mites, and ticks. They have daggerlike mouthparts that are used for tearing food.

**Arthropods are a diverse group of animals. Millions of years of evolution has led to many different body forms and functions.**

| CRUSTACEANS | CHELICERATES | INSECTS | MYRIAPODS |
|---|---|---|---|
|  |  |  |  |
| Crab | Spider | Beetle | Centipede |

- **Insects** make up 80 percent of all known animal species. Ants, bees, butterflies, moths, cockroaches, flies, and mosquitoes are all insects. Insects have six legs.
- **Myriapods** are centipedes and millipedes. They have long bodies and many pairs of legs. Myriapods usually live in humid environments. The first pair of legs in centipedes has poisonous fangs* that are used for capturing and killing prey.

 Explain why jointed appendages became important adaptations for arthropods. _____

## Arthropod exoskeletons serve a variety of functions.

The exoskeleton protects the arthropod but also makes certain activities more difficult. These include movement, growth, and maintaining homeostasis, or keeping conditions inside the body stable. Arthropods have evolved ways of getting around the limits of their exoskeletons.

**Movement** How do arthropods move? Very stiff cuticle plates are separated by more flexible ones. The flexible cuticle plates act as joints so the animal can move.

**Molting, or growth** The cuticle cannot grow. An arthropod must shed its exoskeleton in a process called molting, which has three steps.

1. Before molting, the animal forms a new layer of cuticle underneath its exoskeleton.

2. Enzymes from the animal begin to digest and soften the old cuticle. In time, the exoskeleton splits open, and the animal crawls out of it. The animal must shed every surface of its body, including the lining of its gut. This step can be so difficult that the animal can die trying to get out of its old cuticle.

---

**\* ACADEMIC VOCABULARY**

**fang** long, sharp structure with a hollow center through which poison flows

**3.** The new exoskeleton is filled with fluid while it is still soft. It takes time for the new exoskeleton to harden. During this time the animal is very vulnerable* to predators.

**Managing internal functions—circulation** Arthropods have open circulatory systems. Blood is pumped through a tubelike heart to the body cavity, where it comes in direct contact with organs and tissues. The hard exoskeleton keeps the blood contained, while body movements keep it circulating.

**Managing external functions—senses** Arthropod sensory organs are made of a slightly softer type of cuticle. Temperature, touch, sound, and smell are sensed through the antennae and body hairs.

Most arthropods also have compound eyes. A compound eye has thousands of tiny lenses, each of which sees only a small part of the scene. These images combine to form a larger picture that isn't as clear as what humans see.

 Highlight the molting process for an arthropod.

# Arthropod diversity evolved over millions of years.

The oldest arthropod fossils are 540-million-year-old trilobites. The oldest known chelicerates and crustaceans appeared a few million years later. Myriapod fossils are younger, but they are still 415 million years old. Because the major groups of arthropods appeared so long ago, it is difficult to determine the relationships between them. Many of today's arthropods are very similar to arthropods that lived hundreds of millions of years ago.

Some scientists think that arthropods are most closely related to annelid worms because both groups have segmented bodies. But segmentation may have evolved separately in each group. Scientists think that members of the phylum Ecdysozoa may be the closest living relatives of the arthropods.

Arthropods must molt their old exoskeletons in order to grow.

 List the appearance of the four major arthropod groups in the fossil record, from youngest to oldest. _____

_____

_____

* ACADEMIC VOCABULARY

**vulnerable** can be attacked or damaged

**Mark It Up**

Go back and highlight each sentence that has a vocabulary word in **bold**.

arthropod            appendage
exoskeleton          segmentation
chitin

**Fill in the blanks with the correct term from the list above.**

1. _____ is an organic molecule that forms a hard surface.

2. An extension of an animal's body is called a(n) _____

3. A(n) _____ supports an animal's tissues against gravity.

4. The characteristics of a(n) _____ include paired, jointed appendages.

## 24.1 The Big Picture

5. Explain how chitin makes an exoskeleton tough. _____
   _____

6. List three activities that an exoskeleton makes more difficult for arthropods. _____
   _____
   _____

7. How does an arthropod gather sensory information? _____
   _____
   _____

# 24.2 Crustaceans

**KEY CONCEPT** Crustaceans are a diverse group of ancient arthropods.

Shrimp and lobsters are crustaceans. The tiny brine shrimp known as "sea monkeys" and pill bugs that live under rocks are also crustaceans.

## Crustaceans evolved as marine arthropods.

**Crustaceans** are arthropods with two distinct body sections, a hard exoskeleton, two pairs of antennae, and one pair of appendages per segment. They evolved in the oceans, and most still live there. Freshwater species also exist, and a few have evolved to live on land.

**Ecosystem Role** Crustaceans are important organisms in aquatic* ecosystems. Some species are predators. Others scavenge dead animals and plants. Shrimp, lobsters, and crabs are eaten by fish, birds, seals, and even humans. Thousands of microscopic species, such as krill, copepods, and zooplankton, are an important food source for fish, whales, and filter-feeding crustaceans.

**Anatomy** The two sections of a crustacean's body are the cephalothorax and the abdomen. The front section, the **cephalothorax,** includes both the head and trunk parts. It is covered by an area of cuticle called the carapace. The **carapace** also protects the sides of the body and the gills. The rear section of the animal is called the **abdomen.**

 List the four physical characteristics of crustaceans. _____

_____

_____

## Crustacean appendages can take many forms.

All crustaceans have appendages that share a common origin. For example, your arm and a bat wing share a common origin because humans and bats have a common ancestor who lived millions of years ago. In bats, the appendage became a winglike structure. In humans, it became an arm. Crustacean appendages have also been modified for different jobs, such as sensing, fighting, walking, feeding, and attracting mates.

**Claws** You are probably familiar with the large claws found on many crabs and lobsters. Lobster claws are used to collect and hold food. But they can be specialized for other jobs. Male fiddler crabs use their large claws to attract females.

* ACADEMIC VOCABULARY

**aquatic** taking place in or on water

## CRUSTACEAN ANATOMY

The anatomy of a crustacean is well suited to its underwater habitat. Crustacean appendages are adapted for many different purposes.

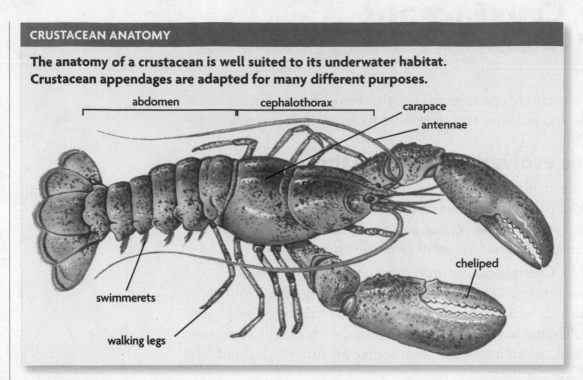

Antennae  All crustaceans have two pairs of antennae on their head that are covered with tiny hairs full of chemical sensors. The antennae are used to smell food, find mates, and avoid predators. The tiny water flea *Daphnia* uses its antennae as oars to move through the water.

Mandibles  Crustaceans, like other arthropods, have mouths made of a pair of hard appendages called mandibles. **Mandibles** bite and crush food. Other appendages near the mouth also act as jaws and tear food.

Legs  Jointed legs allow a crustacean to walk along the ocean floor as it looks for food. Other specialized appendages called swimmerets allow the organism to move through the water.

This diversity of appendages allows crustaceans to specialize. As a result, crustaceans have moved into a wide range of environments and have different ways of surviving.

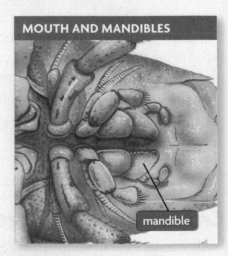

## MOUTH AND MANDIBLES

Instead of teeth, crustaceans have hard mandibles and other mouth parts to bite, tear, and crush food.

What are four types of crustacean appendages? _____

_____

_____

# There are many different types of crustaceans.

Crustaceans vary widely in their anatomy and structures. However, they can be grouped into decapods and non-decapods.

## Decapods

The name *decapod* means "ten legs," and all decapods have five pairs of jointed appendages. This group includes lobsters, crabs, shrimp, and hermit crabs. Most live in saltwater, but crayfish live in fresh water.

## Barnacles, Isopods, and Tongue Worms

Other species of crustaceans do not look like a decapod at all. Scientists have learned that most young crustaceans have a free-swimming larval stage with certain characteristics. Barnacles and tongue worms have this stage, which identifies them as crustaceans.

- **Barnacles** are sessile, or nonmoving, filter feeders covered by a heavy shell that is hard because of the calcium in it. They live attached to rocks, boats, sea turtle shells, and even humpback whales.
- **Isopods** have flat bodies and seven pairs of legs. Most species live in water. Pill bugs and wood lice belong to a group that lives on land.
- **Tongue worms** are parasites that live in the lungs and nasal passages of vertebrates. They have no eyes, mandibles, or antennae. They have lost most of their limbs. But molecular evidence shows tongue worms are most closely related to crustaceans.

 Highlight three crustaceans that are not decapods, and highlight one characteristic about each.

---

### 24.2 Vocabulary Check

**Mark It Up**

Go back and highlight each sentence that has a vocabulary word in **bold**.

crustacean     carapace

cephalothorax     mandible

abdomen

**Choose the correct term from the list for each description.**

1. bite and crush food _____

2. contains the head and trunk regions _____

3. protects the sides of the body and the gills _____

### 24.2 The Big Picture

4. Crustaceans have appendages adapted for different uses. How might this be an advantage? _____
_____

5. Describe one difference and one similarity between decapods and barnacles. _____
_____

# 24.3 Arachnids

KEY CONCEPT   Arachnids include spiders and their relatives.

A person with muscle aches, a stiff neck, and a fever may have the flu. If the person also has an insect bite with a bulls-eye rash around it, then the illness is probably Lyme disease. This disease is caused by a bacteria that is carried and spread by a tiny arachnid called a deer tick.

## Arachnids are the largest group of chelicerates.

Deer ticks are chelicerates. **Chelicerates** are arthropods without mandibles or antennae and have six pairs of appendages. Four pairs are walking legs, and the other two sets help the animal eat.

Three main groups of chelicerates are horseshoe crabs, sea spiders, and arachnids. **Arachnids**—which include spiders—live on land, have eight legs, fanglike pincers that inject venom, and the ability to produce silk. More than 80 percent of all chelicerate species are arachnids.

Arachnids have four adaptations that help them reduce water loss and live on land.

- **Waterproof cuticles** stop water from evaporating across the skin.
- **Book lungs** are structures built of many thin, hollow sheets of tissue that look like the pages of a book. They are found in some arachnid species and help them breathe air. Book lungs provide a large surface for gas exchange. To prevent water loss, book lungs are in a humid chamber, or space, covered by cuticle.
- **Malpighian tubules** let spiders reduce water loss while they get rid of wastes.
- **Spiracles** are used by some arachnids to breathe. Spiracles are tiny holes on the abdomen that open and close to allow oxygen to enter. A series of tubes called **tracheae** (singular, *trachea*) carry the oxygen directly to the arachnid's tissues. Only some species have spiracles.

Underline four features that help an arachnid live on land.

**VOCABULARY**
The word *spiracle* comes from the Latin word *spirare* meaning "to breathe."

## Arachnids have evolved into a diverse group.

All spiders are predators that can make silk and produce venom, or poison. Silk is made by glands in the abdomen. Spiders inject their venom through modified chelicerae.

Mites, ticks, and chiggers are very small arachnids. Many are parasites of plants and animals. Scorpions inject venom from a stinger at the end of their tail, and then use huge pincers to grab the prey.

## ARACHNID ANATOMY

**Arachnids have many unique adaptations for catching and consuming their prey.**

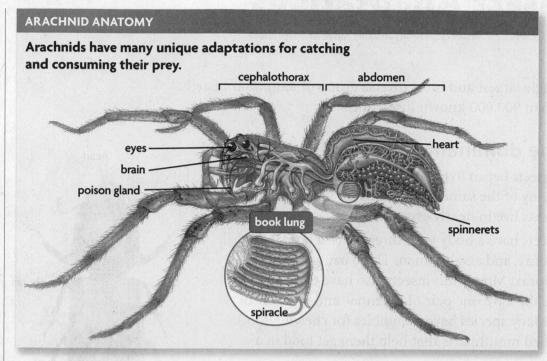

cephalothorax    abdomen

eyes
brain
poison gland

heart

spinnerets

book lung

spiracle

Arachnids are important both as predators and as prey species for vertebrates. Arachnids eat a lot of insects, such as mites and ticks, each year. Mites damage crops, and ticks carry diseases.

**INSTANT REPLAY**    Highlight two identifying characteristics of spiders.

## 24.3    Vocabulary Check

chelicerate        spiracle

arachnid           tracheae

book lung

**Mark It Up**

Go back and highlight each sentence that has a vocabulary word in **bold**.

**Choose the correct term from the list for each description.**

1. carries oxygen to an arachnid's tissues _____

2. lacks antennae and mandibles and has four pairs of legs _____

3. hole in the abdomen that lets in oxygen _____

## 24.3    The Big Picture

4. Explain how book lungs help arachnids breathe air. _____

_____

_____

5. List one similarity and one difference between spiders and scorpions.

_____

# 24.4 Insect Adaptations

**KEY CONCEPT**   Insects show an amazing range of adaptations.

Insects are the single largest and most diverse group of animals on Earth. There are more than 900,000 known insect species.

## Insects are the dominant terrestrial arthropods.

Like arachnids, insects began living on land around 400 million years ago. They have many of the same adaptations for life on land that arachnids do. Insects live in nearly every environment on Earth.

**Anatomy**   All insects have a body with three parts: a head, a middle part called the thorax, and an abdomen. Three pairs of legs are attached to the thorax. Most adult insects also have two pairs of wings. Insects usually have one pair of antennae and one pair of compound eyes. Many species have mandibles for chewing food. Some have modified mouthparts that help them get food in a variety of ways.

**Social structure**   Some insect species live in colonies of hundreds or thousands of individuals. These large groups have complex social organizations. Certain individuals have specific jobs, such as guarding the colony, which help the colony to survive. Scientists think that an insect's genes determine which job it does within the colony.

head

thorax

abdomen

This beetle illustrates the three-part body structure of all insects: head, thorax, and abdomen.

 **INSTANT REPLAY**   Describe the body of a typical insect. _____

_____

_____

## Insects undergo metamorphosis.

As a human being, you were born with all the same body parts as an adult. This fact is not true of many insects. For example, butterflies and mosquitoes go through major physical changes from their younger to their adult forms.

However, some insects, such as grasshoppers and cockroaches, look like tiny adults when they hatch. They have six legs and a head, thorax, and abdomen; but they do not have wings and sex organs. This pattern of development is called **incomplete metamorphosis,** or direct development. The young insects are called nymphs. Nymphs get larger with each molt, but only grow wings and sexual organs during the later molting stages.

**VOCABULARY**

The word *metamorphosis* comes from the Greek word *metamorphoun*, which means "to transform."

In **complete metamorphosis,** young insects do not look like the adults. Instead, they hatch out of eggs as wormlike larvae. Their bodies are not clearly divided into a head, thorax, and abdomen, and they do not have legs or antennae. As larvae grow, they molt several times until they reach an inactive form called a **pupa.** Inside the pupa, some tissues are reorganized to produce a new body form. The adult that comes out looks nothing like a larva. It has wings, legs, compound eyes, sex organs, and three body sections.

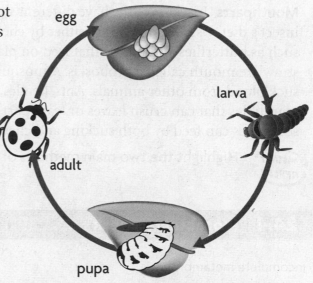

Some insects must go through complete metamorphosis to reach the adult stage.

 What is the difference between incomplete metamorphosis and complete metamorphosis? _____

_____

_____

## Insects have adapted to life on land.

Insects have developed several adaptations that help explain why they are so successful on land.

**Reducing water loss** Like arachnids, insects reduce water loss because of their exoskeleton, Malpighian tubules, spiracles, and tracheae. These structures are shared by insects and arachnids. In earlier times, individuals that could survive long periods without water were the ones that lived to reproduce. Natural selection moved both groups toward having similar water-saving features.

**Flight** Only four groups of animals have evolved true flight: insects, the extinct pterosaurs, bats, and birds. Insects started flying before any other group and have been flying for nearly 400 million years.

Insect wings are long, flat extensions of the exoskeleton that stick out of the animal's back. Muscles at the base of each wing move it up and down, which takes a lot of energy. The insect exoskeleton has evolved in a way that saves the energy needed for flight: it reuses stored kinetic energy created by wing movement. This means the muscles do only part of the work.

For example, when a diver uses a springboard, kinetic energy is created as the diver pushes the board down. When the board springs back, this energy is released, and the diver is thrown into the air. Like the springboard, the insect cuticle is slightly flexible. When the wing moves, it bends the exoskeleton. When the cuticle springs back, the stored kinetic energy pushes the wing back to its original position.

**Mouthparts** Insect mouths have different shapes depending on the insect's diet. Usually, insects eat either by chewing or sucking. Insects such as butterflies and moths that feed on plant nectar have a long, strawlike mouth called a proboscis. A mosquito uses its proboscis to suck blood from other animals. Ants, beetles, and dragonflies have mandibles that can crush leaves or tear apart flesh. Bees, wasps, and some flies can feed by both sucking and chewing.

 Highlight the two main methods of feeding used by insects.

---

## 24.4   Vocabulary Check

**Mark It Up**

Go back and highlight each sentence that has a vocabulary word in **bold**.

incomplete metamorphosis          pupa
complete metamorposis

**Choose the correct term from the list for each description.**

1. Young insects must molt several times to develop their adult form
   _____

2. Inactive form during development _____

3. Young insects look like adults as soon as they hatch
   _____

---

## 24.4   The Big Picture

4. How might the social organization of some insects contribute to their being so successful? _____
   _____
   _____

5. Describe the process of complete metamorphosis in four steps. _____
   _____
   _____
   _____

6. Briefly explain how insects are able to fly without using too much energy. _____
   _____
   _____

# 24.5 Arthropods and Humans

**KEY CONCEPT** Arthropods and humans interact in many ways.

The relationship between arthropods and humans can be beneficial or harmful. Some arthropods are important pollinators that fertilize crops. Others are pests that destroy crops and invade homes. Insects are used for food in some cultures, but they can also spread diseases.

## Arthropods and humans share many of the same resources.

Many arthropods are herbivores, or plant eaters, and eat many of the same plants that people use for food, clothing, and building materials. These arthropods compete with humans for the same resources.

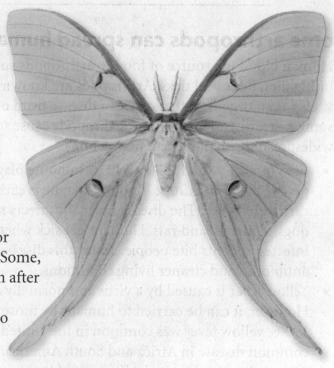

Each year, arthropods cause millions of dollars in damage to important crops such as corn, wheat, and soybeans. To prevent this, farmers use insecticides to reduce arthropod populations. An **insecticide** is a chemical compound that kills insects and other arthropods.

Spraying insecticides on plants can have unwanted results. Many insecticides are toxic, or poisonous, to other animals, including people. Some, such as chlordane and DDT, do not break down after use and collect in the soil and water. They also collect in prey animals and in the predators who eat them.

Some arthropods may survive the insecticide. When they reproduce, their offspring will also survive the insecticide. Through natural selection, more and more of these resistant arthropods will be born, and new insecticides will need to be developed.

Scientists want to avoid all of these unwanted side effects. They have discovered three ways to use the arthropods' own characteristics to control their populations.

- Insecticides can be developed that harm only arthropods.
- Integrated pest management, or IPM, reduces the number of insect pests by managing their ecology. For instance, scientists can use insect traps, physical barriers, and introduced predators such as ladybugs and parasitic wasps.
- Genetically modified plants can be made to resist particular pest species. For example, Bt corn has been made to include a gene from a soil bacterium inserted into its DNA. The gene makes a protein that kills caterpillar pests but is harmless to most other animals.

 **INSTANT REPLAY** What three ways can arthropod pests be controlled with few unwanted side effects? _____

_____

_____

Some types of ladybugs are used to control aphids which damage crops and garden plants.

## Some arthropods can spread human diseases.

Human blood is a source of food to arthropods such as mosquitoes, biting flies, fleas, and ticks. Arthropods are known as disease vectors. A **vector** is an organism that carries a disease from one host to another. In some cases, diseases carried by arthropods cause serious illnesses and widespread death in human populations.

- Between the years 1347 and 1350, bubonic plague killed millions of people living in Europe. Bubonic plague is caused by a bacterium carried by a flea. The disease normally affects rodents such as prairie dogs, squirrels, and rats. Humans get sick when fleas that have fed on infected rodents bite people. Today this disease is controlled by antibiotics and cleaner living conditions.
- Yellow fever is caused by a virus and normally affects monkeys. However, it can be carried to humans by mosquitoes. Until the early 1900s, yellow fever was common in the United States. It is still a common disease in Africa and South America.
- Malaria is caused by a parasite carried by mosquitoes. In the 1950s, DDT was used to eliminate the disease in some areas. Malaria is still common in tropical regions of Africa, Asia, and Central and South America.
- West Nile virus is carried by mosquitoes that have fed on infected birds. It was first discovered in Africa, West Asia, and the Middle East. It has now spread throughout the world and is found in 46 states in the U. S. It causes fever, headache, and skin rashes. It can also lead to serious infections in the brain that can cause death. Scientists are working to control the spread of West Nile virus.

Researchers have developed various methods for controlling arthropod vectors. Vaccinations can protect people from many types of diseases. The use of pesticides that harm only specific arthropods can also help slow the spread of disease.

 Name two diseases carried by arthropod vectors that have been or still are a big concern in the United States. _____

_____

## 24.5 Vocabulary Check

**Mark It Up**

Go back and highlight each sentence that has a vocabulary word in **bold**.

insecticide

vector

1. Circle the word that refers to something that kills arthropods.

2. Underline the word that means an organism that carries a disease from one host to another.

## 24.5 The Big Picture

3. Why was it important for scientists to develop new ways of controlling pest populations? _____

_____

_____

4. Explain how Integrated Pest Management works. _____

_____

5. Name four arthropod vector diseases and describe how they are spread. _____

_____

_____

_____

_____

_____

# Chapter 24 Review

1. Arthropod appendages have been adapted for different functions over time. What are these functions? _____
   _____

2. What are four ways that an exoskeleton helps an animal to survive?
   _____
   _____

3. Why is it difficult to accurately determine the relationships between the different groups of arthropods? _____
   _____

4. A crustacean's body sections are the
   **a.** abdomen and carapace.
   **b.** carapace and mandibles.
   **c.** abdomen and cephalothorax.
   **d.** cephalothorax and cheliped.

5. Lobsters have ten jointed appendages and fused body segments that contain two sections. Barnacles are sessile filter feeders with a hard shell. How do scientists know that both these animals are crustaceans?
   _____

6. How do spiracles and tracheae help an arachnid breathe on land?
   _____

7. What are three adaptations that help insects live on land? _____
   _____
   _____

8. As larvae develop into adults during complete metamorphosis, they molt into an inactive form called a
   **a.** pupa          **c.** larva
   **b.** nymph         **d.** worm

9. Why do humans and arthropods interact so often? _____
   _____
   _____

10. Why is it important to know which arthropods are vectors? _____
    _____
    _____

# 25 Vertebrate Diversity

## GETTING READY TO LEARN

### Preview Key Concepts

**25.1 Vertebrate Origins**
All vertebrates share common characteristics.

**25.2 Fish Diversity**
The dominant aquatic vertebrates are fish.

**25.3 A Closer Look at Bony Fish**
Bony fish include ray-finned and lobe-finned fish.

**25.4 Amphibians**
Amphibians evolved from lobe-finned fish.

**25.5 Vertebrates on Land**
Reptiles, birds, and mammals are adapted for life on land.

### Review Academic Vocabulary

**Write the correct word for each definition.**

| exoskeleton | appendage | mandibles |
|---|---|---|
| book lung | complete metamorphosis | |

1. _____ : parts that crush and bite food

2. _____ : structure built of thin, hollow sheets of tissue

3. _____ : body part used for movement

4. _____ : young go through several changes to become adults

5. _____ : support that is outside the body

### Preview Biology Vocabulary

**Try to guess the meaning of each boldfaced word from its context.**

| PHRASE | MY GUESS |
|---|---|
| 1. One river flows north and another flows south—an example of **countercurrent flow**. | |
| 2. Frogs and turtles are **amphibian** animals. | |

# 25.1 Vertebrate Origins

**KEY CONCEPT** All vertebrates share common characteristics.

You are a vertebrate. So are birds, tigers, lizards, and squirrels. While the vertebrates you most often see live on land, the first vertebrates were fish. Even today, the largest group of vertebrates is fish.

## The phylum Chordata contains all vertebrates and some invertebrates.

The phylum Chordata is made up of three groups. One group includes all vertebrates, which are animals with a well-developed brain inside of a hard skull. The other two groups, tunicates and lancelets, are invertebrates. All **chordates** share four features at some stage of their development.

- **Notochord** A **notochord** is a flexible skeletal support rod in the animal's back.
- **Hollow nerve cord** A hollow nerve cord runs along the animal's back.
- **Pharyngeal slits** Pharyngeal slits are slits through the animal's body in the pharynx, which is the part of the gut just behind the mouth. Water enters through the mouth and goes out through the slits without passing through the digestive system.
- **Tail** A tail extends beyond the anal opening and has muscles for movement.

The larvae and embryos of all chordate groups have these characteristics. However, most groups lose some or all of these structures as adults.

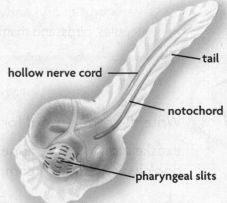

A sea squirt is a tunicate. This sea squirt larva shows all four chordate features.

Underline four characteristics that all chordates share at some stage of their development.

## All vertebrates share common features.

Vertebrates tend to be large, active animals. Even the smallest vertebrate, an Indonesian fish the size of a fingernail, is larger than most invertebrates.

### Vertebrate Endoskeleton

An **endoskeleton** is an internal skeleton built of bone or cartilage. These tissues are made of collagen* fibers mixed in with harder materials. The endoskeleton allows vertebrates to grow to large sizes. Vertebrate skeletons can be divided into distinct parts.

* ACADEMIC VOCABULARY

**collagen** a type of protein that combines with other materials to form hard structures, such as bones.

- **Braincase** A braincase or cranium protects the brain.
- **Vertebrae** A series of short, stiff vertebrae form the backbone, which protects the spinal cord. The vertebrae are separated by joints that let the backbone bend as the animal moves.
- **Bones** Bones support and protect the body's soft tissues. Muscles attach to certain points on the bones.
- **Gill arches** Gill arches support the gills. These arches are found in the pharynx of fish and some amphibians. Gills are the organs that fish use to breathe, just as land vertebrates use their lungs.

The endoskeleton forms a frame that supports muscles and protects internal organs. It contains cells that can break down and rebuild the skeleton to make it larger and stronger as the animal grows. In contrast, arthropod skeletons cannot grow and must be shed.

## Vertebrate Classes

There are seven classes of vertebrates in the phylum Chordata.

- **Agnatha** are jawless fishes.
- **Chondrichthyes** are fish with cartilage skeletons, such as sharks, rays, and chimeras.
- **Osteichthyes** are fish with bony skeletons. The ray-finned fish in this group are the most diverse group of vertebrates.
- **Amphibia** were the first vertebrates adapted to live in water and on land. They must reproduce in water or on moist land. They include salamanders, frogs (and toads), and caecilians.
- **Reptilia** have ways to reduce water loss so they can live entirely on land. Reptiles include snakes, lizards, crocodiles, alligators, and turtles.
- **Aves** are the birds, the only vertebrates that can fly. Only birds have feathers.
- **Mammalia** are animals with hair, mammary glands, and three middle ear bones.

 Highlight four features that all vertebrates share.

# Fossil evidence sheds light on the origins of vertebrates.

Scientists have learned about early vertebrates mostly from fossils found in the Burgess Shale in the Canadian Rocky Mountains. The fossils date from the Cambrian explosion about 550 million years ago.

Different classes of vertebrates include aves (birds) and mammalia (mammals).

**Closest relatives of vertebrates** Recent research indicates that tunicates may be the closest relatives to the vertebrates. All vertebrate embryos have a group of cells called the neural crest, which develops into parts of the nervous system and into the head, bones, and teeth. Fossils show that tunicates had cells that resemble the neural crest.

**Early vertebrates** The oldest fossil fish are 530 million years old. These fish did not have jaws. Most of these early vertebrates were extinct by 360 million years ago. Today, the two living relatives of the jawless fish are the lampreys and the hagfish.

- **Lampreys** are specialized fish parasites. They have long, thin bodies without paired fins, mouths surrounded by a sucker, and tongues covered with toothlike projections. They hold onto fish with their suckers and use their tongues to scrape holes in their prey.
- **Hagfish** are jawless, eel-like animals with a part of a skull but no vertebrae. Hagfish also have a notochord.

 What structure shows that tunicates may be the closest relatives of vertebrates? _____

| 25.1 | Vocabulary Check |
|---|---|

**Mark It Up**

Go back and highlight each sentence that has a vocabulary word in **bold**.

chordate          endoskeleton
notochord

**Choose the correct term from the list for each description.**

1. flexible skeletal support rod _____

2. can be made of bones or cartilage _____

3. larva or embryo has pharyngeal slits _____

| 25.1 | The Big Picture |
|---|---|

4. How is the vertebrate endoskeleton different from the arthropod exoskeleton? _____

5. Why are some invertebrates classified as chordates? _____

_____

6. Which feature of the endoskeleton is not found in humans? _____

_____

# 25.2 Fish Diversity

KEY CONCEPT   The dominant aquatic vertebrates are fish.

Swimming long distances requires endurance* and a lot of energy. If you swim just a few laps in a pool, you will soon get tired. Fish spend their entire lives moving through water. But fish are more energy-efficient than you are because their bodies and internal structures are adapted to live in a watery environment.

## Fish are vertebrates with gills and paired fins.

You get the oxygen you need by breathing air into and out of your lungs. Because fish live underwater, they get oxygen in a completely different way. Fish use specialized organs called gills to breathe. **Gills** are large sheets of thin tissue filled with capillaries that take in dissolved oxygen from the water and release carbon dioxide. The capillaries give gills a very large surface area for gas exchange.

A fish circulatory system pumps blood in a single loop through a heart that has only two main chambers. The smaller chamber, the atrium, collects oxygen-poor blood returning from the body and pumps it into the ventricle. The ventricle, the larger chamber, pumps blood through the capillaries in the gills. Here, carbon dioxide is released, and oxygen is picked up by the blood.

### Countercurrent Flow

The arteries in the gills are arranged so that blood flows in one direction. In contrast, water entering the gills flows in the opposite direction. The opposite movements of water and blood are known as **countercurrent flow.**

There is always a greater concentration of oxygen in the water than in the fish's blood. In countercurrent flow, blood always passes by water that contains more oxygen than the blood does. Recall that oxygen always diffuses from an area of higher concentration to an area of lower concentration. Water entering the gills and water leaving the gills pass by blood low in oxygen. As a result, oxygen diffuses into the blood along the entire length of the gills.

**VISUAL VOCAB**

**Countercurrent flow** maximizes the amount of oxygen the fish can pull from the water.

water flow

oxygen exchange

blood flow

* ACADEMIC VOCABULARY

**endurance**  the ability to perform a long, hard activity

## Swimming and Changing Directions

Most fish swim by using large muscles on each side of their body that run from head to tail. These muscles contract and produce repeated S-shaped waves that move down the fish's body and push it forward through the water. These body movements also move the fish from side to side, which wastes energy. Fish reduce this energy loss by using their fins.

**Types of fins** Most fish have dorsal fins on their backs and anal fins on their bellies. Most fish also have a pair of pectoral fins just behind the head and a pair of pelvic fins near the middle of the belly. The caudal fin is another name for the tail fin.

**Fins at work** Fins keep fish steady in the water. Their movements move water around the fish as it swims. The dorsal and anal fins keep the fish from rolling over. The caudal fin moves the fish in a forward direction. The pectoral and pelvic paired fins help the fish to change direction, stop, and hover* in the water.

 Highlight the different types of fins and what each type does.

Fins help fish move easily through the water to search for food or to escape predators.

# Jaws evolved from gill supports.

Jaws evolved from gill arches nearest the mouth. These arches are made of bone or cartilage. Over time, the upper section of the third gill arch attached to the fish's cranium and formed the upper jaw. Because gill arches are jointed, the bottom part of the gill arch could bend to open and close the mouth. This bottom part became the lower jaw.

In most fish, the fourth gill arch also supports the jaws. Most jawed vertebrates have teeth on their upper and lower jaws to capture and shred food. But capturing food may not have been the first function of jaws. Evidence suggests that closing the front pair of arches prevented oxygen-rich water from flowing out of the mouth as water was pumped over the gills. The closed gill arches also kept prey from escaping once they were in the predator's mouth.

 Describe how a jaw formed from gill arches. _____

_____

_____

**JAW EVOLUTION**

Evidence from fossils supports the idea that jaws evolved from fish gills.

cranium

mouth

gill arches

**Agnatha** Jawless fish such as lampreys evolved from filter-feeding ancestors. In jawless fish, the filters were modified to function as gills.

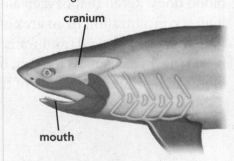

cranium

mouth

**Modern fish** In modern fish such as sharks, the fourth set of gill arches fused to the cranium.

* ACADEMIC VOCABULARY

**hover** stay in one place

# Only two groups of jawed fish still exist.

Jawed fish diversified very quickly after they first appeared about 440 million years ago. Four groups of fish appeared at this time.

- **Acanthodians** were fish covered with spines. They became extinct about 250 million years ago.
- **Placoderms** were heavily armored with huge bony plates. They became extinct about 350 million years ago.
- **Cartilaginous fish** are one of the two groups of fish that survive today. They include sharks, rays, and chimeras.
- **Bony fish** are the group that includes all other fish living in the world today.

## Cartilaginous Fish

Cartilaginous fish are members of the phylum Chondrichthyes. They have skeletons made of cartilage, but their ancestors had bony skeletons. These fish have lost the ability to make bone. There are two groups within the Chondrichthyes.

Sharks are one of the oldest living groups of fish in the world. Most species are highly efficient hunters.

- **Chimeras, or ratfish** are in one group. Chimeras are a small group of deep-sea fish with platelike grinding teeth. They feed on crustaceans and other invertebrates.
- **Sharks, rays, and skates** are in the other group. Most sharks hunt other animals. But whale sharks and basking sharks are filter feeders.

Cartilaginous fish fertilize their eggs inside their bodies and many give birth to live young. Oil stored in their livers provides buoyancy* that keeps them from sinking. They are powerful swimmers with good eyesight and an unusually keen sense of smell.

All fish have a **lateral line** system on their sides. This is a series of shallow canals made of cells that sense small changes in water movement caused by swimming prey animals. Many fish also have sensory organs called electroreceptive cells. These cells receive signals from the electrical currents made by muscular contractions in other animals. In cartilaginous fish, these highly sensitive cells are on the nose. For example, a shark can detect the tiny electric currents produced by the heartbeat of an animal that is hiding.

---

**\* ACADEMIC VOCABULARY**

**buoyancy** ability to float or rise in a fluid

## Bony Fish

All other living fish have skeletons made of bone. These bony fish are called the Osteichthyes. They live in nearly every water environment on Earth.

The gills of all bony fish are in a chamber, or space, covered by a protective plate called the **operculum.** The operculum's movements create a low-pressure area just outside of the gills. Water flows from the high-pressure area in the mouth, through the gills, and toward the operculum.

 Highlight two characteristics found in all bony fish.

---

### 25.2    Vocabulary Check

**Mark It Up**

Go back and highlight each sentence that has a vocabulary word in **bold.**

gill                                    lateral line
countercurrent flow          operculum

**Fill in the blanks with the correct term from the list above.**

1. A(n) _____ is a protective plate.

2. The movements of a prey animal in the water is sensed by the
   _____.

3. A(n) _____ maximizes the amount of oxygen a fish
   can get from the water.

4. A(n) _____ is a large sheet of thin tissue filled with
   capillaries.

### 25.2    The Big Picture

5. Explain why countercurrent flow helps a fish get more oxygen from
   the water. _____
   _____

6. What advantages did jaws bring to vertebrates? _____
   _____

7. What similar functions are performed by the lateral line system and
   electroreceptive cells? _____
   _____
   _____

# 25.3 A Closer Look at Bony Fish

**KEY CONCEPT** Bony fish include ray-finned and lobe-finned fish.

You are probably most familiar with bony fish. The goldfish in pet stores and the tuna fish that you eat for lunch are bony fish. So are the trout and bass found in many lakes, rivers, and streams.

## Ray-finned fish have a fan of bones in their fins.

Some fish have fins supported by a fan-shaped set of bones called a **ray-fin.** Ray-fin bones are covered by a thin layer of skin and connective tissue. Muscles in the fish's body move the bones. The fin is lightweight, can fold up, and is easy to move. Ray-fins enable a fish to turn, dive, stay in one place, and make other movements. But the fins are thin and cannot support the fish out of water.

### Diversity of Body Plans

Ray-finned fish are the most diverse group of living vertebrates. They make up nearly half of all vertebrate species on Earth. Most have stream-lined bodies, but others look quite different.

- Long, torpedo-shaped fish, such as the barracuda, can swim more easily through the water. They are predators that can suddenly swim fast and surprise their prey.
- Some fish are flattened from side to side, such as butterfly fish. They cannot swim quickly, but they are very maneuverable*.
- Fish that feed on the surface of the water have flattened heads and mouths that point up. This body plan allows them to eat invertebrates on the surface and makes it hard for predators to see them.
- Flatfish are flat-shaped. They lie on the sea floor and wait for prey to swim by. As this fish develops its flattened shape, one eye gradually moves to the top of its head so it can see prey with both eyes.
- Some slow-swimming fish use camouflage to hide from predators or prey. For example, a leafy sea dragon looks like the seaweed it lives in.

**\* ACADEMIC VOCABULARY**

**maneuverable**  able to make changes easily in direction and position

## Staying Afloat

Most ray-finned fish have lungs modified into a buoyancy organ called a **swim bladder.** The swim bladder helps a fish float higher or lower in the water. Because the fish does not have to swim to keep from floating to the surface or sinking, the swim bladder saves the fish energy. For the fish to rise higher in the water, oxygen from the blood is added to the swim bladder. To reduce buoyancy, oxygen is reabsorbed into the blood.

Some ray-finned fish still have lungs. The bichir, which lives in slow-moving streams in West Africa, has gills but can also breathe air. This trait enables it to survive out of water for several hours.

 How does the structure of a ray-fin help a fish swim? _____

_____

---

**BONY FISH ANATOMY**

The unique features of the anatomy of a bony fish include a swim bladder that maintains buoyancy and gills used to breathe.

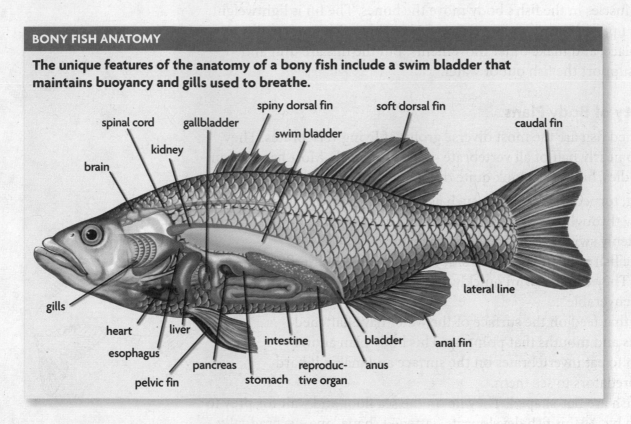

## Lobe-finned fish have paired rounded fins supported by a single bone.

The lobe-finned fish include the ancestors of all land-based vertebrates. Only seven species are still living today. **Lobe-fins** are rounded, paired pectoral and pelvic fins. They are arranged around a series of bony supports, like the limb of a land vertebrate. There is always one bone at the base of the fin. It is attached to smaller bones arranged in a fan shape. Muscles in the fin and across the bones make the fin thick and fleshy. Lobe-fins are less maneuverable but can support a fish's weight.

**Coelacanths** Coelacanths are odd-looking fish with thick, fleshy fins and a tail with three lobes. They breathe with gills. Their swim bladder is filled with fat and provides buoyancy. Scientists thought they were extinct; but in 1938, a coelacanth was caught in the Indian Ocean near South Africa.

**Lungfish** Lungfish live in streams and swamps in Australia, South America, and Africa. They can breathe with either gills or lungs and can live in oxygen-poor water.

Recent research suggests that lungfish are the closest living relatives of land-based vertebrates. Both lungfish and land vertebrates are the only animals with separate blood circuits—one circuit for the lungs and one for the rest of the body.

Highlight the features that make a lobe-fin different from a ray-fin.

**VISUAL VOCAB**

**Lobe-fins** are paired limblike fins that are round in shape.

lobe fin

---

### 25.3 Vocabulary Check

ray-fin  lobe-fin
swim bladder

**Mark It Up**

Go back and highlight each sentence that has a vocabulary word in **bold**.

1. Circle the fin that is more maneuverable in the water.

2. Underline the structure that helps with buoyancy.

3. Put a box around the fin that is rounded and can support a fish's weight.

---

### 25.3 The Big Picture

4. Explain what a swim bladder is and how it works. _____

_____

_____

5. What characteristic of lobe-fins links these fish to land-based vertebrates? _____

_____

6. What evidence suggests that lungfish are the closest living relatives of land vertebrates? _____

_____

_____

# 25.4 Amphibians

**KEY CONCEPT** Amphibians evolved from lobe-finned fish.

Suppose you were a real "fish out of water." How long would you last? The air cannot support your body as the water does. Your lateral line does not work. It is so dry that you start losing water through your skin. You cannot take in oxygen. These are a few of the problems animals faced when they first moved out of the water and onto land.

## Amphibians were the first animals with four limbs.

One of the oldest known fossils of a four-limbed vertebrate shows the animal had lungs. But it also had gills and a lateral line system. These structures work only in water. This suggests that the first animals with four limbs lived in water and used their limbs for swimming.

All vertebrates that live on land are **tetrapods,** that is, they have four limbs. Even their descendants that returned to the water, such as dolphins and whales, are tetrapods. Each limb evolved from a lobe-fin. Tetrapod legs contain bones arranged in the same pattern as lobe-fins. However, the fan of bones at the end is replaced by a set of jointed fingers, wings, or toes. Snakes, which do not have four limbs, are still tetrapods because they evolved from limbed ancestors.

**Leaving the water** Limbs and lungs made these animals successful in oxygen-poor water. Over time, these adaptations enabled tetrapods to climb out of the water and search for food or escape predators. These animals gave rise to the first amphibians. **Amphibians** are animals that can live both on land and in water.

**Living on land** A number of adaptations help amphibians live on land.

- large shoulder and hip bones help support more weight
- vertebrae that interlock so the backbone doesn't twist or sag
- a mobile, muscular tongue to capture food
- a middle ear that helps some amphibians to hear while on land
- ability to breathe through the skin, or through gills or lungs
- a three-chambered heart with one ventricle and two atria. The atria keep oxygen-rich and oxygen-poor blood separate.

Over time, these adaptations enabled amphibians to live partly on land. However, amphibians had not evolved ways to keep themselves or their eggs from drying out in the air. They still needed to spend part of their lives in water.

 Highlight three adaptations that help amphibians live on land.

> **VOCABULARY**
>
> In the word *amphibian*, the root *amphi* comes from a Greek word meaning "on both sides." The suffix *–bian* comes from a Greek word meaning "life." *Amphibian* literally means "life that can live on both sides" (in water and on land).

# Amphibians return to the water to reproduce.

An amphibian's skin is thin and wet. Amphibians might die if they move too far from water. A few species are able to live in the desert by burrowing underground. They come out only during the rainy season.

## Reproduction Strategies

Amphibian eggs do not have a shell. The embryos will dry out and die unless they stay moist. To keep their eggs wet, some amphibians lay eggs directly in water or on moist ground. Others wrap eggs in leaves. Still others, such as frogs, brood* eggs in pockets on the female's back.

## Amphibian Metamorphosis

Some frogs start their lives as tadpoles living in water. **Tadpoles** are the larvae of frogs. They have gills and a broad-finned tail but no limbs. To grow into frogs, tadpoles undergo metamorphosis, that is, they change from one form with certain habits into a different form with different habits.

During metamorphosis, the tadpole's gills are reabsorbed, and its lungs develop. The circulatory system is reorganized to send blood to the lungs. The tail fin, or the entire tail, is also reabsorbed. The body grows limbs and reorganizes its skeleton, muscles, and parts of its nervous system into the adult form. The digestive system is rebuilt so digestion occurs in the stomach, and wastes are eliminated through the cloaca.

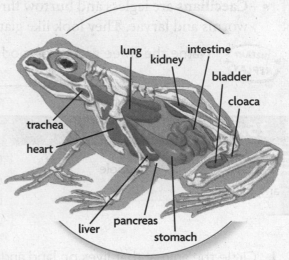

Tadpoles go through metamorphosis to become adult frogs.

Many amphibians, however, do not go through metamorphosis. Adult females lay eggs on the ground or keep them in their bodies. The young develop directly into their adult forms that can live on land.

How does an amphibian's breathing change after metamorphosis? _____

# Modern amphibians can be divided into three groups.

Three groups of modern amphibians are found in the world today. They are salamanders, frogs, and caecilians.

---

\* ACADEMIC VOCABULARY

**brood** to cover up and protect eggs and young

- **Salamanders** have a long body, four walking limbs, and a tail. Members of the largest family do not have lungs. Instead, they exchange gases through the lining of their skin and mouth. Salamanders eat insects, worms, and snails. Large species prey on fish and frogs.
- **Frogs** are the largest amphibian group, with more than 3,000 species. Adult frogs have no tails, long muscular hind legs, webbed feet, exposed eardrums, and bulging eyes. The long bones in the hips, legs, and feet are adapted for jumping. Toads are one family of frogs. They have bumps on their skin and shorter legs. Glands in the skin of toads and frogs make toxins that protect them from predators. Adult frogs will eat any animal they can catch.
- **Caecilians** are legless and burrow through the soil looking for earthworms and larvae. They look like giant earthworms themselves.

 Name the three groups of modern amphibians. _____

_____

| 25.4 **Vocabulary Check** | **Mark It Up** |
|---|---|

Go back and highlight each sentence that has a vocabulary word in **bold.**

tetrapod        tadpole
amphibian

1. Circle the animal that lives on land and in water.
2. Underline the first animal to have four limbs.
3. Put a box around the animal that is a larva.

### 25.4   The Big Picture

4. How is a lobe-fin different from a tetrapod limb? _____

_____

5. Why are interlocking vertebrae important? _____

_____

6. Describe three ways that an amphibian can keep its eggs wet. _____

_____

_____

7. What does a frog's leg structure say about its habits? _____

_____

_____

# 25.5 Vertebrates on Land

**KEY CONCEPT** Reptiles, birds, and mammals are adapted for life on land.

About 350 million years ago, one group of amphibians evolved traits that enabled them to leave the water forever. They diversified into reptiles, birds, and mammals, which is the class that includes you.

## Amniotes can retain moisture.

An **amniote** is a vertebrate whose embryo or fetus is protected by a thin, tough, membranelike sac around it. Amniotes have evolved into thousands of different forms, and they live in nearly every ecosystem.

**Amniotes today** Modern amniotes are predators or prey in the tropics, arid deserts, the Arctic, and freshwater and marine environments. They have become burrowers, runners, sit-and-wait predators, and slow pursuers. Some species never leave the trees. Others have developed powered flight. Many species alive today are survivors of larger groups whose members are extinct. Birds, for instance, are the descendants of the dinosaurs.

**Retaining moisture** All amniotes share a set of characteristics that prevent water loss. One characteristic is skin cells waterproofed with keratin. **Keratin** is a protein that attaches to fats inside the cell. This forms a waterproof layer that prevents water contained inside the animal's body from reaching the skin, where it would evaporate. Also, the kidneys and large intestines are bigger in amniotes than in amphibians. These organs contain tissues that reabsorb water. Such adaptations are ways that amniotes lose less water than do amphibians.

Amniotes include mammals, reptiles, and birds. The embryos of all amniotes are protected by membranes.

**INSTANT REPLAY** Highlight two characteristics that help amniotes retain water.

## Amniotes do not need to return to water to reproduce.

Over time, amniote adults adapted to living on land. But it was the evolution of the amniotic egg that enabled them to stay on land even to reproduce. The **amniotic egg** is an almost completely waterproof container that keeps an embryo from drying out as it develops.

An amniote egg requires a lot of energy from the mother. She must not only build a shell for the egg but also make enough yolk and egg white to feed the embryo until it hatches. For example, a bird may lose 5 to 30 percent of its body weight making an egg.

Other amniotes, such as rattlesnakes and garter snakes, make eggs but keep them in their bodies until they hatch. This protects the eggs from predators. Some amniotes give birth to well-developed young.

Most mammal embryos develop inside the mother's body. The eggs have no shells, but they do have the same membranes found in typical amniotic eggs. One of these membranes, the **placenta,** is an organ that develops in the uterus of female mammals during pregnancy. The placenta carries nutrients from the mother to the embryo and also removes wastes from the embryo.

The amniotic egg allows an embryo to develop without drying out.

 How does an amniotic egg protect the embryo from water loss? _____

## 25.5 Vocabulary Check

| | |
|---|---|
| amniote | amniotic egg |
| keratin | placenta |

**Mark It Up**

Go back and highlight each sentence that has a vocabulary word in **bold**.

Choose the correct term from the list for each description.

1. carries nutrients from the mother to the embryo _____

2. protein that is part of a waterproof layer of cells _____

3. waterproof container with yolk and white _____

4. vertebrate with a thin, tough sac around the embryo or fetus
_____

## 25.5 The Big Picture

5. Why is it important for an amniote to have waterproof skin? _____

_____

6. How do bigger kidneys and large intestines help an amniote prevent water loss? _____

_____

7. Name one difference and one similarity between reproduction in mammals and reproduction in other amniotes. _____

_____

# Chapter 25 Review

1. Name four characteristics that all chordates share at some stage of their development. _____

   _____

2. What feature of an endoskeleton enables a vertebrate to change size and shape as it grows? _____

3. Countercurrent flow increases the amount of oxygen a fish can pull from the water because _____
   a. the ventricle pumps blood through the gills.
   b. there is more oxygen in water than in a fish's blood.
   c. oxygen diffuses into areas of higher concentration.
   d. blood and water move in the same direction.

4. What is the function of the paired fins in a fish? _____

   _____

5. What is the difference between the bone arrangements in a ray-fin and in a lobe-fin? _____

   _____

6. Lobe-finned fish include the ancestors of _____
   a. cartilagenous fish.
   b. ray-finned fish.
   c. chimeras.
   d. terrestrial vertebrates.

7. Describe an amphibian's heart. _____

   _____

   _____

8. Describe two changes that occur in a frog's metamorphosis from a tadpole. _____

   _____

   _____

9. Name three types of amniotic reproduction. _____

   _____

   _____

10. What is the purpose of the placenta? _____

   _____

   _____

# 26 A Closer Look at Amniotes

## GETTING READY TO LEARN

### Preview Key Concepts

**26.1 Amniotes**
Reptiles, birds, and mammals are amniotes

**26.2 Reptiles**
Reptiles were the first amniotes.

**26.3 Birds**
Birds have many adaptations for flight.

**26.4 Mammals**
Evolutionary adaptations allowed mammals to succeed dinosaurs as a dominant terrestrial vertebrate.

## Review Academic Vocabulary

Write the correct word for each definition.

endoskeleton    chordate    tetrapod    amniotic egg    placenta

1. _____ : waterproof container that keeps embryo moist

2. _____ : vertebrates with four legs

3. _____ : membrane that nourishes an embryo

4. _____ : support that is inside the body

5. _____ : animal with notochord, tail, gills, hollow nerve cord

## Preview Biology Vocabulary

Two key terms from this chapter share the same word part. Read the definitions and guess what the word part means.

| TERM | DEFINITION | WHAT I THINK -therm MEANS |
|------|-----------|---------------------------|
| ectotherm | animal whose body temperature depends on the surrounding environment | |
| endotherm | animal that can maintain its own body temperature | |

# 26.1 Amniotes

**KEY CONCEPT**  Reptiles, birds, and mammals are amniotes.

Before you were born, you grew and developed inside a fluid-filled membrane, or amniotic sac. There are many different types of amniote animals, but each of them, like you, begins inside an amniotic sac.

## Amniote embryos develop in a fluid-filled sac.

All reptiles, birds, and mammals are amniotes, which means they develop inside a sac made of layers of membranes. In some amniotes, the sac is inside the mother's body. In others, the tough outer shell of an egg protects the embryo as it develops outside of the mother's body. This shell is semipermeable. It allows oxygen and carbon dioxide to pass through but holds water inside, so the embryo will not dry out.

Inside the shell of an amniotic egg, four membranes protect and nourish the embryo. The amnion surrounds and cushions the embryo from changes in temperature or physical blows. The chorion allows gas exchange with the outside environment. The yolk sac contains the nutrient supply. The allantois holds waste materials from the embryo.

  How does an embryo get oxygen while it is inside an egg?

_____

_____

## Anatomy and circulation differ among amniotes.

Over time, amniotes evolved many different body shapes and sizes. This led to differences in anatomy and blood circulation among species.

**Anatomy**  The first amniotes moved like a lizard. A lizard's legs stick out from the sides of its body. The elbows and knees are bent as it walks. Muscles around the ribs move the body forward, but the contractions make the body sway from side to side. These muscles also inflate the lungs. Animals that move like this cannot run and breathe at the same time.

Amniotes such as mammals, dinosaurs, and birds evolved a more upright stance. A cat, for example, has straighter limbs set underneath its body. When it walks, its legs swing back and forth like a pendulum.*

The lizard has a sprawling walk. The cat walks upright—a feature that enables the cat to move and breathe at the same time.

---

**\* ACADEMIC VOCABULARY**

**pendulum**  an object that swings back and forth in a straight line

The cat's body does not sway from side to side. This type of movement uses less energy and enables the animal to breathe as it walks.

**Circulation** As amniotes evolved, their bodies required more energy for movement and growth. To get this energy, their tissues needed efficient ways of receiving oxygen. This led to the development of different types of circulatory systems. All amniotes have a centralized heart and two circuits of blood vessels. Separate circuits allow amniotes to conserve energy. The two circuits are the pulmonary and systemic circuits.

- The **pulmonary circuit** moves oxygen-poor blood from the heart to the lungs, and then moves oxygen-rich blood from the lungs back to the heart.
- The **systemic circuit** moves oxygen-rich blood from the heart to the rest of the body. It then moves oxygen-poor blood back to the heart where it can be pumped to the lungs.

Like amphibians, reptiles have a three-chambered heart with two atria and one ventricle. One atrium collects oxygen-poor blood from the body. The other collects oxygen-rich blood from the lungs. Both atria send blood into the ventricle, which pumps blood into the pulmonary and systemic circuits. The single ventricle can keep blood away from the lungs when the animal needs to stop breathing as it runs or swims.

Mammals and birds have a four-chambered heart with two atria and two ventricles. These chambers keep oxygen-poor and oxygen-rich blood separate. As a result, more oxygen-rich blood goes to the tissues. This adaptation gave mammals and birds a large and constant supply of oxygen for their energy needs. Eventually, this type of heart also gave them more control over their body temperature.

 How does a four-chambered heart provide more energy for tissues?

_____

_____

_____

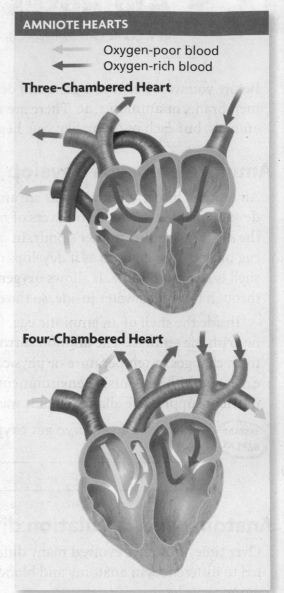

**AMNIOTE HEARTS**

← Oxygen-poor blood
← Oxygen-rich blood

**Three-Chambered Heart**

**Four-Chambered Heart**

Reptiles have three-chambered hearts. Birds and mammals have four-chambered hearts that keep oxygen-rich and oxygen-poor blood completely separate.

# Amniotes can be ectothermic or endothermic.

Like all organisms, amniotes are more active when they are warm. The term **ectotherms** refers to organisms whose body temperatures are determined by their surrounding environment. Ectotherms can adjust their body temperature by changing their external environment. For example, many reptiles lie in the sun to warm up and move into the shade to cool down.

**Endotherms** are organisms that can increase or decrease their own metabolism to keep themselves warm or cool. When they are cold, they shiver by rapidly contracting their muscles to make more heat. Most endotherms also have hair, fat cells, or feathers to prevent heat loss. If endotherms get too warm, they cool off by sweating and panting.

Endotherms and ectotherms have two different ways of managing energy use. Endotherms can be active in all types of temperatures, but they need more energy to keep their tissues warm. As a result, they have to eat more. Ectotherms are less active when it is cold, but they can survive on less food than can endotherms.

 Underline three ways in which an endotherm maintains a stable body temperature.

---

## 26.1 Vocabulary Check

| Mark It Up |
|---|
| Go back and highlight each sentence that has a vocabulary word in **bold**. |

pulmonary circuit          ectotherm

systemic circuit           endotherm

**Fill in the blanks with the correct term from the list above.**

1. An organism whose body temperature depends on the environment is an _____.

2. Oxygen-poor blood moves back to the heart through the _____.

3. An _____ can be active in a cold or warm environment.

## 26.1 The Big Picture

4. What are the four membranes in an amniotic egg? _____

5. Why can't reptiles run and breathe at the same time? _____

_____

6. How does a mammal's heart compare to a reptile's heart?

_____

# 26.2 Reptiles

**KEY CONCEPT** Reptiles were the first amniotes.

The eastern water lizard may look slow, but it has a top speed of 20 kilometers per hour and strong jaws filled with sharp teeth. It may never compare to the crocodile as a threat to humans, but it hunts, kills, and eats in the same way. What makes reptiles unique?

## Reptiles are a diverse group of amniotes.

About 200 million years ago, many of Earth's plant and animal species became extinct. One group of organisms that survived—the reptiles— have thrived for millions of years. **Reptiles** are ectotherms that are covered with dry scales or plates and reproduce by laying amniotic eggs covered with a tough outer shell.

An egg allows a young reptile to develop fully before it is born. There are two ways that reptile eggs develop.

- **Oviparous** reptiles put their eggs into a nest, and the eggs develop completely outside of the adult reptile's body.
- **Viviparous** reptiles hold the eggs inside of their body while the young develop. These reptiles give birth to live offspring.

Reptiles have evolved a wide variety of shapes, sizes, and features. Some reptiles, such as snakes, have no legs and move by rippling their muscles. Others run swiftly on land or spend most of their time in the water. Still others, like the turtles, carry their homes on their backs.

In spite of these differences, all reptiles share a few similar features. All living reptiles are ectotherms. Recall that an ectotherm's body temperature changes based on the surrounding environment. As a result, many reptiles spend a lot of time lying in the sun to absorb heat. Their dry scales or plates help absorb and retain the heat they need.

 Underline two ways in which reptile eggs develop.

> **VOCABULARY**
> The name *reptile* comes from the Latin word *reptilis*, which means "creeping."

## Reptiles have been evolving for millions of years.

Reptiles became the dominant vertebrate during the Mesozoic era, which lasted from about 238 million years ago to 65 million years ago.

### Synapsids, Anapsids, and Diapsids

Over time, reptile amniotes evolved into three different groups.

- **Synapsids** had one hole on each side of the skull. Eventually, they gave rise to modern mammals.
- **Anapsids** have skulls without any holes on the sides. The anapsids of today are turtles and tortoises.

- **Diapsids** have two holes on each side of the skull, one above the other. Diapsid skulls came about as reptiles began to move onto land. For the next 200 million years, diapsid reptiles ruled Earth. This group gave rise to many of the modern reptiles and birds of today.

Skull holes may have started out as weight-reducing adaptations. Less bone would have made the skull lighter, easier to move, and provided more space for muscle attachment.

## Diversity of Extinct Amniotes

- Pelycosaurs were synapsids that included meat-eaters (carnivores) and plant-eaters (herbivores). Some of their descendants gave rise to the mammals.
- Ichthyosaurs were some of the first diapsid reptiles. Their long bodies, flipper-shaped limbs, and dorsal fin were similar to modern-day dolphins.
- Plesiosaurs were marine reptiles. They "flew" through the water moving four limbs as flippers. Some had small heads and long necks. Others had short necks and long heads.
- Dinosaurs were the dominant land vertebrates for 150 million years. The largest, such as the huge sauropods, ate only plants. The carnivorous theropod dinosaurs gave rise to modern-day birds.
- Pterosaurs were the first vertebrates to evolve powered flight. Fossils show that pterosaurs may have had hair and were endothermic.

pterosaur

ichthyosaur

dinosaur

Ancient amniotes appeared first in the oceans then moved onto the land. Eventually some animals achieved powered flight.

 **INSTANT REPLAY** What are the three amniote skull types?

_____

_____

_____

# There are four modern groups of reptiles.

Only four groups of reptiles are alive today: turtles, sphenodonts, snakes and lizards, and crocodilians.

**Turtles** Turtles, tortoises, and terrapins are the only remaining anapsid amniotes. The rounded back of a turtle's shell is the carapace. The smooth belly part is the plastron. The shell is covered with tough, flattened plates made of keratin that are attached to the rib cage and vertebrae. Turtles are toothless but have sharp, horny beaks. They eat plants and animals. Terrestrial turtles are called tortoises.

**Sphenodonts** The only living sphenodonts are two species of tuatara that live on a few small islands near New Zealand. Tuataras are closely related to lizards and snakes. They have a diapsid skull and a light-sensitive eyespot in the center of their head.

**Snakes and lizards** These reptiles all shed their skins on a regular basis, have flexible skulls that let them swallow prey larger than their heads, and have a specialized organ that allows them to "taste" the air. When a snake or a lizard sticks its forked tongue out of its mouth, the tongue collects particles from the air. These particles are interpreted by the specialized organ, called a Jacobson's organ, found in the top of a reptile's mouth. The organ helps the reptile locate prey and avoid predators.

Most lizards are carnivores, but iguanas eat only plants. All snakes are predators. Some kill by squeezing their prey, while others inject poisons into their prey through fangs.

**Crocodilians** These reptiles include alligators, crocodiles, and caimans. All are semiaquatic* predators that live in swamps and rivers in the tropics and subtropics. They are ambush* predators. It may surprise you to know that crocodilians are more closely related to modern-day birds than they are to lizards and snakes.

 Underline the only modern reptiles that are anapsids.

---

**\* ACADEMIC VOCABULARY**

**semiaquatic** spends part of the time in the water

**ambush** lie in wait and then attack

---

## 26.2 Vocabulary Check

reptile     viviparous

oviparous

**Mark It Up**

Go back and highlight each sentence that has a vocabulary word in **bold.**

1. Circle the reproduction method in which females use a nest.

2. Underline the reproductive method in which females keep their eggs inside of their bodies.

## 26.2 The Big Picture

3. Why is it important that a reptile's scales absorb heat from the sun?

_____

4. What is the difference among synapsid, anapsid, and diapsid skulls?

_____

5. Which extinct amniotes gave rise to some modern-day animals?

_____

# 26.3 Birds

**KEY CONCEPT** Birds have many adaptations for flight.

The birds that you see all around you are actually related to a ferocious dinosaur known as a *Velociraptor*. In fact, birds are dinosaurs that evolved powered flight.

## Birds evolved from theropod dinosaurs.

Most paleontologists agree that birds are the descendants of one group of theropod dinosaurs. Theropods were bipedal, or two-legged, dinosaurs. Most were carnivorous and some, such as *Allosaurus* and *Tyrannosaurus*, were huge. Birds and many theropods share five anatomical features: hollow bones; fused collarbones that form a V-shaped wishbone, or furcula; rearranged muscles in the hips and legs that improve bipedal movements; "hands" that have lost their fourth and fifth fingers; and feathers.

Theropods had feathers, but they did not have wings. They were running animals. This means that feathers did not evolve for flight. They may have helped to keep the animals warm or been used for courtship displays or to scare off rivals. As birds evolved, they developed feathered wings.

The oldest fossil bird is *Archaeopteryx*, a chicken-sized animal that lived about 150 million years ago. It had feathers and a furcula. Like a reptile, it also had clawed fingers, a tail, and teeth. Its feathers make it an important link between flightless dinosaurs, dinosaurs that could fly, and the modern birds of today.

The feathered *Archaeopteryx* is an important link between dinosaurs and modern-day birds.

 Underline five shared features of birds and theropods.

## A bird's body is specialized for flight.

Birds have specialized adaptations for powered flight, including wings; flight muscles; a metabolism that provides a lot of energy; hollow bones; and reproductive adaptations.

**Wings** Wings are structures that allow birds to fly. Their curved shape is similar to an airplane wing. This kind of surface is called an **airfoil**. An airfoil is curved down on the top surface (convex) and curved up on the bottom (concave). This shape makes air move faster on top than below. The difference in air speed produces a pressure difference that lifts the wing up.

**VISUAL VOCAB**

An **airfoil** is convex on the top and concave on the bottom. Differences in air pressure above and below the airfoil create lift.

**Muscles** A bird's chest muscles provide the power for flight. In almost all vertebrates, chest muscles attach to the arms and the breastbone, or **sternum.** But a bird's chest muscles are so big that the sternum has evolved a larger surface called a keel, or ridge.

**Metabolism** Flying takes a lot of energy. Maintaining an active metabolism to produce large amounts of ATP during flight requires a huge amount of oxygen. To meet this challenge, a bird's body is filled with a series of **air sacs** that connect to the lungs. Air sacs store air as the bird breathes. Inhaled air travels through the lungs and air sacs in such a way that oxygen-rich air is always available.

**Bone structure** Birds have evolved bones that are hollow. Inside bird bones there is a system of support structures. Many bones are connected to the air sacs, and air fills the cavities in the bones. This adaptation decreases the bird's weight and increases the amount of air in a bird's body to make flying easier.

**Reproductive adaptations** The reproductive organs of male and female birds are active only for a few months during mating season. The rest of the year, the organs shrink to reduce the bird's weight.

AIR SAC
trachea
lungs
air sac

Air sacs and hollow bones give birds enough oxygen for flight and decrease the bird's weight.

 INSTANT REPLAY   What are five adaptations that help birds fly?

_____

_____

_____

## Birds have spread to many ecological niches.

Modern birds are the descendants of the one dinosaur group that survived when all other dinosaurs became extinct. Over time, this group diversified into more than 9000 species. Through natural selection, birds adapted to different habitats and gradually developed different wings, beaks, and feet.

**Differences in wing shape** The shape of a bird's wing reflects the way it flies. Short, wide wings allow a bird to maneuver easily. Gulls have long, narrow wings for soaring long distances over water. Hawks, eagles, and condors have long, broad wings for soaring slowly over land. Many types of songbirds have short, slightly pointed wings to maneuver through tight spaces. The wings of flightless birds, such as ostriches, are too small to lift the bird into the air.

**Differences in beak shape** The shape of a bird's beak, or bill, reflects how it eats. A bird's beak is a layer of keratin that covers the jaw bones. The long, spearlike beak of a heron can capture fish. The hooked beak of an eagle can tear flesh from its prey. Thin, pointed bills can catch insects. A parrot's thick beak can crack nuts.

**Differences in foot shape** With few exceptions, bird feet have four toes. Aquatic birds have webbed feet, with skin connecting the toes to form paddles. Birds of prey, such as eagles, have heavy claws to capture and kill prey. Woodpeckers have two toes pointing forward and two pointing backward, so they can cling to vertical tree trunks.

 Underline three features that help you know where a bird lives and how it feeds.

---

**26.3  Vocabulary Check**

airfoil          air sac

sternum

**Mark It Up**

Go back and highlight each sentence that has a vocabulary word in **bold.**

1. Underline the word that describes a bird's wing.

2. Circle the word that refers to a place where chest muscle can attach.

3. Put a box around the word that refers to a structure that helps a bird get more oxygen for flying.

---

**26.3  The Big Picture**

4. What are three adaptations that decrease weight and make flight easier?

_____

_____

_____

5. How do scientists know that feathers did not evolve for flight? _____

_____

_____

_____

6. Turkey vultures can soar for hours over the countryside. What shape do you think their wings are? Explain your answer. _____

_____

7. Would you expect to find a large keel on an ostrich? Explain.

_____

_____

_____

# 26.4 Mammals

**KEY CONCEPT** Evolutionary adaptations allowed mammals to succeed dinosaurs as a dominant terrestrial vertebrate.

You might style your hair with braids, gel, beads, and combs. Even with no decorations or styling, however, your hair is special. It sets humans and other mammals apart from reptiles, birds, amphibians, and fish. What other traits make mammals unique?

## All mammals share several common characteristics.

All **mammals** are active, large-brained, endothermic animals with complex social, feeding, and reproductive behaviors. Mammals are the only group of synapsids alive today. Fossil evidence suggests that early mammals had long noses and short legs, similar to shrews.

The ability to regulate their own body temperature gave mammals an advantage over reptiles. Mammals could adapt better to changes in climate. When the dinosaurs became extinct, mammals took their places in various habitats. In time, mammals succeeded dinosaurs as a dominant terrestrial life form.

Modern mammals share four characteristics. All species have hair, mammary glands, a middle ear containing three bones, and a jaw that lets them chew their food.

**Hair** Mammals are furry. Most species are covered with a layer of hair that helps them stay warm. Each hair is a long, thin, shaft or stick of dead cells with keratin that grows out of a follicle in the skin. The hair traps a layer of air next to the skin to provide insulation, much like a down vest insulates you.

Hair also has other uses. Have you ever seen a frightened cat fluff up to look bigger? Colored hairs, such as in a tiger's stripes, can provide camouflage. Many mammals also have long, stiff whiskers that collect sensory information.

This mammal, a raccoon, has a thick, furry coat of hair that helps it stay warm in the winter.

**Mammary glands** All female mammals feed their babies a fluid called milk. **Mammary glands** are specialized glands that produce this milk, which contains water, sugars, protein, fats, minerals, and antibodies. Some mammals, such as cats, dogs, and pigs, have a series of glands along the belly to feed several young at a time.

**Middle ear** Mammals have three small middle ear bones. One bone, the stapes, is found in other tetrapods. But the malleus and incus are unique to mammals. They were derived from reptilian jaw bones. Sounds collect in the ear canal and vibrate against the eardrum. These adaptations allow mammals to hear a wider range of sounds to find prey or avoid predators.

**Chewing** Adaptations in the jaw enable mammals to chew their food instead of just biting and swallowing it. A secondary palate* in the mouth separates the nose and mouth passages so that mammals can chew and breathe at the same time. Muscles move the jaw from side to side.

 Underline four characteristics that all mammals share.

# Modern mammals are divided into three main groups.

More than 4500 species of mammal are alive today. They can be classified into three groups: monotremes, marsupials, and eutherians.

### Monotremes

The **monotremes** are mammals that lay eggs. They have characteristics of both mammals and reptiles. Australia's duck-billed platypus and two types of echidna are the only species that survive today.

Monotremes have kept reptilian characteristics such as a sprawling posture; a single external opening, the cloaca, for their urinary, digestive, and reproductive tracts; and amniotic eggs with leathery shells that develop outside the body. Like mammals, they have mammary glands, but they don't have nipples. The babies lick milk from pools on the mother's belly.

### Marsupials

Kangaroos, wombats, koalas, and opossums are a few species of marsupials. **Marsupials** are mammals that give birth to very underdeveloped young that must grow inside a marsupium, or pouch. The embryos spend only a short time inside the mother, attached to a placenta. Most of them are born a few weeks after fertilization. The tiny babies then crawl through the mother's fur until they reach the pouch. They attach themselves to a nipple and nurse for up to six months before coming out of the pouch.

**REPTILIAN EAR BONE**

eardrum    inner ear
middle ear

stapes

**MAMMALIAN EAR BONES**

eardrum    inner ear
malleus
incus

ear canal    stapes

Unlike reptiles, mammals have three bones in their middle ear that help them detect higher pitched sounds.

The opossum is the only marsupial in North America. It can sleep while hanging by its tail.

## Eutherian Mammals

**Eutherian** mammals give birth to young that are far more developed. In most eutherians, the baby is attached to the mother's uterus by an organ called the placenta. Through the placenta, the baby receives oxygen and nutrients, and waste products are removed.

Gestation* in eutherians lasts longer than in most marsupials. In some species, such as tigers, newborns are nearly helpless and need a lot of care from the parents. In others, such as deer and horses, the young are able to run a few hours after being born to avoid predators.

Eutherian mammals are diverse. Whales, manatees, and seals evolved from land-dwelling mammals. Bats evolved powered flight. And one group, humans, evolved the ability to think about their ancestors.

 Underline the reptilian reproductive traits of monotremes.

* ACADEMIC VOCABULARY

**gestation** carrying offspring in the uterus

## 26.4 Vocabulary Check

mammal                 marsupial
mammary gland          eutherian
monotreme

**Mark It Up**

Go back and highlight each sentence that has a vocabulary word in **bold**.

Choose the correct term from the list above for each description.

1. babies grow to maturity inside a pouch _____

2. has mammal and reptile characteristics _____

3. contains milk for developing young _____

4. young are more completely developed at birth _____

## 26.4 The Big Picture

5. Name one difference between a mammal's jaw and other animal jaws.

_____

6. Describe one similarity and one difference between development of offspring in marsupials and eutherians. _____

_____

7. How does the mammalian middle ear help mammals to survive better?

_____

# Chapter 26 Review

1. Name the four membranes of an amniotic egg and describe what each one does. _____
_____
_____

2. Describe basic amniote circulation. _____
_____

3. Explain the functions of the pulmonary and the systemic circuits. _____
_____
_____

4. One possible explanation for skull holes is that they _____
   a. help regulate an animal's body temperature.
   b. strengthen the overall structure of the skull.
   c. provide more space for circulation.
   d. make a skull lighter and more flexible.

5. Explain the difference between viviparous and oviparous reptiles. _____
_____

6. What is the evidence that birds descended from theropod dinosaurs?
_____
_____

7. Choose the word that completes the following sentence:

   When a bird breathes, inhaled air travels through the lungs and
   _____ in such a way that oxygen-rich air is always available.
   a. air foils
   b. hollow bones
   c. keel
   d. air sacs

8. How does an airfoil wing shape help a bird to fly? _____
_____
_____

9. What are four characteristics that mammals share? _____
_____

10. What is a marsupium used for? _____
_____

# 27 Animal Behavior

## GETTING READY TO LEARN

### Preview Key Concepts

**27.1 Adaptive Value of Behavior**
Behavior lets organisms respond rapidly and adaptively to their environment.

**27.2 Instinct and Learning**
Both genes and environment affect an animal's behavior.

**27.3 Evolution of Behavior**
Every behavior has costs and benefits.

**27.4 Social Behavior**
Social behaviors enhance the benefits of living in a group.

**27.5 Animal Cognition**
Some animals other than humans exhibit behaviors requiring complex cognitive abilities.

### Review Academic Vocabulary

Write the correct word for each definition.

mammal    evolution    natural selection    omnivore

1. _____ : some organisms survive to reproduce

2. _____ : has hair, inner ear bones, glands that produce milk

3. _____ : changes in species over time

### Preview Biology Vocabulary

See how many key terms from this chapter you already know. Rewrite each phrase, using a different word or words for the **words in bold.**

| PHRASE | REWRITTEN WITH DIFFERENT WORDS |
|---|---|
| 1. A spider building a web for the first time is an example of **instinct**. | A spider building a web for the first time is an example of _____ _____ |
| 2. Young animals often learn by **imitation**. | Young animals often learn by _____ _____ |
| 3. **Altruism** is a behavior that can help a species to survive. | _____ _____ is a behavior that can help a species to survive. |

# 27.1 Adaptive Value of Behavior

**KEY CONCEPT** Behavior lets organisms respond rapidly and adaptively to their environment.

A lizard moves into the shade on a hot day. A cat comes running when it hears a can opener. What do these observations have in common? They are examples of organisms responding to stimuli in a way that helps them.

## Behavioral responses to stimuli may be adaptive.

Animal behaviors can be complex, especially in animals with complex nervous systems. But all behavior can be broken down into the relationship between a stimulus and a response.

### Stimulus and Response

A **stimulus** (plural, *stimuli*) is a type of information that can make an organism change its behavior. Internal stimuli tell an animal what is happening in its own body. For example,

- Hunger or thirst causes an animal to search for food or water.
- Pain in a part of its body causes an animal to take some action to avoid injury.

External stimuli give an animal information about its surroundings.

- The sound of a predator can cause an animal to hide or run away.
- The sight of a possible mate can trigger courtship behaviors.
- Longer or shorter days can trigger migration.

Animals have specialized cells that detect changes in physical or chemical stimuli. The cells transfer information to an animal's nervous system. The nervous system activates other systems, such as muscles. An animal's ability to move, for example, is one way it responds to stimuli.

Thirsty zebras may walk for miles to find pools of water where they can drink.

### The Function of Behavior

Recall that homeostasis refers to the maintenance of constant internal conditions. Many behaviors help an animal maintain homeostasis. For example, temperature receptors cause a lizard to move to a sunnier spot if it is too cold.

Kinesis and taxis are behaviors that describe how an animal moves from an uncomfortable location to a better location. **Kinesis** is an increase in random movement that lasts until the animal finds a better environment. For example, when a pill bug begins to dry out, it becomes more active and moves around until it reaches a moist area. Then, its activity decreases again. On the other hand, **taxis** is simply a movement toward or away from a stimulus.

Animals with more successful behaviors tend to survive and have more offspring. If the behaviors can be inherited, their offspring will probably behave in similar ways. Behaviors, like any characteristic, can evolve by natural selection.

 **INSTANT REPLAY** Highlight three examples of internal stimuli and three examples of external stimuli.

## Internal and external stimuli usually interact to trigger specific behaviors.

Some behaviors are triggered by a single stimulus, but most behaviors are responses to both internal and external stimuli. An example is the reproductive behavior of green anoles, a type of lizard.

Most of the year, female anoles ignore the males. But in spring, two external stimuli change their behavior: (1) exposure to long days and short nights and (2) seeing males that are ready to reproduce. These males move their bodies up and down and extend their dewlap. The dewlap is a flap of bright red skin under the chin. Seeing the dewlap makes females release sex hormones, an internal signal that makes them receptive to courtship by males.

 **INSTANT REPLAY** What internal and external stimuli change a female anole's behavior?

## Some behaviors occur in cycles.

Most animals respond to daily, monthly, or yearly cycles. In order to be active every day, for instance, your body needs to sleep every night. This daily pattern of activity and sleep is a **circadian rhythm,** a cycle of activity that occurs over a 24-hour period.

These activity patterns are controlled by an internal mechanism called a **biological clock.** This biological clock is run by chemicals in the brain and proteins in the body that can detect changes in light.

**Hibernation** Some animals avoid cold temperatures by entering into hibernation, which is like a very deep sleep. During this time, an animal has a lower body temperature, reduced heartbeat, and a slower breathing rate. Shorter days and cooler temperatures cause an animal to enter hibernation in the fall. In the spring, longer days and warmer temperatures stimulate hormones that awaken the animal.

**Migration** If you've seen a flock of geese flying southward during the fall, you've seen bird migration in action. Like hibernation, migratory behavior allows animals to avoid harsh conditions for part of the year.

Grizzly bears store up fat in the summer, then hibernate through the bitter northern winters.

 **INSTANT REPLAY** Name a behavior pattern that occurs in a regular cycle.

_____

_____

## 27.1 Vocabulary Check

stimulus            circadian rhythm

kinesis             biological clock

taxis

**Mark It Up**

Go back and highlight each sentence that has a vocabulary word in **bold**.

**Fill in the blanks with the correct term from the list above.**

1. _____ is simply the movement toward or away from a stimulus.

2. An internal mechanism that controls activity patterns is called a _____.

3. A _____ is information that can make an organism change its behavior.

## 27.1 The Big Picture

4. How can stimulus and response behaviors help a species to survive?

_____

_____

5. What is the relationship between a circadian rhythm and a biological clock? _____

# 27.2 Instinct and Learning

**KEY CONCEPT** Both genes and environment affect an animal's behavior.

Genetic and environmental factors interact in most behaviors. "Nature (genetic) versus nurture (environmental)" is not the best way to look at behavior. Most behaviors are a mixture of both nature *and* nurture.

## Innate behaviors are triggered by specific internal and external stimuli.

A spider can build a web the first time it tries. This kind of behavior is an **instinct.** An instinct is innate and mostly inflexible, or unchanging. An **innate** behavior is performed correctly the first time an animal tries it. An inflexible behavior is performed in roughly the same way each time.

**Instinctive behaviors** These behaviors are especially important in newborns, who have had no time to learn how to act. Mistakes could be life threatening. For example, baby mammals that do not suckle die of starvation.

The moment they are born, these piglets know instinctively how to suckle from their mother.

**Innate behaviors** These behaviors are triggered by a signal called a **releaser.** Releasers make an animal run through a particular pattern of behavior. Releasers can be an image, a sound, a smell, or a touch. For example, hungry herring gull chicks will peck at a red spot at the tip of a parent's bill. The parent usually responds by spitting up a bit of half-digested fish for the chick to eat.

Biologists think that innate behaviors are hard-wired into an animal's nervous system. Innate behaviors can be inherited and are affected by gene expression. But they can also be changed by environmental factors. As young herring gulls grow older, for instance, they become more accurate at pecking at the red spot on their parent's bill. The parent then responds more quickly.

What is a releaser?

_____

_____

# Many behaviors have both innate and learned parts.

Animals often change their behavior as they gain real-world experience. In other words, animals learn. Most animal behaviors are a combination of innate behaviors influenced by learning and experience. Two examples are habituation and imprinting.

## Habituation

Garden shops sell plastic owls to scare away animals that eat garden plants. But a gardener must move the owls every few days or the animals stop being afraid of them. This is an example of **habituation,** which occurs when an animal learns to ignore a repeated stimulus. This can happen even if the stimulus normally triggers innate behaviors. When the animals see owls in the same place in the garden every day, they get used to the stimulus and ignore it.

A "scarecrow" owl has to be moved every few days, or the animals will begin to ignore it.

## Imprinting

**Imprinting** is a learning process that occurs only during a short time in an animal's life. During this critical period, the animal learns skills such as how to identify its parents, its siblings, its offspring, characteristics of its own species, or the place where it was born.

Austrian zoologist Konrad Lorenz studied imprinting in greylag geese, who follow their mother during the first two days after hatching. He divided a group of goose eggs in half. Some eggs were left with the mother, and the rest he raised himself. The baby geese raised by their mother behaved normally. The babies that were with Lorenz during the critical period did not recognize other geese as members of their own species. Instead, they thought they were humans. They followed Lorenz and tried to mate with humans when they grew up. This experiment showed that imprinting is an innate process and cannot be changed. This is true even though the stimulus for the behavior is learned.

## Imitation

In **imitation,** animals learn by observing the behavior of other animals. Young male songbirds learn to sing by listening to adult males and trying to repeat what they hear. Human babies imitate adults in a number of ways, such as learning to speak their native language.

Not all imitated behaviors are passed from adult to younger animals. Sometimes younger animals teach older ones. An example is the potato washing behavior of a troop of Japanese macaques, or snow monkeys. A young female discovered that it was easier to get sand off a potato by dipping it in water. Before, all the monkeys had brushed the sand off with their hands. Over a period of time, a number of older individuals in the troop began washing their potatoes as well.

Explain the difference between imprinting and imitation.

_____

_____

# Learning is adaptive.

Animals that are able to learn can modify, or change, their behavior to adapt to new situations. The ability to learn gives animals an advantage in survival and reproduction.

### Associative Learning

In associative learning, an animal learns to associate, or connect, a specific action with its results. For example, young blue jays do not identify prey by instinct. Instead, they eat every new insect they find. Insects that taste good, such as grasshoppers, are eaten again and again. But after only one experience with a bad-tasting monarch butterfly, the jays avoid them for the rest of their lives. The jays learn to associate the monarch's orange and black markings with its bad taste.

One type of associative learning is conditioning. Conditioning is a way to change an animal's behavior in response to certain stimuli. An animal is presented with a pair of stimuli, and then it is conditioned to give a specific response. The two main types of conditioning are called classical conditioning and operant conditioning.

### Classical Conditioning

**Classical conditioning** is a process in which an animal learns to associate a previously neutral stimulus, such as a bell, with a behavior that used to be triggered by a different stimulus, such as a can of food being opened. Ivan Pavlov, a Russian physiologist, used the concept of classical conditioning in his experiments with dogs.

- Normally, the presence of food makes a dog salivate, or drool.

- A bell is rung when food is presented to the dog.

- The dog salivates because of the presence of food.

- After hearing the bell and being presented with food at the same time repeatedly, the dog salivates when the bell is rung even if there is no food.

A stimulus can be used to condition behavior, such as training a dog to sit up.

The bell was a neutral stimulus. The dog was conditioned to salivate when the bell was rung because the dog now expected to receive food.

## Operant Conditioning

In **operant conditioning,** specific behaviors can be made to happen more often or less often by offering an animal positive or negative reinforcement. Positive reinforcement refers to offering something good, such as a food reward. Negative reinforcement refers to removing something good, such as taking away a toy. Giving food to a dog after it performs a trick is positive reinforcement.

 Highlight two types of associative learning.

| 27.2 | Vocabulary Check | Mark It Up |
|---|---|---|

Go back and highlight each sentence that has a vocabulary word in **bold.**

instinct      imprinting

innate      imitation

releaser      classical conditioning

habituation      operant conditioning

**Choose the correct term from the list for each description below.**

1. signal that makes an animal run through a pattern of behavior

   _____

2. an animal learns to ignore a repeated stimulus _____

3. inborn behavior that is inflexible _____

4. learning by observing and copying others _____

5. behavior performed correctly the first time an animal tries it

   _____

| 27.2 | The Big Picture |
|---|---|

6. How might a behavior be a result of genetics and environmental factors?

   _____

   _____

7. Why is it important that a young animal imprint on its own species?

   _____

   _____

8. How could you use negative reinforcement to stop a dog from biting when it plays? _____

# 27.3 Evolution of Behavior

**KEY CONCEPT** Every behavior has costs and benefits.

A thirsty zebra walks carefully to the edge of a river. Just in time, it spots a crocodile waiting in the shallows. Crocodiles are large enough to drag a full-grown zebra into the water and drown it. Recognizing the danger, the zebra quickly turns and trots away. It needs water, but the risk to its life is too great.

## Even beneficial behaviors have associated costs.

Every behavior has benefits* and costs. Shorebirds travel thousands of miles during their migration, which requires a lot of energy. But migration increases a bird's chances of survival by escaping from cold temperatures to warmer locations.

### Benefits of Behavior

From an evolutionary point of view, the most important benefits of a behavior include increased survivorship and reproduction rates. **Survivorship** refers to the number of individuals that live from one year to the next. Behaviors that increase an individual's fitness will increase its chances of survival and reproduction. These behaviors will be favored by natural selection, but they still have associated costs.

### Costs of Behavior

Behavioral costs can be broken down into three basic categories.

**Energy costs** Every animal behavior, such as running away from a predator, uses up ATP. When an animal uses this metabolic energy for one behavior, such as searching for a mate, that energy is not available for other needs, such as searching for food.

**Opportunity costs** Every behavior takes time. For example, when a songbird defends its territory from other birds, it is using time that it could have spent eating or mating.

**Risk costs** Many behaviors expose an individual to possible injury or death. All animals have to look, or forage, for food. But foraging also increases the chances that an animal will be caught by a predator.

Songbirds, like this nuthatch, spend energy and time to defend their territory against intruders.

 Highlight the three categories of behavioral costs.

---

**\* ACADEMIC VOCABULARY**

**benefits** things that are useful

# Animals perform behaviors whose benefits are greater than their costs.

Behavior responses evolve only if they improve the fitness of those individuals that perform them. Territoriality and optimal foraging show how the benefits of a behavior can be greater than the costs.

**Territoriality** refers to the control of a specific area—or territory—by one or more individuals of a species. The benefit is access to resources such as food and mates. The costs include the energy and time required to control a territory that can be used for feeding or mating.

The theory of **optimal foraging** states that natural selection should favor behaviors where animals get the most, or optimal amount of, calories for the cost. The benefits of foraging are measured by the amount of energy an animal gains. The costs of foraging include the energy used to catch and eat food; the risk of capture by a predator; and the loss of time that could have been spent on other activities.

 Highlight the benefits of territoriality and optimal foraging.

---

## 27.3 Vocabulary Check

survivorship        optimal foraging

territoriality

### Mark It Up

Go back and highlight each sentence that has a vocabulary word in **bold**.

---

**Choose the correct term from the list for each description below.**

1. getting the most calories for the cost of finding the food _____

2. number of individuals that live from one year to the next _____

3. control of a specific area _____

## 27.3 The Big Picture

4. What are two important benefits of a behavior? _____

_____

5. Describe one energy, one opportunity, and one risk cost of territoriality.

_____

_____

6. How would optimal foraging increase an animal's survivorship?

_____

# 27.4 Social Behavior

**KEY CONCEPT** Social behaviors enhance the benefits of living in a group.

Many factors determine whether animals live alone or in groups. Even closely related species have different living patterns. For example, woodchucks in the eastern United States live alone. Their close cousins in the West, the marmots, live in groups.

## Living in groups also has benefits and costs.

Animals gain advantages living in groups, but they also pay a price in terms of their individual lives.

### Benefits of Social Behavior

Living in a social group provides benefits to individuals within the group. An individual can follow other members to good feeding sites. Immature animals or animals who have no offspring can help gather food and protect the young. Having more eyes and ears in the group makes it easier to detect predators. Also, a predator can usually capture only one member of a group, allowing the rest to escape.

Living in groups helps individual penguins survive in their harsh Antarctic environment.

### Costs of Social Behavior

Living in a group also comes at some cost to an individual. Groups cannot hide from predators as easily as an individual can. Members also compete for resources such as food or mates. This can lead to conflicts between group members. Finally, animals in groups have an increased chance of catching diseases or passing parasites to each other.

 Describe two benefits and two costs of living in a group.

_____

_____

## Social behaviors are interactions between members of the same or different species.

Social behaviors are behaviors animals use when interacting with members of their own or other species. These behaviors include communication, selecting a mate, and defense.

## Communication

Animals use communication as a way to keep in touch with each other, signal when danger is near, and attract a mate.

**Visual**  Gestures* or postures may help to identify an animal's status in the group. A dog with its tail between its legs has a lower rank than a dog that holds its tail high.

**Sound**  Animals often use calls to identify their offspring. Alarm calls and distress calls tell others that danger is near. Mating calls are used to communicate that an animal is ready to mate.

**Touch**  A bee performs a waggle dance that gives the location of a food source. Other bees touch the bee with their antennae to interpret this dance.

**Chemical**  Some animals communicate by using pheromones. Pheromones are chemicals released by an animal that affect the behavior of others of the same species. These chemicals can announce an animal's readiness to mate, identify group members, and mark territory.

Bees that find a food source can communicate that information to other bees by performing a waggle dance.

## Mate Selection

Courtship displays are behaviors most often used by males of a species to attract females. Scientists think that females observe courtship displays to judge the condition of the male or the quality of his genes. By being choosy about a mate, a female can help ensure that her offspring have the best chance of survival.

## Defense

Defensive behaviors include aggressive action to protect both the individual and the group. For instance, when lions are in elephant territory, an elephant herd will form a protective circle around younger members of the group. Watching for signs of danger is another defensive behavior.

 **INSTANT REPLAY**  Highlight four types of communication.

## Some behaviors benefit other group members at a cost to the individual performing them.

Individuals that live in a social group often help one another. Sometimes these social behaviors seem to reduce the fitness of the individuals that perform them. How could such behaviors evolve?

**Types of helpful social behavior** Helpful social behaviors are cooperation, reciprocity, and altruism.

- Cooperation involves behaviors that improve the fitness of both individuals. Lionesses hunt in a group and share the prey they catch, even though only one member of the pride may have killed the prey.
- Reciprocity involves behaviors in which individuals help other group members and are helped in return. Vampire bats, which must eat every few nights, will regurgitate blood for other bats that are hungry. In return, other bats will give the donor some of their food on another night.
- **Altruism** is a behavior in which an animal reduces its own fitness to help other members of its group. In other words, the animal appears to sacrifice itself for the group. Black-tailed prairie dogs live in colonies. When one animal sees a hawk overhead, it will sound an alarm call. This benefits other colony members but calls attention to the individual, who may be killed by the hawk.

**Evolution of altruism** Alleles involved in altruistic behavior can spread through a population in two ways. They can spread directly from an individual to its offspring or indirectly when an individual helps close relatives survive. When an animal reproduces:

- Parents and siblings share 50 percent of the animal's alleles.
- Nephews and nieces share 25 percent of its alleles.
- First cousins share 12.5 percent of its alleles.

The total number of genes an animal and its relatives contribute to the next generation is called its **inclusive fitness.** It includes both direct fitness from reproduction and indirect fitness from helping kin, or relatives, survive. When natural selection acts on alleles that favor the survival of close relatives, it is called **kin selection.** In fact, prairie dog colonies are populated by closely related females and only one or two territorial males.

 Highlight three kinds of helpful social behaviors.

# Eusocial behavior is an example of extreme altruism.

**Eusocial species** Species that live in large groups made up of many individuals, mostly workers or soldiers who do not reproduce, are called **eusocial** species. All young are the offspring of one female, called the queen. The other adults devote their lives to foraging, defending the colony, caring for the queen, and raising her offspring. Eusocial behaviors probably evolved by kin selection.

**Social Species** Some species live in colonies of many individuals that work together for the survival of the group. These are called social species. In many social insects, such as bees, ants, and wasps, the males

**VOCABULARY**

Reciprocity can be thought of in a "You scratch my back, I'll scratch yours" kind of relationship. Each animal performing the behavior will eventually benefit when another animal performs it in return.

**VOCABULARY**

The term *eusocial* comes from the Greek prefix *eu-*, which means "good, well, or true," and the Latin word *socius*, which means "companion."

are haploid and females are diploid. Females use sperm to produce only daughters. They lay unfertilized eggs to produce sons. Sisters share half of their mother's alleles and all of their father's alleles. Therefore, sisters share 75 percent of their alleles. The close relationship between sisters may increase eusociality in these insects.

**Other eusocial animals** Eusocial termites, snapping shrimp, and naked mole rats are diploid animals. But their colonies are still made of closely related animals. Kin selection still favors working together.

What is the connection between eusocial behaviors and how closely members of a group are related?

_____

_____

_____

---

## 27.4 Vocabulary Check

pheromone      kin selection

altruism      eusocial

inclusive fitness

**Mark It Up**

Go back and highlight each sentence that has a vocabulary word in **bold**.

**Choose the term that best completes each sentence.**

1. A behavior in which an animal reduces its own fitness to help other members of its group is _____.

2. A _____ is a chemical that affects the behavior of other animals.

3. _____ occurs when natural selection favors the survival of close relatives.

---

## 27.4 The Big Picture

4. A group can be easily seen by predators. Despite this cost, why do some animals still live in a group? _____

_____

5. What is the difference between cooperation and reciprocity?

_____

_____

6. If altruism is observed in a group, what would you expect to find when studying the social structure of that group?

_____

_____

# 27.5 Animal Cognition

**KEY CONCEPT** Some animals other than humans exhibit behaviors requiring complex cognitive abilities.

Where did human cognition, or reasoning, come from? Do other animals share our ability to think about the world?

## Animal intelligence is difficult to define.

Today, scientists do not compare an animal's level of intelligence with a human's. Instead, scientists study an animal's cognitive, or reasoning, abilities. **Cognition** is the mental process of knowing through perception* and reasoning. Cognition also includes awareness and the ability to judge. Animals that have a higher level of cognition can solve more complex problems. Intelligence is difficult to define and measure. Cognitive abilities, however, can be described and measured more objectively.

 Highlight four aspects of cognition.

## Some animals can solve problems.

Scientists sometimes study how animals think by giving them problems to solve. Cognition involves the ability to invent new behaviors in new situations. As a result, animals with cognitive abilities should be able to solve problems they've never seen before.

Dolphins can easily learn how to perform complex tasks, such as catching and tossing a ball.

**Problem-solving behavior** Researchers have observed complex problem-solving behaviors in primates, dolphins, and the corvids, a group of birds that includes crows, ravens, and jays. In one study, a chimpanzee was put in a room containing boxes, sticks, and a banana hung out of reach. At first, the chimp did nothing. After a while, it suddenly piled up the boxes and climbed up to knock down the fruit with a stick. Solving a problem mentally without repeated trial and error is called **insight.**

**Tool use** Tools help an animal perform a task. Australian bottlenose dolphins use sponges to protect their snouts when foraging. Chimps trim sticks to insert into termite mounds. Tool use itself is not a sign of cognition. But making tools suggests that an animal understands cause and effect, and it can make predictions about its own behavior.

 Why is insight an example of a cognitive ability?

_____

* **ACADEMIC VOCABULARY**

**perception** understanding something by using the senses

## Cognitive ability may provide an adaptive advantage for living in social groups.

Animals we recognize as the most "intelligent" often have two things in common. They have large brains for their body size, and they live in complex social groups. Elephants are an example. In an elephant herd, surviving and reproducing require that the animals identify other individuals in the group; remember who their friends and enemies are; keep track of changing relationships; and use all this information to their advantage.

Living in complex societies may also help individuals to develop and pass on cultural behaviors. **Cultural behavior** is a behavior that is spread by learning, rather than by natural selection. The key to cultural behavior is that it is taught to one generation by another. For example, each elephant herd teaches its young the special calls of the herd.

 Highlight two characteristics of "intelligent" animals.

### 27.5 Vocabulary Check

| | |
| --- | --- |
| cognition | cultural behavior |
| insight | |

**Mark It Up**

Go back and highlight each sentence that has a vocabulary word in **bold**.

1. Circle the word that means solving a problem without trial and error.

2. Box the word that means knowing through perception or reasoning.

### 27.5 The Big Picture

3. Why is cognition the focus of scientific studies instead of intelligence?

_____

_____

4. A capuchin monkey grabs a rock and uses it to break open a nut. A chimpanzee takes the leaves off a stick before putting it into a termite hole. Which animal has demonstrated tool use? Explain.

_____

5. What is the difference between insight and cultural behavior?

_____

_____

# Chapter 27 Review

1. Explain how kinesis or taxis can help an animal maintain homeostasis. Give an example of each behavior. _____
_____
_____

2. What stimuli cause an animal to enter hibernation and what stimuli awaken it? _____
_____

3. Choose the word that best completes the following sentence:

   Imprinting is a(n) _____ process, even though the stimulus for the behavior is learned.
   **a.** inflexible
   **b.** habituation
   **c.** imitative
   **d.** innate

4. Explain how operant conditioning is a type of associative learning.
_____

5. Why would an animal engage in a behavior that might attract a predator?
_____

6. Which of the following best describes optimal foraging?
   **a.** Animals face the greatest costs when foraging.
   **b.** Animals get the most calories for the cost.
   **c.** Animals get enough calories to avoid predators.
   **d.** Animals have more time to spend on other activities.

7. What is the relationship between altruism and kin selection?
_____
_____

8. What types of communication might be used in courtship and to attract a mate? _____

9. Why is altruism always seen in eusocial animals? _____
_____

10. Write a definition of *cognition* for someone who does not understand the words *perception* and *reasoning*. _____
_____

# 28 Human Systems and Homeostasis

## GETTING READY TO LEARN

### Preview Key Concepts

**28.1 Levels of Organization**
The human body has five levels of organization.

**28.2 Mechanisms of Homeostasis**
Homeostasis is the regulation and maintenance of the internal environment.

**28.3 Interactions Among Systems**
Systems interact to maintain homeostasis.

### Review Academic Vocabulary

Write the correct word for each definition.

cell      system      mitosis      cell cycle

1. _____ : regular pattern of cell growth

2. _____ : organized group of parts that form a whole

3. _____ : process of cell division

4. _____ : basic unit of life

### Preview Biology Vocabulary

To see how many key terms you already know from this chapter, choose the word that makes sense in each sentence.

organ      homeostasis      feedback      tissue

1. Your arm is made up of four different types of _____.

2. _____ is what tells a furnace to turn on or off to maintain a specific temperature.

3. Maintaining an internal environment within set limits is known as _____.

4. The heart or the brain is an example of a(an) _____ in the body.

# 28.1 Levels of Organization

**KEY CONCEPT** The human body has five levels of organization.

Humans, like plants and other animals, are multicellular organisms. This means our bodies are made up of many cells. However, these cells are not all the same. Human bodies include many different types of cells. Each type of cell has a specialized function*. For example, red blood cells deliver oxygen to all the parts of the body. Muscle cells contract to make it possible for the body to move. Neurons transmit and receive messages from other neurons. The body needs all these types of cells to survive.

## Specialized cells develop from a single zygote.

Before a human being develops, an egg and sperm unite to form a zygote. A zygote is a fertilized egg. It is made of just one cell. Then the zygote begins to divide, and the cells that it forms also divide. This process continues for a few weeks. The cells that form during this time are called embryonic stem cells. At this point these cells are all the same. Every embryonic stem cell contains all the information it needs to become any kind of specialized cell in the body.

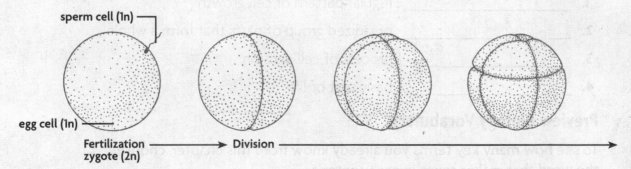

sperm cell (1n)

egg cell (1n)

Fertilization → Division →
zygote (2n)

Embryonic stem cells all look alike. Later they can become blood cells, muscle cells, neurons, skin cells, or any other kind of specialized cell.

### Determination

A few weeks after the zygote forms, a process called **determination** begins. In this process, each stem cell commits* to becoming one type of cell, such as a muscle cell or a neuron. Each stem cell still contains all the genetic information it would need to become any type of specialized cell. However, the stem cells no longer use all that information. Now, they will become only one type of specialized cell. For example, a cell that is going to become a neuron cannot become a blood cell later.

* ACADEMIC VOCABULARY

**function** action, role

**commit** to follow a course of action

## Differentiation

Once a cell has committed to becoming a particular specialized cell, it must develop into that cell. This process is called **differentiation,** because it is the process in which cells develop their specialized shapes and functions. The diagram on the right shows some cells that have gone through differentiation.

sperm cells

bone cells

zygote

epithelial cells

connective cells

Different types of cells need different structures. Sperm cells need whiplike tails to help them swim. Other cells, such as those in the stomach, skin, and bones, do not need to move.

What is the difference between determination and differentiation?

_____

_____

_____

# Specialized cells function together in tissues, organs, organ systems, and the whole organism.

If you think about your body, you cannot help but notice that there is more to you than individual cells. You also have tissues and organs. In fact, there are five levels of organization in a human body.

1. **Cells** Each type of specialized cell has its own job to do. Blood cells carry oxygen to all the parts of the body. Some lung cells make mucus that traps particles and protects the lungs from bacteria and viruses.

2. **Tissues** Groups of cells working together are called **tissues.** There are four types of tissues: epithelial (skin and lining of many organs); connective (ligaments and tendons); muscle; and nervous tissues.

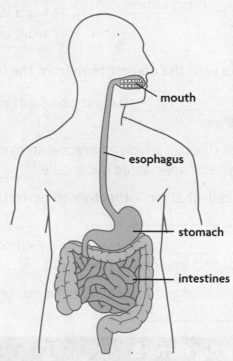

mouth

esophagus

stomach

intestines

Your digestive system is an organ system. It includes your mouth, esophagus, stomach and intestines.

3. **Organs** Different types of tissue that work together form an **organ.** Your heart, lungs, liver, and stomach are only a few of the organs in your body.

4. **Organ systems** Two or more organs working together form an **organ system.** For example, one organ system allows you to breathe. This organ system includes your lungs, sinuses, nasal passages, pharynx, and larynx.

5. **Organism** Together, all of the organ systems make up an organism. You are an organism.

 Which of the following is a cell, a tissue, an organ, or an organ system? sperm, heart and blood vessels, liver, lining of the stomach

_____

_____

## 28.1    Vocabulary Check

determination          organ
differentiation        organ system
tissue

**Fill in the blanks with the correct term from the list above.**

1. A(An) _____ is made up of different types of tissue that work together.

2. The process through which embryonic stem cells commit to becoming only one type of specialized cell is called _____.

3. Groups of cells that work together to perform a specialized function are called _____.

4. _____ is the process by which committed cells develop their specialized shapes and functions.

5. Together, your lungs, nasal passages, larynx, pharynx, and sinuses form a(an) _____.

## 28.1    The Big Picture

6. Put the following five terms in order from simplest to most complex: tissue, organ system, organ, cell, organism. _____

7. How do specialized cells differ from each other? _____

_____

# 28.2 Mechanisms of Homeostasis

**KEY CONCEPT** Homeostasis is the regulation and maintenance of the internal environment.

The tissues, organs, and organ systems in your body all work together to accomplish one goal: keeping you alive. To do this, they must respond to conditions* in the world around you.

## Conditions within the body must remain within a narrow range.

A car will not operate properly unless it is in good condition. It needs its oil changed, its engine tuned up, and its tires rotated from time to time. Cars also respond to conditions on the road. It is harder to control a car when the road is wet, slippery, or covered with ice. Your body is much more complicated than a car, but it also responds to conditions inside the body and in the environment. The organs in your body will work well only in certain conditions.

**Temperature** One of the conditions your body requires is that its temperature remain between 36.7°C and 37.1°C (98.2°F and 98.8°F). If it rises past 41°C (106°F), you could die from overheating. If your temperature drops below 27°C (80°F), your heart could stop.

**Minerals** The trace minerals in your body must also stay within certain limits. If your levels of a mineral are too high or too low, you could get sick or die.

**Chemical reactions** The work that your cells, tissues, and organs do depends on chemical reactions. Trillions of chemical reactions take place in your body every second. Chemical reactions depend on the actions of enzymes. However, enzymes stop working if the temperature inside the body rises too high. This is why keeping a stable temperature is so important.

substrates (reactants)

enzyme

Enzymes need to be a certain size and shape. Without the right conditions, enzymes stop working.

---

*ACADEMIC VOCABULARY

**conditions** circumstances, situations

## Homeostasis and the Internal Environment

Your temperature and your levels of fluids, nutrients, salts, and gases are part of your internal environment. Your body has control* systems that keep your internal environment stable*. Your body's ability to maintain a stable internal environment is called **homeostasis.**

## Control Systems in the Body

Control systems in the body are composed of four parts.

**Sensors** Sensors collect information about conditions inside and outside your body.

**Control center** Sensors send this information to a control center, such as your brain. The control center compares this information to the conditions that are necessary for the body to be at its best. When conditions change too much, the control center sends messages through a communication system to respond to the change.

**Communication systems** There are two main communication systems in your body. One is the nervous system, which uses nerve impulses to send information. The other is the endocrine system, which sends messages by releasing hormones.

brain

spinal cord

nerves

The nervous system, which includes your brain, uses nerve impulses to send information throughout your body.

**Targets** Nerve impulse or hormone messages are sent to targets in the body. The target is any organ, tissue, or cell that changes its activity in response to a message. For example, when it is cold outside, a message might cause your muscles to contract and shake, or shiver, to generate heat.

Why is it so important that control systems maintain your body's homeostasis?

_____

_____

**\* ACADEMIC VOCABULARY**

**control** command, regulate

**stable** steady, constant

# Negative feedback loops are necessary for homeostasis.

The flow of information from sensors to control centers, to communication systems, and to targets forms a feedback loop. This means that information constantly moves back and forth between different parts of the body. **Feedback** is information from sensors that allows a control center to compare current conditions to a set of ideal values.*

## Negative Feedback

Most functions in the body are ruled by negative feedback loops. In **negative feedback,** a control system sends instructions to a target to counteract* changes. The target responds to bring conditions back to normal.

## Positive Feedback

Negative feedback loops help your body to maintain homeostasis. They work to bring the body back to its normal conditions. Sometimes, though, the body needs to make adjustments. It must, at least for a short time, take an action that moves it further away from ideal conditions. Instructions from a control center to make this kind of a change is called **positive feedback.** For example, if you cut your finger, a control system increases the clotting factors in your blood until the wound has been sealed.

If you inhale and hold your breath, sensors in your body send feedback to your brain stem: oxygen levels are falling too low and carbon dioxide levels are rising too high.

Your brain sends messages to the muscles of your diaphragm and rib cage to counteract these changes. You are forced to exhale and then inhale deeply until conditions return to normal.

---

**\* ACADEMIC VOCABULARY**

**ideal values**  the best conditions

**counteract**  to take action against something

Suppose you have an ear infection. A feedback loop in your body increases your temperature until you have a fever. Is this an example of positive feedback or negative feedback? Explain.

_____

_____

## 28.2 Vocabulary Check

homeostasis    negative feedback
feedback       positive feedback

**Mark It Up**

Go back and highlight each sentence that has a vocabulary word in **bold.**

**Choose the correct term from the list for each description.**

1. Your body's control over its internal environment _____

2. Feedback from a control center that increases the amount of change away from ideal values _____

3. Information from sensors that allows a control center to compare current conditions to a set of ideal values _____

4. Feedback from a control center that counteracts change away from ideal values _____

## 28.2 The Big Picture

5. What four parts of a control system must work together in a feedback loop?

_____

6. Suppose you are caught out in the rain and get drenched and cold. Which type of feedback loop would cause your body to start shivering to keep warm? Explain your answer.

_____

_____

7. In question 7 above, the muscles that start shivering represent which part of the control system?

_____

# 28.3 Interactions Among Systems

**KEY CONCEPT**  Systems interact to maintain homeostasis.

## Each organ system affects other organ systems.

Each organ system in your body has its own job to do. But it is not enough for your organ systems to do their own jobs well. If you are to stay healthy, your organ systems must all work together.

### Vitamin D Production

You may know that your body can make its own vitamin D if you spend a few minutes in the sun every day. The ultraviolet rays of sunlight cause a substance in the skin to turn into an inactive* form of vitamin D. But your body cannot use the vitamin D until it is made active*. First your blood carries the inactive vitamin D to your liver. The liver changes it into another compound. Then it is carried to the kidneys, which change it into active vitamin D.

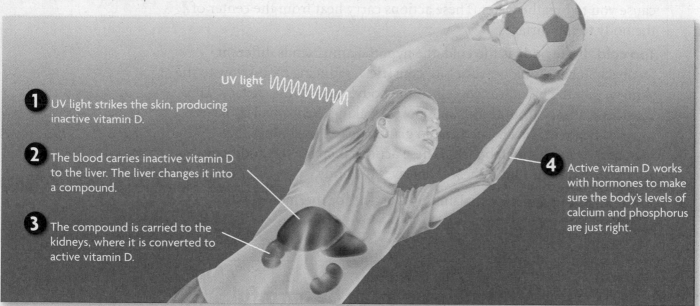

**UV light**

**1** UV light strikes the skin, producing inactive vitamin D.

**2** The blood carries inactive vitamin D to the liver. The liver changes it into a compound.

**3** The compound is carried to the kidneys, where it is converted to active vitamin D.

**4** Active vitamin D works with hormones to make sure the body's levels of calcium and phosphorus are just right.

Once the vitamin D is active, the blood carries it throughout the body. Everywhere it goes, vitamin D interacts with hormones. These hormones control the levels of calcium and phosphorus, which help build strong bones. If the skin, liver, kidneys, or blood fail to do their

**\* ACADEMIC VOCABULARY**

**inactive**  not working

**active**  working

jobs, the levels of vitamin D in the body decrease. If this happens to a child, the child's bones will not develop normally. If it happens to an adult, the adult may lose bone mass and break bones more easily.

### Regulation of Body Temperature

Remember that temperature is one condition that the body controls as part of homeostasis. The process of keeping body temperature steady, no matter how cold or hot it may be outside, is called **thermoregulation.** One of the brain's control centers, the hypothalamus, is in charge of thermo-regulation. Sensors in the skin and blood vessels send infor-mation about body temperature to the hypothalamus. If the body's temperature is too hot or too cold, the hypothalamus sends feedback to the respiratory, circulatory, nervous, and endocrine systems.

**Too hot** If the body is too hot, the hypothalamus sends feedback through the nervous and endocrine systems. These messages cause the body to sweat. They cause blood vessels to dilate*, increasing the flow of blood to the skin. They also cause the heart to beat faster, and cause you to breathe faster. These actions carry heat from the center of the body to the surface.

**Too cold** If the body is too cold, the hypothalamus sends different feedback. It causes blood vessels to constrict*, reducing blood flow to the skin, so that the blood carries less of the body's heat to the surface. Tiny muscles contract around the skin's pores, making them smaller. Skeletal muscles begin to shiver. The thyroid gland releases hormones that increase the body's metabolism. These actions increase the body's heat and reduce the amount of heat that leaves the body.

How is the hypothalamus important for thermoregulation?

_____

_____

## A disruption of homeostasis can be harmful.

The body does not always succeed in maintaining homeostasis. Some-times injuries or illnesses can overwhelm the body's control systems. Other times sensors do not detect changes, wrong messages are sent, or messages do not reach their targets.

---

**\* ACADEMIC VOCABULARY**

**dilate** to grow larger or wider

**constrict** to get smaller or narrower

### VISUAL VOCAB

**Thermoregulation** maintains a stable body temperature under a vari-ety of conditions, just as a thermostat regulates a furnace. Both mechanisms use feedback to keep temperatures within set ranges.

control — THERMOSTAT — messages — FURNACE — target — info to control

**Short-term effects** Your body can usually cope with a short-term disruption of homeostasis. A cold or flu may make you feel sick for a few days or weeks. Eventually, your body's immune system begins to kill the virus or bacteria that are making you sick. Homeostasis is restored, and you are back to normal.

**Long-term effects** Some very serious diseases, such as diabetes, can cause a long-term disruption of homeostasis. One form of diabetes occurs when the body does not produce enough of the hormone insulin. Without insulin, glucose cannot enter the cells. The excess glucose leaves the body in the urine. The body must then burn fat for fuel, but the breakdown of fat makes the blood more acidic. Acidic blood harms every cell in the body. Eventually, if untreated, diabetes can lead to heart disease, blindness, nerve damage, kidney damage, and even coma and death.

Why would a long-term disruption in homeostasis tend to be more harmful than a short-term one?

_____

_____

## 28.3 Vocabulary Check

**Mark It Up**

Go back and highlight each sentence that has a vocabulary word in **bold**.

thermoregulation

**1.** Define *thermoregulation* in your own words.

_____

_____

_____

## 28.3 The Big Picture

**2.** If the hypothalamus fails to do its job, what might happen to your body's internal temperature?

_____

_____

**3.** Do you think that giving insulin to people with diabetes would help to restore their homeostasis? Why or why not?

_____

# Chapter 28 Review

1. What single cell do specialized cells develop from?_____

2. Write the terms *organ, cell, organism, tissue,* and *organ system* onto the diagram in order of the smallest to largest.

3. What is the difference between determination and differentiation?

_____

_____

_____

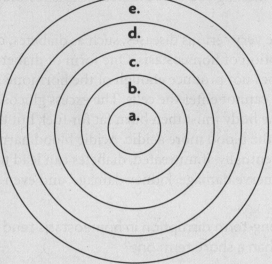

e.

d.

c.

b.

a.

4. Which of the following compares information about conditions in the body to a set of ideal values?
   a. sensors
   b. control center
   c. communication systems
   d. targets

5. Why is it important for the body to maintain homeostasis?

_____

6. Which of the following is likely to be the result of a negative feedback loop?
   a. blood clotting
   b. pain
   c. shivering
   d. growth

7. What organs need to work together to produce vitamin D in a form that our bodies can use?

_____

8. Give an example of a short-term disruption of homeostasis._____

_____

# 29 Nervous and Endocrine System

## GETTING READY TO LEARN

### Preview Key Concepts

**29.1 How Organ Systems Communicate**
The nervous system and the endocrine system provide the means by which organ systems communicate.

**29.2 Neurons**
The nervous system is composed of highly specialized cells.

**29.3 The Senses**
The senses detect the internal and external environments.

**29.4 Central and Peripheral Nervous Systems**
The central nervous system interprets information, and the peripheral nervous system gathers and transmits information.

**29.5 Brain Function and Chemistry**
Scientists study the functions and chemistry of the brain.

**29.6 Endocrine System and Hormones**
The endocrine system produces hormones that affect growth, development, and homeostasis.

### Review Academic Vocabulary

Write the correct word for each definition.

differentiation      tissue      negative feedback

**1.** _____ : similar cells working together

**2.** _____ : cells acquiring specialized structures

**3.** _____ : counteracts change away from set values

### Preview Biology Vocabulary

Read the definitions and guess what the word part *cerebro-* means.

| TERM | DEFINITION |
|------|------------|
| cerebrum | part of the brain that interprets and responds to signals from the body |
| cerebellum | part of the brain that coordinates the body's movements |

What I think *cerebro-* means: _____

# 29.1 How Organ Systems Communicate

**KEY CONCEPT** The nervous system and the endocrine system provide the means by which organ systems communicate.

## The body's communication systems help maintain homeostasis.

To maintain homeostasis, the different parts of your body must be able to communicate with each other. The body has two communication systems that transmit messages between different parts of the body: the nervous and endocrine systems.

### The Nervous System

The **nervous system** is a physically connected network of cells, tissues, and organs. It controls thoughts, movements, and simple processes such as swallowing. This system has two parts. The **central\* nervous system (CNS)** includes the brain and spinal cord. The **peripheral\* nervous system (PNS)** is a network of nerves that extends throughout your body. The PNS carries messages to and from the CNS. It sends messages that affect thoughts, movements, and simple tasks such as swallowing.

### The Endocrine System

The **endocrine system** is a collection of physically separate organs. This system sends messages that tell the body how and when to grow and develop. It also sends messages that control how the body responds to changes in its environment. For example, when the weather is hot, the system signals your body to sweat.

Both systems provide a way for the body to respond to a **stimulus** in the environment. A stimulus is anything that causes the body to make a change. A ringing alarm clock could stimulate you to wake up.

 Highlight two differences between the nervous and endocrine systems.

The cells, tissues, and organs of the nervous system are physically connected to each other.

---

**\* ACADEMIC VOCABULARY**

**central**  located at the center
**peripheral**  located along the edges

# The nervous and endocrine systems have different methods and rates of communication.

The nervous system can send signals along a physical network of specialized tissues. Getting a message from the nervous system is like getting your email through a computer connected to a high-speed cable. These messages arrive very fast. The nervous system controls your heart rate, breathing, and reflexes.

The organs in the endocrine system are separate from each other. They release chemicals that are carried by the blood throughout the body. Only certain cells will respond to the chemicals sent by the endocrine system. Some messages from the endocrine system arrive slowly, like a letter in the mail. These chemicals control processes that happen over long periods of time, like aging. Other messages from the endocrine system arrive more quickly, like an overnight package.

 Highlight the ways that the nervous and endocrine systems communicate.

The organs in the endocrine system are physically separated from each other.

## 29.1 Vocabulary Check

nervous system
endocrine system
stimulus

central nervous system (CNS)
peripheral nervous system (PNS)

**Mark It Up**

Go back and highlight each sentence that has a vocabulary word in **bold**.

Choose the correct term from the list for each description.

1. a communication network that involves the brain, spinal cord, and nerves throughout the body _____

2. a set of organs that are not connected to each other and control growth, development, and responses to the environment

_____

3. something that causes your body to respond _____

## 29.1 The Big Picture

4. What is the central nervous system? _____

5. How can messages from the endocrine system reach cells throughout the body? _____

_____

6. Your hand jerks away from a hot surface. Do you think the message was sent by the nervous or endocrine system? Explain.

_____

# 29.2 Neurons

**KEY CONCEPT** The nervous system is composed of highly specialized cells.

## Neurons are highly specialized cells.

The nervous system is made up of specialized cells called neurons. A **neuron** is a cell that can store information and send and receive messages. Together, neurons make up an information network, somewhat like the Internet. As shown in the diagram, neurons have three parts:

1. The cell body contains the cell's nucleus and organelles.

2. **Dendrites** are branches of the cell that extend out to receive messages from other cells. Each dendrite can have many branches. Each neuron has several dendrites.

3. An **axon** is a long branch that transmits messages to other cells. Each neuron has only one axon.

---

**STRUCTURE OF A NEURON**

**A neuron is a specialized cell of the nervous system that produces and transmits signals.**

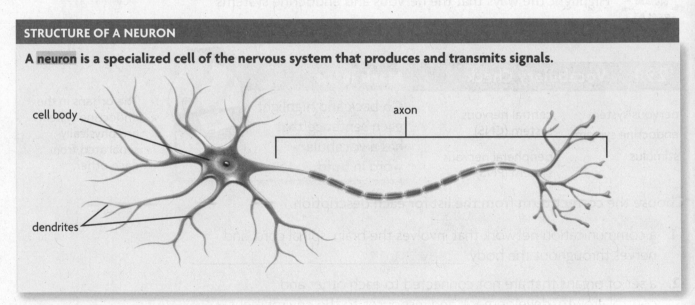

cell body

dendrites

axon

Neurons have branches that extend in all directions so they can send and receive messages.

---

All neurons have this same basic structure, but they are not all the same. There are three types of neurons:

1. Sensory neurons keep track of stimuli and send messages to interneurons.

2. Interneurons receive messages from sensory neurons, and pass them on to other interneurons. They also process* the information they receive, and send messages to targeted body parts, telling them how to respond. The brain and spinal cord are made up of interneurons.

**\* ACADEMIC VOCABULARY**

**process** to figure out or come to understand

**3.** Motor neurons receive messages from interneurons. Then they pass the signals on to other tissues in the body, such as muscles.

 Underline the structure that allows neurons to receive messages from other neurons.

## Neurons receive and transmit signals.

Neurons send information in the form of electrical and chemical signals.* When a neuron receives a stimulus, it produces an electrical impulse* that travels from one end of the neuron to the other. But before the impulse can travel to the next neuron, it must be transformed into a chemical signal.

### Before a Neuron is Stimulated

Even a neuron that is at rest must be ready to send a signal. To do this, it must have a more negative charge on the inside than it does on the outside. The difference between the charge on the inside and the charge on the outside is called the **resting potential.*** It contains the potential energy needed to send a signal.

How do neurons maintain their resting potential? Neurons contain two kinds of ions: sodium ions ($Na^+$) and potassium ions ($K^+$). Notice that both $Na^+$ and $K^+$ ions are positively charged. There are more $Na^+$ ions outside of the neuron, and more $K^+$ ions on the inside of the neuron.

The inside of the neuron is negative compared with its surroundings. This is because there are fewer positive ions inside of the neuron than there are outside of it.

Each neuron's cell membrane works to maintain the neuron's resting potential. The membrane opens channels that allow ions to enter and leave the cell. But some positively charged ions find their way into the neuron. To maintain resting potential, a neuron uses a **sodium-potassium pump,** a kind of protein that pumps $Na^+$ out of the cell and pumps $K^+$ ions in.

## Transmission within a Neuron

When a neuron is stimulated, it produces a moving electrical impulse called an **action potential.** What causes this electrical impulse, and how does it move? Once stimulated, channels in the neuron's membrane open quickly, and $Na^+$ ions rush into the cell. The increase in $Na^+$ ions in the cell causes a part of the neuron's inner membrane to become positively charged. This is the electrical impulse. It moves because the change in charge stimulates channels next to the positive charge to open. These channels open, $Na^+$ ions rush in, the next channels open, $Na^+$ ions rush in.

At the same time, $K^+$ channels open and close more slowly. When $K^+$ channels open, $K^+$ ions leave the cell. This makes the cell more negative, as during resting potential. Because these channels open and close more slowly, $K^+$ ions appear to leave the neuron at the tail-end of the action potential, as you can see in the diagram.

## Transmission Between Neurons

Before the action potential can be passed to another neuron, it reaches the axon **terminal,** the end of the axon. Then it must pass through a tiny gap between the neurons, called a **synapse.** As the action potential reaches the terminal, the terminal releases chemicals into the synapse. These chemicals, called **neurotransmitters,** are the nervous system's chemical signals. They connect to the next neuron, stimulating it to open its $Na^+$ channels. This produces another action potential.

What happens when the inner cell membrane becomes positively charged?

_____

_____

**ACTION POTENTIAL**

$Na^+$

$K^+$

As the action potential moves along the axon, $Na^+$ channels open. $Na^+$ rushes into the cell, and the cell becomes positive. As the impulse moves forward, $K^+$ channels open. $K^+$ flows out of the cell, and it becomes negative again, returning to its resting potential.

**CHEMICAL SYNAPSE**

$Na^+$

synapse

neurotransmitter

receptor

vesicles

The action potential stimulates the axon terminal to release its neurotransmitters.

The neurotransmitters attach themselves to the dendrite of the next neuron, so that it will open its $Na^+$ channels.

**Mark It Up**

Go back and highlight each sentence that has a vocabulary word in **bold**.

neuron                    action potential

dendrite                  synapse

axon                      terminal

resting potential         neurotransmitter

sodium-potassium pump

**Fill in the blanks with the correct term from the list above.**

1. A neuron uses a(n) _____ to receive messages.

2. A message moves from one end of a neuron to another in the form of a(n) _____.

3. Neurotransmitters are released from an axon's _____.

4. To maintain its resting potential, a neuron uses a(n) _____.

5. A specialized cell that stores information and carries messages is called a(n) _____.

6. When there are more $K^+$ ions inside the neuron than outside it, the neuron is at its _____.

7. A message jumps from one neuron to another in the form of a chemical signal called a(n) _____.

8. A(n) _____ is the space between two neurons.

9. A(n) _____ carries messages away from a neuron and passes them to other cells.

## 29.2 The Big Picture

10. You knock over the first domino in a long chain of dominoes. Each domino knocks the next one down. How does this resemble an action potential?

_____

_____

_____

11. What kind of neuron processes information in the brain and spinal cord? _____

12. How do action potentials move from one neuron to another?

_____

_____

# 29.3 The Senses

**KEY CONCEPT** The senses detect the internal and external environments.

## The senses help to maintain homeostasis.

The human body has five senses: vision, hearing, touch, taste, and smell. These senses rely on specialized sensory organs: the eyes, ears, skin, tongue, and nose. When your brain receives information from your sense organs, it triggers responses that help to maintain homeostasis. Your sensory organs help to protect you and also affect how you behave. If food smells rotten, you will choose something else to eat. If you feel cold, you may put on a sweater or coat.

 Underline the five senses and their sensory organs.

## The senses detect physical and chemical stimuli.

Your sensory organs contain sensory receptors, specialized cells that detect* stimuli. These stimuli can come from inside or outside of your body.

### Vision

Light enters the eye through the pupil. The iris controls the size of the pupil, so the eye can let in the right amount of light. First light passes through the cornea, a clear layer that protects the eye. Then it passes through the lens.

The lens focuses light on the retina, where it stimulates photoreceptors called rod and cone cells. **Rod cells** sense brightness of light, and can see black and white. **Cone cells** detect color. Rod cells work better in low light, and cone cells work better in bright light. That's why it is hard to see colors in the dark. The rod and cone cells produce nerve impulses. The impulses move along a bundle of axons, which form the optic nerve. The nerve carries the impulses to the brain, which interprets* them as images.

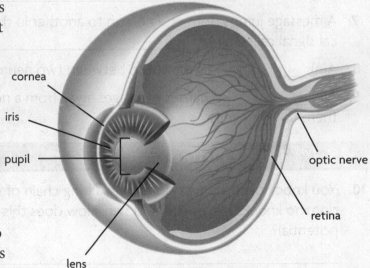

Light enters the eye through the pupil. It stimulates rod cells and cone cells on the retina.

---

**\* ACADEMIC VOCABULARY**

**detect** to sense or discover something

**interpret** to figure out the meaning of something

## Hearing

Sound enters the ear through the pinna, the part of the ear you can see. The pinna funnels vibrations into the auditory canal. There, the sound waves strike the eardrum, making it vibrate. The vibrations enter the cochlea, a snail-shaped group of canals. The cochlea holds fluid and **hair cells,** which contain mechanoreceptors to detect vibrations. Vibrations move the fluid in the cochlea, which makes the hair cells bend. The hair cells send electrical impulses through the auditory nerve to the brain. The brain interprets these impulses as sound.

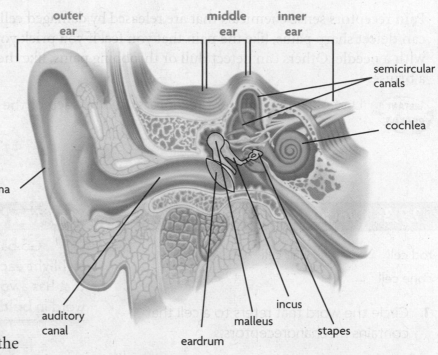

The ear has three parts: the outer ear, the middle ear, and the inner ear.

## Smell and Taste

Both your nose and tongue contain receptors that can sense molecules that are dissolved in liquid or become a vapor or gas in the air. When chemical molecules enter your nose, they dissolve in mucus and are detected by olfactory* cells. The receptors in your tongue are part of your taste buds. As a substance dissolves in your saliva, the receptors sense it and send electrical impulses to the brain.

## Touch, Temperature, and Pain

Your skin contains receptors that can detect touch, temperature, and pain. Gentle touches are detected by receptors in the top layer of your skin. Deeper pressure is detected by heavy pressure receptors deeper within the skin. Other receptors detect heat and cold.

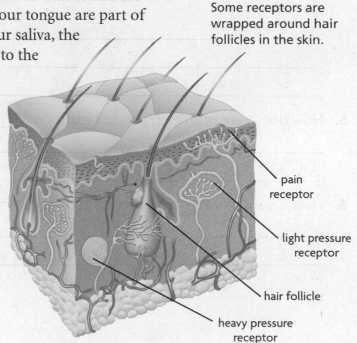

Some receptors are wrapped around hair follicles in the skin.

* ACADEMIC VOCABULARY

**olfactory** related to the sense of smell

Pain receptors sense chemicals that are released by damaged cells. Some can detect sharp pains, like the pain that you feel if you prick your finger with a needle. Others can detect dull or throbbing pains, like the pain of a bruise.

 Underline the different receptors used by each of the senses.

## 29.3 Vocabulary Check

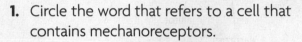

**Mark It Up**

Go back and highlight each sentence that has a vocabulary word in **bold**.

rod cell        hair cell

cone cell

1. Circle the word that refers to a cell that contains mechanoreceptors.

2. Put a box around the word that means a cell that can detect colors.

3. Underline the word that means a cell that can detect brightness of light.

## 29.3 The Big Picture

4. How are the rod and cone cells in the eye similar to the taste buds in your tongue?

_____

_____

_____

5. How does your brain help you to hear sounds? _____

_____

_____

6. How is your skin able to detect both temperature and pain?

_____

_____

# 29.4 Central and Peripheral Nervous Systems

**KEY CONCEPT** The central nervous system interprets information, and the peripheral nervous system gathers and transmits information.

## The nervous system's two parts work together.

You already know that the nervous system has two parts: the central nervous system (CNS) and the peripheral nervous system (PNS). The two parts of the nervous system are connected, and they work together.

- The central nervous system (CNS) includes the brain and spinal cord. It is made up of interneurons. These neurons receive information, interpret it, and send signals to the PNS.
- The peripheral nervous system (PNS) connects the CNS to all of your organs and organ systems. It reaches every part of your body. Sensory neurons in the PNS detect stimuli inside and outside your body and send signals to the CNS. Motor neurons carry messages from the CNS to target cells in your muscles or other organs.

 What part of the nervous system is made up of interneurons?

## The CNS processes information.

The interneurons in the brain and spinal cord are arranged in a special way. All the cell bodies are clustered together, and all the axons are clustered together. The cell bodies as a group have a dark gray color and are called gray matter. The axons are called white matter because their myelin sheaths appear white.

### The Brain

Your brain contains more than 100 billion neurons. They are protected by three layers of tissue, called the meninges. Fluid between the layers cushions the brain, so it does not bang against the skull. The brain itself has three parts: the cerebrum, the cerebellum, and the brain stem.

**Cerebrum** The **cerebrum** interprets signals from your body. It forms responses such as hunger, thirst, emotions, motion, or pain. The two halves of the cerebrum are called hemispheres. The left hemisphere controls the right side of the body, while the right hemisphere controls the left.

Your nervous system is your body's information superhighway. It connects your brain and spinal cord to the rest of your body.

The outer layer of the cerebrum is called the **cerebral cortex.** It interprets signals from your sensory organs. The cerebral cortex is about as thick as a pencil, but its folded surface area can hold more than 10 billion neurons. The neurons in the cerebral cortex are arranged in groups that perform different tasks. Each hemisphere of the cerebral cortex can be divided into four areas, called lobes.

**FRONTAL LOBE**
Personality, reasoning, and judgment are controlled in the frontal lobe. It also coordinates voluntary movement and speech production.

motor cortex (movement)

sensory cortex (touch)

**PARIETAL LOBE**
The sensory cortex, which interprets and coordinates information regarding the sense of touch, is contained in this lobe.

multisensory information

planning

speech production

vision (entire lobe)

hearing

**TEMPORAL LOBE**
Speech interpretation and hearing are functions carried out by the temporal lobe. It also plays a role in memory.

speech interpretation

**OCCIPITAL LOBE**
Visual information is processed in this lobe.

Each hemisphere of the brain has four lobes.

Underneath the cerebral cortex are many smaller groups of neurons. For example, the limbic system controls learning and emotions. The thalamus sorts out information from your sensory organs and passes signals between the spinal cord and other parts of the brain. The hypothalamus keeps track of temperature, hunger, and thirst.

**Cerebellum** The **cerebellum** is the part of the brain that coordinates your movements. It helps you keep your balance, to stand up straight, and to move smoothly.

**Brain stem** The brain is connected to the spinal cord by the **brain stem.** It controls the activities that are the most basic to life, such as breathing and heartbeat. The brain stem has three parts.

- The midbrain controls some reflexes.
- The pons controls breathing, and passes signals back and forth between the brain and the spinal cord.
- The medulla oblongata physically connects the brain and spinal cord. It controls your heart, and tasks such as vomiting, swallowing, and coughing.

**VISUAL VOCAB**

cerebrum

cerebellum

You can learn the location of the **cerebellum** by remembering that it hangs below the large part of the brain, just as a bell hangs from the ceiling.

## The Spinal Cord

The interneurons of the spinal cord, like those of the brain, are protected by meninges and fluid. The spinal cord itself is a bundle of neurons about as wide as your thumb. It connects the brain to the nerves in the rest of the body. If the spinal cord is hurt, messages cannot flow back and forth between the brain and the rest of the body. This is why spinal cord injuries can cause paralysis.

However, not all nerve signals need to travel all the way up to the brain. Some travel along **reflex arcs.** These pathways allow interneurons in the spinal cord to receive and send messages to motor neurons. This is why you can pull your hand away from a hot stove before you get burned. You do not have to think about it first.

 Underline the main function(s) of each of the three parts of the brain.

## The PNS links the CNS to muscles and other organs.

The peripheral nervous system (PNS) includes all the nerves that are not part of the CNS. It includes 12 pairs of nerves in the head, such as the nerves in your face, nose, eyes, and ears. It also includes 31 pairs of spinal nerves.

The PNS includes sensory neurons and motor neurons. The sensory neurons collect information about the body and its environment. The motor neurons trigger responses to that information. Some of the responses are involuntary,* such as jerking your leg when a doctor taps your knee. Other responses are voluntary,* such as moving your hand to eat.

Your voluntary movements are controlled by the **somatic nervous system.** Your **autonomic nervous system** controls functions that happen automatically, such as breathing. The autonomic nervous system includes two systems: the sympathetic nervous system and the parasympathetic nervous system.

Each part of the nervous system has a different function.

* ACADEMIC VOCABULARY

**involuntary**  something you have no choice about

**voluntary**  something that you choose to do

# Drugs alter brain chemistry.

Drugs can affect the amount of a neurotransmitter in the nervous system's synapses. This is why medicines often have side effects. They can make you sleepy, change your appetite, or reduce your ability to feel pain. If a drug increases the amount of a neurotransmitter in your synapses, neurons may send more impulses to your brain. If a drug lessens the amount of a neurotransmitter, neurons may not send all the messages that they normally would.

## Some Drugs Cause Addiction

The physical need to have a substance is called **addiction.** Addiction occurs because the brain adapts* to a drug, and neurons send normal amounts of impulses even though the levels of neurotransmitters are not normal. There are two ways the brain can start to depend on a drug.

- **Desensitization** occurs when a drug causes the body to produce more neurotransmitter than usual. Neurons adapt by removing some receptors, so they receive less neurotransmitter. In this way, the body increases its **tolerance** for the drug. It takes larger and larger doses to produce the same effect.
- **Sensitization** occurs when drugs lower the amount of a neurotransmitter in the synapses. Fewer action potentials are produced than normal. In this case, neurons adapt by adding more receptors, so they can receive more of the neurotransmitter.

## How Drugs Work

Drugs can change your behavior by changing the number of action potentials that your neurons produce. For instance, **stimulants** cause your neurons to produce more action potentials. Some increase the amount of neurotransmitter in your synapses. As a result, you feel happy and alert.

### NEURONS ADAPT

**When the amount of neurotransmitter becomes abnormal, the adjacent neuron adapts.**

synapse

**Normal**
Neurons release the correct amount of each neurotransmitter.

receptor

neurotransmitter

**Desensitization**
When there is too much neurotransmitter, neurons adapt by removing some receptors.

**Sensitization**
When there is too little neurotransmitter, neurons adapt by adding neurons.

**Depressants** make you feel relaxed and tired. They stop your neurons from producing so many action potentials. Some do this by lowering the amounts of neurotransmitter in your synapses.

Some drugs work a little differently. They might bind to a neuron's receptors themselves, taking the place of the neurotransmitters. Or they stop neurotransmitters from being removed from the receptors. The neurotransmitters cannot flow back into the neurons that released them. As a result, an action potential is more likely to occur.

 Underline the ways that drugs interfere with the neurons.

---

## 29.5 Vocabulary Check

**Mark It Up**

Go back and highlight each sentence that has a vocabulary word in **bold**.

addiction          sensitization

desensitization    stimulant

tolerance          depressant

**Fill in the blanks with the correct term from the list above.**

1. Desensitization can cause the body to develop a(an) _____ for a drug.

2. A _____ drug increases the number of action potentials that neurons produce.

3. A(an) _____ can make a person feel relaxed and tired.

4. When a synapse has more neurotransmitter in it than usual, neurons undergo _____.

5. When a synapse has less neurotransmitter in it than usual, neurons undergo _____.

## 29.5 The Big Picture

6. How can doctors look at a patient's brain without doing surgery?

_____

7. If you have to take more aspirin each time you get a headache, what has happened to increase your tolerance for this drug? _____

_____

8. What is the difference between a stimulant and a depressant?

_____

_____

## SECTION
# 29.6 The Endocrine System and Hormones

**KEY CONCEPT** The endocrine system produces hormones that affect growth, development, and homeostasis.

## Hormones influence a cell's activities by entering the cell or binding to its membrane.

The endocrine system, like the nervous system, can send signals to cells, causing them to change their activity. However, the endocrine system sends chemical signals, called **hormones.**

The endocrine system is made up of organs called **glands.** These organs release hormones into the bloodstream, which carries hormones throughout the body. Only certain cells are affected by hormones. These cells have receptors that interact* only with specific hormones that match those receptors.

All hormones are either steroid or nonsteroid. Steroid hormones are made of a type of fat and can enter their target cells. Nonsteroid hormones are made of amino acids and bind to receptors outside the cell.

Hormones only affect cells that have receptors matching the specific hormones.

 Why don't hormones affect every cell?

## Endocrine glands secrete hormones that act throughout the body.

Even though the endocrine system does not have its own connected network of tissues, its hormones can travel to any cell in the body. Some glands make hormones that target other glands and stimulate them to make hormones. Other glands release hormones that prompt* cells to divide and take up nutrients or that control the body's blood pressure. Some of the major glands in the endocrine system include:

- The **hypothalamus** is in the middle of the brain. It makes hormones that stimulate other glands to release hormones. It stimulates the production of hormones controlling growth, reproduction, and body temperature.

* ACADEMIC VOCABULARY

**interact** to act on each other

**prompt** to cue, to stimulate into action

488  McDougal Littell Biology

- The **pituitary gland** is also in the middle of the brain. It makes hormones that control cell growth and the amount of water in the blood. It also releases hormones that stimulate other glands to produce hormones. Hormones from the hypothalamus must pass through the pituitary before they enter the bloodstream.
- The thyroid gland wraps around the windpipe on three sides. Its hormones control metabolism, growth, and development.
- The thymus is in the chest. It makes hormones that help white blood cells to mature and fight off infection.
- The adrenal glands are above the kidneys. They release hormones that control the parasympathetic nervous system. Adrenal hormones make you breath faster, increase your blood pressure, and make you feel alert.
- The pancreas lies between the stomach and intestines. It makes enzymes that help you digest your food. It also makes hormones that control the body's glucose levels.
- The gonads include women's ovaries and men's testes. They make steroid hormones that affect sexual development. Men's and women's gonads make the same hormones, but they make them in different amounts.

1. HYPOTHALAMUS
2. PITUITARY
3. THYROID
4. THYMUS
5. ADRENAL GLANDS
6. PANCREAS
7. FEMALE GONADS: OVARIES
7. MALE GONADS: TESTES

The endocrine glands are not connected to each other. But their hormones can travel throughout the body.

 **INSTANT REPLAY** Underline the endocrine glands that control growth.

## The hypothalamus interacts with the nervous and endocrine systems.

The nervous system and the endocrine system are joined together by the hypothalamus. The hypothalamus is part of the central nervous system (CNS). It receives, sorts, and interprets signals from neurons. It is also part of the endocrine system and produces hormones. The hormones made by the hypothalamus are called **releasing hormones.** They stimulate other glands to release other hormones.

Most of the releasing hormones made by the hypothalamus affect the pituitary gland. Since both glands are in the middle of the brain, they can quickly pass hormones back and forth to each other. They work together to help the body maintain homeostasis. One task the hypothalamus and pituitary glands work on together is maintaining body temperature:

1. The body gets cold. Thermoreceptors in the nervous system send signals to the hypothalamus.

2. The hypothalamus releases a hormone called TRH (TSH-releasing hormone).

3. TRH stimulates the pituitary to release TSH (thyroid-stimulating hormone).

4. TSH stimulates the thyroid gland to release a hormone that makes cells more active.

5. As cells become more active, the body's internal temperature rises. The hypothalamus stops releasing TRH, and the other glands stop releasing their hormones. The cycle has ended.

 How can the hypothalamus receive signals from both the nervous and endocrine systems?

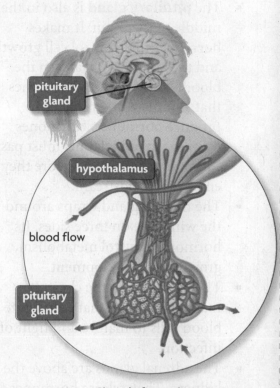

pituitary gland

hypothalamus

blood flow

pituitary gland

Signals from the nervous and endocrine systems can stimulate the hypothalamus to release hormones. These hormones stimulate the pituitary gland, which affects other glands.

## Hormonal imbalances can cause severe illness.

Hormones help the body to maintain homeostasis. Too much or too little of a hormone can affect the entire body and cause disease. For example, diabetes can occur when the pancreas does not make enough of the hormones that control glucose levels in the blood. If the thyroid does not make enough hormones, a person can develop hypothyroidism (*hypo-* means "low"). This disease can slow the physical growth and mental development of children. It can cause adults to become weak, gain weight, get depressed, and develop sensitivity to cold. The opposite condition is hyperthyroidism (*hyper-* means "high"), in which the thyroid makes too many hormones. In adults this disease can cause rapid heartbeat, sleeplessness, fatigue, hair loss, and sensitivity to heat.

The adrenal glands can also cause illness if they produce too much or too little of a hormone, cortisol. When the level of cortisone in the body is right, the body breaks sugar down well, and controls its blood pressure. When the adrenal glands release too much cortisol, a person can develop obesity, high blood pressure, diabetes, and muscle weakness. If the adrenal glands produce too little cortisol, a person can develop low blood pressure, weight loss, and loss of appetite.

**INSTANT REPLAY** What disease can occur when the pancreas is not working properly?

_____

## 29.6    Vocabulary Check

**Mark It Up**
Go back and highlight each sentence that has a vocabulary word in **bold**.

| | |
|---|---|
| hormone | pituitary gland |
| gland | releasing hormones |
| hypothalamus | |

**Fill in the blanks with the correct term from the list above.**

1. The _____ works closely with the pituitary gland.

2. _____ stimulate other glands to release other hormones.

3. A chemical signal made by the endocrine system is called a _____.

4. A _____ is an organ of the endocrine system.

5. Hormones from the hypothalamus stimulate the _____ to release its own hormones.

## 29.6    The Big Picture

6. How do hormones get to their target cells?

_____

7. Why don't hormones affect all the cells in the body?

_____

8. What organ of the endocrine system also interacts with the nervous system? _____

# Chapter 29 Review

1. What are the body's two communication systems? _____
   _____

2. Which of the body's communication systems operates the most
   quickly? Why? _____
   _____

3. List the parts of a neuron.
   _____
   _____

4. Which of the following kinds of neurons collects information about
   the body's environment?
   **a.** sensory neurons    **c.** motor neurons
   **b.** interneurons       **d.** all of the above

5. What is the difference between a resting potential and an action
   potential? _____
   _____

6. Choose the word that completes the following sentence:

   Before an action potential can enter another neuron, the axon
   terminals must release _____ into the synapse.
   **a.** dendrites      **c.** neurotransmitters
   **b.** axons         **d.** hormones

7. List the body's five specialized sense organs. _____
   _____

8. What is the difference between the central nervous system and the
   peripheral nervous system?
   _____
   _____
   _____
   _____

9. How do drugs affect your body's neurons? _____
   _____

10. Compare how the nervous and endocrine systems communicate.
    _____
    _____

# 30 Respiratory and Circulatory Systems

## GETTING READY TO LEARN

### Preview Key Concepts

**30.1 Respiratory and Circulatory Functions**
The respiratory and circulatory systems bring oxygen and nutrients to the cells.

**30.2 Respiration and Gas Exchange**
The respiratory system exchanges oxygen and carbon dioxide.

**30.3 The Heart and Circulation**
The heart is a muscular pump that moves the blood through two pathways.

**30.4 Blood Vessels and Transport**
The circulatory system transports materials throughout the body.

**30.5 Blood**
Blood is a complex tissue that transports materials.

**30.6 Lymphatic System**
The lymphatic system provides another type of circulation in the body.

### Review Vocabulary

Write the correct word for each definition.

nervous system          brain stem          hypothalamus

1. _____ : connects brain to spinal cord

2. _____ : stores and carries information to and from cells

3. _____ : network that controls thoughts and movements

### Preview Biology Vocabulary

Try to guess the meaning of each boldfaced word from its context.

| PHRASE | MY GUESS |
|---|---|
| 1. The speed of the heartbeat is controlled by the **pacemaker**. | |
| 2. The tiny **alveoli** give the lungs a large surface area for gas exchange. | |
| 3. **Plasma** is composed of 95 percent water; it makes up half your blood. | |

# 30.1 Respiratory and Circulatory Functions

**KEY CONCEPT** The respiratory and circulatory systems bring oxygen and nutrients to the cells.

## The respiratory and circulatory systems work together to maintain homeostasis.

The cells in your body cannot work well unless they have nutrients and oxygen. They also need to get rid of waste products.* The circulatory and respiratory systems supply all the cells with what they need.

- The **circulatory system** carries blood to all parts of the body. Blood brings nutrients and oxygen ($O_2$) to the cells, and takes away waste. Blood vessels also keep blood that is low in $O_2$ from mixing with blood that is rich* in $O_2$.

- The **respiratory system** is the part of the body where the blood picks up $O_2$ and drops off extra carbon dioxide ($CO_2$) and water vapor. The lungs are part of the respiratory system. They are the only place in the body where gas from the blood is exchanged with gas from the atmosphere.

The respiratory and circulatory systems work together. They respond to your body's changing needs. For example, if you exercise, your cells need more $O_2$. You breathe faster to take in more $O_2$, and your heart beats faster to carry it more quickly to your cells.

When you exercise, the cells in your body need more oxygen.

 **INSTANT REPLAY** How does $O_2$ travel from your lungs to your muscles?

## The respiratory system moves gases into and out of the blood.

The respiratory system brings $O_2$ into the body and expels* $CO_2$. Air enters the body mainly through the nose. Mucus in the nose warms the air and makes it moist. The mucus works with tiny hairs, called cilia, to filter dust and pathogens from the air.

---

**\* ACADEMIC VOCABULARY**

**waste products** things that will not be used

**rich** having a lot of something

**expel** to get rid of something

Air then flows into the throat and the **trachea,** or windpipe. The trachea is made of soft tissue, but it is supported by C-shaped rings of cartilage. When you swallow, a small piece of tissue, the epiglottis, closes off the entrance to the trachea. This keeps food and liquid from going down the trachea and entering the lungs. The trachea divides into two branches, called the bronchi. One branch goes to each lung. The **lungs** collect $O_2$ from the air you inhale. Inside the lungs, the bronchi divide into smaller branches, called bronchioles. The bronchioles end in clusters of tiny air sacs called **alveoli.** There are between 300 and 600 million alveoli in the lungs. The alveoli collect $O_2$ and release $CO_2$ and water vapor.

Air flows into and out of your lungs with help from special muscles in your chest and belly. One of these muscles is the **diaphragm,** a dome-shaped muscle at the bottom of the rib cage. These muscles contract and relax, changing the air pressure in your lungs. The changes in air pressure cause air to flow into or out of your lungs as you inhale or exhale.

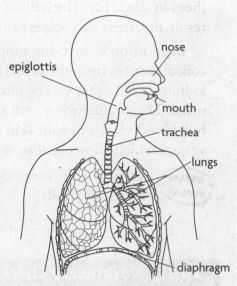

The respiratory system moves air into and out of the body.

 What major organs collect $O_2$ from the air you breathe?

_____

# The circulatory system moves blood to all parts of the body.

The circulatory system circulates* blood in your body. It carries $O_2$ and nutrients to the body's cells. It also takes $CO_2$ and water vapor back to the heart and lungs.

The circulatory system has several parts. The **heart** pumps blood, keeping it moving to every part of the body. It takes your blood about 60 seconds to move from your heart, throughout your body, and back to your heart. As it flows, your blood moves through three types of blood vessels: arteries, veins, and capillaries. **Arteries** carry blood away from the heart to the rest of the body. This blood is rich in oxygen. **Veins** carry blood from the rest of the body back to the heart. This blood contains much less oxygen. Arteries and veins are like major highways that carry materials to and from all parts of the body.

Arteries and veins are connected by a network of **capillaries.** These are tiny blood vessels that carry blood to and from the body's cells. These vessels are so small that blood cells must move through

The heart is a muscle about the size of your fist.

* ACADEMIC VOCABULARY

**circulate** to move around and around (in a circle)

them in single file. The walls of the capillaries are only one cell thick. As a result, nutrients and wastes can move easily into and out of the capillaries.

In addition to carrying supplies to the cells, the circulatory system collects wastes from the cells. It carries these wastes to the liver and kidneys, where they can be filtered and taken out of the body in the urine. The circulatory system also distributes heat. When you are too hot, blood vessels in your skin expand. More blood flows into these vessels, which allows heat to escape through the skin.

 What blood vessels do nutrients pass through in order to reach the body's cells?

_____

_____

## 30.1 Vocabulary Check

**Mark It Up**

Go back and highlight each sentence that has a vocabulary word in **bold**.

| | |
|---|---|
| circulatory system | diaphragm |
| respiratory system | heart |
| trachea | artery |
| lung | vein |
| alveoli | capillary |

The arteries, veins, and capillaries of the circulatory system extend throughout the body.

**Choose the correct term from the list for each description.**

1. In the list above, circle the body part that pumps blood throughout the body.

2. Put a box around the body system where gas exchange takes place.

3. Underline the word that means "tiny air sacs in the lungs."

4. Draw a triangle around the dome-shaped muscle at the base of the rib cage.

5. Draw a wavy line under the structure that carries air to your lungs.

## 30.1 The Big Picture

6. Put the following terms in the order that oxygen passes through them to reach your blood: alveoli, lung, trachea, nose, bronchi. _____

_____

7. What is the difference between an artery, a vein, and a capillary?

_____

_____

# 30.2 Respiration and Gas Exchange

**KEY CONCEPT** The respiratory system exchanges oxygen and carbon dioxide.

## Gas exchange occurs in the alveoli of the lungs.

The cells in your body carry out cellular respiration. This means that they need $O_2$, and they produce $CO_2$ as a waste product. The body gets $O_2$ from air in the atmosphere and expels* $CO_2$ into the atmosphere. The place where the body exchanges gases with the atmosphere is the lungs.

### Diffusion of $O_2$ and $CO_2$

The process of gas exchange involves both the respiratory system and the circulatory system. $O_2$ must move from the lungs into the blood, and $CO_2$ must move from the blood into the lungs. When you inhale, air flows from the bronchi into the bronchioles and finally into the alveoli.

A network of capillaries is around and inside the alveoli. The blood that flows into these capillaries contains little $O_2$. As a result, $O_2$ diffuses* from areas of high concentration* (in the alveoli) to areas of low concentration (in the capillaries). In each capillary, **red blood cells** pick up the $O_2$ and deliver it to all the body's cells.

Inside the red blood cells, the $O_2$ binds to an iron-rich protein called **hemoglobin.** Each molecule of hemoglobin binds with four $O_2$ molecules. The iron in hemoglobin is what makes blood red. Blood becomes bright red only when it absorbs oxygen. Blood leaves the alveoli with almost three times the $O_2$ it had when it came in.

The blood that enters the lungs carries $CO_2$ that cells produce as a waste product. In the blood, $CO_2$ and water combine to form carbonic acid. When the blood reaches the alveoli, carbonic acid diffuses into the alveoli. There, it separates into $CO_2$ and water vapor. Each time you exhale, you are expelling $CO_2$ and water vapor.

### Gas Exchange and the Nervous System

Gas exchange is one of the most important functions in the body. It helps to maintain homeostasis and keep you alive. You do not have to think about gas exchange for it to happen. It is controlled for you by two areas in the brain stem, the medulla and pons.

* ACADEMIC VOCABULARY

**expel** to force to leave
**diffuse** to spread out freely
**concentration** the amount of a substance in a solution, such as oxygen in the blood

**Diffusion of gases into and out of the alveoli maintains $O_2$ and $CO_2$ homeostasis.**

ALVEOLI

capillaries

GAS EXCHANGE

alveolus

capillary

$CO_2$ diffuses into alveolus.

$CO_2$

$O_2$

$O_2$ diffuses into blood.

The medulla and pons keep track of the concentration of gases in your blood, especially $CO_2$. When you exercise, the level of $CO_2$ in your blood goes up. Sensors in the respiratory and circulatory systems alert the brain stem that the blood has too much $CO_2$. The medulla uses the nervous and endocrine systems to send messages to the diaphragm and to the muscles in your rib cage. These muscles begin to contract and relax more often, making you breathe faster and more deeply.

Why does $O_2$ diffuse from the alveoli into the capillaries?

Air inhaled.

Muscles contract and rib cage expands.

Diaphragm flattens and moves downward.

Air exhaled.

Muscles and rib cage relax.

Diaphragm relaxes and rises.

Signals from the medulla in the brain stem stimulate the diaphragm and the muscles in the rib cage to contract and relax.

# Respiratory diseases interfere with gas exchange.

Any illness that attacks the respiratory system makes it harder for the body to carry out gas exchange. If gas exchange is reduced, every cell in the body can be harmed. Smoking is the biggest cause of respiratory disease. Tobacco smoke contains more than 4800 chemicals that can paralyze cilia and damage the alveoli.

If smokers do not quit, they may develop a disease known as **emphysema.** In this disease, many alveoli are destroyed. Over time, less and less $O_2$ can enter the blood. There is no cure for emphysema, and eventually the lungs fail.

**Asthma** is another common respiratory disease. It causes muscle spasms that constrict the bronchioles. A person having a severe asthma attack can die from lack of $O_2$. The attacks can be treated with drugs that relax the bronchioles.

 Highlight how smoking affects a person's lungs.

## 30.2 Vocabulary Check

red blood cell      emphysema
hemoglobin          asthma

**Fill in the blanks with the correct term from the list above.**

1. _____ pick up $O_2$ in the alveoli and carry it to the body's cells.

2. _____ causes muscle spasms that constrict the bronchioles.

3. Smokers are at risk for developing _____.

4. In red blood cells, $O_2$ binds to an iron-rich protein called _____.

## 30.2 The Big Picture

5. How are gases exchanged in the alveoli? _____
_____
_____

6. What is the leading cause of respiratory disease? _____
_____

# 30.3 The Heart and Circulation

**KEY CONCEPT** The heart is a muscular pump that moves the blood through two pathways.

## The tissues and structures of the heart make it an efficient pump.

Your heart beats about 100,000 times each day. In that time, it circulates blood through 96,000 kilometers of blood vessels—roughly one quarter of the distance from Earth to the moon. In your lifetime, your heart may beat as many as 2.5 billion times. And it never stops. Why doesn't the heart get tired and need to rest? It is made of cardiac muscle tissue. Unlike the tissues of skeletal muscles, cardiac muscle tissue can work continuously* and never get tired. The heart is a very efficient* pump.

### Structures of the Heart

Your heart has four chambers. The smallest are the right **atrium** and left atrium. The largest are the right and left **ventricles.** The septum, a thick wall of tissue, separates the ventricles from each other.

The heart also has **valves,** flaps of tissues that stop blood from flowing backward. They open when the atria or ventricles contract and close when the atria or ventricles relax. After blood fills each chamber, the cardiac muscle contracts, pumping the blood out of the chamber.

The heart is small but strong. Cardiac muscles can squeeze each chamber with a great deal of force. The heart can also pump faster as you become more active or pump slower when you sit or lie down.

**HEART CHAMBERS AND VALVES**

aortic valve

pulmonary valve

left atrium

mitral valve

right atrium

tricuspid valve

left ventricle

right ventricle

septum

Your heart has four chambers. It also has valves that keep the blood flowing in only one direction.

---

* ACADEMIC VOCABULARY

**continuously** without stopping

**efficient** able to get something done without wasting time or effort

## The Heartbeat

Even though the heart has four chambers, it only contracts twice in each heartbeat. First the atria contract together. Then the ventricles contract together.

How does the heart know when to contract? It receives a signal from a group of cells in the heart's right atrium. These cells are known as the sinoatrial (SA) node, or **pacemaker.** When the SA node is damaged, people must get an artificial* pacemaker to keep the heart beating. The pacemaker sends an electrical signal that starts a wave of contractions in the atria. After the atria have contracted, the signal is passed to a group of cells known as the atrioventricular (AV) node. This node is located in the right ventricle. The AV node sends a signal, and the two ventricles contract.

## Blood Flow in the Heart

Blood flows in a certain pathway through the heart. Blood always enters the heart through an atrium and leaves through a ventricle.

**1** Oxygen-poor blood from the body enters the **right atrium.** The atria contract, and blood flows into the right ventricle.

**2** The ventricles contract and pump blood from the **right ventricle** into the pulmonary* artery. From there, blood flows directly to the lungs, where $CO_2$ is exchanged for $O_2$.

**3** Oxygen-rich blood leaves the lungs, returning to the **left atrium** of the heart through the pulmonary vein. The atria contract and pump blood into the left ventricle.

**4** The ventricles contract, and pump blood from the **left ventricle** into a large artery, the aorta. From there, blood circulates to the rest of the body.

 What are the main structures of the heart? Include the structures that regulate the heartbeat in your answer.

_____

_____

* ACADEMIC VOCABULARY

**artificial** made by humans

**pulmonary** belonging to or connected with the lung

# The heart pumps blood through two main pathways.

The diagram on the right shows how blood circulates through two pathways in the body. In **pulmonary circulation,** the heart pumps blood to and from the lungs, giving the blood a chance to exchange its gases. In **systemic circulation** the heart pumps blood to and from the rest of the body, carrying nutrients to cells and waste products away from cells.

Trace your finger along the path taken by the blood as it is pumped into and out of the heart. Find the place where the blood switches from pulmonary to systemic circulation.

**PULMONARY**

**SYSTEMIC**

Pulmonary and systemic circulation each have their own pathways into and out of the heart.

## 30.3  Vocabulary Check

**Mark It Up**

Go back and highlight each sentence that has a vocabulary word in **bold.**

atrium          pacemaker
ventricle       pulmonary circulation
valve           systemic circulation

**Fill in the blanks with the correct term from the list above.**

1. The heart's SA node is located in the right _____.

2. _____ makes sure that blood in the heart flows in only one direction.

3. _____ occurs only between the heart and the lungs.

4. _____ occurs between the heart and the rest of the body, except the lungs.

5. The heart's _____ produces an electrical signal that tells the heart when to beat.

6. The heart's left _____ pumps oxygen-rich blood to all the parts of the body.

## 30.3  The Big Picture

7. The heart is located near the lungs. How does this show that the circulatory and respiratory systems work closely together? _____

_____

8. What is the pathway that blood follows through the heart?

_____

_____

# 30.4 Blood Vessels and Transport

**KEY CONCEPT** The circulatory system transports materials throughout the body.

## Arteries, veins, and capillaries transport blood to all parts of the body.

The circulatory system uses three types of vessels to transport blood throughout the body. Each vessel has its own structure and function.

### Arteries

Arteries carry blood from the heart to the rest of the body. Blood coming from the heart is under a great deal of pressure, so arteries must be strong and flexible. The wall of each artery has three layers. The inside layer consists* of endothelium coated with a protein that stops blood from clotting. The middle layer is made of muscle and elastic fibers. The walls of the arteries can expand and contract to help keep the blood moving. The outer layer consists of connective tissue and more elastic fibers. Small arteries, called arterioles, have the same three layers but have much smaller diameters.

---

**THREE TYPES OF BLOOD VESSELS**

**Arteries, veins, and capillaries transport the blood to every cell.**

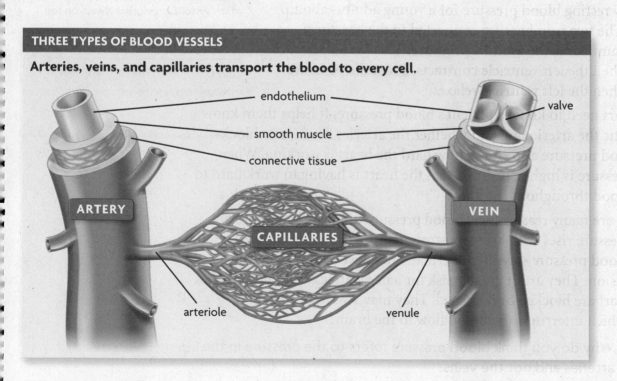

endothelium

valve

smooth muscle

connective tissue

ARTERY

CAPILLARIES

VEIN

arteriole

venule

---

\* ACADEMIC VOCABULARY

**consist** to be made of

## Veins

Veins carry blood from the rest of the body back to the heart. This blood is under much less pressure. Veins are larger and have thinner walls than arteries do. Veins cannot expand and contract to keep blood moving. Instead, they have valves that keep blood from flowing backwards. Also, when you move, muscles in the skeletal system squeeze the veins to help the blood circulate. That is why if you sit too long, your blood does not move as well in your veins.

## Capillaries

Capillary walls do not contain muscles or elastic fibers. Their walls are only one cell thick, so materials can easily diffuse into and out of the blood. Some parts of the body, such as the lungs, kidneys, and liver, are very active and need large quantities of blood. In these organs, the capillaries form thick networks called capillary beds. The beds can move large amounts of blood into and out of these organs.

## Circulation and Blood Pressure

As blood flows through the arteries, it pushes against the arterial walls. The force blood exerts on the artery walls is called **blood pressure.** Blood pressure is written as a fraction. A healthy resting blood pressure for a young adult is about 120/70. The two numbers are connected to the heartbeat. The top number is the **systolic pressure.** This blood pressure occurs when the left ventricle contracts. **Diastolic pressure** occurs when the left ventricle relaxes.

> ### VISUAL VOCAB
>
> **Systolic pressure** occurs when the left ventricle contracts. **Diastolic pressure** occurs when the ventricle relaxes. You can write these numbers as a fraction in which systolic pressure is always on top.
>
> | 120 | **systolic** = numerator |
> | --- | --- |
> | 70 | **diastolic** = denominator |

Doctors need to know a patient's blood pressure. It helps them know how elastic the arteries are and whether the arteries have many blockages. Blood pressure also shows how hard the heart is working. When blood pressure is higher, it shows that the heart is having to work hard to pump blood throughout the body.

There are many reasons why blood pressure might rise temporarily. Blood pressure rises with exercise, stress, and strong emotions. People whose blood pressure stays high permanently have a condition called hypertension. They are at greater risk for a heart attack, in which arteries to the heart are blocked or damaged. They may also be at risk for a stroke, which interrupts the blood flow to the brain.

 Why do you think blood pressure refers to the pressure in the arteries and not the veins?

_____

_____

# Lifestyle plays a key role in circulatory diseases.

The choices you make about how to live your life affect the health of your circulatory system. Several circulatory diseases are related to smoking, to lack of exercise, and to stress. On the other hand, eating fruits and vegetables and avoiding foods that are high in saturated fat can help you keep your circulatory system healthy.

One of the most common diseases of the circulatory system is arteriosclerosis. This disease makes the artery walls thick and rigid. Another disease, atherosclerosis, is caused by a buildup of sticky plaque* on the artery walls. Plaque can reduce blood flow in the artery.

It is possible to treat diseases of the arteries. Some patients have surgery to replace part of the artery. Others have a balloon angioplasty. In this surgery, a device is inserted* into the artery and inflated like a balloon. The plaque is pushed against the artery walls, which allows more blood to flow through. Doctors say that people can help avoid these diseases by maintaining a healthy weight, exercising regularly, and not smoking.

 **Give an example of a heart-healthy meal.**

_____

## 30.4 Vocabulary Check

**Mark It Up**

Go back and highlight each sentence that has a vocabulary word in **bold**.

blood pressure

systolic pressure

diastolic pressure

Choose the correct term from the list for each description.

1. The bottom number in a blood pressure reading _____

2. The top number in a blood pressure reading _____

3. The force with which blood pushes against an artery wall _____

## 30.4 The Big Picture

4. What blood vessels carry blood to the heart? away from the heart?

_____

5. Give an example of one thing you can do to help prevent heart disease.

_____

# 30.5 Blood

**KEY CONCEPT** Blood is a complex tissue that transports materials.

An adult human body contains about 5 liters (more than 5 quarts) of blood. Blood transports supplies to your cells and takes waste products away from them. Some components* of blood help to fight infections and to control bleeding.

## Blood is composed mainly of cells, cell fragments, and plasma.

Blood looks like a single substance. Actually, it is a mixture of cells, cell fragments, and fluid. It also contains particles of fat, other nutrients, and dissolved gases.

If you spin blood in a centrifuge*, it separates into two main parts. One part contains a red-brown mix of red blood cells, white blood cells, and platelets. **Platelets** are made in bone marrow. They are cell fragments that help the blood clot to stop bleeding. The other part is a clear, pale yellow fluid, called **plasma.** About 55% of the blood is plasma. Plasma is about 90% water. However, it also contains amino acids, glucose, hormones, vitamins, salts, and waste products.

Plasma plays an important role in homeostasis. When concentrations of certain molecules are high in plasma, they diffuse out of the blood through the capillaries. When those concentrations are low, molecules diffuse into the blood. These substances include water, gases, nutrients, and ions. Proteins in the plasma also help to maintain homeostasis. They keep blood volume stable, so fluid in the blood does not leak out of blood vessels. The proteins also work with platelets to stop bleeding.

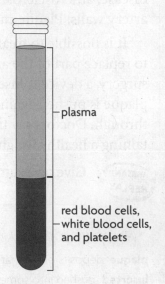

plasma

red blood cells, white blood cells, and platelets

Blood can be separated into two main parts.

 **INSTANT REPLAY** What do you think might happen to your blood if you don't drink enough water?

_____

_____

## Platelets and different types of blood cells have different functions.

Blood contains red blood cells, white blood cells, and platelets. All three are made in the bone marrow. But they have different shapes and different functions.

* ACADEMIC VOCABULARY

**component** part of something

**centrifuge** machine that spins materials until they separate into parts

## Red Blood Cells

About 45 percent of the blood's cells are red blood cells. They are shaped like an inner tube with a solid center. Red blood cells are made from stem cells in bone marrow. When they mature, they fill with hemoglobin and lose their nuclei and other important organelles. They cannot divide and reproduce. Instead, they circulate through the body for about 120 days, and then begin to degrade.* The blood then carries them to the liver and spleen. These organs break up and recycle what is left of the red blood cells.

normal red blood cell

The most important function of red blood cells is to carry $O_2$ to cells and carry $CO_2$ away from them. $O_2$ binds to the hemoglobin in red blood cells, and is carried to all the body's cells. When the blood returns to the heart, it carries $CO_2$ from the cells to the lungs. Here it can be exchanged for more $O_2$.

When red blood cells are healthy, they function well. But if they are damaged or the wrong shape, they cannot transport $O_2$ as easily. In sickle cell disease, for example, red blood cells are shaped like the letter "C". They carry less $O_2$ and survive only 10 to 20 days. They also tend to clump in blood vessels. Sickle cell disease is a genetic disorder.

sickle cell

## ABO Blood Groups and Rh Factors

Not all red blood cells are the same. The surface of each red blood cell contains specialized protein markers*. Your blood type is based on the protein markers on your red blood cells. When people receive blood transfusions, they can only receive blood types that are compatible* with their own red blood cells.

There are about 26 different blood types. The most common protein markers are A and B, which produce three blood types: A, B, and AB. Type O does not have a protein marker. Altogether, these blood types are called the **ABO blood group.** Type O can be given to a person with any other blood type. Type AB blood has both A and B markers. People with AB blood can receive blood from any other blood type. But people with type A and type B blood can receive only their own blood type or type O blood. Otherwise, the wrong blood types will clump together and block important blood vessels.

**\* ACADEMIC VOCABULARY**

**degrade**  to wear away or fall apart

**marker**  something that shows when a substance, such as a protein, is present

**compatible**  able to exist or work together

Another blood protein, called the **Rh factor,** is also important to know. People either have the Rh factor or they don't. So you are either Rh positive (Rh⁺) or Rh negative (Rh⁻). Anyone can receive Rh⁻ blood. But if you are Rh⁻, and you receive Rh⁺ blood, your immune system will attack the Rh⁺ blood cells. You can see why blood used in a transfusion must be the right ABO type and the right Rh type.

| ABO and Rh BLOOD COMBINATIONS | | |
| --- | --- | --- |
| **BLOOD TYPE** | **CAN DONATE TO** | **CAN RECEIVE FROM** |
| A | A, AB | A, O |
| B | AB, B | B, O |
| AB | AB | A, B, AB, O |
| O | A, B, AB, O | O |
| **Rh FACTOR** | **CAN DONATE TO** | **CAN RECEIVE FROM** |
| **Rh⁺ factor** | Rh⁺ | Rh⁺, Rh⁻ |
| **Rh⁻ factor** | Rh⁺, Rh⁻ | Rh⁻ |

If you know your blood type and Rh factor, use this chart to figure out to whom you can give blood or from whom you can receive blood.

## White Blood Cells

**White blood cells** are part of the immune system as well as the circulatory system. Unlike red blood cells, white blood cells contain no hemoglobin. White blood cells fight infection. They also remove foreign* particles and dead cells. Different white blood cells have different functions. Some surround microorganisms and ingest* them. Some produce proteins that destroy pathogens. Some white blood cells—unlike red blood cells—can pass through capillary walls into the lymphatic system. There, they can attack pathogens.

## Platelets and Blood Clotting

When you cut or tear a blood vessel, platelets cluster around the wound. They help the blood to clot. First they form long spikes to make a net. Then they release proteins called clotting factors. The clotting factors produce a sticky thread called fibrin, which traps platelets and white blood cells. The tangle of fibrin, platelets, and white blood cells forms a plug, or clot, which seals the wound and stops the bleeding.

Blood clotting is an example of a positive feedback loop. The body increases the release of clotting factors until the wound is sealed.

* ACADEMIC VOCABULARY

**foreign** introduced from outside
**ingest** to eat and destroy a pathogen

Sometimes blood clots form inside blood vessels. When this happens, clots become a serious health risk. They can cause a heart attack or a stroke. But being unable to form clots can be equally serious. Hemophilia is a disorder in which a clotting factor is missing from the blood. People with hemophilia risk bleeding to death every time they get even a minor cut or bruise. If they do get injured, they must receive an injection of the missing clotting factor so the wound can be sealed.

Why is hemophilia such a serious disease?

_____

_____

## 30.5 Vocabulary Check

**Mark It Up**

Go back and highlight each sentence that has a vocabulary word in **bold**.

platelet

plasma

ABO blood group

Rh factor

white blood cell

**Choose the correct term from the list for each description.**

1. In the list above, circle the term that refers to the four blood types.

2. Put a box around the pale fluid that makes up about 55% of the blood.

3. Underline the cell fragment that helps with blood clotting.

4. Draw a wavy line under the cell that fights infection.

## 30.5 The Big Picture

5. What are the main functions of plasma?

_____

_____

6. Describe two differences between red and white blood cells.

_____

_____

# 30.6 Lymphatic System

**KEY CONCEPT** The lymphatic system provides another type of circulation in the body.

You already know that the circulatory system distributes blood throughout the body, bringing gases and nutrients to every cell. Your body also has a second network to circulate fluids throughout the body. This system is the **lymphatic system.** Like the circulatory system, the lymphatic system brings nutrients to cells and carries waste products away. But it also absorbs extra fluid in the body and fights disease.

## Lymph is collected from tissues and returned to the circulatory system.

The capillaries of the circulatory system leak fluid into the area between the cells. This fluid is called interstitial fluid. It carries nutrients to the cells, and removes their wastes. About 90% of this fluid makes its way back into the capillaries. The remaining fluid is collected by the lymphatic system. If the lymphatic system did not collect this fluid, it would remain trapped in your tissues. Within a few hours, your body would begin to swell.

Like the circulatory system, the lymphatic system also has capillaries, called lymphatic capillaries. When interstitial fluid enters these capillaries, it is called **lymph.** The heart does not pump lymph through the lymphatic system. Instead, skeletal muscles in the body squeeze the lymph vessels and move the fluid. One-way valves, like the valves in veins, keep the lymph from flowing backwards.

Lymph is carried to special structures called lymph **nodes.** The nodes filter the lymph by trapping bacteria, viruses, fungi, and cell fragments. These are destroyed by the immune system. From the nodes, the cleaned lymph flows into large veins located under each collarbone. The fluid is then returned to the circulatory system.

When lymphatic nodes or vessels are damaged or removed, the lymph cannot drain and the area swells. People sometimes use exercise, pressure bandages, or massage to push lymph out of damaged areas.

tonsils

thymus

spleen

lymph nodes

Like the circulatory system, the lymphatic system extends throughout the entire body.

**INSTANT ►◄ REPLAY** Where does lymph come from?

_____

## The lymphatic system is a major part of the immune system.

The lymphatic system includes three structures that are also part of the immune system: the tonsils, the thymus, and the spleen. Each of these structures helps the body fight infection. The tonsils are lymph nodes that are in the back of the throat. They filter out bacteria and viruses. The thymus is located behind the breastbone. It produces special white blood cells, called **lymphocytes** that fight against infection. The spleen is the lymphatic system's largest organ. It filters the lymph, cleaning out any abnormal tissue. The spleen contains many lymphocytes and other white blood cells that destroy harmful organisms.

 Where are lymphocytes produced?

_____

| 30.6 | Vocabulary Check |
|------|------------------|

**Mark It Up**

Go back and highlight each sentence that has a vocabulary word in **bold**.

lymphatic system     node

lymph     lymphocyte

**Fill in the blanks with the correct term from the list above.**

1. Where is lymph filtered? _____

2. What system collects excess fluid from between the body's cells?

   _____

3. What kind of white blood cells are made in the thymus? _____

4. What fluid circulates through the lymphatic system? _____

| 30.6 | The Big Picture |
|------|-----------------|

5. How are the lymphatic system and the circulatory system similar?

   _____

   _____

6. How are the lymphatic system and the circulatory system different?

   _____

   _____

# Chapter 30 Review

1. What two body systems work together to provide $O_2$ to cells?

   _____

2. What do the alveoli do in the respiratory system?

   _____

   _____

3. How do respiratory diseases interfere with gas exchange?

   _____

4. Which of the following tells the heart when to contract?
   a. atrium
   b. valve
   c. ventricle
   d. pacemaker

5. Draw a sketch showing the two main pathways through which the heart pumps blood.

6. Choose the word that completes the following sentence:

   Blood pressure is the force that blood places on the _____ walls.
   a. artery
   b. vein
   c. capillary
   d. lymph

7. Give an example of a lifestyle choice that can help prevent circulatory diseases. _____

   _____

   _____

8. Name two components of blood. _____

9. Why do you need to know your blood type before receiving blood?

   _____

   _____

10. Where is lymphatic fluid filtered and cleaned in the lymphatic system?

    _____

    _____

# 31 Immune System and Disease

## GETTING READY TO LEARN

### Preview Key Concepts

**31.1 Pathogens and Human Illness**
Germs cause many diseases in humans.

**31.2 Immune System**
The immune system consists of organs, cells, and molecules that fight infections.

**31.3 Immune Responses**
The immune system has many responses to pathogens and foreign cells.

**31.4 Immunity and Technology**
Living in a clean environment and building immunity help keep a person healthy.

**31.5 Overreactions of the Immune System**
An overactive immune system can make the body very unhealthy.

**31.6 Diseases That Weaken the Immune System**
When the immune system is weakened, the body cannot fight off diseases.

### Review Academic Vocabulary

Write the correct word for each definition.

lymphatic system     lymphocyte     hemoglobin

1. _____ : network that collects excess fluid between the cells

2. _____ : white blood cell

### Preview Biology Vocabulary

See how many key terms from this chapter you already know. Rewrite each phrase, using a different word or words for the **words in bold.**

| PHRASE | REWRITTEN WITH DIFFERENT WORDS |
|---|---|
| 1. **Allergens** such as pollen and animal dander can trigger sneezing and itching in people. | Pollen and animal dander are examples of _____ _____ |
| 2. Insects are common **vectors** for diseases. | Insects are _____ _____ |

# 31.1 Pathogens and Human Illness

**KEY CONCEPT**  Germs cause many diseases in humans.

Diseases have played a major role in human history. For example, in the 14th century, the Black Death killed nearly one-fourth of Europe's population. In 1918, the Spanish flu killed millions of people worldwide. Today, air travel can spread disease quickly around the globe. That is why scientists are concerned whenever a new disease appears.

## Germ theory states that microscopic particles cause certain diseases.

Today, scientists know that there are two different kinds of diseases: noninfectious and infectious. Noninfectious diseases are impossible to pass from one person to another. Cancer and heart disease are examples of noninfectious diseases. Infectious diseases can be passed from one person to another. These diseases are caused by germs, usually bacteria and viruses. Flu and polio are infectious diseases caused by viruses.

In the 1850s, French scientist Louis Pasteur proposed the **germ theory** of disease. In his theory, he stated that diseases are caused by microorganisms, called **pathogens.** At the time, not all scientists agreed with Pasteur. But two scientists, British surgeon Joseph Lister and German scientist Robert Koch, used Pasteur's research in their own work.

**1857**
Germ theory  Louis Pasteur hypothesizes that disease is caused by small "animals."

**1883**
Koch's postulates  Robert Koch finds four conditions that prove a pathogen causes a disease.

1800    1900

**1865**
Antiseptic technique Joseph Lister finds that cleaning his surgical tools reduces patients' infections.

**1900s**
Applying antiseptic technique Cities around the world start treating drinking water with chlorine, reducing the cases of cholera.

Scientists did not always know that germs can cause disease.

Lister had noticed that half his patients died from infections after surgeries that should have been successful. He heard about Pasteur's germ theory and began cleaning his operating tools and his patients' wounds before surgery. The number of patients who died from infections after surgery dropped to nearly zero.

Koch decided to try making healthy animals sick by injecting them with pathogens from a sick animal. He found that four conditions* must be met before one can be certain that a particular pathogen causes disease. His conditions are called Koch's postulates*:

- The pathogen must be present in every case in which a disease is found.
- The pathogen must be isolated* and grown in the lab to make a pure, uncontaminated* culture.
- Healthy animals infected with a pure culture of the pathogen must become sick with the disease.
- The pathogen must be re-isolated and cultured from the newly sick animals. This pathogen must be the same type as the original pathogen.

 Which type of disease does a pathogen cause: infectious or noninfectious?

## There are different types of pathogens.

How is it possible to isolate a pathogen? At first, scientists strained bacteria and larger pathogens through a ceramic filter with tiny holes. The pathogens remained on the filter, while the liquid solution passed through it. The solution that passed through was harmless. Yet sometimes there would be no pathogens on the filter, and the solution still caused disease. They called these pathogens filterable viruses.

Over time, scientists discovered a huge number of tiny pathogens. All pathogens attack healthy cells but in different ways.

- **Bacteria** are single-celled organisms. Some bacteria release chemicals that are toxic to their host. Others destroy healthy cells. Food poisoning is caused by bacteria.

Bacteria are large enough to be isolated by ceramic filters.

* ACADEMIC VOCABULARY

**condition** requirement

**postulate** something that is assumed to be true without needing proof

**isolated** separated from anything else

**uncontaminated** pure, not mixed with anything else

Interactive Reader **515**

- **Viruses** are strands of DNA or RNA that are surrounded by protein coats. They are so small that they can be seen only with an electron microscope. Viruses enter healthy cells and take them over, forcing the healthy cells to produce more viruses. Viruses cause illnesses such as colds and AIDS.
- **Fungi** can have one cell or more than one cell. They can invade healthy cells and take the cells' nutrients. Fungal infections usually occur in places that are warm and damp. For example, athlete's foot is a fungus that invades skin cells between the toes.
- **Protists** are single-celled organisms. They can prey on healthy body cells. Malaria is a disease of the red blood cells that is caused by a protist.
- **Parasites** are organisms that grow on a host and feed off it. Some parasites even kill their host. Intestinal worms are one kind of parasite.

Pathogens come in many shapes and sizes.

fungi (microscopic)

parasitic protist

parasitic roundworm

**INSTANT REPLAY** Name a method scientists can use to find larger pathogens.

_____

| COMMON INFECTIOUS DISEASES WORLDWIDE | | | | |
|---|---|---|---|---|
| **DISEASE** | **PATHOGEN TYPE** | **HOW IT SPREADS** | **AFFECTED BODY SYSTEMS** | **DEATHS ANNUALLY** |
| HIV | virus | body fluids | immune | 3,100,000 |
| Pneumonia | virus, bacteria | airborne | respiratory | 2,000,000 |
| Tuberculosis | bacteria | airborne | respiratory, digestive | 1,800,000 |
| Malaria | protozoa | mosquito bite | digestive, circulatory, muscular | 1,000,000 |
| Hepatitis B | virus | contaminated food/water | digestive, immune | 1,000,000 |
| Measles | virus | airborne | respiratory, nervous | 500,000 |
| Influenza | virus | airborne, direct contact | respiratory | 400,000 |

Source: World Health Organization

## Pathogens can enter the body in different ways.

Pathogens have to enter the body before they can make a person sick. Pathogens can be spread in several ways.

- Direct contact means that a pathogen is spread through physical touch. For example, rabies can be transmitted when a sick animal bites a healthy one. HIV can be transmitted during sexual intercourse or while sharing infected needles.

- Indirect contact means a pathogen can infect a person without that person touching an infected person. Pathogens that are spread by indirect contact can survive on nonliving surfaces, such as tables or doorknobs. For example, the fungi that cause athlete's foot can survive on a bathroom floor for some time. Pathogens that spread by indirect contact can be passed in the air or by eating contaminated food.
- Some pathogens are spread by vectors. A **vector** is anything that can carry a pathogen and pass it to other organisms. Vectors can include insects, birds, and other animals. Mosquitoes can carry West Nile virus. In the 1300s, the Black Death, or bubonic plague, was carried by the fleas of rats.

Salmonella, a disease that causes vomiting and diarrhea in humans, can be found in the intestines of some pigs.

Name one method you could use to try to prevent pathogens from entering your body.

_____

---

## 31.1 Vocabulary Check

**Mark It Up**

Go back and highlight each sentence that has a vocabulary word in **bold**.

germ theory      vector

pathogen

Fill in the blanks with the correct term from the list above.

1. A _____ is anything that carries a pathogen and transmits it to healthy cells.

2. According to _____, diseases are caused by microorganisms.

3. An organism that causes disease is called a _____.

---

## 31.1 The Big Picture

4. Give an example of something you think doctors might have done differently after learning that germs cause disease.

_____

_____

5. What do viruses do after they invade your body? _____

_____

6. Give an example of one way that a pathogen can enter your body.

_____

# 31.2 Immune System

**KEY CONCEPT** The immune system consists of organs, cells, and molecules that fight infections.

## Many body systems protect you from pathogens.

Your body has organs, cells, and tissues to protect you from pathogens. The body system that fights off infection is the **immune system.** The immune system works with other body systems to prevent infection.

Your skin is your body's first physical defense. It prevents pathogens from entering your body. Your skin also secretes* oil and sweat, which make it hard for pathogens to survive on the skin's surface.

Openings in the skin, such as cuts or scrapes, provide an entrance for pathogens. Also, your eyes, ears, nose, and mouth could provide an entrance. Fortunately, these openings have extra protection. Tears, sticky mucous membranes, and hairlike cilia trap and remove pathogens before they can enter the rest of the body.

Where is a pathogen most likely to enter your body?

_____

## Cells and proteins fight the body's infections.

Even if pathogens do enter your body, you may not get sick. The immune system sends special cells, like defending warriors, to attack the pathogens. These cells travel through the lymphatic and circulatory systems in search of invading pathogens.

### White Blood Cells

White blood cells attack pathogens that have gotten through the body's external* barriers. When a pathogen first enters the body, cells in the blood and other tissues send out chemical signals. These warning signals draw the white blood cells to the site of the infection.

If the pathogen is a virus, bacterium, or fungus, a phagocyte will destroy them. A **phagocyte** is a white blood cell that destroys pathogens by surrounding and engulfing them.

**VISUAL VOCAB**

A **phagocyte** is a cell that engulfs and destroys other cells. It comes from Greek words that translate to mean "cell eater."

phagocyte      bacterium

* ACADEMIC VOCABULARY

**secrete** to produce and release

**external** outer

The next white blood cells to arrive at the infection site are lymphocytes. There are two kinds of lymphocytes: T-lymphyocytes (called **T cells**) and B-lymphocytes (called **B cells**). T cells destroy body cells that have been infected by pathogens. B cells produce proteins that stop pathogens from infecting body cells.

### Proteins

The immune system uses three types of proteins to fight pathogens.

- **Complement proteins** are made by white blood cells and by some organs. These proteins work in different ways. Some weaken a pathogen's cell membrane. Then water can enter the cell and cause it to burst. Other proteins attract phagocytes to the infection site. Still others cause pathogens to stick to the walls of blood vessels, where phagocytes can more easily find and destroy them.
- **Antibodies** are proteins made by B cells. An antibody can destroy pathogens in one of three ways. They can bind to proteins on the pathogen's cell membrane. They can cause pathogens to stick together in a clump, making them easier for phagocytes to find and destroy. Some antibodies activate proteins that weaken the pathogen's cell membrane and cause it to burst.
- **Interferons** are proteins produced by body cells that have been infected by a virus. The interferons stimulate other body cells to release enzymes that can prevent viruses from entering and infecting them. Viruses cannot reproduce if they cannot enter healthy cells.

 Underline two immune system proteins that can cause a pathogen's cell membrane to burst.

Some antibodies cause pathogens to stick together in clumps. This helps phagocytes find and destroy several pathogens at once.

# Immunity prevents a person from getting sick from a pathogen.

You can become immune to a pathogen. If you are immune, you will not get sick even if the pathogen infects your body. There are two types of immunity: passive and active.

**Passive immunity** is immunity that occurs without your body having to become sick. Mothers pass immunity to their children during pregnancy and through breastfeeding. Passive immunity can also be passed from one generation to the next in DNA.

**Active immunity** is immunity that the body produces in response to an infection. After your body has been infected by a pathogen once, it is less likely to become sick if the same pathogen enters your body again. The immune system will attack it more quickly the second time.

 Would passive or active immunity protect you from a bacterial infection you have had before?

_____

| 31.2 | Vocabulary Check | **Mark It Up** |

immune system          antibodies
phagocyte              interferons
T cells                passive immunity
B cells                active immunity

**Mark It Up**

Go back and highlight each sentence that has a vocabulary word in **bold**.

**Fill in the blanks with the correct term from the list above.**

1. _____ can be passed from mother to child.

2. Body cells infected with a virus produce _____.

3. _____ produce proteins that stop pathogens from infecting cells.

4. _____ destroy body cells that are infected with a pathogen.

5. A _____ surrounds and engulfs a pathogen.

6. The body system that fights infection is called the _____.

7. The proteins made by B cells are called _____.

8. After recovering from an infection, you often have _____.

| 31.2 | The Big Picture |

9. What are some of your body's internal and external defenses against infection? _____

_____

_____

10. What kind of white blood cell can engulf a pathogen? _____

# 31.3 Immune Responses

**KEY CONCEPT** The immune system has many responses to pathogens and foreign cells.

## Many body systems work to produce nonspecific responses.

When individual cells respond to pathogens, the response is called specific. Specific responses are different for each pathogen. But the body can also respond to pathogens in other, nonspecific* ways. Nonspecific responses are the same for every pathogen. These responses include inflammation and fever.

### Inflammation

One kind of nonspecific response is **inflammation.** Inflammation is characterized by swelling, redness, pain, itching, and increased warmth. For example, if you scrape your knee, it will become inflamed. The body is trying to stop pathogens from entering through the newly broken skin.

How does inflammation begin? First a pathogen enters the body. Then two kinds of white blood cells—mast cells and basophils—begin to respond. These cells release chemicals called histamines. Histamines stimulate the cells in blood vessel walls to spread out. Then fluid can move out of the blood vessels, into the nearby tissues. White blood cells squeeze out of the capillaries, moving toward the site of the infection. There, they can fight the pathogens. Once the pathogens are destroyed, the body repairs its tissues, stopping the inflammation. (The six types of white blood cells are shown in the chart below.)

| WHITE BLOOD CELLS | |
| --- | --- |
| **NAME** | **FUNCTION** |
| Basophil | makes chemicals that cause inflammation in the bloodstream |
| Mast cell | makes chemicals that cause inflammation in other body tissues |
| Neutrophil | engulfs pathogens and foreign invaders; phagocyte |
| Macrophage | engulfs dead or damaged body cells and some bacteria; phagocyte |
| Lymphocyte | destroys infected body cells or produces proteins that inactivate pathogens |
| Eosinophil | injects poisonous packets into parasites, such as protozoa |

There are six types of white blood cells. They help the body to trigger specific and nonspecific responses to pathogens.

---

*  ACADEMIC VOCABULARY

**nonspecific**  general

## Fever

Like inflammation, fever is a general response to pathogens. It begins when mast cells or macrophages, another kind of white blood cell, release chemicals. These chemicals are carried by the blood to the hypothalamus, which controls the body's temperature. The hypothalamus signals the body to increase its internal temperature.

Why does heat help the body to fight pathogens? A low fever, around 37.7°C (100°F), stimulates body cells to produce interferons. Interferons stop viruses from reproducing. Low fevers also cause white blood cells to mature* more quickly, so that there are more mature white blood cells available to destroy pathogens. With more white blood cells, the body can recover quickly from infection.

Low fevers help the body to fight infections, but high fevers are dangerous. A fever of more than 39°C (103°F) can prevent the hypothalamus from being able to control the body's temperature. Enzymes that control chemical reactions in the body stop working. A very high fever can cause seizures, brain damage, and even death.

  Underline two ways that inflammation and fever help the body fight pathogens.

**WHITE BLOOD CELL MATURATION**

Legend: 38.5°C (101.3°F) / 37°C (98.6°F)

White blood cells mature faster when the body has a low fever (black line).

## Cells of the immune system produce specific responses.

The cells of the immune system can respond to pathogens in ways that are specific, or custom-made, for each pathogen. This response gives the body acquired immunity to the pathogen. For this to work, the body must be able to tell the difference between its own cells and pathogens. **Antigens** are protein markers on the surface of pathogens that white blood cells use to identify pathogens.

When your body fights off an infection, it produces **memory cells,** which are specialized T and B cells that "remember" an antigen. If they meet this antigen a second time, they will quickly destroy it. As a result, the pathogen will not be able to reproduce and cause illness.

There are two kinds of specific immune system responses that can cause the body to produce memory cells. The two responses are cellular immunity and humoral immunity.

* ACADEMIC VOCABULARY

**mature** to become fully developed and able to function independently

# Cellular Immunity

**Cellular immunity** is an immune response that depends on T cells. Before T cells can destroy body cells that are infected by pathogens, they must be activated. This process is shown in the figure below.

1. A phagocyte swallows a pathogen. The pathogen's antigens are removed and displayed on the phagocyte's cell membrane. The phagocyte is now called an "antigen-presenting" cell.

2. A T cell binds to this antigen-presenting cell, which releases proteins that activate the T cell.

3. The activated T cell divides into activated T cells and memory T cells. The activated T cells fights the infection. The memory T cells are kept in reserve for future infections.

4. The activated T cells bind to infected cells and cause them to burst.

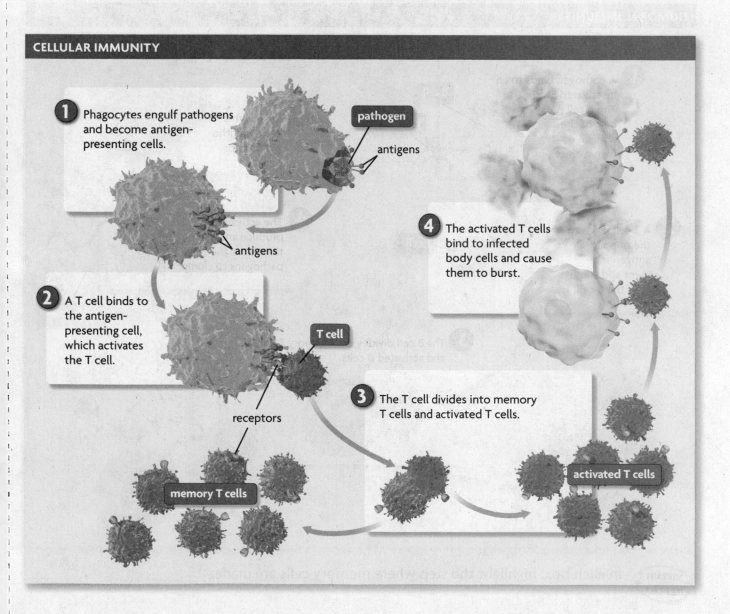

**CELLULAR IMMUNITY**

1. Phagocytes engulf pathogens and become antigen-presenting cells.

   pathogen
   antigens
   antigens

2. A T cell binds to the antigen-presenting cell, which activates the T cell.

   T cell
   receptors

3. The T cell divides into memory T cells and activated T cells.

   memory T cells
   activated T cells

4. The activated T cells bind to infected body cells and cause them to burst.

## Humoral Immunity

**Humoral immunity** is an immune response that depends on B cells and antibodies. Before B cells can fight pathogens, they must be activated by T cells, as the figure below shows.

1. A pathogen binds to a B cell. The B cell engulfs the pathogen and puts part of the antigen on its surface.

2. A T cell binds to the antigen, releasing proteins to activate the B cell.

3. The activated B cell divides into activated and memory B cells.

4. Activated B cells produce up to 2000 pathogen-specific antibodies. Different antibodies fight pathogens by causing them to burst, inactivating them, or cause them to clump, as in the example below.

5. Phagocytes engulf and destroy the pathogen clumps.

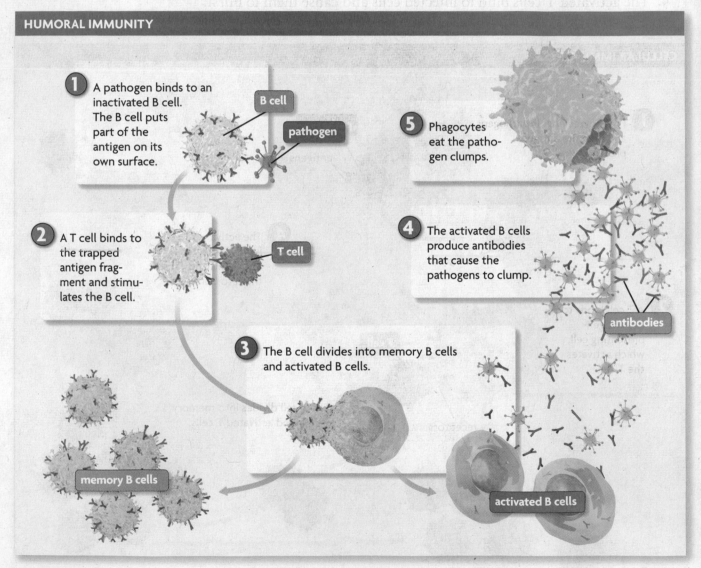

**HUMORAL IMMUNITY**

1. A pathogen binds to an inactivated B cell. The B cell puts part of the antigen on its own surface.

B cell

pathogen

5. Phagocytes eat the pathogen clumps.

2. A T cell binds to the trapped antigen fragment and stimulates the B cell.

T cell

4. The activated B cells produce antibodies that cause the pathogens to clump.

antibodies

3. The B cell divides into memory B cells and activated B cells.

memory B cells

activated B cells

 **INSTANT REPLAY**  In each box, highlight the step where memory cells are made.

# The immune system rejects foreign tissues.

If you receive an organ transplant, your body must learn to treat the new cells as if they were its own. Otherwise, your immune system will attack the new cells and destroy them, a process called **tissue rejection.** If the new organ is from a close relative, the cells are more like your own. Your body would be less likely to attack them.

To prevent tissue rejection, people who receive a new organ take drugs that make their immune systems less active. These drugs, however, also put people at risk from infections caused by viruses, bacteria, and fungi because, with a less active immune system, the body is less able to defend against pathogens.

In some cases, the body stops recognizing its own cells and attacks them as "foreign" cells. Diseases caused by these attacks are called auto-immune diseases. As yet, scientists do not know what causes the body to attack its own cells.

Why are people who receive new organs at risk for infections?

_____

## 31.3    Vocabulary Check

inflammation          cellular immunity
antigens              humoral immunity
memory cells          tissue rejection

### Mark It Up

Go back and highlight each sentence that has a vocabulary word in **bold.**

**Fill in the blanks with the correct term from the list above.**

1. _____ occurs after T cells destroy infected body cells.

2. The protein markers that help the body tell the difference between its own cells and foreign cells are called _____.

3. _____ are specialized T and B cells that provide acquired immunity by "remembering" antigens.

4. Redness, itching, and warmth are examples of _____.

## 31.3    The Big Picture

5. Why is it important for the body to recognize its own cells?

_____

6. Give an example of a nonspecific response to a pathogen.

_____

# 31.4 Immunity and Technology

**KEY CONCEPT** Living in a clean environment and building immunity help keep a person healthy.

## Many methods are used to control pathogens.

Infectious diseases are spread from one person to another. Scientists have developed many ways to kill pathogens.

### Outside the Body

Many pathogens outside the body can be killed with heat or chemicals. **Antiseptics** are chemicals, such as soap, vinegar, and rubbing alcohol, that kill pathogens. For example, rubbing alcohol weakens cell membranes, so that a pathogen's nutrients leak out and it bursts. Antiseptics are not specific, meaning they can kill a wide range of pathogens.

### Inside the Body

Inside the body, pathogens can sometimes be killed with medicines. Antibiotics are medicines that target bacteria or fungi. Unlike antiseptics, antibiotics target one type of bacteria or fungus. But because antibiotics are used so much, antibiotic-resistant bacteria have evolved. **Antibiotic resistance** occurs when bacteria that are not affected by antibiotics survive and reproduce. When this happens, scientists must find new ways to kill these bacteria that survive.

 How are antibiotics and antiseptics alike?

_____

## Vaccines artificially produce acquired immunity.

Vaccines cannot cure a person who is sick. However, they can prevent a person from getting sick. Vaccination allows a person to acquire immunity to a disease without actually becoming infected with it.

A **vaccine** is a substance that contains the antigen of a pathogen. When your immune system meets the antigen, your body undergoes a specific immune response and produces memory cells against that pathogen. The vaccine does not make you sick because the pathogen it contains is too weak to reproduce or to attack your cells.

Suppose the same type of pathogen enters your body after you have been vaccinated. Your memory cells become activated right away, as you can see in the figure. The pathogens will be destroyed before you even get sick.

What does a vaccine cause your immune system to produce?

_____

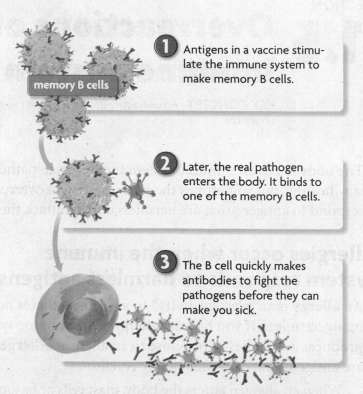

**1** Antigens in a vaccine stimulate the immune system to make memory B cells.

**2** Later, the real pathogen enters the body. It binds to one of the memory B cells.

**3** The B cell quickly makes antibodies to fight the pathogens before they can make you sick.

Vaccines help the body to respond quickly when a pathogen enters.

## 31.4 Vocabulary Check

**Mark It Up**

Go back and highlight each sentence that has a vocabulary word in **bold**.

antiseptics

antibiotic resistance

vaccine

**Choose the correct term from the list for each description.**

1. A substance that contains the antigen of a pathogen _____

2. Ability of surviving bacteria to be unaffected by antibiotics

   _____

3. Chemicals that kill pathogens outside the body _____

## 31.4 The Big Picture

4. Why can't a vaccine help a person who is already sick? _____

   _____

5. How can pathogens be killed outside or inside of your body?

   _____

   _____

# 31.5 Overreactions of the Immune System

**KEY CONCEPT** An overactive immune system can make the body very unhealthy.

The body needs an immune system that reacts to pathogens in order to stay healthy. But sometimes the immune system overreacts. It may respond to antigens that are harmless or even attack the body's own cells.

## Allergies occur when the immune system responds to harmless antigens.

An **allergy** is an oversensitivity* to an antigen that is normally harmless. If you have an allergy, your immune system produces antibodies in response to an allergen. **Allergens** are antigens that cause an allergic reaction.

When an allergen enters the body, mast cells or basophils release histamine. (Recall that mast cells and basophils are two kinds of white blood cells.) Histamine causes inflammation. Another type of white blood cell, eosinophils, also produce chemicals that cause inflammation. Allergens can be found in food, in the air, and in many chemicals.

### Food Allergens

Many foods can cause allergic reactions. The most common food allergens are milk, eggs, peanuts and tree nuts, soy, wheat, fish, and shellfish. A severe allergic reaction can cause a condition known as **anaphylaxis.** During anaphylaxis, the immune system releases so much histamine that airways tighten and blood vessels become porous.* Air cannot reach the lungs or other tissues. Blood leaks out of the circulatory system. A person experiencing anaphylaxis may die if he or she is not treated right away.

More than half of Americans have allergies to substances that are normally harmless, such as the dander in a dog's fur.

### Airborne Allergens

Some people have allergic reactions to allergens in the air they breathe. Some plants and molds release pollen and spores into the air at certain times of the year. The dander of animals and the feces of dust mites can also enter a person's body through the air he or she inhales.

---

**\* ACADEMIC VOCABULARY**

**oversensitivity** tending to react even to the smallest amount of stimulation

**porous** full of small holes

## Chemical Allergens

Many kinds of chemicals can cause allergic reactions. Some people are allergic to nickel, a metal that is used in jewelry. Others react to drugs prescribed for them by their doctors or to the venom in bee stings.

 How is an allergic response different from a normal inflammation response?

_____

_____

# In autoimmune diseases, white blood cells attack the body's healthy cells.

You read in Section 31.3 that an autoimmune disease occurs when the body attacks its own healthy cells. For example, in Type 1 diabetes, the immune system destroys cells in the pancreas. Scientists do not know why some people develop autoimmune diseases. However, they have developed treatments to help people control and live with these diseases.

 What is an autoimmune disease?

_____

_____

## 31.5    Vocabulary Check

**Mark It Up**

Go back and highlight each sentence that has a vocabulary word in **bold**.

allergy
allergen
anaphylaxis

Choose the correct term from the list for each description.

1. A condition that occurs when the immune system releases enough histamine to tighen airways _____

2. An antigen that causes an allergic reaction _____

3. An oversensitivity to a normally harmless antigen _____

## 31.5    The Big Picture

4. What cells in the body release the chemicals that cause allergic reactions? _____

5. Why are severe allergic reactions dangerous? _____

_____

_____

# 31.6 Diseases that Weaken the Immune System

**KEY CONCEPT** When the immune system is weakened, the body cannot fight off diseases.

Some fatal illnesses do not kill people directly. Instead, they prevent the body from carrying out normal functions. Diseases, such as leukemia and AIDS, make the body too weak to fight off pathogens.

## Leukemia is characterized by abnormal white blood cells.

Red blood cells, white blood cells, and platelets are made in the bone marrow, a tissue found inside bones, shown in the figure. When bone marrow is healthy, it produces new blood cells to replace the ones that die.

Cancer of the bone marrow is called **leukemia.** Unlike other cancers, it does not form tumors. Leukemia can cause the bone marrow to produce white blood cells that do not mature properly. These white blood cells cannot fight infections. Here is what usually happens:

red bone marrow

- Bone marrow produces white blood cells that cannot mature. These cells are smaller than mature ones. They also have less cytoplasm.
- The bone marrow keeps trying to produce healthy white blood cells. Instead, it makes more of the defective ones.
- Eventually, the bone marrow spends all its resources trying to make new white blood cells. It cannot make enough red blood cells and platelets to replace those that die or are damaged.

It is possible to cure leukemia with a bone marrow transplant. First, the recipient is given large doses of radiation and chemotherapy to kill the abnormal bone marrow cells. Then new marrow from another person, usually a family member, is inserted into the bones.

If a bone marrow transplant is successful, the patient will begin making healthy blood cells. However, there can be problems. Sometimes the body attacks the new tissues, making antibodies against them. Also having a weak immune system can leave the body at risk for an opportunistic infection. An **opportunistic infection** is caused by a pathogen that a healthy immune system could destroy but a weak immune system cannot.

 How does leukemia weaken the immune system?

_____

_____

# HIV targets the immune system.

HIV is the **human immunodeficiency virus.** It is a retrovirus that attacks and weakens the immune system. A retrovirus is a virus that contains RNA instead of DNA. Because HIV weakens the immune system, a person with an HIV infection is more likely to get opportunistic infections.

## HIV Transmission

Although HIV is very dangerous, it does not pass easily from one person to another. It lives only in human blood. You cannot get HIV by shaking hands with someone who is infected. But you can become infected if your blood or other body fluids mix with those of someone who has HIV. You can get it through sexual intercourse. A mother can pass it on to her baby during pregnancy. People can also get HIV by sharing needles used for drugs or for body piercing and tattooing. For this reason, doctors and nurses use a new needle for every patient when they give shots or take blood.

This illustration of an HIV virus is about 500,000 times its actual size. The bumps are its antigens.

## HIV Reproduces in T-cells

HIV does not infect all blood cells. It infects only T cells, the white blood cells that trigger the body's immune system's specific responses to invading pathogens. When HIV enters a T cell, the T cell stops working properly. Instead, HIV uses it to produce more HIV viruses.

Once infected, a T cell can produce thousands of HIV viruses before it dies. The body cannot make new T cells fast enough to replace those that HIV has killed. The immune system gets weaker, and opportunistic infections begin to take over the body. This may not happen right away. Some individuals have HIV infections for 10 or more years before they notice any symptoms. But eventually, the body will develop opportunistic infections and AIDS.

## HIV Leads to AIDS

**Acquired immune deficiency syndrome (AIDS)** is the final stage of a HIV infection. Having AIDS means that a person has a worn-out immune system. A person with AIDS may have many opportunistic infections: fungal infections, tuberculosis, pneumonia, viral infections, and cancers.

HIV targets and eventually destroys T cells, weakening the body's immune system.

AIDS always causes death because the body is too weak to fight off its infections. It is possible to treat an HIV infection and to reduce or delay its symptoms. But at present, there is no cure for AIDS.

**Why do people die of AIDS?**

_____

_____

## 31.6 Vocabulary Check

**Mark It Up**

Go back and highlight each sentence that has a vocabulary word in **bold**.

leukemia

opportunistic infection

human immunodeficiency virus (HIV)

acquired immune deficiency syndrome (AIDS)

**Fill in the blanks with the correct term from the list above.**

1. An infection that the immune system would normally be able to fight off is called an _____.

2. _____ is a retrovirus that attacks and weakens the immune system.

3. _____ is the final stage of the decline caused by HIV.

4. Cancer of the bone marrow is called _____.

## 31.6 The Big Picture

5. How can leukemia be cured?

_____

_____

6. Why is it so difficult for the immune system to fight an HIV infection?

_____

_____

_____

# Chapter 31 Review

1. Who first proposed the germ theory of disease? _____

2. Name three kinds of pathogens. _____
   _____

3. What body system fights off infection? _____

4. What kind of white blood cell destroys pathogens by engulfing them?
   **a.** phagocytes
   **b.** lymphocytes
   **c.** T cells
   **d.** B cells

5. What is an antibody, and what does it do? _____
   _____
   _____

6. Choose the word that completes the following sentence:
   _____ immunity can be passed from mother to child
   during breastfeeding.
   **a.** Acquired
   **b.** Active
   **c.** Passive
   **d.** Opportunistic

7. Why do scraped knees and insect bites become red and painful
   or itchy? _____
   _____

8. How can antiseptics keep you from getting sick? _____
   _____

9. What is an allergy? _____
   _____

10. Name one risk that leukemia patients face after a bone marrow
    transplant. _____
    _____
    _____

# 32 Digestive and Excretory Systems

## GETTING READY TO LEARN

### Preview Key Concepts

**32.1 Nutrients and Homeostasis**
Cells require many different nutrients.

**32.2 Digestive System**
The digestive system breaks down food into simpler molecules.

**32.3 Absorption of Nutrients**
Nutrients are absorbed and solid wastes eliminated after digestion.

**32.4 Excretory System**
The excretory system removes wastes and helps to maintain homeostasis.

## Review Academic Vocabulary

Write the correct word for each definition.

inflammation    allergy    pathogen    immune system    tissue rejection

1. _____ : antibodies attacking a donated organ

2. _____ : fights off infection and pathogens

3. _____ : oversensitivity to a harmless antigen

4. _____ : swelling, redness, itching, increased warmth

5. _____ : disease-causing agent

## Preview Biology Vocabulary

To see how many key terms you already know from this chapter, choose the word that makes sense in each sentence.

kidney    absorption    mineral    stomach    esophagus

1. Food travels from the mouth down the _____.

2. The main organ for cleaning and filtering the blood is the _____.

3. _____ is the movement of nutrients from the digestive system into the blood.

4. The _____ is an organ that holds food.

5. Calcium is a _____ that makes bones strong.

# 32.1 Nutrients and Homeostasis

**KEY CONCEPT** Cells require many different nutrients.

## Six types of nutrients help to maintain homeostasis.

To maintain homeostasis in your body, you must consume* six kinds of nutrients almost every day. If any of these nutrients is missing for too long, your body's cells will stop working properly. Over time, your organs will not work well either.

**Water** Your body is more than half water. Almost every chemical reaction in your body uses water. Water also helps you to digest food and excrete wastes, makes up much of the volume of your blood, helps to control your body's temperature, and keeps your skin from drying out. You need at least 2 liters (8 cups) every day, to replace the water you lose in sweat, urine, and respiration.

**Carbohydrates** Your body gets energy from carbohydrates. Simple carbohydrates are those found in sugar and fruit. Complex carbohydrates are starches found in vegetables, grains, and potatoes. These foods also contain fiber. Fiber cannot be digested, but it helps to move food through your digestive system.

**Proteins** Your body uses proteins to grow and repair cells and tissues. The enzymes and hormones used in cell metabolism are also made of protein. Proteins are made of chains of amino acids. Your body can make about 12 of the 20 amino acids it needs. The other eight are called essential amino acids, and they must come from the food you eat.

**Fats** Fats are made of long strings of fatty acids. They give your body energy and are important in many cell functions. There are two kinds of fats: saturated and unsaturated. Saturated fats are solid at room temperature and come from animal products. Unsaturated fats are usually liquid at room temperature. They are found in plant oils, such as olive oil, and in some fish, such as cod and salmon. Unsaturated fats are better for your health than are saturated fats.

Meat and eggs contain all eight essential amino acids. Plant foods must be combined to provide all essential amino acids.

* ACADEMIC VOCABULARY

**consume** eat or drink

To fuel this growth, your body needs more nutrients and more Calories. A calorie, with a lower case c, is the amount of energy needed to make one gram of water warmer by one degree Celsius. One **Calorie** (with an upper case C) of food equals that same amount of energy, multiplied by 1000. It is the same as a kilocalorie.

 Why is it so important to eat a well-balanced diet during the teenage years?

_____

_____

## 32.1    Vocabulary Check

**Mark It Up**

Go back and highlight each sentence that has a vocabulary word in **bold**.

mineral
vitamin
Calorie

**Fill in the blanks with the correct term from the list above.**

1. A _____ is a measure of the energy contained in food.

2. A _____ works with enzymes to control the functions, growth, and development of cells.

3. An inorganic material the body uses to carry out cellular processes and to build or repair tissues is called a _____.

## 32.1    The Big Picture

4. Why should protein be included in your diet every day?

_____

5. What nutrient makes up more than half of your body? _____

6. What type of nutrient is your main source of energy? _____

7. What are the different types of fat found in foods? _____

_____

SECTION

# 32.2 Digestive System

**KEY CONCEPT** The digestive system breaks down food into simpler molecules.

## Several digestive organs work together to break down food.

**Digestion** is the process by which your body breaks down the large molecules in your food into simpler molecules that it can use. The **digestive system** is the organ system that breaks food down into energy that can be used by cells.

The organs of the digestive system include the mouth, esophagus, stomach, pancreas, liver, gallbladder, large and small intestines, rectum, and anus. Each section is separated by a ring of muscle, called a **sphincter.** These rings of muscles open and close to allow food to pass through. The smooth muscles in the walls of digestive organs contract* and relax to keep food moving in only one direction.

Some organs, such as the mouth, stomach, and small intestine, secrete different substances to help break food apart. Salivary glands in the mouth secrete an enzyme that breaks down starches. Stomach acid includes enzymes that break down proteins. Once food is completely digested, nutrients move into the circulatory and lymphatic systems and are carried to all cells. Undigested material leaves the body as liquid and solid wastes. The process takes about 24 to 33 hours.

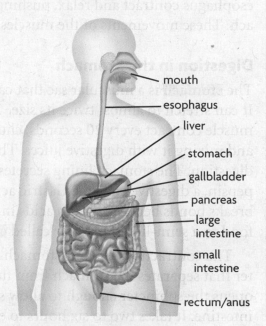

mouth
esophagus
liver
stomach
gallbladder
pancreas
large intestine
small intestine
rectum/anus

The organs of the digestive system are like an assembly line in a factory that takes food apart, rather than putting it together.

**INSTANT REPLAY** What keeps food moving in only one direction through the digestive system?

## Digestion begins in the mouth and continues in the stomach.

### Digestion in the Mouth

Digestion begins when you take a bite of food. Your teeth provide mechanical* digestion as you chew your food, shredding it into small pieces. Chemical digestion also occurs in the mouth. Your salivary glands

---

**\* ACADEMIC VOCABULARY**

**contract**  to pull together or shorten
**mechanical**  something that works through physical forces and not chemical ones

make saliva, which contains an enzyme called amylase. Amylase breaks complex starch molecules into simple sugars.

When you swallow your food, it moves into your **esophagus,** a tube that connects the mouth and stomach. The muscles in the walls of the esophagus contract and relax, pushing the food down toward the stomach. These movements of the muscles are called **peristalsis.**

### Digestion in the Stomach

The **stomach** is a muscular sac that can hold about 2 liters (2 qt) of food. It can stretch to almost twice its size. The stomach's three layers of muscle contract every 20 seconds, churning the food into small pieces and mixing it with digestive juices. This action is also part of mechanical digestion. The stomach lining secretes hydrochloric acid (HCl) and pepsin, a digestive enzyme. Gastric acid kills bacteria, while pepsin breaks bonds between amino acids in proteins. Together, they reduce food to a semi-liquid mixture called **chyme.**

The contractions of your stomach push chyme up against the sphincter that separates the stomach from the small intestine. Each contraction opens the sphincter enough to allow some chyme to squirt into the small intestine. It takes two to six hours to empty the stomach after a meal.

 How does peristalsis help you to digest your food?

_____

_____

## Digestion is completed in part of the small intestine.

Most digestion takes place in the **small intestine,** a long, narrow tube that is attached at one end to the stomach. There, muscle contractions continue to churn the food, and chemical digestion breaks complex molecules into simpler molecules.

The section of small intestine closest to the stomach is called the duodenum. The duodenum finishes the process of digestion, with help from the pancreas, liver, and gallbladder. The pancreas makes an alkaline fluid to neutralize the pepsin that comes with chyme from the stomach. The pancreas also releases enzymes that help break down fats. The liver makes **bile,** a substance that also breaks down fats.

Fluids from the pancreas, liver, and gallbladder flow through ducts into the duodenum.

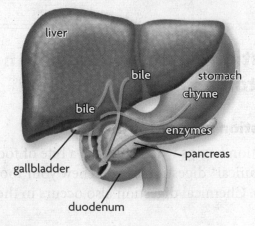

liver

bile

stomach

chyme

bile

enzymes

pancreas

gallbladder

duodenum

The gallbladder stores the bile, releasing it into the duodenum. By the time chyme passes through the duodenum, it has been broken into simple molecules that the body can use.

 What organs help to complete digestion in the small intestine?

_____

## 32.2   Vocabulary Check

**Mark It Up**

Go back and highlight each sentence that has a vocabulary word in **bold**.

| | |
|---|---|
| digestion | stomach |
| digestive system | chyme |
| sphincter | small intestine |
| esophagus | bile |
| peristalsis | |

**Fill in the blanks with the correct term from the list above.**

1. Food moves from the stomach into the _____.

2. _____ is a chemical substance produced by the liver.

3. _____ describes the contractions of smooth muscle that keep food moving.

4. The _____ connects the mouth and stomach.

5. Organs that break down food into energy form the _____.

6. _____ is the process of breaking large food molecules down into simpler molecules.

7. In the stomach, solid food becomes a semi-liquid mixture called _____.

8. The _____ can stretch to twice its original size.

9. A _____ separates each digestive organ from the next.

## 32.2   The Big Picture

10. Where does digestion begin? _____

11. Where is digestion completed? _____

# 32.3 Absorption of Nutrients

**KEY CONCEPT** Nutrients are absorbed and solid wastes eliminated after digestion.

## Most absorption of nutrients occurs in the small intestine.

Breaking food apart is only the first part of digestion. Once food is digested, the body must absorb* its nutrients. **Absorption** is the process by which the nutrients in your food move from the digestive organs into the circulatory and lymphatic systems. The small intestine has three structures that help your body absorb nutrients from chyme: the lining, the villi, and the micovilli.

### Specialized Structures for Absorption

The small intestine is lined with ridges and folds. These folds increase the surface area of the small intestine, and slow chyme down as it passes through. If chyme passes through the small intestine more slowly, then more nutrients can be absorbed. The folds in the intestine's lining are covered with **villi,** small finger-like structures. The villi are covered with epithelial cells that absorb nutrients. Every epithelial cell is covered with thousands of **microvilli,** or tiny villi no larger than the period at the end of this sentence.

Each of the villi is covered with thousands of microvilli.

### Absorption of Different Nutrients

The small intestine is about 6 meters (about 20 feet) long. It has three different sections, and each section absorbs different nutrients.

**Duodenum** Most simple sugars, amino acids, and minerals are absorbed in the duodenum. These nutrients diffuse into the circulatory system and are carried to the liver.

**Jejunum** Glucose, some amino acids, vitamin C, most B vitamins, and some water are absorbed in the jejenum. These nutrients also diffuse into the circulatory system and are carried to cells all over the body.

**Ileum** Fat-soluble vitamins, vitamin B12, fatty acids, cholesterol, and some water are absorbed in the ileum. These nutrients diffuse into lymph and blood vessels and are distributed to cells all over the body.

---

**\* ACADEMIC VOCABULARY**

**absorb** to soak up

### Absorbed Nutrients and the Liver

Blood that is rich in nutrients leaves the small intestine and enters the liver. There, enzymes use these simple molecules to build more complex molecules that cells need. The liver also stores some nutrients, such as glucose, for future use.

 How can the small intestine absorb so many nutrients from chyme?

_____

_____

## Water is absorbed and solid wastes are eliminated from the large intestine.

The large intestine, or colon, is about 1.5 meters (5 ft) long and wider than the small intestine. Every day, the large intestine absorbs about 1 liter of water, along with some salts. The remaining material forms a solid mass, called feces. Feces are made of undigested plant fiber, dead bacteria, and bits of undigested fat and protein. Feces are stored in the rectum, a tube connecting the large intestine to the anus. About 24 to 33 hours after you eat a meal, feces pass through the anus and leave the body.

 Circle a nutrient that is absorbed in the large intestine.

### 32.3 Vocabulary Check

**Mark It Up**

Go back and highlight each sentence that has a vocabulary word in **bold**.

absorption        microvilli
villi

Choose the correct term from the list for each description.

1. Tiny fingerlike projections on epithelial cells in the small intestine

   _____

2. The process by which nutrients move from the digestive system into the circulatory and lymphatic systems _____

3. Projections that extend out of the folds of the small intestine and are covered with epithelial cells _____

### 32.3 The Big Picture

4. Where does the body absorb most nutrients? _____

5. Which digestive organs absorb water? _____

# 32.4 Excretory System

**KEY CONCEPT** The excretory system removes wastes and helps maintain homeostasis.

## The excretory system eliminates nonsolid wastes from the body.

The skin, lungs, kidneys, ureters, urinary bladder, and urethra make up the **excretory system.** This system eliminates* nonsolid wastes from the body in sweat, urine, and exhaled breath. Wastes can include toxins, water, salts, $CO_2$, urea, minerals, and vitamins. Urea is a waste product made when proteins break down.

By eliminating wastes, the excretory system helps the body maintain homeostasis.

- The lungs remove extra $CO_2$ and some water vapor from the body, releasing them with each breath that you exhale. Releasing extra $CO_2$ helps to maintain the proper balance of $O_2$ and $CO_2$ in your blood.

- Sweat glands in the skin release extra water and salts. Sweat also cools the body.

- The **kidneys** filter and clean the blood and produce urine. Urine moves through the **ureter,** a tube connecting each kidney to the bladder. The bladder is also called the **urinary bladder.** It is shaped like a sac and can hold up to half a liter (more than 2 cups) of urine at a time. The urine is released from the body through the urethra.

Look at the drawing of the excretory system. Which organs are involved in producing and releasing urine?

## The kidneys help to maintain homeostasis by filtering the blood.

One quarter of your blood passes through your kidneys every minute. Your kidneys filter and clean the blood and make sure that it is chemically balanced.

**\* ACADEMIC VOCABULARY**

**eliminate** to remove or get rid of

## Structure of the Kidneys

The kidneys are located in the lower back—one on the left and one on the right. Most people have two kidneys, but it is possible to live with one.

The inside layer of a kidney is called the medulla. The outside layer is called the cortex. The cortex is packed with nephrons, which also extend into the medulla. A **nephron** is the filtering unit in the kidneys. Each kidney contains about one million nephrons.

## Kidneys and Homeostasis

The kidneys help maintain homeostasis in three ways:

- They remove waste products from the blood.
- They help maintain the balance of electrolytes, pH, and fluid in the body.
- They release hormones that help keep the bones healthy, produce red blood cells, and regulate blood pressure.

If the kidneys stop working properly, waste products build up in the blood. The homeostasis of organ systems is disrupted, and some organs may fail.

 Highlight the three ways that the kidneys help to maintain homeostasis.

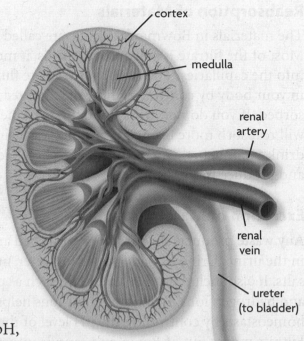

The kidneys filter, clean, and chemically balance your blood.

# Nephrons clean the blood and produce urine.

Nephrons clean the blood and produce urine in three steps: filtration, reabsorption, and excretion.

## Filtration

Each nephron is attached to an arteriole, a venule, and a ball of capillaries called the **glomerulus.** Each glomerulus is tucked into a cup-shaped structure called Bowman's capsule. Blood flows into the arterioles and moves into each nephron's glomerulus. There, blood pressure pushes water, amino acids, salts, glucose, electrolytes, and urea out of the capillaries into Bowman's capsule. Blood cells, plasma proteins, and platelets are too big to move out of the capillaries, so they stay in the blood.

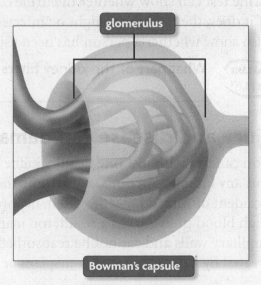

The glomerulus acts as a filter for your blood. Only small molecules move out of the capillaries to form the filtrate.

## Reabsorption of Materials

The materials in Bowman's capsule are called the filtrate. Most of the filtrate is reabsorbed, that is, it moves back into the capillaries. The nephrons regulate fluid balance in your body by controlling how much water is reabsorbed. If you do not drink enough water, the nephrons will reabsorb more fluid and produce less urine. If you drink too much, the nephrons will reabsorb less fluid and produce more urine.

## Excretion of Materials

Any waste products that are not reabsorbed are excreted in the urine. Urine is made mostly of water, urea, and salts. It also includes other materials, such as potassium and hydrogen ions. Removing these ions helps maintain homeostasis by controlling the pH level of the blood. Filtrate moves out of Bowman's capsule into a structure called the loop of Henle. There, more water is reabsorbed.

Next, the urine moves into the collecting ducts. It then flows into the ureter and collects in the urinary bladder. When the bladder empties, urine flows out of the body through the urethra. In a healthy person, urine is pale yellow. It contains 95% water and 5% waste products.

## Urine Testing

Doctors sometimes ask for a urine sample during a routine checkup. A urine test can show whether the urine contains sugar, protein, or blood. If it does, the nephrons might be infected or injured. A urine test can also show whether a person has been using drugs.

 What part of the kidney filters blood?

NEPHRON

from body

Filtration

Reabsorbtion

to body

collecting duct

from other nephrons

loop of Henle

Excretion

# Injury and disease can damage kidney function.

You can live with just one healthy kidney, but you cannot survive without any kidney functions. Sometimes the kidneys are injured by an accident or infection. More often, nephrons are damaged by diabetes or high blood pressure. As a result, too many molecules pass through the capillary walls and cannot be reabsorbed. Serious kidney diseases can be treated by having a kidney transplant or by receiving dialysis.

## Kidney Transplant

A person who has two healthy kidneys can donate one. The person receiving the kidney should be a close relative, such as a sibling, parent, or child. The tissues of relatives are enough alike that the patient's body might not reject the new kidney. However, the patient still has to take drugs to stop the immune system from attacking the new organ. With a weakened immune system, the patient is at risk for getting other infections.

## Kidney Dialysis

Dialysis can save a person's life when a kidney transplant is not possible. **Dialysis** is a mechanical process that cleans and filters a person's blood. It must be done three times a week and takes 3 to 5 hours per session. Some people do not use a machine for dialysis. They have peritoneal dialysis instead. Blood is pumped through tubes into the abdomen, where the abdominal lining can act as a filter.

 How can doctors treat a patient whose kidneys fail?

_____

| 32.4 Vocabulary Check | Mark It Up |
| --- | --- |

Go back and highlight each sentence that has a vocabulary word in **bold.**

excretory system    nephron

kidney    glomerulus

ureter    dialysis

urinary bladder

**Choose the correct term from the list for each description.**

1. A ball of capillaries in a kidney _____

2. The body system that eliminates nonsolid wastes _____

3. A filtering unit in a kidney _____

4. A tube that carries urine from the kidney to the bladder _____

5. A saclike organ that stores urine before it is released _____

## 32.4   The Big Picture

6. What part of the kidney produces urine? _____

7. Why can't people live without kidneys? _____

_____

_____

# Chapter 32 Review

1. What six types of nutrients help to maintain homeostasis in the body?

   _____

2. What unit is used to measure the amount of energy in food? _____

3. Label the parts of the digestive system in the drawing at right.

   a. _____

   b. _____

   c. _____

   d. _____

   e. _____

   f. _____

   g. _____

4. Give an example of mechanical and chemical digestion.

   _____

   _____

5. What is peristalsis? _____

   _____

6. Nutrients are absorbed in the _____.
   a. stomach
   b. small intestine
   c. large intestine
   d. kidneys

7. What do the villi and microvilli do? _____

8. What organ eliminates solid waste? _____

9. What do the kidneys do? _____

   _____

10. Why might a doctor want to test a person's urine during a checkup?

    _____

    _____

# CHAPTER

# 33 Protection, Support, and Movement

## GETTING READY TO LEARN

### Preview Key Concepts

**33.1 Skeletal System**
The skeletal system includes bones and tissues that are important for supporting, protecting, and moving your body.

**33.2 Muscular System**
Muscles are tissues that can contract, enabling movement.

**33.3 Integumentary System**
The integumentary system has many tissues that protect the body.

### Review Academic Vocabulary

Write the correct word for each definition.

mineral     absorption     nephron     excretory system     small intestine

1. _____ : place where most digestion occurs

2. _____ : filtering unit in the kidney

3. _____ : network that eliminates nonsolid wastes

4. _____ : inorganic nutrient

5. _____ : moving nutrients from digestive system to blood

### Preview Biology Vocabulary

See how many key terms from this chapter you already know. Rewrite each phrase, using a different word or words for the **words in bold**.

| PHRASE | REWRITTEN WITH DIFFERENT WORDS |
|---|---|
| 1. **Cartilage** connects the rib bones so they can move more easily. | The rib bones are connected by _____ _____ |
| 2. Fingernails and hair are made up of **keratin**. | Fingernails and hair are made up of _____ _____ |
| 3. The first layer of protection for the body is the **epidermis**. | The first layer of protection for the body is _____ _____ |

549

# 33.1 Skeletal System

**KEY CONCEPT** The skeletal system includes bones and tissues that are important for supporting, protecting, and moving your body.

When you jog, your body absorbs a force of more than twice your body weight. When you jump, you land with about 12 times your body weight. Your bones and muscles must be strong enough to handle these forces along with the everyday stresses your body experiences.

## Your skeletal system is made up of the appendicular and axial skeletons.

The **skeletal system** is the organ system that supports your body. It protects your internal organs and allows the body to keep its shape. The skeletal system includes the bones and the connective tissues that hold the bones together. The human skeleton has 206 bones.

### Appendicular Skeleton

The **appendicular skeleton** is the part of your skeleton that can move easily. It includes all the bones that extend* out from the trunk of your body—your arms, legs, feet, and hands.

The appendicular skeleton also includes two sets of bones, called girdles, that connect your arms and legs to your body. The girdles allow your arms and legs to have a wide range of motion,* such as throwing or kicking a ball, and moving sideways.

### Axial Skeleton

The bones in the body's trunk and head make up the **axial skeleton.** These bones move less but support the body's weight and protect internal tissues. The bones of the skull protect the brain. The ribs and breastbone protect the heart and lungs. The bony **vertebrae** surround and protect the spinal cord.

The axial skeleton does allow some movement. The ribs are connected by flexible tissue that enables the chest to expand when you breathe in. Flexible tissue in the spine gives people the ability to bend, turn, and look behind them.

The skeletal system is made up of an appendicular skeleton (light blue) and an axial skeleton (dark blue).

---

**\* ACADEMIC VOCABULARY**

**extend**  reach out

**range of motion**  how much you can move a part of your body

## Cartilage

The bones in your body are connected to each other, but they cannot be connected bone-to-bone. Such hard materials would not allow you to move. Instead, bones are connected to each other with **cartilage,** a flexible connective tissue. Cartilage is found between your bones. It allows for smooth movement and prevents bones from rubbing against each other, which would wear down or damage their surfaces.

 Name one part of your body that is part of the appendicular skeleton. Name another part that is part of the axial skeleton.

# Bones connect to form joints.

The place where two bones meet is called a **joint.** Some joints give bones a full range of movement while others allow little or no movement.

**No movement.** Joints that allow no movement are called fibrous joints. They are made of the same dense material as your bones. For example, fibrous joints hold your teeth in place and hold the plates of your skull together to protect the brain.

**Some movement** Joints that allow some movement are called cartilaginous joints. These joints are held together by cartilage. The vertebrae in your spine are separated by discs of cartilage, giving the spine some flexibility. For example, you can bend to the side, forward, and backward.

**Full range of movement** Other joints, called synovial joints, allow a full range of movement. These joints are cushioned with cartilage but held together with ligaments. A **ligament** is a long, flexible band of connective tissue. It holds bones together but is loose enough to allow bones to move. There are several different types of synovial joints:

 **Gliding joints** allow flat bone surfaces to slide across each other. The ankle and wrist contain gliding joints.

 **Pivot joints** allow two bones to rotate against each other. The skull's top two vertebrae form a pivot joint, allowing the head to turn from left to right.

 **Ball and socket joints** include a ball-shaped end of a bone, and a cup. The ball can move and rotate inside the cup. The hips and shoulders contain ball and socket joints.

 **Saddle joints** allow a bone to move front to back and left to right. One bone rides inside the other, as if the second bone were a saddle. Your thumbs are connected to your hands with saddle joints.

**VISUAL VOCAB**

A **ligament** is a long band of connective tissue that connects two bones across a joint.

ligament

**Hinge joints** allow bones to move in one direction, like a swinging door. The knees, fingers, and toes contain hinge joints.

Some bones are connected with more than one type of synovial joint. These are called compound joints. In your elbow, for example, a hinge joint connects your forearm to your upper arm. Your elbow also has a pivot joint that allows you to turn your hand upward or downward.

 Find one of each kind of joint on your own body. Explore the range of motion that you have for each joint.

## Bones are living tissue.

Bones may seem hard and unchanging, but they are actually living tissue. They produce blood cells and store minerals. Each bone is coated with a layer of connective tissue called periosteum. This tissue holds and protects blood vessels. Like the body's other tissues, bones rely on blood vessels to bring nutrients and carry away wastes.

### Bone Structure

There are two types of bone tissue: compact and spongy. Compact bone is the outer layer of a bone and protects the body against jolts and bumps. It is made up of rings of calcium-rich tissue.

Spongy bone is porous, like a sponge. It is located at the center of the bone. Spongy bone is surrounded by hard, dense, compact bone. A young person's spongy bone is mostly red bone marrow. Red bone marrow, which is part of the circulatory system, produces red blood cells. As a person grows, some red bone marrow is replaced by yellow bone marrow, which is mostly fat. It can change back into red bone marrow to produce blood cells if the body suddenly loses blood.

compact bone

periosteum

yellow bone marrow

spongy bone, contains red bone marrow

Bones have many layers for protection and support.

### Bone Growth

At first, human embryos have a skeleton made only of flexible cartilage. As they develop, the cartilage becomes hard bone.

Bones cannot form without the help of cells called osteoblasts. These cells release collagen, a strong connective tissue that forms fibers. They also release calcium phosphate, a mineral that hardens the collagen. The collagen combines with calcium phosphate to form bone. This process is called **calcification**. Once calcification occurs, the osteoblast is trapped in the bone. It is then called an osteocyte.

Bones grow from their ends, where the cartilage is located. Children's bones grow longer, wider, and thicker until puberty. During the teenage years, sex hormones stimulate bones to become more dense. Bones are strongest when a person is between 18 and 30 years old. After age 30, calcium is taken from the bones and used in the rest of the body. As a result, the bones become less dense. But even after you stop growing, the osteoblasts in your bone can still create new tissue to heal broken bones.

Bones store calcium for the body to use. The process of moving calcium into and out of the bones is controlled by hormones and helps to maintain chemical homeostasis in your body. The thyroid gland releases a hormone that stimulates osteoblasts to take calcium out of the blood and put it into bone tissue. The parathyroid gland releases a hormone that stimulates other bone cells to take calcium out of bone tissue so the body can use it.

What materials are needed for calcification?

_____

## 33.1    Vocabulary Check

| | |
|---|---|
| skeletal system | cartilage |
| appendicular skeleton | joint |
| axial skeleton | ligament |
| vertebrae | calcification |

### Mark It Up

Go back and highlight each sentence that has a vocabulary word in **bold**.

**Choose the correct term from the list for each description.**

1. A flexible band of tissue that connects bones across a joint _____

2. The bones that surround the spinal cord _____

3. The place where two bones meet _____

4. The organ system that includes the bones _____

5. Making hard bone by combining collagen and calcium _____

6. The bones found in the trunk and head _____

7. Bones found in the arms, legs, hands, and feet _____

8. Flexible connective tissue found between bones _____

## 33.1    The Big Picture

9. Why is cartilage such an important part of the skeletal system?

_____

10. Name one way spongy bone differs from compact bone. _____

_____

# 33.2 Muscular System

**KEY CONCEPT** Muscles are tissues that can contract, enabling movement.

## Humans have three types of muscle.

The **muscular system** is the body system that makes movement possible. It moves bones at joints and moves blood, food, and fluids throughout the body. Muscle contractions also help to generate* heat. Muscles are made up of long fibers. **Muscle fibers** are muscle cells that contract, or shorten, when the nervous system stimulates them. There are three types of muscle tissue: skeletal, smooth, and cardiac.

### Skeletal Muscle

A **skeletal muscle** is a muscle attached to the skeleton by tendons. A **tendon** is a connective tissue that attaches muscle to muscle or muscle to bone. Tendons help muscles move the skeleton.

**Voluntary and involuntary control** Most skeletal muscles are under your voluntary control. That is, you can choose to contract them. A few are involuntary, or move without you having to think about moving them. For example, muscles in your spine and legs move involuntarily, adjusting your weight, to help you keep your balance.

**Fast- and slow-twitch fibers** There are two kinds of fibers in skeletal muscle: fast-twitch and slow-twitch fibers. Fast-twitch fibers respond quickly to nerve impulses and make sudden movements. Slow-twitch fibers respond slowly and make longer-lasting movements. Your leg contains both kinds of fibers. When you walk slowly, the slow-twitch fibers contract over several seconds. You use fast-twitch fibers when you sprint.

The body's muscles do more than move body parts. They also move blood, food, and fluids throughout the body.

### Smooth Muscle

**Smooth muscle** helps to control the movement of blood, food, and fluids throughout the body. It can be found in many body systems. For example, smooth muscles contract to push food through the digestive system and regulate the width of blood vessels in the circulatory system.

The movements of smooth muscles are involuntary—controlled by hormones and nerve impulses. Smooth muscles contract more slowly than skeletal muscles do and can hold their contractions longer.

### Cardiac Muscle

**Cardiac muscle** is found only in the heart. Cardiac muscles use large amounts of energy (ATP) and have more mitochondria than do skeletal

**\* ACADEMIC VOCABULARY**

**generate** cause or bring about

muscles. Like smooth muscles, cardiac muscles are under involuntary control. A collection of cells, called the pacemaker, sends impulses to the heart, causing it to contract.

**Name two ways in which cardiac and smooth muscles differ from skeletal muscle.**

_____

_____

# Muscles contract when the muscle system causes muscle filaments to move.

When you play tug-of-war, your team must hold onto a rope and pull the other team toward you. Each player grabs onto the rope and pulls. When your muscles contract, their long, thin strands, or filaments, work like a team during a game of tug-of-war. Some filaments pull at other filaments, which are like the ropes connecting the teams. The smallest "players" in a muscle are myofibrils and sarcomeres.

## Muscle Structure

**Myofibrils** are long strands of protein found within a muscle fiber. Each myofibril contains a set of filaments that are arranged in a regular pattern. These filaments cause muscles to contract. A **sarcomere** is a section of a myofibril that contains all the filaments needed to make that section of muscle contract.

Sarcomeres contain two kinds of filaments. **Actin** filaments are thin protein fibers. They are attached to the ends of the sarcomere, so pulling them causes muscles to contract. They are like the rope in the tug-of-war game. **Myosin** filaments are protein fibers that pull actin. They are like the players pulling the rope. Each myosin filament is attached to the center of the sarcomere, so it can pull the actin without moving itself.

## Muscle Contraction

When a muscle is relaxed, actin and myosin filaments are not connected to each other. Actin filaments have binding sites, like knots on the tug-of-war rope. Myosin filaments have extensions that act like little hands. When the nervous system stimulates a muscle to contract, myosin filaments reach out and grab actin filaments, pulling them in.

Filaments in muscle cells cause the muscle to contract.

muscle fiber

myofibril

sarcomere

muscle

When the nervous system stops stimulating the muscle, myosin and actin filaments separate. The muscle relaxes again.

How can myosin grab actin? First a neuron releases neurotransmitters that bind to receptors on a muscle fiber. The neurotransmitters stimulate calcium ion ($Ca^{2+}$) channels to open. $Ca^{2+}$ ions rush into the sarcomere, and expose binding sites on the actin filament. Myosin can then grab onto the binding site and pull the actin.

When myosin has moved actin as far as it can, it uses ATP to break its bond with actin. Then it reaches farther down the actin filament, grabs it again, and pulls it in a hand-over-hand type of motion. When the nervous system stops stimulating the muscle, the $Ca^{2+}$ channels close. As a result, the binding sites on the actin are covered again.

  What two filaments cause muscles to contract?

_____

## FILAMENT ACTION

actin    $Ca^{2+}$

myosin

The nervous system causes $Ca^{2+}$ ions to diffuse toward and bind to actin.

regulatory protein

$Ca^{2+}$ ions loosen regulatory proteins. Now, myosin can grab and pull actin.

Actin and myosin work together to contract a muscle.

---

## 33.2 Vocabulary Check

| | |
|---|---|
| muscular system | cardiac muscle |
| muscle fiber | myofibril |
| skeletal muscle | sarcomere |
| tendon | actin |
| smooth muscle | myosin |

**Mark It Up**

Go back and highlight each sentence that has a vocabulary word in **bold**.

**Mark the correct term and fill in the blanks with the correct term from the list above.**

1. Put a box around the tissue that connects muscle to bone or muscles.

2. Underline the word that means long strands of protein divided into sarcomeres.

3. A muscle under voluntary control _____

4. A filament that grabs another filament to contact a muscle

   _____

## 33.2 The Big Picture

5. What is a sarcomere? _____

   _____

6. How do Ca+ channels help in muscle contraction? _____

   _____

# 33.3 Integumentary System

**KEY CONCEPT** The integumentary system has many tissues that protect the body.

## The integumentary system helps maintain homeostasis.

The **integumentary system** includes your skin, hair, nails, oil glands, and sweat glands. This body system surrounds and protects all other organ systems and helps to maintain homeostasis.

How does your skin protect your body? Oil glands release acidic oils that stop fungi and bacteria from infecting the skin. Your fingernails, toenails, and hair are made of **keratin,** a tough, waterproof protein. Nails help protect sensitive fingertips and toes. Hair insulates your head, keeping you warm. Your integumentary system removes water, salts, and urea from the blood through your sweat glands. These glands also help to cool the body when its internal temperature rises too high.

 Highlight the ways that your integumentary system helps to protect you.

## The integumentary system consists of many different tissues.

All the tissues in your integumentary system are located in your skin. Your skin is your body's largest organ. It has three layers: the epidermis, the dermis, and the subcutaneous fat.

### Epidermis

The outer layer of the skin is the **epidermis.** It contains pores, or openings, that can release sweat, salt, and oils. The surface of the epidermis is mostly dead skin cells that flake off. Below the surface are new, living cells that are constantly dividing. The new cells push up to the surface over two to four weeks, replacing the old dead cells.

Cells in the epidermis also contain proteins that protect the skin, such as keratin and melatonin. Almost every type of cell in the epidermis makes keratin. Keratin can cause the skin to thicken to form a callus, such as where a foot rubs against the inside of a shoe. Melanin, however, is produced only by specialized cells called melanocytes.

Skin has three layers that contain organs to protect you, to maintain homeostasis, and to sense the world around you.

epidermis

dermis

fat layer

hair follicle

oil gland

pressure receptors

sweat gland

Melanin is a dark pigment* that protects the internal organs from the sun's harmful radiation. When your skin is exposed to a lot of sunlight, melanocytes produce more melanin. Your skin then darkens, or tans.

## Dermis and Subcutaneous Fat

The middle layer of skin is the **dermis.** It contains glands and cells that make elastin and collagen. Elastin makes the skin flexible, so it can stretch without tearing. Collagen is a dense protein that gives the skin shape. When it breaks down, wrinkles form.

Hair follicles are also found in the dermis. A **hair follicle** is a long pit where keratin is produced, making hair. The dermis also includes sweat and oil glands. Oil lubricates* the skin and makes it waterproof.

The deepest layer of the skin is the subcutaneous fat. This layer protects and insulates the rest of the body.

 Give an example of a place where your skin might have a callus built out of keratin.

_____

_____

### * ACADEMIC VOCABULARY

**pigment**   a substance that adds color

**lubricate**   to make something slippery or smooth

## 33.3   Vocabulary Check

### Mark It Up

Go back and highlight each sentence that has a vocabulary word in **bold**.

| | |
|---|---|
| integumentary system | dermis |
| keratin | hair follicle |
| epidermis | |

1. Underline the word meaning the middle layer of the skin.

2. Put a box around the term for the top layer of the skin.

3. Put a wave line under the term for a tough, waterproof protein.

## 33.3   The Big Picture

4. In what ways does the integumentary system help to protect the body? _____

_____

5. How is the outer layer of the skin replaced as cells die? _____

_____

# Chapter 33 Review

1. What is the difference between the appendicular and the axial skeletons?

   _____

   _____

2. What kind of tissue connects bones to each other? _____

3. Label the five types of joints in the drawing.

   a. _____

   b. _____

   c. _____

   d. _____

   e. _____

4. Calcification is the mixing of _____ and calcium phosphate to form bone.

   a. elastin

   b. melanin

   c. collagen

   d. actin

5. What are the two types of bone tissue?

   _____

6. Some _____ muscles are under your control.

   a. skeletal

   b. smooth

   c. cardiac

   d. involuntary

7. What are actin and myosin filaments? What does myosin do?

   _____

   _____

8. What parts of your body are made of keratin? _____

9. Name two substances found in the dermis. _____

   _____

10. Name one way that the integumentary system helps maintain homeostasis. _____

   _____

# 34 Reproduction and Development

## GETTING READY TO LEARN

### Preview Key Concepts

**34.1 Reproductive Anatomy**
Female and male reproductive organs fully develop during puberty.

**34.2 Reproductive Processes**
Human reproductive processes depend on cycles of hormones.

**34.3 Fetal Development**
Development progresses in stages from zygote to fetus.

**34.4 Birth and Development**
Physical development continues through adolescence and declines with age.

### Review Academic Vocabulary

Write the correct word for each definition.

skeletal system     dermis     calcification     hair follicle     vertebrae

1. _____ : bones around the spinal cord

2. _____ : process of creating hard bone

3. _____ : layer that maintains skin's structure

4. _____ : includes the bones and connective tissues

5. _____ : pit that contains cells producing keratin

### Preview Biology Vocabulary

Two key terms from this chapter share the same word part: *mensis*.
Read the definitions and guess what the word part means.

| TERM | DEFINITION | WHAT I THINK *mensis* MEANS |
|------|------------|------------------------------|
| menstrual cycle | series of monthly changes in the female reproductive system | |
| menopause | when the monthly cycle becomes irregular and finally stops | |

# 34.1 Reproductive Anatomy

**KEY CONCEPT** Female and male reproductive organs fully develop during puberty.

The **reproductive system** includes the organs, glands, and hormones that help to produce a new human being. Humans can reproduce after puberty. **Puberty** occurs when your hypothalamus and pituitary glands release hormones, causing you to develop sexual characteristics.

## The female reproductive system produces ova.

The female reproductive system produces egg cells and provides a place where fertilized eggs, called ova, can develop. One egg cell is called an **ovum.** The ova are made by the **ovaries,** organs on either side of the uterus. The **uterus** is a muscular organ that protects and nourishes a developing egg.

During puberty, the ovaries release **estrogen,** a steroid hormone. Estrogen causes the female pelvis to widen, the breasts to enlarge, and fat deposits and bone mass to increase. Estrogen helps egg cells to mature before they leave the ovaries. It also helps to prepare the uterus for pregnancy and to maintain a pregnancy once it occurs.

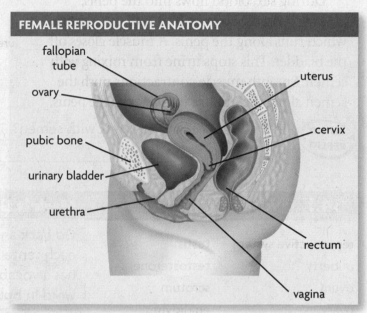

**FEMALE REPRODUCTIVE ANATOMY**

fallopian tube

ovary

uterus

pubic bone

cervix

urinary bladder

urethra

rectum

vagina

After puberty, the ovaries release an egg every month. For several days, the egg travels through a **fallopian tube,** an organ that ends in the uterus. During that time, sperm can fertilize the egg. A fertilized egg will develop into a baby over nine months. During normal birth, a baby is pushed out through the vagina. If the egg is not fertilized, it will break down.

 As you read through the text, underline the label of each part of the female reproductive system on the drawing.

## The male reproductive system produces sperm.

When males reach puberty, **testosterone,** a steroid hormone, is released. Testosterone helps stimulate the testicles, or **testes,** to produce sperm. One testicle is called a testis. Each testis produces millions of sperm cells. The testes are enclosed in a pouch called the **scrotum.** The scrotum hangs outside the body, below the pelvis, keeping the testes cool. Sperm cannot develop if they are kept too warm.

When immature sperm leave the testes, they travel to a long tube called the **epididymis** where they mature. Here the sperm remain until they are expelled or reabsorbed by the body. During sexual stimulation, the sperm travel into the **vas deferens.** Glands secrete fluids that protect the sperm and help it move. These fluids, and the sperm, form a white fluid called **semen.**

During sex, blood flows into the penis, making it rigid. Semen moves into the urethra, which runs along the penis. A muscle closes off the bladder. This stops urine from mixing with semen. Smooth muscle contractions push the semen along the urethra until it exits the penis.

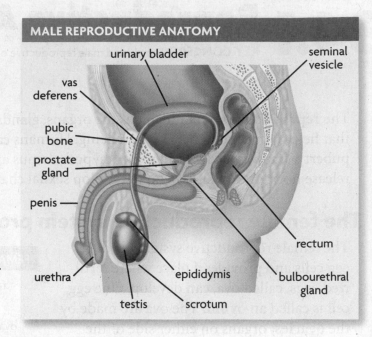

**MALE REPRODUCTIVE ANATOMY**

urinary bladder
seminal vesicle
vas deferens
pubic bone
prostate gland
penis
rectum
urethra
epididymis
bulbourethral gland
testis
scrotum

**INSTANT REPLAY** Why doesn't urine ever mix with semen?

_____

## 34.1 Vocabulary Check

**Mark It Up**

Go back and highlight each sentence that has a vocabulary word in **bold.**

| | |
|---|---|
| reproductive system | testis |
| puberty | testosterone |
| ovum | scrotum |
| ovary | epididymis |
| uterus | vas deferens |
| estrogen | semen |
| fallopian tube | |

1. In the list above, circle the word that describes the place where sperm mature.
2. Put a box around the word that means an egg cell.
3. Underline the word that refers to the time period when males and females develop sexual characteristics.

## 34.1 The Big Picture

4. At what point in an egg's journey to the uterus can the egg be fertilized? _____
5. What happens to sperm in the epididymis? _____
_____

# 34.2 Reproductive Processes

**KEY CONCEPT** Human reproductive processes depend on cycles of hormones.

Several hormones regulate the reproductive cycles in your body. Feedback loops among these hormones help ensure that each process occurs at the right time and in the right order.

## Eggs mature and are released according to hormonal cycles.

Female reproduction occurs in a cycle. Every month, the hypothalamus, pituitary gland, and ovaries release hormones. As hormone levels rise and fall, an egg matures and is released.

### Production of Eggs

When females are born, their ovaries already contain partly developed eggs. At puberty, the second stage of egg production begins. Every 28 days or so, hormones stimulate a potential egg to complete meiosis I. The potential egg divides unevenly, producing two sex cells. The smaller cell breaks down. The larger one receives most of the organelles that the embryo will need if the egg is fertilized. If a sperm fertilizes the egg, it will begin meiosis II. It will divide again, producing an ovum, and another small cell that also breaks down. Both the ovum and the second cell contain 23 chromosomes from the mother.

potential egg

Meiosis I completed

Meiosis II completed only after sperm enters

ovum (egg)

Potential eggs go through meiosis I and II to produce mature ova.

### Release of Eggs

In the ovaries, each developing egg is surrounded by a group of cells called a **follicle.** The follicle helps the egg to mature. When the egg is ready, the follicle ruptures*, and the egg breaks through the ovary wall. The release of an egg from an ovary is called **ovulation.** The egg is swept into the fallopian tube. During the next five to seven days, it travels through the tube toward the uterus. If it is not fertilized by a sperm, it is discarded.

### The Menstrual Cycle

The monthly changes that occur in the female reproductive system are called the **menstrual cycle.** These changes include producing and releasing an egg and preparing the uterus to receive it. The average length of

* ACADEMIC VOCABULARY

**rupture** break open

the menstrual cycle is 28 days. But many females have cycles that are shorter or longer. Every cycle has three phases: flow phase, follicular phase, and luteal phase.

1. **Flow phase** Day 1 of the menstrual cycle is the day the menstrual flow begins. The lining of the uterus, called the **endometrium,** detaches from the uterus. Contractions of the uterus push the endometrium out of the body. These contractions, called cramps, can be painful. The endometrium leaves the body through the vagina. A few ounces of blood, mucus, and fluid go with it. During this phase, the level of follicle-stimulating hormone (FSH) starts to rise. As a result, a follicle in the ovaries begins to mature.

2. **Follicular phase** Days 6–14 of the menstrual cycle are the follicular phase. The pituitary releases more FSH, along with luteinizing hormone (LH). Rising levels of FSH and LH cause the egg and follicle to mature. The follicle releases estrogen, causing the endometrium to thicken. Estrogen stimulates LH levels to rise higher. As a result, the follicle ruptures, and ovulation occurs at about day 14.

## MENSTRUAL CYCLE

**Hormones cause changes in the follicle, egg, and lining of the uterus.**

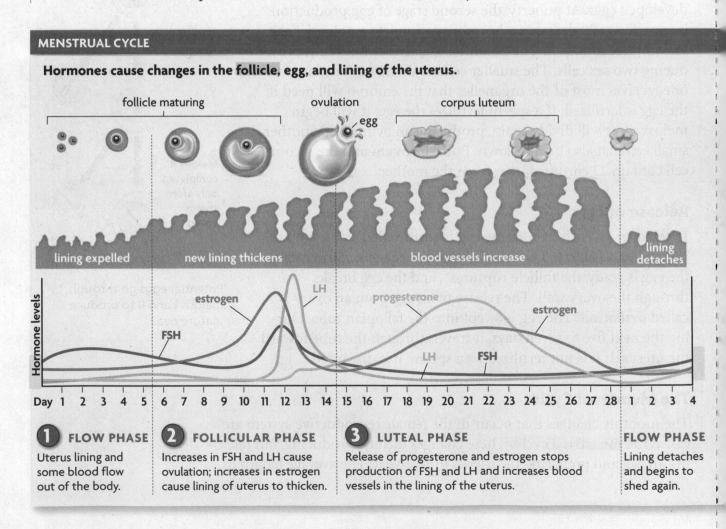

1 **FLOW PHASE**
Uterus lining and some blood flow out of the body.

2 **FOLLICULAR PHASE**
Increases in FSH and LH cause ovulation; increases in estrogen cause lining of uterus to thicken.

3 **LUTEAL PHASE**
Release of progesterone and estrogen stops production of FSH and LH and increases blood vessels in the lining of the uterus.

**FLOW PHASE**
Lining detaches and begins to shed again.

3. **Luteal phase** After ovulation, the empty follicle turns yellow and is called the **corpus luteum,** which means "yellow body." Days 14–28 are the luteal phase. During this time, the corpus luteum releases estrogen and another hormone, progesterone, which slows production of LH. Progesterone and estrogen also increase the number of blood vessels in the endometrium. If the egg is not fertilized, FSH and LH levels fall. The corpus luteum breaks down and stops releasing estrogen and progesterone. The endometrium detaches from the uterus, and the next flow phase begins.

A female's reproductive years can last from the preteen years to the late 50s. As women age, their hormone levels fall. In a process called **menopause,** the menstrual cycle becomes more irregular and finally stops completely.

How does the corpus luteum affect the menstrual cycle?

_____

_____

# Sperm production in the testes is controlled by hormones.

Females produce one egg each month, but males produce millions of sperm every day. Sperm production begins when hormones from the hypothalamus stimulate the pituitary to release FSH and LH. These hormones travel to the testes, stimulating the testes to release testosterone. Testosterone causes specialized cells to begin meiosis and develop into mature sperm. As testosterone rises, FSH and LH levels decline. This feedback loop helps control the number of sperm that are produced.

When sperm undergo meiosis, they divide into equal cells. Each cell has 23 chromosomes. The newly formed sperm cells mature in the epididymis. Each sperm has a head, midpiece, and tail. The head contains a nucleus and a cap region, called the acrosome. The acrosome contains enzymes that allow the sperm to penetrate an egg's membrane.

When sperm are released from the penis, testosterone levels decline. These low levels stimulate the hypothalamus. As a result, sperm production increases again. Males can produce sperm throughout their lives, beginning in puberty. As they grow older, however, they produce fewer sperm.

**Sperm cell**

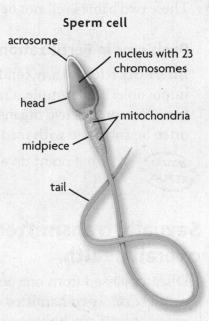

A mature sperm has a head, midpiece, and whip-like tail that enables it to move.

How are sperm and eggs alike?

_____

## Fertilization occurs when a sperm cell joins an egg cell.

During sexual intercourse, the penis is inserted into the vagina until the tip is near the opening of the uterus. Semen is ejaculated through the penis, and sperm are released into the vagina. Sperm then swim up through the uterus and into the fallopian tubes where an egg may be fertilized.

### Process of Fertilization

Usually only one of the millions of sperm released fertilizes an egg. Why only one? When a sperm enters an egg, the egg's membrane changes right away to stop other sperm from entering. The egg's 23 chromosomes then join with the 23 chromosomes in the sperm. This produces a fertilized egg called a zygote.

In rare cases, a woman can give birth to more than one baby. If a single fertilized egg splits into two zygotes, the woman will have genetically identical twins. In even rarer cases, a fertilized egg may split into three, four, or more genetically identical embryos. On the other hand, if two eggs are released and fertilized, the woman may have fraternal twins. These two babies will not be genetically identical.

### Problems in Fertilization

Infertility refers to any condition that makes reproduction difficult or impossible. For example, a male's vas deferens may be blocked, or a female's reproductive organs may be damaged by disease. Infertility can often be corrected with medication, surgery, or dietary changes.

 At what point do a sperm and an egg become a zygote?

## Sexually transmitted diseases affect fertility and overall health.

Diseases passed from one person to another during sexual contact are called sexually transmitted diseases or STDs. People who have STDs may not have any symptoms, but they can still infect other people. STDs can be bacterial, such as chlamydia and syphilis. Bacterial STDs attack the reproductive organs and can cause infertility. Antibiotics can cure these bacterial diseases. STDs can also be viral, such as human immunodeficiency virus (HIV). There are no cures for viral STDs.

It is possible to avoid STDs. One way is to abstain from sex. Couples who do not have STDs can avoid them by being faithful to each other. The next safest choice is to use a condom, but a condom can break.

Name one way you can avoid STDs.

_____

_____

## 34.2　Vocabulary Check

| | |
|---|---|
| follicle | menopause |
| ovulation | zygote |
| menstrual cycle | infertility |
| endometrium | sexually transmitted disease |
| corpus luteum | |

**1.** In the list above, circle the word that refers to a fertilized egg.

**2.** Put a box around the term that means the lining of the uterus.

**3.** Underline the phrase that refers to a ruptured follicle.

**4.** a series of monthly changes in females _____

**5.** cells that surround each egg in the ovaries _____

## 34.2　The Big Picture

**6.** What hormones stimulate the testes to release testosterone? _____

**7.** How many chromosomes do eggs and sperm contain? _____

**8.** What happens during the menstrual cycle if an egg is not fertilized?

_____

_____

## The mother affects the fetus, and pregnancy affects the mother.

Throughout the pregnancy, the mother and fetus continually affect each other's health.

**Health of the fetus** The fetus gets all of its nutrients from the mother, so it is important that the mother eat well during the pregnancy. For example, nutrients such as folic acid help prevent defects in the spinal cord. The mother should also avoid drugs and alcohol, because these substances can cause birth defects.

**Health of the mother** To supply enough energy for herself and her developing baby, a mother needs to add about 300 more Calories a day to her diet. Most mothers gain about 12 kilogram (26 lbs). Gaining too much or too little weight can interfere with the fetus's development.

The mother's health is also affected by hormones during pregnancy. Sometimes these hormones make it hard for the mother's body to maintain homeostasis. Women may develop morning sickness or even pregnancy-related diabetes. To protect her health during pregnancy, the mother should have regular medical checkups, eat well, and exercise.

 Highlight one way that pregnancy can affect a woman's health.

Pregnant women should talk to their doctors before taking any medication.

---

### 34.3 Vocabulary Check

blastocyst    umbilical cord
embryo    trimester
amniotic sac    fetus
placenta

**Mark It Up**

Go back and highlight each sentence that has a vocabulary word in **bold**.

Choose the correct term from the list for each description.

1. the fertilized egg after three cell layers develop _____

2. the fertilized egg after nine weeks _____

3. three months of pregnancy _____

4. the structure that connects the embryo to the placenta _____

### 34.3 The Big Picture

5. When is a fetus most at risk for birth defects? _____

6. Name two things a mother can do to protect her fetus. _____

_____

# 34.4 Birth and Development

**KEY CONCEPT** Physical development continues through adolescence and declines with age.

## Birth occurs in three stages.

When the fetus is fully developed, the placenta can no longer provide enough nourishment. It is time for the baby to be born. There are three stages in the process of birth: dilation of the cervix, emergence of the baby, and expulsion of the placenta. The physical changes the mother's body goes through are called labor.

### Dilation of the Cervix

Labor begins with regular contractions of the uterus. The mother and fetus release a hormone, oxytocin, that stimulates the muscles in the walls of the uterus. However, not all contractions mean that the baby is about to be born. True labor does not begin until the contractions are frequent, intense, and painful. In the early stages of labor, the amniotic sac may break, releasing amniotic fluid through the vagina (also called the birth canal).

Labor contractions push the walls of the cervix apart. The baby cannot be born until the cervix dilates, or widens, to at least 10 centimeters (4 inches). This space allows most babies to pass through. If the cervix does not dilate enough, a doctor can deliver the baby by Cesarean section, or C-section. During a C-section, the doctor makes an incision in the abdominal wall and removes the baby.

**STAGE 1**

During the first stage of labor, the uterus contracts, the cervix dilates, and the baby turns head down.

### Emergence of the Baby

The contractions of the uterus cause the baby to turn so that its head is toward the cervix. (Sometimes babies are born feet first, which is more difficult.) The muscles of the uterus push the baby into the birth canal. Once the baby's head emerges,* the rest of the body slips out easily.

Soon after birth, the baby begins to breathe on its own. The hormone oxytocin stimulates the mother's breasts to produce milk and makes her want to bond* with the baby.

**STAGE 2**

During the second stage, the baby emerges from the mother's body.

---

**\* ACADEMIC VOCABULARY**

**emerges** comes out

**bond** become emotionally attached to someone or something

### Expulsion of the Placenta

When the baby emerges, birth is still not complete. The placenta must detach from the uterus and be expelled through the vagina. The uterus continues to contract, constricting blood vessels. This reduces bleeding from the uterus. A nurse or doctor cuts the baby's umbilical cord, leaving a few inches of it attached to the baby's abdomen. Later, the umbilical cord dries up and falls off. It leaves behind a scar called the navel, or belly button.

What role does oxytocin play in the birth process?

_____

_____

_____

**STAGE 3**
In the third stage, contractions of the uterus expel the placenta and help to control bleeding.

## Human growth and aging also occur in stages.

Hormones do not stop affecting a child's growth after it is born. Instead, they continue to regulate how a child grows and develops.

### Infancy and Childhood

**Infancy** lasts from birth to age 2. At birth, a baby's ability to maintain homeostasis is not fully developed. During the first year, the baby gets better at controlling its heart rate, temperature, and breathing. Babies grow dramatically during infancy. They learn to sit, stand, walk, and speak a few words.

**Childhood** begins at age 2 and lasts until about age 12. Growth slows down during this period. The nervous system matures, and children develop more fine motor skills, such as writing. They also develop more language and reasoning skills.

### Puberty and Adolescence

At puberty, children begin to mature sexually. For girls, puberty begins between the ages of 10 and 14. For boys, puberty begins between the ages of 10 and 16. During this time, young people grow very fast, averaging 5 to 7 centimeters (2 to 3 inches) per year. The brain also develops rapidly during this period.

**Adolescence** begins with sexual maturity. For girls, sexual maturity occurs with ovulation and the beginning of the menstrual cycle. For boys, it begins when sperm start to appear in the semen. Adolescents continue to grow and become more coordinated. Their brains also continue to develop, making more neural connections.

## Adulthood and Aging

You might think that **adulthood** is a period of time in which humans are fully developed and at their peak. This is partly true. Adults become independent, and may raise families of their own. However, the body continues to change as people age. The immune system begins to decline, and the body produces lower levels of key hormones, such as testosterone and estrogen. Women go through menopause, and men's sperm count drops. The body's metabolism and digestion slow down. Skin becomes thinner, bones lose calcium, and muscle mass decreases as fat deposits increase.

The picture is not all gloomy, however. Scientists are finding that genetics, lifestyle, and environment make a big difference in how people age. Eating a healthy diet, getting lots of exercise, and continuing to learn can slow down the effects of aging. Exercise helps the body maintain bone and muscle mass. Learning new things allows the brain to continue making new neural connections, just as it did during a person's youth.

 Name one way that people can slow down the aging process.

_____

## 34.4 Vocabulary Check

| | |
|---|---|
| infancy | adolescence |
| childhood | adulthood |

**Mark It Up**

Go back and highlight each sentence that has a vocabulary word in **bold**.

Fill in the blanks with the correct term from the list above.

1. _____ begins with sexual maturity.

2. During _____, people become independent and may raise families.

3. _____ lasts from birth to age 2.

4. _____ lasts from age 2 until about age 12.

## 34.4 The Big Picture

5. List the three stages of birth. _____

_____

6. People grow the fastest during which stages of life? _____

_____

# Chapter 34 Review

1. Label the parts of the male reproductive system in the drawing.

    a. _____

    b. _____

    c. _____

    d. _____

    e. _____

    f. _____

2. Where in the female reproductive system does fertilization of an egg usually take place? _____

3. A fertilized egg matures in
    _____

    a. a follicle.
    b. the epididymis.
    c. a fallopian tube.
    d. the uterus.

4. The menstrual cycle's three phases are _____
    _____.

5. What structure helps sperm to penetrate an egg's membrane?
    a. vas deferens
    b. acrosome
    c. testes
    d. tail

6. When the zygote becomes a ball of cells and implants itself into the lining of the uterus, it is called a _____.

7. What does the placenta do? _____
    _____

8. When is a fetus most at risk for developing birth defects?
    _____

9. How are the second and third stages of birth similar?
    _____

10. What is the difference between puberty and adolescence?
    _____

# Glossary

## A

**abdomen** part of an arthropod's body that is farthest from the head. (p. 399)
**abdomen** parte del cuerpo de un artrópodo situada detrás del tórax.

**abiotic** nonliving factors in the environment, such as moisture, temperature, wind, sunlight, soil, and minerals. (p. 224)
**abiótico** factor inerte de un ecosistema, como la humedad, la temperatura, el viento, la luz solar, el suelo y los minerales.

**ABO blood group** four common blood types (A, B, AB, and O) and the proteins that make them different from each other. (p. 507)
**grupo sanguíneo ABO** sistema que contiene los cuatro tipos de sangre comunes (A, B, AB y O) y los marcadores proteicos que los distinguen.

**absorption** process by which nutrients move out of one system and into another. (p. 542)
**absorción** proceso mediante el cual los nutrientes pasan de un sistema del organismo a otro.

**abyssal zone** (uh-BIHS-uhl) part of the ocean that lies below 2000 meters and is completely dark. (p. 262)
**zona abisal** región del océano por debajo de los 2000 metros de profundidad que se encuentra en total oscuridad.

**acid** compound that gives up a proton (H+) when dissolved in a solution. (p. 23)
**ácido** compuesto que cede un protón (H+) al ser disuelto en una solución.

**acid rain** rain with a decreased pH that is caused by pollutants in the atmosphere. (p. 272)
**lluvia ácida** precipitación que se produce cuando los contaminantes de la atmósfera hac el pH de la lluvia disminuya.

**acquired immune deficiency syndrome (AIDS)** condition characterized by having several infections and very few T cells; caused by HIV. (p. 531)
**síndrome de inmunodeficiencia adquirida (SIDA)** enfermedad caracterizada por falta de defensa contra varias infecciones y muy pocas células T; causada por el VIH.

**actin** filament that helps cause muscle contraction. (p. 555)
**actina** filamento que al ser accionado por los filamentos de miosina provoca una contracción muscular.

**action potential** fast change in electrical charge across a neuron's membrane; also called an impulse. (p. 476)
**potencial de acción** cambio rápido en la descarga eléctrica a a lo largo de la membrana de las neuronas; también llamado impulso.

**activation energy** the lowest amount of energy needed to start a chemical reaction. (p. 31)
**energía de activación** energía necesaria para iniciar una reacción química.

**active immunity** resistance to disease that occurs after the body responds to an antigen. (p. 520)
**inmunidad activa** inmunidad que se produce después de que el cuerpo haya respondido a un antígeno.

**active transport** movement of molecules across a membrane from a region of lower concentration to a region of higher concentration; requires energy input by a cell. (p. 49)
**transporte activo** desplazamiento de moléculas a través de una membrana desde un medio de baja concentración a un medio de alta concentración.

**adaptation** inherited trait that is passed on to offspring because it allows organisms to better survive in their environment. (pp. 7; 167)
**adaptación** rasgo heredado durante un periodo de tiempo mediante selección natural, que facilita la supervivencia de los organismos en su medio ambiente.

**adaptive radiation** process by which one species evolves and gives rise to many descendant species that occupy different ecological niches. (p. 197)
**radiación adaptativa** proceso evolutivo mediante el cual una especie da lugar a varias nuevas especies que ocupan distintos nichos ecológicos.

**addiction** uncontrollable physical and mental need for something. (p. 486)
**adicción** necesidad física y mental incontrolable de alguna sustancia o actividad.

**adenosine diphosphate (ADP)** low-energy molecule that can be converted to ATP. (p. 53)
**adenosín difosfato (ADP)** molécula con poca energía que puede convertirse en ATP.

**adenosine triphosphate (ATP)** high-energy molecule that contains, within its bonds, energy that cells can use. (p. 53)
**adenosín trifosfato (ATP)** molécula de alta energía en cuyos enlaces se almacena energía para las células.

**adhesion** attraction between molecules of different substances. (p. 22)
**adhesión** atracción que se produce entre moléculas de diferentes sustancias.

**adolescence** period of life beginning at puberty and ending at adulthood. (p. 572)
**adolescencia** periodo de la vida que comienza en la pubertad y que termina en la edad adulta.

**ADP** see adenosine diphosphate. (p. 53)
**ADP** véase adenosín difosfato.

**adulthood** period of life when a person is fully developed and physical growth stops. (p. 573)
**edad adulta** período de la vida en el que un individuo alcanza su completo desarrollo y en el que cesa el crecimiento.

**aerobic** (ay-ROH-bihk) process that requires oxygen to occur. (p. 62)
**aeróbico** proceso que requiere la presencia de oxígeno para ocurrir.

**airfoil** surface, such as a bird's wing, whose shape allows for flight by moving air faster over the top than underneath it. (p. 435)
**superficie aerodinámica** superficie de ala cuya forma, como en el caso de las aves, permite que el aire se mueva más rápido por arriba que por abajo, facilitando así el vuelo.

**air sac** air-filled space that connects to a bird's lungs, which helps in breathing. (p. 436)
**sacos aéreos** órganos llenos de aire conectados a los pulmones de las aves para facilitar la respiración.

**algae** (singular: alga) plantlike protists that carry out photosynthesis. (p. 321)
**alga** protista fotosintética de aspecto vegetal.

**alkaloid** nitrogen-containing chemical produced by plants, many of which are used in medicines. (p. 343)
**alcaloide** compuesto químico, producido por las plantas, que contiene nitrógeno y es usado en muchos medicamentos.

**allele** (uh-LEEL) an alternative form of a gene; occurs at a specific place on a chromosome. (p. 99)
**alelo** cualquier variante de un gen que ocupa la misma posición en un cromosoma.

**allele frequency** proportion of one allele, compared with all the alleles for that trait, in the gene pool. (p. 181)
**frecuencia alélica** proporción de un alelo determinado con respecto a los demás alelos del mismo rasgo en una misma población.

**allergen** antigen that does not cause disease but still produces an immune response. (p. 528)
**alérgeno** antígeno que, si bien no causa una enfermedad, produce una respuesta inmune.

**allergy** immune response that occurs when the body responds to a nondisease-causing antigen, such as pollen or animal dander. (p. 528)
**alergia** respuesta inmune producida cuando el organismo responde a aquellos antígenos que no causan enfermedades, como el polen o la caspa de ciertos animales.

**alternation of generations** plant life cycle in which the plant alternates between haploid and diploid phases. (p. 360)
**alternancia generacional** ciclo de vida de las plantas en el que la planta alterna fases haploides y diploides.

**altruism** behavior in which an animal may decrease its chance of survival to help the other members of its social group. (p. 454)
**altruismo** patrón de comportamiento animal, en el cual un individuo sacrifica su integridad para beneficiar a otros miembros de su grupo social.

**alveolus** (al-VEE-uh-luhs) (plural: alveoli) tiny, thin-walled structure where gas exchange occurs in the lungs. (p. 495)
**alvéolo** pequeña estructura de paredes delgadas a través de la cual se absorbe oxígeno gaseoso y se libera dióxido de carbono en los pulmones.

**amino acid** molecule that makes up proteins; made of carbon, hydrogen, oxygen, nitrogen, and sometimes sulfur. (p. 28)
**aminoácido** molécula que forma las proteínas; está compuesta de carbono, hidrógeno, oxígeno, nitrógeno y, a veces, de azufre.

**amniote** vertebrate whose embryo or fetus is enclosed by a thin, tough sac. (p. 425)
**amniota** vertebrado cuyo embrión o feto está envuelto en un saco membranoso delgado y resistente.

**amniotic egg** waterproof container that allows an embryo to develop out of water and outside the mother without drying out. (p. 425)
**huevo amniótico** envoltura impermeable que permite el desarrollo del embrión fuera del agua y de la propia madre sin que éste se deshidrate.

**amniotic sac** fluid-filled organ that cushions and protects the developing embryo of some vertebrates. (p. 568)
**saco amniótico** membrana que contiene líquido y que amortigua y protege el embrión de ciertos vertebrados.

**amphibian** vertebrate that can live on land and in water. (p. 422)
**anfibio** vertebrado que puede vivir en el agua y en tierra firme.

**anaerobic** process that does not require oxygen to occur. (p. 62)
**anaeróbico** proceso que no requiere oxígeno para ocurrir.

**analogous structure** body part that is similar in function to a body part of another organism but is structurally different. (p. 174)
**estructura análoga** parte del cuerpo que cumple una función similar a la parte del cuerpo de un organismo diferente, pero que tiene una estructura diferente.

**anaphase** third phase of mitosis during which chromatids separate and are pulled to opposite sides of the cell. (p. 78)
**anafase** tercera fase de la mitosis, en la cual las cromátidas se separan y se dirigen hacia los polos opuestos de la célula.

**anaphylaxis** (AN-uh-fuh-LAK-sihs) severe allergic reaction that causes airways to tighten and blood vessels to leak. (p. 528)
**anafilaxis** reacción alérgica grave que produce rigidez de las vías aéreas y el drenaje de líquido de los vasos sanguíneos.

**angiosperm** (AN-jee-uh-SPURM) seed plant whose embryos are enclosed by fruit. (p. 337)
**angiosperma** planta cuyos embriones se encuentran encerrados en el fruto.

**anthropoid** humanlike primate. (p. 215)
**antropoide** primate semejante al ser humano.

**antibiotic** chemical that kills or slows the growth of bacteria. (p. 311)
**antibiótico** compuesto químico que mata o inhibe el desarrollo de las bacterias.

**antibiotic resistance** process by which bacteria mutate and are no longer affected by an antibiotic. (p. 526)
**resistencia antibiótica** proceso mediante el cual una bacteria sufre mutaciones y para hacerse resistente a los antibióticos.

**antibody** protein produced by B cells that helps destroy pathogens. (p. 519)
**anticuerpo** proteína producida por las células B que contribuye a la destrucción de los patógenos.

**anticodon** set of three nucleotides in a tRNA molecule that binds to a complementary mRNA codon during translation. (p. 136)
**anticodón** grupo de tres nucleótidos de la molécula de ARNt que se acopla a un codón complementario de ARNm durante la traslación.

**antigen** (AN-tih-juhn) foreign substance that brings about an immune response. (p. 522)
**antígeno** marcador proteico que ayuda al sistema inmune a identificar sustancias extrañas tales como los virus.

**antiseptic** (AN-tih-SEHP-tihk) chemical, such as soap, vinegar, or rubbing alcohol, that destroys pathogens outside of the body. (p. 526)
**antiséptico** compuesto químico, como el jabón, el vinagre o el alcohol, que destruyen los patógenos fuera del cuerpo.

**apoptosis** (AP-uhp-TOH-sihs) programmed cell death. (p. 80)
**apoptosis** muerte celular programada.

**appendage** extension, such as an antenna or arm, that is attached to the body. (p. 395)
**apéndice** prolongación del cuerpo, como una antena o un brazo, unida o contigua al mismo.

**appendicular skeleton** part of the skeletal system that allows for most of the body's movements; includes bones of the arms, shoulders, legs, and pelvis. (p. 550)
**esqueleto apendicular** parte del sistema esquelético que permite la mayor parte de los movimientos del cuerpo; consta, entre otros, de los huesos de los brazos, hombros, piernas y la pelvis.

**arachnid** chelicerate that lives on land, such as a spider. (p. 402)
**arácnido** quelicerado terrestre, como la araña.

**Archaea** one of the three domains of life, containing single-celled prokaryotes in the kingdom Archaea. (p. 293)
**Arqueas** uno de los tres dominios de la vida, compuesto de procariontes unicelulares del reino Archaea.

**artery** large blood vessel that carries blood away from the heart. (p. 495)
**arteria** gran vaso sanguíneo que transporta la sangre desde el corazón.

**arthropod** invertebrate with an exoskeleton, jointed appendages, and a segmented body. (p. 395)
**artrópodo** invertebrado con exoesqueleto, apéndices articulados y cuerpo segmentado.

**artificial selection** process by which humans modify a species by breeding it for certain traits. (p. 169)
**selección artificial** proceso mediante el cual los seres humanos modifican una especie al criarla para obtener ciertos rasgos.

**asexual reproduction** process by which offspring are produced from a single parent; does not involve the joining of egg and sperm. (p. 82)
**reproducción asexual** proceso mediante el cual se producen descendientes de un solo progenitor, sin necesidad de la unión de gametos.

**asthma** (AZ-muh) condition marked by tightening in the lungs, making breathing difficult. (p. 499)
**asma** enfermedad que, al estrechar las vías aéreas de los pulmones, dificulta la respiración.

**atmosphere** air blanketing Earth's solid surface. (p. 255)
**atmósfera** envoltura de aire que rodea la superficie sólida de la Tierra.

**atom** smallest basic unit of matter. (p. 19)
**átomo** unidad básica más pequeña de la materia.

**ATP** see adenosine triphosphate. (p. 53)
**ATP** véase adenosín trifosfato.

**ATP synthase** enzyme that adds a high-energy phosphate group to ADP to form ATP. (p. 60)
**ATP sintetasa** enzima que cataliza la reacción para enlazar un grupo fosfato de alta energía al ADP y formar así el ATP.

**atrium** (plural: atria) small chamber in the human heart that receives blood from the veins. (p. 500)
**aurícula** pequeña cavidad del corazón humano que recibe sangre de las venas.

**autonomic nervous system** part of the peripheral nervous system that controls involuntary functions. (p. 483)
**sistema nervioso autónomo** parte del sistema nervioso periférico que controla las funciones involuntarias.

**autosome** chromosome that contains genes for characteristics not directly related to the sex of the organism. (p. 91)
**autosoma** cromosoma cuyos genes no rigen los rasgos relacionados directamente con el sexo del organismo.

**autotroph** organism that gets its energy from nonliving sources, such as sunlight or inorganic chemicals. (p. 226)
**autótrofo** organismo que obtiene su energía a partir de fuentes abióticas como, por ejemplo, la luz solar o sustancias inorgánicas.

**auxin** (AWK-sihn) plant hormone that causes cells in the growing tip to grow longer. (p. 373)
**auxina** hormona vegetal que estimula la elongación de las células y regula el crecimiento de las plantas.

**axial skeleton** part of the skeletal system that supports the body's weight and protects the body's internal tissues; includes the bones of the skull, spinal column, and rib cage. (p. 550)
**esqueleto axial** parte del sistema esquelético que da soporte al peso corporal y que protege los tejidos internos del organismo; consta de los huesos del cráneo, la columna vertebral y la caja torácica.

**axon** long extension of the neuron membrane that carries impulses from one neuron to another. (p. 474)
**axón** prolongación de la membrana de la neurona que transmite impulsos eléctricos de una neurona a otra.

# B

**Bacteria** one of the three domains of life, containing single-celled prokaryotes in the kingdom Bacteria. (p. 293)
**Bacteria** uno de los tres dominios en los que se dividen los seres vivos, que consta de procariontes unicelulares del reino Bacteria.

**bacteriophage** virus that infects bacteria. (pp. 124; 300)
**bacteriófago** virus que infecta a las bacterias.

**base** compound that takes up a proton (H+) when dissolved in solution. (p. 23)
**base** compuesto que al disolverlo en una solución acepta un protón (H+).

**base pairing rules** describe how nucleotides form bonds in DNA; adenine (A) always bonds with thymine (T), and guanine (G) always bonds with cytosine (C). (p. 127)
**reglas de apareamiento de bases** regla que describe cómo se enlazan los nucleótidos en el ADN; la adenina (A) siempre se enlaza con la timina (T), y la guanina (G) siempre se enlaza con la citosina (C).

**bathyal zone** (BATH-ee-uhl) part of the ocean that extends from the edge of the neritic zone to the base of the continental shelf. (p. 262)
**zona batial** región oceánica que se extiende desde el límite de la zona nerítica hasta la base de la plataforma continental.

**B cell** white blood cell that matures in the bone marrow and makes antibodies that fight off infection; also called a B-lymphocyte. (p. 519)
**célula B** glóbulo blanco que madura en la médula osea y que produce los anticuerpos que combaten las infecciones; también se conoce como linfocito B.

**behavioral isolation** isolation between populations that results from differences in courtship or mating behavior. (p. 193)
**aislamiento etológico** aislamiento entre poblaciones debido a diferencias en los rituales de cortejo o apareamiento.

**benign** having no dangerous effect on health, especially referring to an abnormal growth of cells that are not cancerous. (p. 81)
**benigno** que no tiene efectos graves sobre la salud; se refiere particularmente al crecimiento anormal de células que no son cancerosas.

**benthic zone** lake or pond bottom, which receives little to no sunlight. (p. 266)
**zona béntica** fondo de un lago o estanque, adonde llega poca o ninguna luz.

**bilateral symmetry** body plan in which the body can be divided into identical halves in only one direction. (p. 380)
**simetría bilateral** se observa en los organismos que pueden dividirse en partes iguales a lo largo de un plano único.

**bile** fluid released by the liver and gallbladder into the small intestine that helps the body digest and absorb fats. (p. 540)
**bilis** fluido segregado por el hígado y almacenado en la vesícula biliar, y que es liberado al intestino delgado para facilitar la digestión y la absorción de las grasas.

**binary fission** (BY-nuh-ree FIHSH-uhn) asexual reproduction in which a single-celled organism divides into two equal parts. (p. 82)
**fisión binaria** reproducción asexual en la que una célula se divide en dos partes iguales.

**binomial nomenclature** naming system that gives each species a two-part scientific name (genus and species) using Latin words. (p. 284)
**nomenclatura binomial** sistema de denominación de especies mediante el cual se les otorga un nombre científico que consta de dos palabras en latín (género y especie).

**biodiversity** variety of life within an area. (pp. 2; 224)
**biodiversidad** variedad de las formas de vida en una zona determinada.

**biogeochemical cycle** movement of a chemical through the living (biological) and nonliving (geological) parts of an ecosystem. (p. 233)
**ciclo biogeoquímico** movimiento de una sustancia química a través de los componentes biológicos y geológicos, o vivos e inertes, de un ecosistema.

**biogeography** study of the distribution of organisms around the world. (p. 173)
**biogeografía** estudio de la distribución de los organismos en el mundo.

**bioinformatics** use of computer databases to organize and analyze biological data. (p. 158)
**bioinformática** utilización de bases de datos de computación para organizar y analizar datos biológicos.

**biological clock** internal mechanism that controls an animal's activity patterns. (p. 444)
**reloj biológico** mecanismo interno que controla el ritmo de actividad de un animal.

**biology** scientific study of all forms of life. (p. 3)
**biología** estudio científico de todas las formas de vida.

**biomagnification** describes the higher concentration of toxic substances in the tissues of organisms higher on the food chain than ones lower in the food chain. (p. 275)
**biomagnificación** condición en la cual la concentración de sustancias tóxicas en los tejidos de los organismos que pertenecen a eslabones más altos de la cadena alimentaria es mayor que la concentración en los organismos de los eslabones más bajos.

**biomass** total dry mass of all organisms in a given area. (p. 237)
**biomasa** masa deshidratada total de todos los organismos de un área determinada.

**biome** regional or global community of organisms characterized by the climate conditions and plant communities that thrive there. (p. 221)
**bioma** comunidad regional o global de organismos caracterizada por las condiciones climáticas y el tipo de vegetación del área.

**bioremediation** process by which humans use living things to break down pollutants. (p. 310)
**biorremediación** proceso mediante el cual los seres humanos emplean organismos vivos para descomponer sustancias contaminantes.

**biosphere** all organisms and the part of Earth where they exist. (pp. 2; 255)
**biosfera** todos los seres vivos y las partes de la Tierra en las que existen.

**biota** collection of living things. (p. 255)
**biota** conjunto de seres vivos.

**biotechnology** use and application of living things and biological processes. (p. 14)
**biotecnología** aprovechamiento y aplicación de los seres vivos y de sus procesos biológicos.

**biotic** living things, such as plants, animals, fungi, and bacteria. (p. 224)
**biótico** referente a los seres vivos, tales como las plantas, los animales, los hongos y las bacterias.

**bipedal** animal that walks on two legs. (p. 216)
**bípedo** animal que camina sobre dos patas.

**blade** broad part of a leaf where most of the photosynthesis of a plant takes place. (p. 355)
**lámina** parte ancha de la hoja donde ocurre la mayor parte de la fotosíntesis de una planta.

**blastocyst** stage of development during which the zygote consists of a ball of cells. (p. 568)
**blastocisto** fase de desarrollo en la que el cigoto consta de células apelotonadas.

**blood pressure** force with which blood pushes against the wall of an artery. (p. 504)
**presión sanguínea** fuerza que ejerce la sangre contra las paredes de las arterias.

**bond energy** amount of energy needed to break a bond between two particular atoms; or the amount of energy released when a bond forms between two particular atoms. (p. 30)
**energía de enlace** energía necesaria para romper un enlace entre dos partículas atómicas; energía liberada al formarse un enlace entre dos átomos determinados.

**book lung** respiratory organ that has membranes arranged like the pages in a book. (p. 402)
**pulmón en libro** órgano respiratorio compuesto por una serie de membranas dispuestas como las páginas de un libro.

**botany** study of plants. (p. 342)
**botánica** estudio de las plantas.

**bottleneck effect** genetic drift resulting from an event that kills a large part of a population. (p. 187)
**efecto de cuello de botella** deriva genética resultante de un acontecimiento que reduce drásticamente el tamaño de una población.

**brain stem** part that connects the brain to the spinal cord and controls breathing and heartbeat. (p. 482)
**tronco del encéfalo** estructura que conecta el cerebro con la médula espinal y que controla la respiración y los latidos del corazón.

# C

**calcification** process that hardens bones by adding calcium phosphate and collagen. (p. 552)
**calcificación** proceso que endurece los huesos mediante depósitos de fosfato cálcico y colágeno.

**Calorie** measure of energy released from digesting food; one Calorie equals one kilocalorie of heat. (p. 538)
**caloría** medida de energía liberada al digerir la comida; una caloría equivale a una kilocaloría de calor.

**Calvin cycle** process by which a photosynthetic organism uses energy to make simple sugars from $CO_2$. (p. 60)
**ciclo de Calvin** proceso mediante el cual un organismo fotosintético usa energía para sintetizar monosacáridos a partir del $CO_2$.

**Cambrian explosion** earliest part of the Paleozoic era, when a huge diversity of animal species evolved. (p. 213)
**explosión Cámbrica** periodo inicial de la era paleozoica, en la que surgió una enorme diversidad de especies animales.

**cancer** common name for a class of diseases characterized by uncontrolled cell division. (p. 81)
**cáncer** nombre común de una clase de enfermedades caracterizadas por una división descontrolada de las células.

**canopy** thick covering formed by the uppermost branches of trees. (p. 259)
**cobertura arbórea** tupido entramado formado por las ramas más altas de los árboles.

**capillary** tiny blood vessel that moves blood between larger blood vessels and other tissues in the body. (p. 495)
**capilar** diminuto vaso sanguíneo que transporta la sangre entre vasos sanguíneos más grandes y otros tejidos del cuerpo.

**capsid** protein shell that surrounds a virus. (p. 299)
**cápsida** cubierta proteica que envuelve al virus.

**carapace** (KAR-uh-PAYS) plate of exoskeleton that covers the head and thorax of a crustacean. (p. 399)
**caparazón** parte del exoesqueleto de los crustáceos que cubre la cabeza y el tórax.

**carbohydrate** molecule made of carbon, hydrogen, and oxygen; includes sugars and starches. (p. 26)
**carbohidrato** molécula compuesta de carbono, hidrógeno y oxígeno; incluye los azúcares y los almidones.

**carcinogen** substance that causes cancer. (p. 81)
**carcinógeno** sustancia que estimula o contribuye a inducir el cáncer.

**cardiac muscle** muscle tissue that is only found in the heart. (p. 554)
**músculo cardíaco** tejido muscular, también conocido como miocardio, que sólo se halla en el corazón.

**carnivore** organism that gets energy by eating only animals. (p. 228)
**carnívoro** organismo que obtiene energía al alimentarse únicamente de otros animales.

**carpel** female structure of flowering plants; made of the ovary, style, and stigma. (p. 364)
**carpelo** estructura reproductora femenina de las plantas con flor; consta de ovario, estilo y stigma.

**carrier** organism who has a gene for a certain trait or disease that does not show up in the organism's phenotype. (p. 109)
**portador** organismo cuyo genoma contiene un gen de cierto rasgo o enfermedad que no se encuentra expresado en el fenotipo de dicho organismo.

**carrying capacity** number of individuals that can be persistently supported by the resources of an environment. (p. 249)
**capacidad de carga de población** número de individuos que los recursos de un ambiente pueden sustentar normalmente de manera continua.

**cartilage** tough, elastic, and fibrous connective tissue found between bones. (p. 551)
**cartílago** tejido conectivo resistente, fibroso y elástico que se encuentra entre los huesos.

**catalyst** (KAT-uhl-ihst) substance that decreases activation energy and increases reaction rate in a chemical reaction. (p. 33)
**catalizador** sustancia que disminuye la energía de activación y aumenta la tasa de reacción de una reacción química determinada.

**catastrophism** theory that states that natural disasters such as floods and volcanic eruptions shaped Earth's landforms and caused extinction of some species. (p. 165)
**catastrofismo** teoría según la cual la configuración actual de los accidentes geográficos de la Tierra y la extinción de algunas especies se debió a inundaciones, erupciones volcánicas y otras catástrofes naturales.

**cell** basic unit of life. (p. 3)
**célula** unidad básica de la vida.

**cell cycle** pattern of growth, DNA replication, and cell division that occurs in a eukaryotic cell. (p. 74)
**ciclo celular** proceso de crecimiento, replicación de ADN y división celular que ocurre en las células eucarióticas.

**cell differentiation** processes by which unspecialized cells develop into their mature form and function. (p. 85)
**diferenciación celular** proceso mediante el cual las células no especializadas adquieren una forma y una función determinada.

**cell membrane** double-layer of phospholipids that forms a boundary between a cell and the surrounding environment and controls the movement of substances into and out of a cell. (p. 43)
**membrana celular** capa doble de fosfolípidos que forma una barrera entre la célula y el medio que la rodea, y que controla el flujo de materiales hacia dentro y hacia fuera de la célula.

**cell theory** theory that states that all organisms are made of cells, all cells are produced by other living cells, and the cell is the most basic unit of life. (p. 37)
**teoría celular** establece que todos los organismos están formados por células, que todas las células proceden de otras células vivas y que la célula es la unidad básica de la vida.

**cellular immunity** immune response that relies on T cells to destroy infected body cells. (p. 523)
**inmunidad celular** respuesta inmune que depende de las células T para atacar las células infectadas del cuerpo.

**cellular respiration** process that makes ATP by breaking down carbon-based molecules when oxygen is present. (p. 62)
**respiración celular** proceso de producción de ATP mediante la descomposición de moléculas de carbono en presencia de oxígeno.

**cell wall** rigid structure that gives protection, support, and shape to cells in plants, algae, fungi, and bacteria. (p. 42)
**pared celular** estructura rígida que proteje, sustenta y da forma a las células de las plantas, algas, hongos y bacterias.

**Cenozoic** geologic time period that began 65 million years ago and continues today. (p. 214)
**Cenozoico** período geológico que empezó hace 65 millones de años y que se extiende hasta la actualidad.

**central dogma** theory that states that, in cells, information only flows from DNA to RNA to proteins. (p. 132)
**dogma central** teoría que formula que la información en las células siempre fluye del ADN al ARN y luego a las proteínas.

**central nervous system (CNS)** part of the nervous system that interprets messages from other nerves in the body; includes the brain and spinal cord. (p. 472)
**sistema nervioso central** parte del sistema nervioso encargada de interpretar los mensajes recibidos de otros nervios del cuerpo; consta del cerebro y de la médula espinal.

**centriole** (SEHN-tree-OHL) small cylinder-shaped organelle made of protein tubes arranged in a circle; divided in mitosis. (p. 40)
**centriolo** orgánulo celular con forma de pequeño cilindro formado por una serie de tubos de proteínas en disposición circular; participa en la reproducción celular.

**centromere** (SEHN-truh-MEER) part of a condensed chromosome that looks pinched; where spindle fibers attach during meiosis and mitosis. (p. 78)
**centrómero** región de condensación del cromosoma donde se une el huso durante la meiosis y la mitosis.

**cephalothorax** (SEHF-uh-luh-THAWR-AKS) region of a crustacean body where the head and thorax meet. (p. 399)
**cefalotórax** región del cuerpo de los crustáceos donde se unen la cabeza y el tórax.

**cerebellum** (SEHR-uh-BEHL-uhm) part of the brain that coordinates and directs all voluntary muscle movement and controls posture and balance. (p. 482)
**cerebelo** parte del encéfalo que coordina y regula todos los movimientos musculares voluntarios, y que permite mantener la postura y el equilibrio.

**cerebral cortex** layer of gray matter on the surface of the cerebrum that receives information and produces responses. (p. 482)
**corteza cerebral** capa de material gris situada en la superficie del cerebro que se encarga de recibir información y de generar respuestas.

**cerebrum** (SEHR-uh-bruhm) largest part of the brain, coordinating movement, thought, reasoning, and memory; includes the cerebral cortex and the white matter beneath it. (p. 481)
**cerebro** la parte más grande del encéfalo que se encarga de coordinar el movimiento, el pensamiento, el razonamiento y la memoria; incluye la corteza cerebral y la materia blanca que se encuentra debajo de ésta.

**chaparral** (SHAP-uh-RAL) biome characterized by hot, dry summers and cool, moist winters; also called Mediterranean shrubland. (p. 260)
**chaparral** bioma caracterizado por veranos secos y calurosos e inviernos frescos y húmedos; también se conoce como matorral mediterráneo.

**chelicerate** arthropod that lacks antennae and has four pairs of walking legs and a pair of fanglike mouth parts. (p. 402)
**quelicerado** artrópodo sin antenas con cuatro pares de patas y una boca de dos piezas en forma de colmillos.

**chemical reaction** process by which substances change into different substances through the making and breaking of chemical bonds. (p. 30)
**reacción química** proceso mediante el cual una sustancia se transforma en otra sustancia diferente al romperse sus enlaces químicos y formarse otros nuevos.

**chemosynthesis** (KEE-mo-SIHN-thih-sihs) process by which ATP is made using chemicals as an energy source instead of light. (pp. 55; 227)
**quimiosíntesis** proceso de síntesis del ATP cuya fuente de energía no es la luz, sino determinadas sustancias químicas.

**childhood** period of life from age two until puberty. (p. 572)
**infancia** periodo de la vida comprendido entre los dos años y la pubertad.

**chitin** tough, protective polysaccharide that makes up arthropod skeletons and the cell walls of some fungi. (pp. 324; 395)
**quitina** polisacárido duro que forma los exoesqueletos de los artrópodos y las paredes celulares de algunos hongos.

**chlorophyll** (KLAWR-uh-fihl) light-absorbing pigment molecule in photosynthetic organisms. (p. 56)
**clorofila** molécula pigmentaria de los organismos fotosintéticos que absorbe la luz.

follicle after ovu-
of its yellow color.

ués de la ovulación; se
causa de su color.

nic leaf inside of a
a en el interior de la

s opposite of the flow

n sentido opuesto al
peces.

en two atoms share

se forma cuando dos
lectrones.

anismos.

segments between
sis I. (p. 105)
mentos de
gos durante la meiosis

, such as lobsters, crabs,
, an exoskeleton, and

s langostas, los
riza por tener un
ares de extremidades

l between members of
t by natural selection.

miento que se
sma población, no por
ceso de aprendizaje.

n moisture; in insects, a
aterial. (pp. 332; 389)
cera que mantiene la
luro de material inerte.

n) bacteria that can
ar la fotosíntesis.

ess by which the cell
citoplasma celular se

one that stimulates
s; also involved in the

nula la última fase
bién participa en el

that contains molecules
terior de las células
s y, en algunas células,

---

up of numer-
ergy into

s membranes
energía

lopment, a
412)
de su
duras faríngeas

cated chromo-

s that is pres-
manifiesta

t consists of
77)
ADN formado
n genética.

re that passes
la que pasa del

cover some or
and capture

cubren total
las y que
tos.

s over a
arca 24 horas.
utrients and
rt, blood, and
o de trans-
corporales;
os.

nary relation-
e order that

según su
upadas en el

onary rela-
parentescos
e especies.

sm learns to
rd or punish-

cual un
viamente

---

**climate** average long-term weather pattern of a region. (p. 257)
**clima** promedio de valores del tiempo en una región a largo plazo.

**clone** genetically identical copy of a single gene or an entire organism. (p. 154)
**clon** copia genéticamente exacta de un gen o de un organismo completo.

**codominance** heterozygous genotype that equally expresses the traits from both alleles. (p. 112)
**codominancia** genotipo heterocigoto que expresa equitativamente los rasgos de ambos alelos.

**codon** sequence of three nucleotides that codes for one amino acid. (p. 136)
**codón** secuencia de tres nucleótidos que codifica un aminoácido.

**coelom** fluid-filled space that is completely covered by mesoderm. (p. 388)
**celoma** cavidad llena de líquido cubierta enteramente por el mesodermo.

**coevolution** process in which two or more species evolve in response to changes in each other. (p. 196)
**coevolución** proceso mediante el cual dos o más especies evolucionan a consecuencia de cambios producidos en cada uno de ellas.

**cognition** mental process of knowing, including aspects such as awareness, perception, reasoning, and judgment. (p. 456)
**cognición** conjunto de procesos mentales cuya función es el conocimiento y que incluyen la conciencia, la percepción, el razonamiento y el juicio.

**cohesion** attraction between molecules of the same substance. (p. 22)
**cohesión** atracción entre moléculas de una misma sustancia.

**cohesion tension theory** theory that explains how the physical properties of water allow it to move through the xylem of plants. (p. 349)
**teoría de la tensión-cohesión** teoría que explica el modo en que las propiedades físicas del agua permiten que ésta fluya a través del xilema de las plantas.

**collagen** three-stranded protein, found only in animals, that combines to form strong, flexible fibers. (p. 377)
**colágeno** proteína animal compuesta por tres cadenas que se enlazan para formar fibras resistentes y flexibles.

**collenchyma cell** elongated cells with unevenly thick walls that form a supportive tissue of plants. (p. 346)
**célula del colénquima** célula alargada con paredes de grosor irregular que forma el tejido de sostén de las plantas.

**commensalism** ecological relationship in which one species receives a benefit but the other species is not affected one way or another. (p. 243)
**comensalismo** relación ecológica entre dos especies en la que una se beneficia sin perjudicar ni beneficiar a la otra.

**community** collection of all of the different populations that live in one area. (p. 221)
**comunidad** conjunto de todas las poblaciones que viven en un área determinada.

**competition** ecological relationship in which two organisms try to obtain the same resource. (p. 243)
**competencia** relación ecológica en la que dos organismos tratan de obtener el mismo recurso.

**competitive exclusion** theory that states that no two species can occupy the same niche at the same time. (p. 242)
**exclusión competitiva** teoría según la cual dos especies distintas no pueden ocupar el mismo nicho al mismo tiempo.

**complete digestive tract** digestive system that has two openings, a mouth and an anus, that are at opposite ends of a continuous tube. (p. 387)
**tubo digestivo completo** sistema digestivo con dos aperturas, la boca y el ano, situadas en los extremos opuestos de un tubo continuo.

**complete metamorphosis** process by which immature organisms change their body form before becoming an adult. (p. 405)
**metamorfosis completa** proceso mediante el cual se van produciendo cambios en los organismos inmaduros antes de llegar a adultos.

**compound** substance made of atoms of different elements that are bonded together in a set ratio. (p. 20)
**compuesto** sustancia formada por átomos de diversos elementos combinados en una proporción determinada.

**concentration gradient** difference in the concentration of a substance from one location to another. (p. 46)
**gradiente de concentración** diferencia en la concentración de una sustancia entre un lugar y otro.

**cone** reproductive structure of gymnosperms inside of which the female gamete is fertilized and seeds are produced. (p. 337)
**cono** estructura reproductora de las gimnospermas en cuyo interior se fertiliza el gameto femenino y se producen semillas.

**cone cell** sensory neuron in the eye that detects color. (p. 478)
**cono (célula)** neurona sensorial del ojo que detecta el color.

**coniferous** tree that keeps its needles year-round and reproduces with cones. (p. 260)
**conífera** árbol que mantiene sus hojas durante todo el año y que se reproduce mediante conos.

**conjugation** process by which a prokaryote transfers part of its chromosome to another prokaryote. (p. 307)
**conjugación** proceso mediante el cual un procarionte transfiere parte de su cromosoma a otro procarionte.

**constant** condition that is controlled so that it does not change during an experiment. (p. 10)
**constante** condición controlada de un experimento que no varía en el transcurso del mismo.

**consumer** organism that gets its energy and nutrients by eating other organisms. (p. 226)
**consumidor** organismo que obtiene su energía y nutrientes mediante la ingestión de otros organismos.

**convergent evolution** evolution toward similar characteristics in unrelated species, resulting from adaptations to similar environmental conditions. (p. 195)
**evolución convergente** evolución hacia características similares en especies no relacionadas, que resulta de adaptaciones a condiciones ambientales similares.

**coral reef** ocean habitat found in the shallow coastal waters in a tropical climate. (p. 263)
**arrecife de coral** hábitat oceánico que se encuentra en aguas costeras poco profundas de climas tropicales.

**corpus luteum** (KAWR-puhs LOO-tee-u lation; also called a yellow body because (p. 565)
**cuerpo lúteo** folículo que aparece des conoce también como cuerpo amarillo

**cotyledon** (KAHT-uhl-EED-uhn) embry seed. (p. 340)
**cotiledón** hoja embriónica que se for semilla.

**countercurrent flow** flow of water that of blood in a fish's gills. (p. 415)
**flujo contracorriente** flujo de agua flujo de la sangre en las branquias de lo

**covalent bond** chemical bond formed w one or more pairs of electrons. (p. 21)
**enlace covalente** enlace químico qu átomos comparten uno o más pares de

**cross** mating of two organisms. (p. 96)
**cruzamiento** apareamiento de dos or

**crossing over** exchange of chromosome homologous chromosomes during mei
**entrecruzamiento** intercambio de se cromosomas entre cromosomas homól I.

**crustacean** any of the aquatic arthropod and shrimps, that has a segmented body paired, jointed limbs. (p. 399)
**crustáceo** artrópodo acuático, como l cangrejos y los camarones, que se carac cuerpo segmentado, un exoesqueleto y articuladas.

**cultural behavior** behavior that is passe the same population by learning and n (p. 457)
**comportamiento cultural** comport transmite entre los miembros de una m selección natural, sino mediante un pr

**cuticle** in plants, a waxy layer that holds tough exoskeleton made of nonliving m
**cutícula** en las plantas, es una capa de humedad; en los insectos, exoesqueleto

**cyanobacteria** (singular: cyanobacteriu carry out photosynthesis. (p. 210)
**cianobacteria** bacteria capaz de reali

**cytokinesis** (sy-toh-kuh-NEE-sihs) pro cytoplasm divides. (p. 74)
**citocinesis** proceso mediante el cual divide.

**cytokinin** (sy-tuh-KY-nihn) plant horm the final stage of cell division, cytokine growth of side branches. (p. 372)
**citoquinina** hormona vegetal que est de la división celular: la citocinesis; tan crecimiento de las ramas laterales.

**cytoplasm** jellylike substance inside cells and, in some cells, organelles. (p. 38)
**citoplasma** sustancia gelatinosa del i que contiene diversos tipos de molécul orgánulos.

**cytoskeleton** network of proteins, such as microtubules and microfilaments, inside a eukaryotic cell that supports and shapes the cell. (p. 39)

**citoesqueleto** red proteica, como los microtúbulos y los microfilamentos, dentro de una célula eucariótica que da soporte y define la forma de la célula.

# D

**data** (singular: datum) observations and measurements recorded during an experiment. (p. 9)

**datos** observaciones y medidas registrados en el transcurso de un experimento.

**deciduous** tree that has adapted to winter temperatures by dropping its leaves and going dormant during the cold season. (p. 260)

**caducifolio** árbol que pierde su foliaje y entra en un período de letargo para adaptarse a las temperaturas invernales.

**decomposer** detritivore that breaks down organic matter into simpler compounds, returning nutrients back into an ecosystem. (p. 228)

**descomponedor** detritívoro que, al descomponer la materia orgánica en compuestos más sencillos, devuelve al ecosistema sus nutrientes básicos.

**dendrite** branchlike extension of a neuron that receives impulses from neighboring neurons. (p. 474)

**dendrita** prolongación ramificada de la neurona que recibe impulsos eléctricos de las neuronas adyacentes.

**density-dependent limiting factor** environmental resistance that affects a population that has become overly crowded. (p. 249)

**factor limitativo dependiente de la densidad** resistencia ambiental que afecta a una población sometida a una densidad demográfica excesiva.

**density-independent limiting factor** environmental resistance that affects a population regardless of population density. (p. 249)

**factor limitativo independiente de la densidad** resistencia ambiental que afecta a una población sin importar su densidad demográfica.

**dependent variable** experimental data collected through observation and measurement. (p. 10)

**variable dependiente** datos de una investigación recolectados por medio de la observación y de la medición.

**depressant** drug that causes fewer signals to be transmitted between neurons. (p. 487)

**depresor** medicamento que reduce la transmisión de señales entre las neuronas.

**derived characteristic** trait that differs in structure or function from that found in the ancestral line for a group of species; used in constructing cladograms. (p. 287)

**carácter derivado** rasgo que difiere, en su estructura o función, del hallado en un linaje ancestral de un grupo de especies; se usa para crear cladogramas.

**dermal tissue** tissue system that covers the outside of plants and animals. (p. 347)

**tejido dérmico** sistema de tejidos que cubre la superficie de los animales y las plantas.

**dermis** second layer of skin that includes structural proteins, blood vessels, glands, and hair follicles. (p. 558)

**dermis** segunda capa de piel formada por proteínas estructurales, vasos sanguíneos y folículos capilares.

**desensitization** process by which neurons in the brain break down neurotransmitter receptors in response to a larger amount of neurotransmitter in the synapse than usual. (p. 486)

**desensibilización** proceso mediante el cual las neuronas del cerebro inactivan los receptores de los neurotransmisores como respuesta a una cantidad de neurotransmisores mayor de lo habitual en la sinapsis.

**desert** biome characterized by a very dry climate. (p. 260)

**desierto** bioma caracterizado por un clima muy seco.

**determination** process by which stem cells become committed to develop into only one type of cell. (p. 460)

**determinación celular** proceso mediante el cual las células madre se desarrollan en un tipo específico de célula.

**detritivore** organism that eats dead organic matter. (p. 228)

**detritívoro** organismo que se alimenta de materia orgánica muerta.

**deuterostome** animal development in which the animal's anus develops before the mouth. (p. 380)

**deuterostomia** desarrollo animal en el que el ano del animal se desarrolla antes que la boca.

**dialysis** treatment in which a patient's blood is filtered through a machine, the waste is removed, and the cleaned blood is returned to the patient's body. (p. 547)

**diálisis** tratamiento médico que consiste en filtrar la sangre del paciente mediante una máquina que elimina los desechos y devuelve la sangre purificada al cuerpo del paciente.

**diaphragm** thin muscle below the rib cage that controls the flow of air into and out of the lungs. (p. 495)

**diafragma** músculo delgado situado debajo de la caja torácica que controla el flujo de aire hacia el interior y el exterior de los pulmones.

**diastolic pressure** (DY-uh-STAHL-ihk) pressure in an artery when the left ventricle relaxes. (p. 504)

**presión diastólica** presión en la arteria en el momento en que se relaja el ventrículo izquierdo.

**dicot** (DY-KAHT) flowering plant whose embryos have two cotyledons. (p. 340)

**dicotiledónea** planta con flor cuyos embriones tienen dos cotiledones.

**differentiation** process by which committed cells acquire the structures and functions of highly specialized cells. (p. 461)

**diferenciación celular** proceso mediante el cual ciertas células adquieren estructuras y funciones altamente especializadas.

**diffusion** movement of dissolved molecules in a fluid or gas from a region of higher concentration to a region of lower concentration. (p. 46)

**difusión** movimiento de las moléculas disueltas en un líquido o gas desde una región de alta concentración a otra región de menor concentración.

**digestion** process by which large, complex molecules are broken down into smaller molecules that can be used by cells. (p. 539)

**digestión** proceso mediante el cual grandes y complejas moléculas se descomponen en moléculas más pequeñas que pueden ser absorbidas por las células.

**digestive system** body system that digests food; includes mouth, esophagus, stomach, pancreas, intestines, liver, gallbladder, rectum, and anus. (p. 539)

**sistema digestivo** sistema corporal encargado de la digestión de los alimentos; consta de la boca, el esófago, el estómago, el páncreas, los intestinos, el hígado, la vesícula biliar, el recto y el ano.

**dihybrid cross** cross, or mating, between organisms involving two pairs of contrasting traits. (p. 103)

**cruzamiento dihíbrido** cruzamiento o apareamiento entre organismos que tienen dos pares de rasgos opuestos.

**diploid** (DIHP-loyd) cell that has two copies of each chromosome, one from an egg and one from a sperm. (p. 91)

**diploide** celula que tiene dos copias de cada cromosoma, una proveniente de un óvulo y la otra de un espermatozoide.

**directional selection** pathway of natural selection in which one uncommon phenotype is selected over a more common phenotype. (p. 183)

**selección direccional** proceso de selección natural en el que se favorece un fenotipo menos común sobre un fenotipo más común.

**disruptive selection** pathway of natural selection in which two opposite, but equally uncommon, phenotypes are selected over the most common phenotype. (p. 184)

**selección disruptiva** proceso de selección natural en el que se favorece a dos fenotipos opuestos, pero igualmente poco comunes, sobre el fenotipo común.

**divergent evolution** evolution of one or more closely related species into different species; resulting from adaptations to different environmental conditions. (p. 195)

**evolución divergente** evolución de una o más especies afines que lleva a la formación de especies diferentes como resultado de adaptaciones a diversas condiciones ambientales.

**DNA; deoxyribonucleic acid** (dee-AHK-see-RY-boh-noo-KLEE-ihk) molecule that stores genetic information in all organisms. (p. 4)

**ADN (ácido desoxirribonucleico)** molécula que almacena la información genética de todos los organismos.

**DNA fingerprint** unique sequence of DNA base pairs that can be used to identify a person at the molecular level. (p. 152)

**identificación por ADN** secuencia única de pares de bases de ADN que permite la identificación de una persona a nivel molecular.

**DNA microarray** research tool used to study gene expression. (p. 158)

**micromatriz de material genético (biochip)** instrumento de investigación usado para estudiar la expresión de los genes.

**DNA polymerase** (PAHL-uh-muh-RAYS) enzyme that makes bonds between nucleotides, forming an identical strand of DNA during replication. (p. 129)

**ADN polimerasa** enzima que establece enlaces entre los nucleótidos y que permite la formación de cadenas idénticas de ADN durante el proceso de replicación.

**dominant** allele that is expressed when two different alleles are present in an organism's genotype. (p. 99)

**dominante** el alelo que se expresa de entre dos alelos diferentes que integran el genotipo de un organismo determinado.

**dormancy** state of inactivity during which an organism or embryo is not growing. (p. 368)

**letargo** periodo de inactividad durante el cual un organismo o embrión no crece.

**double fertilization** process by which two sperm of a flowering plant join with an egg and a polar body, forming an embryo and endosperm. (p. 366)

**fertilización doble** proceso mediante el cual dos gametos masculinos de una planta angiosperma se combinan con un óvulo y un núcleo polar para dar lugar al embrión y al endosperma.

**double helix** model that compares the structure of a DNA molecule, in which two strands wind around one another, to that of a twisted ladder. (p. 127)

**doble hélice** modelo mediante el cual se representa la estructura molecular del ADN como dos cadenas que giran sobre sí mismas, como una escalera espiroidal.

# E

**ecological equivalents** organisms that share a similar niche but live in different geographical regions. (p. 242)

**equivalentes ecológicos** organismos que tienen nichos ecológicos similares, pero que viven en diferentes zonas geográficas.

**ecological footprint** amount of land necessary to produce and maintain enough food, water, shelter, energy, and waste. (p. 270)

**huella ecológica** espacio que requiere una población humana para producir y mantener suficiente alimento, agua, alojamiento y energía, y para contener sus desperdicios.

**ecological niche** all of the physical, chemical, and biological factors that a species needs to survive, stay healthy, and reproduce in an ecosystem. (p. 241)

**nicho ecológico** conjunto de factores físicos, químicos y biológicos que una especie requiere para sobrevivir de manera saludable y reproducirse en un ecosistema determinado.

**ecology** study of the interactions among living things and their surroundings. (p. 221)

**ecología** estudio de las interacciones entre los seres vivos y su entorno.

**ecosystem** collection of organisms and nonliving things, such as climate, soil, water, and rocks, in an area. (pp. 5; 221)

**ecosistema** conjunto de organismos y factores físicos, como el clima, el suelo, el agua y las rocas, que caracterizan una zona determinada.

**ectotherm** organism that regulates its body temperature by exchanging heat with its environment. (p. 431)

**poiquilotermo** organismo que regula su temperatura corporal mediante el intercambio de calor con el ambiente.

**egg** female gamete. (p. 95)

**óvulo** gameto femenino.

**electron transport chain** series of proteins in the thylakoid and mitochondrial membranes that aid in converting ADP to ATP by transferring electrons. (p. 59)
**cadena de transporte de electrones** serie de proteínas de las membranas de las mitocondrias y los tilacoides que contribuyen a transformar ADP en ATP mediante la transferencia de electrones.

**element** substance made of only one type of atom that cannot be broken down by chemical means. (p. 19)
**elemento** sustancia formada por un solo tipo de átomo que no se puede descomponer por medios químicos.

**embryo** stage of development after the fertilized cell implants into the uterus but before the cells take on a recognizable shape. (p. 568)
**embrión** fase de desarrollo a partir de la implantación del óvulo fertilizado en el útero, anterior a la etapa en que las células adquieren una forma reconocible.

**emigration** movement of individuals out of a population. (p. 248)
**emigración** flujo de individuos que abandonan una población.

**emphysema** (EHM-fih-SEE-muh) condition of the lungs in which the surface area of aveoli decreases, making breathing difficult. (p. 499)
**enfisema** enfermedad de los pulmones que causa una reducción en la superficie de los alvéolos y, en consecuencia, dificulta la respiración.

**endocrine system** (EHN-duh-krihn) body system that controls growth, development, and responses to the environment by relcasing chemical signals into the bloodstream. (p. 472)
**sistema endocrino** sistema corporal que controla el crecimiento, el desarrollo y las respuestas al entorno, mediante la liberación de señales químicas al torrente sanguíneo.

**endocytosis** (EHN-doh-sy-TOH-sihs) uptake of liquids or large molecules into a cell by inward folding of the cell membrane. (p. 49)
**endocitosis** captación celular de líquidos o de grandes moléculas mediante una invaginación de la membrana hacia el interior de la célula.

**endometrium** (EHN-doh-MEE-tree-uhm) lining of the uterus. (p. 564)
**endometrio** recubrimiento interior del útero.

**endoplasmic reticulum** (EHN-duh-PLAZ-mihk rih-TIHK-yuh-luhm) interconnected network of thin, folded membranes that produce, process, and distribute proteins. (p. 39)
**retículo endoplasmático** red de finas membranas interconectadas y plegadas que producen, procesan y distribuyen proteínas.

**endoskeleton** internal skeleton built of bone or cartilage. (p. 412)
**endoesqueleto** esqueleto interno formado por huesos y cartílagos.

**endosperm** tissue within seeds of flowering plants that nourishes an embryo. (p. 366)
**endosperma** tejido de reserva dentro de las semillas de las plantas con flor que abastece el embrión.

**endospore** prokaryotic cell with a thick, protective wall surrounding its DNA. (p. 308)
**endospora** célula procariótica cuyo ADN está protegido por una gruesa pared.

**endosymbiosis** ecological relationship in which one organism lives inside the body of another organism. (p. 210)
**endosimbiosis** relación ecológica en la que un organismo vive en el interior de otro.

**endotherm** organism that produces its own heat through metabolic processes. (p. 431)
**endotermo** organismo que regula la temperatura de su cuerpo mediante sus propios procesos metabólicos.

**endothermic** chemical reaction that requires a net input of energy. (p. 32)
**endotérmica** reacción química que requiere un aporte neto de energía.

**energy pyramid** diagram that compares energy used by producers, primary consumers, and other trophic levels. (p. 236)
**pirámide de energía** diagrama mediante el cual se compara la energía usada por los productores, los consumidores primarios y otros niveles tróficos.

**enzyme** protein that catalyzes chemical reactions for organisms. (p. 34)
**enzima** proteína que cataliza reacciones químicas para los organismos.

**epidemic** rapid outbreak of a disease that affects many people. (p. 303)
**epidemia** aparición repentina de una enfermedad que afecta a muchas personas.

**epidermis** outermost layer of skin that consists mainly of dead skin cells, and provides a barrier to pathogens. (p. 557)
**epidermis** primera capa de piel, que consta principalmente de células epiteliales muertas y que constituye una barrera para los patógenos.

**epididymis** coiled tube through which sperm leave the testes and enter the vas deferens. (p. 562)
**epidídimo** tubo enrollado a través del cuál los espermatozoides salen de los testículos y pasan al conducto deferente.

**epoch** smallest unit of geologic time, lasting several million years. (p. 204)
**época** unidad más pequeña de tiempo geológico, que dura varios millones de años.

**equilibrium** (EE-kwuh-LIHB-ree-uhm) condition in which reactants and products of a chemical reaction are formed at the same rate. (p. 31)
**equilibrio químico** estado en el que los reactivos y los productos de una reacción química se forman a la misma velocidad.

**era** second largest unit of geologic time, lasting tens to hundreds of millions of years and consisting of two or more periods. (p. 204)
**era** segunda unidad más amplia de tiempo geológico; que abarca entre decenas y cientos de millones de años y consta de dos o más períodos.

**esophagus** (ih-SAHF-uh-guhs) tube-shaped tissue of the digestive system that connects the mouth to the stomach. (p. 540)
**esófago** tejido en forma de tubo del sistema digestivo que conecta la boca con el estómago.

**estrogen** steroid hormone that is found in greater quantities in women than in men and contributes to female sexual characteristics and development. (p. 561)
**estrógeno** hormona esteroide que abunda más en las mujeres que en los hombres, y que contribuye al desarrollo de las características sexuales femeninas.

**estuary** partially enclosed body of water found where a river flows into the ocean. (p. 264)

**estuario** masa de agua parcialmente cerrada donde un río desemboca en el océano.

**ethnobotany** study of how various cultures use plants. (p. 342)

**etnobotánica** estudio del conocimiento que tienen las culturas sobre el uso de las plantas.

**ethylene** (EHTH-uh-LEEN) plant hormone that is produced in fruits and causes them to ripen. (p. 372)

**etileno** hormona vegetal que se produce en las frutas y que las hace madurar.

**Eukarya** one of the three domains of life, contains all eukaryotes in kingdoms Protista, Plantae, Fungi, and Animalia. (p. 293)

**Eukarya** uno de los tres dominios de la vida; consta de todos los eucariotas de los reinos protistas, plantashongos y animales.

**eukaryotic cell** (yoo-KAR-ee-AHT-ihk) cell that has a nucleus and other membrane-bound organelles. (p. 38)

**célula eucariota** célula que consta de un núcleo y de otros orgánulos limitados por una membrana.

**eusocial** organism population in which the role of each organism is specialized and not all of the organisms will reproduce. (p. 454)

**eusocial** población de organismos en la que todos tienen una función especializada y en la que algunos de ellos no se reproducen.

**eutherian** mammal that gives birth to live young that have completed fetal development. (p. 440)

**euterio** mamífero cuyas crías nacen tras un desarrollo fetal completo.

**evolution** change in a species over time (p. 7); process of biological change by which descendents come to differ from their ancestors. (p. 164)

**evolución** proceso de cambio de las especies a través del tiempo; proceso de cambios biológicos a través del cual los descendientes se diferencian de sus ancestros.

**excretory system** body system that collects and gets rid of wastes from the body; includes the kidneys and bladder. (p. 544)

**sistema excretor** sistema corporal que recoge y elimina los desechos del organismo; consta de los riñones y la vejiga urinaria.

**exocytosis** (EHK-soh-sy-TOH-sihs) release of substances out a cell by the fusion of a vesicle with the membrane. (p. 50)

**exocitosis** expulsión de sustancias de una célula mediante la fusión de una vesícula citoplasmática con la membrana celular.

**exon** sequence of DNA that codes information for protein synthesis. (p. 140)

**exón** secuencia de ADN que codifica la información para la síntesis de las proteínas.

**exoskeleton** hard outer structure, such as the shell of an insect or crustacean, that provides protection and support for the organism. (p. 395)

**exoesqueleto** estructura exterior dura como, por ejemplo, el caparazón de un crustáceo, que protege y sustenta al organismo.

**exothermic** chemical reaction that yields a net release of energy in the form of heat. (p. 32)

**exotérmica** reacción química que, al producirse, libera energía en forma calor.

**experiment** process that tests a hypothesis by collecting information under controlled conditions. (p. 10)

**experimento** procedimiento mediante el cual se trata de comprobar una hipótesis mediante la recolección de datos bajo condiciones controladas.

**exponential growth** dramatic increase in population over a short period of time. (p. 248)

**crecimiento exponencial** intenso incremento de población en un breve espacio de tiempo.

**extinction** elimination of a species from Earth. (p. 197)

**extinción** desaparición de una especie o grupo de especies de la Tierra.

# F

**facilitated diffusion** diffusion of molecules assisted by protein channels that pierce a cell membrane. (p. 48)

**difusión facilitada** difusión de moléculas asistida mediante canales de proteínas que perforan la membrana celular.

**facultative aerobe** organism that can live with or without oxygen. (p. 306)

**aerobio facultativo** organismo capaz de vivir con o sin oxígeno.

**fallopian tube** tube of connective tissue that attaches the ovary to the uterus in the female reproductive system and in which fertilization occurs. (p. 561)

**trompa de Falopio** conducto de tejido conjuntivo que conecta el ovario con el útero en el sistema reproductor femenino, y donde se produce la fertilización.

**fatty acid** hydrocarbon chain often bonded to glycerol in a lipid. (p. 27)

**ácido graso** cadena de hidrocarbono que suele enlazarce con los glicéridos de un lípido.

**feedback** information that is compared with a set of ideal values and aids in maintaining homeostasis. (p. 465)

**retroalimentación** información que se compara con un grupo de valores ideales y que contribuye al mantenimiento de la homeóstasis.

**fermentation** anaerobic process by which ATP is produced by glycolysis. (p. 70)

**fermentación** proceso anaeróbico que da lugar al ATP mediante la glicólisis.

**fertilization** fusion of an egg and sperm cell. (p. 91)

**fertilización** fusión de un gameto masculino y uno femenino.

**fetus** unborn offspring from the end of the eighth week after conception to the moment of birth. (p. 569)

**feto** cría no nacida desde el final de la octava semana después de la concepción hasta el momento del nacimiento.

**fibrous root** root system made up of many threadlike members of more or less equal length. (p. 352)

**raíces fibrosas** sistema radical compuesto de una multitud de filamentos que tienen una longitud aproximadamente igual.

**filter feeder** animal that eats by straining particles from water. (p. 383)

**organismo filtrador** animal que se alimenta mediante la filtración de partículas del agua.

**fitness** measure of an organism's ability to survive and have off-spring relative to other members of a population. (p. 171)
**aptitud biológica** capacidad de un organismo determinado para sobrevivir y producir descendencia en relación con los demás miembros de una población.

**flagellum** (plural: flagella) whiplike structure outside of a cell that is used for movement. (p. 306)
**flagelo** estructura en forma de látigo del exterior de determinadas células que les permite moverse en su medio.

**flower** female reproductive structure of an angiosperm. (p. 337)
**flor** sistema reproductor femenino de una angiosperma.

**fluid mosaic model** model that describes the arrangement and movement of the molecules that make up a cell membrane. (p. 44)
**modelo de mosaico fluido** modelo que describe la disposición y movimiento de las moléculas que conforman la membrana celular.

**follicle** group of cells that surrounds and nourishes an egg while it is in the ovary. (p. 563)
**folículo** conjunto de células que rodean y nutren al óvulo mientras éste permanece en el ovario.

**food chain** model that links organisms by their feeding relation-ships. (p. 228)
**cadena alimentaria** modelo que relaciona los organismos según sus interacciones alimentarias.

**food web** model that shows the complex network of feeding relationships within an ecosystem. (p. 229)
**red alimentaria** modelo que representa una red compleja de relaciones alimentarias en un ecosistema determinado.

**fossil** trace of an organism from the past. (p. 165)
**fósil** huella de un organismo del pasado.

**founder effect** genetic drift that occurs after a small number of individuals colonize a new area. (p. 187)
**efecto fundador** deriva genética que se produce cuando un pequeño número de individuos coloniza una nueva región.

**frameshift mutation** mutation that involves the insertion or deletion of a nucleotide in the DNA sequence. (p. 142)
**mutación del marco de lectura** mutación que implica la incorporación o la eliminación de un nucleótido en una secuencia de ADN.

**fruit** fertilized and mature ovary of a flower. (p. 337)
**fruto** ovario fertilizado y maduro de una flor.

**fruiting body** spore-producing part of a fungus that grows above ground. (p. 324)
**esporocarpo** estructura productora de esporas de un hongo que crece sobre la tierra.

# G

**gamete** sex cell; an egg or a sperm cell. (p. 90)
**gameto** célula sexual; óvulo o espermatozoide.

**gametogenesis** (guh-MEE-tuh-JEHN-ih-sihs) process by which gametes are made through the combination of meiosis and other maturational changes. (p. 95)
**gametogénesis** proceso de producción de gametos mediante una combinación de meiosis y otros cambios de maduración.

**gametophyte** (guh-MEE-tuh-FYT) haploid, gamete-producing phase in a plant life cycle. (p. 360)
**gametofito** fase de producción de gametos o células sexuales haploides en el ciclo de vida de las plantas.

**gastrovascular cavity** saclike digestive space. (p. 384)
**cavidad gastrovascular** espacio digestivo en forma de bolsa.

**gel electrophoresis** (ih-LEHK-troh-fuh-REE-sihs) method of separating various lengths of DNA strands by applying an elec-trical current to a gel. (p. 148)
**electroforesis en gel** método de separación de fragmentos de ADN mediante la aplicación de una corriente eléctrica a un gel.

**gene** specific region of DNA that codes for a particular protein. (pp. 13; 99)
**gen** parte específica del ADN con información codificada para sintetizar una proteína.

**gene flow** physical movement of alleles from one population to another. (p. 186)
**flujo génico** desplazamiento físico de alelos de una población a otra.

**gene knockout** genetic manipulation in which one or more of an organism's genes are prevented from being expressed. (p. 156)
**supresión génica** manipulación genética mediante la cual se anula la capacidad de expresarse de uno o más genes de un organismo determinado.

**gene pool** collection of alleles found in all of the individuals of a population. (p. 181)
**población genética** colección de alelos de todos los individuos de una población determinada.

**generalist** species that does not rely on a single source of prey. (p. 229)
**generalista** especie que no depende de un solo tipo de presa.

**gene sequencing** process of determining the order of DNA nucleotides in genes and genomes. (p. 157)
**secuenciación génica** proceso de determinación del orden de los nucleótidos de ADN en los genes y en los genomas.

**gene therapy** procedure to treat a disease in which a defective or missing gene is replaced or a new gene is put into a patient's genome. (p. 160)
**terapia génica** procedimiento para el tratamiento de una enfermedad en el que un gen defectuoso o ausente se reemplaza por uno sano que se inserta en el genoma del paciente.

**genetic drift** change in allele frequencies due to chance alone, occurring most commonly in small populations. (p. 187)
**deriva genética** cambio en las frecuencias de alelos que se produce, sobre todo, en poblaciones pequeñas.

**genetic engineering** process of changing an organism's DNA to give the organism new traits. (p. 154)
**ingeniería genética** proceso de modifación del ADN de un organismo con el fin de dotarlo de nuevos rasgos.

**genetic linkage** tendency for genes located close together on the same chromosome to be inherited together. (p. 106)
**ligamiento genético** tendencia de los genes que se encuentran muy próximos en un cromosoma a ser transmitidos juntos a la descendencia.

**genetics** study of the heredity patterns and variation of organ-isms. (p. 96)
**genética** estudio de los patrones hereditarios y de la variación de los organismos.

**genetic screening** process of testing DNA to determine the chance that a person has, or might pass on, a genetic disorder. (p. 160)
**análisis genético** proceso de análisis de ADN para determinar las probabilidades que tiene una persona de contraer o transmitir una enfermedad genética.

**genome** all of an organism's genetic material. (p. 100)
**genoma** todo el material genético de un organismo determinado.

**genomics** (juh-NOH-mihks) study and comparison of genomes within a single species or among different species. (pp. 13; 157)
**genómica** estudio comparativo de los genomas de una misma especie y de especies diferentes.

**genotype** (JEHN-uh-TYP) collection of all of an organism's genetic information that codes for traits. (p. 100)
**genotipo** conjunto de todos los rasgos codificados en la información genética de un organismo.

**genus** first name in binomial nomenclature; the second-most specific taxon in the Linnaean classification system that includes one or more physically similar species, which are thought to be closely related. (p. 284)
**género** primera palabra de la nomenclatura binomial; segundo taxón más específico del sistema de clasificación de las especies de Linneo, que consta de dos o más especies físicamente semejantes consideradas muy próximas.

**geographic isolation** isolation between populations due to physical barriers. (p. 194)
**aislamiento geográfico** separación entre poblaciones debido a barreras físicas.

**geologic time scale** time scale representing the history of Earth. (p. 204)
**escala de tiempo geológico** escala de tiempo para representar la historia de la Tierra.

**geosphere** features of Earth's surface—such as continents and the sea floor—and everything below Earth's surface. (p. 255)
**geosfera** componentes de la superficie de la Tierra, es decir, los continentes, el suelo oceánico y el interior mismo de la Tierra.

**germination** process by which seeds or spores sprout and begin to grow. (p. 369)
**germinación** proceso mediante el cual las semillas o esporas brotan y empiezan a crecer.

**germ theory** theory that states that diseases are caused by microscopic particles called pathogens. (p. 514)
**teoría de los gérmenes** teoría según la cual las enfermedades son causadas por unas partículas microscópicas llamadas patógenos.

**gibberellin** (JIHB-uh-REHL-ihn) plant hormone that stimulates cell growth. (p. 372)
**giberelina** hormona vegetal que estimula el crecimiento celular.

**gill** respiratory organ of aquatic animals that allows breathing underwater. (p. 415)
**branquia** órgano respiratorio de numerosos animales acuáticos que permite respirar bajo el agua.

**gland** organ that makes and releases chemicals that affect the activities of other tissues. (p. 488)
**glándula** órgano que produce y secreta compuestos químicos que afectan el funcionamiento de otros tejidos.

**global warming** worldwide trend of increasing average temperatures. (p. 273)
**calentamiento global** incremento del promedio de la temperatura en toda la Tierra.

**glomerulus** (gloh-MEHR-yuh-luhs) tangled ball of capillaries that circulates blood in the kidneys. (p. 545)
**glomérulos** ovillo de vasos capilares por los que circula la sangre en los riñones.

**glycolysis** (gly-KAHL-uh-sihs) anaerobic process in which glucose is broken down into two molecules of pyruvate and two net ATP are produced. (p. 62)
**glicólisis** proceso anaeróbico en el que la glucosa se descompone en dos moléculas de piruvato y se producen dos moléculas de ATP.

**Golgi apparatus** (GOHL-jee) stack of flat, membrane-enclosed spaces containing enzymes that process, sort, and deliver proteins. (p. 40)
**aparato de Golgi** conjunto de sacos apilados y aplanados rodeados de una membrana que contienen enzimas que procesan, clasifican y distribuyen proteínas.

**gradualism** principle that states that the changes in landforms result from slow changes over a long period of time. (p. 165)
**gradualismo** principio que postula que los cambios en los accidentes geográficos resultan de pequeños cambios graduales durante extensos períodos de tiempo.

**grassland** biome in which the primary plant life is grass. (p. 260)
**pradera** bioma en la que las forma de vida vegetal predominante son las hierbas y los pastos.

**gravitropism** growth of plants in response to gravity; plant stems grow upward, against gravity, and roots grow toward the gravitational pull. (p. 373)
**gravitropismo** crecimiento de las plantas condicionado por la gravedad; el tallo crece hacia arriba, en sentido inverso a la fuerza de gravedad, y las raíces crecen hacia abajo, en el mismo sentido que la gravedad.

**greenhouse effect** normal warming effect produced when gases, such as carbon dioxide and methane, trap heat in Earth's atmosphere. (p. 273)
**efecto invernadero** calentamiento producido cuando ciertos gases, como el dióxido de carbono y el metano, atrapan el calor en la atmósfera terrestre.

**ground tissue** tissue system that makes up the majority of a plant. (p. 347)
**tejido fundamental** sistema de tejidos que comprende la parte principal del cuerpo de la planta.

**growth factor** broad group of proteins that stimulate cell division. (p. 80)
**factor de crecimiento** grupo numeroso de proteínas que estimulan la división celular.

**guard cell** one of a pair of cells that controls the opening and closing of a stoma in plant tissue. (p. 355)
**células oclusivas** las dos células que controlan la apertura y cierre de los estomas en el tejido vegetal.

**gymnosperm** (JIHM-nuh-SPURM) seed plant whose seeds are not enclosed by fruit. (p. 337)
**gimnosperma** planta productora de semillas que no están encerradas en una fruta.

# H

**habitat** combined biotic and abiotic factors found in the area where an organism lives. (p. 241)
**hábitat** conjunto de factores bióticos y abióticos de la zona donde vive un organismo determinado.

**habitat fragmentation** process by which part of an organism's preferred habitat range becomes inaccessible. (p. 277)
**fragmentación del hábitat** proceso mediante el cual una parte del hábitat de un organismo se hace inaccesible.

**habituation** process of eventually ignoring a repeated stimulus. (p. 447)
**habituación** proceso que eventualmente conduce a ignorar un estímulo que se repite.

**hair cell** mechanoreceptor in the inner ear that detects sound waves when it is bent. (p. 479)
**célula ciliada** mecanoreceptor del oído interno que detecta las ondas sonoras que lo accionan.

**hair follicle** pit in the dermis of the skin that contains cells that produce hair. (p. 558)
**folículo piloso** estrecha cavidad de la piel que contiene células que forman el cabello.

**half-life** amount of time it takes for half of the isotope in a sample to decay into its product isotope. (p. 202)
**vida mitad** intervalo de tiempo necesario para que la mitad de los átomos de una muestra de isótopos se desintegren.

**haploid** (HAP-loyd) cell that has only one copy of each chromosome. (p. 91)
**haploide** célula que sólo tiene una copia de cada cromosoma.

**Hardy-Weinberg equilibrium** condition in which a population's allele frequencies for a given trait do not change from generation to generation. (p. 189)
**equilibrio de Hardy-Weinberg** condición en la que las frecuencias alélicas de un rasgo determinado en una población determinada se mantienen constantes de una generación a otra.

**heart** muscle in the chest that moves blood throughout the body. (p. 495)
**corazón** músculo situado en el pecho que hace circular la sangre por el cuerpo.

**hemocoel** open space between cells in animal tissues. (p. 387)
**hemocele** cavidad intracelular de los tejidos animales.

**hemoglobin** (HEE-muh-GLOH-bihn) iron-rich protein in red blood cells that allows the cell to absorb oxygen gas. (p. 497)
**hemoglobina** proteína rica en hierro de los glóbulos rojos que permite a las células absorber oxígeno gaseoso.

**herbivore** organism that eats only plants. (p. 228)
**herbívoro** organismo que sólo se alimenta de plantas.

**heritability** ablity of a trait to be passed from one generation to the next. (p. 169)
**heredabilidad** propiedad de un rasgo determinado de ser transmitido de una generación a la siguiente.

**heterotroph** organism that gets its energy and nutrients by consuming other organisms. (p. 226)
**heterótrofo** organismo que obtiene su energía y sus nutrientes alimentándose de otros organismos.

**heterozygous** characteristic of having two different alleles that appear at the same locus of homologous chromosomes. (p. 99)
**heterocigoto** característica que consiste en tener dos alelos diferentes en el mismo locus de cromátidas hermanas.

**histone** protein that organizes chromosomes and around which DNA wraps. (p. 77)
**histona** proteína que ordena los cromosomas y alrededor de la cual se enrolla el ADN.

**homeobox** (HOH-mee-uh-BAHKS) genes that define the head-to-tail pattern of development in animal embryos; also called *Hox* genes. (p. 378)
**homeobox** genes que definen el desarrollo de los embriones animales organizado de cabeza a cola; también se conocen como genes Hox.

**homeostasis** (HOH-mee-oh-STAY-sihs) regulation and maintenance of constant internal conditions in an organism. (pp. 6; 464)
**homeostasis** regulación y mantenimiento de condiciones internas constantes en un organismo determinado.

**homeotic** (hoh-mee-AH-tihk) genes that control early development in animals. (p. 378)
**homeóticos** genes que controlan la primera fase del desarrollo de los animales.

**hominid** primate that walks upright, has long lower limbs, thumbs that oppose the other four fingers, and a relatively large brain. (p. 215)
**homínido** primate que camina erguido, que tiene extremidades inferiores largas, pulgar desarrollado y alineado con los cuatro dedos restantes y un cerebro relativamente grande.

**homologous chromosomes** chromosomes that have the same length, appearance, and copies of genes, although the alleles may differ. (p. 90)
**cromosomas homólogos** cromosomas de la misma longitud, aspecto y secuencia de genes, aunque los alelos de uno y otro cromosoma pueden ser distintos.

**homologous structure** body part that is similar in structure on different organisms but performs different functions. (p. 174)
**estructura homóloga** estructura anatómica similar de organismos diferentes pero que cumplen funciones diferentes.

**homozygous** characteristic of having two of the same alleles at the same locus of homologous chromosomes. (p. 99)
**homocigoto** característica que consiste en tener los mismos alelos en el mismo locus de cromátidas hermanas.

**hormone** chemical signal that is produced in one part of an organism and affects cell activity in another part. (pp. 372; 488)
**hormona** señal química producida en una parte del organismo que afecta a la actividad celular en otra parte del cuerpo.

**Human Genome Project** project whose goal is to map, sequence, and identify all of the genes in the human genome. (p. 157)
**Proyecto Genoma Humano** proyecto cuya meta consiste en cartografiar un mapa, identificar y hallar la secuencia de todos los genes del genoma humano.

**human immunodeficiency virus (HIV)** virus that weakens the immune system by reproducing in and destroying T cells; causes AIDS. (p. 531)
**virus de inmunodeficiencia humana (VIH)** virus que debilita el sistema inmune al reproducirse en las células T y destruirlas; causa el SIDA.

**humoral immunity** immune response that relies on B cells to produce antibodies to help fight infection. (p. 524)

**inmunidad humoral** respuesta inmune basada en los anticuerpos producidos por las células B para combatir las infecciones.

**hydrogen bond** attraction between a slightly positive hydrogen atom and a slightly negative atom. (p. 22)

**enlace de hidrógeno** atracción entre un átomo de hidrógeno con una carga parcial positiva y otro con una carga parcial negativa.

**hydrologic cycle** pathway of water from the atmosphere to Earth's surface, below ground, and back. (p. 232)

**ciclo hidrológico** movimiento del agua desde la atmósfera hasta la superficie de la Tierra, al subsuelo y de vuelta a la atmósfera.

**hydrosphere** collection of Earth's water bodies, ice, and water vapor. (p. 255)

**hidrosfera** conjunto de las masas de agua líquida, sólida y gaseosa de la Tierra.

**hypertonic** solution that has a higher concentration of dissolved particles compared with another solution. (p. 47)

**hipertónica** solución con una concentración mayor de partículas disueltas que otra solución.

**hypha** (plural: hyphae) threadlike filament forming the body and mycelium of a fungus. (p. 324)

**hifa** filamento que forman el cuerpo y el micelio de los hongos.

**hypothalamus** small area of the midbrain that plays a role in the nervous and endocrine systems. (p. 488)

**hipotálamo** área reducida del cerebro medio que participa en las funciones de los sistemas nervioso y endocrino.

**hypothesis** (plural: hypotheses) proposed explanation or answer to a scientific question. (p. 9)

**hipótesis** proceso de explicación o respuesta a una pregunta científica.

**hypotonic** solution that has a lower concentration of dissolved particles compared with another solution. (p. 47)

**hipotónica** solución con una concentración menor de partículas disueltas que otra solución.

# I

**imitation** process by which an organism learns a behavior by observing other individuals. (p. 447)

**imitación** proceso mediante el cual un organismo aprende un determinado comportamiento mediante la observación de otros individuos.

**immigration** movement of individuals into a population. (p. 248)

**inmigración** desplazamiento de individuos hacia una población establecida.

**immune system** body system that fights off infections. (p. 518)

**sistema inmune** sistema encargado de combatir las infecciones.

**imprinting** process by which a newborn animal quickly learns to recognize another animal, such as a parent. (p. 447)

**impronta filial** proceso mediante el cual un animal recién nacido aprende rápidamente a reconocer a otro como, por ejemplo, su progenitor.

**inclusive fitness** total number of genes an animal contributes to the next generation. (p. 454)

**aptitud inclusiva** número total de genes que un animal transmite a la siguiente generación.

**incomplete dominance** heterozygous phenotype that is a blend of the two homozygous phenotypes. (p. 112)

**dominancia incompleta** fenotipo heterocigoto que resulta de la mezcla de dos fenotipos homocigotos.

**incomplete metamorphosis** process by which immature arthropods look similar to their adult form. (p. 404)

**metamorfosis incompleta** proceso mediante el cual los especímenes jóvenes de los artrópodos son muy similares en forma a los adultos.

**independent variable** condition or factor that is manipulated by a scientist during an experiment. (p. 10)

**variable independiente** condición o factor que es manipulado en el transcurso de un experimento científico.

**index fossil** fossil of an organism that existed during only specific spans of geologic time across large geographic areas. (p. 204)

**fósil índice** fósil de un organismo que existió en el pasado geológico durante un intervalo corto con una amplia distribución geográfica.

**indicator species** species whose presence in an ecosystem gives clues about the condition of that ecosystem. (p. 275)

**especies indicadoras** especies cuya presencia en un ecosistema proporcionan claves sobre el estado en que se encuentra dicho ecosistema.

**infancy** period of life from birth until the ability to walk has been acquired. (p. 572)

**infancia** periodo de vida comprendido entre el nacimiento y los primeros pasos.

**infertility** persistent condition in which offspring cannot be produced. (p. 566)

**esterilidad** incapacidad recurrente de un individuo para reproducirse.

**inflammation** immune response that is characterized by swelling, redness, pain, and itching. (p. 521)

**inflamación** respuesta inmune caracterizada por hinchazón, rubor, dolor y picazón.

**innate** behavior that is not learned through experience. (p. 446)

**innato** comportamiento que no se aprende a través de la experiencia.

**insecticide** chemical that is used to kill insects. (p. 407)

**insecticida** compuesto químico usado para matar insectos.

**insight** ability to solve a problem without repeated trial and error. (p. 456)

**perspicacia** capacidad para resolver un problema sin necesidad de pasar por procesos reiterados de prueba y error.

**instinct** inborn pattern of behavior that is characteristic of a species. (p. 446)

**instinto** patrón innato de comportamiento característico de cada especie.

**integumentary system** body system that separates the other body systems from the external environment; includes the skin and the tissues found within it. (p. 557)

**sistema tegumentario** sistema que delimita los sistemas corporales del medio exterior; consta de la piel y de los tejidos que la conforman.

**interferon** type of protein, produced by body cells, that prevents viruses from making more copies of themselves in infected cells. (p. 519)

**interferón** tipo de proteína generada por las células corporales que impide la replicación de los virus en el interior de las células infectadas.

**intertidal zone** strip of land between the high and low tide lines. (p. 262)

**zona intermareal** banda de tierra comprendida entra las líneas de pleamar y de bajamar.

**introduced species** species that is not native and was brought to an area a result of human activities. (p. 278)

**especie introducida** especie no autóctona que llega a otras regiones como resultado de actividades humanas.

**intron** segment of a gene that does not code for an amino acid. (p. 140)

**intrón** región de un gen que no participa en la codificación de amino ácidos.

**invertebrate** animal without a backbone. (p. 379)

**invertebrado** animal sin columna vertebral.

**ion** atom that has gained or lost one or more electrons. (p. 20)

**ión** átomo que ha ganado o perdido uno o más electrones.

**ionic bond** chemical bond formed between oppositely charged ions. (p. 21)

**enlace iónico** enlace químico que se establece mediante la fuerza eléctrica ejercida entre dos iones de cargas opuestas.

**isotonic** solution that has an equal concentration of dissolved particles compared with another solution. (p. 47)

**isotónica** solución que tiene la misma concentración de partículas disueltas que otra solución.

**isotope** form of an element that has the same number of protons but a different number of neutrons as another element. (p. 202)

**isótopo** átomo de un elemento químico que tiene el mismo número de protones, pero una cantidad diferente de neutrones que otro átomo del mismo elemento.

# J

**joint** location in the body where two bones meet. (p. 551)

**articulación** área del cuerpo en la que se unen dos huesos.

# K

**karyotype** (KAR-ee-uh-TYP) image of all of the chromosomes in a cell. (p. 120)

**cariotipo** imagen de todos los cromosomas de una célula.

**kelp forest** ocean habitat that exists in cold, nutrient-rich shallow coastal waters, made up of large communities of kelp, a seaweed. (p. 263)

**bosques de quelpo** hábitat oceánico de frías aguas costeras de poca profundidad que son ricas en nutrientes y en las que abundan grandes comunidades de algas pardas llamadas quelpos.

**keratin** protein that binds to lipids inside a skin cell, forming a waterproof layer within the skin. (pp. 425; 557)

**queratina** proteína que se enlaza con los lípidos dentro de las células epiteliales creando una capa impermeable en el interior de la piel.

**keystone species** organism that has an unusually large effect on its ecosystem. (p. 224)

**especie clave** organismo que tiene una rol dominante en su ecosistema.

**kidney** organ of the excretory system that removes waste from the blood and helps to maintain stable water levels in the body. (p. 544)

**riñón** órgano del sistema excretor que elimina los desechos de la sangre y contribuye a mantener niveles estables de agua en el organismo.

**kinesis** random movement that results from an increase in activity levels due to a stimulus. (p. 444)

**quinesia** movimiento aleatorio que resulta de un incremento en los niveles de actividad producidos por un estímulo.

**kin selection** natural selection that acts on alleles that favor the survival of close relatives. (p. 454)

**nepotismo** selección natural de los alelos que favorece la supervivencia de los familiares más próximos.

**Krebs cycle** process during cellular respiration that breaks down a carbon molecule to produce molecules that are used in the electron transport chain. (p. 63)

**ciclo de Krebs** proceso de respiración celular en el que se desintegra una molécula de carbono para generar moléculas que intervienen en la cadena de transporte dc electrones.

# L

**lactic acid** product of fermentation in many types of cells, including human muscle cells. (p. 70)

**ácido láctico** producto de fermentación de muchos tipos de células como, por ejemplo, las células musculares humanas.

**lateral line** sensory system in fish that allows them to sense distant movements in the water. (p. 417)

**línea lateral** sistema sensorial de los peces que les permite captar movimientos lejanos en el agua.

**law of independent assortment** Mendel's second law, stating that allele pairs separate from one another during gamete formation. (p. 103)

**ley de transmisión independiente** segunda ley de Mendel, según la cual los pares de alelos se separan durante la formación de los gametos.

**law of segregation** Mendel's first law, stating that (1) organisms inherit two copies of genes, one from each parent, and (2) organisms donate only one copy of each gene in their gametes because the genes separate during gamete formation. (p. 98)

**ley de la segregación** primera ley de Mendel, según la cual (1) los organismos heredan dos copias de cada gen, una de cada progenitor, y (2) que los organismos sólo reciben una copia de cada gen de los gametos de sus progenitores ya que los genes se separan durante la formación de gametos.

**leukemia** cancer of the bone marrow that weakens the immune system by preventing white blood cells from maturing. (p. 530)
**leucemia** cáncer de la medula ósea que debilita el sistema inmune al impedir que maduren los glóbulos blancos.

**lichen** fungus that grows symbiotically with algae, resulting in a composite organism that grows on rocks or tree trunks. (p. 328)
**liquen** organismo compuesto por un hongo y una alga que viven en y que crece sobre las rocas y los troncos de los árboles.

**ligament** long, flexible band of connective tissue that joins two bones across a joint. (p. 551)
**ligamento** tira alargada y flexible de tejido conjuntivo que une dos huesos a través de una articulación.

**light-dependent reactions** part of photosynthesis that absorbs energy from sunlight and transfers energy to the light-independent reactions. (p. 56)
**reacciones lumínicas** etapa de la fotosíntesis en la que se absorbe energía solar para luego usarse en las reacciones oscuras.

**light-independent reactions** part of photosynthesis that uses energy absorbed during the light-dependent reactions to make carbohydrates. (p. 57)
**reacciones oscuras** etapa de la fotosíntesis en que se aplica la energía absorbida durante las reacciones lumínicas para la síntesis de carbohidratos.

**lignin** (LIHG-nihn) complex polymer that hardens the cell walls of some vascular tissues in plants. (p. 333)
**lignina** polímero complejo que endurece las paredes celulares de determinados tejidos vasculares de las plantas.

**limiting factor** environmental factor that limits the growth and size of a population. (p. 249)
**factor limitante** factor ambiental que limita el crecimiento y tamaño de una población determinada.

**limnetic zone** open water of a lake or pond that is located away from shore. (p. 265)
**zona limnética** aguas abiertas de un lago o estanque alejadas de las orillas.

**linkage map** diagram that shows the relative locations of genes on a chromosome. (p. 115)
**mapa de ligamiento** diagrama que representa la situación relativa de los genes en un cromosoma determinado.

**lipid** nonpolar molecule made up of carbon, hydrogen, and oxygen; includes fats and oils. (p. 27)
**lípido** molécula apolar compuesta de carbono, hidrógeno y oxígeno; las grasas y los aceites son lípidos.

**littoral zone** area between the high and low water marks along the shoreline of a lake or pond. (p. 265)
**zona litoral** área de aguas de profundidad intermedia a lo largo de la orilla de un lago o estanque.

**lobe-fin** paired limblike fin that is round in shape. (p. 420)
**aleta lobulada** tipo de aleta de forma redondeada que se presenta en pares y que se asemeja a una extremidad.

**logistic growth** population growth that is characterized by a period of slow growth, followed by a period of exponential growth, followed by another period of almost no growth. (p. 248)
**crecimiento logístico** crecimiento de población que se caracteriza por un período de crecimiento lento, seguido por un período de crecimiento exponencial al que le sigue un período de crecimiento insignificante.

**lung** organ that absorbs oxygen gas from air that an organism inhales. (p. 495)
**pulmón** órgano que absorbe el oxígeno gaseoso que inhala un organismo.

**lymph** collection of interstitial fluid and white blood cells that flows through the lymphatic system. (p. 510)
**linfa** conjunto de los fluidos intersticiales y de glóbulos blancos que circulan por el sistema linfático.

**lymphatic system** (lihm-FAT-ihk) body system that consists of organs, vessels, and nodes through which lymph circulates. (p. 510)
**sistema linfático** sistema corporal que consta de órganos, vasos y nódulos a través de los cuales circula la linfa.

**lymphocyte** (LIHM-fuh-SYT) white blood cell that plays a role in an immune response; *see* B cell and T cell. (p. 511)
**linfocito** glóbulo blanco que participa en la respuesta inmune; véanse célula B y célula T.

**lysogenic infection** infectious pathway of a virus in which host cells are not immediately destroyed. (p. 300)
**infección lisogénica** infección vírica en la que las células huésped no son destruidas de inmediato.

**lysosome** (LY-suh-SOHM) organelle that contains enzymes. (p. 40)
**lisosoma** orgánulo que contiene enzimas.

**lytic infection** infectious pathway of a virus in which host cells are destroyed. (p. 300)
**infección lítica** infección vírica en la que se destruyen las células huésped.

#  M

**malignant** cancerous tumor in which cells break away and spread to other parts of the body, causing harm to the organism's health. (p. 81)
**maligno** tumor canceroso en el que las células se desprenden y se diseminan a otras partes del cuerpo provocando daños a la salud del organismo.

**mammal** endothermic organism that has hair, mammary glands, bones in the ear that allow for hearing, and a jaw for chewing food. (p. 438)
**mamífero** organismo endotérmico que tiene pelo y glándulas mamarias, además de huesos en el oído que le permiten oír y una mandíbula para masticar.

**mammary gland** gland that produces milk. (p. 438)
**glándula mamaria** glándula productora de leche.

**mandible** appendage that is used to crush and bite food. (p. 400)
**mandíbula** apéndice empleado para triturar y morder la comida.

**marsupial** mammal whose young complete fetal development in the mother's external pouch. (p. 439)
**marsupial** mamífero cuyas crías terminan su desarrollo fetal en una bolsa exterior de la madre.

**medusa** umbrella-shaped body form of a cnidarian in which the mouth and tentacles are on the underside. (p. 384)
**medusa** organismo cnidario en forma de paraguas que tiene la boca y los tentáculos en la superficie cóncava.

**meiosis** (my-OH-sihs) form of nuclear division that divides a diploid cell into haploid cells; important in forming gametes for sexual reproduction. (p. 91)

**meiosis** forma de división nuclear en la que una célula diploide se divide en células haploides; importante en la formación de gametos para la reproducción sexual.

**memory cell** specialized white blood cell that contributes to acquired immunity by acting quickly to a foreign substance that infected the body previously. (p. 522)

**célula de memoria** glóbulo blanco que participa en el proceso de inmunización mediante una respuesta rápida ante una sustancia extraña que ya había infectado el organismo anteriormente.

**menopause** period of life when the female reproductive system permanently stops the menstrual cycle. (p. 565)

**menopausia** período de la vida en que el sistema reproductor femenino deja de producir el ciclo menstrual.

**menstrual cycle** series of changes in the female reproductive system that take place over the course of one month. (p. 563)

**ciclo menstrual** sucesión de cambios en el sistema reproductor femenino que ocurre en el plazo de un mes.

**meristem** undifferentiated plant tissue from which new cells are formed. (p. 352)

**meristemo** tejido indiferenciado de las plantas en el que se forman nuevas células.

**mesoglea** jellylike material that separates the two tissue layers of a cnidarian. (p. 384)

**mesoglea** matriz gelatinosa que separa las dos capas de tejidos de un cnidario.

**mesophyll** photosynthetic tissue of a leaf, located between the upper and lower epidermis. (p. 355)

**mesófilo** tejido fotosintético de la hoja, situado entre la epidermis superior y la epidermis inferior de la hoja.

**Mesozoic** era during which dinosaurs roamed Earth (from 248 million years ago to 65 million years ago). (p. 213)

**Mesozoico** era de la Tierra que se inició hace unos 248 millones de años y que finalizó hace 65 millones de años en la que abundaron los dinosaurios.

**messenger RNA (mRNA)** form of RNA that carries genetic information from the nucleus to the cytoplasm, where it serves as a template for protein synthesis. (p. 134)

**ARN mensajero (ARNm)** forma de ARN que transporta la información genética del núcleo al citoplasma, donde sirve de patrón para la síntesis de las proteínas.

**metabolism** all chemical processes that make or break down materials within an organism. (p. 3)

**metabolismo** conjunto de procesos químicos que sintetizan o descomponen sustancias en el interior de los organismos.

**metaphase** second phase of mitosis when spindle fibers line up the chromosomes along the cell equator. (p. 78)

**metafase** segunda fase de la mitosis en la que las fibras de los husos alinean los cromosomas en el plano ecuatorial de la célula.

**metastasize** (mih-TAS-tuh-syz) to spread by transferring a disease-causing agent from the site of the disease to other parts of the body. (p. 81)

**metástasis** diseminación de una enfermedad causada por un agente patógeno del foco en que se origina a otras partes del cuerpo.

**microclimate** climate of a specific location within a larger area. (p. 257)

**microclima** clima de un lugar específico enclavado en un área más extensa.

**microevolution** observable change in the allele frequencies of a population over a few generations. (p. 183)

**microevolución** cambio observable en las frecuencias alélicas de una población en el transcurso de unas pocas generaciones.

**microscope** tool that provides an enlarged image of an object. (p. 12)

**microscopio** instrumento que permite ver una imagen amplificada de un objeto.

**microvillus** (plural: microvilli) small hairlike projection on the surface of a villus in the small intestine. (p. 542)

**microvellosidad** proyección pilosa muy pequeña que recubre las vellosidades del intestino delgado.

**mineral** inorganic material, such as calcium, iron, potassium, sodium, or zinc, that is essential to the nutrition of an organism. (p. 537)

**mineral** material inorgánico, como el calcio, el hierro, el potasio, el sodio o el zinc, que resulta esencial en la nutrición de los organismos.

**mitochondrial DNA** DNA found only in mitochondria, often used as a molecular clock. (p. 291)

**ADN mitocondrial** ADN propio de las mitocondrias que suele actuar a modo de reloj molecular.

**mitochondrion** (MY-tuh-KAHN-dree-uhn) (plural: mitochondria) bean-shaped organelle that supplies energy to the cell and has its own ribosomes and DNA. (p. 40)

**mitocondria** orgánulo en forma de fríjol que suministra energía a la célula y que tiene sus propios ribosomas y ADN.

**mitosis** (my-TOH-sihs) process by which a cell divides its nucleus and contents. (p. 74)

**mitosis** proceso en el cual tanto el núcleo como los demás elementos de la célula se duplican.

**molecular clock** theoretical clock that uses the rate of mutation to measure evolutionary time. (p. 290)

**reloj molecular** reloj teórico que emplea la tasa de mutación para medir el tiempo evolutivo.

**molecular genetics** study of DNA structure and function on the molecular level. (p. 13)

**genética molecular** estudio de la estructura y función del ADN a nivel molecular.

**molecule** two or more atoms held together by covalent bonds; not necessarily a compound. (p. 21)

**molécula** dos o más átomos unidos mediante enlaces covalentes; no forman necesariamente un compuesto.

**monocot** (MAHN-uh-KAHT) flowering plant whose embryos have one cotyledon. (p. 340)

**monocotiledónea** planta angiosperma cuyos embriones tienen un solo cotiledón.

**monohybrid cross** cross, or mating, between organisms that involves only one pair of contrasting traits. (p. 101)

**cruzamiento monohíbrido** cruzamiento o apareamiento entre dos organismos que sólo involucra un par de rasgos diferentes.

**monomer** molecular subunit of a polymer. (p. 25)
**monómero** subunidad molecular del polímero.

**monotreme** mammal whose offspring complete fetal development in laid eggs. (p. 439)
**monotrema** mamífero que pone huevos donde sus crías completan su desarrollo fetal.

**muscle fiber** cell of the muscular system that shortens when it is stimulated by the nervous system. (p. 554)
**fibra muscular** célula del sistema muscular que se contrae al ser estimulada por el sistema nervioso.

**muscular system** body system that moves bones within and substances throughout the body. (p. 554)
**sistema muscular** sistema corporal que mueve los huesos y que hace circular sustancias a través del cuerpo.

**mutagen** agent that can induce or increase the frequency of mutations in organisms. (p. 144)
**mutágeno** agente que puede inducir mutaciones en un organismo o incrementar la frecuencia de éstas.

**mutation** change in the DNA sequence. (p. 142)
**mutación** cambio en la secuencia de ADN.

**mutualism** ecological relationship between two species in which each species gets a benefit from the interaction. (p. 243)
**mutualismo** relación ecológica entre dos especies que resulta beneficiosa para ambas.

**mycelium** vegetative part of a fungus, consisting of a mass of branching, threadlike hyphae that grows underground. (p. 324)
**micelio** parte vegetativa del hongo compuesta de un entramado de filamentos ramificados, llamados hifas, que crece bajo tierra.

**mycorrhizae** ecological relationship between the mycelium of a fungus and the roots of certain plants. (p. 325)
**micorriza** relación ecológica entre el micelio de un hongo y las raíces de determinadas plantas.

**myofibril** long strand of protein within a muscle fiber. (p. 555)
**miofibrilla** larga cadena proteica dentro de una fibra muscular.

**myosin** filament that pulls actin filaments to cause muscle contraction. (p. 555)
**miosina** filamento que al tensar los filamentos de actina causa la contracción muscular.

# N

**natural selection** mechanism by which individuals that have inherited beneficial adaptations produce more offspring on average than do other individuals. (p. 169)
**selección natural** mecanismo mediante el cual los organismos que han heredado adaptaciones beneficiosas producen un promedio más alto de descendientes que los demás individuos.

**nebula** rotating cloud of gas and dust. (p. 207)
**nébula** nube giratoria de polvo y gases.

**negative feedback** control system for homeostasis that adjusts the body's conditions when the conditions vary from the ideal. (p. 465)
**retroalimentación negativa** sistema de control de la homeostasis que regula las condiciones del cuerpo cuando éstas no son óptimas.

**nematocyst** capsule containing a thin, coiled tubule with a poisonous barb at one end. (p. 384)
**nematocisto** cápsula que contiene un fino túbulo enrollado con un aguijón venenoso en la punta.

**nephron** (NEHF-rahn) individual filtering unit of the kidney that removes waste from the blood. (p. 545)
**nefrona** unidad de filtración del riñón que retira los desechos de la sangre.

**neritic zone** zone of the ocean that extends from the intertidal zone out to the edge of the continental shelf. (p. 262)
**zona nerítica** zona del océano que se extiende desde la zona intermareal hasta el límite de la plataforma continental.

**nervous system** body system that controls sensation, interpretation, and response; includes the brain, spinal cord, and nerves. (p. 472)
**sistema nervioso** sistema corporal que controla las sensaciones, las interpretaciones y las respuestas; incluye el encéfalo, la médula espinal y los nervios.

**neuron** cell of the nervous system that sends impulses between the body systems and interprets and stores some messages in the brain. (p. 474)
**neurona** célula del sistema nervioso que transmite impulsos entre los diversos sistemas del organismo y que, además, interpreta y almacena información en el cerebro.

**neurotransmitter** (NUR-oh-TRANS-miht-uhr) chemical that sends a nervous system's signal across a synapse. (p. 476)
**neurotransmisor** compuesto químico que transmite una señal del sistema nervioso a través de la sinapsis.

**nitrogen fixation** process by which certain types of bacteria convert gaseous nitrogen into nitrogen compounds. (p. 234)
**fijación del nitrógeno** proceso mediante el cual ciertos tipos de bacterias transforman el nitrógeno gaseoso en compuestos nitrogenados.

**node** organ located along the lymphatic vessels that filters bacteria and foreign particles from lymph. (p. 510)
**ganglio linfático** órgano situado a lo largo de los vasos linfáticos encargado de filtrar bacterias y sustancias extrañas de la linfa.

**nonrenewable resource** natural resource that is used more quickly than it can be formed. (p. 270)
**recurso no renovable** recurso natural que se consume con más rapidez de la que se puede reponer.

**normal distribution** distribution in a population in which allele frequency is highest near the mean range value and decreases progressively toward each extreme end. (p. 183)
**distribución normal** distribución de la población en la que la frecuencia alélica es mayor en la zona de valor medio y disminuye progresivamente hacia ambos extremos.

**notochord** flexible skeletal support rod embedded in an animal's back. (p. 412)
**notocordio** bastón esqueletal flexible que proporciona sostén y que está situado en el dorso de los animales.

**nucleic acid** polymer of nucleotides; the genetic material of organisms. (p. 28)
**ácido nucleico** polímero de nucleótidos; material genético de los organismos.

**nucleotide** (NOO-klee-oh-TYD) monomer that forms DNA; made up of a phosphate group, a sugar, and a nitrogen-containing base. (p. 126)
**nucleótido** monómero que forma el ADN y que tiene un grupo fosfato, un azúcar y una base nitrogenada.

**nucleus** (NOO-klee-uhs) (plural: nuclei) organelle made up of a double membrane that acts as the storehouse for most of a cell's DNA. (p. 39)
**núcleo** orgánulo compuesto de una doble membrana que almacena la mayor parte del ADN de la célula.

**obligate aerobe** prokaryote that cannot survive without the presence of oxygen. (p. 306)
**aerobio obligado** procariota que no puede sobrevivir en un entorno sin oxígeno.

**obligate anaerobe** prokaryote that cannot survive in the presence of oxygen. (p. 306)
**anaerobio obligado** procariota que no puede sobrevivir en un entorno oxigenado.

**observation** using the senses to study the world; using tools to collect measurements; examining previous research results. (p. 9)
**observación** utilización de los sentidos para estudiar el mundo; uso de instrumentos de medición; análisis de resultados de investigación.

**omnivore** organism that eats both plants and animals. (p. 228)
**omnívoro** organismo que se alimenta tanto de animales como de plantas.

**operant conditioning** process by which a behavior increases or decreases as the result of a reward or punishment. (p. 449)
**condicionamiento operante** proceso mediante el cual varía la frecuencia de un comportamiento como resultado de un premio o un castigo.

**operculum** protective bony plate that covers a fish's gills. (p. 418)
**opérculo** placa protectora ósea que recubre las branquias de los peces.

**operon** section of DNA that contains all of the code to begin transcription, regulate transcription, and build a protein; includes a promotor, regulatory gene, and structural gene. (p. 139)
**operon** sección de ADN que contiene todos los códigos necesarios para iniciar y regular el proceso de transcripción y para sintetizar una proteína: consta de un promotor, de un gen regulador y de un gen estructural.

**opportunistic infection** infection caused by a pathogen that a healthy immune system would normally be able to fight off. (p. 530)
**infección oportunista** infección causada por un patógeno que un sistema inmune saludable podría combatir con eficacia.

**optimal foraging** theory that states that natural selection will favor organisms that have behaviors that can gather the best food sources. (p. 451)
**abastecimiento óptimo** teoría según la cual la selección natural favorece a aquellos organismos cuyos comportamientos les permiten acceder a las mejores fuentes de alimento.

**organ** group of different types of tissues that work together to perform a specific function or related functions. (pp. 84; 462)
**órgano** grupo de diversos tipos de tejidos que funcionan de manera coordinada para desarrollar una función específica o funciones relacionadas.

**organelle** structure that is specialized to perform a distinct process within a cell. (p. 38)
**orgánulo** estructura intracelular que se especializa en una función específica.

**organism** any individual living thing. (p. 3)
**organismo** cualquier ser vivo.

**organ system** two or more organs that work in a coordinated way to carry out similar functions. (pp. 84; 462)
**sistema de órganos** dos o más órganos que funcionan de manera coordinada para realizar funciones similares.

**osmosis** diffusion of water molecules across a semipermeable membrane from an area of higher water concentration to an area of lower water concentration. (p. 46)
**ósmosis** difusión de moléculas de agua a través de una membrana semipermeable, desde un área de mayor concentración de agua a otra de menor concentración de agua.

**ossicle** small bone, especially one of the three found in the middle ear of mammals. (p. 391)
**huesecillo** en los mamíferos, cada uno de los tres huesos pequeños que se encuentran en el oído medio.

**ovary** organ in which female gametes develop before fertilization. (pp. 364; 561)
**ovario** órgano en el que se desarrollan los gametos femeninos antes de la fertilización.

**oviparous** reproductive strategy in which the embryos develop outside of the mother's body. (p. 432)
**ovíparo** organismo que se reproduce mediante un sistema en el que los embriones se desarrollan fuera del cuerpo materno.

**ovulation** process by which an egg is released from the ovary and becomes available for fertilization. (p. 563)
**ovulación** proceso mediante el cual se libera un óvulo del ovario, quedando susceptible a ser fertilizado.

**ovum** (plural: ova) egg cell that is produced by the female reproductive system. (p. 561)
**óvulo** ovocito producido en el sistema reproductor femenino.

**P**

**pacemaker** collection of cells that stimulates the pumping action of the heart. (p. 501)
**nódulo sinusal** conjunto de células que estimula los latidos del corazón; también conocido como marcapaso natural.

**paleontology** study of fossils or extinct organisms. (p. 176)
**paleontología** estudio de los fósiles o de los organismos extintos.

**Paleozoic** era of geologic time (from 544 to 248 million years ago) during which members of every major animal group alive today evolved. (p. 213)
**Paleozoico** era geológica (desde hace 544 a 248 millones de años) durante la cual evolucionaron especies de los principales grupos de animales de la actualidad.

**parasitism** ecological relationship in which one organism benefits by harming another organism. (p. 243)
**parasitismo** relación ecológica en la que un organismo se beneficia perjudicando al otro organismo.

**parasympathetic nervous system** division of the peripheral nervous system that calms the body and helps the body to conserve energy. (p. 484)
**sistema nervioso parasimpático** parte del sistema nervioso periférico encargado de mantener un estado corporal de descanso y ayudar al cuerpo a conservar energía.

**parenchyma cell** cell with thin walls that forms tissues within leaves, roots, stems, and fruit of plants. (p. 346)
**célula del parénquima** célula de paredes delgadas que forma tejidos en el interior de las hojas, raíces, tallos y frutas de las plantas.

**particulate** microscopic bits of dust, metal, and unburned fuel produced by industrial processes. (p. 272)
**materia particulada** partículas microscópicas de polvo, metal y combustibles sin quemar, que se generan en los procesos industriales.

**passive immunity** immunity that occurs without the body undergoing an immune response. (p. 519)
**inmunidad pasiva** inmunidad que tiene lugar sin que el cuerpo experimente una reacción inmune.

**passive transport** movement of molecules across the cell membrane without energy input from the cell. (p. 46)
**transporte pasivo** movimiento de moléculas a través de la membrana celular, que se produce sin aporte de energía celular.

**pathogen** agent that causes disease. (pp. 297; 514)
**patógeno** agente que causa una enfermedad.

**pedigree** chart of the phenotypes and genotypes in a family that is used to determine whether an individual is a carrier of a recessive allele. (p. 118)
**pedigrí** diagrama de los fenotipos y genotipos de una familia que se emplea para determinar si un individuo es portador de un alelo recesivo.

**period** unit of geologic time that lasts tens of millions of years and is associated with a particular type of rock system. (p. 204)
**periodo** unidad de tiempo geológico que abarca decenas de millones de años y que suele asociarse a tipos determinados de formaciones rocosas.

**peripheral nervous system (PNS)** part of the nervous system that transmits impulses between the central nervous system and other organs in the body. (p. 472)
**sistema nervioso periférico (SNP)** división del sistema nervioso que transmite impulsos entre el sistema nervioso central y otros órganos del cuerpo.

**peristalsis** (PEHR-ih-STAWL-sihs) wavelike involuntary muscle contractions that push food through the organs of the digestive system. (p. 540)
**peristaltismo** contracciones involuntarias en forma de ondas que impulsan los alimentos a través de los órganos del sistema digestivo.

**petal** modified leaf that surrounds a flower's reproductive structures. (p. 364)
**pétalo** hoja modificada que rodea las estructuras reproductivas de la flor.

**petiole** stalk that attaches a leaf blade to a stem. (p. 355)
**peciolo** rabillo que une la lámina de la hoja al tallo.

**pH** measurement of acidity; related to the concentration of free hydrogen ions in solution. (p. 23)
**pH** medida de acidez; relacionada con la concentración de los iones libres de hidrógeno en una solución.

**phagocyte** cell that destroys other cells by surrounding and engulfing them. (p. 518)
**fagocito** célula que destruye a otras células rodeándolas y engulléndolas.

**phagocytosis** (FAG-uh-sy-TOH-sihs) uptake of a solid particle into a cell by engulfing the particle; see endocytosis. (p. 49)
**fagocitosis** absorción de una partícula sólida por parte de una célula que la envuelve: véase endocitosis.

**pharmacology** study of drugs and their effects on the body. (p. 343)
**farmacología** estudio de los medicamentos y de los efectos que causan en el cuerpo.

**phenotype** collection of all of an organism's physical characteristics. (p. 100)
**fenotipo** conjunto de todas las características físicas de un organismo determinado.

**pheromone** chemical released by an organism that stimulates a behavior in other organisms of the same species. (p. 453)
**feromona** compuesto químico liberado por un organismo que estimula ciertos comportamientos en otros organismos de la misma especie.

**phloem** tissue that transports sugars in vascular plants. (p. 347)
**floema** tejido transportador de azúcares en las plantas vasculares.

**phospholipid** molecule that forms a double-layered cell membrane; made up of a glycerol, a phosphate group, and two fatty acids. (p. 43)
**fosfolípido** molécula que forma una membrana de capa doble; consta de glicerol, un grupo fosfato y dos ácidos grasos.

**photoperiodism** response of an organism to changes in the length of the day. (p. 374)
**fotoperiodismo** respuesta de un organismo a las variaciones de luz en un período de 24 horas.

**photosynthesis** process by which light energy is converted to chemical energy; produces sugar and oxygen from carbon dioxide and water. (p. 56)
**fotosíntesis** proceso mediante el cual la energía del sol se convierte en energía química; produce azúcar y oxígeno a partir de dióxido de carbono y agua.

**photosystem** series of light-absorbing pigments and proteins that capture and transfer energy from sunlight in the thylakoid membrane. (p. 59)
**fotosistema** conjunto de pigmentos y proteínas que capturan y transfieren luz en la membrana tilacoide.

**phototropism** growth of a plant toward a light source. (p. 373)
**fototropismo** crecimiento de la planta hacia la luz.

**phylogeny** evolutionary history of a group of related species. (p. 287)
**filogenia** historia evolutiva de un grupo de especies relacionadas.

**phylum** group of animals defined by structural and functional characteristics that are different from every other animal phylum. (p. 379)

**división** grupo de animales definidos por una serie de características estructurales y funcionales que se diferencian de cualquier otra división; también se conoce como filum.

**phytoplankton** photosynthetic microscopic protists, such as algae. (p. 262)

**fitoplancton** colonia de protistas microscópicas fotosintéticas, como las algas.

**pioneer species** organism that is the first to live in a previously uninhabited area. (p. 251)

**especie pionera** primer organismo que vive en una zona hasta entonces deshabitada.

**pituitary gland** area in the middle of the brain that makes and releases hormones that control cell growth and osmoregulation, or water levels in the blood. (p. 489)

**glándula pituitaria** zona en el centro del cerebro que produce y segrega hormonas que controlan el crecimiento celular y la osmorregulación, es decir, la regulación de los niveles de líquidos en la sangre.

**placenta** (pluh-SEHN-tuh) organ that develops in female mammals during pregnancy and carries nutrients from the mother to the embryo. (pp. 426; 568)

**placenta** órgano que se desarrolla en las hembras de los mamíferos durante la gestación y que lleva nutrientes de la madre al embrión.

**plankton** microscopic, free-floating organisms, which may be animals or protists, that live in the water. (p. 262)

**plancton** organismos microscópicos, animales o protistas, que flotan libremente en el agua.

**plant** multicellular eukaryote that produces its own food through photosynthesis. (p. 332)

**planta** organismo eucariota multicelular que produce su propio alimento mediante la fotosíntesis.

**plasma** clear yellowish fluid, about 90 percent water, that suspends cells in the blood. (p. 506)

**plasma** líquido de color amarillento pálido que consisten en un 90 por ciento deagua en el que están suspendidas las células sanguíneas.

**plasmid** circular piece of DNA found in bacteria that can replicate separately from the DNA of the main chromosome. (pp. 154; 306)

**plásmido** cadena de material genético en forma circular que se encuentra en las bacterias y que se replica independientemente del ADN cromosómico.

**platelet** cell fragment that is made in the bone marrow and is important for blood clotting. (p. 506)

**plaqueta** fragmento celular que se produce en la médula ósea y que cumple una función importante en la coagulación de la sangre.

**point mutation** mutation that involves a substitution of only one nucleotide. (p. 142)

**mutación puntual** mutación que involucra la sustitución de un solo nucleótido.

**polar body** haploid cell produced during meiosis in the female of many species; these cells have little more than DNA and eventually break down. (p. 95)

**cuerpo polar** célula haploide producida durante la meiosis en las hembras de muchas especies; esta célula tiene poco más que ADN y termina por desintegrarse.

**pollen grain** two-celled structure that contains the male form of the plant's gamete. (p. 333)

**grano de polen** estructura formada por dos células que contiene el gameto masculino de la planta.

**pollination** process by which seed plants become fertilized without the need for free-standing water. (p. 336)

**polinización** proceso mediante el cual las plantas con semillas se fertilizan sin depender del agua del suelo.

**pollution** anything that is added to the environment and has a negative affect on the environment or its organisms. (p. 272)

**contaminación** cualquier sustancia que se libera en el medio ambiente con efectos negativos para los organismos que lo habitan y su entorno.

**polygenic trait** trait that is produced by two or more genes. (p. 113)

**rasgo poligénico** rasgo producido por dos o más genes.

**polymer** large, carbon-based molecule formed by smaller subunits called monomers. (p. 25)

**polímero** gran molécula de carbono formada por monómeros.

**polymerase chain reaction (PCR)** method for increasing the quantity of DNA by separating it into two strands and adding primers and enzymes. (p. 150)

**reacción en cadena de la polimerasa (RCP)** método para obtener un gran número de copias de ADN separándolo en dos hebras y añadiendo cebadores y enzimas.

**polyp** tube-shaped body form of a cnidarian in which the mouth and tentacles face upward. (p. 384)

**pólipo** cuerpo de forma tubular de un cnidario con la boca y los tentáculos orientados hacia arriba.

**population** all of the individuals of a species that live in the same area. (p. 170)

**población** conjunto de individuos de la misma especie que viven en la misma zona.

**population crash** dramatic decline in the size of a population over a short period of time. (p. 249)

**colapso poblacional** reducción drástica del tamaño de una población en un breve período de tiempo.

**population density** measure of individuals living in a defined area. (p. 245)

**densidad de población** cantidad de habitantes que viven en un área determinada.

**population dispersion** way in which individuals of a population are spread out over an area or volume. (p. 245)

**dispersión de población** manera en la que los individuos de una población determinada se han distribuido en una área o en un volumen.

**positive feedback** control system in which sensory information causes the body to increase the rate of change away from homeostasis. (p. 465)

**retroalimentación positiva** sistema de control mediante el cual la información sensorial estimula el cuerpo a incrementar la tasa de cambio, alejándola de valores homeostáticos.

**predation** process by which one organism hunts and kills another organism for food. (p. 243)
**predación** proceso mediante el cual un organismo acecha, mata y se come a otro organismo.

**pressure-flow model** model for predicting how sugars are moved from photosynthetic tissue to the rest of a plant. (p. 350)
**modelo de flujo de presión** modelo para predecir la forma en que los azúcares son transportados del tejido fotosintético al resto de una planta.

**primary growth** growth in vascular plants that causes elongation of the plant body. (p. 353)
**crecimiento primario** crecimiento de las plantas vasculares que resulta de la elongación del cuerpo de la planta.

**primary succession** establishment and development of an ecosystem in an area that was previously uninhabited. (p. 251)
**sucesión primaria** establecimiento y desarrollo de un ecosistema en una zona hasta entonces deshabitada.

**primate** mammal with flexible hands and feet, forward-looking eyes, and enlarged brains relative to body size. (p. 215)
**primate** mamífero de manos y pies flexibles, mirada frontal y un cerebro grande en relación con el tamaño del cuerpo.

**primer** short segment of DNA that starts replication by DNA polymerase. (p. 150)
**cebador** pequeño segmento de ADN que inicia la replicación mediante ADN polimerasa.

**prion** infectious agent that is made up of a protein fragment that can cause other proteins to fold incorrectly. (p. 298)
**prión** agente infeccioso que consta de una partícula proteica que induce a otras proteínas a plegarse de forma incorrecta.

**probabilty** likelihood that a particular event will happen. (p. 103)
**probabilidad** posibilidad de que ocurra un suceso en particular.

**producer** organism that gets its energy from abiotic sources, such as sunlight or inorganic chemicals. (p. 226)
**productor** organismo que obtiene su alimento de fuentes abióticas, como la luz solar o compuestos inorgánicos.

**product** substance formed by a chemical reaction. (p. 30)
**producto** sustancia formada por una reacción química.

**prokaryotic cell** (proh-KAR-ee-AHT-ihk) cell that does not have a nucleus or other membrane-bound organelles. (p. 38)
**célula procarionta** célula que no tiene núcleo ni orgánulos limitados por membranas.

**promoter** section of DNA to which RNA polymerase binds, starting the transcription of mRNA. (p. 139)
**promotor** sección de ADN a la que se enlaza el ARN polimerasa al inicio del proceso de transcripción de ARNm.

**prophage** DNA of a bacteriophage inserted into a host cell's DNA. (p. 300)
**profago** ADN de un bacteriófago insertado en el ADN de la célula huésped.

**prophase** first phase of mitosis when chromatin condenses, the nuclear envelope breaks down, the nucleolus disappears, and the centrosomes and centrioles move to opposite sides of the cell. (p. 78)
**profase** primera fase de la mitosis, en la que la cromatina se condensa, la membrana nuclear se desintegra, el nucleolo desaparece y los centrosomas y los centriolos migran a lados opuestos de la célula.

**prosimian** oldest primate group that includes mostly small, nocturnal primates such as lemurs. (p. 215)
**prosimio** grupo de primates más antiguo que consta, principalmente, de pequeños primates nocturnos, como los lemures.

**protein** polymer made up of amino acids linked by peptide bonds; folds into a particular structure depending on bonds between amino acids. (p. 28)
**proteína** polímero compuesto de aminoácidos unidos por enlaces peptídicos; se pliega formando una estructura determinada según sean los enlaces que hay entre los aminoácidos.

**proteomics** (PROH-tee-AH-mihks) study and comparison of all the proteins made by an organism's genome. (p. 158)
**proteómica** estudio y comparación de todas las proteínas producidas por el genoma de un organismo determinado.

**protist** eukaryote that is not an animal, plant, or fungus. (p. 316)
**protista** organismo eucariota que no es un animal, una planta, ni un hongo.

**protostome** animal development in which the animal's mouth develops before the anus. (p. 380)
**protóstomo** animal en el que la boca se desarrolla antes que el ano.

**protozoa** animal-like protist. (p. 319)
**protozoo** protista con características animales.

**pseudocoelom** fluid filled space with mesoderm only on one side of the space. (p. 389)
**pseudoceloma** cavidad llena de fluido que tiene mesodermo en un solo lado de la cavidad.

**pseudopod** temporary extension of cytoplasm and plasma membrane that helps protozoa move and feed. (p. 319)
**pseudópodo** extensión temporal del citoplasma y de la membrana plasmática que permite a los protozoos moverse y alimentarse.

**puberty** stage of adolescence that is marked by the production of hormones involved in reproduction. (p. 561)
**pubertad** fase de la adolescencia marcada por la producción de hormonas involucradas en la reproducción.

**pulmonary circuit** (PUL-muh-NEHR-ee) collection of blood vessels that carries blood between the lungs and heart. (pp. 430; 502)
**circuito pulmonar** conjunto de vasos sanguíneos que transporta sangre entre los pulmones y el corazón.

**pulmonary circulation** see pulmonary circuit.
**circulación pulmonar** véanse circuito pulmonar.

**punctuated equilibrium** theory that states that speciation occurs suddenly and rapidly followed by long periods of little evolutionary change. (p. 197)
**equilibrio puntuado** teoría según la cual la especiación se produce repentinamente y va seguida de largos períodos de escasa actividad evolutiva.

**Punnett square** model for predicting all possible genotypes resulting from a cross, or mating. (p. 101)
**cuadrado de Punnet** modelo de predicción de todos los genotipos posibles que se pueden obtener a partir de un determinado cruzamiento o apareamiento.

**pupa** stage of metamorphosis in which the organism reorganizes into a completely new body form. (p. 405)
**pupa** fase de la metamorfosis en la que el organismo adopta una nueva forma corporal.

**purebred** type of organism whose ancestors are genetically uniform. (p. 97)
**pura raza** organismo de ancestros con uniformidad genética.

# R

**radial symmetry** arrangement of body parts in a circle around a central axis. (p. 380)
**simetría radial** disposición de las partes del cuerpo en un círculo que rodea un eje central.

**radiometric dating** technique that measures the amount of radioactive material that has decayed. (p. 202)
**fechado radiométrico** técnica para medir la tasa natural de degradación de los isótopos para calcular la edad de los materiales.

**radula** filelike feeding organ found in mollusks. (p. 387)
**rádula** órgano raspador con el que se alimentan los moluscos.

**ray-fin** fan-shaped arrangement of bones in a fish's fin. (p. 419)
**aleta radial** disposición en abanico de las espinas de una aleta de pez.

**reactant** substance that is changed by a chemical reaction. (p. 30)
**reactante** sustancia que cambia a consecuencia de una reacción química.

**receptor** protein that detects a signal molecule and performs an action in response. (p. 44)
**receptora** proteína que detecta la señal de una molécula y responde con una acción concreta.

**recessive** allele that is not expressed unless two copies are present in an organism's genotype. (p. 99)
**recesivo** alelo que no se expresa, a menos que en el genotipo del organismo en cuestión estén presentes dos copias de dicho gen.

**recombinant DNA** (ree-KAHM-buh-nuhnt) genetically engineered DNA that contains genes from more than one organism or species. (p. 154)
**ADN recombinante** ADN manipulado genéticamente que contiene genes de más de un organismo o especie.

**red blood cell** cell that carries oxygen gas from the lungs to the rest of the body. (p. 497)
**glóbulo rojo célula** encargada de transportar oxígeno gaseoso de los pulmones al resto del cuerpo.

**reflex arc** nerve pathway in which an impulse crosses only two synapses before producing a response. (p. 483)
**arco reflejo** circuito nervioso en el que un impulso sólo atraviesa dos simpasis antes de producir una respuesta.

**regeneration** process by which a new plant can grow from a fragment of a nonreproductive structure, such as a root, stem, or leaf. (p. 370)
**regeneración** proceso mediante el cual una nueva planta puede desarrollarse a partir de un fragmento de una estructura no reproductora, como una raíz, un tallo o una hoja.

**relative dating** estimate of the age of a fossil based on the location of fossils in strata. (p. 202)
**datación relativa** estimación de la edad de un fósil según la ubicación de los fósiles en los estratos.

**releaser** stimulus that triggers a specific behavior. (p. 446)
**estímulo liberador** que suscita un comportamiento específico.

**releasing hormone** chemical that stimulates other glands to release their hormones. (p. 490)
**hormona liberadora** sustancia química que estimula otras glándulas para que secreten hormonas.

**renewable resource** resource that replaces itself quickly enough so that it will not be used faster than it can be made. (p. 270)
**recurso renovable** recurso natural que se restablece a un ritmo superior del ritmo al que se consume.

**replication** process by which DNA is copied. (p. 129)
**replicación** proceso mediante el cual se copian las moléculas de ADN.

**reproductive isolation** final stage in speciation, in which members of isolated populations are either no longer able to mate or no longer able to produce viable offspring. (p. 193)
**aislamiento reproductor** fase final de la especiación en la que los miembros de poblaciones aisladas pierden la capacidad de aparearse o no pueden producir crías viables.

**reproductive system** body system that allows for sexual reproduction; includes testes, ovaries, uterus, and other male and female sex organs. (p. 561)
**sistema reproductor** sistema corporal que permite la reproducción sexual; consta de testículos, ovarios, útero y otros órganos sexuales masculinos y femeninos.

**reptile** ectotherm that is covered with dry scales, breathes with lungs, and reproduces by laying eggs. (p. 432)
**reptil** vertebrado ectotermo con la piel cubierta de escamas, que respira con pulmones y que pone huevos para reproducirse.

**respiratory system** body system that brings oxygen into the body and removes carbon dioxide; includes the nose, trachea, and lungs. (p. 494)
**sistema respiratorio** sistema corporal que lleva oxígeno al cuerpo y elimina el dióxido de carbono; consta de nariz, tráquea y pulmones.

**resting potential** difference in electrical charge between the inside and outside of a neuron; contains the potential energy needed to transmit the impulse. (p. 475)
**potencial de reposo** diferencia de carga eléctrica entre el interior y el exterior de una neurona; energía potencial necesaria para transmitir un impulso.

**restriction enzyme** enzyme that cuts DNA molecules at specific nucleotide sequences. (p. 147)
**enzima de restricción** enzima que fragmenta moléculas de ADN en secuencias específicas de nucleótidos.

**restriction map** diagram that shows the lengths of fragments between restriction sites in the strand of DNA. (p. 149)
**mapa de restricción** diagrama que representa las longitudes de los fragmentos entre los sitios de corte de una hebra de ADN.

**retrovirus** virus that contains RNA and uses the enzyme called reverse transcriptase to make a DNA copy. (p. 303)
**retrovirus** virus que contiene ARN y que usa una enzima llamada transcriptasa para hacer una copia del ADN.

**Rh factor** surface protein on red blood cells in the ABO blood group; people can be Rh+ or Rh-. (p. 508)

**factor Rh** proteína de la superficie de los glóbulos rojos de los grupos sanguíneos ABO; el factor Rh de las personas puede ser Rh+ o Rh-.

**ribosomal RNA (rRNA)** RNA that is in the ribosome and guides the translation of mRNA into a protein; also used as a molecular clock. (pp. 134; 291)

**ARN ribosómico (ARNr)** ARN presente en los ribosomas que guía el proceso de síntesis de las proteínas a partir del ARNm; también denominado reloj molecular.

**ribosome** (RY-buh-sohm) organelle that links amino acids together to form proteins. (p. 40)

**ribosoma** orgánulo que enlaza las moléculas de aminoácidos para formar proteínas.

**ribozyme** RNA molecule that can catalyze specific chemical reactions. (p. 209)

**Ribozima** molécula de ARN que tiene la capacidad de catalizar determinadas reacciones químicas.

**RNA** nucleic acid molecule that allows for the transmission of genetic information and protein synthesis. (p. 132)

**ARN** molécula de ácido nucleico encargada de la transmisión de información genética y de la síntesis de las proteínas.

**RNA polymerase** enzyme that brings about the synthesis of a complementary strand of RNA from a DNA template. (p. 132)

**ARN polimerasa** enzima que cataliza la síntesis de una hebra complementaria de ARN a partir de un patrón de ADN.

**rod cell** photoreceptor in the eye that detects light intensity and contributes to black and white vision. (p. 478)

**bastoncillo** célula fotosensible del ojo que detecta la intensidad de la luz y contribuye a la visión en blanco y negro.

**root cap** mass of cells that covers and protects the tips of plant roots. (p. 352)

**ápice de la raíz** masa de células que cubre y protege las puntas de las raíces de las plantas.

**root hair** thin hairlike outgrowth of an epidermal cell of a plant root that absorbs water and minerals from the soil. (p. 352)

**pelos radicales** finas extensiones de la célula epidérmica en las raíces de una planta encargada de absorber agua y minerales del suelo.

# S

**sarcomere** section of a muscle fiber that contains all of the filaments necessary to cause muscle contraction. (p. 555)

**sarcómero** sección de fibra muscular con todos los filamentos necesarios para generar una contracción muscular.

**sclerenchyma cell** thick-walled, lignin-rich cells that form supportive plant tissue. (p. 346)

**esclereida célula** rica en lignina que constituye el esclerénquima, un tejido de sostén de las plantas.

**scrotum** skin that encloses the testes outside of the male body. (p. 561)

**escroto** piel que envuelve las gónadas masculinas en el exterior del cuerpo.

**secondary growth** growth in woody plants resulting in wider roots, branches, and stems. (p. 353)

**crecimiento secundario** crecimiento de las plantas que produce un engrosamiento de las raíces, de las ramas y de los tallos.

**secondary succession** reestablishment of a damaged ecosystem in an area where the soil was left intact. (p. 252)

**sucesión secundaria** desarrollo de un ecosistema dañado en una zona donde el suelo permanece inalterado.

**seed** structure used by some land plants to store and protect the embryo. (p. 333)

**semilla** estructura empleada por algunas plantas para almacenar y proteger al embrión.

**segmentation** repeated sections of an annelid's long body that contain the same set of body structures, apart from its distinct head and tail region. (pp. 388; 395)

**segmentación** secciones repetidas del cuerpo alargado de un anélido, cada una de las cueles contiene el mismo conjunto de estructuras corporales, con excepción de la cabeza y de la cola.

**selective permeability** condition or quality of allowing some, but not all, materials to cross a barrier or membrane. (p. 44)

**permeabilidad selectiva** condición o cualidad que permite discriminar el flujo de determinados materiales a través de una membrana o barrera.

**semen** white substance that contains sperm and fluids produced by sex glands of the male reproductive system. (p. 562)

**semen** sustancia blanca que contiene espermatozoides y fluidos generados por las glándulas sexuales del sistema reproductor masculino.

**sepal** modified leaf that covers and protects the flower while it develops. (p. 364)

**sépalo** hoja modificada que cubre la flor durante su desarrollo.

**sensitization** process by which a neuron adds more receptors to its surface in response to consistently lower amounts of a neurotransmitter in the synapse. (p. 486)

**sensibilización** proceso mediante el cual una neurona incorpora a su superficie más receptores en respuesta a una insuficiencia sostenida de neurotransmisores en el espacio sináptico.

**sessile** unable to move. (p. 383)

**sésil** fijo a un punto, que no se mueve.

**sex chromosome** chromosome that directly controls the development of sexual characteristics. (p. 91)

**cromosoma sexual** cromosoma que controla directamente el desarrollo de las características sexuales.

**sex-linked gene** gene that is located on a sex chromosome. (p. 110)

**gen ligado al sexo** gen ubicado en un cromosoma sexual.

**sexually transmitted disease (STD)** disease that is passed from one person or another during sexual contact. (p. 566)

**enfermedad de transmisión sexual (ETS)** enfermedad que se transmite de una persona a otra durante el contacto sexual.

**sexual reproduction** process by which two gametes fuse and offspring that are a genetic mixture of both parents are produced. (p. 91)

**reproducción sexual** proceso mediante el cual se unen dos gametos que dan lugar a crías cuyo genoma es una mezcla del de los dos progenitores.

**sexual selection** selection in which certain traits enhance mating success; traits are, therefore, passed on to offspring. (p. 188)
 **selección sexual** selección en la que determinados rasgos incrementan el éxito del apareamiento; en consecuencia, tales rasgos se transmiten a las crías.

**skeletal muscle** muscle tissue that is attached to the skeletal system and, when contracted, moves bones. (p. 554)
 **músculo esquelético** tejido muscular adherido al sistema esquelético que, al contraerse, mueve los músculos.

**skeletal system** body system that includes bones and the connective tissues that hold the bones together in the body. (p. 550)
 **sistema esquelético** sistema que consta de los huesos y de los tejidos conjuntivos que mantienen unidos a los huesos.

**slime mold** protist with a slimelike amoeboid stage that grows on decaying vegetation and in moist soil. (p. 323)
 **moho mucoso** protista de aspecto gelatinoso con una fase ameboide, que crece en material vegetal en descomposición y en la tierra húmeda.

**small intestine** organ of the digestive system that connects the stomach to the large intestine and in which chemical digestion takes place. (p. 540)
 **intestino delgado** órgano del sistema digestivo que conecta el estómago al intestino grueso y en el que se produce la digestión química.

**smog** air pollution in which gases released from burning fossil fuels form a fog when they react with sunlight. (p. 272)
 **smog** contaminación atmosférica en la que los gases liberados por la combustión de hidrocarburos reaccionan con la luz creando una niebla.

**smooth muscle** muscle tissue that moves substances, such as food and blood, through organs and tissues, such as the digestive system organs and blood vessels. (p. 554)
 **músculo liso** tejido muscular que mueve los alimentos y la sangre por los órganos y los tejidos como, por ejemplo, los órganos del sistema digestivo y los vasos sanguíneos.

**sodium potassium pump** active transport protein in neurons that carries sodium (Na+) ions out of the cell and bring potassium (K+) ions into the cell. (p. 475)
 **bomba sodio-potasio** transporte activo de proteínas en las neuronas, en el que se extrae de la célula iones de sodio (Na+) y se mete iones de potasio (K+).

**solute** substance that dissolves in a solvent and is present at a lower concentration than the solvent. (p. 23)
 **soluto** sustancia que se disuelve en un solvente y que aparece en menor concentración que éste.

**solution** mixture that is consistent throughout; also called a homogeneous mixture. (p. 23)
 **solución** mezcla uniforme en toda su extensión; también se conoce como mezcla homogénea.

**solvent** substance in which solutes dissolve and that is present in greatest concentration in a solution. (p. 23)
 **solvente** sustancia en la que se disuelve un soluto y que se presenta en mayor concentración que éste.

**somatic cell** (soh-MAT-ihk) cell that makes up all of the body tissues and organs, except gametes. (p. 90)
 **célula somática** célula que conforma todos los tejidos y órganos del organismo, excepto los gametos.

**somatic nervous system** part of the peripheral nervous system that sends signals from the brain to the muscles that produce voluntary movements. (p. 483)
 **sistema nervioso somático** parte del sistema nervioso periférico que transporta señales del encéfalo a los músculos para producir los movimientos voluntarios.

**specialist** consumer that eats only one type of organism. (p. 229)
 **especialista** consumidor que se alimenta de un solo tipo de organismo.

**speciation** evolution of two or more species from one ancestral species. (p. 193)
 **especiación** evolución de dos o más especies a partir de una sola especie ancestral.

**species** group of organisms so similar to one another that they can breed and produce fertile offspring. (pp. 3; 164)
 **especie** grupo de organismos tan semejantes entre sí que pueden reproducirse y tener descendencia fértil.

**sperm** male gamete. (p. 95)
 **espermatozoide** gameto masculino.

**sphincter** (SFIHNGK-tuhr) ring of muscle that separates the different organs of the digestive system. (p. 539)
 **esfínter** músculo en forma de anillo que separa a los diversos órganos del sistema digestivo.

**spiracle** (SPIHR-uh-kuhl) hole on the body of an insect's exoskeleton through which air can be taken in or released. (p. 402)
 **espiráculo** orificio en el cuerpo del exoesqueleto de los insectos a través del cual entra y sale aire.

**sporangia** spore-forming structures found in fungi, algae, and some plants. (p. 325)
 **esporangio** estructura que produce esporas y que se encuentra en los hongos, las algas y algunas plantas.

**sporophyte** (SPAWR-uh-FYT) diploid, spore-producing phase of a plant life cycle. (p. 360)
 **esporofita** fase diploide de producción de esporas en el ciclo de vida de una planta.

**stabilizing selection** pathway of natural selection in which intermediate phenotypes are selected over phenotypes at both extremes. (p. 184)
 **selección estabilizadora** proceso de selección natural en el que se da preferencia a los fenotipos intermedios sobre los fenotipos de ambos extremos.

**stamen** male structure of flowering plants; includes the stalk and anther, which produces pollen. (p. 364)
 **estambre** estructura floral masculina de las gimnospermas; consiste de una antera productora de polen unida a un pedicelo.

**start codon** codon that signals to ribosomes to begin translation; codes for the first amino acid in a protein. (p. 136)
 **codón de iniciación** codón que da la señal a los ribosomas para que inicien el proceso de traducción; codifica el primer aminoácido de la proteína.

**stem cell** cell that can divide for long periods of time while remaining undifferentiated. (p. 85)
 **célula madre** célula capaz de dividirse durante largos periodos de tiempo sin diferenciarse.

**sternum** long, flat bone that connects the ribs in front of the chest and to which the chest muscle attaches. (p. 436)
**esternón** hueso plano y alargado que conecta las costillas a la altura del pecho y al que van adheridos los músculos pectorales.

**stimulant** drug that increases the number of impulses that neurons generate. (p. 486)
**estimulante** droga que incrementa el número de impulsos que generan las neuronas.

**stimulus** (STIHM-yuh-luhs) (plural: stimuli) something that causes a physiological response. (pp. 443; 472)
**estímulo** cualquier cosa capaz de provocar una respuesta fisiológica.

**stomach** muscular sac in the digestive system that breaks down food into a liquidlike mixture. (p. 540)
**estómago** saco muscular del sistema digestivo donde se descompone la comida en una mezcla líquida.

**stomata** (singular: stoma) pores in the cuticle of a plant through which gas exchange occurs. (p. 332)
**estoma** poro en la cutícula de una planta a través del cual se produce el intercambio gaseoso.

**stop codon** codon that signals to ribosomes to stop translation. (p. 136)
**codón de terminación** codón que indica a los ribosomas que detengan el proceso de traducción.

**substrate** reactant in a chemical reaction upon which an enzyme acts. (p. 34)
**sustrato** reactivo de una reacción química sobre el que actúa un enzima.

**succession** sequence of biotic changes that regenerate a damaged community or start a community in a previously uninhabited area. (p. 251)
**sucesión** secuencia de cambios bióticos que regeneran una comunidad dañada o que crean una nueva comunidad en una zona hasta entonces deshabitada.

**survivorship** probability of surviving to a particular age. (p. 450)
**supervivencia** probabilidad de sobrevivir hasta una edad determinada.

**survivorship curve** graph showing the surviving members of each age group of a population over time. (p. 246)
**curva de supervivencia** gráfica que representa los sobrevivientes de una población por grupos de edad durante un periodo determinado.

**sustainable development** practice of not using natural resources more quickly than they can be replenished. (p. 280)
**desarrollo sostenible** práctica que consiste en no utilizar los recursos naturales más rápidamente de lo que pueden ser generarlos.

**swim bladder** buoyancy organ that helps fish to swim at different depths in the water. (p. 420)
**vejiga natatoria** órgano de flotación que permite a los peces nadar a diferentes profundidades.

**symbiosis** ecological relationship between members of at least two different species that live in direct contact with one another. (p. 243)
**simbiosis** relación ecológica en la que los miembros de al menos dos especies diferentes viven en contacto directo.

**sympathetic nervous system** part of the autonomic nervous system that prepares the body for action and stress. (p. 484)
**sistema nervioso simpático** sistema que forma parte del sistema nervioso autónomo y que se encarga de preparar el cuerpo para situaciones de acción y de estrés.

**synapse** tiny gap between neurons through which chemical signals are sent. (p. 476)
**sinapsis** pequeño espacio entre las neuronas a través del cual se envían señales químicas.

**system** changing, organized group of related parts that interact to form a whole. (p. 5)
**sistema** conjunto organizado y dinámico de partes que interactúan entre sí para formar un todo.

**systemic circuit** (sihs-STEHM-ihk) collection of blood vessels that carries blood between the heart and the rest of the body, except for the lungs. (pp. 430; 502)
**circuito sistémico** conjunto de vasos sanguíneos que transporta la sangre entre el corazón y el resto del cuerpo, excepto los pulmones.

**systemic circulation** see systemic circuit.
**circulación sistémica** véanse circuito sistémico.

**systolic pressure** (sih-STAHL-ihk) measure of pressure on the walls of an artery when the left ventricle contracts to pump blood through the body. (p. 504)
**presión sistólica** medida de la presión de las paredes arteriales cuando el ventrículo izquierdo se contrae para bombear sangre a través del cuerpo.

# T

**tadpole** aquatic larva of frogs or toads. (p. 423)
**renacuajo** larva acuática de las ranas y los sapos.

**taiga** (TY-guh) biome with long and cold winters, lasting up to six months; also called a boreal forest. (p. 260)
**taiga** bioma propio de zonas de largos y fríos inviernos de hasta seis meses de duración; también se conoce como bosque boreal.

**taproot** main root of some plants, usually larger than other roots and growing straight down from a stem. (p. 352)
**raíz pivotante** raíz principal de determinadas plantas, normalmente más grande que las demás raíces y que crece en en lína recta hacia abajo a partir del tallo.

**taxis** movement in a particular direction, either toward or away from a stimulus. (p. 444)
**taxismo** movimiento en una dirección determinada, ya sea hacia un estímulo o en sentido opuesto a éste; conocido también como taxis.

**taxon** (plural: taxa) level within the Linnaean system of classification (kingdom, phylum, class, order, family, genus, or species) that is organized into a nested hierarchy. (p. 284)
**taxón** cualquiera de los niveles del sistema de clasificación jerárquico de Linneo, (reino, división, clase, orden, familia, género o especie).

**taxonomy** science of classifying and naming organisms. (p. 284)
**taxonomía** ciencia dedicada a la clasificación y nomenclatura de los organismos.

**T cell** white blood cell that matures in the thymus and destroys infected body cells by causing them to burst; also called a T-lymphocyte. (p. 519)
**célula T** glóbulo blanco que madura en el timo y que destruye las células infectadas haciéndolas reventar; también se conoce como linfocito T.

**telomere** (TEHL-uh-MEER) repeating nucleotide at the ends of DNA molecules that do not form genes and help prevent the loss of genes. (p. 77)
**telómero** extremo de la molécula de ADN compuesto de nucleótidos repetidos que no producen genes pero que ayudan a prevenir la pérdida de éstos.

**telophase** last phase of mitosis when a complete set of identical chromosomes is positioned at each pole of the cell, the nuclear membranes start to form, the chromosomes begin to uncoil, and the spindle fibers break apart. (p. 78)
**telofase** última fase de la mitosis en que un conjunto completo de cromosomas idénticos se sitúa en los polos opuestos de la célula; empiezan a formarse las membranas nucleares; los cromosomas empiezan a desenrollarse y el huso mitótico se desintegra.

**temporal isolation** isolation between populations due to barriers related to time, such as differences in mating periods or differences in the time of day that individuals are most active. (p. 194)
**aislamiento temporal** aislamiento entre poblaciones que se produce por motivos de índole temporal como, por ejemplo, diferencias en los períodos de apareamiento o de las horas del día en que los individuos son más activos.

**tendon** band of connective tissue that joins a muscle to the bone that it moves. (p. 554)
**tendón** banda de tejido conjuntivo que conecta cada músculo con el hueso que mueve.

**terminal** end of the neuron's axon from which neurotransmitters are released to stimulate an adjacent cell. (p. 476)
**terminal** extremo del axón de la neurona desde el cual se segregan neurotransmisores para estimular a la célula adyacente.

**territoriality** behavior pattern in which an organism controls and defends a specific area. (p. 451)
**territorialidad** patrón de comportamiento mediante el cual un organismo determinado controla y defiende un área específica.

**testcross** cross between an organism with an unknown genotype and an organism with a recessive phenotype. (p. 102)
**cruzamiento de prueba** cruzamiento entre un organismo de genotipo desconocido y un organismo de fenotipo recesivo.

**testis** (plural: testes) organ of the male reproductive system that produces sperm. (p. 561)
**testículo** órgano del sistema reproductor masculino encargado de la producción de espermatozoides.

**testosterone** (tehs-TAHS-tuh-ROHN) steroid hormone that is found in greater quantities in men than women and contributes to male sexual characteristics and development. (p. 561)
**testosterona** hormona esteroide que se encuentra en mayor cantidad en el hombre que en la mujer y que contribuye al desarrollo de las características sexuales masculinas.

**tetrapod** vertebrate with four limbs. (p. 422)
**tetrápodo** vertebrado con cuatro extremidades.

**theory** proposed explanation for a wide variety of observations and experimental results. (p. 10)
**teoría** explicación de un fenómeno a partir de una amplia gama de observaciones y resultados experimentales.

**thermoregulation** (THUR-moh-REHG-yoo-LAY-shuhn) process of the body maintaining a stable internal temperature under various conditions. (p. 468)
**termorregulación** proceso que permite mantener una temperatura interna constante bajo diferentes condiciones.

**thigmotropism** turning or bending of a plant in response to contact with an object. (p. 373)
**tigmotropismo** giro o flexión de una planta como respuesta al contacto con un objeto.

**thylakoid** (THY-luh-KOYD) membrane-bound structure within chloroplasts that contains chlorophyll and other light-absorbing pigments used in the light-dependent reactions of photosynthesis. (p. 56)
**tilacoide** estructura de la membrana interna de los cloroplastos que contiene clorofila y otros pigmentos fotoabsorbentes que intervienen en las reacciones captadoras de luz de la fotosíntesis.

**tissue** group of cells that work together to perform a similar function. (pp. 84; 461)
**tejido** grupo de células similares que trabajan juntas para desempeñar la misma función.

**tissue rejection** process by which a transplant recipient's immune system makes antibodies against the protein markers on the donor's tissue; can result in the destruction of the donor tissue. (p. 525)
**rechazo de tejidos** proceso mediante el cual el sistema inmune de un individuo receptor de un transplante genera anticuerpos contra los marcadores proteicos del tejido donante; puede producir la destrucción del tejido donante.

**tolerance** drug resistance that occurs when cells adapt, requiring larger doses of the drug to produce the same effect. (p. 486)
**tolerancia** resistencia a una droga producida cuando las células se adaptan a ella, lo cual requiere un aumento de la dosis para producir el mismo efecto.

**toxin** poison released by an organism. (p. 311)
**toxina** sustancia tóxica producida por un organismo.

**trachea** (TRAY-kee-uh) (plural: tracheae) long structure made of soft tissue that connects the mouth and nose to the lungs in humans (p. 495); a system of thin branching tubes in the bodies of insects that allow for breathing. (p. 402)
**tráquea** tubo alargado de tejido blando que conecta la boca y la nariz con los pulmones de los humanos; sistema de finos tubos ramificados en el cuerpo de los insectos que les permite respirar.

**trait** characteristic that is inherited. (p. 96)
**rasgo** característica heredada.

**transcription** process of copying a nucleotide sequence of DNA to form a complementary strand of mRNA. (p. 132)
**transcripción** proceso donde se copia una secuencia de ADN para formar una cadena complementaria de ARNm.

**transfer RNA (tRNA)** form of RNA that brings amino acids to ribosomes during protein synthesis. (p. 134)
**ARN de transferencia (ARNt)** tipo de ARN que transporta aminoácidos a los ribosomas durante el proceso de síntesis proteica.

**transgenic** organism whose genome has been altered to contain one or more genes from another organism or species. (pp. 15; 155)

**transgénico** organismo cuyo genoma ha sido alterado mediante la incorporación de uno o más genes de otro organismo o especie.

**translation** process by which mRNA is decoded and a protein is produced. (p. 135)

**traducción** proceso mediante el cual se decodifica el ARNm y se produce una proteína.

**transpiration** release of vapor through the pores of the skin or the stomata of plant tissue. (p. 349)

**transpiración** liberación de vapor a través de los poros de la piel o, en los tejidos vegetales, de los estomas.

**trimester** one of three periods of approximately three months each into which a human pregnancy is divided. (p. 569)

**trimestre** uno de los períodos de aproximadamente tres meses en que se divide la gestación humana.

**trophic level** level of nourishment in a food chain. (p. 229)

**nivel trófico** nivel de alimentación de la cadena trófica.

**tropism** movement or growth of a plant in response to an environmental stimulus. (p. 373)

**tropismo** movimiento o crecimiento determinado por un estímulo ambiental.

**tundra** biome found at far northern latitudes where winters last as long as ten months per year. (p. 260)

**tundra** bioma de latitudes septentrionales extremas donde los inviernos duran hasta diez meses.

# U

**umbilical cord** structure that connects an embryo to its mother and provides the embryo with nourishment and waste removal. (p. 568)

**cordón umbilical** estructura que conecta el embrión con su madre y que le suministra alimento y un sistema de eliminación de residuos.

**umbrella species** species whose protection under the Endangered Species Act leads to the preservation of its habitat and all of the other organisms in its community. (p. 280)

**especie paraguas** especie protegida por la Ley de Especies en Peligro de Extinción cuya salvaguarda conlleva la protección de su hábitat y la de todos los otros organismos que viven en él.

**uniformitarianism** theory that states that the geologic processes that shape Earth are uniform through time. (p. 166)

**uniformitarismo** teoría según la cual los procesos geológicos que dan forma a la Tierra se producen de manera uniforme a lo largo del tiempo.

**ureter** (yu-REE-tuhr) tube of connective tissue that carries urine from each of the kidneys to the bladder. (p. 544)

**uréter** tubo de tejido conjuntivo que transporta la orina desde los riñones hasta la vejiga.

**urinary bladder** saclike organ that collects and stores urine before it is excreted from the body. (p. 544)

**vejiga urinaria** órgano en forma de bolsa donde se recoge y se almacena la orina antes de ser excretada del cuerpo.

**uterus** organ of the female reproductive system in which a fertilized egg attaches and a fetus develops. (p. 561)

**útero** órgano del sistema reproductor femenino al que se adhiere el huevo fertilizado y dónde se desarrolla el feto.

# V

**vaccine** substance that stimulates an immune response, producing acquired immunity without illness or infection. (pp. 303; 527)

**vacuna** sustancia que estimula una respuesta inmune y que proporciona inmunidad ante una enfermedad o infección determinada sin provocarla.

**vacuole** (VAK-yoo-OHL) organelle that is used to store materials, such as water, food, or enzymes, that are needed by the cell. (p. 40)

**vacuola** orgánulo encargado de almacenar diversos materiales necesarios para la célula, como el agua, nutrientes o enzimas.

**valve** flap of tissue that prevents blood from flowing backward into a blood vessel or heart chamber. (p. 500)

**válvula** tejido membranoso encargado de evitar que la sangre refluya por el vaso sanguíneo en que circula o hacia una cavidad del corazón.

**variation** differences in physical traits of an individual from the group to which it belongs. (p. 167)

**variación** diferencia en rasgos físicos que presenta un individuo con respecto al grupo al que pertenece.

**vascular cylinder** center of a root or stem that contains phloem and xylem. (p. 352)

**cilindro vascular** cilindro en el centro de una raíz o tallo que contiene el floema y el xilema.

**vascular system** collection of specialized tissues in some plants that transports mineral nutrients up from the roots and brings sugars down from the leaves. (p. 333)

**sistema vascular** conjunto de tejidos especializados de determinadas plantas que transportan nutrientes minerales desde las raíces hacia arriba y que conducen el azúcar de las hojas hacia abajo.

**vascular tissue** supportive and conductive tissue in plants, consisting of xylem and phloem. (p. 347)

**tejido vascular** tejido conductor y de sostén de las plantas que consta de xilema y de floema.

**vas deferens** duct in which sperm mixes with other fluids before reaching the urethra. (p. 562)

**conducto deferente** conducto en el que el esperma se mezcla con otros fluidos antes de alcanzar la uretra.

**vector** organism, such as a mosquito or tick, that carries pathogens from one host to another. (pp. 408; 517)

**vector** organismo, como o el mosquito o la garrapatas que puede transferir patógenos de un huésped a otro.

**vegetative reproduction** asexual reproduction in which a stem, leaf, or root will produce a new individual when detached from a parent plant. (p. 370)

**reproducción vegetativa** reproducción asexual en la que un tallo, una hoja o una raíz producen un nuevo individuo cuando se separan de la planta de la cual forman parte.

**vein** large blood vessel that carries blood from the rest of the body to the heart. (p. 495)

**vena** vaso sanguíneo de gran caudal que transporta la sangre desde todas las partes del cuerpo hasta el corazón.

**ventricle** large chamber in the heart that receives blood from an atrium and pumps blood to the rest of the body. (p. 500)

**ventrículo** amplia cámara del corazón que recibe sangre de la aurícula y la impulsa al resto del cuerpo.

**vertebra** (plural: vertebrae) bone that makes up the spinal column. (p. 550)

**vértebra** hueso que compone la columna vertebral.

**vertebrate** animal with an internal segmented backbone. (p. 379)

**vertebrado** animal con una columna vertebral interna y segmentada.

**vesicle** (VEHS-ih-kuhl) small organelle that contains and carries materials within the cytoplasm. (p. 40)

**vesícula** pequeño argánulo que contiene y transporta materiales en el interior del citoplasma.

**vestigial structure** remnants of an organ or structure that functioned in an earlier ancestor. (p. 174)

**estructura vestigial** restos de algún órgano o estructura en una especie determinada que cumplieron alguna función en un ancestrode ésta.

**villus** (VIHL-uhs) (plural: villi) small fingerlike projection in the small intestine that absorbs nutrients. (p. 542)

**vellosidades** pequeñas proyecciones en forma de dedo del intestino delgado encargadas de absorber los nutrientes.

**viroid** infectious particle made of single-stranded RNA without a protein coat, that almost always use plants as their host. (p. 297)

**viroide** partícula infecciosa que consta de un solo filamento de ARN sin envoltura de proteínas, que casi siempre se hospeda como parásito en las plantas.

**virus** infectious particle made only of a strand of either DNA or RNA surrounded by a protein coat. (p. 297)

**virus** partícula infecciosa que consta de un sólo filamento de ADN o ARN y rodeado por una envuelta de proteína.

**vitamin** organic molecule that works with enzymes to regulate cell function, growth, and development. (p. 536)

**vitamina** molécula orgánica que funciona con enzimas para regular el funcionamiento, el crecimiento y el desarrollo de las células.

**viviparous** reproductive strategy in which the embryo develops within the mother's body. (p. 432)

**vivíparo** modalidad de reproducción en la que los embriones se desarrollan en el interior de la madre.

# W

**water mold** fungus that is either a parasite or decomposer and lives in fresh water or moist soil. (p. 323)

**moho acuático** hongo acuático o de suelos húmedos que actúa como parásito o descomponedor de materia orgánica.

**watershed** region of land that drains into a river, river system, or other body of water. (p. 265)

**cuenca hidrográfica** área terrestre que vierte sus aguas hacia un río, una red fluvial o cualquier otra masa acuática.

**water vascular system** system of water-filled canals that extend down each arm of a echinoderm, such as a sea star. (p. 391)

**sistema ambulacral sistema** formado por una serie de tubos llenos de agua que se prolongan por los brazos de los equinodermos como, por ejemplo, la estrella de mar.

**white blood cell** cell that attacks pathogens. (p. 508)

**glóbulo blanco** célula cuya función es atacar a los patógenos.

**wood** fibrous material made of dead cells that are part of the vascular system in some plants. (p. 340)

**madera** material fibroso formado por células muertas que forman parte del sistema vascular de algunas plantas.

# X

**X chromosome inactivation** process that occurs in female mammals in which one of the X chromosomes is randomly turned off in each cell. (p. 111)

**inactivación X** proceso en los mamíferos del sexo femenino en que uno de los cromosomas X de cada célula se desactiva aleatoriamente.

**xylem** tissue that transports water and dissolved minerals in vascular plants. (p. 347)

**xilema** tejido de las plantas vasculares que transporta agua y sales minerales disueltas.

# Z

**zooplankton** animal plankton. (p. 262)

**zooplancton** plancton animal.

**zygote** cell that forms when a male gamete fertilizes a female gamete. (p. 566)

**cigoto** célula formada cuando un gameto masculino fertiliza un gameto femenino.

# Acknowledgements

## Photography

2 © PhotoDisc/Getty Images; 21 © Getty Images; 27 © Stockbyte/Getty Images; 30 © Getty Images; 166 © Richard Hamilton Smith/Corbis; 169 *all,* 170 © Getty Images; 176, 186 © Royalty-Free/Corbis; 205 *top* © Comstock; *middle* © Getty Images; 207, 215, 216 © Getty Images; 243 © Ingram Publishing/Superstock; 246 © Getty Images; 258 NASA; 259 © Royalty-Free/Corbis; 267 © NASA; 277, 280 © Getty Images; 337 © Ingram Publishing/Superstock; 350 © Olga Shelego/ShutterStock; 353, 355 *all,* 370 © Getty Images; 404, 407 © Stockbyte; 408 © Artville; 413 *both* © Getty Images; 417 © Comstock; 438, 439 © Corbis; 443, 445, 446, 448, 452 © Getty Images; 453 © Artville: Bugs and Insects; 456 *both,* 485, 494, 517, 528, 535, 570 © Getty Images.

## Maps

186, 194, 221 © MapQuest.com, Inc.; 259 © GeoNova LLC.